REA

RELIGIOUS

AMERICAN RELIGIOUS CREEDS

Volume I

Old Catholicism
Orthodoxy
Lutheranism
Reformed
Methodism
Twentieth-Century Holiness
—and many others

Volume II

Pentecostalism
Black Trinitarianism
German Mennonites
Primitive Baptists
Quakerism
Fundamentalism
British Israelism
—and many others

Volume III

Liberalism
Mail Order Churches
Mormonism
Christian Science
Spiritualism
Theosophy
Judaism
Islam
Hinduism
—and many others

AMERICAN RELIGIOUS CREEDS

VOLUME II

J. GORDON MELTON, EDITOR

Triumph™ Books
New York, New York

TRIUMPH BOOKS EDITION 1991
An Imprint of Gleneida Publishing Group, Inc.

This edition published by special arrangement with
Gale Research Inc.

Library of Congress Cataloging-in-Publication Data

Encyclopedia of American religions, religious creeds.
    American religious creeds : an essential compendium of more than
450 statements of belief and doctrine / J. Gordon Melton, editor.
      p.   cm.
    Reprint. Originally published: The Encyclopedia of American
religions, religious creeds. Detroit, Mich. : Gale Research Co.,
1988.
    Includes indexes.
    ISBN 0-8007-3014-3 (v. 1). — ISBN 0-8007-3015-1 (v. 2). — ISBN
0-8007-3016-X (v. 3)
    1. Creeds—Encyclopedias. 2. United States—Religion—1960—
Encyclopedias. I. Melton, J. Gordon. II. Title.
BL427.E52 1991
291.2'0973—dc20   90-47872
                                             CIP

Acknowledgments

Grateful acknowledgment is due to the
following publishers for use of their material.

"Account of Our Religion, Doctrine and Faith [Hutterite Brethren]." Reprinted from *Baptist Confessions of Faith,* edited by William L. Lumpkin, copyright © 1959 by Judson Press.

"Affirmations for Humanistic Jews [Sherwin T. Wine, Society for Humanistic Judaism]." Reprinted from *Judaism Beyond God: A Radical New Way to Be Jewish* by Sherwin T. Wine (copyright © 1985 by Sherwin T. Wine; reprinted by permission of the Society for Humanistic Judaism, 28611 W. Twelve Mile Rd., Farmington Hills, Mich. 48334), Society for Humanistic Judaism, 1985, p. 244.

Confessions [of the General Church of the New Jerusalem]. Reprinted from *Liturgy and Hymnal for the Use of the General Church of the New Jerusalem* (copyright 1916, 1921, 1939, and 1966 by the General Church of the New Jerusalem; reprinted by permission of the publisher), General Church of the New Jerusalem, 1966, pp. 217–20.

Creed of the Church of Scientology © 1954 L. Ron Hubbard. All Rights Reserved. Grateful acknowledgment is made to L. Ron Hubbard Library for permission to reprint a selection from the copyrighted works of L. Ron Hubbard.

"Dogma" and "Doctrine [Church of Seven Arrows]." Reprinted from *Shaman's Notes 2: Structure of Complete Belief-Systems* (copyright 1985 by Church of Seven Arrows; reprinted by permission of the publisher), Church of Seven Arrows, 1985, pp. 14–26.

"I Believe [Rabbi Joseph H. Gelberman, Little Synagogue]." Reprinted from *To Be . . . Fully Alive: A Collection of Essays for Life Enhancement on the Spiritual and Psychological Potential of Man* by Dr. Joseph H. Gelberman (copyright © 1983 by Dr. Joseph H. Gelberman; reprinted by permission of the publisher), Coleman Graphics, 1983, pp. xxiii–xxv.

"Our Message [Family of Love (Children of God)]." Reprinted from *The Basic Mo Letters* by Moses David (© Children of God, 1976), Children of God, 1976, pp. 27–31.

"Principles of Miracles." Reprinted from *A Course in Miracles* (copyright © 1975 by the Foundation for Inner Peace; reprinted by permission of the publisher), Foundation for Inner Peace, 1975, pp. 1–4.

"Statement of Principles" and "Affirmations of the Ethical Movement [American Ethical Union]." Reprinted from *Ethical Perspectives: Statements of the Ethical Culture Movement* (© 1972 New York Society for Ethical Culture; reprinted by permission of the publisher), New York Society for Ethical Culture, 1972.

"The Theological Declaration of Barmen." Reprinted from *The Church's Confession Under Hitler* by Arthur C. Cochrane, Westminster Press, 1962, pp. 237–42.

Contents

AMERICAN RELIGIOUS CREEDS—VOLUME II

Contents

Contents

Contents

Contents

Introduction

Just as *The Encyclopedia of American Religions* provided the first comprehensive study of religious and spiritual groups in the United States since the U.S. Census Bureau's last edition of *Religious Bodies* (1936), *American Religious Creeds* represents the first comprehensive compilation of the creeds, confessions, and statements of belief of America's religious groups in over a century. *American Religious Creeds* presents more than 450 creedal texts, covering not only Christian churches, but also the hundreds of Jewish, Islamic, Buddhist, Hindu, and other traditions possessing a following in the United States and Canada. In addition, historical notes and comments are provided to help researchers, librarians, students, and other information seekers understand the context in which creeds were written, revised, or discarded.

Authentic Text Used for All Creeds

The texts of the religious creeds presented in this volume are in their authentic form, although obvious typographical errors have been corrected. The authentic wording, grammar, and punctuation of each statement remains intact. In some cases, a creed's format was altered slightly for stylistic consistency and clarity. No attempt was made to introduce foreign material or explanatory notes into the body of the creed's text. Where alternate readings of a statement's text have been available, the editor chose an English language text currently in use by the church. Further, no attempt has been made to provide theological exposition, detailed textual analysis, or variant readings of a text, except in those few cases in which contemporary Christian churches disagree over the exact wording of the older creeds.

Types of Creeds and Statements Covered

Creeds are formal statements of belief to which members of a church are expected to give their intellectual assent. The writing of religious creeds is primarily an activity of Christian churches. At the same time, some other churches publish less rigid statements of belief reflecting a consensus of church teachings, while recognizing some variance of belief among members (and even leaders). A number of religious groups publish statements with an understanding that such beliefs are entirely secondary in the life of the group; emphasis is placed more upon piety, religious experience, liturgy, behavior (ethics), or membership in an ethnic group. On the other hand, some churches are strictly anti-creedal. Nevertheless, even the most anti-creedal and experience-oriented groups usually have a small body of assumed intellectual content (a system of beliefs that can be put into words) and, on occasion, official group statements are written for members' use. Such statements are considered to fall within the scope of this work.

Each creedal statement presented in this volume is acknowledged by at least one existing church or religious group described in the second edition of *The Encyclopedia of American Religions* (or its supplement). While the latter contains 1,550 entries, this work contains over 450. This difference is due to several factors. First, many creedal statements serve a variety of individual churches. For example, the Nicene Creed is the basic statement of faith for all Eastern Orthodox groups; divisions in this tradition have been based on nondoctrinal issues such as ethnicity, language, and political allegiances. Second, some groups simply have no summary statement of belief. The Plymouth Brethen groups, for example, are noncreedal, and many Hindu and Buddhist groups are centered more on experience than doctrine. Finally, some groups' statements are not listed because the editor, after repeated attempts, could not locate those creeds.

Contemporary Focus

Unlike previous collections, *American Religious Creeds* seeks to maintain a contemporary focus by presenting primarily creeds currently acknowledged by those religious groups operating in the United States and Canada. This volume makes no attempt to gather creedal statements from the various religious traditions, especially the older Christian families and, therefore, it is not intended to replace previously published works on Christian creeds, such as Philip Schaff's 1877 compilation, *The Creeds of Christendom* (Harper & Brothers, 1877); *Creeds of the Churches* (John H. Leith, editor; Doubleday, 1963); Arthur C. Cochrane's *Reformed Confessions of the 16th Century* (Westminster, 1966); Williston Walker's *Creeds and Platforms of Congregationalism* (Pilgrim, 1969); and William L. Lumpkin's *Baptist Confessions of Faith* (Judson, 1959).

Religious statements for *American Religious Creeds* were compiled from a variety of sources located in the files of the Institute for the Study of American Religion, including sources gathered over the years directly from the religious groups. Other material was obtained through mailings during the compilation of material for production of the most recent edition of *The Encyclopedia of American Religions*.

Contents and Arrangement

American Religious Creeds comprises 23 chapters organized into three volumes. The first chapter covers the four ancient Christian creeds (acknowledged and used by a majority of existing Christian groups and not associated with one in particular). The remaining chapters cover the statements of the individual churches, religious bodies, and spiritual groups that constitute the major religious families operating in the United States and Canada. Material within each chapter is arranged alphabetically by name of religious group or church, not by name of creed. Some material has been rearranged to highlight those creeds and confessions serving an entire religious family or group of churches. In addition, statements that partially define religious families or subfamilies are placed at the beginning of the appropriate chapter or subchapter. (See the detailed contents pages preceding this Introduction for an overview of the arrangement of each of the chapters in this volume.)

Creeds presented in *American Religious Creeds* contain the following elements:

> *Creed Title.* The actual or descriptive title, followed by the name of the primary group related to the statement. (Where no formal title was given, a descriptive title was assigned.) Names of primary religious groups not contained in the creed's formal title are added parenthetically. (Other religious groups that acknowledge the particular statement are mentioned in the notes following the text.)

> *Text of Religious Creed.* The full text of the creed in its authentic form.

> *Notes.* These appear in italic type following the text of individual creeds. When applicable, these remarks provide data about the origin of the creed, call attention to particular ideas and emphases covered (or, in some cases, omitted) by the text, discuss variant readings of the text as used by different churches, and point out relationships to other religious statements. Also mentioned here are other religious groups that acknowledge the particular creed.

Name and Keyword Index Provided

To facilitate access to the material, *American Religious Creeds* contains a Creed/Organization Name and Keyword Index. This index lists, in a single alphabetic sequence, full titles of all the creeds presented in the volume as well as the names of all the religious traditions and individual churches mentioned in the text and notes. In addition, creed title and church name citations also appear in the index rotated by key word in title/name. Creed names appear in italic type to distinguish them from religious organizations. Citations refer users to the volume and page where the indexed creed or religious group appears.

Institute for the Study of American Religion

The Institute for the Study of American Religion was founded in 1969 for the purpose of researching and disseminating information about the numerous religious groups in the United States. More recently, the Institute's scope has been expanded to include religious groups in Canada, making it the only research facility of its kind to cover so broad a range of activity. After being located for many years in Evanston, Illinois, the Institute moved to Santa Barbara, California, in 1985. At that time, its collection of more than 25,000 books and its extensive files were donated to the Special Collections department of the library of the University of California—Santa Barbara.

Suggestions Are Welcome

Users of this volume with inquiries, additional information, corrections of inadvertent errors, or other suggestions for improvements are invited to write the Institute in care of its director. The Institute is particularly interested in obtaining copies of statements missing from this volume for inclusion in future editions.

Dr. J. Gordon Melton
Institute for the Study of American Religion
Box 90709
Santa Barbara, CA 93190-0709

AMERICAN RELIGIOUS CREEDS

CREEDS

VOLUME II

Chapter 1

Pentecostal Family

White Trinitarian Holiness Pentecostal

DOCTRINAL TEACHINGS [APOSTOLIC FAITH (KANSAS)]

TRINITY OF THE GOD-HEAD

(God the Father, Jesus Christ the Son, the Holy Ghost) "For there are THREE that bear record in heaven, the Father, the Word (Jesus) and the Holy Ghost: . . . " 1 John 5-7

REPENTANCE

(Act of Man) "Now after that John was put in prison, Jesus came into Galilee, preaching the gospel of the kingdom of God, And saying, The time is fulfilled, and the kingdom of God is at hand: REPENT YE, and believe the gospel." Mark 1:14-15

"The Lord is not slack concerning His promise, as some men count slackness; but is longsuffering to us-ward, not willing that any should perish, but that ALL SHOULD COME TO REPENTANCE." 2 Pet. 3:9

"REPENT YE therefore, and BE CONVERTED, that your sins may be blotted out, when the times of refreshing shall come from the presence of the Lord." Acts 3:19

CONVERSION

(Justification) (Act of God) ". . . Verily I say unto you, EXCEPT YE BE CONVERTED, and become as little children ye shall not enter into the kingdom of heaven." Matt. 18:3

"Be it known unto you therefore, men and brethren, that through this man (Jesus) is preached unto you the FORGIVENESS OF SINS: And by Him all that believe are JUSTIFIED from all things, from which we could not be justified by the law of Moses." Acts 13:38-39

"Therefore if any man be in Christ, he is a NEW CREATURE: old things are passed away, behold, all things are become new." 2 Cor. 5:17

CONSECRATION

(Act of Man) "I beseech you therefore, brethren, by the mercies of God, that YE PRESENT YOUR BODIES a living sacrifice, holy acceptable unto God, which is your reasonable service. And be not conformed to this world, but be ye transformed by the renewing of your mind, that ye may prove what is that good, and acceptable, and perfect will of God." Rom. 12:1-2

SANCTIFICATION

(Act of God) (a second, definite work of grace) "Wherefore Jesus also, that He might SANCTIFY the people with His own blood, suffered without the gate. Let us go forth therefore unto Him without the camp, bearing His reproach." Heb. 13:12-13

"Husbands, love your wives, even as Christ also loved the CHURCH, and gave Himself for it; That He might SANCTIFY and CLEANSE it with washing of the water by the word, that He might present it unto HIMSELF a glorious church, not having spot or wrinkle, or any such thing; but that it should be HOLY and without blemish. Eph. 5:25-27

"And the very God of peace SANCTIFY YOU WHOLLY; and I pray God, your WHOLE SPIRIT AND SOUL AND BODY be preserved blameless unto the coming of our Lord Jesus Christ." 1 Thes. 5:23

BAPTISM OF HOLY GHOST

"John answered, saying unto them all, I indeed baptize you with water; but one mightier than I cometh, the latchet of whose shoes I am not worthy to unloose: He shall BAPTIZE YOU WITH THE HOLY GHOST and with fire." Luke 3:16

"For John truly baptized with water; but ye shall be baptized with the Holy Ghost not many days hence." Acts 1:5

The EVIDENCE of the baptism of the Holy Ghost is the speaking with other tongues. (No fanaticism)

"And they were all filled with the Holy Ghost and began to speak with other tongues, as the spirit gave them utterance." Acts 2:4

"And they of the circumcision which believed were astonished, as many as came with Peter, because that on the Gentiles also was poured out the gift of the Holy

1

Ghost. For they heard them speak with tongues, and magnify God." Acts 10:45-46

DIVINE HEALING

"And Jesus went about all Galilee, teaching in their synagogues, and preaching the gospel of the kingdom, and HEALING ALL MANNER OF SICKNESS AND ALL MANNER OF DISEASES among the people." Matt. 4:23

"Who His own self (Jesus) bare our sins in His own body on the tree, that we, being dead to sins, should live unto righteousness: by whose stripes YE ARE HEALED." 1 Peter 2:24

"Is any sick among you? let him call for the elders of the church; and let them pray over him, annointing him with oil in the name of the Lord: And the prayer of faith shall save the sick and the Lord shall raise him up; and if he have committed sins, they shall be forgiven him. Confess your faults one to another, and pray one for another, that ye may be healed. The effectual fervent prayer of a righteous man availeth much." James 5:14-16

ORDINANCES

WATER BAPTISM (by immersion). "Go ye therefore, and teach all nations, baptizing them in the name of the Father, and of the Son, and of the Holy Ghost." Matt. 28:19

"Know ye not, that so many of us as were baptized into Jesus Christ were baptized into His death? Therefore we are buried with Him by baptism into death: that like as Christ was raised up from the dead by the glory of the Father, even so we also should walk in newness of life." Rom. 6:3-4

THE LORD'S SUPPER. "And as they were eating, Jesus took bread, and blessed it, and brake it, and gave it to the disciples, and said, Take, eat; this is my body. And He took the cup, and gave thanks, and gave it to them, saying, Drink ye all of it. For this is my blood of the new testament, which is shed for many for the remission of sins." Matt 26:26-28 (Read 1 Cor. 11:23-30)

FEET WASHING. "He (Jesus) riseth from supper, and laid aside His garments; and took a towel, and girded Himself, After that He poured water into a basin, and began to wash the disciples feet, and to wipe them with the towel wherewith He was girded . . . " "If I then, your Lord and Master, have washed your feet; ye also ought to wash one another's feet." John 13:4-5, 14

NO DIVORCE AND REMARRIAGE

"Whosoever putteth away his wife, and marrieth another, committeth adultery: and whosoever marrieth her that is put away from her husband committeth adultery." Luke 16-18

"The wife is bound by the law as long as her husband liveth; but if her husband be dead, she is at liberty to be married to whom she will; only in the Lord." 1 Cor. 7:39

SECOND COMING OF CHRIST

"And if I go and prepare a place for you, I WILL COME AGAIN, and receive you unto Myself; that where I am, there ye may be also." John 14:3

". . . Ye men of Galilee, why stand ye gazing into heaven? this same Jesus which is taken up from you into heaven, SHALL SO COME in like manner as ye have seen Him go into heaven." Acts 2:11

"And then shall appear the sign of the Son of man in heaven: and then shall all the tribes of the earth mourn, and they shall see the SON OF MAN COMING IN THE CLOUDS OF HEAVEN with power and great glory." Matt. 24:30

THOUSAND YEAR REIGN OF CHRIST

"And I saw thrones, and they sat upon them, and judgment was given unto them: and I saw the souls of them that were beheaded for the witness of Jesus — and they lived and REIGNED WITH CHRIST A THOUSAND YEARS." Rev. 20:4

"Blessed and holy is he that hath part in the first resurrection: on such the second death hath no power, but they shall be priests of God and of Christ and shall REIGN WITH HIM A THOUSAND YEARS." Rev. 20-6

CONDITIONAL IMMORTALITY

(Life through Christ) ". . . I am come that they might have LIFE, and that they might have it more abundantly." John 10:10

"And this is the record, that God has given to us ETERNAL LIFE, and this life IS IN HIS SON. HE THAT HATH THE SON HATH LIFE, and he that hath not the Son of God hath not life." 1 John 5:11-12

"To them who by patient continuance in well doing SEEK FOR glory and honor and IMMORTALITY, eternal life." Rom. 2:7

(Immortality is yet future. Read 1 Cor. 15:51-54)

DESTRUCTION OF THE WICKED

"Enter ye in at the strait gate: for wide is the gate, and broad is the way that leadeth to DESTRUCTION, and many there be which go in thereat: . . . " Matt. 7:13

. . . In flaming fire taking vengeance on them that know not God, and that obey not the gospel of our Lord Jesus Christ: who shall BE PUNISHED WITH EVERLASTING DESTRUCTION from the presence of the Lord, and from the glory of His power." 2 Thes. 1:7-9

"For the wages of sin is DEATH; but the gift of God is ETERNAL LIFE through Jesus Christ our Lord." Rom. 6:23

"For, behold, the day cometh, that shall burn as an oven; and all the proud, yea, all that do wickedly, shall be stubble: and the day that cometh shall BURN THEM UP, saith the Lord of hosts, that it shall LEAVE THEM NEITHER ROOT NOR BRANCH." Mal. 4:1

TITHES AND OFFERINGS

"Will a man rob God? Yet ye have robbed me. But ye say, Wherein have we robbed thee? In TITHES AND OFFER-

INGS. — Bring ye all the tithes into the storehouse, that there may be meat in mine house, and prove me herewith, saith the Lord of hosts, if I will not open you the windows of heaven, and pour you out a blessing, that there be not room enough to receive it." Mal. 3:8, 10.

"But woe unto you, Pharisees! for ye tithe mint and rue and all manner of herbs, and pass over judgment and the love of God: THESE OUGHT YE TO HAVE DONE, and not to leave the other undone." Luke 11:42.

Notes: The Pentecostal Movement arose in the early twentieth century simultaneously with fundamentalism. However, while the movement participated in the general conservative evangelical Christian world view, fundamentalists rejected pentecostals because of their holiness leanings and their doctrine of the baptism of the Holy Spirit. Pentecostals derived their beliefs directly and literally from the Bible, with little reference to the authority of Christian tradition. Hence the authority of the Bible became crucial to their theological position. Any doctrinal statements are considered, at best, summaries of the major Biblical teachings, and churches have consistently prefaced such statements with some affirmation of the authority of the Bible.

The crucial item found throughout the pentecostal statements is a belief in the baptism of the Holy Spirit. Most modern pentecostals believe that the believer's experience of baptism, like that which occurred at the first Christian Pentecost, is initially accompanied by the gift of speaking-in-tongues and followed by the emergence of other gifts (such as healing or prophecy).

The Holiness-Pentecostal Churches share a belief in three major experiences in the pilgrimage of the Christian life, each initiated by the action of the Holy Spirit in the individual's life. First, the sinner, by repentence of sin and faith in Christ, can be justified. Second, the Christian can be cleansed of inbred sin and made perfect in love, an experience termed santification. Third, the sanctified believer can be baptized in the Holy Spirit and begin to manifest the gifts of the spirit.

The Apostolic Faith derives from the original pentecostal work in Topeka, Kansas in 1901. Its doctrinal statement is primarily a compilation of texts from the Bible.

* * *

DOCTRINE (APOSTOLIC FAITH BIBLE COLLEGE)

It is recognized that the true church of Jesus Christ consists of all believers in the saving grace of our Lord and Saviour Jesus Christ who have accepted him as their personal Saviour. It is recognized and agreed that no organization or man has been granted authority by the Lord to exclude from or accept anyone into the Kingdom of Heaven, as this is done by Jesus Christ only. It is further recognized and agreed that we as Christians are to love all members of the Body of Christ (Christians), and this love and fellowship derives from the unity instilled by the Holy Spirit. Although differences in doctrinal beliefs and interpretations should not influence our love for one another,

adherence to similar doctrinal beliefs and modes of worship have bonded together those of the Apostolic Faith Movement as founded by Charles F. Parham in the early 1900's. The scripture teaches us to adhere to the truth and proper doctrine.

These common doctrinal beliefs are essentially as follows:

Triune God; Father, Son and Holy Spirit.

Creation and Formation.

Man is basically sinful and in need of Salvation.

Salvation by Grace upon repentance toward God and acceptance of Jesus Christ as one's personal Saviour, which is the conception of Spiritual Life.

Sanctification of the Spirit, Soul and Body. A second definite work of Grace by the Lord Jesus Christ.

Baptism of the Holy Spirit; evidenced by speaking in other languages.

Water Baptism (of all believers) by immersion in water in the name of the Father, and of the Son, and of the Holy Spirit.

Sacrament of the Lord's Supper.

Washing of Feet.

Divine Healing through Jesus Christ for all believers.

Do not condone divorce and remarriage. Matthew 19:8-9

Destruction of the Wicked.

Conditional Immortality.

Rapture of the Man Child Class.

Return of Jesus Christ to earth again; bodily and visibly.

A Ministry supported by tithes and offerings.

These basic doctrines shall be adhered to in the teaching of the Apostolic Faith Bible College, which in addition to other doctrinal teachings approved by the Board from time to time if they are not inconsistent with the above listed basic doctrines.

Notes: *This oldest school in the pentecostal movement has a statement in agreement with its sponsoring body, the Apostolic Faith (Kansas).*

* * *

BIBLE DOCTRINES (APOSTOLIC FAITH CHURCH)

THE DIVINE TRINITY. The Godhead consists of three Persons in one: the Father, the Son, and the Holy Ghost. These are separate and distinct Persons not merely three names for one Person. "For there are three that bear record in heaven, the Father, the Word, and the Holy Ghost: and these three are one" (I John 5:7). (See Matthew 3:16,17.)

REPENTANCE TOWARD GOD. Repentance is a godly sorrow for sin with a renunciation of sin. Isaiah 55:7; Mark 1:15; Acts 3:19; 20:21; II Corinthians 7:10

RESTITUTION. Restitution includes restoring where you have defrauded, stolen, or slandered; paying back debts,

**BIBLE DOCTRINES (APOSTOLIC FAITH
    CHURCH) (continued)**

and making confession. Leviticus 6:4; Ezekiel 33:15;
Matthew 5:23, 24; Luke 19:8,9

JUSTIFICATION AND REGENERATION. Justification is the act of God's grace whereby we receive remission
of sins and stand before God as though we had never
sinned. John 1:12,13; 3:3,16; II Corinthians 5:17

ENTIRE SANCTIFICATION (Holiness). Entire sanctification is the act of God's grace by which we are made
holy. It is the second, definite work wrought by the Blood
of Jesus through faith, and subsequent to salvation and
regeneration. Luke 1:74,75; John 17:15-17; II Corinthians
7:1; Ephesians 5:25-27

THE BAPTISM OF THE HOLY GHOST. The baptism
of the Holy Ghost is the enduement of power from on
High upon the clean, sanctified life. Matthew 3:11; Luke
24:49; John 7:38,39; 14:16,17,26; Acts 1:5-8

When we receive the gift of the Holy Ghost, it is
accompanied by the same sign as the disciples had on the
Day of Pentecost, viz., speaking with tongues as the Spirit
gives utterance. Mark 16:17; Acts 2:4; 10:45,46; 19:6; I
Corinthians 14:21,22

DIVINE HEALING. The healing of sickness and disease
is provided for God's people in the Atonement. "With his
stripes we are healed" (Isaiah 53:5). Matthew 8:17; Mark
16:18; Luke 13:16; Acts 10:38; James 5:14-16

THE SECOND COMING OF JESUS. The return of Jesus
will be just as literal and visible as His going away. John
14:3; Acts 1:9-11

There will be two appearances under one coming: first, to
catch away His waiting Bride. Matthew 24:40-44; I
Thessalonians 4:15-17; second, to execute judgment upon
the ungodly. Zechariah 14:3,4; II Thessalonians 1:7-10;
Jude 14,15

THE TRIBULATION. During the interim between
Christ's coming for His Bride and His return in judgment,
there is to be the Great Tribulation, or the time of Jacob's
trouble. Isaiah 26:20,21; Jeremiah 30:7; Daniel 12:1;
Matthew 24:21,22,29; Mark 13:19; Revelation 9 and 16

CHRIST'S MILLENNIAL REIGN. Christ's Millennial
Reign is the 1000 years' literal reign of Jesus on earth,
which will be ushered in by the coming of Jesus back to
earth with ten thousands of His saints. At this time He will
judge the nations that dwell upon the face of the earth. II
Thessalonians 1:7-10; Jude 14, 15

During this time the devil will be bound. Revelation 20:2-6

THE GREAT WHITE THRONE JUDGMENT. God
will finally judge the quick and the dead according to their
works. Daniel 12:2; Acts 10:42; Revelation 20:11-15

THE NEW HEAVEN AND THE NEW EARTH. The
Word teaches that this earth which has been polluted by
sin shall pass away after the White Throne Judgment, and
God will create a new heaven and a new earth in which
righteousness shall dwell. Isaiah 65:17; 66:22; II Peter
3:12,13; Revelation 21:1-3

ETERNAL HEAVEN AND ETERNAL HELL. The
Bible teaches that hell is as eternal as Heaven. Matthew
25:41-46. The wicked shall be cast into a burning hell, a
lake of fire burning with brimstone forever and ever. Mark
9:43,44; Luke 16:24; Revelations 14:10,11

NO DIVORCE AND REMARRIAGE. The Word
teaches that marriage is binding for life. Under the New
Testament law, the law of Christ, there is but one cause for
separation—fornication; and no right to marry again while
the first companion lives. Matthew 5:31,32; 19:3-9; Mark
10:11,12; Luke 16:18; Romans 7:2,3

WATER BAPTISM. One immersion (not three) "in the
name of the Father, and of the Son, and of the Holy
Ghost," as Jesus commanded. Matthew 28:19. Examples:
Matthew 3:16; Acts 8:38,39. Types: Romans 6:4,5; Colossians 2:12

THE LORD'S SUPPER. Jesus instituted the Lord's
Supper that we might "shew the Lord's death till he
come." I Corinthians 11:23-26; Matthew 26:26-29

WASHING THE DISCIPLES' FEET. Jesus said, "If I
then, your Lord and Master, have washed your feet; ye
also ought to wash one another's feet. For I have given you
an example, that ye should do as I have done to you." John
13:14,15

Notes: *The doctrinal statement of the Apostolic Faith
Church is an expansion of that of the Apostolic Faith
(Kansas), the original pentecostal organization. The statement commits the church to belief in divine healing,
premillennialism, and foot washing, and contains a specific
denial of triune immersion.*

*　　　*　　　*

**DECLARATION OF FAITH (AND RELATED
DOCUMENTS) [CHURCH OF GOD (CLEVELAND,
TENNESSEE)]**

DECLARATION OF FAITH

We believe:

1. In the verbal inspiration of the Bible.

2. In one God eternally existing in three persons;
    namely, the Father, Son, and Holy Ghost.

3. That Jesus Christ is the only begotten Son of the
    Father, conceived of the Holy Ghost, and born of the
    Virgin Mary. That Jesus was crucified, buried, and
    raised from the dead. That He ascended to heaven
    and is today at the right hand of the Father as the
    Intercessor.

4. That all have sinned and come short of the glory of
    God and that repentance is commanded of God for
    all and necessary for forgiveness of sins.

5. That justification, regeneration, and the new birth
    are wrought by faith in the blood of Jesus Christ.

6. In sanctification subsequent to the new birth,
    through faith in the blood of Christ; through the
    Word, and by the Holy Ghost.

7. Holiness to be God's standard of living for His
    people.

8. In the baptism with the Holy Ghost subsequent to a clean heart.

9. In speaking with other tongues as the Spirit gives utterance and that it is the initial evidence of the baptism of the Holy Ghost.

10. In water baptism by immersion and all who repent should be baptized in the name of the Father, and of the Son, and of the Holy Ghost.

11. Divine healing is provided for all in the atonement.

12. In the Lord's Supper and washing of the saints' feet.

13. In the premillennial second coming of Jesus. First, to resurrect the righteous dead and to catch away the living saints to Him in the air. Second, to reign on the earth a thousand years.

14. In the bodily resurrection; eternal life for the righteous, and eternal punishment for the wicked.

CHURCH OF GOD TEACHINGS

The Church of God stands for the whole Bible rightly divided. The New Testament is the only rule for government and discipline. Below are given some of the teachings that are made prominent:

1. Repentance. Mark 1:15; Luke 13:3; Acts 3:19.

2. Justification. Rom. 5:1; Titus 3:7.

3. Regeneration. Titus 3:5.

4. New birth. John 3:3; 1 Peter 1:23; 1 John 3:9.

5. Sanctification subsequent to justification. Rom. 5:2; 1 Cor. 1:30; 1 Thess. 4:3; Heb. 13:12.

6. Holiness. Luke 1:75; 1 Thess. 4:7; Heb. 12:14.

7. Water baptism. Matt. 28:19; Mark 1:9, 10; John 3:22, 23; Acts 8:36, 38.

8. Baptism with the Holy Ghost subsequent to cleansing; the enduement of power for service. Matt. 3:11; Luke 24:49, 53; Acts 1:4-8.

9. The speaking in tongues as the Spirit gives utterance as the initial evidence of the baptism of the Holy Ghost. John 15:26; Acts 2:4; 10:44-46; 19:1-7.

10. Spiritual gifts. 1 Cor. 12:1, 7, 10, 28, 31; 1 Cor. 14:1.

11. Signs following believers. Mark 16:17-20; Rom. 15:18, 19; Heb. 2:4.

12. Fruits of the Spirit. Rom. 6:22; Gal. 5:22, 23; Eph. 5:9; Phil. 1:11.

13. Divine healing provided for all in the atonement. Psa. 103:3; Isa. 53;4, 5; Matt. 8:17; Jas. 5:14-16; 1 Pet. 2:24.

14. The Lord's Supper. Luke 22:17-20; 1 Cor. 11:23-26.

15. Washing the saints' feet. John 13:4-17; 1 Tim. 5:9, 10.

16. Tithing and giving. Gen. 14:18-20; 28:20-22; Mal. 3:10; Luke 11:42; 1 Cor. 9:6-9; 16:2; Heb. 7:1-21.

17. Restitution where possible. Matt. 3:8; Luke 19:8.

18. Premillennial second coming of Jesus. First, to resurrect the dead saints and to catch away the living saints to Him in the air. 1 Cor. 15:52; 1 Thess. 4:15-17;2 Thess. 2:1. Second, to reign on the earth a thousand years. Zech. 14:4; 1 Thess. 4:14; 2 Thess. 1:7-10; Jude 14, 15; Rev. 5:10; 10:11-21; 20:4-6.

19. Resurrection. John 5:28, 29; Acts 24:15; Rev. 20:5, 6.

20. Eternal life for the righteous. Matt. 25:46; Luke 18:30; John 10:28; Rom. 6:22; 1 John 5:11-13.

21. Eternal punishment for the wicked. No liberation nor annihilation. Matt. 25:41-46; Mark 3:29; 2 Thess. 1:8, 9; Rev. 20:10-15; Rev. 21:8.

22. Total abstinence from all liquor or strong drinks. Prov. 20:1; 23:29-32; Isa. 28:7; 1 Cor. 5:11; 6:10; Gal. 5:21.

23. Against the use of tobacco in any form, opium, morphine, etc. Isa. 55:2; 1 Cor. 10:31, 32; 2 Cor. 7:1; Eph. 5:3-8; Jas. 1:21.

24. Meats and drinks. Rom. 14:2, 3, 17; 1 Cor. 8:8; 1 Tim. 4:1-5.

25. The Sabbath. Rom. 14:5, 6; Col. 2:16, 17; Rom. 13:1, 2.

26. Against members wearing jewelry for ornament or decoration, such as finger rings (this does not apply to wedding bands), bracelets, earrings, lockets, etc. 1 Tim. 2:9; 1 Pet. 3:3.—31st A., 1936, p. 34; Amended 47th A., 1958, p. 31.

27. Against members belonging to lodges. John 18:20; 2 Cor. 6:14-17.

28. Against members swearing. Matt. 5:34; Jas. 5:12.

29. Divorce and remarriage. Mat. 19:7-9; Mark 10:11, 12; Luke 16:18; 1 Cor. 7:2, 10, 11.—45th A., 1954, p. 29.

RESOLUTION RELATIVE TO PRINCIPLES OF HOLINESS OF CHURCH OF GOD

The foundation of the Church of God is laid upon the principles of Biblical holiness. Even before the Church experienced the outpouring of the Holy Ghost, its roots were set in the holiness revival of the past century. It was, and is, a holiness church—holiness in fact and holiness in name.

The passing of three-quarters of a century has not diminished our holiness position or convictions. The years have, instead, strengthened our knowledge that without holiness it is impossible to please God.

We, hereby, remind ourselves that the Scriptures enjoin us at all times to examine our own hearts. The continuing and consistent life of holiness require this. Conditions of our day desperately require it. The subtle encroachment of worldliness is a very real and unrelenting threat to the Church. We must therefore beware lest *we* become conformed to the world, or lest a love for the world take root in *our* hearts and manifest itself as lust of the flesh, lust of the eye, or the pride of life.

For these reasons, we present the following:

Whereas, the Church of God is historically a holiness church, and

Whereas, we are enjoined by the Scriptures to be so and

DECLARATION OF FAITH (AND RELATED DOCUMENTS)
[CHURCH OF GOD (CLEVELAND,
TENNESSEE)] (continued)

Whereas, a tide of worldliness threatens the spirituality of the Church,

Be it resolved that we, the Church of God, reaffirm our standard of holiness, in stated doctrine, in principles of conduct, and as a living reality in our hearts.

Be it further resolved that we, as ministers, maintain this standard in our own lives, in our homes, and in our pulpits

Be it further resolved that we, as ministers and members, rededicate ourselves to this purpose, and guard our lives against conformity to the world in appearance, in selfish ambition, in carnal attitudes, and in evil associations

Be it further resolved that we, as ministers and members, seek to conform to the positive virtues of love, mercy, and forgiveness as taught by Jesus Christ.

Notes: *The Church of God (Cleveland, Tennessee) is one of the older pentecostal bodies, having existed as a holiness church for several decades before the message of pentecost was brought from California to the mountains of Tennessee. The basic doctrinal statement is the church's Declaration of Faith. It is expanded upon by a second doctrinal item, Church of God Teachings, which offers scriptural references to the prominent teachings of the church. The Teachings also refer to specific matters not covered in the Declaration such as prohibitions on secret lodges, alcohol, tobacco, drugs, and jewelry (apart from wedding rings). A slightly modified form of this statement is also used by the Church of God (World Headquarters). A third item, the Holiness Resolution, expands the church's stance on holiness.*

*　　*　　*

DOCTRINE (CHURCH OF GOD, HOUSE OF PRAYER)

DOCTRINE

The apostles who preached Christ—not creed—gave the body of Christ its doctrine as they were inspired by the Holy Ghost, therefore, it shall be our purpose to continue in the apostles' doctrine and fellowship, "for we preach not ourselves, but Christ Jesus the Lord." Acts 2:42; 2 Cor. 4:5.

We believe the body of Christ should have unity on essentials, liberty on non-essentials, and charity toward all men.

We believe the Bible sets forth the following as being essential in our day. Acts 15:28.

THE BIBLE

We accept both divisions of the Bible as the inspired Word of God, but rely on the New Testament for church government and rule of Christian conduct. We believe the New Testament is God's last message spoken by His Son for the day and age in which we live, revealing the church with its gifts, graces, and government; therefore, the New Testament shall be our all-sufficient rule of faith and practice. Heb. 1:1, 2.

"Therefore leaving the principles of the doctrine of Christ, let us go on to perfection; not laying again the foundation of repentance from dead works, and of faith toward God, of the doctrine of baptisms, and of laying on of hands, and of resurrection of the dead, and of eternal judgment. And this will we do, if God permit." Heb. 6:1-3.

REPENTANCE

Repentance is impelled by godly sorrow and followed by restitution and conversion. It is the entrance into the way of salvation and there must be repentance before sins can be remitted. Mark 1:4; Luke 3:8; Acts 2:38; 3:19; 17:30; 26:20; 2 Cor. 7:10.

FAITH TOWARD GOD

REGENERATION. The Spiritual or new birth is made possible by the vicarious atonement and where there is no spiritual birth, there is no spiritual life.

We accept the teaching of Christ in His discourse to Nicodemus as fundamental, and rely on the fact that when a man is regenerated he is born of God, and made a new creature in Christ. St. John 3:1-8; Eph. 2:8; Gal. 6:15.

JUSTIFICATION. The Bible teaches that those who are born (Gr. begotten) of God doth not commit sin, therefore they are justified by faith in the blood of Jesus Who was "delivered for our offences, and was raised again for our justification." Acts 13:38, 39; Rom. 4:25, 5:9; 1 John 3:9.

SANCTIFICATION. All who have been born of God, and are justified by faith in the blood, may also be sanctified with the blood. Heb. 13:12. Regeneration or the "new birth" is the impartation of divine life; justification is the accounting of one just in the sight of God; sanctification is cleansing.

DIVINE HEALING BY FAITH. The atonement provides healing for the body and complete deliverance for those who are possessed with evil spirits. The gifts of healing and power over demons is transmitted to the church through Christ by the power of the Holy Ghost. Isaiah 53:4, 5; Matt. 8:17; Mark 16:18; James 5:14-16; 1 Peter 2:24.

LAYING ON OF HANDS

DIVINE HEALING BY LAYING ON OF HANDS. Concerning the believers, Jesus said: "They shall lay hands on the sick, and they shall recover." Mark 16:18; Acts 9:12.

BAPTISM WITH THE HOLY GHOST BY LAYING ON OF HANDS. In the great revival at Samaria the apostles, Peter and John, layed their hands on the believers and prayed for them to receive the Holy Ghost. Acts 8:17, 18. The apostle Paul did likewise on finding certain believers at Ephesus. Acts 19:6.

ORDINATION TO CHRISTIAN SERVICE BY LAYING ON OF HANDS. The apostles layed their hands on and prayed for the seven men who had been chosen to look after the church business in the early church. Acts 6:1-6.

Paul and Barnabas were ordained to go forth into the work to which the Holy Ghost had specifically called them. Acts 13:1-3.

Timothy's calling and work was recognized by the laying on of the hands of the presbytery. 1 Timothy 4:14.

RESURRECTION

There are two resurrections mentioned in the New Testament, the first, being the resurrection of life and the second, the resurrection of damnation. Saint Paul speaks of the resurrection from the dead which is proof that some will be raised from among the dead at the first resurrection, while others will remain in their graves until the second resurrection, which takes place at the close of the thousand years reign with Christ. John 5:28, 29; Acts 4:2; 24:15; Rom. 1:4; 1 Cor. 15:12-55; Rev. 20:5, 6, 13.

DOCTRINE OF BAPTISMS

BAPTISM WITH WATER. We accept immersion in the name of the Father, and of the Son, and of the Holy Ghost, as the scriptural mode of water baptism. Matt. 28:19; Mark 1:9, 10; Acts 8:36-39; 1 Peter 3:21.

BAPTISM WITH THE SPIRIT. Those who are sanctified may tarry for and receive the baptism of the Holy Ghost, which is the gift of power for service upon a sanctified life. Luke 24:49; Acts 1:8.

On the day of Pentecost when the first disciples were baptized with the Holy Ghost, God gave the sign of speaking with other tongues as the initial evidence. This sign also followed when the Holy Ghost fell on the Gentiles at the house of Cornelius, and is positive proof that the same spiritual baptism and the same evidence of said baptism is for both Jews and Gentiles. Matt. 3:11; Mark 16:17; Acts 1:5-8; 2:4; 10:44-46; 19:6.

CHRIST'S SECOND ADVENT. The Bible specifically announces the return of our Lord to this earth. John 14:1-3; Acts 1:11; Heb. 9:28. He will first descend into the air, where the saints will meet Him and be kept during the great tribulation period. 1 Thes. 4:14-17; Rev. 3:10; 4:1-5; 5:5-10. When the tribulation is past, He will come to earth with all the saints who meet Him in the air, and will reign with His people for one thousand years upon the earth. 2 Thes. 1:7-10; Rev. 1:7; 19:11-16; 20:6.

SACRAMENT. Jesus instituted the sacrament or Lord's Supper the same night in which He was betrayed of Judas Iscariot. Its purpose is to show the Lord's death until He comes again; therefore, all true believers should participate in the communion of the body and blood of Christ, the elements consisting of bread and the unfermented fruit of the vine. Unbelievers should not partake. The Communion should not be neglected, but should be observed often. We encourage believers to observe this ordinance quarterly, and especially the night preceding Good Friday of every year and as often as the churches decide to do so. Matt. 26:17-29; Luke 22:19, 20; 1 Cor. 10:16; 11:23-29.

FEET WASHING. Following the supper, Jesus poured water into a basin and washed the disciples' feet saying, "I have given you an example that ye should do as I have done unto you." This ordinance is also for believers and only believers should be invited to be present when it is observed. John 13:2-17; 1 Tim. 5:10.

ETERNAL JUDGMENT

The Bible plainly teaches that every man must stand before God to be judged. The righteous on that day shall go into life eternal and the unrighteous shall go away into everlasting punishment.

"For we must all appear before the judgment seat of Christ; that every one may receive the things done in his body, according to that he hath done, whether it be good or bad." 2 Cor. 5:10. See also Romans 2:2-11; Matt. 25:46; Rev. 20:11-15; 21:7, 8.

Approved this 18th day of August, 1963, at Markleysburg, Pennsylvania, U.S.A., by the General Assembly of the Church of God House of Prayer.

Notes: *This statement was adopted in 1963.*

* * *

ARTICLES OF FAITH [CHURCH OF GOD (JERUSALEM ACRES)]

1.   WE BELIEVE in the eternal existence of one God in three Persons—namely, God the Father (Yahweh), God the Son (Yahshua or Jesus), and God the Spirit (Ruach Hachodesh).

2.   WE BELIEVE in the eternal pre-existence of the Son of God as the Lamb slain from the foundation of the world and as the Creator of all things, both visible and invisible.

3.   WE BELIEVE that Jesus Christ was miraculously conceived of the Holy Spirit by the Virgin Mary and that He was both God and man—God in the sense of the ever-inherent divinity shown by His resurrection from the dead, and man in the sense that He voluntarily made Himself lower than the angels that He might suffer and taste death for every man.

4.   WE BELIEVE that Jesus Christ lived a sinless life, overcoming every temptation that is common to man; that He died on the cross to atone for the sins of all men; that He was buried on the day of Passover; that He was in the heart of the earth for three days and three nights; that at the end of the Sabbath He arose again; and that He ascended into heaven, to sit at the right hand of God as the only Mediator between God and man.

5.   WE BELIEVE that on the Day of Pentecost Jesus confirmed His High Priest ministry by filling the Church with the Holy Spirit, thereby giving them power for service.

6.   WE BELIEVE that the whole Bible is the inspired Word of God and that true doctrine for faith,

ARTICLES OF FAITH [CHURCH OF GOD (JERUSALEM ACRES)] (continued)

practice, government, and discipline must be determined from the New Testament, witnessed by the law and the prophets.

7. WE BELIEVE that God is the Author of one eternal religion set forth and systematized at Sinai by Moses, reformed and perfected at Calvary by Jesus Christ, believed and practiced by the New Testament Church, and restored and observed among the Gentiles by the last days' Church.

8. WE BELIEVE in the total brotherhood of the Christian community and in the higher calling of the Church which distinguishes it within the Kingdom of God.

9. WE BELIEVE that Jesus Christ came into the earth not only to die for man's sins but also to establish the Church of God according to the divine pattern.

10. WE BELIEVE that the Church was and is an organism for the fulfillment of prophecy and that prophecy is the primary witness and identification of the Church.

11. WE BELIEVE that Jesus established the theocratic order of government for the Church with one Anointed Leader, Twelve Apostles, Seventy Prophets, and Seven Men of Wisdom, and that this order is to be restored in the last days.

12. WE BELIEVE that all matters of doctrine and polity of the Church (called Apostles' Doctrine) have been and must be settled in the Council of Apostles and Elders, in which the Anointed Leader is the moderator and final authority.

13. WE BELIEVE that all men err and that Jesus Christ alone proved to be infallible; therefore, we do not equate verbal utterances (prophesying) with the written Word of God.

14. WE BELIEVE that both the Old and New Testaments predicted the apostasy of the early Church and that although the Kingdom of God continued through the Dark Ages, the Church as an organism ceased to exist in 325 A.D. with the uniting of Church and State.

15. WE BELIEVE that following the restoration of the fundamental doctrines of faith through the Protestant Reformation, The Church of God was resurrected from the Dark Ages according to prophecy in 1903, by A.J. Tomlinson.

16. WE BELIEVE in water baptism by immersion and in the seven spiritual baptisms—namely, the baptism of repentance (born again), the baptism of the blood (sanctification), the baptism of the Holy Spirit (speaking with tongues), the baptism of fire (zeal), the baptism into the Body of Christ (the covenant of church membership), the baptism of suffering, and the baptism of death.

17. WE BELIEVE in the full restoration of the gifts to individuals, both the nine gifts of the Spirit and the five gifts of the ministry.

18. WE BELIEVE in the New Testament observance of the seventh-day Sabbath and of the principal Feasts of the Lord, Passover (the Lord's Supper and washing the saints' feet), Pentecost, and Tabernacles.

19. WE BELIEVE that marriage is an institution of God and that no one has the right to divorce his companion and be remarried except for the cause of fornication (the act of adultery); however, we believe converts should remain in the state in which they are called.

20. WE BELIEVE that Israel will be fully restored, that their land (or inheritance) will be given to them as a nation, and that the remnant of Israel will be saved with an everlasting salvation.

21. WE BELIEVE that the Church will be supernaturally protected during the period of Great Tribulation (Indignation).

22. WE BELIEVE in the pre-millennial second-coming of Christ to establish His Kingdom in Jerusalem, Israel, where the resurrected and living saints will reign with Him for one thousand years.

23. WE BELIEVE in eternal life for the righteous and eternal punishment for the wicked.

24. WE BELIEVE that there will be a new heaven and a new earth after the Millennial Kingdom and that the righteous will inhabit the new earth forever.

Notes: *The Church of God headquartered at Jerusalem Acres (Cleveland, Tennessee) is one of a number of groups deriving from the Church of God (Cleveland, Tennessee). Its beliefs, however, differ in a number of respects from the other churches of that lineage. The influence of the Sacred Name Movement is evident in the use of the Hebrew transliterations of God's name (Yahweh) and Jesus's (Yahshua), in the church's sabbatarianism, and in the adoption of the Old Testament feasts. Among the church's unique beliefs is that of the seven spiritual baptisms.*

*   *   *

TWENTY-NINE IMPORTANT BIBLE TRUTHS (CHURCH OF GOD OF PROPHECY)

These twenty-nine vital points of New Testament doctrine are some of the prominent teachings of the Church of God of Prophecy. These teachings are all based on the Scripture; they were taught and practiced by the early Church; and they have been searched out in these last days by Godly men not concerned with their own opinions. However, the Church does not make a "hobby horse" of any one teaching or group of teachings, but accepts the whole Bible rightly divided with the New Testament as the only rule for government and discipline.

REPENTANCE. Repentance is both a condition and an act; it is the state of being in Godly sorrow for sins committed and the act of turning from and forsaking those sins. "For godly sorrow worketh repentance to salvation not to be repented of: but the sorrow of the world worketh death." 2 Corinthians 7:10. Also, read Mark 1:15; Luke 13:3; Acts 3:19. Repentance is a prerequisite for justification.

JUSTIFICATION. Justification is both a state and an act; it is the state of being void of offense toward God brought about by the act of God in forgiving actual transgressions for which one has repented. It is the result of repentance and faith. "Therefore being justified by faith, we have peace with God through our Lord Jesus Christ." Romans 5:1. Also, read Romans 5:2-9; Titus 3:7. Justification precedes regeneration.

REGENERATION. Regeneration is an act of God performed in the justified heart whereby new, spiritual life is generated. Man is dead in trespasses and sin through Adam; he must be quickened or regenerated through Christ. It is a vital part of the plan of salvation by faith. "Not by works of righteousness which we have done, but according to his mercy he saved us, by the washing of regeneration, and renewing of the Holy Ghost." Titus 3:5. Other Scriptures are Matthew 19:28; Ephesians 2:1, 4, 5. Regeneration is simultaneous with the new birth.

BORN AGAIN. To be born again is to become a new creature in Christ and a child of God. This new birth is the result of repentance, justification and regeneration. It is a definite and instantaneous experience wrought in the heart accompanied by a definite inner witness. There is no other way to enter the kingdom of God. (However, the new birth does not make one a member of the Church of God.) "Marvel not that I said unto thee, Ye must be born again." John 3:7. Read John 3:3-8; 1 Peter 1:23; 1 John 3:9; Romans 8:16; 1 John 3:14. The new birth is a prerequisite for the experience of sanctification.

SANCTIFICATION. Sanctification is the second definite work of grace, an instantaneous work wrought in the regenerated heart by the Holy Ghost with the blood of Christ. Whereas in regeneration actual transgressions are blotted out, in sanctification the Adamic nature, or inbred sin, is eradicated. "Wherefore Jesus also, that he might sanctify the people with his own blood, suffered without the gate. Let us go forth therefore unto him without the camp, bearing his reproach." Hebrews 13:12, 13. Read Romans 5:2; 1 Corinthians 1:30; 1 Thessalonians 4:3; 1 John 1:9. Sanctification restores man to the holy estate of Adam before the fall gives him the grace to live a life of holiness, and makes him eligible for the indwelling of the Holy Ghost.

HOLINESS. Holiness is the state of being free from sin, a condition made possible by the experience of sanctification. God requires man to live without sin in this present world and provided the means through the shed blood of Christ. "For the grace of God that bringeth salvation hath appeared to all men, Teaching us that, denying ungodliness and worldly lusts, we should live soberly, righteously, and godly, in this present world." Titus 2:11, 12. "Follow peace with all men, and holiness, without which no man shall see the Lord." Hebrews 12:14. Read Luke 1:74, 75; 1 Thessalonians 4:7; Ephesians 4:24; 1 Peter 1:15, 16. Holiness is a necessity not only for the individual but also for the Church, the body of Christ. Read Ephesians 1:4; 5:27; 2 Corinthians 7:1; Psalm 93:5.

WATER BAPTISM. Water baptism is the act of being immersed in water according to the commandment and instructions of Christ. This ordinance has no power to wash away sin but is the answer of a good conscience toward God, representing the death, burial and resurrection of Christ through which one has obtained new life. Only those who have already been born again are eligible for water baptism. "The like figure whereunto even baptism doth also now save us (not the putting away of the filth of the flesh, but the answer of a good conscience toward God,) by the resurrection of Jesus Christ." 1 Peter 3:21. Water baptism has divine approval only when it is done "in the name of the Father, and of the Son, and of the Holy Ghost." Read Matthew 28:19; Mark 1:8-10; John 3:22, 23; Acts 10:47, 48.

BAPTISM WITH THE HOLY GHOST. When a person is sanctified wholly he is eligible for the indwelling of the Holy Ghost. This indwelling is a definite and instantaneous experience described in the Scripture by the word "baptism," and always accompanied by the evidence of speaking in other tongues as the Spirit gives the utterance. It has no reference to water baptism, regeneration or sanctification. It is the filling of the temple already made clean by sanctification. It is not a work of grace but a gift of God in answer to the prayer of Christ. The baptism of the Holy Ghost is an enduement of power for service. "But ye shall receive power, after that the Holy Ghost is come upon you: and ye shall be witnesses unto me both in Jerusalem, and in all Judaea, and in Samaria, and unto the uttermost part of the earth." Acts 1:8. Read 1 Corinthians 3:16, 17.

SPEAKING IN TONGUES. Speaking in tongues as the Spirit gives utterance is the initial, physical evidence of the baptism of the Holy Ghost. No one ever receives the Holy Ghost without speaking in tongues. This is separate and distinct from the gift of tongues which is one of the nine gifts of the Spirit. "And they were ALL filled with the Holy Ghost, and began to speak with other tongues, as the Spirit gave them utterance." Acts 2:4. Also read John 15:26; Acts 10:44-46 and 19:6.

FULL RESTORATION OF THE GIFTS TO THE CHURCH. The nine gifts of the Spirit were set in the Church and are operated through individuals by the prompting of the Spirit. Since these gifts were given to the Church, they are subject to its government and cannot be taken away by any individual who leaves the Church. Although these gifts were lost when the Church went into the dark ages, they were fully restored to the Church when it arose out of darkness. 1 Corinthians 12:28, "And God hath set some in the church, first apostles, secondarily prophets, thirdly teachers, after that miracles, then gifts of healings, helps, governments, diversities of tongues." Read 1 Corinthians 12:1, 4-11; 1 Corinthians 14:1.

SIGNS FOLLOWING BELIEVERS. Miraculous signs and wonders will accompany the work and ministry of true believers. These signs are recorded in Mark 16:17-20, "And these signs shall follow them that believe; In my name shall they cast out devils; they shall speak with new tongues; They shall take up serpents; and if they drink any deadly thing, it shall not hurt them; they shall lay hands on the sick, and they shall recover . . . And they went forth, and preached everywhere, the Lord working with

TWENTY-NINE IMPORTANT BIBLE TRUTHS (CHURCH OF
GOD OF PROPHECY) (continued)

them, and confirming the word with signs following.
Amen." Also read Romans 15:18, 19; Hebrews 2:4.

FRUIT OF THE SPIRIT. The Spirit-filled life will
manifest the fruit of the Spirit. Galatians 5:22, 23, "But the
fruit of the Spirit is love, joy, peace, longsuffering,
gentleness, goodness, faith, Meekness, temperance: against
such there is no law." These virtues cannot be manifested
by the flesh or by human nature. They are divine in origin
and must spring from a Spirit-filled heart. Read Romans
6:22; Ephesians 5:9; Philippians 1:11.

DIVINE HEALING. Christ's atoning sacrifice on the
cross provided not only for the salvation of the souls of
men but also for the healing of man's physical ailments.
Psalm 103:2, 3, "Bless the Lord, O my soul, and forget not
all his benefits: Who forgiveth all thine iniquities; who
healeth all thy diseases." Divine healing is healing accomplished by the power of God without the aid of medicine
or surgical skills. This healing virtue is available to all who
believe, the same as salvation. Read also Isaiah 53:4, 5;
Matthew 8:17; James 5:14-16; 1 Peter 2:24.

THE LORD'S SUPPER. The Lord's Supper was instituted by Christ and is a sacred ordinance which we are
commanded to observe. The Supper consists of unleavened
bread, which represents His body broken on the cross for
our sins, and the wine (unfermented grape juice), which
represents the blood of Christ shed for our sanctification.
This ordinance is observed in commemoration of Christ
and His death. Only sinless and consecrated Christians are
eligible to partake of this Supper. Read Luke 22:17-20; 1
Corinthians 11:23-33.

WASHING THE SAINTS' FEET. Feet washing was
instituted by Jesus on the night of the Last Supper and is a
New Testament ordinance we are enjoined to observe—as
much so as communion. Its observance was taught by the
apostles and practiced by the early Church. Charity and
good works do not fulfill this obligation. "If I then, your
Lord and Master, have washed your feet; ye also ought to
wash one another's feet." John 13:14. Read John 13:4-17; 1
Timothy 5:10.

TITHING AND GIVING. Tithing is the paying of one
tenth of our increase into the treasury of the Church. It
began with Abraham, continued under the law and
received Christ's approval. "Woe unto you, scribes and
Pharisees, hypocrites! for ye pay tithe of mint and anise
and cummin, and have omitted the weightier matters of
the law, judgment, mercy, and faith: these ought ye to have
done, and not to leave the other undone." Matthew 23:23.
The obligation for tithing is not fulfilled by giving ten
percent to the poor or to some good cause but only by
paying it into the Church treasury.

Giving differs from and is in addition to tithing. Both are
parts of God's plan to finance His work on earth. Read
Genesis 14:18-20; Malachi 3:10; Luke 11:42; 1 Corinthians
16:2; 2 Corinthians 9:6-9; Hebrews 7:1-21.

RESTITUTION WHERE POSSIBLE. Restitution is the
act of restoring something wrongfully taken or the
satisfying of one who has been wronged. God requires

those who become converted to perform such tasks if at all
possible. "And Zacchaeus stood, and said unto the Lord;
Behold, Lord, the half of my goods I give to the poor; and
if I have taken any thing from any man by false accusation,
I restore him fourfold. And Jesus said unto him, This day
is salvation come to this house, forsomuch as he also is a
son of Abraham." Luke 19:8, 9. Read Matthew 3:8;
Romans 13:8.

PRE-MILLENNIAL SECOND COMING OF JESUS.
Christ is coming back to earth again. First, to resurrect the
dead saints and to catch away the living saints to meet
Him in the air, where they will attend the marriage supper
of the Lamb. "For the Lord himself shall descend from
heaven with a shout, with the voice of the archangel, and
with the trump of God: and the dead in Christ shall rise
first: Then we which are alive and remain shall be caught
up together with them in the clouds, to meet the Lord in
the air: and so shall we ever be with the Lord." 1
Thessalonians 4:16, 17. Read Matthew 24:27, 28; 1
Corinthians 15:51, 52.

Second, to return with the saints to reign on earth a
thousand years. ". . . And they lived and reigned with
Christ a thousand years. But the rest of the dead lived not
again until the thousand years were finished. This is the
first resurrection." Revelation 20:4, 5. Read Zechariah
14:4, 5; Luke 1:32; 1 Thessalonians 4:14; 2 Thessalonians
1:7-10; Jude 14, 15; Revelation 5:10; 19:11-21.

RESURRECTION. All the dead, both righteous and
wicked, will be resurrected. The righteous dead will be
raised in the first resurrection which is at Christ's
appearing. The resurrection of the wicked dead will occur
after the thousand years reign of Christ on earth. "And
have hope toward God, which they themselves also allow,
that there shall be a resurrection of the dead, both of the
just and unjust." Acts 24:15. Read Daniel 12:2; John 5:28,
29; 1 Corinthians 15:12-23; 41-58; Revelation 20:5, 6.

ETERNAL LIFE FOR THE RIGHTEOUS. Those who
die in the Lord and those who are serving Him when He
returns will receive a reward of eternal life—eternal
happiness in the presence of the Lord. "And these shall go
away into everlasting punishment: but the righteous into
life eternal." Matthew 25:46. Read Luke 18:30; John
10:28; Romans 6:22; 1 John 5:11-13.

ETERNAL PUNISHMENT FOR THE WICKED. Our
life in this present world determines our eternal reward.
The unconverted and the wicked are doomed to eternal
punishment, from which there is no escape—no liberation
or annihilation. "And these shall go away into everlasting
punishment: but the righteous into life eternal." Matthew
25:46. Read Mark 3:29; 2 Thessalonians 1:8, 9; Revelation
20:10-15; 21:8.

TOTAL ABSTINENCE FROM LIQUOR OR STRONG
DRINK. The Bible expressly forbids the use of intoxicating beverages. Even slight indulgence is sinful and not in
keeping with Scriptural standards of holiness. "Wine is a
mocker, strong drink is raging: and whosoever is deceived
thereby is not wise." Proverbs 20:1. Read also Isaiah 28:7;
1 Corinthians 5:11; 6:10; Galatians 5:21.

AGAINST USE OF TOBACCO, OPIUM, MORPHINE, ETC. The use of tobacco in any form is forbidden as well as the habitual use of narcotics. These sinful practices defile the body, the temple of the Holy Ghost, and are outward evidence of an impure heart. "Having therefore these promises, dearly beloved, let us cleanse ourselves from all filthiness of the flesh and spirit, perfecting holiness in the fear of God." 2 Corinthians 7:1. Read Isaiah 55:2; 1 Corinthians 10:31, 32; Ephesians 5:3-8; James 1:21.

ON MEATS AND DRINKS. The New Testament makes no rigid rule concerning what the Christian shall eat or drink (with the exception of strong drink). Thus, we have no right to judge what our brother eats or what he drinks. The legal restrictions of Jewish law concerning these were not extended into the Grace Dispensation. "For the kingdom of God is not meat and drink; but righteousness, and peace, and joy in the Holy Ghost." Romans 14:17. Read Romans 14:2, 3; 1 Corinthians 8:8; 1 Timothy 4:1-5.

ON THE SABBATH. The observance of the Sabbath was a requirement of Jewish law and as such was not carried over into the Grace Dispensation. Sunday is not the Sabbath but is merely a day set aside to give special attention to the worship of God. Instead of keeping only the Sabbath day holy, we are required in this dispensation to keep every day holy. The Jewish Sabbath is a type of Christ, who is our rest, rather than the day. "Let no man therefore judge you in meat, or in drink, or in respect of an holyday, or of the new moon, or of the sabbath days: Which are a shadow of things to come; but the body is of Christ." Colossians 2:16, 17. Read Hosea 2:11; Romans 13:1, 2; Romans 14:5, 6; Hebrews 4:1-11.

AGAINST WEARING GOLD FOR ORNAMENT. Ornaments of gold or other precious metals are a useless and frivolous waste of money, for they do not benefit the wearer either physically or spiritually. For this reason, and because they are evidences of a prideful heart, they are unbecoming to a child of God. Isaiah 55:2, "Wherefore do ye spend money for that which is not bread? and your labour for that which satisfieth not? hearken diligently unto me, and eat ye that which is good, and let your soul delight itself in fatness." Read 1 Timothy 2:9; 1 Peter 3:3; 1 John 2:16.

AGAINST BELONGING TO LODGES. The Bible is opposed to the people of God being unequally yoked together with unbelievers; it is opposed to deeds done in secret; and it demands the complete and undivided loyalty of God's children. John 18:20, "Jesus answered him, I spake openly to the world; I ever taught in the synagogue, and in the temple, whither the Jews always resort; and in secret have I said nothing." Read 2 Corinthians 6:14-17; Ephesians 5:12, 13; 2 Corinthians 11:2. Also many secret societies require the taking of an oath which is expressly forbidden by Scripture. (See next paragraph.)

AGAINST SWEARING. The taking of an oath is a vain thing and condemned by the Scripture. An affirmation to the truth of anything is sufficient. Matthew 5:34, "But I say unto you, Swear not at all; neither by heaven; for it is God's throne." Also, the use of profanity is forbidden. Read Exodus 20:7; James 5:12.

AGAINST DIVORCE AND REMARRIAGE EVIL. Divorce and remarriage constitute the sin of adultery. Matthew 5:32, "But I say unto you, That whosoever shall put away his wife, saving for the cause of fornication, causeth her to commit adultery: and whosoever shall marry her that is divorced commiteth adultery." The only allowable causes for remarriage are fornication and death. However, fornication is not unfaithfulness or simple adultery, but is a state of being married to another's wife or husband. 1 Corinthians 7:2, "Nevertheless, to avoid fornication, let every man have his own wife, and let every woman have her own husband." Read Romans 7:2, 3; 1 Corinthians 5:1-5, 13; 1 Corinthians 6:16-18; Revelation 2:22.

Notes: *The Church of God of Prophecy continues in the lineage of the Church of God as established in Cleveland, Tennessee by A.J. Tomlinson, who split with the group now referred to as the Church of God (Cleveland, Tennessee). There is no difference of doctrinal position between the two bodies. However, the Church of God of Prophecy has prepared its own presentation of the prime teachings. In summarizing its teachings, the Church of God of Prophecy emphasizes that it accepts the whole Bible as the Word of God. New members assume an obligation by affirmatively answering a question: "Will you sincerely promise in the presence of God and these witnesses that you will accept the Bible as the Word of God—believe and practice its teachings rightly divided—the New Testament as your rule of faith and practice, government and discipline, and walk in the light to the best of your knowledge and ability?" Thus, this statement of twenty-nine items is considered not a creed, but a presentation of prominent Biblical teachings.*

As with the Church of God (Cleveland, Tennessee), there is an acceptance of divine healing, premillennialism, and foot washing, and a rejection of secret lodges, intoxicating drinks, tobacco, narcotics, and jewelry (the exception clause for wedding rings does not appear).

*   *   *

TEACHINGS (CHURCH OF GOD OF THE MOUNTAIN ASSEMBLY)

Regeneration—St. John 3:3-8.

Water Baptism—By immersion in the name of the Father, and of the Son, and of the Holy Ghost.—St. Matt. 28:19; Rom. 6:4.

Sanctification—Following regeneration—St. John 17:17; I Cor. 1:30 I Cor. 5:11; Eph. 5:26; Heb. 10:20, 13:12.

Baptism of the Holy Ghost—Following sanctification, with the Bible evidence of speaking in tongues. St. John 15:26: Acts 2:4; 10:44-47.

Holiness—St. Luke 1:74-75; Heb. 12:14.

Fruit of the Spirit—Gal. 5:22-23.

Spiritual Gifts of the Church—I Cor. 12:8-10.

Signs following the Believers—St. Mark 16:17-18.

Divine Healing—St. Mark 16:18; I Cor. 12:9; James 5:14.

The Lord's Supper—I Cor. 11:23-24.

TEACHINGS (CHURCH OF GOD OF THE MOUNTAIN
ASSEMBLY) (continued)

Washing the Saints' Feet—St. John 13:4-17.

Tithing and Giving—Gen. 14:20, 28:22; Mal. 3:10; I Cor.
16:2; II Cor. 8:11-15; Gal. 6:6.

Restitution When Possible—St. Luke 19-8.

Thousand Year Reign with Christ—Rev. 20:4.

Resurrection of the Dead—St. John 5:28-29; I Cor. 15.

Eternal Life for the Righteous—St. Matt. 25-46; Rom
6:22.

Eternal Punishment for the Wicked—St. Matt. 25:41; Rev.
14:10-11.

Total Abstinence from Strong Drink—Pr. 20:1; Gal. 5:21.

Keeping the Sabbath Day Holy—Ex. 20:8.

Against Pride—Wearing of gold for decoration, such as
finger rings, bracelets, lockets, etc.—Pr. 16:18; I Pet. 3:3; I
John 2:15-16.

Against Uncleanness—(This includes the use of tobacco in
any form.)—II Cor. 7:1; James 1:21.

Against Women Members Cutting Their Hair—I Cor.
11:5-15.

Against Swearing—St. Matt. 5:34; James 5:12.

Modesty Is Required of the Sisters of the Church—I Tim.
2:9-10; I Pet. 3:3-5.

Against Going to War and Killing—Ex. 20-13; St. Luke
3:14; St. John 18:36; St. Luke 18-20.

Against Infants Being Taken into the Church—All children under twelve years of age are under question by the
Church.

The New Testament Is Our Creed and Teachings—And
we further believe all scripture as being given by inspiration of God, is profitable for doctrine, for reproof, for
correction, and for instruction in righteousness.—2 Tim.
3:16.

We Prefer the King James Version of the Bible—and
therefore advise our members to use this version.

Notes: *These teachings derive directly from the Church of
God Teachings of the Church of God (Cleveland, Tennessee); however, there have been a number of additions and
deletions. Additions include statements on pacifism, women
cutting their hair, and the preference for the King James
Version of the Bible. Deletions include the prohibition on
secret lodges.*

* * *

COVENANT AND BIBLE DOCTRINE (CHURCH OF GOD OF THE UNION ASSEMBLY)

FIRST—REPENTANCE. For you to repent you must be
sorry enough to quit the things that are wrong. II Cor. 7
ch., 9 and 10 verses; Jonah 3 ch., 8-10 verses; Matt. 3 ch., 2
verse; Mark 1 ch., 15 verse; Luke 24 ch., 47 verse; Acts 2
ch., 38 verse. Goodness of God leadeth to repentance—
Rom. 2 ch., 4 verse. Repentance toward God, Acts 20 ch.,
21 verse.

SECOND—WATER BAPTISM BY IMMERSION.
Matt. 3 ch., 13 through 17 verses; Mark 16 ch., 16 verse;
Rom. 6 ch., 4 and 5 verses; Col. 2 ch., 11 thru 13 verses.

THIRD—JUSTIFICATION BY FAITH IN JESUS
CHRIST. Rom. 5 ch., 1 and 9 verses; Titus 3 ch., 7 verse;
Rom. 3 ch., 25 and 26 verses; Acts 13 ch., 39 verse.

FOURTH—SANCTIFICATION THROUGH THE
BLOOD. St. John 17 ch., 17 and 19 verses; Eph. 5 ch., 25
and 26 verses; I Thess. 4 ch., 3 verses; Heb. 2 ch., 11 verse;
Heb. 13 ch., 12 verse.

FIFTH—BAPTISM OF THE HOLY GHOST. Matt. 3
ch., verse 11; Luke 24 ch., 49 verse; St. John 7 ch., 37 thru
39 verses; St. John 14 ch., 16 and 26 verses.

SIXTH—EVIDENCE THAT YOU HAVE RECEIVED
THE HOLY GHOST IS STAMMERING LIPS AND
OTHER TONGUES. FRUIT OF THE SPIRIT. Gal. 5
ch., 22 to 24 verses; Isaiah 28 ch., 11 and 12 verses; I Cor.
14 ch., 21 verse; Acts 2 ch., 4 verse; Acts 10 ch., 46 and 47
verses; Acts 19 ch., 6 verse.

SEVENTH—LORD'S SUPPER. Matt. 26 ch., 26 thru 30
verses; Luke 22 ch., 17 and 20 verses; I Cor. 11 ch., 23 thru
26 verses; I Cor. 5 ch., 7 and 8 verses.

EIGHTH—FEET WASHING. St. John 13 ch., 4 thru 17
verse; I Tim. 5 ch., 9 and 10 verses; I Peter 2 ch., 21 verse.

NINTH—HEALING OF THE BODY. Mark 6 ch., 13
verse; Mark 16 ch., 18 verse; James 5 ch., 14 and 15 verses.

FOR MEMBERS WHO ARE SOLDIERS

All members are forbidden to take up arms and go to
war.

The nature of our belief is as follows:

The Word of God said "Thou Shalt Not Kill." Mark 10
ch., 17 thru 19 verses reads "And when he was gone forth
into the way, there came one running, and kneeled to him,
and asked him, Good Master, what shall I do that I may
inherit eternal life?

"And Jesus said unto him, Why callest thou me good?
There is none good but one, that is, God.

"Thou knowest the commandments, Do not commit
adultery, Do not kill, Do not steal, Do not bear false
witness, Defraud not, Honor they father and mother."

WHY WE DON'T BELIEVE IN KILLING. Mark 3 ch.,
4 verse reads "And he saith unto them, Is it lawful to do
good on the sabbath days, or to do evil? to save life or to
kill? But they held their peace."

James 2 ch., 11 thru 13 verses reads "For he that said, Do
not commit adultery, said also, Do not kill. Now if thou
commit no adultery, yet if thou kill, thou art become a
transgressor of the law."

"So speak ye, and so do, as they that shall be judged by the
law of liberty."

"For he shall have judgment without mercy, that hath
shewed no mercy, and mercy rejoiceth against judgment."

Matthew 26 ch., 51 and 52 verses reads "And, behold, one
of them which were with Jesus stretched out his hand, and
drew his sword, and struck a servant of the high priest's
and smote off his ear.

"Then said Jesus unto him, Put up again thy sword into his place: for all they that take the sword shall perish with the sword."

II Cor. 10 ch., 3 and 4 verses reads "For though we walk in the flesh, we do not war after the flesh:

"For the weapons of our warfare are not carnal, but mighty through God to the pulling down of strong holds."

Romans 12 ch., 17 thru 21 verses reads "Recompence to no man evil for evil. Provide things honest in the sight of all men.

"If it be possible, as much as lieth in you, live peaceably with all men.

"Dearly beloved, avenge not yourselves, but rather give place unto wrath: for it is written, Vengeance is mine; I will repay, saith the Lord.

"Therefore if thine enemy hunger, feed him; if he thirst, give him drink: for in so doing thou shalt heap coals of fire on his head.

"Be not overcome of evil, but overcome evil with good."

I Thess. 5 ch., verse 15 reads, "See that none render evil for evil unto any man; but ever follow that which is good both among yourselves, and to all men."

HOW WE WILL SERVE AS A SOLDIER FOR OUR COUNTRY. We will proudly serve our country in any way we can except doing violence to any man. We don't believe in being forced to do anything contrary to our God and our conscience. Some of our boys have been man-handled, held by Sergeants and others, and forced to take shots, vaccinations and medicine contrary to Rule 23 set forth in the Minutes of this Church and Assembly.

We are not trying to change the Army. We ask them not to try to change us. We ask no special favor but to be treated as other Americans. We are proud to go to the battle fronts and help the wounded and be of service in any other way that is not contrary to our conscience and belief as set forth in the above.

Luke 3 ch.—13 and 14 verses reads "And he said unto them, Exact no more than that which is appointed you.

"And the soldiers likewise demanded of him saying, And what shall we do. And he said unto them, Do violence to no man, neither accuse any falsely; and be content with your wages."

If we can be a soldier under these conditions, we will proudly do so.

Rule 23 of the General Rules of this Minute

All members of the Church are forbidden to use medicine, vaccinations or shots of any kind but are taught by the Church to live by faith. However, new members who have recently taken up fellowship with the Church or future members will be given time to grow in the faith until they attain to the teaching of the Church of God of the Union Assembly as found in James 5 ch.—13 thru 15 verses. "Is any among you afflicted? let him pray. Is any merry? let him sing psalms.

"Is any sick among you? let him call for the elders of the church; and let them pray over him, annointing him with oil in the name of the Lord:

"And the prayer of faith shall save the sick, and the Lord shall raise him up; and if he have committed sins, they shall be forgiven him."

Romans 14 ch., 1 verse reads "Him that is weak in faith receive ye, but not to doubtful disputations."

Notes: *The Covenant of the Church of God of the Union Assembly is a statement binding upon all pastoral leaders (ministers and evangelists) of the church. The brief summary of nine important biblical teachings introduces a more complete exposition of the church's teachings on a wide variety of matters. In general, the church follows the teachings of the Church of God of the Mountain Assembly and has produced a lengthy statement against war and killing. It has also added a statement on its controversial position against the use of medicine.*

* * *

ADDITION TO THE TWENTY-NINE IMPORTANT BIBLE TRUTHS [CHURCH OF GOD (WORLD HEADQUARTERS)]

30. The Kingdom of God on Earth as it is in Heaven—Matt. 6:10; Matt. 6:28-34; Mark 1:14-15; Luke 4:43; Luke 12-31-32; Luke 16:16; Luke 22:29; Matt. 13th Chapter; Daniel 2:44; Daniel 7:27; Rev. 11:15; Matt. 21:43.

Notes: *This branch of the Church of God movement follows the Church of God Teachings adopted by the Church of God (Cleveland, Tennessee). To these teachings, however, it has added a thirtieth statement on the Kingdom of God, which is reproduced here. For a more complete exposition of this branch's unique emphases, see* The Book of Doctrines, 1903-1970 *(Huntsville, AL: Church of God Publishing House, 1970).*

* * *

WE BELIEVE (CONGREGATIONAL HOLINESS CHURCH)

There is but one living and true God, the great Creator, and there are three persons in the Godhead: the Father, the Son and the Holy Ghost. Genesis 1:1-27; Matthew 28:19; I John 5:7.

The Holy Bible to be the inspired Word of God. 2 Timothy 3:16; 2 Peter 1:20, 21.

We are justified when we repent of our sins and believe in Jesus Christ. Mark 1:5; Acts 13:38, 39; Romans 5:1.

Sanctification to be a definite work of grace subsequent to salvation. St. John 15:2; 17:16, 17; Ephesians 5:25-27; 1 John 1:9.

In the baptism with the Holy Ghost, and speaking with other tongues as the Spirit gives utterance to be the initiatory evidence of this experience. Acts 2:4; 19:6; 10:44-46.

In divine healing for the body. Acts 3:2-12; 9:32-43; 5:15, 16; James 5:14. We do not condemn medical science.

Every blessing we receive from God, including divine healing, comes through the merits of the atonement. Romans 5:11; James 1:16, 17.

13

In the operation of the nine Gifts of the Spirit and encourage our people to so live that these gifts may be manifest in their lives. 1 Corinthians 12:1-12.

Notes: *These brief statements of belief are derived from the Articles of Faith of the International Pentecostal Holiness Church, from which the Congregational Holiness Church derived.*

* * *

COVENANT, BASIS OF UNION, AND ARTICLES OF FAITH (EMMANUEL HOLINESS CHURCH)

COVENANT

We, having been called out of the world by the blessed spirit of God, and accepted the Lord Jesus Christ as our Saviour and Preserver, and become acquainted with the articles of faith and policy of the Emmanuel Holiness Church, and believing it to be of God, we do solemnly, but cheerfully and with joy and gladness enter into this covenant with you. We will watch over each other and walk together in brotherly love and kindness, sharing each other's joys and sorrows, praying for ourselves and others. Not forsake the assembling of ourselves together as the manner of some is. Endeavoring to bring up those under our care in the nurture and admonition of the Lord.

We will minister to each other in sickness and affliction, in distress and imprisonment, in poverty and want.

Never speak of anyone as we would not have them speak of us. Defend one another in things that are right. Bearing one anothers burdens, prefer one another in honor, affiliate with no party nor faction in the measures of evil. Strive in all things to exemplify our profession by corresponding practice.

We will abstain from all sinful conformity to the world and be just in all our dealings, and endeavor to pay all our debts, be exemplary in all deportment, having family worship in our homes, and offering thanks for our daily food.

We will contribute cheerfully, according to our ability to the support of the ministry, the expense of the church, the relief of the poor, and the general spread of the gospel. And will sustain the worship, ordinance, discipline, and the doctrines of this church. In keeping this solemn covenant may we ever enjoy the blessings and presence of the Lord and the fellowship of the saints.

CHAPTER II. BASIS OF UNION

Art. 1. We believe that Jesus Christ shed His blood for the remission of sins that are past; and for the regeneration of penitent sinners, and for salvation from sin, and from sinning. (Rom. 3:25, I John 3:5-10, Eph. 2:1-10.)

Art. 2. We believe, teach and firmly maintain the scriptural doctrine of justification by faith alone. (Rom. 5:1.)

Art. 3. We believe also that Jesus Christ shed His blood for the complete cleansing of the justified believer from all indwelling sin and from its pollution. Subsequent to regeneration. (I John 1:7-9.)

Art. 4. We believe also that entire sanctification is an instantaneous, definite, second work of grace, obtainable by faith on the part of the fully justified believer. (John 15:2, Acts 26:18, II Cor. 1:15, Luke 24:30-33, 50-53, John 17, I Thes. 5:16-23.)

Art. 5. We believe also that the Pentecostal Baptism of the Holy Ghost and fire is obtainable by a definite act of appropriating faith on the part of the fully cleansed believer, and that the initial evidence of the reception of this experience is speaking with other tongues as the spirit gives utterance. (Luke 11:13, Acts 1-5, Acts 2:1-4, Acts 8:17, Acts 10:44-46, Acts 19:6).

Art. 6. We believe also in divine healing as in the atonement. (Isaiah 53:4-5, Matt. 8:16-17, Mark 16:14-18, Jas. 5:14-16, I Peter 2:24.)

Art. 7. We believe in the imminent, personal, premillennial second coming of our Lord Jesus Christ. (I Thes. 4:15-18, Titus 2:13, II Peter 3:1-4, Matt. 24:29-44) and we love and wait for His appearing. (II Tim. 4:8.)

Art. 8. We forbid that our members participate in actual combat service, in taking of arms in war, if their conviction is objective.

Art. 9. The Emmanuel Holiness Church is utterly opposed to the teachings of the so-called Christian Scientists, Spiritualists, Unitarians, Universalists and Mormons. We deny as false and unscriptural Seventh Day Adventism, Annihilation of the wicked, conditional immortality, and antinomianism, absolute perfection, so-called comeoutism, the so-called resurrection in this life, the redemption or glorification of the body in this life, the doctrine of the restitution of all things (as set forth in the millennial-dawnism), and the teaching that we are not born of God until we are sanctified wholly.

Art. 10. No subsequent General Assembly shall have the authority to change the Basis of Union without a full representation of the General officers, elder body and its ministerial members and one lay delegate from each local church present at its General Assembly.

CHAPTER III. ARTICLES OF FAITH

Art. 1. We believe there is but one living and true God, everlasting, of infinite power, wisdom and goodness; Maker and preserver of all things, both visible and invisible. And in the unity of this Godhead, there are three persons of one substance, of eternal beings, and equal in holiness, justice, wisdom, power and dignity; the Father, the Son, and the Holy Ghost.

Art. 2. We believe that the Son, who is the word of the Father, the very and eternal God, of one substance with the Father, took Man's nature in the womb of the blessed Virgin; so that two whole and perfect natures, that is to say, the Godhead and the Manhood, were joined together in one Person, never to be divided, whereof is one Christ, very God and perfect Man, who actually suffered, was crucified, dead and buried, to reconcile the Father to us and to make atonement, not only for our actual guilt, but also for original sin.

Art. 3. We believe that Christ did truly rise again from the dead, and took again His body, with all things appertaining to the perfections of man's nature. And ascending into heaven and there sitteth until He shall return to judge all men at the last day.

Art. 4. We believe the Holy Ghost, proceeding from the Father and the Son, is of one substance, majesty and glory with the Father and the Son, Very and Eternal God.

Art. 5. We believe that eternal life with God in heaven is a portion of the reward of the finally righteous; and that everlasting banishment from the presence of the Lord, and unending torture in hell, the wages of the persistently wicked. (Matt. 25:46, Psalm 9:17, Rev. 21:7,8.)

Notes: *There have been four basic doctrinal documents adopted by the Emmanuel Holiness Church. The creed of the church is the Apostles' Creed. The covenant is identical to the one used by the (Original) Church of God. The basis of union was taken from that of the Pentecostal Fire-Baptized Holiness Church, from which the Emmanuel Holiness Church came. The articles of faith are identical to those of the International Pentecostal Holiness Church, from which the Pentecostal Fire-Baptized Holiness Church came.*

The three doctrinal statements of the Emmanuel Holiness Church, along with the Apostles' Creed, are found at the beginning of the church's book of Discipline and Doctrine. *Besides these statements, an additional set of general rules advocate the exclusive use of the King James Version of the Bible and prescribe a lengthy set of behavioral norms. In the basis of union, pacifism is advocated.*

*   *   *

FAITH (FREE WILL BAPTIST CHURCH OF THE PENTECOSTAL FAITH)

1. THE HOLY SCRIPTURES

These are the Old and New Testaments. They were written by men divinely inspired, and contain God's will as revealed to man. They are a sufficient and infallible guide in religious faith and practice, and the supreme standard by which all human conduct, creeds and opinions should be tried. II Timothy 3:16-19

2. THE TRUE GOD

The Scriptures teach that there is only one true and living God (Deut. 6:4; 1 Cor. 8:4; Jer. 10:10; John 7:28; II Cor. 1:18; I John 5:20; I Tim. 6:17), who is a Spirit (John 4: 24; II Cor. 3:17), self-existent (Ex. 3:14; Psalm 83:18; John 5:26; Rev. 1:4), eternal (Psalm 90:2; Deut. 33:27; Isa. 57:15; Rom. 1:20; I Tim. 1:17), Immutable (Mal. 3:6; Num. 23:19; James 1:17), omnipresent (I Kings 8:27; Jer. 23:24; Psalm 139:7-10; Isa. 57:15; Acts 17:24), omniscient (Acts 15:18; I Chron. 28:9; Psalm 94:9, 10; Acts 1:24), Omnipotent (Rev. 19:6; Job 42:2; Psalm 135:6; Matt. 19:26; Mark 14:36; Luke 18:27), independent (Eph. 4:6; Job 9:12; Isa. 14:13, 14; Daniel 4: 35; Rom. 11:33-36), good (Psalm 119:68; 25: 8; 106:1; 145:9; Matt. 19:17), wise (Rom. 16: 27; Daniel 2:20; I Tim. 1:17; Jude 25), holy (Lev. 19:2 Job 6:10); just (Deut. 32:4; Psalm 92:15; 119:137; Zeph. 3:5), and merciful (Eph. 2:4; Ex. 34:6; Neh.

9:17; Psalm 100:5), the Creator (Gen. 1:1; Ex. 20:11; Psalm 33:6, 9; Col. 1:16; Heb. 11:3), Preserver (Neh. 9:6; Job 7:20; Col. 1:17; Heb. 13) and Governor (Psalm 47:7; II Chron. 20:6; Psalm 95:3) of the Universe; the Redeemer (Isa. 47:4; Psalm 73: 35; Prov. 23:11; Isa. 41:14; 59:20; Jer. 50:34), Saviour (Isa. 45:21; 43:3, 11; 49:26), Sanctifier (Ex. 31:13; I Thess. 5:23; Jude 1), and Judge (Heb. 12:23; Gen. 18:25; Psalm 50:6; II Tim. 4:8) of men; and the only proper object of divine worship (Ex. 34:14; 20:4, 5; Matt. 4:10; Rev. 19:10).

The mode of His existence, however, is a subject far above the understanding of man (Job 11:7; Isa. 40:28; finite beings can not comprehend Him (Rom. 11:33; Job 26:14). There is nothing in the universe that can justly represent Him for there is none like Him (Ex. 9:14; 8:10; I Chron. 17:20). He is the foundation of all perfection and happiness. He is glorified by the whole inanimate creation, and is worthy to be loved and served by all intelligences (Psalm 19:1, 2; 145:10; 150:6).

3. DIVINE GOVERNMENT AND PROVIDENCES

God exercises a providential care and superintendence over all His creatures (Acts 17:28; Matt. 10:20; Psalm 104:13, 14; Job 14:5, Eph. 1:11), and governs the world in wisdom and mercy, according to the testimony of His Word (Psalm 22:28; 97:2; Isa. 33:22; Ex. 34:6; Job 36:5). God has endowed man with power of free choice, and governs him by moral laws and motives; and the power of free choice is the exact measure of his responsibility (Deut. 30:19; Isa. 1:18-20; John 5:40; Rom. 2:14, 15; Prov. 1:24-28).

All events are present with God from everlasting to everlasting, but His knowledge of them does not in any way cause them, nor does He decree all events which He knows will occur (Ezek. 33:11; Acts 15:11; I Sam. 2:30; Ezek. 18:20, 25, 31; Jer. 44:4).

4. CREATION, PRIMITIVE STATE OF MAN AND HIS FALL

God created the world and all things that it contains, for His own pleasure and glory, and for the enjoyment of His creatures (Rev. 4:11; Isa. 43:7; I Tim. 6:17). The angels were created by God (Col. 1:16), to glorify Him (Rev. 7:11), and obey His commandments (Psalm 103:20).

Those who have kept their first estate, He employs in ministering blessings to the heirs of salvation (Heb. 1:14; Jude 6), and in executing His judgments upon the world (II Sam. 24:16; Rev. 16:1).

God created man, consisting of a material body and a thinking, rational soul (Gen. 2:7). He was made in the image of God to glorify his Maker (Gen. 1:26, 27; I Cor. 6:20).

Our first parents, in their original state of probation, were upright; they naturally preferred and desired to obey their Creator, and had no preference or desire to transgress His will (Eccl. 7:29; Eph. 4:24; Col. 3:10), till they were influenced and inclined by the tempter to disobey God's commands. Previously to this, the only tendency of their nature was to do righteousness. In consequence of the first transgression, the state under which the posterity of Adam came into the world is so far different from that of Adam,

15

FAITH (FREE WILL BAPTIST CHURCH OF THE
PENTECOSTAL FAITH) (continued)

that they have not that righteousness and purity which
Adam had before the fall; they are not naturally willing to
obey God, but are inclined to evil (Psalm 51:5; Rom. 8:7;
Eph. 2:4; Psalm 58:3; Gen. 8:21; John 3:6; Gal. 5:19-21;
Rom. 5:12).

Hence, none by virtue of any natural goodness and mere
work of their own, can become the children of God (John
6:44; I Cor. 2:14); but all are dependent for salvation upon
the redemption effected through the blood of Christ, and
upon being created anew unto obedience through the
operation of the Spirit (John 3:25; 1:13; Heb. 12:14; Col.
1:14; Titus 3:5), both of which are freely provided for every
descendant of Adam.

5. CHRIST

Jesus Christ, the Son of God, possesses all Divine
perfections. As He and the Father are one, He in His
Divine nature filled all the offices and performed the
works of God to His creatures that have been the subject
of revelation to us. As man, He performed all the duties
toward God that we are required to perform, repentance of
sin excepted.

His divinity is proved from His titles, His attributes and
His works. The Bible ascribes to Christ the title of Saviour
(Isa. 45:25; 43:10; 11; John 4:42; Phil. 3:20; II Tim. 1:10;
Titus 2:13), Jehovah (Psalm 83:18; Isa. 40: 3; Luke 1:76),
Lord of Hosts (Isa. 8:13, 14; I Peter 2:4-6; Isa. 6:5; John
12:41), the first and the last (Rev. 21:13; 1:1, 11; Isa. 44:6),
God (I Tim. 3:16; I John 3:16; John 1:1; Heb. 1:8; John
20:28, 29) true God (I John 5:20), great God (Titus 2:13),
God over all (Rom. 9:5), Mighty God, and the everlasting
Father (Isa. 9:6).

He is eternal (Col. 1:17; Micah 5:2; Heb. 1:8), unchangeable (Heb. 13:8; 1:12), omnipresent (John 3:13; Matt. 18:20;
28:20; Eph. 1:23), omniscient (John 16:30; 2:25, 26; 21:17;
Rev. 2:23), omnipotent (Col. 2:8, 10; Matt. 28:18; Heb.
1:3; Rev. 1:8), holy (Acts 3:14; Luke 1:35; Heb. 7:26; Rev.
3:7), and is entitled to Divine worship (Heb. 1:6; John
5:23; Phil. 2:10, 11; Matt. 28:9; Luke 24:52).

By Christ the world was created (Heb. 1:8, 10; John 1:3,
10; Col. 1:16), He preserves (Heb. 1:3; Col. 1:17), and
governs it (Isa. 9:6; I Peter 3:22; Eph. 1:21); He has
provided redemption for all men (Eph. 1:7; Heb. 9:12; Gal.
3:13; Isa. 44:6; I Peter 1:18, 19; Rev. 5:9), and He will be
their final Judge (II Tim. 4:1; Matt. 25:31-46; John 5:22).

The Word, which in the beginning was with God, and
which was God, by whom all things were made, condescended to a state of humiliation in becoming like us,
pollution and sin excepted (John 1:14; Phil. 2:6, 7; II Cor.
8:9; Heb. 4:15). In this state, as a subject of the law, He
was liable to the infirmities of our nature (Heb. 2:17; Matt.
8:17; 4:2; 8:24; John 11:33, 35; 19:28; Isa. 53:3; Luke
22:44); was tempted as we are (Heb. 4:15; Matt. 4:1-11);
but He lived our example, and rendered perfect obedience
to the Divine requirements (I Peter 2:21; John 13:15; I
John 2:6). As Christ was made of the seed of David
according to the flesh, He is called The Son of Man (Isa.
42:21; Matt. 5:17; 3:15; Gal. 4:4); and as the Divine

existence is the fountain from which He proceeded, and
was the only agency by which He was begotten (Luke
19:10), He is called the Son of God (John 16:27; Matt.
1:18, 20), being the only begotten of the Father (Luke 1:35;
Mark 1:1; John 1:34; 20:31), and the only incarnation of
the Divine Being (John 3:16; 1:18).

6. THE HOLY SPIRIT

The Scriptures ascribe to the Holy Spirit the acts of an
intelligent being. He is said to guide (John 16:13), to know
(I Cor. 2:11), to move (Gen. 1:2; Acts 8:39), to give
information (Acts 10:19; I Cor. 2:13; Acts 21:11; John
14:26), to command (Acts 13:2), to forbid (Acts 16:6), to
send forth (Acts 13:4), to reprove (John 16:8; Gen. 6:3),
and to be sinned against (Mark 3:29; Isa. 63:10; Acts 7:51;
Eph. 4:30). The attributes of God are ascribed to the Holy
Spirit; such as eternity (Heb. 9:14), omnipresence (Psalm
139:7), omniscience (I Cor. 2:10), goodness (Neh. 9:20;
Psalm 143:10), and truth (John 14:17). The works of God
are ascribed to the Holy Spirit; creation (Job 33:4; 26:13;
Psalm 104:30), inspiration (II Peter 1:21), giving of life (I
Peter 3:18; Rom. 8:11), and sanctification (I Cor. 6:11).

The same acts which in one part of the Bible are attributed
to the Holy Spirit are in other parts said to be performed
by God (Isa. 6:8, 9; Acts 28:25, 26; John 3:16; Matt. 1:18).
The apostles assert that the Holy Spirit is Lord and God
(II Cor. 3:17; Acts 5:3, 4). From the foregoing the
conclusion is, that the Holy Spirit is in reality God, and
one with the Father in all Divine perfections. It has also
been shown that Jesus Christ is God, one with the Father.
Then these three, the Father, Son, and Holy Spirit, are one
God.

The truth of this doctrine is also proved from the fact that
the Father, the Son, and the Holy Ghost are united in the
authority by which believers are baptized, and in the
benedictions pronounced by the apostles (Matt. 28:19; II
Cor. 13:14; I Peter 1:2), which are acts of the highest
religious worship.

7. THE ATONEMENT AND MEDIATION OF
CHRIST

As sin cannot be pardoned without a sacrifice, and the
blood of beasts could never wash away sin, Christ gave
Himself a sacrifice for the sins of the world (I John 2:2;
Isa. 53:5; 10:11; Rom. 4:25; Matt. 20:28; I Peter 3:18; John
1:29; Heb. 9:26; Rom. 5:6-8), and thus made salvation
possible for all men (Titus 2:11; Heb. 2:9; I Tim. 2:6; Isa.
45:22; II Peter 3:9; II Cor. 5:14, 15; I Tim. 4:10).

He died for us, suffering in our stead, to make known the
righteousness of God, that He might be just in justifying
sinners who believe in His Son (Rom. 3:25, 26; 5:9, 18;
Matt. 26:28; Eph. 1:7; Rev. 1:9; I Peter 2:24). Through the
redemption effected by Christ, salvation is actually enjoyed
in this world, and will be enjoyed in the next, by all who do
not in this life refuse obedience to the known requirements
of God (Rom. 5:18; 8:1; Mark 16:15; Rom. 2:14, 15). The
atonement for sin was necessary (Heb. 9:22; Eph. 1:7;
Rom. 5:19). For present and future obedience can no more
blot out past sins than past obedience can remove the guilt
of present and future sins. Had God pardoned the sins of
men without satisfaction for the violation of His law, it

would follow that transgressions might go on with impunity, government would be abrogated and the obligation of obedience to God would be, in effect, removed. Our Lord not only died for our sins, but He arose for our justification (Rom. 4:25; I Cor. 15:17), and ascended to heaven (Acts 1:11; Mark 16:19), where as Mediator between God and man He will make intercession for men until the final judgment (Heb. 7:25; Rom. 8:34; Heb. 9:24; I Tim. 2:5; I Cor. 15:24).

8. THE GOSPEL CALL

The call of the Gospel is coextensive with the atonement of all men (Mark 16:15; Isa. 45:22; Prov. 8:4; Isa. 55:1; Rev. 22:17), both by the Word and the Striving of the Spirit (Joel 2:28; John 16:18; 1:9; Isa. 55:11; Luke 2:10; so that salvation is rendered equally possible to all (I Tim. 2:4; Acts 10:34; Ezek. 33:11; II Peter 3:9), and if any fail of eternal life, the fault is wholly their own (Hosea 13:9; Prov. 1:24-31; Isa. 65; 12; Jer. 7:13, 14; Zech. 7:11, 13; John 5:40; Matt. 23:37).

9. REPENTANCE

The repentance which the Gospel requires includes a deep conviction, a penitential sorrow, an open confession, a decided hatred, and an entire forsaking of all sin (II Cor. 7:10; Psalm 51:17; Prov. 28:13; Psalm 32:3, 5; Ezek. 36:31; Psalm 51:3, 4; Ezek. 18:30). This repentance God has enjoined on all men; and without it in this life, the sinner must perish eternally (Acts 17:30; Luke 13:5; Acts 3:19).

10. FAITH

Saving faith is an assent of the mind to the fundamental truths of revelation (Heb. 11:1, 6; John 5:46, 47; Rom. 10:9), an acceptance of the Gospel through the influence of the Holy Spirit (Rom. 10:10; Gal. 5:22; I Cor. 12:8, 9); and a firm confidence and trust in Christ (Acts 16:31; John 3:16; Rom. 4:20, 22; Eph. 3:12). The fruit of faith is obedience to the Gospel (James 2:17; Gal. 5:6; I Tim. 1:5). The power to believe is the gift of God (Phil. 1:29; II Peter 1:1; Eph. 2:8); but believing is an act of the creature which is required as a condition for pardon, and without which the sinner can not obtain salvation (John 3:36; Mark 16:16; John 18:21, 24; Heb. 11:6). All men are required to believe in Christ; and those who yield obedience to His requirements become the children of God by faith (John 1:7; Gal. 3:26; Acts 10:43; Rom. 5:1; John 3:15).

11. REGENERATION

As man is a fallen and sinful being, he must be regenerated in order to obtain salvation (John 3:3; Heb. 12:14; Rev. 21:27; Gal. 5:19-21). This change is an instantaneous renewal of the heart by the Holy Spirit (John 3:5; 1:13; Ezek. 36:26, 27; Titus 3:5; Eph. 2:10), whereby the penitent sinner receives new life, becomes a child of God (Rom. 8:16; John 1:12; 5:25; James 1:18; II Cor. 5:17), and disposed to serve Him (Ezek. 11:19, 20; I Peter 2:5). This is called in Scripture being born again, born of the Spirit (John 3:5, 6, 8; I John 4:7; 5:1), being quickened (Eph. 2:1; Psalm 119:50, 93; Eph. 2:5; Col. 2:13), passing from death unto life (John 5:24; I John 3:14), and a partaking of Divine nature (II Peter 1:4; Heb. 3:14).

12. JUSTIFICATION

Personal justification implies that the person justified has been guilty before God; and in consideration of the atonement of Christ, accepted by faith, the sinner is pardoned and absolved from the guilt of sin, and restored to the Divine favor (Rom. 5:1, 16; Acts 13:39; Isa. 53:11). Though Christ's atonement is the foundation of the sinner's redemption, yet without repentance and faith it can never give him justification and peace with God (Acts 13:19; Heb. 4:2; 11:6; Rom. 9:31, 32; Acts 13:38, 39).

13. SANCTIFICATION

MAN'S SIDE. A complete consecration of himself and all his to God and His service (Rom. 12:1; I Cor. 6:19, 20; Lev. 20:7; II Cor. 7:1; I Cor. 10:31; Mal. 3:10; Luke 12:22, 23; 14:25-33).

GOD'S SIDE. Is an instantaneous work of God's grace in a believer's heart whereby the heart is cleansed from all sin and made pure by the blood of Christ; it is obtained by faith and is subsequent to regeneration. The Christian can and should abide in this state unto the end of life, constantly growing in grace and in the knowledge of our Lord Jesus Christ (I Thess. 4:3; John 17:17; I Thess. 5:23; Heb. 13:12; Eph. 5:26; I John 1:7; Lev. 20:8; Heb. 9:13, 14; II Tim. 2:20, 21; Heb. 2:11; 10:1-22; Luke 24:49; Acts 2:1-4; 15:8, 9; 26:16-18; I Cor. 1:30; I John 4:16-18).

14. BAPTISM OF THE HOLY GHOST

We believe that the baptism of the Holy Ghost may be obtained by a definite act of appropriating faith on the part of the fully cleansed believer, and that the first evidence of the reception of this experience is the speaking with other tongues as the Spirit gives utterance (Luke 11:13; Acts 1:5; 2:1-4; 8:17).

15. GIFTS OF THE SPIRIT

We believe that it is the privilege of the Spirit-baptized believer to enjoy the benefits of spiritual gifts—wisdom, knowledge, faith, gifts of healing, working of miracles, prophecy, discerning of spirits, divers kinds of tongues, and the interpretation of tongues (I Cor. 12:1-14), and that these gifts are separate and apart from the baptism.

16. PERSEVERANCE OF THE SAINTS

There are strong grounds to hope that the truly regenerate will persevere unto the end and be saved through the power of Divine grace which is pledged for their support (Rom. 8:38, 39; I Cor. 10:13; II Cor. 12:9; Job 17:9; Matt. 16:18; John 10:27, 28; Phil. 1:6), but their future obedience and final salvation are neither determined nor certain, since through infirmity and manifold temptations, they are in danger of falling; they ought therefore to watch and pray lest they make shipwreck of their faith and be lost (II Chron. 15:2; II Peter 1:10; Ezek. 33:18; John 15:6; I Cor. 10:12; Heb. 6:6; 12:15; I Chron. 28:9; Rev. 2:4; I Tim. 1:19; II Peter 2:20, 21; I Cor. 9:27; Matt. 24:13).

17. THE LORD'S DAY

Before the death and resurrection of Christ, under the old dispensation, the seventh day of the week, as commemorative of the work of creation, was set apart for the Sabbath (Ex. 20:8-11). Under the Gospel, the first day of the week,

FAITH (FREE WILL BAPTIST CHURCH OF THE
    PENTECOSTAL FAITH) (continued)

in commemoration of the resurrection of Christ, and by authority of the apostles, is observed as the Christian Sabbath or The Lord's Day. (Luke 24:1-7; 33:36; John 20:19-26; Acts 2:1; 20:7; I Cor. 16:2; Rev. 1:10).

In these days when The Lord's Day is being desecrated by so many, we as a church feel it our duty to take a stand against the practice of buying and selling on Sunday, attending meetings for worldly amusement, visiting pleasure resorts, promiscuous and questionable, joy-riding, etc., on The Lord's Day.

18. WORLDLY AND SINFUL AMUSEMENTS

We believe that it is decidedly against the Christian character and influence of all people to engage in dancing, card playing, attend fairs, shows, carnivals, etc.; going to swimming lakes and pools and bathing with mixed crowds.

19. TEMPERANCE

To be temperate is to abstain from the use of all intoxicating liquors, be moderate in eating, avoiding immodest styles and fashions of the world; leaving off those things that will make us conform to the ways of the world. "Abstain from all appearance of evil" is a good motto.

Members of the Free-Will Baptist Church who persist in the use of intoxicating liquors, after they have been admonished, are to be excluded.

We believe that the use of tobacco in any form is in direct opposition to the principles of gospel temperance. Our churches and Sunday schools should discourage every form of intemperance, and do what they can to encourage the enforcement of the prohibition laws and regulations.

20. TITHING

While the individual member of the church is left free to decide for himself the amount he should give to God's cause, we believe that one-tenth of our net income belongs to God. While this was practiced under the law, instead of repealing, as some would have us believe, Jesus endorsed it (Matt. 23:23). For other Scriptures on tithing, see Gen. 28:22; Lev. 27:30; Mal. 3:8-10.

21. DIVORCE

We believe that there is only one Scriptural reason for divorce, and that is, fornication on the part of the person from whom the divorce is desired. We do not believe that there is any Scripture that sets either the husband or wife free to marry again so long as both parties live (Matt. 5:32; 19:9; Luke 16:18; Rom. 7:3; I Cor. 7:10).

22. THE CHURCH

The Church is an organized body of believers in Christ, who stately assemble to worship God, and who sustain the ordinances of the Gospel agreeably to His Word (I Cor. 1:2; Acts 2:41, 47; 20:7; I Cor. 16:1, 2; Rev. 1:4). In a more general sense it is the whole body of Christians throughout the world, and none but the regenerate are its real members (Eph. 5:25, 27; 1:22, 23; I Cor. 12:27, 28; Col. 1:18, 24; I Peter 2:5; John 18:36; 15:2, 6). Believers are admitted to a particular Church on their giving

evidence of faith, being baptized and receiving the hand of fellowship (Acts 2:41; 8:12; Gal. 3:27).

23. THE GOSPEL MINISTRY

QUALIFICATIONS OF MINISTERS. They must possess good natural and acquired abilities (II Tim. 2:15; I Tim. 4:13-16; Titus 1:9; 2:7, 8; II Tim. 1:7; 2:2; I Tim. 3:2-7, deep and ardent piety (Psalm 50:16; II Tim. 1:8-11, 14; 2:22; 3:5; Titus 1:5-9; I Cor. 2:12-16), be specially called by God to the work (Acts 20:28; Heb. 5:4; I Cor. 9:16; Acts 13:2), and ordained by the laying on of hands (I Tim. 4:14; II Tim. 1:6; Acts 13:3).

DUTIES OF MINISTERS. They are to preach the Word (Mark 16:15; II Tim. 4:2; II Cor. 4:5; Ezek. 33:7;), administer the ordinances of the Gospel (Matt. 28:19; Luke 22:19, 20; Acts 20:11; 27:35; I Cor. 11:23-28; 10:16), visit their people, and otherwise perform the work of faithful pastors (Heb. 13:17; I Peter 5:2; Acts 20:28, 31; Jer. 3:15). (See "The Pastor" under Government.)

24. ORDINANCES OF THE GOSPEL

CHRISTIAN BAPTISM. This is the immersion of believers in water in the name of the Father, the Son, and the Holy Ghost (Matt. 28:19; Col. 2:12; Acts 8:36-39; Matt. 3:16; Mark 1:5; John 3:23; Acts 16:32-34; 2:41), in which are represented the burial and resurrection of Christ, the death of Christians to the world, the washing of their souls from the pollution of sin, their rising of newness of life, their engagement to serve God, and their resurrection at the last day (Rom. 6:4; Col. 3:3; 2:12; Titus 3:5; Gal. 3:27; I Cor. 15:29).

THE LORD'S SUPPER. This is a commemoration of the death of Christ for our sins, in the use of bread, which He made the emblem of His broken body; and the cup, the emblem of His shed blood (I Cor. 11:23-26; Matt. 26:26-28; Luke 22:19, 20). And by it the believer expresses his love for Christ, his faith and hope in Him, and pledges to Him perpetual fidelity (I Cor. 10:16, 21; 11:27-29). It is the privilege and duty of all who have spiritual union with Christ thus to commemorate His death; and no man has a right to forbid these tokens to the least of His disciples (I Cor. 10:17; Matt. 26:27; Rom. 14:1, 10; I Cor. 12:12-27; Acts 2:42; 20:7).

FEET-WASHING. This is a sacred ordinance of humility, instituted by our Lord Jesus Christ and enjoined upon His disciples as a duty to be observed by them. In this He set the example (Matt. 28:19, 20; John 13:1-17).

LAYING ON OF HANDS. In this the believer is taught to receive the gift of the Holy Ghost (Acts 8:14-17; 19:6).

25. DEATH AND THE INTERMEDIATE STATE

DEATH. As the result of sin, all mankind are subject to the death of the body (Rom. 5:12; Heb. 9:27; I Cor. 15:22; Psalm 89:48; Eccl. 8:8).

INTERMEDIATE STATE. The soul does not die with the body; but immediately after death, it enters into a conscious state of happiness or misery, according to the moral character here possessed (Eccl. 12:7; Phil. 1:23; Luke 23:43; Matt. 17:3; 22:31, 32; Acts 7:59; Matt. 10:28; II Cor. 5:8; Luke 16:22-26; Rev. 6:9).

26. SECOND COMING OF CHRIST

The Lord Jesus, who ascended on high and sits at the right hand of God, will come again to close the gospel dispensation, glorify His saints, and judge the world (Acts 1:11; Matt. 25:31; I Cor. 15:24-28; I Thess. 4:15-17; II Thess. 1:7, 10; II Peter 3:3-13; Matt. 24:12-14).

27. THE RESURRECTION

The Scriptures teach the resurrection of the bodies of all men at the last day, each in its own order; they that have done good will come forth to the resurrection of life, and they that have done evil, unto the resurrection of damnation (John 5:28, 29; Acts 24:15; I Cor. 15:22, 23; II Tim. 2:18; Phil. 3:21; I Cor. 15:35-44; Daniel 12:2).

28. THE GENERAL JUDGMENT AND FUTURE RETRIBUTION

There will be a general judgment, when time and man's probation will close forever (Acts 17:31; I Cor. 15:24; Rev. 10:6; 22:11; II Peter 3:11, 12; Eccl. 9:10). Then all men will be judged according to their works (II Cor. 5:10; Eccl. 12:14; Matt. 12:36; Rev. 20:12; Rom. 2:16). Immediately after the general judgment the righteous will enter into eternal life, and the wicked go into a state of endless punishment (Matt. 25:40; II Thess 1:8-10; Rom. 6:23; II Peter 1:11; Mark 3:29; 9:43, 44; Jude 7; Rev. 14:11; 21:7, 8; Matt. 13:41-43; Rom. 2:6-10).

CHURCH COVENANT

Having been brought, as we believe, by Divine grace to accept the Lord Jesus as our Savior and Preserver, we do now solemnly and joyfully covenant and agree, by God's help, to walk together in brotherly love.

We, therefore, enter into covenant as members of this Church and as Christians, that we will watch over each other in love, sharing together each other's joys and sorrows; that we will not forsake the assembling of ourselves together, nor omit the great duty of prayer for ourselves and others; that by Divine assistance we will endeavor to bring up those under our care in the nurture and admonition of the Lord; that in all things we will strive to exemplify our profession by a corresponding practice; to abstain from all sinful conformity to the world; to be just in our dealings, faithful in our engagements, and exemplary in all our deportment; that we will abstain from the sale and use of intoxicating liquors; that we will abstain from remarriage as long as a former husband or wife lives; that we will sustain the worship, ordinances, discipline and doctrines of this Church; that we will contribute cheerfully, according to our ability, to the support of the ministry, the expense of the church, the relief of the poor and the general spread of the Gospel.

In keeping this solemn Covenant, may we ever enjoy the blessings and presence of the Great Head of the Church.

Notes: *This statement is closely related to the Faith of Free Will Baptists of the National Association of Free Will Baptists, even though it differs on a number of significant points. Most importantly, the section on sanctification has been rewritten, and statements on the baptism of the Holy Spirit and the gifts of the Spirit have been added. Quite apart from these central doctrinal issues, statements have also been added on worldly and sinful amusements, temperance, and divorce. There is an important addition in the item on ordinances where beside baptism, the Lord's Supper, and foot washing, the laying-on-of-hands is accepted as a fourth ordinance. The Free Will Baptist Church of the Pentecostal Faith has not seen the necessity of adding the statement on the inerrancy of scripture, which has been placed at the beginning of the statement by the National Association of the Free Will Baptists.*

* * *

STATEMENT OF FAITH OF THE GENERAL CONFERENCE OF THE EVANGELICAL BAPTIST CHURCH

THE BIBLE INSPIRED. The Bible is the Word of God, verbally inspired and inerrable in the original writings. 2 Timothy 3:16-17; 2 Peter 1:21.

THE HOLY TRINITY. God, the Father, God, the Son, and God, the Holy Spirit; co-existent, eternal, omniscient, all powerful. Deuteronomy 6:4-5; Matthew 28:19; 2 Corinthians 13:14; Luke 1:35; John 1:14.

JUSTIFICATION. Through the fall we all become "dead in trespasses and sins." Through Christ we are "made alive," "born again," and "justified by faith through the atonement." Acts 2:38; John 3:3-8; Romans 5:1-12; Psalms 51:5; Ephesians 2:1-3.

SANCTIFICATION. A work of grace subsequent to justification. "Wherefore Jesus also, that He might sanctify the people with His own blood, suffered without the gate," Hebrews 13:12. "For He hath made Him to be sin for us, who knew no sin; that we might be made the righteousness of God in Him." 2 Corinthians 5:21. "Knowing this, that our old man is crucified with Him, that the body of sin might be destroyed, that henceforth we should not serve sin." Romans 6:6. There is therefore a holy and victorious life for the believer, as we fully consecrate ourselves to Him, and "reckon ourselves to be dead unto sin, but alive unto God." Romans 6:11; Ephesians 4:22-24.

BAPTISM OF THE HOLY SPIRIT. There is for every believer whose heart has been cleansed, an enduement of "power from on high" according to Acts 2:1-4; Acts 1:4-8; Acts 15-8; Acts 19:1-6; I Corinthians 14:22.

SPIRITUAL GIFTS. If "we abide in Him" and "follow on to know the Lord" it is possible to have the "signs" that are promised to follow believers in Mark 16:17-20, and the spiritual gifts spoken of in the 12 chapter of I Corinthians in operation in our assemblies. "For the perfecting of the saints, for the work of the ministry, for the edifying of the body of Christ." Ephesians 4:12.

HEALING IN THE ATONEMENT. "Himself took our infirmities and bare our sicknesses," Matthew 8:17; and

STATEMENT OF FAITH OF THE GENERAL CONFERENCE
OF THE EVANGELICAL BAPTIST CHURCH (continued)

"with His stripes we are healed," Isaiah 53:5. It is our blessed privilege to "lay hands on the sick and to anoint them with oil in the Name of the Lord," and "the prayer of faith shall save the sick." Matthew 16:18; James 5:14-16.

THE PRE-MILLENNIAL RETURN OF OUR LORD.

The rapture of the prepared and waiting saints, the great tribulation, the return of our Lord with His saints and the Holy angels in power and great glory to reign on earth a thousand years. I Thessalonians 4:14-17; Matthew 25:31; Acts 1:11; Revelation 20:4; Jude 1:14-15.

THE RESURRECTION.

The resurrection of the crucified body of our Lord and the bodily resurrection of the just before the thousand years and of the unjust after the thousand years. Acts 2:22-24; I Corinthians 15:4-8; Romans 8:34; Daniel 12:2-3; John 5:25-29; Revelation 20:4-5.

HEAVEN AND HELL.

The everlasting blessedness and reward of the righteous and the everlasting punishment of the wicked. Matthew 25:46; Revelation 21:8; Luke 16:19-25.

A PERSONAL DEVIL.

Called Satan, who accomplished the fall of man, and who is now the prince of the power of the air, the accuser of the brethren, and the tempter of all mankind. I Peter 5:8; Revelation 12:9-10; 2 Thessalonians 3:5; Ephesians 2:1-2.

SUNDAY.

We accept and observe Sunday as the Lord's rest day under the new covenant. Revelation 1:10; Acts 20:7.

ORDINANCES

We observe the Lord's Supper, Luke 22:19-20; I Corinthians 11:23-26; and Water Baptism by immersion "in the Name of the Father, the Son, and the Holy Spirit," Matthew 28:19; Matthew 3:15-17; Acts 2:38; Romans 6:3-4; Colossians 2:12.

HOLY COMMUNION.

As instructed by the Holy Scriptures the Holy Communion shall be an ordinance of this Church and all Evangelical Baptist churches. The Holy Communion shall be small particles of bread representing the body of Christ; and wine (grapejuice) representing the Blood of Christ, which shall be blest by a prayer offered by the minister of the church, or the officiating minister. This service shall be held as often as the pastor of the church might feel disposed, and the service shall be in remembrance of Jesus Christ, the Son of God, Who was crucified on the middle cross. Luke 22:19-20; I Corinthians 11:23-26; All Christians, irrespective to their church affiliation, or whether they belong to any church or not, shall be invited by the officiating minister to participate in this service. The minister having the right to officiate shall be an ordained minister. The custom in which the participants shall follow shall be either about the altar or served in the pews by members of the board of deacons and deaconess. As to the number of times the Lord's Supper shall be observed during a church year shall be left entirely to the discretion of the pastor of the church.

WATER BAPTISM.

This Church, and all Evangelical Baptist churches, has adopted the mode of baptism as immersion, and every person uniting with the church for the first time shall be baptized by immersion within six months following their reception into the church. If they do not, they are automatically regarded as persons not in good and regular standing of the church, and do not have any right to vote on any issue that might be brought before the church until they meet all requirements of the church.

If a person comes to this Church by letter or profession of faith and has been baptized by any ordained minister and is satisfied with their baptism, they are received into full fellowship of the church. Matthew 3:1-17; Mark 1:8; Matthew 28:18-20; Acts 2:38-42; Acts 10:44-48; Romans 6:3-4; Acts 16:13-15; Acts 16:25-34; Colossians 2:12; Galatians 3:27. The baptismal service shall be a public service, and all candidates shall be immersed in the Name of the Father, the Son and the Holy Ghost. Only ordained ministers shall have the authority to perform this Gospel rite.

DEDICATION OF CHILDREN.

It is the belief of this Church, and all Evangelical Baptist churches, that children should be publicly dedicated to God, in which an ordained minister officiates. In this service parents promise to bring up their children in the "nurture and admonition of the Lord," Ephesians 6:4. This custom was adopted when they learned that men and women of old dedicated their children to Almighty God. Instead of using water, as is generally done in the christening of a child, the Evangelical Baptists use flowers in the dedicatory service, in which a child is dedicated to Almighty God. Every parent belonging to this Church, and any other Evangelical Baptist church, is urged to dedicate their children publicly to God, and the service can be arranged by negotiating with the pastor of the church.

TITHING.

It shall be expected that all members of the church shall give one-tenth of their income to the support of the church as instructed in Malachi 3:10, "bring ye all the tithes into the storehouse (church) that there may be meat (funds) in mine house and prove me now herewith, saith the Lord of hosts, if I will not open you the windows of heaven, and pour you out a blessing that there shall not be room enough to receive it." Genesis 14:20; Malachi 3:8; Hebrows 7:5; 2 Chronicles 31:5. The time instructed by the Word of God to bring the tithe is on the first day of the week, which is the Lord's Day, I Corinthians 16:2.

* * *

STATEMENT OF FAITH (INTERNATIONAL PENTECOSTAL CHURCH OF CHRIST)

1. THE SCRIPTURES INSPIRED

The Bible is the revealed Word of God to man: The New Testament is our sole rule for discipline and government (II Timothy 3:15-17; II Peter 1:21).

2. THE ONE TRUE GOD

The triune Godhead consists of one true God the Father, Jesus Christ His Son, and the Holy Ghost the third person of the Godhead (John 10:36; 14:26; 20:21).

3. THE FALL OF MAN

Man was created good and upright: for God said, "Let us make man in our image, after our likeness!" However, man by voluntary transgression fell and thereby incurred not only physical death but also spiritual death, which is separation from God (Genesis 1:26, 27; 2:17; 3:6; Romans 5:12-19).

4. THE SALVATION OF MAN

Man's only hope of redemption is through the shed blood of Jesus Christ the Son of God.

(a) Conditions to Salvation. Salvation is received through repentance toward God and faith toward the Lord Jesus Christ. By the washing of regeneration and renewing of the Holy Ghost, being justified by grace through faith, man becomes an heir of God according to the hope of eternal life (Luke 24:47; John 3:3; Romans 10:13-15; Ephesians 2:8; Titus 2:11; 3:5-7).

(b) The Evidences of Salvation. The inward evidence of salvation is the direct witness of the Spirit (Romans 8:16). The outward evidence to all men is a life of righteousness and true holiness (Ephesians 4:24; Titus 2:12).

5. SANCTIFICATION

Sanctification is an act of separation from that which is evil, and of dedication unto God (Romans 12:1,2; I Thessalonians 5:23; Hebrews 13:12).

Sanctification is obtainable as a second definite work of grace, received by faith in the blood of Christ.

Sanctification is realized in the believer by recognizing his identification with Christ in His death and resurrection, and by faith reckoning daily upon the fact of that union, and by offering every faculty continually to the dominion of the Holy Spirit (Romans 6:1-11, 13; 8:1, 2, 13; Galatians 2:20; Philippians 2:12, 13; I Peter 1:5).

6. THE BAPTISM IN THE HOLY GHOST

All believers are entitled to, should ardently expect and earnestly seek the promise of the Father, the baptism in the Holy Ghost and fire, according to the command of our Lord Jesus Christ. The Bible evidence of the Baptism in the Holy Ghost is witnessed by the physical sign of speaking with other tongues as the Spirit of God gives utterance. (Acts 2:4; 10:46; 19:6). This was the normal experience of all in the early Christian Church. With it comes the enduement of power for life and service, the bestowment of the gifts and their uses in the work of the ministry (Luke 24:49; Acts 1:4; I Corinthians 12:1-31). With the baptism in the Holy Ghost comes such experiences as an overflowing fullness of the Spirit (John 7:37-39; Acts 4:8), a deepened reverence for God (Acts 2:42), and a more active love for Christ, for His Word, and for the lost (Mark 16:20).

7. THE ORDINANCES OF THE CHURCH

(a) Baptism in Water. The ordinance of baptism by immersion in the name of the Father, and of the Son and of the Holy Ghost is commanded in the Scriptures. All who repent and believe on Christ as Saviour and Lord are to be baptized. Thus they declare to the world that they died with Christ and that they also have been raised with Him to walk in newness of life (Matthew 28:19; Mark 16:16; Acts 10:47, 48: Romans 6:4).

(b) Holy Communion. The Lord's Supper, consisting of the elements—bread and fruit of the vine—is the symbol expressing our sharing the divine nature of our Lord Jesus Christ (II Peter 1:4); a memorial of His suffering and death (I Corinthians 11:26); and a prophecy of His second coming (I Corinthians 11:26); and is enjoined on all believers "till He comes!"

(c) Foot Washing. The ordinance of washing the saints feet is scripturally sound, and its practice in the local assembly is left optional. (John 13:4-17).

(d) Child Dedication. Since water baptism is an outward expression of an inward work of grace, we do not practice infant baptism. However, we do encourage presenting our children to the Lord in child dedication and blessing until they are old enough to make their own choice and decision (Luke 2:27; Mark 10:13-16).

8. THE CHURCH AND ITS MISSION

The Church is the Body of Christ, the habitation of God through the Spirit, with divine appointments for the fulfillment of her great commission. Each believer, born of the Spirit, is an integral part of the General Assembly and Church of the Firstborn, which are written in heaven (Ephesians 1:22, 23; 2:22; Hebrews 12:23).

Since God's purpose concerning man is to seek and to save that which is lost, to be worshipped by man, and to build a body of believers in the image of His Son, the priority reason-for-being of the International Pentecostal Church of Christ as part of the Church is:

(a) To be an agency of God for evangelizing the world (Acts 1:8; Matthew 28:19, 20; Mark 16:15, 16).

(b) To be a corporate body in which man may worship God (I Corinthians 12:13).

(c) To be a channel of God's purpose to build a body of saints being perfected in the image of His Son (Ephesians 4:11-16; I Corinthians 12:28; I Corinthians 14:12).

The International Pentecostal Church of Christ exists expressly to give continuing emphasis to this reason-for-being in the New Testament apostolic pattern by teaching and encouraging believers to be baptized in the Holy Spirit. This experience:

(a) Enables them to evangelize in the power of the Spirit with accompanying supernatural signs (Mark 16:15-20; Acts 4:29-31; Hebrews 2:3, 4).

(b) Adds a necessary dimension to worshipful relationship with God (I Corinthians 2:10-16; I Corinthians 12, 13, and 14).

(c) Enables them to respond to the full working of the Holy Spirit in expression of fruit and gifts and ministries as in New Testament times for the edifying of the body of Christ (Galatians 5:22-26; I Corinthians 14:12; Ephesians 4:11, 12; I Corinthians 28; Colossians 1:29).

9. THE MINISTRY

A divinely called and scripturally ordained ministry has been provided by our Lord for the threefold purpose of leading the Church in: (1) Evangelization of the world (Mark 16:15-20); (2) Worship of God (John 4:23, 24); (3) Building a body of saints being perfected in the image of His Son (Ephesians 4:11-16).

10. DIVINE HEALING

Divine healing is an integral part of the gospel. Deliverance from sickness is provided for in the atonement, and is the privilege of all believers (Isaiah 53:4, 5; Matthew 8:16, 17; James 5:14-16).

11. THE BLESSED HOPE

The resurrection of those who have fallen asleep in Christ and their translation together with those who are alive and remain unto the coming of the Lord is the imminent and blessed hope of the church (I Thessalonians 4:16, 17; Romans 8:23; Titus 2:13; I Corinthians 15:51, 52).

12. THE MILLENNIAL REIGN OF CHRIST

The Word of God promises the catching away of the prepared and waiting saints. Followed by the great tribulation, and then the return of our Lord with His saints and holy angels in power and great glory to reign on earth a thousand years. This millennial reign will bring the salvation of national Israel (Ezekiel 37:21, 22; Zephaniah 3:19, 20; Romans 11:26, 27) and the establishment of universal peace (Isaiah 11:6-9; Psalm 72:3-8; Micah 4:3, 4).

13. THE FINAL JUDGMENT

There will be a final judgment in which the wicked dead will be raised and judged according to their works. Whosoever is not found written in the Book of Life, together with the devil and his angels, and the beast and false prophet, will be consigned to everlasting punishment in the lake which burneth with fire and brimstone, which is the second death (Matthew 25:46; Mark 9:43-48; Revelation 19:20; 20:11-15; 21:8).

14. THE NEW HEAVENS AND THE NEW EARTH

"We, according to His promise, look for new heavens and a new earth wherein dwelleth righteousness" (II Peter 3:13; Revelation 21:22).

15. TITHES AND OFFERINGS

The needs of the New Testament Church, its varied ministries along with its God ordained leadership are to be met by the tithes and offerings of the believers (Matthew 23:23; I Corinthians 16:1, II Corinthians 9:6, 7).

Notes: *This statement replaces the Basis of Fellowship of the former International Pentecostal Assemblies and the Statement of Faith of the former Pentecostal Church of Christ. It is unique for its position on child dedication, a fourth ordinance beside baptism, holy communion, and foot washing. Not included from the International Pentecostal Assemblies statement is the item against war.*

ARTICLES OF FAITH (INTERNATIONAL PENTECOSTAL HOLINESS CHURCH)

1. We believe there is but one living and true God, everlasting, of infinite power, wisdom and goodness; Maker and Preserver of all things, both visible and invisible. And in the unity of this Godhead, there are three Persons of one substance, of eternal being, and equal in holiness, justice, wisdom, power, and dignity: the Father, the Son, and the Holy Ghost.

2. We believe that the Son, who is the Word of the Father, the very and eternal God, of one substance with the Father, took man's nature in the womb of the blessed Virgin; so that two whole and perfect natures, that is to say, the Godhead and manhood, were joined together in one person, never to be divided, whereof is one Christ, very God and perfect man, who actually suffered, was crucified, dead, and buried, to reconcile the Father to us, and to make atonement, not only for our actual guilt, but also for original sin.

3. We believe that Christ did truly rise again from the dead, and took again His body, with all things appertaining to the perfections of man's nature, and ascended into heaven and there sitteth until He shall return to judge all men at the last day.

4. We believe the Holy Ghost proceeding from the Father and the Son, is of one substance, majesty and glory, with the Father and the Son, very and eternal God.

5. We believe in the verbal and plenary inspiration of the Holy Scriptures, known as the Bible, composed of sixty-six books and divided into two departments, Old and New Testaments. We believe the Bible is the Word of God, the full and complete revelation of the plan and history of redemption.

6. We believe that eternal life with God in heaven is a portion of the reward of the finally righteous; and that everlasting banishment from the presence of the Lord, and unending torture in hell, the wages of the persistently wicked (Matt. 25:46; Psalm 9:17; Rev. 21:7, 8).

7. We believe that Jesus Christ shed His blood for the remission of sins that are past; and for the regeneration of penitent sinners, and for salvation from sin and from sinning (Rom. 3:25; I Jno. 3:5-10; Eph. 2:1-10).

8. We believe, teach and firmly maintain the scriptural doctrine of justification by faith alone (Rom. 5:1).

9. We believe that Jesus Christ shed His blood for the complete cleansing of the justified believer from all indwelling sin and from its pollution, subsequent to regeneration (I John 1:7-9).

10. We believe that entire sanctification is an instantaneous, definite second work of grace, obtainable by faith on the part of the fully justified believer (John 15:2; Acts 26:18).

11. We believe that the Pentecostal baptism of the Holy Ghost and fire is obtainable by a definite act of

appropriating faith on the part of the fully cleansed believer, and the initial evidence of the reception of this experience is speaking with other tongues as the Spirit gives utterance (Luke 11:13; Acts 1:5; 2:1-4; 8:17; 10:44-46; 19:6).

12. We believe in divine healing as in the atonement (Isa. 53:4, 5; Matt. 8:16, 17; Mark 16:14-18; Jas. 5:14-16; Ex. 15:26).

13. We believe in the imminent, personal, premillennial second coming of our Lord Jesus Christ (I Thess. 4:15-18; Titus 2:13; II Peter 3:1-4; Matt. 24:29-44), and we love and wait for His appearing (II Timothy 4:8).

CHANGES IN ARTICLES OF FAITH

No subsequent General Conference shall have authority to change the Articles of Faith until the proposed change has been submitted to each local church, the majority voting favorable to the change.

Notes: *One of the oldest of the pentecostal church bodies, the International Pentecostal Holiness Church (formerly the Pentecostal Holiness Church) has adopted a variety of doctrinal statements. The church's creed is the Apostles' Creed. The Articles of Faith have been adopted by the Emmanuel Holiness Church and used by the Congregational Holiness Church as a basis for its statement of doctrine. The first four of these articles were taken verbatim from the Twenty-five Articles of Religion of the Methodist Episcopal Church. The remaining statements incorporate the church's particular doctrinal emphases such as the baptism of the Holy Ghost, divine healing, and premillennialism. The present statement was derived from two others, the Articles of Faith and the Basis of Union, which dated to the 1911 union of the Fire-Baptized Holiness Church and the Pentecostal Holiness Church.*

In addition to the Articles of Faith, the International Pentecostal Holiness Church has added two lengthy statements which offer elaboration on the church's beliefs and the history of the articles' development. Only the articles are reproduced here.

*   *   *

CHURCH COVENANT AND BASIS OF FELLOWSHIP [(ORIGINAL) CHURCH OF GOD]

CREED AND COVENANT

"We believe in God the Father Almighty, maker of heaven and earth; and in Jesus Christ, His only Son, our Lord: which was conceived by the Holy Ghost, born of the virgin Mary, suffered under Pontius Pilate, was crucified, dead and buried: the third day He arose from the dead; He ascended into heaven and sitteth on the right hand of God the Father Almighty: from thence He shall come to judge the quick and dead. We believe in the Holy Ghost, The Church of God, the Communion of the saints, the forgiveness of sins, Sanctification by the Blood of Jesus Christ, the filling of the Holy Ghost, the resurrection of the body, and life everlasting" Amen.

CHURCH COVENANT

We, having been called out from the world by the blessed Spirit of God, and being acquainted with the articles of faith and pality of "The (Original) Church of God," and believing it to be The "True" Church of God, and having given our names, and thereby become members of the same, do solemnly, but cheerfully, and with joy and gladness enter into this covenant:

We will watch over one another with brotherly love and kindness, that we may with meekness assist in sustaining each other to the extent of our ability.

We will abstain (refrain) from frivolous conversations, foolish talking and jesting, from backbiting, tattling, taking up a reproach against any one, especially of our union. We will endeavor to walk worthy of the vocation wherewith we are called, with meekness and long-suffering, forbearing one another in love, doing all in our power to keep the unity of the Spirit in the bonds of peace.

We will share one another's burdens, and "so fulfill the law of Christ." We will also heed 1 Thes. 5:12, "And we beseech you, brethren, to know them which labor among you, and are over you in the Lord, and admonish. . . . And be at peace among yourselves." "We exhort you, brethren, warn them that are unruly, comfort the feebleminded, support the weak, be patient toward all men. See that none render evil for evil unto any man." Read Romans 12:17, also Ephesians 4:32.

We will endeavor to engage in some kind of Christian work, visiting the sick and distressed, and to all who will accept our deed of charity, so far as in our power lies, avoiding all sin. Eph. 5:11; 1 Peter 4:5; James 1:27; and all this we do, the Lord helping us. We will pay our Tithes, and give offerings, as the Lord has prospered us.

We accept this obligation of this Covenant in the name of the Father, and of the Son, and of the Holy Ghost.

DOCTRINE—BASIS OF FELLOWSHIP

The Following is a Summary of the Teachings, Precepts and Examples of our Lord, which The (Original) Church of God stands for and practices.

We stand for the whole Bible, rightly divided as set forth by the prophets, Jesus Christ and the Apostles, accepting nothing but the plainly written Word of God on all subjects.

1. REPENTANCE TOWARD GOD. A godly sorrow which arises from love to God and is accompanied with a hatred of sin, a love for holiness, and a fixed resolution to forsake sin, and an expectation of favor and forgiveness through the words of Christ. This is evangelistic or Gospel Repentance. Matt. 3: 2-8; 2 Cor. 7:10; Acts 20:21; Luke 13:3; Acts 3:19.

2. RESTITUTION. The blood of Jesus will never blot out any sin that we can make right: We must have a conscience void of offence toward God and man. Restitution includes restoring where one has defrauded, paying back debts, and confessing when necessary. Luke 19:8, 9; Psalms 69:4; Exodus 22:3; Luke 3:14.

CHURCH COVENANT AND BASIS OF FELLOWSHIP
[(ORIGINAL) CHURCH OF GOD] (continued)

3. REGENERATION. A change and renovation of the soul by the Spirit and grace of God. Matt. 19:28; Titus 3:4, 5. Born again, or from above, to receive spiritual life in the soul, enabling us to perform spiritual actions and live to God. To be Regenerated, renewed, to receive spiritual life, John 3:3, 5; 6:1; 1 Peter 1:23.

4. JUSTIFICATION. A state of being justified before God at any time in the Christian experience. It is that act of God's free grace by which we receive remission of sins. James 2:24; Rom. 5:1; 2 Cor. 5:21; Phil. 3:9; Romans 3:24-26; St. John 1:12.

5. SANCTIFICATION. Sanctification is subsequent to regeneration. Romans 5:2; 1 Cor. 1:30. Sanctification is that act of God's free grace, by which He makes us holy: and is the *Second Definite Work of Grace*, wrought with the blood of Christ through faith in Him. Heb. 10:10; therefore believers are saints. Heb. 13:12; 1 John 1:9; 1 Thes. 4:3; Heb. 2:11. Holiness, a life hid with Christ in God. Col. 3:3; Gal. 5:24; Luke 1:74-76; 1 Thes. 4:7; Heb. 12:14. Sanctification and holiness, with their equivalents are mentioned in the Word of God over five hundred times.

6. ENTIRE SANCTIFICATION. Entire Sanctification is by the work of the Holy Ghost through the knowledge of the Scriptures. St. John 17:17; 1 Thes. 5:23, 24. This is obtained by knowledge of the Scriptures and perfect obedience to them, and retained by the same method. The redemption of the body in the First Resurrection, and the uniting of redeemed soul and spirit into a redeemed body: then both soul and body is redeemed, made like unto the glorious body of Christ. 1 John 3:2, and we shall see Him and be like Him.

7. BAPTISM, OR FILLING WITH THE SPIRIT. Baptism with the Holy Ghost is subsequent to cleansing: the enduement of power for service and holy living which comes upon Sanctified believers only, and is Jesus Christ's baptism (Matt. 3:11), and is received through faith in the Word of God, and obtained through perfect obedience with a full surrender and complete sacrifice. John 20:22; Luke 24:49; John 7:38, 39; 14:16, 17, 26; Acts 1:5-8; 2:1-4; 10:44-46; 19:1-6.

8. SPEAKING WITH OTHER TONGUES. As the initiating evidence of the filling of the Holy Ghost to an overflowing: you will have the same sign or evidence that the disciples had on the day of Pentecost at Jerusalem (Acts 2:4), and the Gentiles had at the home of Cornelius (Acts 10:44-49), and at Ephesus (Acts 19:1-8). It is one of the signs that shall follow believers (Mark 16:17), and is one of the gifts of the Spirit to "The Church of God," for the day of grace until the return of the Bridegroom (1 Cor. 12:10). And, it was "other tongues" for it had to be interpreted.

The above Scriptures correctly read and prayerfully studied should convince every honest seeker of the truth that when one is filled with the Holy Ghost to overflowing, as were the saints at Jerusalem, he will "speak with other tongues as the Spirit gives the utterance." Every man, woman or child who is filled with the Holy Ghost *WILL Speak With Other Tongues.*

9. DIVINE HEALING. Jesus not only made provision for the salvation of the soul in His suffering on earth, but for the healing of the body as well. Isaiah 53:4, 5; Matt. 8:16-17; Mark 16:14-18; James 5:14-16; Exodus 15:26. Divine healing is obtained by faith, laying on of hands, the anointing of oil, and by special gift (1 Cor. 12:9).

The (Original) Church of God considers it not as a test of fellowship, but as an individual matter between themselves and God. It can clearly be seen through the Scriptures, that provision was made for body afflictions. This is a great blessing to those who can exercise the faith. 1 Peter 2:24; Heb. 12:12, 13.

10. GIFTS ACCOMPANYING GOD'S CHURCH. The full working of ALL the gifts in the Church. 1 Cor. 12:1-12; 28:32; 14:1.

11. SIGNS FOLLOWING BELIEVERS. We believe this exactly as the 16th chapter of Mark sets forth, and we believe every one of them will follow the ministry of God's Word. Mark 16:17-20; Heb. 2:4; Romans 15:18-19.

12. FRUITS OF THE SPIRIT. John 15:1-11. By our fruits all will know and judge whether we have what we profess. Romans 6:22; Gal. 5:22-23; Eph. 5:9; Phil. 1:11. May all take heed that the Spirit we manifest is a stronger evidence of the kind of spirit we possess than is our testimony or profession in words. It is a reflection on the plan of salvation to manifest one kind of spirit and profess another (1 Thes. 4:4).

13. WORKS OF THE FLESH. The (Original) Church of God stands against ALL the works of the flesh as in Gal. 5:19-21. By these are the unsaved dominated and controlled, and they can be seen on the surface by expressions and acts (2 Cor. 12:20.)

14. PRE-MILLENNIAL SECOND COMING OF CHRIST. The return of Jesus is just as literal as His going away (Acts 1:11; John 14:3). There will be two appearances under one coming: first, to resurrect the sleeping saints, and to catch away His waiting Bride (both the living and the dead) to meet Him in the air (Matt. 24:40-44; 1 Thes. 4:16-17).

In the First Resurrection every soul shall come out of Paradise, and shall enter their immortal bodies to live forever with Christ (Rev. 20:4). Verse 6 tells us who will have a part in the first resurrection. Second. Christ's coming on down to earth at the close of the great tribulation.

The Millineum will be a reign of peace and blessing with Jesus Christ our King and Ruler, and takes place between the resurrection of the saints and the resurrection of the wicked.

15. ETERNAL LIFE FOR THE RIGHTEOUS. Matt. 25:46; Luke 18:29-30; John 10:28; Romans 6:22; 1 John 5:11-13; Matt. 25:34-46.

16. THE WHITE THRONE JUDGEMENT. At the end of the Millineum or the one thousand years have expired, the ungodly and sinner will be called into judgement (Rev. 20:7, 10; 2 Thes. 1:7-9; Rev. 20:13-15). This is the resurrection of the wicked dead only, the second death.

17. ETERNAL PUNISHMENT FOR THE WICKED. Concerning the punishment for the wicked we read the following Scriptures and let the Word of God decide the question. On one thing we can be assured, that God will do right and give justice to every one, Matt. 25:41-46; Mark 3:29; Rev. 20:10-15; 21:18-19.

The foregoing Scriptures teach that the lake of fire is just as eternal as heaven. The wicked shall be cast into the lake of fire where the beast and false prophet are. Read the above Scriptures and flee the wrath to come on all them that know not God and who obey not His commandments.

18. TOTAL ABSTINENCE FROM ALL LIQUORS AND STRONG DRINKS. Christian people should be "temperate in all things" lawful; they should abstain from the use of intoxicants, tobacco and kindred carnal habits; they should not seek popularity, worldly power, nor offices, nor desire any of the follies of this world; "Wherefore come ye out from among them, and be ye separate, saith the Lord, and touch not the unclean thing; and I will receive you." 2 Cor. 6:17; Rev. 18:4; 1 Cor. 9:25; Gal. 5:25; 1 Thes. 5:22; Judges 13:4; Hab. 2:15; Prov. 23:29-32.

19. AGAINST ALL UNCLEANNESS AND FILTHI-NESS OF THE FLESH. God's people should be pure, holy, devout, reverent, with "Chaste Conversation coupled with fear" not yeilding to the lust of the flesh; therefore vulgar conversation, secret vice, and other improper and sinful conduct which give rise to social evils are entirely outside of the realms of Christian living (1 Peter 1:15; 2:12; 3:1; 2 Peter 3:11-14; 2 Cor. 7:1; Gal. 5:19-25; 1 John 3:3; Heb. 12:14; 1 Cor. 10:21; 2 Cor. 6:17-18; 1 Thes. 4:7). We, The (Original) Church of God, are *against and Forbid* the use of tobacco in any form either by ministers or laymen, and No One should be taken into the church until they have cleansed themselves from this and other sinful habits!

20. AGAINST MEMBERS GOING TO WAR. The Letter and the Spirit of the Gospel are emphatically against strife, contention, and carnal warfare, and therefore, no Christian should have part in carnal strife, whether among individuals, in suits of law, or in conflicts among nations. The nonresistant doctrine was taught and exemplified by Christ and the apostles and adhered to by true Christians until the present time. Matt. 5:38-45; 26:52; John 18:36; 1 Cor. 6:1-8; Romans 12:17-21; 2 Cor. 10:4; Luke 22:49-52; 3:10-14.

We believe it to be wrong for Christians to take up arms and go to war, as Jesus said: "Thou shalt not kill"; therefore, we would rather our members not engage in war.

21. SABBATH. The Sabbath (cessation) appears in the Scriptures as a day of God's rest in the finishing work of creation (Genesis 2:2, 3). For the next 2500 years of human life, there is absolutely no mention made of it in the Scripture. At Sinai the Sabbath was revealed (see Neh. 9:13, 14). This important passage fixes beyond all cavil the time when the Sabbath, God's rest (Gen. 2:1-3) was given to man. The seventh day Sabbath was never made a day of sacrificial worship, or any manner of religious service: it was simply and only a day of complete rest for man and beast—a humane provision for man's needs. In Christ's words, "The Sabbath was made for man, and not man for the Sabbath" (Mark 2:27). Christ, Himself, was held to be a Sabbath-breaker by the religious authorities of that day.

The Christians' first day perpetuates in the dispensation of Grace the principles that one-seventh of the time is especially sacred, but in all other respects is in contrast with the Sabbath: one is the seventh day, the other the first. The Sabbath commemorates God's Creation Rest; the First Day, Christ's Resurrection from the dead. On the seventh day God rested: on the first day Christ was busy all day. Jesus appeared to His disciples eight times that day. The Sabbath was a day of legal obligation, the first day one of voluntary worship service.

22. AGAINST MEMBERS SWEARING. Matt. 5:34; James 5:12.

23. MARRIAGE AND DIVORCE. Marriage was divinely instituted for the propagation, purity and happiness of the human race; it receives divine sanction between one man and one woman; the bond is dissoluable only by death or fornication, and there should be no marriage between a believer and an unbeliever, nor between members of The Church of God and other denominations (1 Cor. 7:39). "She is at liberty to be married to whom she will: only in the Lord" (Gen. 2:18; Mark 10:2-12; Rom. 7:2; Matt. 5:32; 19: 3-12).

We, The (Original) Church of God, accept as a Bible reason only one cause for divorce and remarriage as given in Matthew 5:32; but this is solely to God's children, having no reference to sinners or unbelievers. We do not go back of one's conversion, nor hold anything against them, inasmuch as the Word says "Old things have passed away, and, behold, all things are become new." Isaiah 43:18; 2 Cor. 5:17; Rev. 21:5. We accept both men and women where God accepts them, and hold them responsible from that time forward, as does God's Holy Word, and not from that time backward. God's law does not govern sinners. Jesus told the Samaritan woman (John 4: 10, 14, 39) that she had had five husbands,

CHURCH COVENANT AND BASIS OF FELLOWSHIP
[(ORIGINAL) CHURCH OF GOD] (continued)

and she admitted it, and the man she was now living with was not her husband. Jesus offered her salvation: told her she could have it by asking, as all the past was done in sin.

A Hint to the Wise is Sufficient!

Deacons and Bishops are not to have more than one living wife under any circumstances.

24. THE TRIBULATION. Jesus prophesied a great tribulation, such as was not since the beginning of the world (Matt. 24: 21, 29; Rev. 9th and 16th chapters). This will come under the ten-toe government of Daniel just ahead.

25. CHRIST'S MILLENNIAL REIGN. One thousand years of a literal reign of Jesus on earth. It will be ushered in by the coming of Jesus back to earth with ten thousands of His saints (Jude 14, 15; 2 Thes. 1:5-10). During this time the devil will be bound (Rev. 20: 2, 3). This will be a reign of peace and blessing. Read the prophesy which shows the quality of the kingdom during this time (Isaiah 11: 6-9; 65:25; Hosea 2:18; Isaiah 2: 2-4; Micah 4:3).

26. DOOM OF THE UNBELIEVING DEAD. The last judgement of the Great White Throne. God will judge the quick and dead according to their works (Rev. 20: 11-15; Acts 10:42; Daniel 12:2.)

27. A NEW HEAVEN AND A NEW EARTH. The Word teaches that this earth, which has been polluted by sin, shall pass away, or be regenerated, cleansed, purified and made holy, after the Great White Throne Judgement, and God will make a new heaven and a new earth in which dwelleth righteousness. This will be a glorious scene. The heaven and the earth like as they were before there was any sin (Matt. 24: 35; 2 Peter 3: 12-13; Rev. 21:3).

28. AGAINST MEMBERS WEARING GOLD FOR DECORATION. Such as finger rings, ear rings, bracelets, lockets, etc. (1 Peter 3:3: 1 John 2: 15-16).

29. CHRISTIANS TO BE CLOTHED IN MODEST APPAREL. Christian people should be clothed in modest apparel: the wearing of jewelry, costly array, fashionable attire, gaudy dress, and bodily ornamentation should be strictly avoided by all believers; "Be not conformed to this world; but be ye transformed, by the renewing of your mind" (Romans 12.1, 2; Isaiah 3:16-24; 1 Tim. 2:9, 10; 1 Peter 3:3-5; 1 John 2:15-17).

Under no consideration should Christian women be guilty of putting on men's apparel, or dressing like men, as this is strictly forbidden in God's Word, and it is unthinkable that a Christian woman would put on shorts, etc. Man is not to put on a woman's garment under any circumstance (Deut. 22:5): "The woman shall not wear that which pertaineth unto a man (pants, shorts, shirts, etc.), neither shall a man put on a woman's garment: for all that do so ARE ABOMINATION unto the Lord thy God."

30. PRIDE GOETH BEFORE DESTRUCTION. We believe that pride is an abomination in the sight of God; that humility and contrition characterize God's people in whom is not found an haughty, overbearing spirit. "For whosoever exalteth himself shall be abased; and he that humbleth himself shall be exalted." (Luke 14:11; Prov. 6:16, 17;) "Pride goeth before destruction" (1 John 2:15-17; Prov. 16:18; James 4:6).

31. COMPLETE SEPARATION OF CHURCH AND STATE. We believe that there should be a complete separation of Church and State; that though "Strangers and Pilgrims on the earth," we should be subject unto the higher powers. "Submit yourselves to every ordinance of man for the Lord's sake." Nevertheless we owe our first allegiance to God. John 18:36; Acts 5:29; Rom. 13:1-5; Heb. 11:13.

Notes: *The (Original) Church of God has three doctrinal statements. The Basis of Union (not reproduced here) is derived from the Church of God Teachings and the Twenty-nine Important Bible Truths used by other branches of the Church of God. The Church Covenant has been adopted by the Emmanuel Holiness Church.*

* * *

BASIS OF UNION (PENTECOSTAL FIRE-BAPTIZED HOLINESS CHURCH)

1. We believe that Jesus Christ shed His blood for the remission of sins that are past (Rom. 3:25), and for the regeneration of penitent sinners, and for salvation from sin and sinning (1 John 3:5-10; Eph. 2:1-10).

2. We believe, teach and firmly maintain the Scriptural doctrine of justification by faith (Rom. 5:1).

3. We believe also that Jesus Christ shed His blood for the complete cleansing of the justified believer from all indwelling sin, and from its pollution subsequent to regeneration (1 John 1:7-9).

4. We believe also that entire sanctification is an instantaneous, definite, second work of grace, obtainable by faith on the part of the justified believer (John 15:2; Acts 26:18; 2 Cor. 13:15; Luke 24:30-33, 50-54; John 17).

5. We believe also that the Pentecostal baptism of the Holy Ghost and fire is obtainable by a definite act of appropriating faith on the part of the fully cleansed believer, and that the initial evidence of the reception of this experience is speaking with other tongues as the Spirit gives utterance (Luke 11:13; Acts 1:5; 2:1-4; 8:17; 10:44-46; 19:6; St. John 15:26).

6. We also believe in divine healing as in the atonement (Isa. 53:4-5; Matt. 8:16-17; Mark 16:14-18; James 5:14-16; Ex. 15:26).

7. We believe in the imminent, personal, premillenial second coming of our Lord Jesus Christ (1 Thess. 4:15-18; Titus 2:13; 2 Peter 3:1-14; Matt. 24:29-44), and we love and wait for His appearing (2 Tim. 4:8).

8. The Pentecostal Fire-Baptized Holiness Church is utterly opposed to the teaching of the so-called Christian Scientists, Spiritualists, Unitarians, Universalists and Mormons. We deny as false and unscriptural, Seventh-Day Adventism, annihilation of the wicked, conditional immortality anti-nomianism; absolute perfection, so-called come-outism, the so-called resurrection life, the so-called redemption or glorification of the body in life, the doctrine of the restitution of all things (as set forth in millenialdawnism), and the teaching that we are not born of God until we are sanctified wholly.

9. No subsequent General Council shall have authority to change the Basis of Union without a full representation from the local churches.

Notes: *This statement is derived from the Basis of Union of the Pentecostal Holiness Church prior to the rewriting of its Articles of Faith in 1941. The Pentecostal Holiness Church had merged with the Fire-Baptized Holiness Church in 1911, and the Pentecostal Fire-Baptized Holiness Church broke away in 1918.*

* * *

THIS WE BELIEVE (PENTECOSTAL FREE WILL BAPTIST CHURCH)

We believe the BIBLE to be the inspired Word of God.

We believe that there is ONE GOD, eternally existing in three persons: Father, Son, and Holy Ghost.

We believe in the DEITY OF JESUS CHRIST; that Christ is the only begotten Son of God, and born of the Virgin Mary. That Christ died for our sins, was buried, and raised from the dead. That He ascended to heaven and is today at the right hand of the Father as our intercessor.

We believe that "ALL HAVE SINNED and come short of the glory of God," and that repentance is necessary for the forgiveness of sins.

We believe that JUSTIFICATION IS BY FAITH ALONE, and that regeneration or the new-birth through faith in the blood of Christ is absolutely essential.

We believe that SANCTIFICATION IS SUBSEQUENT TO REGENERATION AND IS A SECOND DEFINITE, INSTANTANEOUS WORK OF GRACE; obtained by faith on the part of the fully justified believer.

We believe that the PENTECOSTAL BAPTISM OF THE HOLY GHOST IS AN ENDUEMENT OF POWER FOR THOSE WHO HAVE CLEAN HEARTS, and the initial evidence of the reception of this experience is speaking with other tongues as the Spirit gives utterance.

We believe that the SAVED SHOULD RECEIVE WATER BAPTISM, in the name of the Father, and the Son, and the Holy Ghost, as a testimony to the world that he has accepted Christ as Saviour and Lord.

WE BELIEVE IN DIVINE HEALING as provided in the Atonement.

WE BELIEVE IN THE SACRAMENT of the LORD'S SUPPER as commemorating Christ's death and anticipating His Second Coming, and feet washing.

WE BELIEVE IN THE PERSONAL, PREMILLENNIAL, SECOND COMING OF JESUS; First, to resurrect the righteous dead and to catch away the living saints to meet Him in the air; second, to reign with His saints on earth a thousand years.

We believe in the bodily resurrection OF BOTH THE SAVED AND THE LOST; the saved to life eternal and the lost to everlasting punishment.

* * *

White Trinitarian Pentecostal

STATEMENT OF FUNDAMENTAL TRUTHS [(GENERAL COUNCIL OF THE) ASSEMBLIES OF GOD]

The Bible is our all-sufficient rule for faith and practice. This Statement of Fundamental Truths is intended simply as a basis of fellowship among us (i. e., that we all speak the same thing, 1 Cor. 1:10; Acts 2:42). The phraseology employed in this Statement is not inspired or contended for, but the truth set forth is held to be essential to a full Gospel ministry. No claim is made that it contains all Biblical truth, only that it covers our need as to these fundamental doctrines.

1. THE SCRIPTURES INSPIRED

   The Scriptures, both the Old and New Testaments, are verbally inspired of God and are the revelation of God to man, the infallible, authoritative rule of faith and conduct (2 Tim. 3:15-17; 1 Thess. 2:13; 2 Peter 1:21).

2. THE ONE TRUE GOD

   The one true God has revealed Himself as the eternally self-existent "I AM," the Creator of heaven and earth and the Redeemer of mankind. He has further revealed Himself as embodying the principles of relationship and association as Father, Son and Holy Ghost (Deut. 6:4; Isaiah 43:10,11; Matthew 28:19; Luke 3:22).

   THE ADORABLE GODHEAD

   (a) TERMS DEFINED

   The terms "Trinity" and "persons," as related to the Godhead, while not found in the Scriptures, are words in harmony with Scripture, whereby we may convey to others our immediate understanding of the doctrine of Christ respecting the Being of God, as distinguished from "gods many and lords many." We therefore may speak with propriety of the Lord our God, who is One Lord, as a trinity or as one Being of three persons, and still be absolutely scriptural (examples, Matt. 28:19; 2 Cor. 13:14; John 14:16, 17).

   (b) DISTINCTION AND RELATIONSHIP IN THE GODHEAD

   Christ taught a distinction of Persons in the Godhead which He expressed in specific terms of relationship, as Father, Son, and Holy Ghost, but

STATEMENT OF FUNDAMENTAL TRUTHS [(GENERAL COUNCIL OF THE) ASSEMBLIES OF GOD] (continued)

that this distinction and relationship, as to its mode is *inscrutable* and *incomprehensible*, because *unexplained*. Luke 1:35; 1 Cor. 1:24; Matt. 11:25-27; 28:19; 2 Cor. 13:14; 1 John 1:3,4.

(c) UNITY OF THE ONE BEING OF FATHER, SON AND HOLY GHOST

Accordingly, therefore, there is *that* in the Son which constitutes Him *the Son* and not the Father; and there is *that* in the Holy Ghost which constitutes Him *the Holy Ghost* and not either the Father or the Son. Wherefore the Father is the Begetter, the Son is the Begotten; and the Holy Ghost is the one proceeding from the Father and the Son. Therefore, because these three persons in the Godhead are in a state of unity, there is but one Lord God Almighty and His name one. John 1:18; 15:26; 17:11,21; Zech. 14:9.

(d) IDENTITY AND CO-OPERATION IN THE GODHEAD

The Father, the Son and the Holy Ghost are never *identical* as to *Person*; nor *confused* as to *relation*; nor *divided* in respect to the Godhead; nor *opposed* as to *co-operation*. The Son is *in* the Father and the Father is *in* the Son, as to relationship. The Son is *with* the Father and the Father is *with* the Son, as to fellowship. The Father is not *from the Son, but the Son is from* the Father, as to authority. The Holy Ghost is *from* the Father and the Son proceeding, as to nature, relationship, co-operation and authority. Hence, neither Person in the Godhead either exists or works separately or independently of the others. John 5:17-30, 32, 37; John 8:17, 18.

(e) THE TITLE, LORD JESUS CHRIST

The appellation, "Lord Jesus Christ," is a proper name. It is never applied, in the New Testament, either to the Father or to the Holy Ghost. It therefore belongs exclusively to the *Son of God*. Rom. 1:1-3,7; 2 John 3.

(f) THE LORD JESUS CHRIST, GOD WITH US

The Lord Jesus Christ, as to His divine and eternal nature, is the proper and only Begotten of the Father, but as to His human nature, He is the proper Son of Man. He is, therefore, acknowledged to be both God and man; who because He is God and man, is "Immanuel," God with us. Matt. 1:23; 1 John 4:2, 10, 14; Rev. 1:13, 17.

(g) THE TITLE, SON OF GOD

Since the name "Immanuel" embraces both God and man in the one Person, our Lord Jesus Christ, it follows that the title, Son of God, describes His proper deity, and the title Son of Man, His proper humanity. Therefore, the title, Son of God, belongs to the *order of eternity*, and the title, Son of Man, to the *order of time*. Matt. 1:21-23; 2 John 3; 1 John 3:8; Heb. 7:3; 1:1-13.

(h) TRANSGRESSION OF THE DOCTRINE OF CHRIST

Wherefore, it is a transgression of the Doctrine of Christ to say that Jesus Christ derived the title, Son of God, solely from the fact of the incarnation, or because of His relation to the economy of redemption. Therefore, to deny that the Father is a real and eternal Father, and that the Son is a real and eternal Son, is a denial of the distinction and relationship in the Being of God; a denial of the Father and the Son; and a displacement of the truth that Jesus Christ is come in the flesh. 2 John 9; John 1:1, 2, 14, 18, 29, 49; 1 John 2:22, 23; 4:1-5; Heb. 12:2.

(i) EXALTATION OF JESUS CHRIST AS LORD

The Son of God, our Lord Jesus Christ, having by Himself purged our sins, sat down on the right hand of the Majesty on high; angels and principalities and powers having been made subject unto Him. And having been made both Lord and Christ, He sent the Holy Ghost that we, in the name of Jesus, might bow our knees and confess that Jesus Christ is Lord to the glory of God the Father until the end, when the Son shall become subject to the Father that God may be all in all. Heb. 1:3; 1 Peter 3:22; Acts 2:32-36; Rom. 14:11; 1 Cor. 15:24-28.

(j) EQUAL HONOR TO THE FATHER AND TO THE SON

Wherefore, since the Father has delivered all judgment unto the Son, it is not only the *express duty* of all in heaven and on earth to bow the knee, but it is an *unspeakable* joy in the Holy Ghost to ascribe unto the Son all the attributes of Deity, and to give Him all the honor and the glory contained in all the names and titles of the Godhead (except those which express relationship. See paragraphs b, c, and d), and thus honor the Son even as we honor the Father. John 5:22, 23; 1 Peter 1:8; Rev. 5:6-14; Phil. 2:8, 9; Rev. 7:9, 10; 4:8-11.

3. THE DEITY OF THE LORD JESUS CHRIST

The Lord Jesus Christ is the eternal Son of God. The Scriptures declare:

(a) His virgin birth (Matthew 1:23; Luke 1:31, 35).

(b) His sinless life (Hebrews 7:26; 1 Peter 2:22).

(c) His miracles (Acts 2:22; 10:38).

(d) His substitutionary work on the cross (1 Cor. 15:3; 2 Cor. 5:21).

(e) His bodily resurrection from the dead (Matthew 28:6; Luke 24:39; 1 Cor. 15:4).

(f) His exaltation to the right hand of God (Acts 1:9, 11; 2:33; Philippians 2:9-11; Hebrews 1-3).

4. THE FALL OF MAN

Man was created good and upright; for God said, "Let us make man in our image, after our likeness." However, man by voluntary transgression fell and thereby incurred not only physical death but also spiritual death, which is separation from God (Genesis 1:26, 27; 2:17; 3:6; Romans 5:12-19).

5. THE SALVATION OF MAN

Man's only hope of redemption is through the shed blood of Jesus Christ the Son of God.

(a) CONDITIONS TO SALVATION

Salvation is received through repentance toward God and faith toward the Lord Jesus Christ. By the washing of regeneration and renewing of the Holy Ghost, being justified by grace through faith, man becomes an heir of God according to the hope of eternal life (Luke 24:47; John 3:3; Romans 10:13-15; Ephesians 2:8; Titus 2:11; 3:5-7).

(b) THE EVIDENCES OF SALVATION

The inward evidence of salvation is the direct witness of the Spirit (Romans 8:16). The outward evidence to all men is a life of righteousness and true holiness (Eph. 4:24; Titus 2:12).

6. THE ORDINANCES OF THE CHURCH

(a) BAPTISM IN WATER

The ordinance of baptism by immersion is commanded in the Scriptures. All who repent and believe on Christ as Saviour and Lord are to be baptized. Thus they declare to the world that they have died with Christ and that they also have been raised with Him to walk in newness of life (Matthew 28:19; Mark 16:16; Acts 10:47, 48; Romans 6:4).

(b) HOLY COMMUNION

The Lord's Supper, consisting of the elements—bread and the fruit of the vine—is the symbol expressing our sharing the divine nature of our Lord Jesus Christ (2 Peter 1:4); a memorial of His suffering and death (1 Cor. 11:26); and a prophecy of His second coming (1 Cor. 11:26); and is enjoined on all believers "till He come!"

7. THE BAPTISM IN THE HOLY GHOST

All believers are entitled to and should ardently expect and earnestly seek the promise of the Father, the baptism in the Holy Ghost and fire, according to the command of our Lord Jesus Christ. This was the normal experience of all in the early Christian Church. With it comes the enduement of power for life and service, the bestowment of the gifts and their uses in the work of the ministry (Luke 24:49; Acts 1:4,8; 1 Cor. 12:1-31). This experience is distinct from and subsequent to the experience of the new birth (Acts 8:12-17; 10:44-46; 11:14-16; 15:7-9). With the baptism in the Holy Ghost come such experiences as an overflowing fullness of the Spirit (John 7:37-39; Acts 4:8), a deepened reverence for God (Acts 2:43; Heb. 12:28), an intensified consecration to God and dedication to His work (Acts 2:42), and a more active love for Christ, for His Word and for the lost (Mark 16:20).

8. THE EVIDENCE OF THE BAPTISM IN THE HOLY GHOST

The Baptism of believers in the Holy Ghost is witnessed by the initial physical sign of speaking with other tongues as the Spirit of God gives them utterance (Acts 2:4). The speaking in tongues in this instance is the same in essence as the gift of tongues (1 Cor. 12:4-10, 28), but different in purpose and use.

9. SANCTIFICATION

Sanctification is an act of separation from that which is evil, and of dedication unto God (Rom. 12:1, 2; 1 Thess. 5:23; Heb. 13:12). The Scriptures teach a life of "holiness without which no man shall see the Lord" (Heb. 12:14). By the power of the Holy Ghost we are able to obey the command: "Be ye holy, for I am holy" (1 Pet. 1:15, 16).

Sanctification is realized in the believer by recognizing his identification with Christ in His death and resurrection, and by faith reckoning daily upon the fact of that union, and by offering every faculty continually to the dominion of the Holy Spirit (Rom. 6:1-11, 13; 8:1,2,13; Gal. 2:20; Phil. 2:12,13; 1 Pet. 1:5).

10. THE CHURCH

The Church is the Body of Christ, the habitation of God through the Spirit, with divine appointments for the fulfillment of her great commission. Each believer, born of the Spirit, is an integral part of the General Assembly and Church of the First-born, which are written in heaven (Ephesians 1:22,23; 2:22; Hebrews 12:23).

11. THE MINISTRY

A divinely called and scripturally ordained ministry has been provided by our Lord for a twofold purpose: 1) The evangelization of the world, and 2) The edifying of the Body of Christ (Mark 16:15-20; Ephesians 4:11-13).

12. DIVINE HEALING

Divine healing is an integral part of the gospel. Deliverance from sickness is provided for in the atonement, and is the privilege of all believers (Isaiah 53:4,5; Matt. 8:16,17; James 5:14-16).

13. THE BLESSED HOPE

The resurrection of those who have fallen asleep in Christ and their translation together with those who are alive and remain unto the coming of the Lord is the imminent and blessed hope of the Church (1 Thess. 4:16,17; Romans 8:23; Titus 2:13; 1 Cor. 15:51,52).

14. THE MILLENNIAL REIGN OF CHRIST

The second coming of Christ includes the rapture of the saints, which is our blessed hope, followed by the visible return of Christ with His saints to reign on the earth for one thousand years (Zech. 14:5; Matt. 24:27, 30; Revelation 1:7; 19:11-14; 20:1-6). This millennial reign will bring the salvation of national Israel (Ezekiel 37:21, 22; Zephaniah 3:19-20; Romans 11:26,27) and the establishment of universal peace (Isaiah 11:6-9; Psalm 72:3-8; Micah 4:3, 4).

15. THE FINAL JUDGMENT

There will be a final judgment in which the wicked dead will be raised and judged according to their works. Whosoever is not found written in the Book of Life, together with the devil and his angels, the beast and the false prophet, will be consigned to everlasting punishment in the lake which burneth with fire and brimstone, which is the second death (Matt. 25:46; Mark 9:43-48; Revelation 19:20; 20:11-15; 21:8).

16. THE NEW HEAVENS AND THE NEW EARTH

"We, according to His promise, look for new heavens and a new earth, wherein dwelleth righteousness" (2 Peter 3:13; Revelation 21:22).

(At the 33rd General Council of the Assemblies of God (1969) the following paragraphs were adopted to replace paragraphs 10 and 11 of the *Statement* of Fundamental Truths. The change incorporates the statement of mission, which was also adopted at that time.)

10. THE CHURCH AND ITS MISSION

The Church is the Body of Christ, the habitation of God through the Spirit, with divine appointments for the fulfillment of her great commission. Each believer, born of the Spirit, is an integral part of the General Assembly and Church of the Firstborn, which are written in heaven (Ephesians 1:22, 23; 2:22; Hebrews 12:23).

Since God's purpose concerning man is to seek and to save that which is lost, to be worshiped by man, and to build a body of believers in the image of His Son, the priority reason-for-being of the Assemblies of God as part of the Church is:

a. To be an agency of God for evangelizing the world (Acts 1:8; Matthew 28:19,20; Mark 16:15,16).

b. To be a corporate body in which man may worship God (1 Corinthians 12:13).

c. To be a channel of God's purpose to build a body of saints being perfected in the image of His Son (Ephesians 4:11-16; 1 Corinthians 12:28; 1 Corinthians 14:12).

The Assemblies of God exists expressly to give continuing emphasis to this reason-for-being in the New Testament apostolic pattern by teaching and encouraging believers to be baptized in the Holy Spirit. This experience:

a. Enables them to evangelize in the power of the Spirit with accompanying supernatural signs (Mark 16:15-20; Acts 4:29-31; Hebrews 2:3,4).

b. Adds a necessary dimension to worshipful relationship with God (1 Corinthians 2:10-16; 1 Corinthians 12, 13, and 14).

c. Enables them to respond to the full working of the Holy Spirit in expression of fruit and gifts and ministries as in New Testament times for the edifying of the body of Christ (Galatians 5:22-26; 1 Corinthians 14:12; Ephesians 4:11, 12; 1 Corinthians 12:28; Colossians 1:29).

11. THE MINISTRY

A divinely called and scripturally ordained ministry has been provided by our Lord for the threefold purpose of leading the Church in: (1) Evangelization of the world (Mark 16:15-20), (2) Worship of God (John 4:23, 24), (3) Building a body of saints being perfected in the image of His Son (Ephesians 4:11-16).

Notes: *The earliest doctrinal division in the Pentecostal Movement became manifest in Los Angeles during the midst of the revival taking place at the Azusa Street Mission. The pastor, William Seymour, was firmly committed to the holiness pentecostal position that one must be saved and sanctified before receiving the baptism of the Holy Spirit. He was opposed by William Durham, a Chicago Baptist minister who had received the baptism at Azusa but believed that baptism was the immediate prospect of all Christians.*

Durham's position was termed the "finished work," referring to the Reformation theological position that sanctification and justification were included in Christ's finished work on the cross. To all who had faith in Christ, his atonement imputed justification (freedom from the divine wrath of sin) and sanctification (holiness in God's eyes). Believers considered to be both justified and sanctified faced the task of ending their participation in sin of thought and action and becoming holy; a lifelong process to be completed only after death. The "finished work" appealed especially to those who had come into the pentecostal experience from non-Methodist backgrounds. It had been adopted by those who came together in 1914 to organize the General Council of the Assemblies of God, the first prominent group to formally align itself with Durham's understanding.

The Statement of Fundamental Truths by the (General Council of the) Assemblies of God was hammered out in such a way as to distinguish the Assemblies of God from both the holiness-pentecostal groups and the non-Trinitarian pentecostal bodies. Particular note should be made of the statements on the baptism of the Holy Ghost and sanctification (7 and 9), as well as the detailed statements on the Trinity (2). In 1969 new statements on the church and the ministry (10 and 11) were adopted.

* * *

TENETS OF FAITH (CALIFORNIA EVANGELISTIC ASSOCIATION)

TENETS OF FAITH

This corporation shall accept the Holy Scriptures as the revealed will of God, the all-sufficient rule for faith and practice, and for the purpose of maintaining general unity, adopts the statement of Fundamental Truths approved by the Board of Trustees.

FUNDAMENTAL TRUTHS

The human phraseology employed in this statement is not inspired or contended for, but the truth set forth is held to be essential to a full gospel ministry. No claims are made that it contains all truth in the Bible, only that it covers our present needs as to those fundamental matters.

1. THE SCRIPTURES INSPIRED.

   The Bible is the inspired Word of God, a revelation from God to man, the infallible rule of faith and conduct, and is superior to conscience and reason. II. Tim. 3:16; II. Pet. 1:21; Heb. 4:12.

2. THE ONE TRUE GOD.

   The one true God has revealed Himself as the eternally self-existent, self-revealed creator of the universe and is the Father of our Lord Jesus Christ. Deut. 6:4; Mark 12:29; Isa. 43:10; Matt. 28:19.

3. MAN, HIS FALL AND REDEMPTION.

   Man was created good and upright, for God said, "Let us make man in our image, after our likeness." But man, by voluntary transgression fell, and his only hope of redemption is in Jesus Christ the Son of God. Gen. 1:26, 31; 3:1-7, Rom. 5:12,21.

4. THE SALVATION OF MAN.

   (a) Conditions to salvation: The grace of God, which bringeth salvation hath appeared to all man through the preaching of repentance toward God and faith toward the Lord Jesus Christ; man is saved by the washing of regeneration and renewing of the Holy Ghost, and being justified by grace through faith, he becomes an heir of God according to the hope of eternal life. Titus 2:11; Rom. 8:16,15; Luke 24:47; Titus 3:5,7.

   (b) The Evidences of Salvation: The inward evidence to the believer of his salvation is the direct witness of the Spirit. Rom. 8:16. The outward evidence to all men is a life of righteousness and true holiness.

5. BAPTISM IN WATER.

   The ordinance of baptism by burial with Christ should be observed as commanded in the Scriptures, by all who have really repented and in their hearts have truly believed on Christ as Savior and Lord. In so doing, they declare to the world that they have been buried with Jesus Christ and that they have also been raised with Him to walk in newness of life. Mat. 28:19; Acts 10:47,48; Rom. 6:4.

6. THE LORD'S SUPPER.

   The Lord's Supper, consisting of the elements, bread and the fruit of the vine, is the symbol expressing our sharing the divine nature of our Lord Jesus Christ, a memorial of His suffering and death and a prophecy of His second coming, and is enjoined on all believers, "until He comes." John 6:48, 51-58; Luke 22:19, 20; II. Pet. 1:4; I. Cor. 11:26.

7. THE PROMISE OF THE FATHER.

   All believers are entitled to and should ardently expect and earnestly seek, the promise of the Father, the Baptism of the Holy Ghost according to the Command of our Lord Jesus Christ. This was the normal experience of all in the early Christian Church. With it comes the enduement of power for life and service, the bestowment of the gifts and their uses in the work of the ministry. Luke 24:49; Acts 1:4,8; I. Cor. 12:1,31. This wonderful experience is distinct from and subsequent to the experience of the new birth. Acts 2:38; 10:44,46; 15:7-9.

8. THE EVIDENCE OF THE BAPTISM IN THE HOLY GHOST.

   The Full consummation of the Baptism of believers in the Holy Ghost is evidenced by the initial physical sign of speaking with other tongues as the Spirit gives utterance, and by subsequent manifestation of spiritual power in public testimony and service. Acts 2:4; 10:44,46; 1:8; 2:42, 43.

9. ENTIRE SANCTIFICATION.

   The Scriptures teach a life of holiness, without which no man shall see the Lord. By the power of the Holy Ghost we are able to obey the command, "Be ye holy, for I am holy." Entire Sanctification is the will of God for all believers, and should be earnestly pursued by walking in obedience to God's word. Heb. 12:14; I. Pet. 1:15; I. Thess. 5:23,24; I. John 2:6; Rom. 8:3,4.

10. THE CHURCH.

    The Church is the body of Christ, the habitation of God through the Spirit, with divine appointments for the fulfillment of her great commission. Each believer, born of the Spirit, is an integral part of the general Assembly and Church of the First-born, which are written in Heaven. Eph. 1:22; Heb. 12:23; Eph. 2:19,22.

11. THE MINISTRY AND EVANGELISM.

    A divinely called and scripturally ordained ministry has been provided by our Lord for a two-fold purpose: (1) the evangelism of the world, and (2) the edifying of the body of Christ. Mark 16:15, 20; Eph. 4:11,13.

12. DIVINE HEALING.

    Deliverance from sickness is provided for in the Word of God and is the privilege of the believers. Mark 16:18; John 5:14; Matt. 8:16, 17.

13. THE BLESSED HOPE.

    The resurrection of those who have fallen asleep in Christ and their translation, together with those who are alive and remain unto the coming of the Lord, we believe, is imminent and is the blessed hope of the Church. I. Thess. 4:16-18; Rom. 8:23; Titus 2:13; I. Cor. 15:41-52.

14. THE EVERLASTING REIGN OF JESUS.

    The revelation of the Lord Jesus Christ from Heaven, the salvation of spiritual Israel, and the everlasting reign of Christ on the earth is the scriptural promise and the only hope of the church. II. Thess. 1:7; Rev. 19:11-16; Rom. 11:25-27: Rev. 21:1-7.

15. THE LAKE OF FIRE.

The Devil and his angels, and whosoever is not found written in the Book of Life shall be punished with everlasting destruction from the presence of the Lord, which is the second death. II. Thess. 1:9; Rev. 20:10.

16. THE NEW HEAVENS AND NEW EARTH.

We, "according to His promise look for new heavens and a new earth wherein dwelleth righteousness." II. Pet. 3:13; Rev. 21:1.

Notes: *These tenets are derived from the Fundamental Truths of the Assemblies of God. The items on the church and on the ministry and evangelism were part of the Assemblies's statement until 1969. The Assemblies are premillennial in their eschatology.*

*   *   *

WE BELIEVE (CALVARY CHAPEL CHURCH)

The Calvary Chapel Church has been formed as a fellowship of believers in the Lordship of Jesus Christ.

Our supreme desire is to know Christ and to be conformed into His image by the power of the Holy Spirit.

We are not a denominational church, nor are we opposed to denominations as such, only their over-emphasis of the doctrinal differences that have led to the division of the Body of Christ.

We believe that the only true basis of Christian fellowship is His (Agape) love, which is greater than any differences we possess and without which we have no right to claim ourselves Christians.

WE BELIEVE worship of God should be Spiritual.

Therefore: We remain flexible and yielded to the leading of the Holy Spirit to direct our worship.

WE BELIEVE worship of God should be Inspirational.

Therefore: We give a great place to music in our worship.

WE BELIEVE worship of God should be Intelligent.

Therefore: Our services are designed with great emphasis upon teaching the Word of God that He might instruct us how He should be worshipped.

WE BELIEVE worship of God is Fruitful.

Therefore: We look for His love in our lives as the supreme manifestation that we have truly been worshipping Him.

Notes: *As with many of the newer churches, the statement of Calvary Chapel is brief, dealing with only a few essential issues. Rather than emphasize doctrine, the statement centers on the Christian fellowship of love as a uniting force above denominational barriers.*

STATEMENT OF FUNDAMENTAL TRUTHS (CALVARY MINISTRIES, INC.)

1. THE SCRIPTURES INSPIRED

The Scriptures, both the Old and New Testaments, are verbally inspired of God and are the revelation of God to man, the infallible, authoritative rule of faith and conduct (2 Timothy 3:15-17; 1 Thessalonians 2:13: 2 Peter 1:21).

2. THE ONE TRUE GOD

The one true God has revealed Himself as the eternally self-existent "I AM," the Creator of heaven and earth and the Redeemer of mankind. He has further revealed Himself as embodying the principles of relationship and association as Father, Son and Holy Ghost (Deuteronomy 6:4; Isaiah 43:10, 11; Matthew 28:19; Luke 3:22).

THE ADORABLE GODHEAD

(a) TERMS DEFINED. The terms "Trinity" and "persons," as related to the Godhead, while not found in the Scriptures, are words in harmony with Scripture, whereby we may convey to others our immediate understanding of the doctrine of Christ respecting the Being of God, as distinguished from "gods many and lords many." We therefore may speak with propriety of the Lord our God, who is One Lord, as a trinity or as one Being of three persons, and still be absolutely scriptural (examples, Matthew 28:19; 2 Corinthians 13:14; John 14:16, 17).

(b) DISTINCTION AND RELATIONSHIP IN THE GODHEAD. Christ taught a distinction of Persons in the Godhead which He expressed in specific terms of relationship, as Father, Son, and Holy Ghost, but that this distinction and relationship, as to its mode is *inscrutable* and *incomprehensible,* because *unexplained.* (Luke 1:35; 1 Corinthians 1:24; Matthew 11:25-27; 28:19; 2 Corinthians 13:14; 1 John 1:3, 4.)

(c) UNITY OF THE ONE BEING OF FATHER, SON AND HOLY GHOST. Accordingly, therefore, there is *that* in the Son which constitutes Him *the* Son and not the Father, and there is *that* in the Holy Ghost which constitutes him *the Holy Ghost* and not either the Father or the Son. Wherefore the Father is the Begetter, the Son is the Begotten; and the Holy Ghost is the one proceeding from the Father and the Son. Therefore, because these three persons in the Godhead are instate of unity, there is but one Lord God Almighty and His name one. (John 1:18; 15:26; 17:11, 21; Zechariah 14:9.)

(d) IDENTITY AND CO-OPERATION IN THE GODHEAD. The Father, the Son and the Holy Ghost are never *identical* as to *Person;* nor *confused* as to *relation;* nor *divided* in respect to the Godhead; nor *opposed* as to *co-operation.* The Son is *in* the Father and the Father is *in* the Son as to relationship. The Son is *with* the Father and the Father is *with* the Son, as to fellowship. The Father is not *from* the Son, but the Son is *from* the Father, as to authority. The Holy Ghost is *from* the Father and the Son proceeding, as to nature, relationship, co-operation and authority. Hence, neither Person in the Godhead either exists or works separately or independently of the others. (John 5:17-30, 32, 37; 8:17, 18.)

(e) THE TITLE, LORD JESUS CHRIST. The appellation, "Lord Jesus Christ," is a proper name. It is never applied, in the New Testament, either to the Father or to the Holy Ghost. It therefore belongs exclusively to the *Son of God.* (Romans 1:1-3, 7; 2 John 3.)

(f) THE LORD JESUS CHRIST, GOD WITH US. The Lord Jesus Christ, as to His Divine and eternal nature, is the proper and only Begotten of the Father, but as to His human nature. He is the proper Son of Man. He is, therefore, acknowledged to be both God and man: who because He is God, and man, "Immanuel," God with us. (Matthew 1:23; 1 John 4:2, 10, 14; Revelation 1:13, 17.)

(g) THE TITLE, SON OF GOD. Since the name, "Immanuel" embraces both God and man in the one Person, our Lord Jesus Christ, it follows that the title, Son of God, describes His proper deity, and the title Son of Man, His proper humanity. Therefore, the title, Son of God, belongs to the *order of eternity,* and the title, Son of Man, to the *order of time.* (Matthew 1:21-23; 2 John 3; 1 John 3:8; Hebrews 7:3; 1:1-13.)

(h) TRANSGRESSION OF THE DOCTRINE OF CHRIST. Wherefore, it is a transgression of the doctrine of Christ to say that Jesus Christ derived the title, Son of God, solely from the fact of the incarnation, or because of His relation to the economy of redemption. Therefore, to deny that the Father is a real and eternal Father, and that the Son is a real and eternal Son, is a denial of the distinction and relationship in the Being of God; a denial of the Father and the Son; and a displacement of the truth that Jesus Christ is come in the flesh. (2 John 9; John 1:1, 2, 14, 18, 29, 49; 1 John 2:22, 23; 4:1-5; Hebrews 12:2.)

(i) EXALTATION OF JESUS CHRIST AS LORD. The Son of God, our Lord Jesus Christ, having by Himself purged our sins, sat down on the right hand of the Majesty on high; angels and principalities and powers having been made subject unto Him. And having been made both Lord and Christ, He sent the Holy Ghost that we, in the name of Jesus, might bow our knees and confess that Jesus Christ is Lord to the glory of God the Father until the end, when the Son shall become subject to the Father that God may be all in all. (Hebrews 1:3; 1 Peter 3:22; Acts 2:32-36; Romans 14:11; 1 Corinthians 15:24-28.)

(j) EQUAL HONOR TO THE FATHER AND TO THE SON. Wherefore, since the Father has delivered all judgment unto the *Son,* it is not only the *express duty* of all in heaven and on earth to bow the knee, but it is an *unspeakable* joy in the Holy Ghost to ascribe unto the Son all the attributes of Deity, and to give Him all the honor and the glory contained in all the names and titles of the Godhead except those which express relationship (see paragraphs b, c, and d), and thus honor the Son even as we honor the Father. (John 5:22, 23; 1 Peter 1:8; Revelation 5:6-14; Philippians 2:8, 9; Revelation 7:9, 10; 4:8-11.)

3. THE DEITY OF THE LORD JESUS CHRIST

The Lord Jesus Christ is the eternal Son of God. The Scriptures declare:

(a) His virgin birth (Matthew 1:23; Luke 1:31, 35).

(b) His sinless life (Hebrews 7:26; 1 Peter 2:22).

(c) His miracles (Acts 2:22; 10:38).

(d) His substitutionary work on the cross (1 Corinthians 15:3; 2 Corinthians 5:21).

(e) His bodily resurrection from the dead (Matthew 28:6; Luke 24:39; 1 Corinthians 15:4).

(f) His exaltation to the right hand of God (Acts 1:9, 11; 2:33; Philippians 2:9-11; Hebrews 1-3).

4. THE FALL OF MAN

Man was created good and upright; for God said, "Let us make man in our image, after our likeness." However, man by voluntary transgression fell and thereby incurred not only physical death but also spiritual death, which is separation from God (Genesis 1:26, 27; 2:17; 3:6; Romans 5:12-19).

5. THE SALVATION OF MAN

Man's only hope of redemption is through the shed blood of Jesus Christ the Son of God.

(a) CONDITIONS TO SALVATION. Salvation is received through repentance toward God and faith toward the Lord Jesus Christ. By the washing of regeneration and renewing of the Holy Ghost, being justified by grace through faith, man becomes an heir of God according to the hope of eternal life (Luke 24:47; John 3:3; Romans 10:13-15; Ephesians 2:8; Titus 2:11; 3:5-7).

(b) THE EVIDENCES OF SALVATION. The inward evidence of salvation is the direct witness of the Spirit (Romans 8:16). The outward evidence to all men is a life of righteousness and true holiness (Ephesians 4:24; Titus 2:12).

6. THE ORDINANCES OF THE CHURCH

(a) BAPTISM IN WATER. The ordinance of baptism, by immersion is commanded in the Scriptures. All who repent and believe in Christ as Saviour and Lord are to be baptized. Thus they declare to the world that they have died with Christ and that they also have been raised with Him to walk in newness of life. (Matthew 28:19; Mark 16:16; Acts 10:47, 48; Romans 6:4).

(b) HOLY COMMUNION. The Lord's Supper, consisting of the elements—bread and the fruit of the vine—is the symbol expressing our sharing the divine nature of our Lord Jesus Christ (2 Peter 1:4); a memorial of His suffering and death (1 Corinthians 11:26); and a prophecy of His second coming (1 Corinthians 11:26); and is enjoined on all believers "till He come!"

STATEMENT OF FUNDAMENTAL TRUTHS (CALVARY
MINISTRIES, INC.) (continued)

7. THE BAPTISM IN THE HOLY GHOST

All believers are entitled to and should ardently expect and
earnestly seek the promise of the Father, the baptism in the
Holy Ghost and fire, according to the command of our
Lord Jesus Christ. This was the normal experience of all in
the early Christian Church. With it comes the enduement
of power for life and service, the bestowment of the gifts
and their uses in the work of the ministry (Luke 24:49;
Acts 1:4-8; 1 Corinthians 12:1-31). This experience is
distinct from and subsequent to the experience of the new
birth (Acts 8:12-17; 10:44-46; 11:14-16; 15:7-9). With the
baptism in the Holy Ghost come such experiences as an
overflowing fullness of the Spirit (John 7:37-39; Acts 4:8),
a deepened reverence for God (Acts 2:43; Hebrews 12:28),
an intensified consecration to God and dedication to His
work (Acts 2:42), and a more active love for Christ, for
His Word, and for the lost (Mark 16:20).

8. THE EVIDENCE OF THE BAPTISM IN THE HOLY GHOST

The Baptism of believers in the Holy Ghost is witnessed by
the initial physical sign of speaking with other tongues as
the Spirit of God gives them utterance (Acts 2:4). The
speaking in tongues in this instance is the same in essence
as the gift of tongues (1 Corinthians 12:4-10, 28), but
different in purpose and use.

9. SANCTIFICATION

Sanctification is an act of separation from that which is
evil, and of dedication unto God (Romans 12:1, 2; 1
Thessalonians 5:23; Hebrews 13:12). The Scriptures teach
a life of "holiness without which no man shall see the
Lord" (Hebrews 12:14). By the power of the Holy Ghost
we are able to obey the command: "Be ye holy, for I am
holy" (1 Peter 1:15, 16).

Sanctification is realized in the believer by recognizing his
identification with Christ in His death and resurrection,
and by faith reckoning daily upon the fact of that union,
and by offering every faculty continually to the dominion
of the Holy Spirit (Romans 6:1-13; Romans 8:1, 2, 13;
Galatians 2:20; Philippians 2:12, 13; 1 Peter 1:5).

10. THE CHURCH

The Church is the Body of Christ, the habitation of God
through the Spirit, with divine appointments for the
fulfillment of her great commission. Each believer, born of
the Spirit, is an integral part of the General Assembly and
Church of the First-born, which are written in heaven
(Ephesians 1:22, 23; 2:22; Hebrews 12:23).

11. THE MINISTRY

A divinely called and scripturally ordained ministry has
been provided by our Lord for a twofold purpose: (1) The
evangelization of the world, and (2) The edifying of the
Body of Christ (Mark 16:15-20; Ephesians 4:11-13).

12. DIVINE HEALING

Divine healing is an integral part of the gospel. Deliverance from sickness is provided for in the atonement, and is
the privilege of all believers (Isaiah 53:4, 5; Matthew 8:16,
17; James 5:14-16).

13. THE BLESSED HOPE

The resurrection of those who have fallen asleep in Christ
and their translation together with those who are alive and
remain unto the coming of the Lord is the imminent and
blessed hope of the Church (1 Thessalonians 4:16, 17;
Romans 8:23; Titus 2:13; 1 Corinthians 15:51, 52).

14. THE MILLENNIAL REIGN OF CHRIST

The second coming of Christ includes the rapture of the
saints, which is our blessed hope, followed by the visible
return of Christ with His saints to reign on the earth for
one thousand years (Zechariah 14:5; Matthew 24:27, 30;
Revelation 1:7; 19:11-14; 20:1-6). This millennial reign will
bring the salvation of national Israel (Ezekiel 37:21, 22;
Zephaniah 3:19-20; Romans 11:26, 27) and the establishment of universal peace (Isaiah 11:6-9; Psalm 72:3-8;
Micah 4:3, 4).

15. THE FINAL JUDGMENT

There will be a final judgment in which the wicked dead
will be raised and judged according to their works.
Whosoever is not found written in the Book of Life,
together with the devil and his angels, the beast and the
false prophet, will be consigned to everlasting punishment
in the lake which burneth with fire and brimstone, which
is the second death (Matthew 25:46; Mark 9:43-48;
Revelation 19:20; 20:11-15; 21:8).

16. THE NEW HEAVENS AND THE NEW EARTH

"We, according to his promise, look for new heavens and a
new earth, wherein dwelleth righteousness" (2 Peter 3:13;
Revelation 21:22).

Notes: *This statement is based upon that of the General
Council of the Assemblies of God, differing only in its
omission of the most recent revisions of, and additions to,
the Assemblies' statement.*

*　　*　　*

WHAT WE BELIEVE (CHRISTIAN CHURCH OF NORTH AMERICA)

We believe and accept the entire Bible as the infallible
Word of God, inspired by the Holy Ghost; the only and
perfect order of our faith; and manner of living; to which
nothing can be added or taken away, which is the power of
God unto salvation to believers. 2 Pet. 1:21; 2 Tim. 3:16-
17; Rom. 1:16.

We believe there is only one living and true God, eternal
with unlimited power, Creator of all things; and in the one
God are three distinct persons: The Father, the Son, and
the Holy Ghost. Eph. 4:6; Matt. 28:19; 1 John 5:7.

We believe that the Son of God is the Word, made flesh,
who assumed the human body through the virgin Mary,
and so is true God and true man, two natures in one
person, the divine and human; and, therefore, is the only
Saviour, who in reality suffered death, not only for the
primitive transgressions, but also for the actual sins of
man. John 1:14; Lk. 1:27-35; 1 Pet. 3:18.

We believe in the existence of a personal devil, who, with all evil spirits, will be eternally punished in the Lake of Fire. Matt. 25:41.

We believe that regeneration or the new birth is received only through faith in Christ Jesus; who was raised for our justification. They who are in Christ Jesus (cleansed through His blood) are new creatures, and have Him for wisdom and righteousness and sanctification and redemption. Rom. 3:24, 25; 2 Cor. 5:17; 1 Cor. 1:30.

We believe in water baptismal by single immersion, in the name of the Father and of the Son and the Holy Ghost according to Christ's commission. Matt. 28:18,19.

We believe in the baptism in the Holy Ghost as an experience received subsequent to salvation, with the sign of speaking in tongues as the Holy Ghost gives utterance. Acts 2:4; 10:45-47; 19:6.

We believe in the Lord's Supper, when Christ, then, taking bread—"He gave thanks, and brake it and gave unto them Saying: 'This is my body which is given for you: this do in rememberance of me.' Likewise also the cup after supper, saying 'This cup is the new testament in my blood, which is shed for you.'" Luke 22;19,20; I Cor. 11:24.

We believe it is necessary to abstain from things offered to idols, from blood, from things strangled and from fornication, as decreed by the Holy Ghost in the General Assembly held at Jerusalem according to Acts 15:28,29; 16:4; 21.25.

We believe that Jesus Christ, Himself, bore all our infirmities and, therefore, we obey the following commandment: "Is any sick among you? Let him call for the elders of the church: and let them pray over him, anointing him with oil in the name of the Lord; and the prayer of faith shall save the sick, and the Lord shall raise him up; and if he has committed sins, they shall be forgiven him." James 5:14; Matt. 8:17.

We believe that the Lord, Himself, (before the millenium) "shall descend from heaven with a great shout, with the trump of God, and the dead in Christ shall rise first; then we that are left, shall together with them be caught up in the clouds to meet the Lord in the air; and so shall we ever be with the Lord." 1 Thess. 4:16, 17; Rev. 20:6.

We believe there shall be a bodily resurrection of all dead, just and unjust, and these shall go away into everlasting punishment but the righteous into life eternal. Acts 24:16; Matt. 25:46.

* * *

DOCTRINAL STATEMENT (ELIM BIBLE INSTITUTE)

1. We believe the Bible to be the only inspired, infallible Word of God. II Peter 1:21.
2. We believe the Godhead consists of the Father, the Son, and the Holy Spirit. II Cor. 13:14. Three in One and One in Three.
3. We believe in the Deity of Jesus Christ, in His virgin birth, in His atoning death, in His bodily resurrec-

tion, in His ascension to the right hand of the Father. I Timothy 3:16.
4. We believe in evangelistic and missionary fervor and endeavor. Acts 1:18; Mark 16:15-18.
5. We believe in salvation through the redeeming blood of Christ. Hebrews 9:22.
6. We believe in sanctification and holiness of heart and the overcoming life as Scriptural requirements for the Bride of Christ. Eph. 5:25-27.
7. We believe in sanctification and the Holy Spirit according to Acts 2:4, 10:46, 19:6, and the present ministry of the Spirit in and through the believer as manifest in the five ministries as they are being restored in end-time revival (Eph. 4:11), the gifts of the Spirit (I Cor. 12:8-11), and the fruit of the Spirit (Gal. 5:22,23).
8. We believe that divine healing is obtained on the basis of the Atonement. I Peter 2:24.
9. We believe in Christ's imminent personal return in power and great glory, in His millennial reign and in His everlasting dominion. Acts 1:11; Rev. 20:4; Dan. 7:14.
10. We believe in the resurrection of both the saved and the lost; they that are saved unto the resurrection of eternal life and they that are lost unto the resurrection of eternal punishment. John 5:28,29; Rev. 20:15.

Notes: *The Elim Bible Institute is the school affiliated with the Elim Fellowship.*

* * *

ARTICLES OF FAITH (GENERAL ASSEMBLY AND CHURCH OF THE FIRST BORN)

We believe in God, the Eternal Father, and his Son, Jesus Christ, and in the Holy Ghost.

We believe that man will be punished for their own sins, and not for Adam's transgression.

We believe that through the Atonement of Christ, all mankind may be saved, by obedience to the laws and ordinances of the Gospel.

We believe that the first principles and ordinances of the Gospel are: first, Faith in the Lord Jesus Christ; second, Repentance; third, Baptism by immerson for the remission of sins; fourth, Laying on of hands for the gift of the Holy Ghost.

We believe in the same organization that existed in the Primitive Church, viz: apostles, prophets, pastors, teachers, evangelists, etc.

We believe in the gift of tongues, prophecy, revelation, visions, healing, interpretation of tongues, etc.

We believe in being honest, true, chaste, benevolent, virtuous, and in doing good to all men; indeed we may say that we follow the admonition of Paul—We believe all things, we hope all things, we have endured many things, and hope to be able to endure all things. If there is anything virtuous, lovely, or of good report or praiseworthy, we seek after these things.

ARTICLES OF FAITH (GENERAL ASSEMBLY AND CHURCH OF THE FIRST BORN) (continued)

Notes: *This group is noteworthy for its position on the ordinances. It has four, but the Lord's Supper is not among them.*

*　　*　　*

STATEMENT OF FAITH [GOSPEL ASSEMBLIES (SOWDER)]

We believe that the Bible, both the Old and New Testaments, was given by inspiration of God, and is our only rule in matters of faith, doctrine and practice. We believe in creation; that man was created by the direct act of God and in the image of God. We believe that Adam and Eve, in yielding to the temptation of Satan, became fallen creatures. We believe that all men are born in sin, and thus the necessity for repentance. We believe in the Incarnation, the Virgin Birth, and the Deity of our Lord and Saviour, Jesus Christ, the Son of the Living God. We believe in His vicarious and substitutional death on the cross as (the) Atonement for the sins of mankind by the shedding of His own blood at Calvary. We believe that the Atonement also provides deliverance and healing for those who believe in His name. We believe in justification by faith, and sanctification to be the way of holiness. We believe that grace and works as recorded in James, chapter two, are compatible. We believe that justification must be sustained by obedience to God's Word. We believe in the resurrection of His body from the tomb, His ascension to Heaven, and that He is now our Advocate. We believe the church to be a direct result of the first advent and that men are to be actively drawn into it. We believe water baptism to be scriptural when administered to believers only. We believe in the necessity of the New Birth, and that this New Birth is through the regeneration by the Holy Spirit as recorded in the second chapter of Acts. We believe in the restoration of Israel. We believe that He is personally coming again at His glorious premillennial second advent to judge the wicked, to resurrect the righteous dead, and to establish the Kingdom of God upon this earth.

We believe that this statement of faith is a sufficient basis for Christian fellowship and that all born-again men and women who sincerely accept this, can, and should, live together in peace, and that it is their Christian duty to promote harmony among the members of the Body of Christ, and also to work together to get the Gospel to as many people as possible in the shortest period of time.

*　　*　　*

DECLARATION OF FAITH (INDEPENDENT ASSEMBLIES OF GOD INTERNATIONAL)

We Believe:

In the God Head manifested in the Father, Son and the Holy Ghost.

In the virgin birth of Jesus Christ.

In the deity of the Lord Jesus Christ.

Repentance is necessary unto salvation.

In water baptism for the believer after salvation.

In the verbal inspiration of the Holy Scriptures.

In the baptism of the Holy Ghost with the evidence of speaking in other tongues.

In eternal life for the believer in Jesus Christ and the eternal damnation for the lost (wicked).

In the literal return of the Lord Jesus Christ.

Notes: *This brief statement is derived from that of the Assemblies of God.*

*　　*　　*

DECLARATION OF FAITH (INTERNATIONAL CHURCH OF THE FOURSQUARE GOSPEL)

1. THE HOLY SCRIPTURES

We believe that the Holy Bible is the Word of the living God; true, immutable, steadfast, unchangeable, as its author, the Lord Jehovah; that it was written by holy men of old as they were moved upon and inspired by the Holy Spirit; that it is a lighted lamp to guide the feet of a lost world from the depths of sin and sorrow to the heights of righteousness and glory; an unclouded mirror that reveals the face of a crucified Saviour; a plumbline to make straight the life of each individual and community; a sharp two-edged sword to convict of sin and evil doing; a strong cord of love and tenderness to draw the penitent to Christ Jesus; a balm of Gilead, inbreathed by the Holy Spirit, that can heal and quicken each drooping heart; the only true ground of Christian fellowship and unity; the loving call of an infinitely loving God; the solemn warning, the distant thunder of the storm of wrath and retribution that shall overtake the unheeding; a sign post that points to Heaven; a danger signal that warns from Hell; the divine, supreme, and eternal tribunal by whose standards all men, nations, creeds, and motives shall be tried.

Scripture References Where Taught:

Heaven and earth shall pass away, but my words shall not pass away. Matt. 24:35. Forever, O Lord, Thy Word is settled in Heaven. Ps. 119:89.

All Scripture is given by inspiration of God, and is profitable for doctrine, for reproof, for correction, for instruction in righteousness: that the man of God may be perfect, thoroughly furnished unto all good works. II Tim. 3:16, 17.

Thy Word is a lamp unto my feet, and a light unto my path. Ps. 119:105.

We have also a more sure word of prophecy; whereunto ye do well that ye take heed, as unto a light that shineth in a dark place, until the day dawn, and the day star arise in your hearts: knowing this first, that no prophecy of the scripture is of any private interpretation. For the prophecy came not in old time by the will of men: but holy men of God spake as they were moved by the Holy Ghost. II Peter 1:19-21.

Search the scriptures; for in them ye think ye have eternal life: and they are they which testify of me. John 5:39.

Study to show thyself approved unto God, a workman that needeth not to be ashamed, rightly dividing the Word of truth. II Tim. 2:15. . . . Let us walk by the same rule, let us mind the same thing. Phil. 3:16. (Also I John 4:1; Isa. 8:20; I Thess. 5:21; Acts 17:11; I John 4:6; Jude 3; Eph. 6:17; Ps. 119:59, 60; Phil. 1:9-11.)

II. THE ETERNAL GODHEAD

We believe that there is but one true and living God; maker of heaven and earth and all that in them is; the Alpha and Omega, who ever was, and is and shall be time without end, Amen; that He is infinitely holy, mighty, tender, loving and glorious; worthy of all possible love and honor, confidence and obedience, majesty, dominion and might, both now and forever; and that in the unity of the Godhead there are three, equal in every divine perfection executing distinct but harmonious offices in the great work of redemption:

> THE FATHER. Whose glory is so exceeding bright that mortal man cannot look upon His face and live, but whose heart was so filled with love and pity for His lost and sin-benighted children that He freely gave His only begotten Son to redeem and reconcile them unto Himself.

> THE SON. Co-existent and co-eternal with the Father, who, conceived by the Holy Spirit and born of the Virgin Mary took upon Himself the form of man, bore our sins, carried our sorrows, and by the shedding of His precious blood upon the cross of Calvary purchased redemption for all that would believe upon Him: then, bursting the bonds of death and hell rose from the grave and ascended on high leading captivity captive, that as the great Mediator betwixt God and man, He might stand at the right hand of the Father making intercession for those for whom He laid down His life.

> THE HOLY SPIRIT. The third person of the Godhead, the Spirit of the Father shed abroad, omnipotent, omnipresent, performing an inexpressibly important mission upon earth, convicting of sin, of righteousness and of judgment, drawing sinners to the Saviour, rebuking, pleading, searching, comforting, guiding, quickening, teaching, glorifying, baptizing and enduing with power from on high, them who yield to His tender ministrations, preparing them for the great day of the Lord's appearing.

Scripture References Where Taught:

. . . Before me there was no God formed, neither shall there be after me. Isa. 43:10. . . . Is there a God beside me? yea, there is no God; I know not any. Isa. 44:8.

Thou canst not see my face: for there shall no man see me, and live. Ex. 33:20.

For God so loved the world, that He gave His only begotten Son, that whosoever believeth in Him should not perish, but have everlasting life. John 3:16.

In the beginning was the Word, and the Word was with God, and the Word was God. The same was in the beginning with God. All things were made by Him, and without Him was not anything made that was made. John 1:1-3. (Also Job 38:4-7.)

Behold, a virgin shall be with child, and shall bring forth a Son and they shall call his name Emmanuel. Matt. 1:23.

I, even I, am the Lord; and beside me there is no saviour. Isa. 43:11. For there is one God, and one Mediator between God and men, the man Christ Jesus; who gave Himself a ransom for all. I Tim. 2:5. For through Him we both have access by one Spirit unto the Father. Eph. 2:18.

For there are three that bear record in Heaven, the Father, the Word, and the Holy Ghost: and these three are one. I John 5:7.

But when the Comforter is come, whom I will send unto you from the Father, even the Spirit of truth, which proceedeth from the Father, He shall testify of me. John 15:26. (Also II Cor. 13:14; Matt. 28:19; Rom. 8:11; John 16:7-14.)

III. THE FALL OF MAN

We believe that man was created in the image of God, before whom he walked in holiness and purity, but that by voluntary disobedience and transgression, he fell from the Eden of purity and innocence to the depths of sin and iniquity, and that in consequence of this, all mankind are sinners sold unto Satan, sinners not by constraint but by choice, shapen in iniquity and utterly void by nature of that holiness required by the law of God, positively inclined to evil, guilty and without excuse, justly deserving the condemnation of a just and holy God.

Scripture References Where Taught:

God created man in His own image. Gen. 1:27.

Wherefore as by one man sin entered into the world and death by sin; and so death passed upon all men, for all have sinned. Rom. 5:12. By one man's disobedience many were made sinners. Rom. 5:19. (Also John 3:6; Ps. 51:5; Rom. 5:15-19; 8:7.)

We have turned every one to his own way. Isa. 53:6. (Also Gen. 6:12; 3:9-18.)

Among whom also we had our conversation in times past in the lusts of our flesh, fulfilling the desires of the flesh and of the mind; and were by nature the children of wrath, even as others. Eph. 2:3. (See Rom. 1:18, 32; 2:1-16; Matt. 20:15; Gal. 3:10; Ezek. 18:19, 20.)

. . . So that they are without excuse. Rom 1:20. That every mouth may be stopped, and all the world may become guilty before God. Rom. 3:19. (Also Gal. 3:22.)

IV. THE PLAN OF REDEMPTION

We believe that while we were yet sinners Christ died for us, the Just for the unjust; freely, and by divine appointment of the Father taking the sinner's place, bearing his sins, receiving his condemnation, dying his death, fully paying his penalty, and signing with His life's blood, the pardon of every one who should believe upon Him; that upon simple faith and acceptance of the atonement purchased on Mount Calvary, the vilest sinner may be cleansed of his iniquities and made whiter than the driven snow.

DECLARATION OF FAITH (INTERNATIONAL CHURCH OF THE FOURSQUARE GOSPEL) (continued)

Scripture References Where Taught:

He was wounded for our transgressions. He was bruised for our iniquities: the chastisement of our peace was upon Him; and with His stripes we are healed. Isa. 53:5.

Who gave Himself for us, that He might redeem us from all iniquity, and purify unto Himself a peculiar people, zealous of good works. Titus 2:14.

Let the wicked forsake his way, and the unrighteous man his thoughts: and let him return unto the Lord, and He will have mercy upon him; and to our God, for He will abundantly pardon. Isa. 55:7.

Wherefore He is able also to save them to the uttermost that come unto God by Him, seeing He ever liveth to make intercession for them. Heb. 7:25.

Come now, and let us reason together, saith the Lord: though your sins be as scarlet, they shall be white as snow; though they be red like crimson, they shall be as wool. Isa 1:18.

V. SALVATION THROUGH GRACE

We believe that the salvation of sinners is wholly through grace; that we have no righteousness or goodness of our own wherewith to seek divine favor, and must come, therefore, throwing ourselves upon the unfailing mercy and love of Him who bought us and washed us in His own blood, pleading the merits and the righteousness of Christ the Saviour, standing upon His word and accepting the free gift of His love and pardon.

Scripture References Where Taught:

By grace are ye saved. Eph. 2:8.

 . . . There is none righteous, no, not one. Rom. 3:10.

All have sinned, and come short of the glory of God. Rom. 3:23.

We are all as an unclean thing, for all our righteousnesses are as filthy rags, and we all do fade as a leaf; and our iniquities, like the wind, have taken us away. Isa. 64:6.

Verily, verily, I say unto you, He that believeth on me hath everlasting life. John 6:47.

But now in Christ Jesus ye who sometimes were far off are made nigh by the blood of Christ. Eph. 2:13.

For the wages of sin is death; but the gift of God is eternal life through Jesus Christ our Lord. Rom. 6:23.

VI. REPENTANCE AND ACCEPTANCE

We believe that upon sincere repentance, godly sorrow for sin, and a whole-hearted acceptance of the Lord Jesus Christ, they who call upon Him may be justified by faith, through His precious blood and that in place of condemnation they may have the most blessed peace, assurance and favor with God; that with open arms of mercy and pardon the Saviour waits to receive each penitent who will in unfeigned contrition and supplication for mercy, open the door of his heart and accept Him as Lord and King.

Scripture References Where Taught:

If we confess our sins, He is faithful and just to forgive us our sins, and to cleanse us from all unrighteousness. I John 1:9.

Being justified by faith, we have peace with God through our Lord Jesus Christ; by whom also we have access, by faith, into this grace wherein we stand, and rejoice in hope of the glory of God. Rom. 5:1, 2.

There is, therefore, now no condemnation to them which are in Christ Jesus, who walk not after the flesh, but after the spirit. Rom. 8:1.

To give knowledge of salvation unto His people by the remission of their sins, through the tender mercy of our God; whereby the day-spring from on high hath visited us, to give light to them that sit in darkness and in the shadow of death, to guide our feet into the way of peace. Luke 1:77-79.

 . . . Him that cometh to me, I will in no wise cast out. John 6:37.

VII. THE NEW BIRTH

We believe that the change which takes place in the heart and life at conversion is a very real one; that the sinner is then born again in such a glorious and transforming manner that old things are passed away and all things are become new; insomuch that the things once most desired are now abhorred, Whilst the things once abhorred are now held most sacred and dear; and that now having had imputed to him the righteousness of the Redeemer and having received of the Spirit of Christ, new desires, new aspirations, new interests, and a new perspective of life, time, and eternity, fills the blood-washed heart so that his desire is now to openly confess and serve the Master, seeking ever those things which are above.

Scripture References Where Taught:

 . . . Except a man be born again, he cannot see the kingdom of God. John 3:3.

Therefore, if any man be in Christ, he is a new creature: old things are passed away; behold all things are become new. II Cor. 5:17.

If ye were of the world, the world would love its own; but because ye are not of the world, but I have chosen you out of the world, therefore the world hateth you. John 15:19.

I am crucified with Christ: nevertheless I live; yet not I, but Christ liveth in me; and the life which I now live in the flesh I live by the faith of the Son of God, who loved me, and gave Himself for me. Gal 2:20. Being justified freely by His grace, through the redemption that is in Christ Jesus, whom God hath sent forth to be a propitiation through faith in His blood, to declare His righteousness for the remission of sins that are past, through the forbearance of God. Rom. 3:24, 25.

Blessed is the man that walketh not in the counsel of the ungodly, nor standeth in the way of sinners, nor sitteth in the seat of the scornful. But his delight is in the law of the Lord; and in His law doth he meditate day and night. Ps. 1:1, 2.

VIII. DAILY CHRISTIAN LIFE

We believe that having been cleansed by the precious blood of Jesus Christ and having received the witness of the Holy Spirit at conversion, it is the will of God that we be sanctified daily and become partakers of His holiness; growing constantly stronger in faith, power, prayer, love and service, first as babies desiring the sincere milk of the Word; then as dear children walking humbly, seeking diligently the hidden life, where self decreases and Christ increases; then as strong men having on the whole armour of God marching forth to new conquests in His name beneath His blood-stained banner, ever living a patient, sober, unselfish, godly life that will be a true reflection of the Christ within.

Scripture References Where Taught:

For this is the will of God, even your sanctification. I Thess. 4:3. And the very God of peace sanctify you wholly; and I pray God your whole spirit and soul and body be preserved blameless unto the coming of our Lord Jesus Christ. I Thess. 5:23.

Having therefore these promises, dearly beloved, let us cleanse ourselves from all filthiness of the flesh and spirit, perfecting holiness in the fear of God. II Cor. 7:1.

The path of the just is as the shining light that shineth more and more unto the perfect day. Prov. 4:18.

Therefore, leaving the principles of the doctrine of Christ, let us go on unto perfection. Heb. 6:1.

For they that are after the flesh do mind the things of the flesh; but they that are after the Spirit, the things of the Spirit. Rom. 8:5.

A highway shall be there, and a way, and it shall be called the way of holiness; the unclean shall not pass over it; but it shall be for those: the wayfaring men, though fools, shall not err therein. Isa. 35:8. (Also I Peter 2:2.)

IX. BAPTISM AND THE LORD'S SUPPER

We believe that water baptism in the name of the Father and of the Son and of the Holy Ghost, according to the command of our Lord, is a blessed outward sign of an inward work; a beautiful and solemn emblem reminding us that even as our Lord died upon the cross of Calvary so we reckon ourselves now dead indeed unto sin, and the old nature nailed to the tree with Him; and that even as He was taken down from the tree and buried, so we are buried with Him by baptism into death: that like as Christ was raised up from the dead by the glory of the Father, even so we should walk in newness of life.

We believe in the commemoration and observing of the Lord's supper by the sacred use of the broken bread, a precious type of the Bread of Life even Jesus Christ, whose body was broken for us; and by the juice of the vine, a blessed type which should ever remind the participant of the shed blood of the Saviour who is the true Vine of which His children are the branches; that this ordinance is as a glorious rainbow that spans the gulf of the years between Calvary and the coming of the Lord, when in the Father's kingdom, He will partake anew with His children; and that the serving and receiving of this blessed sacrament should be ever preceded by the most solemn heart-searching, self-examination, forgiveness and love toward all men, that none partake unworthily and drink condemnation to his own soul.

Scripture References Where Taught:

Go ye therefore, and teach all nations, baptizing them in the name of the Father, and of the Son, and of the Holy Ghost. Matt. 28:19. (Also Acts 1:47, 48; Gal. 3:27, 28.)

Therefore, we are buried with Him by baptism into death: that like as Christ was raised up from the dead by the glory of the Father, even so we also should walk in newness of life. Rom. 6:4. (Also Col. 2:12; I Peter 3:20, 21; Acts 22:16.)

Then they that gladly heard His Word were baptized: and the same day there were added unto them about three thousand souls. Acts 2:41. (Also Matt. 28:19, 20.)

For as often as ye eat this bread, and drink this cup, ye do show the Lord's death till He come. I Cor. 11:26. But let a man examine himself, and so let him eat of that bread, and drink of that cup. I Cor. 11:28.

Examine yourselves, whether ye be in the faith; prove your own selves. II Cor. 13:5.

X. THE BAPTISM OF THE HOLY SPIRIT

We believe that the baptism of the Holy Spirit is the incoming of the promised Comforter in mighty and glorious fulness to endue the believer with power from on high; to glorify and exalt the Lord Jesus; to give inspired utterance in witnessing of Him; to foster the spirit of prayer, holiness, sobriety; to equip the individual and the church for practical, efficient, joyous, Spirit-filled soul-winning in the fields of life; and that this being still the dispensation of the Holy Spirit, the believer may have every reason to expect His oncoming to be after the same manner as that in which He came upon Jew and Gentile alike in Bible days, and as recorded in the Word, that it may be truly said of us as of the house of Cornelius: the Holy Ghost fell on them as on us at the beginning.

Scripture References Where Taught:

I will pray the Father, and He shall give you another Comforter, that He may abide with you forever; even the Spirit of truth; whom the world cannot receive, because it seeth Him not, neither knoweth Him; for He dwelleth with you, and shall be in you. John 14:16, 17.

For John truly baptized with water, but ye shall be baptized with the Holy Ghost. . . . Ye shall receive power, after that the Holy Ghost is come upon you: and ye shall be witnesses unto me, both in Jerusalem, and in all Judea, and in Samaria, and unto the uttermost part of the earth. Acts 1:5, 8.

And they were all filled with the Holy Ghost, and began to speak with other tongues, as the Spirit gave them utterance. Acts 2:4.

Then they laid their hands on them, and they received the Holy Ghost. Acts 8:17.

While Peter yet spake these words, the Holy Ghost fell on all them which heard the word. And they of the circumcision which believed were astonished, as many as came with Peter because that on the Gentiles also was poured out the gift of the Holy Ghost. For they heard

DECLARATION OF FAITH (INTERNATIONAL CHURCH OF
THE FOURSQUARE GOSPEL) (continued)

them speak with tongues, and magnify God. Acts 10:44-
46.

And when Paul had laid his hands upon them, the Holy
Ghost came on them; and they spake with tongues, and
prophesied. Acts 19:6. Know ye not that ye are the temple
of God, and that the Spirit of God dwelleth in you? I Cor.
3:16.

XI. THE SPIRIT-FILLED LIFE

We believe that while the Holy Spirit is as a mighty
rushing wind and as tongues of living flame that can shake
and set ablaze whole communities for God, He is also as a
gentle dove, easily grieved and wounded by impiety,
coldness, idle conversation, boastfulness, a judging or
criticizing spirit and by thoughts and actions dishonoring
to the Lord Jesus; that it is therefore, the will of God that
we live and walk in the Spirit, moment by moment, under
the precious blood of the Lamb; treading softly as with
unshod feet in the presence of the King; being patient,
loving, truthful, sincere, prayerful, unmurmuring, instant
in season, out of season serving the Lord.

Scripture References Where Taught:

And grieve not the Holy Spirit of God, whereby ye are
sealed unto the day of redemption. Let all bitterness, and
wrath, and anger, and clamor, and evil speaking, be put
away from you, with all malice: and be ye kind one to
another, tender-hearted, forgiving one another, even as
God for Christ's sake hath forgiven you. Eph. 4:30-32.
Praying always with all prayer and supplication in the
Spirit and watching thereunto with all perseverance and
supplication for all saints. Eph. 6:18.

I beseech you, therefore, brethren, by the mercies of God,
that ye present your bodies a living sacrifice, holy,
acceptable unto God, which is your reasonable service.
And be not conformed to this world: but be ye transformed by the renewing of your mind, that ye may prove
what is that good, and acceptable, and perfect, will of God.
Rom. 12:1, 2.

He that saith he abideth in Him ought himself also to
walk, even as He walked. I John 2:6.

Walk in the Spirit, and ye shall not fulfill the lust of the
flesh. If we live in the Spirit, let us also walk in the Spirit.
Gal. 5:16, 25.

If any man defile the temple of God, him shall God
destroy; for the temple of God is holy, which temple ye
are. I Cor. 3:17.

XII. THE GIFTS AND FRUITS OF THE SPIRIT

We believe that the Holy Spirit has the following gifts to
bestow upon the believing church of the Lord Jesus Christ:
wisdom, knowledge, faith, healing, miracles, prophecy,
discernment, tongues, interpretation; that, according to the
degree of grace and faith possessed by the recipient, these
gifts are divided to every man severally, as He, the Holy
Spirit, will; that they are to be most earnestly desired and
coveted, in the order and proportion wherein they prove
most edifying and beneficial to the church; and that the
fruit of the Spirit: love, joy, peace, long-suffering, gent-

leness, goodness, faith, meekness, temperance, should be
put forth, cultivated, and diligently guarded as the
resultant adornment, the constant, eloquent, and irrefuta-
ble evidence of a Spirit-filled life.

Scripture References Where Taught:

Concerning spiritual gifts, brethren, I would not have you
ignorant. . . . Covet earnestly the best gifts. I Cor. 12:1,
31. But all these worketh that one and the selfsame Spirit,
dividing to every man severally as He will. I Cor. 12:11.

Even so ye, forasmuch as ye are zealous of spiritual gifts,
seek that ye may excel to the edifying of the church. I Cor.
14:12. The gifts and calling of God are without repentance.
Rom. 11:29.

Having then gifts according to the grace that is given to us,
whether prophecy, let us prophesy according to the
proportion of faith; or ministry, let us wait upon our
ministering: or he that teacheth, on teaching; or he that
exhorteth on exhortation; he that giveth, let him do it with
simplicity; he that ruleth, with diligence; he that showeth
mercy, with cheerfulness. Rom. 12:6-8.

Herein is My Father glorified, that ye bear much fruit; so
shall ye be My disciples. John 15:8.

And now also the axe is laid upon the root of the trees:
every tree, therefore, which bringeth not forth good fruit is
hewn down, and cast into the fire. Luke 3:9.

XIII. MODERATION

We believe that the moderation of the believer should be
known of all men; that his experience and daily walk
should never lead him into extremes, fanaticisms, unseemly manifestations, back-bitings, murmurings; but that his
sober, thoughtful, balanced, mellow, forgiving, and zealous
Christian experience should be one of steadfast
uprightness, equilibrium, humility, self-sacrifice and
Christ-likeness.

Scripture References Where Taught:

Let your moderation be known unto all men. The Lord is
at hand. Phil. 4:5.

That we, henceforth, be no more children, tossed to and
fro, and carried about with every wind of doctrine. . . . But speaking the truth in love, may grow up
into Him in all things, which is the head, even Christ. Eph.
4:14, 15.

Charity doth not behave itself unseemly. I Cor. 13:5.

Put on therefore, as the elect of God, holy and beloved,
bowels of mercies, kindness, humbleness of mind,
meekness, longsuffering: forbearing one another, and
forgiving one another, if any man have a quarrel against
any: even as Christ forgave you, so also do ye. Col. 3:12,
13.

XIV. DIVINE HEALING

We believe that divine healing is the power of the Lord
Jesus Christ to heal the sick and the afflicted in answer to
believing prayer; that He who is the same yesterday, today
and forever has never changed but is still an all-sufficient
help in the time of trouble, able to meet the needs of, and
quicken into newness of life the body, as well as the soul

and spirit in answer to the faith of them who ever pray with submission to His divine and sovereign will.

Scripture References Where Taught:

Himself took our infirmities, and bare our sicknesses. Matt. 8:17.

Whether is easier, to say, Thy sins be forgiven thee; or to say, Arise, and walk? Matt. 9:5.

These signs shall follow them that believe; in my name shall they cast out devils; they shall speak with new tongues; they shall take up serpents; and if they drink any deadly thing, it shall not hurt them; they shall lay hands on the sick, and they shall recover. Mark 16:17, 18.

And now, Lord, behold their threatenings; and grant unto Thy servants, that with all boldness they shall speak Thy Word, by stretching forth Thine hand to heal; that signs and wonders may be done by the name of Thy holy child Jesus. Acts 4:29, 30.

Is any sick among you? Let him call for the elders of the church: and let them pray over him, anointing him with oil in the name of the Lord and the prayer of faith shall save the sick, and the Lord shall raise him up; and if he have committed sins, they shall be forgiven him. Confess your faults one to another, and pray one for another, that ye may be healed. James 5:14-16.

XV. THE SECOND COMING OF CHRIST

We believe that the second coming of Christ is personal and imminent; that He will descend from Heaven in the clouds of glory with the voice of the archangel and with the trump of God; and that at this hour, which no man knoweth beforehand, the dead in Christ shall rise, then the redeemed that are alive and remain shall be caught up together with them in the clouds, to meet the Lord in the air, and that so shall they ever be with the Lord; that also seeing that a thousand years is as a day with the Lord, and that no man knoweth the hour of His appearance, which we believe to be near at hand, each day should be used as though He were expected to appear at even, yet that in obedience to His explicit command, "Occupy till I come," the work of spreading the gospel, the sending forth of missionaries, and the general duties for the upbuilding of the church should be carried on as diligently, and thoroughly, as though neither ours nor the next generation should live in the flesh to see that glorious day.

Scripture References Where Taught:

For the Lord Himself shall descend from heaven with a shout, with the voice of the archangel, and with the trump of God: and the dead in Christ shall rise first: then we which are alive and remain shall be caught up together with them in the clouds, to meet the Lord in the air: and so shall we ever be with the Lord. I Thess. 4:16, 17.

. . . Denying ungodliness and worldly lusts we should live soberly, righteously, and godly, in this present world; looking for that blessed hope, and the glorious appearing of the great God and our Saviour Jesus Christ. Titus 2:12, 13.

But of that day and hour knoweth no man, no, not the angels of heaven, but my Father only. Watch, therefore: for ye know not what hour your Lord doth come.

Therefore, be ye also ready: for in such an hour as ye think not, the Son of man cometh. Matt. 24:36, 42, 44.

Christ was once offered to bear the sins of many; and unto them that look for Him shall He appear the second time without sin unto salvation. Heb. 9:28.

. . . Occupy till I come. Luke 19:13.

Let your loins be girded about, and your lights burning, and ye yourselves like unto men that wait for their Lord . . . that when He cometh and knocketh, they may open unto Him immediately. Blessed are those servants, whom the Lord when He cometh shall find watching: verily, I say unto you, that He shall gird Himself, and make them to sit down to meat, and will come forth and serve them. Luke 12:35-37.

XVI. CHURCH RELATIONSHIP

We believe that having accepted the Lord Jesus Christ as personal Saviour and King, and having thus been born into the family and invisible body or church of the Lord, it is the sacred duty of the believer, whenever this lieth within his power, to identify himself with, and labor most earnestly for the upbuilding of God's kingdom with the visible church of Christ upon earth; and that such visible church is a congregation of believers, who have associated themselves together in Christian fellowship and in the unity of the Spirit, observing the ordinances of Christ, worshipping Him in the beauty of holiness, speaking to each other in psalms, and hymns and spiritual songs, reading and proclaiming His Word, laboring for the salvation of souls, giving of their temporal means to carry on His work, edifying, encouraging, establishing one another in the most holy faith, and working harmoniously together as dear children who are many members but one body of which Christ is the head.

Scripture References Where Taught:

I will praise the Lord with my whole heart, in the assembly of the upright, and in the congregation. Ps. 111:1.

Let us consider one another to provoke unto love and to good works: not forsaking the assembling of ourselves together, as the manner of some is; but exhorting one another: and so much the more, as ye see the day approaching. Heb. 10:24, 25.

. . . And the Lord added to the church daily such as should be saved. Acts 2:47. And so were the churches established in the faith, and increased in numbers daily. Acts 16:5.

So we, being many, are one body in Christ, and every one members one of another. Rom. 12:5. (Also see Rom. 12:6, 7, 8.)

Then they that feared the Lord spake often one to another; and the Lord hearkened, and heard it, and a book of remembrance was written before him for them that feared the Lord, and that thought upon His name. And they shall be mine, saith the Lord of hosts, in that day when I shall make up my jewels; and I shall spare them, as a man spareth his own son that serveth him. Mal. 3:16, 17.

XVII. CIVIL GOVERNMENT

We believe that civil government is of divine appointment, for the interest and good order of human society; and that

DECLARATION OF FAITH (INTERNATIONAL CHURCH OF
THE FOURSQUARE GOSPEL) (continued)

governors and rulers should be prayed for, obeyed, and
upheld, at all times except only in things opposed to the
will of our Lord Jesus Christ, who is the ruler of
conscience of His people, the King of Kings, and the Lord
of Lords.

Scripture References Where Taught:

. . . The powers that be are ordained of God. . . . For
rulers are not a terror to good works, but to the evil. Rom.
13:1, 3. (Also Deut. 16:18; II Sam. 23:3; Ex. 18:21-23; Jer.
30:21.)

. . . We ought to obey God rather than man. Acts 5:29.
Fear not them which kill the body, but are not able to kill
the soul. Matt. 10:28. (Also Dan. 3:15-18; 6:7-10; Acts
4:18-20.)

. . . One is your Master, even Christ. Matt. 23:10.

And He hath on His vesture and on His thigh a name
written, KING OF KINGS, AND LORD OF LORDS.
Rev. 19:16. (Also Ps. 72:11; Rom. 14:9-13.)

XVIII. THE FINAL JUDGMENT

We believe that the death both small and great shall be
raised up and stand with the living before the judgment
seat of God; and that when a solemn and awful separation
shall take place wherein the wicked shall be adjudged to
everlasting punishment and the righteous to life eternal;
and that this judgment will fix forever the final state of
men in heaven or in hell on principles of righteousness as
set forth in his holy Word.

Scripture References Where Taught:

For we must all appear before the judgment seat of Christ;
that every one may receive the things done in his body,
according to that he hath done, whether it be good or bad.
II Cor. 5:10.

The Son of man shall send forth His angels, and they shall
gather out of His kingdom all things that offend, and them
which do iniquity; and shall cast them into a furnace of
fire: there shall be wailing and gnashing of teeth. Then
shall the righteous shine forth as the sun in the kingdom of
their Father. Who hath ears to hear, let him hear. Matt.
13:41-43.

XIX. HEAVEN

We believe that Heaven is the indescribably glorious
habitation of the living God; and that thither the Lord has
gone to prepare a place for His children; that unto this
four-square city, whose builder and maker is God, the
earnest believers who have washed their robes in the blood
of the Lamb and have overcome by the word of their
testimony will be carried; that the Lord Jesus Christ will
present them to the Father without spot or wrinkle; and
that there in unutterable joy they will ever behold His
wonderful face, in an everlasting kingdom whereunto
comes no darkness nor light, neither sorrow, tears, pain
nor death, and wherein hosts of attending angels sweep
their harps, sing the praise of our King, and bowing down
before the throne, cry: "Holy, holy, holy."

Scripture References Where Taught:

Eye hath not seen nor ear heard, neither have entered into
the heart of man, the things which God hath prepared for
them that love Him. I Cor. 2:9.

In My Father's house are many mansions; if it were not so
I would have told you. I go to prepare a place for you.
John 14:2.

And there shall be no night there; and they need no candle,
neither light of the sun; for the Lord God giveth them
light: and they shall reign forever and ever. Rev. 22:5.

And God shall wipe away all tears from their eyes; and
there shall be no more death, neither sorrow, nor crying,
neither shall there be any more pain; for the former things
are passed away. Rev. 21:4.

Therefore are they before the throne of God, and serve
Him day and night in His temple: and He that sitteth on
the throne shall dwell among them. They shall hunger no
more; neither thirst any more; neither shall the sun light
upon them, nor any heat. For the Lamb, which is in the
midst of the throne, shall feed them, and shall lead them
unto living fountains of water. Rev. 7:15-17.

XX. HELL

We believe that hell is a place of outer darkness and
deepest sorrow, where the worm dieth not and the fire is
not quenched; a place prepared for the devil and his angels
where there shall be weeping and wailing and gnashing of
teeth, a place of grief and eternal regret on the part of them
who have rejected the mercy, love and tenderness of the
crucified Saviour, choosing death rather than life; and that
there into a lake that burns with fire and brimstone shall
be cast the unbelieving, the abominable, the murderers,
sorcerers, idolaters, all liars, and they who have rejected
and spurned the love and sacrifice of a bleeding Redeemer,—passing the cross to their doom, in spite of every
entreaty and warning of the Holy Spirit.

Scripture References Where Taught:

The Son of man shall send forth His angels, and they shall
gather out of His kingdom all things that offend, and them
which do iniquity; and shall cast them into a furnace of
fire: there shall be wailing and gnashing of teeth. Matt.
13:41, 42.

And the devil that deceived them was cast into the lake of
fire and brimstone, where the beast and the false prophet
are, and shall be tormented day and night forever and ever.
And whosoever was not found written in the book of life
was cast into the lake of fire. Rev. 20:10, 15.

The same shall drink of the wrath of God, which is poured
out without mixture into the cup of his indignation; and he
shall be tormented with fire and brimstone in the presence
of the holy angels, and in the presence of the Lamb; and
the smoke of their torment ascendeth up forever and ever.
Rev. 14:10, 11.

Then shall He say unto them . . . Depart from me, ye
cursed, into everlasting fire, prepared for the devil and his
angels. Matt. 25:41. And if thy hand offend thee, cut it off:
it is better for thee to enter into life maimed, than having
two hands to go into hell, into the fire that never shall be

quenched: where their worm dieth not and the fire is not quenched. Mark 9:43, 44.

. . . As I live, saith the Lord God, I have no pleasure in the death of the wicked; but that the wicked turn from his way and live; turn ye, turn ye from your evil ways; for why will ye die, O house of Israel? Ezek. 33:11.

XXI. EVANGELISM

We believe that seeing then that all these things shall be dissolved, and that the end of all things is at hand, the redeemed children of the Lord Jehovah should rise and shine forth as a light that cannot be hid, a city set upon a hill, speeding forth the gospel to the ends of the earth, girding the globe with the message of salvation, declaring with burning zeal and earnestness the whole council of God; that when the Lord of Glory shall appear, they shall be found standing, with their loins girded about with truth, their activities and ministry laden down with the wealth of jewels they have won and guarded for Him, the precious souls, whom, by their faithful testimony they have been instrumental in leading from darkness into light; that soul winning is the one big business of the church upon earth; and that therefore every weight and hindrance which would tend to quench the flame or hamper the efficiency of world-wide evangelism should be cut off and cast away as unworthy of the church, detrimental to the most sacred cause of Christ and contrary to the great commission by our Lord.

Scripture References Where Taught:

I charge thee therefore before God, and the Lord Jesus Christ, who shall judge the quick and the dead at His appearing and His kingdom; preach the word; be instant in season, out of season; reprove, rebuke, exhort with all longsuffering and doctrine. II Tim. 4:1, 2.

Redeeming the time, because the days are evil. Eph. 5:16.

. . . He that winneth souls is wise. Prov. 11:30.

Let him know, that he which converteth the sinner from the error of his way shall save a soul from death, and shall hide a multitude of sins. James 5:20.

Son of man I have made thee a watchman unto the house of Israel; therefore hear the word at my mouth, and give them warning from me. When I say unto the wicked, Thou shalt surely die; and thou givest him not warning, nor speakest to warn the wicked from his wicked way, to save his life; the same wicked man shall die in his iniquity; but his blood will I require at thine hand. Ezek. 3:17, 18.

. . . Lift up your eyes, and look on the fields; for they are white, already to harvest. And he that reapeth receiveth wages, and gathereth fruit unto life eternal; that both he that soweth and he that reapeth may rejoice together. And herein is that saying true, One soweth and another reapeth. John 4:35-37.

Pray ye therefore the Lord of the harvest, that he will send forth labourers into His harvest. Matt. 9:38.

. . . Go ye into all the world, and preach the Gospel to every creature. Mark 16:15.

XXII. TITHING AND OFFERINGS

We believe that the method ordained of God to sustain His ministry and the spread of the gospel after His command is "Tithing" and is generally accepted throughout all Foursquare Churches, not only as God's method to take care of the material and financial needs of His church, but to raise the spiritual morale of His people to the extent that God must bless them. We are commanded in Malachi 3:10 to "Bring ye all the tithes into the storehouse, that there may be meat in mine house, and prove me now herewith, saith the Lord of hosts, if I will not open you the windows of heaven, and pour you out a blessing that there shall not be room enough to receive it."

In the matter of "giving" and "free-will offerings," they are ordered of the Lord and practiced in all Foursquare Churches as part of God's plan for the church's material needs and the spirituality of His people. We are admonished in Luke 6:38, "Give, and it shall be given unto you; good measure, pressed down, and shaken together, and running over, shall men give into your bosom, for with the same measure that ye mete withal it shall be measured to you again."

Being "joint heirs" with Him we know that giving unto His kingdom which is also ours is an enjoyable thing, it being more blessed to give than to receive, for we are commanded in II Corinthians 9:7, "Every man according as he purposeth in his heart, so let him give; not grudgingly, or of a necessity: for the Lord loveth a cheerful giver."

Notes: *This lengthy statement (one of the most detailed by any pentecostal church) was compiled by Aimee Semple McPherson, the founder of the church. It roughly follows the outline of the statement of the Assemblies of God, but covers a variety of additional issues. The church is not specifically premillennial in its eschatology.*

*   *   *

ARTICLES OF FAITH (OPEN BIBLE STANDARD CHURCHES, INC.)

A.   THE BIBLE. We believe the Bible to be the inspired word of God, and accept the same as the only infallible guide and rule of our faith and practice.

Scripture References: Matt. 24:35; Psa. 119:89; II Tim. 3:16-17; II Tim. 2:15; II Pet. 1:19-21.

B.   GOD. We believe in the eternal omnipotent, omniscient, omnipresent, and immutable triune God; maker of heaven and earth, and all that in them is; and in the unity of the Godhead there are three persons, equal in every divine perfection and attribute, executing distinct, but harmonious offices, in the great work of redemption.

Scripture References: I John 5:7; II Cor. 13:14; Gen. 1:26; I Tim. 1:17.

GOD THE FATHER. Isa. 43:10; Isa. 44:8; John 3:16.

GOD THE SON. Coexistent and coeternal with the Father, who, conceived by the Holy Spirit, and born of the Virgin Mary, took upon himself the form of man: and by His becoming obedient unto death, bearing the curse of sin, sickness and sorrow, redeemed us back to God. He arose the third day and ascended unto heaven, where He sits on the right hand of God, the father, where He lives to make intercession for us.

Scripture References: John 1:1-3; Matt. 1:23; I Tim. 2:5; Eph. 2:18; Phil. 2:6-11.

GOD THE HOLY SPIRIT. The third person of the Godhead, coexistent and equal with the Father. Sent by the Father, through the Son, to reprove the world of sin and prepare the bride of Christ.

Scripture References: John 14:26; John 15:26; John 16:8.

C. THE FALL OF MAN. Scripture References: Gen. 1:27; Rom. 5:12; Rom. 5:19; Isa. 53:6; Rom. 3:10; Rom. 3:23.

D. THE PLAN OF REDEMPTION. We believe that Christ was the Lamb of God, foreordained from the foundation of the world, and by the shedding of His blood, on the cross, made provision for salvation for ALL men.

Scripture References: I Pet 1:19-20; Isa. 53:5; Titus 2:14; Heb. 7:25.

E. THE NEW BIRTH. We believe that because of man's total inability to save himself, salvation is by God's grace alone; is received through sincere godly repentance, and a wholehearted acceptance of Jesus Christ as his personal Saviour; through being born again, he becomes a new creature in Christ Jesus. Old things have passed away, behold all things have become new.

Scripture References: John 3:3; II Cor. 5:17; Gal. 2:20; I Pet. 2:24.

F. DAILY CHRISTIAN LIFE. We believe that having been cleansed by the blood, and quickened by the Spirit, it is God's will that we should be sanctified daily, and be made partakers of His holiness; walking not after the flesh but after the Spirit; forsaking the very appearance of evil, such as wordly dress, worldly amusements, worldly conversation, worldly habits, etc.

Scripture References: Rom. 8:1; Rom. 8:5; Rom. 12:1-2; II Cor. 7:1; I Pet. 1:15; I Thess. 5:22.

G. MARRIAGE AND DIVORCE. Knowing that marriage was instituted by God; sanctioned by the Lord Jesus Christ, and was commended of Saint Paul to be honorable among all men, we believe that a Christian man or woman should not marry an unsaved person. Having been united by God in holy matrimony, neither person, as long as both shall live, shall be free to remarry, "Except it be for fornication" (Matt. 19:9).

Scripture References: II Cor. 6:15; Matt. 19:5-6; Luke 16:18; Heb. 13:4.

H. WATER BAPTISM. We believe that water baptism by immersion, in the name of the Father, Son and the Holy Ghost, is commanded by God; that it is subsequent to conversion, that it is not a saving ordinance, but an outward sign of an inward work.

Scripture References: Matt. 28:19; Rom. 6:4; Acts 2:38.

I. THE LORD'S SUPPER. We believe in the commemoration of the Lord's Supper as a type of the broken body and shed blood of our Lord Jesus Christ, and as an ordinance showing forth the death, burial and resurrection of our Lord, and a looking forward to the marriage supper of the Lamb. We believe that all Christian believers, regardless of church affiliation, may partake of the Lord's Supper.

Scripture References: I Cor. 11:23-28; II Cor. 13:5; Luke 22:7-22.

J. BAPTISM OF THE HOLY SPIRIT. We believe the baptism of the Holy Spirit is a definite experience, not identical with conversion. The initial evidence of this experience is the speaking in other tongues as the Spirit gives utterance. The baptism of the Holy Spirit is given to endue the believer with power from on high; to give inspired utterance in witnessing for Christ; to lead the believer into holiness and sobriety; to equip him for a practical, efficient, spiritfilled soul winning ministry and service; that inasmuch as this is the dispensation of the Holy Spirit, every believer has a right to expect His incoming to be after the same manner as recorded by the Word of God in Bible days.

Scripture References: John 14:16; Acts 1:8, 2:4, 2:38-39, 19:6; I Cor. 3:16.

K. SPIRIT FILLED LIFE. We believe that having received the initial filling, the baptism of the Holy Spirit, the believer should experience a continual renewing of the power from on high; that the Holy Spirit is as a gentle dove, easily grieved and wounded by coldness, prayerlessness, idle conversation, worldliness, and a judging and criticizing spirit; therefore, it is the will of God that we walk and abide in the Spirit.

Scripture References: Eph. 5:18; Acts 4:31; Eph. 4:30-32; I Cor. 3:17; Gal. 5:16-25; I John 2:6.

L. GIFTS AND FRUIT OF THE SPIRIT. We believe that for the edification of the saints and the upbuilding of the church of Jesus Christ, the Holy Spirit has the following gifts to bestow upon the individual believer: the word of wisdom, the word of knowledge, faith, gifts of healing, working of miracles, prophecy, discerning of spirits, and divers kinds of tongues, and the interpretation of tongues, dividing to every man severally as He will; that they should be coveted earnestly by all spiritual believers and exercised in the spirit of love. We believe that the fruit of the Spirit is love, joy, peace, longsuffering, gentleness, goodness, faith, meekness, temperance; against such there is no law. These should be cultivated in the life of every believer.

Scripture References: I Cor. 12:7-11; I Cor. 12:31; Gal. 5:22-23; John 15:4; John 15:8.

M. MODERATION. We believe that our moderation should be known to all men. The Christian should be sober, well balanced, and seasoned with love. His zeal should be governed by godly wisdom.

Scripture References: Phil. 4:5; Eph. 4:14-15; I Cor. 13:5; Col. 3:12-13.

N. DIVINE HEALING. We believe that divine healing is the power of God to heal the sick and afflicted in answer to believing prayer, and is provided for in the atonement. We believe that God is willing to, and does, heal the sick today.

Scripture References: Isa. 53:4-5; Matt. 8:16-17; James 5:14-16; Acts 3:16.

O. SECOND COMING OF CHRIST.

(1) RAPTURE. We believe that the second coming of Christ is personal, imminent and premillennial; that the Lord Himself will descend from heaven with a shout, with the voice of the archangel, with the trump of God, and the dead in Christ shall rise first. Then the redeemed which are alive and remain, shall be caught up together with them in the clouds to meet the Lord in the air, and so shall they ever be with the Lord: that we should, therefore, be ready, for in such an hour as we think not, the Son of Man will come.

Scripture References: I Thess. 4:16-17; Titus 2:12-13; Matt. 24:36; 24:44; Acts 1:11.

(2) REVELATION. We believe that the coming of Jesus Christ with His saints will end the great tribulation, and establish the millennial kingdom on earth, when Christ shall rule and reign as King of kings and Lord of lords.

Scripture References: Rev. 1:7; Zech. 14:4; II Thess. 1:7-10, 2:8.

P. CHURCH RELATIONSHIP. We believe that every born again child of God should identify himself with the visible church of Jesus Christ, and should labor diligently, and contribute his temporal means toward the spreading of the gospel here on earth. We believe that all the tithes should be given into the storehouse of the Lord, which is the local church.

Scripture References: Heb. 10:24-25; Ps. 111:1; Acts 2:47, 16:5; Rom. 12:5; Mal. 3:8-10; II Cor. 9:6-7; I Cor. 16:2.

Q. CIVIL GOVERNMENT. We believe that government is ordained of God, and all Christians should be subject to the laws of the land, except those contrary to the revealed will of God. We pledge allegiance and moral and spiritual support of the United States of America. In times of war the individual's participation in actual combat and taking of life shall be governed by his own conscience.

Scripture References: Rom. 13:1-7; Acts 5:29; Matt. 5:39-48; Heb. 12:14.

R. FINAL JUDGMENT. We believe in the final judgment of the wicked at the great white throne, when the dead, both small and great, shall be resurrected to stand before God to receive the reward of their deeds done in the flesh.

Scripture References: Matt. 13:41-43; Rev. 20:11-15.

S. HELL. We believe hell is a literal place of outer darkness, bitter sorrow, remorse, and woe, prepared by God for the devil and his angels and that there, into a lake that burns with fire and brimstone, shall be cast the unbelieving, the abominable, the murderers, sorcerers, idolators, and all liars, and those who have rejected the love of Jesus Christ, whose names are not written in the Lamb's book of life.

Scripture References: Rev. 20:10, 14-15; Rev. 21:7-8; Rev. 14:10-11; Matt. 25:41; Mark 9:43-44.

T. HEAVEN. We believe that heaven is the habitation of the living God, where Christ has gone to prepare a place for all His children, where they shall dwell eternally in happiness and security with Him.

Scripture References: I Cor. 2:9; John 14:2; Rev. 21:4; Rev. 22:5; Rev. 7:15-17.

U. EVANGELISM. We believe that as long as conditions indicate that the coming of Jesus Christ draws near, we, His redeemed children, should put forth our utmost efforts to the promulgation of the gospel to every kindred, tribe, and tongue; that soul winning is the chief mission of the church upon the earth, and that therefore every hindrance and hairsplitting doctrine, which would tend to quench or dampen the flame of worldwide evangelism, should be cut off and cast away as falling short of the church's great commission.

Scripture References: II Tim. 4:1-2; Eph. 5:16; Prov. 11:30; Ezek. 3:17-18; John 4:35-37.

V. MISSIONS. We believe that the great commission of our Lord Jesus Christ to carry the gospel message to the entire world is literal, imperative, and binding today; and that it is the supreme privilege and duty of the church of Jesus Christ to stress the cause of worldwide missions. Furthermore, we believe that the very life and strength of the home church depends on its wholehearted sacrifice for, and support of, the world missions program.

Scripture References: Matt. 9:38; Mark 16:15; Rev. 5:9; Rom. 10:13-15; James 5:20; Ps. 2:8.

Notes: *These articles to a large extent follow the text of the Declaration of Faith of the International Church of the Foursquare Gospel. They differ in being specifically premillennial in eschatology and deleting any statement on tithing.*

* * *

STATEMENT OF FAITH (PENTECOSTAL CHURCH OF GOD)

WE BELIEVE . . .

1. In the verbal inspiration of the Scriptures, both the Old and New Testaments.

2. Our God is a trinity in unity, manifested in three persons: the Father, the Son, and the Holy Ghost.

STATEMENT OF FAITH (PENTECOSTAL CHURCH OF GOD) (continued)

3. In the deity of our Lord Jesus Christ, in His virgin birth, in His sinless life, in His miracles, in His vicarious and atoning death on the cross, in His bodily resurrection, in His ascension to the right hand of the Father, and in His personal return in power and glory.

4. That regeneration by the Holy Ghost for the salvation of lost and sinful man, through faith in the shed blood of Jesus Christ, is absolutely essential.

5. In a life of holiness, without which no man can see the Lord, through sanctification as a definite, yet progressive, work of grace.

6. In the Baptism of the Holy Ghost, received subsequent to the new birth, with the speaking in other tongues, as the Spirit gives utterance, as the initial physical sign and evidence.

7. In water baptism by immersion for believers only, which is a direct commandment of our Lord, in the Name of the Father, and of the Son, and of the Holy Ghost.

8. In the Lord's supper and washing of the saints' feet.

9. That divine healing is provided for in the atonement, and is available to all who truly believe.

10. In the premillennial second coming of Jesus: first, to resurrect the righteous dead and to catch away the living saints to meet Him in the air; and, second, to reign on the earth a thousand years.

11. In the bodily resurrection of both the saved and the lost: they that are saved unto the resurrection of life, and they that are lost unto the resurrection of damnation.

Notes: *The Penecostal Church of God teaches a premillennial eschatology and practices foot washing.*

*   *   *

ARTICLES OF RELIGION (PENTECOSTAL CHURCH OF ZION)

ARTICLE 1. THE BIBLE

The Holy Bible, including the divisions commonly known as the Old and New Testament, is the divinely inspired Word of God. No other writing is so inspired. The Bible is infallible in teaching and containeth all things necessary to salvation: so that whatsoever is not read therein, nor may be proved thereby, is not required of any man, that it should be believed as an article of faith, or thought requisite or necessary to salvation. The Bible thus contains the complete will and revelation of God to man.

II Peter 1:20, 21. Knowing this first, that no prophesy of the scripture is of any private interpretation. For the prophesy of the scripture came not in old time by the will of man; but holy men of God spake as they were moved by the Holy Ghost.

II Timothy 3:16, 17. All scripture is given by inspiration of God, and is profitable for doctrine, for reproof for correction, for instruction in righteousness: That the man of God may be perfect, thoroughly furnished unto all good works.

Isaiah 45:23; Hebrews 4:12; Matthew 24:35.

ARTICLE 2. GOD

The supreme Deity of the universe is God. He is the Almighty Creator and Sustainer of the heaven, the earth, and all things therein. The doctrine of evolution is not scriptural.

Genesis 1:1. In the beginning God created the heaven and the earth. Acts 17:24-28, Acts 14:15, Psalms 124:8; Revelation 14:7.

ARTICLE 3. JESUS

Jesus of Nazareth is the only begotten Son of God, conceived of the Holy Ghost and born of the Holy Virgin Mary. He is the Christ, Messiah, Saviour and Redeemer. He was God manifested in the flesh. Outside of Jesus Christ, God has no body.

I Timothy 3:16. And without controversy great is the mystery of godliness: God was manifested in the flesh, justified in the Spirit, seen of angels, preached unto the Gentiles, believed on in the world, received up into glory.

Col. 2:9. For in him dwelleth all the fullness of the Godhead bodily. Matthew 1:18-25; Isaiah 9:6; 7:14; John 10:30.

ARTICLE 4. HOLY GHOST

The Holy Ghost (Holy Spirit) is the Comforter promised by our Lord, who will abide in the hearts of those who diligently seek Him. He will guide us into all Godly truths and give us power. Speaking in other tongues as the spirit of God giveth utterance is the initial evidence of the presence of the Holy Ghost, however the Holy Ghost must also be manifest both in word and by the "Fruits of the Spirit" and keeping the commandments of God.

Acts 2:4. And they were all filled with the Holy Ghost and began to speak with other tongues, as the Spirit gave them utterance. Acts 1:8; John 14:15-19, 26; Romans 5:5; John 16:13; I Cor. 12:7-11; Gal. 5: 22-26.

ARTICLE 5. THE BLOOD OF CHRIST

The condition of man after the fall of Adam is such that he cannot turn and prepare himself by his own natural strength and works, for eternal life. The blood of Christ was shed on the cross to redeem man from sin. I John 1:7. But if we walk in the light, as He is in the light, we have fellowship one with another, and the blood of Jesus Christ his Son cleanseth us from all sin. I Peter 1:18-19; Matthew 26:28; Rev. 5:9.

ARTICLE 6. ACCEPTING CHRIST

To secure the benefits of the Plan of Salvation, each individual must believe on the Lord Jesus Christ, repent and turn from sin, and accept Him as his personal Saviour; be baptised in the name of the Lord Jesus Christ; by immersion in water; and receive the Holy Ghost with the evidence of speaking in other tongues as did the early church on the day of pentecost.

Romans 10:9-10. That if thou shalt confess with thy mouth the Lord Jesus, and shalt believe in thine heart that God hath raised Him from the dead, thou shall be saved. For with the heart man believeth unto righteousness; and with the mouth confession is made unto salvation.

Acts 4:12. Neither is there salvation in any other; for there is none other name under heaven given among men whereby we must be saved.

Acts 2:38. Then Peter said unto them, Repent, and be baptised every one of you in the name of Jesus Christ for remission of sins, and ye shall receive the gift of the Holy Ghost.

Romans 6:4. Therefore we are buried with him by baptism into death: that like as Christ was raised up from the dead by the Glory of the Father, even so we also should walk in newness of life.

John 3:5. Jesus answered, Verily, verily, I say unto thee, except a man be born of water and of the Spirit, he cannot enter into the Kingdom of God. I John 3:4; Matthew 3:13-17; Acts 10:43-48.

ARTICLE 7. CONCERNING BACKSLIDING

It is possible for a man to sin and lose his status with God in any phase of his experience. If this should happen and said person repent and confess such sin and make restitution where possible and necessary, the Lord will forgive them and so will the church.

Jeremiah 3:14. Turn, O backsliding children, saith the Lord; for I am married unto you: and I will take you one of a city, and two of a family, and I will bring you to Zion.

Galatians 6:1. Brethren, if a man be overtaken in a fault, ye which are spiritual, restore such an one in the spirit of meekness; considering thyself, lest thou also be tempted. Matthew 18:12; Jer. 50:6.

ARTICLE 8. THE TEN COMMANDMENTS

1. "Thou shalt have no other Gods before me."

    This commandment teaches we should give all our love and honor to God and worship only Him.

2. "Thou shalt not make unto thee any graven image, or any likeness of anything that is in heaven above, or that is in the earth beneath, or that is in the water under the earth; thou shalt not bow down thyself to them, nor serve them; for I the Lord thy God am a jealous God, visiting the iniquity of the fathers upon the children unto the third and fourth generation of them that hate me; and showing mercy unto thousands of them that love me and keep my commandments."

    This commandment teaches us that if we worship graven images and idols, not only we, but our descendents will have to pay for it.

3. "Thou shalt not take the name of the Lord thy God in vain; for the Lord will not hold him guiltless that taketh his name in vain."

    This commandment teaches us that we should not take the name of God upon our lips lightly, or in blasphemy or profanity; or in vain oaths and curses; but only in reverence are we to name God.

4. "Remember the Sabbath day, to keep it holy. Six days shalt thou labor and do all thy work; but the seventh day is the sabbath of the Lord thy God; in it thou shalt not do any work, thou, nor thy son, nor thy daughter, thy manservant, nor thy maidservant, nor thy cattle, nor thy stranger that is within thy gates; for in six days the Lord made heaven and earth, the sea, and all that in them is, and rested the seventh day: wherefore the Lord blessed the sabbath day, and hallowed it."

    This commandment teaches us to do our earthly and natural work in the first six days of the week, and to refrain from all labor on the seventh day (Saturday) and set this day aside for rest and worship to God. Christ taught that it is lawful to do good such as healing the sick, or helping the ox out of the ditch on the Sabbath. The Sabbath begins on Friday at sunset and ends at Saturday at sunset. We should impose no labor on those in our employment or under our control on the Sabbath.

5. "Honor thy father and mother, that thy days may be long upon the land which the Lord thy God giveth thee."

    This commandment teaches us that a child is to respect and obey their parents, and that God regards the reverent and dutiful child with special favor.

6. "Thou shalt not kill."

    This commandment teaches us that we should regard human life as sacred and that we should refrain from every act that needlessly endangers the life or physical well being of ourself and our fellowmen. Jesus taught that hating anyone violates this commandment also.

7. "Thou shalt not commit adultery."

    This commandment teaches us to respect the divine institution of marriage; to maintain the sanctity of the home; and to be chaste, pure, and modest in all our behavior and speech. Jesus also stated, "But I say unto you that whosoever looketh upon a woman to lust after her hath committed adultery with her already in his heart." Matthew 5:27-28.

    Concerning divorce Jesus said, "It hath been said Whosoever shall put away his wife, let him give her a writing of divorcement. But I say unto you that whosoever shall put away his wife, saving for the cause of fornication, causeth her to commit adultery: and whosoever shall marry her that is divorced committeth adultery." Matthew 5:31-32.

8. "Thou shalt not steal."

    This commandment teaches us never to take anything that belongs to another; to be honest in all things; and never to deprive anyone of his property or of his rights therein by force or fraud.

9. "Thou shalt not bear false witness against thy neighbor."

    This commandment teaches us to avoid deceit, slander, or falsehood and to rule our tongues always by law of truth and love.

10. "Thou shalt not covet thy neighbor's house, thou shalt not covet thy neighbor's wife, nor his manser-

vant, nor his maidservant, nor his ox, nor his ass, nor anything that is thy neighbors."

This commandment teaches us that we should not envy our neighbor, his property, or his possessions, or desire to deprive him of that which is rightfully his.

ARTICLE 9. CHURCH ORGANIZATION

Salvation is through faith in Christ, but for the purpose of cooperation in the proclamation of the Gospel, and the upholding of true Bible standards and doctrines, and for the fellowship of the saints, the church should be organized in accordance with the Bible plan. Acts 6:1-8, Acts 1:23-26, I Cor. 12:27-30, Eph. 2:19-20, Eph. 4:10-17, I Tim. 5:17, I Tim. 3:1-5, Heb. 13:7-17.

ARTICLE 10. TITHES AND OFFERINGS

The Bible plan of financial support for the Gospel work is the paying of the tithes and offering by the members of the church. The tithe is one-tenth part of the increase, and should be paid as a part of the Christian obligation. Offerings are also a part of the Christian obligation to the Lord, and should be given liberally as one is prospered of Him.

Mal. 3:8-10. Will a man rob God? Yet ye have robbed me. But they say, wherein have we robbed thee? In tithes and offering. Ye are cursed with a curse: for ye have robbed me, even this whole nation. Bring ye all the tithes into the storehouse, that there may be meat in mine house, and prove me now herewith, saith the Lord of hosts, if I will not open you the windows of heaven, and pour you out a blessing, that there shall not be room enough to receive it. Matt 23:23, I Cor. 9:13-14, Lev. 27:30.

ARTICLE 11. LAW OF CLEAN AND UNCLEAN

The people of God and the followers of Christ in this age are to use for food those things which were given by God for that purpose, as distinguished from those things designated as unclean for human use.

Lev. 11:1-46. And the Lord spoke unto Moses and to Aaron, saying unto them, Speak unto the children of Israel, saying these are the beasts which ye shall eat among all the beasts that are on the earth. Whatsoever parteth the hoof, and is clovenfooted, and cheweth the cud, among the beasts, that shall ye eat.

Nevertheless these shall ye not eat of them that chew the cud, or of them that divide the hoof: as the camel, because he cheweth the cud, but divideth not the hoof; he is unclean to you. And the coney, because he cheweth the cud, but divideth not the hoof; he is unclean to you. And the hare, because he cheweth the cud, but divideth not the hoof; he is unclean to you.

And the swine, though he divide the hoof, and be clovenfooted, yet he cheweth not the cud; he is unclean to you. Of their flesh shall ye not eat; and their carcase shall ye not touch; they are unclean to you.

These shall ye eat of all that are in the waters; whatsoever hath fins and scales in the waters, in the seas, and in the rivers, them shall ye eat. And all that have not fins and scales in the seas, and in the rivers, of all that move in the waters, and of any living thing which is in the waters, they shall be an abomination unto you:

They shall be even an abomination unto you; ye shall not eat of their flesh, but ye shall have their carcases in abomination. Whatsoever hath no fins nor scales in the waters, that shall be an abomination unto you.

And these are they which ye shall have in abomination among the fowls; they shall not be eaten, they are an abomination: the eagle, and the ossifrage, and the ospray, and the vulture, and the kite after his kind; Every raven after his kind, and the owl, and the night hawk, and the cuckow, and the hawk after his kind, and the little owl, and the cormat, and the great owl, and the swan, and the pelican, and the gier eagle, and the stork, and heron after her kind, and the lapwing, and the bat. All fowls that creep, going upon all four, shall be an abomination unto you. (Read the next verses of the chapter paying special attention to the last five verses.) I Tim. 4:5, Isa. 65:15-17, Deut. 3:21.

ARTICLE 12. UNCLEAN HABITS

The body is the temple of the Holy Ghost, and God's people should be clean, refraining from any practice which would defile their bodies physically or spiritually. Therefore, the smoking, chewing or snuffing of tobacco; the drinking of intoxicating (alcoholic) liquors, and the habitual use of narcotic drugs, are not to be practiced by the members of the Pentecostal Church of Zion.

I Cor. 3:16-17. Know ye not that ye are the temple of God, and that the Spirit of God dwelleth in you? If any man defile the temple of God, him shall God destroy; for the temple of God is holy, which temple ye are. II Cor. 6:16-18; I John 2:15-18; James 1: 14-15; Gal. 5:19-21; Prov. 23:21-23; Prov. 23:29-32; Eph. 5:18; I Tim. 3:3.

ARTICLE 13. PRAYER FOR THE SICK

The Bible teaches both individual and collective prayer for the healing of the sick, and also the calling for the Elders of the church to anoint and pray for the sick, and that God hears and answers the prayer of faith.

James 5:13-16. Is any among you afflicted? Let him pray. Is any merry? Let him sing psalms. Is any sick among you? Let him call for the elders of the church; and let them pray over him, anointing him with oil in the name of the Lord: and the prayer of faith shall save the sick, and the Lord shall raise him up; and if he have committed sins, they shall be forgiven him. Confess your faults one to another, and pray one for another, that ye may be healed. The effectual fervent prayer of a righteous man availeth much. James 1:6, John 5:14-15, Psalms 103:1-3.

ARTICLE 14. PUNISHMENT OF THE WICKED

The wicked dead will be resurrected at the end of the thousand year reign of Christ, to receive final judgment and to be cast into the lake of fire which is the second death.

Rev. 20:11-15. And I saw a great white throne, and him that sat on it, from whose face the earth and the heaven fled away; and there was found no place for them. And I saw the dead, small and great, stand before God; and the books were opened; and another book was opened, which is the book of life: and the dead were judged out of those things which were written in the books, according to their works. And the sea gave up the dead which were in it; and death and hell delivered up the dead which were in them; and they were judged every man according to their works. And death and hell were cast into the lake of fire. This is the second death. And whosoever was not found written in the book of life was cast into the lake of fire. Matt. 5:22, Matt. 13:41, 42. Matt. 25:41, Mark 9:43-48, Luke 16:22-24.

ARTICLE 15. WORLDLINESS AND WORDLY PLEASURES

The scriptures condemn worldliness, and worldly pleasures, which include the lust of the flesh, the lust of the eye, and the pride of life. We should separate ourselves from the world and come out from among them. Attendance at movie theatres, pool halls, dances, and certain other public so-called recreation centers where there are wicked people, drinking or using profane language should be avoided when possible.

The excessive wearing of jewelry, and make-up, playing cards, mixed swimming (men and women together) is also considered worldly and should not be practiced.

Eph. 5:11, And have no fellowship with the unfruitful works of darkness, but rather reprove them. 2 Thes. 3:6. Now we command you brethren, in the name of our Lord Jesus Christ, that ye withdraw yourselves from every brother that walketh disorderly, and not after the tradition which he received of us. Matt. 13:22, Ex. 23:2, 2 Kings 17:15, Mark 6:22, I John 2:15-17, I Peter 3:3-4.

The following articles of religion are accepted and practiced by most of the members and clergy in the Pentecostal Church of Zion; however some have different opinions on some of the articles.

ARTICLE 16. CONCERNING CHILDREN

Children when born in the natural are under the grace of God until they reach an undetermined age when they are able to understand the way of Salvation. At any age that a child feels the need to come to the altar and repent he should be allowed to do so, and will be accepted as a member of the church when complying with the membership rules.

ARTICLE 17. CONCERNING THE KEEPING OF THE PASSOVER (OR SO CALLED LORD'S SUPPER)

The last passover to be observed was kept by Jesus and the Apostles the night before his death. We believe that his body was the "Bread from Heaven" and his blood was the "Fruit of the Vine." The passover is now celebrated through communion of the Holy Ghost daily and is not to be kept through the symbols literally.

John 13:14. If I then, your master, have washed your feet; ye also ought to wash one another's feet. 1 Tim. 5:9-10, 1 Peter 2:21.

ARTICLE 18. CRUCIFIXION OF JESUS

The Bible teaches that Jesus was crucified on the day of the week commonly known to us as Wednesday (midst of the week), and He was in the tomb three days and three nights, arising in the end of the Sabbath, thus fulfilling the prophesy of His sign as recorded in Matt. 12:39,40. But He answered and said unto them, An evil and adulterous generation seeketh after a sign; and there shall no sign be given to it, but the sign of the prophet Jonas: For as Jonas was three days and three nights in the whale's belly; so shall the Son of Man be three days and three nights in the heart of the earth. Matt. 28:1-8, Dan. 9:27, 1 Cor. 15:3-4, Mark 16:1-6, Mark 15:42, John 20:1-10, John 19:14, Luke 24:1-8, Luke 23:54-56.

ARTICLE 19. SIGNS OF THE TIMES

The regathering of literal Israel to the land of Palestine, as portrayed in the prophesies began to be fulfilled in 1948 when Israel became a state. The fulfillment of the signs in the political, religious, physical and social world lead us to believe that we are living in the time of the end, and that the second coming of Christ is very near.

Ezekiel 37:21-22. And say unto them, Thus saith the Lord God; Behold, I will take the children of Israel from among the heathen, whither they be gone, and will gather them on every side, and bring them into their own land: And I will make them one nation in the land upon the mountains of Israel; and one king shall be king to them all: and they shall be no more two nations, neither shall they be divided into two kingdoms any more at all. Jer. 31:9-11, Isa. 61:4.

Luke 21:24-26. And they shall fall by the edge of the sword, and shall be led away captive into all nations: and Jerusalem shall be trodden down of the Gentiles, until the times of the Gentiles be fulfilled. And there shall be signs in the sun, and in the moon, and in the stars; and upon the earth distress of nations, with perplexity; the sea and the waves roaring, Men's hearts failing them for fear, and for looking after those things which are coming on the earth: for the powers of heaven shall be shaken. Ezek. 21:25-27; Luke 17:26-31, Rev. 11-18, Matt. 24, 2 Tim. 4:3-4, 2 Tim. 3:1-13.

ARTICLE 20. KINGDOM OF HEAVEN

The Kingdom of Heaven is divided into three phases.

(1) The church, built by Christ (and established on the day of Pentecost) (Acts 2) in Matt. 16:18, 19. And I say also unto thee, Thou art Peter, and upon this rock I will build my church; and the gates of hell shall not prevail against it. And I will give unto thee the keys of the kingdom of heaven: and whatsoever thou shalt bind on earth shall be bound in heaven; and whatsoever thou lasht loose on earth shall be loose heaven.

(2) The second phase of the kingdom of heaven will begin at the second coming of Christ, when the dead in Christ is raised and the living saints are changed from mortal to immortality and rise to meet Him in the air, and so shall they ever be with the Lord. The saints will live and reign with him a thousand years.

Rev. 20:4. And I saw thrones, and they sat upon them, and judgment was given unto them: and I saw the souls of them that were beheaded for the witness of Jesus, and for the word of God, and which had not worshipped the beast, neither his image, neither had received his mark upon their foreheads, or in their hands; and they lived and reigned with Christ a thousand years.

(3) The third and final phase of the kingdom will begin after the thousand year reign of Jesus Christ and the resurrection of the wicked dead. There will be a new heaven and a new earth upon which Christ will set up his everlasting Kingdom and will reign with His saints forever.

2 Peter 1:11. For so an entrance shall be ministered unto you abundantly into the everlasting kingdom of our Lord and Saviour Jesus Christ. Rev. 22:14.

ARTICLE 21. STATE OF THE DEAD

When man dies, he is unconscious and in the grave awaits the resurrection. There will be no chance to repent and make restitution for sin after the natural death of a man.

Ecclesiastes 9:5. For the living know that they shall die: but the dead know not anything, neither have they any more reward; for the memory of them is forgotten. Psalms 146:4, I Cor. 15:42-56, Job 17: 13, Rev. 20:11-15, Job 14:13-14.

ARTICLE 22. CONCERNING WEARING APPAREL

Men and ladies alike should dress at all times in modest apparel. They should not dress so laviously that they are conspicuous, nor so odd that they are a public spectacle. The wearing of dresses with no sleeves, or the wearing of shorts by either sex is not considered modest street apparel.

I Tim. 2:9-10. In like manner also that women adorn themselves in modest apparel, with shamefacedness and sobriety; not with braided hair, or gold, or pearls or costly array: But (which becometh women professing Godliness) with good works. Mark 12:38, James 2:3, I Peter 3:3.

Notes: *These articles are unusual for their division following Article 15 into those beliefs held by the whole church and those about which there is some difference of opinion. Among the teachings are those concerning the annual observance of the Lord's Supper at Passover, the dating of Christ's crucifixion on Wednesday instead of Friday, and soul sleep.*

* * *

Deliverance Pentecostal

STATEMENT OF FAITH [ABUNDANT LIVING CHRISTIAN FELLOWSHIP (KINGSPORT, TENNESSEE)]

The church accepts the holy scriptures as the revealed will of God, the all-sufficient rule for faith and practice; and for the purpose of maintaining general unity adopts the following statement of fundamental truths:

1. We believe the Bible to be the inspired and only infallible and authoritative Word of God. II Tim 3:16; Heb 4:12

2. We believe that there is one God, eternally existent in three personalities: God the Father, God the Son, and God the Holy Ghost. II Cor 13:14; Mat 3:16, 17

3. We believe in the deity of our Lord Jesus Christ in His virgin birth, in His bodily resurrection, in His ascension to the right hand of the Father, and in the blessed hope of His personal visible future return to the earth to receive to Himself, His blood-bought church, that it may be with Him forever. Rom 10:9, 10; I Peter 1:18-21

4. We believe that the only means of being cleansed from sin is through repentance and faith in the precious blood of Christ. Eph 1:3-7; Rom 5:9

5. We believe that regeneration by the Holy Spirit is absolutely essential for personal salvation. John 3:5-6; Titus 3:5

6. We believe in baptism by immersion in water (Acts 8:14-16; Acts 19:1-5) to be administered to all those who have repented of their sins and who have believed on the Lord Jesus Christ to the saving of their souls and who give clear evidence of their salvation. Romans 6:3-5; Colossians 2:12

7. We believe that the redemptive work of Christ on the cross provides healing of the human body in answer to believing prayer. I Peter 2:24; Is 53:4, 5

8. We believe that the baptism in the Holy Spirit, according to Acts 2:4, is given to believers who ask for Him. Acts 19:2-6

9. We believe in the sanctifying power of the Holy Spirit by whose indwelling the Christian is enabled to live a holy life. Rom 8:1,2; Acts 13:2-4

10. We believe in the Lord's Supper to be observed regularly as enjoined by the scriptures. Luke 22:19-20; I Corinthians 11:23-26

11. We believe in the resurrection of both the saved and the lost, the one to everlasting life and the other to everlasting damnation. Matt 25:31-46; I Thess 4:15-18

12. We believe that God becomes the Heavenly Father of every person who accepts Jesus Christ as Savior and Lord and that because He is a good Father, He meets all our needs and gives us the desires of our hearts. Phil 4:19; Mark 11:24

Notes: *As a whole, the deliverance churches do not have formal statements of faith or, as is true in most cases, do not make an issue of them. Most of these churches try to work in an interdenominational atmosphere, where too much emphasis upon doctrine leads to unnecessary doctrinal controversy. In spite of a diligent search, only one statement of a local congregation was located.*

The Statement of Faith of the Abundant Living Christian Fellowship, a congregation founded by a student of Kenneth Hagin, summarizes the position presented at greater length in the writings of Hagin and other ministers (such as Fred Price) in the International Convention of Faith Churches.

This statement is typical of, and similar to, those adopted by churches associated with the convention, though it is merely the statement of a single congregation.

*   *   *

Apostolic Pentecostal

CHURCH DOCTRINES [APOSTOLIC FAITH (HAWAII)]

We preach Christ, His birth, His baptism, His works, His teachings, His crucifixion, His resurrection, His ascension, His second coming, His millennial reign, His white throne judgement, and the new heavens and new earth when He shall have put all enemies under His feet, and shall reign eternally, and we shall abide with Him forever and ever.

REPENTENCE TOWARD GOD—Acts 20:21. Repentance is Godly sorrow for sin. II Cor. 7:10. Mark 1:15.

RESTITUTION—The Blood of Jesus will never blot out any sin that we can make right. We must have a conscience void of offense toward God and man. Restitution includes restoring where you have defrauded or stolen, paying back debts and confession. Luke 19:8, 9. Ezekiel 33:15.

THE BAPTISM OF THE HOLY GHOST is the gift of power upon the sanctified. Luke 24:49. Matt. 3:11. John 7:38, 39. John 14:16, 17, 26. Acts 1:5-8.

And when we receive it, we have the same sign or Bible evidence as the disciples had on the day of Pentecost, speaking with tongues, as the Spirit gives utterance. Mark 16:17. I Cor. 14:21, 22. Examples—Acts 2:4. Acts 10:45, 46. Acts 19:6.

HEALING OF THE BODY—Sickness and disease are destroyed through the atonement of Jesus. Isa. 53:4, 5. Matt. 8:17. Mark 16:18. Jas. 5:14-16. All sickness is the work of the devil, which Jesus came to destroy. I John 3:8. Luke 13:16. Acts 10:38. Jesus cast out devils and commissioned His disciples to do the same. Mark 16:17. Luke 10:19. Mark 9:25, 26.

THE SECOND COMING OF JESUS—The return of Jesus is just as literal as His going away. Acts 1:9-11. John 14:3. There will be two appearances under one coming; first, to catch away His waiting bride (Matt. 24:40, 44 and I Thess. 4:15-17), (second), to execute judgment upon the ungodly. II Thess. 1:7-10. Jude 14 and 15. Zech. 14:3, 4.

ORDINANCES.

1st. WATER BAPTISM BY IMMERSION (SINGLE)—Jesus went down into the water and came up out of the water, giving us an example that we should follow. Matt. 3:16. Acts 8:38, 39. Acts 2:38. Rom. 6:4, 5. Col. 2:12.

2nd. THE LORD'S SUPPER—Jesus instituted the Lord's Supper that we might "show His death till He come." I Cor. 11:23, 26. Luke 22:17-20. Matt. 26:26-29.

It brings healing to our bodies if we discern the Lord's body. I Cor. 11:29, 30.

Why we take the Lord's Supper at night, and in the evening he cometh with the twelve. Mark 14:17.

THE TRIBULATION—Jesus prophesied a great tribulation such as was not from the beginning of the world. Matt. 24:21, 22, 29. Rev. 9. Rev. 16. Isa. 26:20, 21. Mal: 4:1.

CHRIST'S MILLENNIAL REIGN is the 1000 years of the literal reign of Jesus on this earth. It will be ushered in by the coming of Jesus back to earth with ten thousands of His saints. Jude 14, 15. II Thess. 1:7-10. During this time the devil will be bound. Rev. 20:2, 3. It will be a reign of peace and blessing. Isa. 11:6-9. Isa. 65:25. Hos. 2:18. Zech. 14:9-20. Isa. 2:2-4.

THE GREAT WHITE THRONE JUDGMENT—God will judge the quick and dead according to their works. Rev. 20:11-14. Dan. 12:2. Acts 10:42.

ETERNAL HEAVEN AND ETERNAL HELL—The Bible teaches that hell is as eternal as heaven. Matt. 25:41-46. The wicked shall be cast into a burning hell, a lake of fire burning with brimstone forever and ever. Rev. 14:10, 11. Luke 16:24. Mark 9:43, 44.

SANCTIFICATION is that act of God's grace by which He makes us holy. It is a second definite work wrought by the Blood of Jesus through faith. John 17:15-17. I Thess. 4:3. Heb. 13:12. Heb. 2:11. Heb. 12:14. I John 1:7.

JUSTIFICATION is that act of God's free grace by which we receive remission of sins. Acts 10:43. Rom. 5:1. Rom. 3:25. Acts 13:38, 39. John 1:12. John 3:3.

NEW HEAVENS AND NEW EARTH—The Word teaches that this earth, which has been polluted by sin, shall pass away after the White Throne Judgment, and God will make a new heaven and new earth in which righteousness shall dwell. Matt. 24:35. II Peter 3:12, 13. Rev. 21:1-3. Isa. 65:17.

CLUBS, SECRET SOCIETIES, ETC.—We firmly believe and hold that God's people should have no connection whatsoever with clubs, secret societies or any organization or body wherein there is fellowship with unbelievers, bound by an oath. Eph. 5:12. II Tim. 2:4. II Cor. 6:14-18. James 4:4.

HUMAN GOVERNMENT—We recognize the institution of human government as being ordained of God. Therefore, we should be loyal to our government and stand ready to fulfill our obligations as loyal citizens. The Word of God commands us to pray for the rulers of our country. There is a growing number of conscientious objectors in our country today who claim that they do so in obedience to the Bible, yet they brazenly defy the law and constituted authority. It is outright disloyalty to established government. In fact that stand is in sympathy with the enemy. Such conduct is based upon a false impression and the true Christian church verily does not condone their action. We, therefore, strongly exhort our members to freely and willingly respond to the call of our government for military service in time of peace and in time of war. I Peter 2:13. Rom. 13:1-3. I Tim. 2:1-3. II Cor. 4:2.

MARRIAGE AND DIVORCE—Marriage is a divine institution, established and sanctified by God. Marriage is honorable in all. Only death dissolves the marriage bond.

CHURCH DOCTRINES [APOSTOLIC FAITH (HAWAII)] (continued)

Divorce is only a privilege permitted by Moses because of the hardness of the human heart. Deut. 24:1-4. Matt. 5:31-32. Matt. 19:7-9. I Cor. 7:1-16 & 39. Rom. 7:1-3.

TITHING & FREE-WILL OFFERING—We believe and teach that tithing and free-will offerings is God's financial plan to provide for this work upon earth. It is a voluntary matter between every believer and God. Matt. 22:21. Malachi. 3:7-11. Heb. 7:1-10. II Cor. 9:6-7.

Notes: *The Non-Trinitarian, Apostolic, or "Jesus Only" Pentecostal churches are defined by their denial of the Trinity. Though the Trinity has been recognized as a central affirmation of Christianity for many centuries, the apostolic churches claim that it is not taught in the Bible and is a later doctrinal accretion. Most of the Apostolic churches have some roots in the Assemblies of God, within which the "Jesus only" issue was raised and discussed most vigorously.*

The church doctrines of the Apostolic Faith are derived from those of the (Original) Church of God, which in turn are derived from the Church of God Teachings of the Church of God (Cleveland, Tennessee). Unlike most apostolic churches, the Apostolic Faith believes in sanctification as a second work of grace. The Apostolic Faith continues the (Original) Church of God's position on secret societies, but has taken an opposite stance on the issue of participation in war.

*　　*　　*

WHAT WE BELIEVE (APOSTOLIC FAITH MISSION CHURCH OF GOD)

WHAT WE BELIEVE. We believe in the resurrection of the dead and the second coming of Christ.

No one shall hold an office in this church who is a member of another church.

No man, woman, boy or girl is a member of this church who uses intoxicants, or uses snuff, tobacco, morphine or any habit forming drugs.

Even foolish talking, jesting or using any slang language is discouraged. We command all members to abstain from all appearances of evil. II Cor. 7:1; I Thes. 5:23; I Cor. 6:1.

DIVINE HEALING. We believe that this is a divine instruction built upon the foundation of the Apostles and Prophets. Jesus Christ the Chief Cornerstone and it is the Christian's right and privilege to trust God for their healing when they are sick and afflicted. James 1:14; Mark 11:22; Mark 9:23; Heb. 11:6; Acts 3:6-16.

We do not condemn those who are weak in the faith for using medicine, but exhort and nourish and cherish them until they become strong: for the Bible says: Him that is weak in the faith receive ye, but not to doubtful disputations. Rom. 14:1 also said, that some would use herbs, but not to judge them. Rom. 14:2.

COMMUNION AND FEET WASHING. On the night of our Lord's betrayal He ate the Passover supper with His Apostles after which He instituted the sacrament.

"And He took bread and gave unto them, saying, This is my body which is given for you: This do in remembrance of me. Likewise also the cup after supper, saying, This cup is the new testament in my blood, which is shed for you." (Luke 22:19-20.)

Paul instructed the church how to observe it. (I Cor. 11:23-34).

Thus was instituted the use of literal bread and the fruit of the vine, which are partaken of, literally as emblems of His broken body and shed blood. There is also a spiritual significance and blessing in partaking of the sacrament.

When the Passover was ended, we read in John 13:4-5, "He riseth from supper and laid aside His garments; and took a towel and girded himself. After that he poureth water into a basin and began to wash the disciples feet, and to wipe them with the towel wherewith he was girded."

Jesus said, "If I then, your Lord and Master washed your feet; ye also ought to wash one another's feet. For I have given you an example that ye should do as I have done to you" (John 13:14-15).

WOMEN PREACHERS. This church believes that a woman has a right to teach or preach. God said He would pour out His spirit upon all flesh. Your sons and daughters shall prophesy. The word prophesy means to utter predictions, to make declarations of events to come, to instruct in religious doctrine. Read Acts 2:17; Joel 2:28; Acts 21:9; Rom. 16:1-2; Phil. 4:3, when God made man he also made a woman to help man. (Gen. 2:19-23).

ARTICLE OF FAITH

SECTION 1. We believe in justification by faith according to Romans 5:1 and that no man is justified with God as long as he is doing what God says not to do.

SECTION 2. We believe that Jesus Christ shed His blood to sanctify the people according to Heb. 13:12; I John 1:7-9; Rom. 6:6; I Thes. 5:23; St. John 17:17; Acts 26:18.

SECTION 3. We believe that sanctification does affect the innermost being according to Matt. 23:26; I Thes. 5:23; and that is instantaneous and is carried on into Holiness, Lev. 11:44.

LAWS OF THE LAND. We believe the magistrates are ordered for peace, safety, welfare of all people. Therefore, under this condition our duty is to be in obedience to all of the laws of the land so long as they are not contrary to the word of God. We do not believe in war, nor going to war, for God is not the author of confusion, but of peace.

THE COMING OF JESUS. That Jesus is coming again in person is a doctrine clearly set forth in apostolic times. Jesus taught it, the Apostles preached it, and the saints expected it. (I Thes. 4:14-17; Titus 2:13-14.)

TRANSLATION OF THE SAINTS. We believe that the time draweth near for the coming of the Lord to make a change in the present order of things. At that time, all the righteous dead shall arise from their graves, and they that are living righteous before God shall be translated or "caught up to meet the Lord in the air." (Matt. 24:36-42;

Luke 17:20-37; I Cor. 15:51-54; Philippians 3:20-21; I Thes. 5:1-10).

FINAL JUDGMENT. When the thousand years shall have passed, there shall be a resurrection of the dead who shall be summoned before the Great White Throne for their final judgment. All those whose names are not found written in the Book of Life shall be cast into the Lake of Fire and brimstone which God has prepared for the Devil and his angels. (Rev. 20:10-15).

SANCTIFICATION. We believe that Sanctification is a work of grace, and it begins in regeneration by the application of the blood of Jesus. I John 1:7; Heb. 12:2; Acts 20:28; Rom. 5:6; Heb. 9:14; I Peter 1:8-19; Rev. 7:14.

We understand the word Sanctified or Sanctification means Separation and Consecration, St. John 17:17; I Cor. 1:30; Eph. 5:25-26; II Tim. 2:21; I Peter 1:2.

We believe that God's church in the early dispensation was Sanctified, Duet. 14:2; Duet. 7:6; Ezek. 36:23; St. John 17:19; Acts 20:32; I Cor. 1:2; I Cor. 6:11; Heb. 2:11; Jer. 1:5; Dan. 7:27.

THE GOD HEAD. We believe that Jesus is God, and there is no other beside Him. (Duet. 4:35; 6:4; II Sam. 7:22; I Chron. 17:20: Psa. 83:18; Isa. 43:10; 44:6; 45:8; Mark 12:29; I Cor. 8:4; Eph. 4:5; I Tim. 2:5; Acts 9:5; Rev. 1:13).

We believe that there are three (3) that bear record in Heaven, Viz: The Father, The Word, The Holy Ghost. These three are one manifested in the person of Jesus Christ and Jesus Christ is image of the Invisible God, the Creator of all things, the Alpha and Omega, the beginning and the ending. Isaiah 9:6; John 14:8-11; Rev. 1:8: John 10:30-38.

WATER BAPTISM. Water Baptism is an essential part of the New Testament Salvation: and not, as some teach. "Just an outward form of an inward cleansing. Without proper baptism it is impossible to enter into the kingdom of God (God's true Church, the Bride of Christ), and therefore, is not merely a part of local church membership.

MANNER OF BAPTISM. Water Baptism can only be administered by immersion (Col. 2:12). Note the following: Jesus said "Born (to bring forth) of the water," (John 3:5); Paul said, "We are buried with Him (Lord Jesus Christ) by baptism," (Rom. 6:4); Jesus "Came up out of the water," (Mark 1:10); Phillip and the eunuch "Went down into the water," and "Came up out of the water" (Acts 8:38-39).

Jesus' death, burial and resurrection was a type of our salvation. "Repent (death to sin), and he baptized (burial) everyone of you in the name of Jesus Christ for the remissions of sins, and ye shall receive the gift of the Holy Ghost" (resurrection).

FORMULA FOR WATER BAPTISM. The Name in which baptism is administered is as important as immersion. This name is Lord Jesus Christ.

Jesus' last command to His disciples was, "Go ye therefore and teach all nations, baptizing them (all nations) in the name of the Father and the Son and of the Holy Ghost." (Matt. 28:19).

You will notice He said name, not names. As we have previously explained, Father, Son, and Holy Ghost are not names but titles of positions held by God. We see quickly that this is true as we hear the angel announce "She shall bring forth a SON, and thou shalt call His name Jesus." (Matt. 1:21).

This name the Apostles understood to be Lord Jesus Christ, and from the first day that the Church of God was established on the day of Pentecost (Act 2:36-41). Until the end of their ministry, they baptized in the name of the Lord Jesus Christ.

"Thou shalt call His name Jesus: for he shall save his people from their sins." (Matt. 1:21).

Are you looking for Salvation? "Neither is there Salvation in any other, for there is none other name under Heaven given among men, whereby we must be saved." (Acts 4:12).

Without this name, water baptism is void.

HOLINESS. Godly living should characterize the life of every child of the Lord, and we should live according to the pattern and example given in the Word of God. "For the grace of God that bringeth salvation hath appeared to all men, teaching us that, denying ungodliness and worldly lusts, we should live soberly, righteously, and Godly, in this present world" (Titus 2:11-12). "For even hereunto were ye called: because Christ also suffered for us, leaving us an example that ye should follow His steps: who did no sin, neither was guile found in His mouth; who, when He was reviled, reviled not again; when He suffered He threatened not; but committed Himself to Him that judgeth righteously" (I Peter 2:21-23).

"Follow peace with all men and holiness, without which no man shall see the Lord" (Heb. 12:14).

But as He which hath called you is holy, so be ye holy in all manner of conversation; because it is written, be ye holy: for I am holy. And if ye call on the Father, who without respect of persons judgeth according to every man's work, pass the time of your sojourning here in fear: forasmuch as ye know that ye were not redeemed with corruptible things, as silver and gold, from your vain conversation received by tradition from your fathers; but with the precious blood of Christ as of a lamb without blemish and without spot" (I Peter 1:15-19).

Notes: *One of the earliest apostolic churches, the Apostolic Faith Mission Church of God teaches sanctification as a second definite work of grace, the necessity of baptism for salvation, and pacifism. It practices foot washing.*

* * *

ARTICLES OF FAITH (ASSEMBLIES OF THE LORD JESUS CHRIST)

INTRODUCTION

We believe the Bible to be the direct and absolute word of God, (II Tim. 3:16) given to us by the inspiration of the Holy Ghost as it moved upon the tongues and pens of men who had received special anointing of God for this express purpose. (II Peter 1:21) "For the prophecy came not in old time by the will of man: But Holy men of God spoke as they were moved by the Holy Ghost." We believe the Bible to be God's means of doctrine, instruction, and comfort to the church today, infallible in its authority, singular in interpretation, and man's only avenue of access to God.

ARTICLES OF FAITH

"THE ONE TRUE GOD"

We believe in the one everliving, eternal God; infinite in power. Holy in nature, attributes and purpose; and possessing absolute, indivisible deity. This one true God has revealed Himself as Father in creation; through His Son in redemption; and as the Holy Spirit, by animation. (I Cor. 8:6; Eph. 4:6; II Cor. 5:19; Joel 2:28).

The scripture does more than attempt to prove the existence of God; it asserts, assumes and declares that the knowledge of God is universal. (Romans 1, 19, 21, 28, 32, 2:15) God is invisible, incorporeal, without parts, without body and therefore free from all limitations. He is Spirit (John 4:24), and "a spirit hath not flesh and bones. . . . " (Luke 24:39).

. . . "The first of all the commandments is, Hear, O Israel; the Lord our God is one Lord" (Mark 12:29; Deut. 6:4). "One God and Father of All, who is above all, and through all, and in you all" (Eph. 4:6).

This one true God manifested Himself in the Old Testament in divers ways; in the Son while He walked among men; as the Holy Spirit after the ascension.

THE SON OF GOD

The one true God, the Jehovah of the Old Testament, took upon Himself the form of man, and as the son of man, was born of the virgin Mary. As Paul says, "And without controversy great is the mystery of godliness; God was manifest in the flesh, justified in the spirit, seen of angels, preached unto the Gentiles believed on in the world, received up into Glory" (I Timothy 3:16; John 1:10).

"He came unto His own, and His own received Him not" (John 1:11). This one true God was manifest in the flesh, that is, in His Son Jesus Christ.

". . . God was in Christ, reconciling the world unto Himself, not imputing their trespasses unto them . . . " (II Cor. 5:19).

We believe that, ". . . in Him (Jesus) dwelleth all the fullness of the Godhead bodily" (Col. 2:9).

THE NAME

". . . unto us a child is born, unto us a son is given; . . . and His name shall be called Wonderful, counselor, The Mighty God, The Everlasting Father, The Prince of Peace" (Isaiah 9:6). This prophecy of Isaiah was fulfilled when the Son of God was named, "And she shall bring forth a son, and thou shalt call His name Jesus: For He shall save His people from their sins" (Matthew 1:21).

Neither is there salvation in any other; for there is none other name under heaven given among men, whereby we must be saved (Acts 4:12).

MAN AND HIS FALL

God created man in His own image (Gen. 1:26,27), innocent, pure and holy. By transgression man lost his standing. (Rom. 5:11; Eph. 2:3). Man needed a redeemer which has been supplied in the seed of the woman, which seed bruised the serpent's head (Gen 3:15; Luke 2:10, 11); that is: Our Lord and Saviour Jesus Christ in whom we have redemption, through his blood, even the forgiveness of sins. (Eph. 1:7; Rev. 1:5).

THE GRACE OF GOD

"For the grace of God that bringeth salvation hath appeared to all men, teaching us that denying ungodliness and worldly lusts, we should live soberly, righteously, and godly in this present world." (Titus 2:11,12).

"For the law was given by Moses, but grace and truth came by Jesus Christ" (John 1:17).

A Christian, to keep saved, must walk with God and keep himself in the love of God (Jude 21) and in the grace of God. The word "grace" means "favor." When a person transgresses and sins against God, He loses His favor. If he continues to commit sin and does not repent, he will eventually be lost and cast into the lake of fire. (Read John 15:2, 6:2; II Peter 2:20, 21, 22). Jude speaks of the backsliders of his day and their reward. (And read Hebrews 6:4-6).

"For by grace are ye saved through faith; and that not of yourselves; it is the Gift of God." (Eph. 2:8)

THE COMMUNION

Melchizedek, the Priest of the Most High God, gave the first Communion to our Father Abraham, consisting of bread and wine. (Gen. 14:18) Christ, being "made a High Priest forever after the order of Melchizedek" evidently administered the same. (Heb. 7:21; Matthew 26:26-29; I Cor. 11:23-32).

On the night of our Lord's betrayal, He ate the Passover Supper with His Apostles, after which He instituted the sacrament. "And He took bread, and gave thanks, and brake it, and gave unto them, saying, this is my body which is given for you: This do in remembrance of me. Likewise also the cup after supper, saying, this cup is the new testament in my blood, which is shed for you." (Luke 22:19, 20)

Paul instructed the church how to observe it: (I Cor. 11:23-24).

THE WASHING OF FEET

This ordinance is as much a divine command as any other New Testament ordinance. Jesus gave us an example that we do even as He had done. He said that we ought to wash one another's feet. And again, "If ye know these things, happy are ye if you do them." (John 13:4-17) There is scriptural evidence that this was practiced by the Church in the days of the Apostle Paul. (I Tim. 5:10)

DIVINE HEALING

The physical suffering of the Lord Jesus Christ purchased healing for our bodies, as His death, burial and resurrection provided for the salvation of our souls, for: . . . "with His stripes we are healed" (Isaiah 53:5). Matthew

8:17 read, ". . . Himself took our infirmities, and bore our sicknesses." (See also I Peter 2:24).

We see from this that healing for the body is in the atonement. That being true, then it is for all who believe. Jesus said of believers, ". . . they shall lay hands on the sick, and they shall recover." Later James wrote in his Epistle to all the churches: "Is any sick among you? Let him call for the elders of the church; and let them pray over him, anointing him with oil in the name of the Lord: and the prayer of faith shall save the sick, and the Lord shall raise him up; and if he have committed sins, they shall be forgiven him. Confess your faults one to another, and pray one for another, that ye may be healed. The effectual fervent prayer of a righteous man availeth much." (James 5:14-16)

REPENTANCE AND REMISSION OF SIN

The only grounds upon which God will accept a sinner is repentance, from the heart, for the sins that he has committed. A broken and contrite heart, He will not despise. (Psa. 51:17) John preached repentance, Jesus proclaimed it, and before His ascension commanded that repentance and remission of sins should be preached in His name, beginning at Jerusalem (Luke 24:47). Peter fulfilled this command on the Day of Pentecost. (Acts 2:38).

WATER BAPTISM

The scriptural mode of baptism is immersion, and is only for those who have fully repented, having turned from their sins and a love of the world. It should be administered by a duly authorized minister of the Gospel in obedience to the Word of God, and in the name of Jesus Christ, according to the Acts of the Apostles 2:38; 8:16; 10:48; 19:5; thus obeying and fulfilling Matthew 28:19.

HOLY SPIRIT BAPTISM

John the Baptist, in Matthew 3:11, said, ". . . He shall baptize you with the Holy Ghost, and with fire."

Jesus, in Acts 1:5, said, ". . . ye shall be baptized with the Holy Ghost not many days hence."

Luke tells us in Acts 2:4, ". . . they were all filled with the Holy Ghost, and began to speak with other tongues (languages) as the Spirit gave them utterance."

The terms "Baptize with the Holy Ghost and fire," "Filled with the Holy Ghost," and the "Gift of the Holy Ghost" are synonymous terms used interchangeably in the Bible.

APOSTOLIC DOCTRINE OF NEW BIRTH

The basic and fundamental doctrine of this Organization shall be the Bible standard of full salvation, which is repentance, baptism in water by immersion in the name of Jesus Christ for the remission of sins, and the baptism of the Holy Ghost with the evidence of speaking with other tongues as the Spirit gives utterance. (Acts 2:4 and 2:38; John 3:5)

HOLINESS

We believe that godly living should characterize the life and walk of all saints according to the sign and example found in (I Peter 2:21; Titus 2:11; Gal. 2:20; Heb. 12:14; I Peter 1:15-17).

We believe we are to cleanse ourselves from all filthiness of the flesh and spirit perfecting holiness in the fear of God (II Cor. 7-1), and to abstain from ALL appearance of EVIL, (I Thes. 5:22) and to turn away from those who have a form of godliness but deny the power thereof. (II Tim. 3:5; I Cor. 11:6; I Tim. 2:9, 10; I Peter 2:3,4)

TITHING

We believe tithing is God's financial plan to provide for His work, and has been since the days of Abraham. Tithing came with faith under Abraham; Moses' law enjoined it, and Israel practiced it when she was right with God; Jesus endorsed it (Matt. 23:23); and Paul said to lay by in store as God has prospered you. Do not rob God of His portion, that is tithes and offerings. (Read Mal. 3).

MARRIAGE AND DIVORCE

"Whosoever shall put away his wife, except it be for fornication, and shall marry another, committeth adultery." (Mat. 5:32 and 19:9)

In order to lift a higher standard in the ministry, no minister, shall be accepted in this organization who has married for the second time, after his conversion, unless the first marriage was terminated by a death.

SECRET SOCIETIES, ETC.

According to the word of God we firmly believe and hold that the people of God should have no connection whatever with secret societies, or any other organization or body wherein is a fellowship of unbelievers bound by an oath.

(James 5:3-7; II Cor. 6:14-18) We are exhorted by the Word of God to "be content with such things as we have," and "be content with our wages." (I Tim. 6:8; Heb. 13:5; Luke 3:14).

THE RETURN OF THE LORD JESUS CHRIST

That the Lord Jesus Christ is to come to earth in person is a doctrine clearly set forth in apostolic times. Jesus taught it; the apostles preached it; the saints expect it. (See Matt. 24:1 etc.; Acts 1:11; 3:19-21; I Cor. 1:7-8; 11:26; Phil. 3:20-21; Titus 2:13).

TRANSLATION OF SAINTS

We believe the catching away of the church draweth nigh, and at that time all the dead in Christ shall arise from their graves, and we that are alive and, remain shall be translated or "caught up" to meet the Lord in the air. (Matt. 24:36-42; Luke 17:20-37; I Cor. 15:51; Phil. 3:20-21; I Thes. 4:13-17)

Whereas, the Word of God teaches the imminent second coming of our Lord Jesus Christ; and that there will be first an appearing or catching away of the church (I Thes. 4:13) preceding His second coming back to earth; and said first appearing we believe to be at hand and likely to occur at any moment.

TRIBULATION

Moreover, we believe that the distress upon the earth is the "beginning of sorrows" and will become more intense until there "shall be a time of trouble such as never was since there was a nation even to that same time" (Matt. 24:1; Hab. 2:14; Rom. 11:25-27).

ARTICLES OF FAITH (ASSEMBLIES OF THE LORD JESUS CHRIST) (continued)

MILLENNIUM

We believe that the period of "Tribulation" will be followed by the dawn of a better day on earth, and that for one thousand years there shall be "peace on earth and good will toward men." (Rev. 20:1-5; Isa. 65:17-25; Matt. 5:5; Dan. 7:27; Mic. 4:1; Hab. 2:14; Rom. 11:25-27).

FINAL JUDGMENT

When the thousand years are finished, there shall be a resurrection of the dead, who shall be summoned before the Great White Throne for their final judgment; and all whose names are not found written in the Book of Life shall be cast into the Lake of Fire, burning with brimstone, which God has prepared for the devil and his angels. Satan being cast in first. (Rev. 20:5-15; Matt. 25:41-46; Rev. 21:8).

CIVIL GOVERNMENT

All civil magistrates are ordained of God for peace, safety and the welfare of all people (Rom. 13:1-10; Titus 3:1-2; I Peter 2:13-14;) therefore, it is our duty to be in obedience to all requirements of the laws that are not contrary to the Word of God, and that do not force one to the violation of the sixth commandment, by bearing arms. Is is our duty to honor them, pay tribute, or such taxation as may be required without murmuring (Matt. 17:24-27; 22:17-21), and show respect to them in all lawful requirements of the civil government.

CONSCIENTIOUS SCRUPLES

We propose to fulfill all the obligations of loyal citizens, but are constrained to declare against participation in combatant service in war, armed insurrection, property destruction, aiding or abetting in or the actual destruction of human life.

Furthermore, we cannot conscientiously affiliate with any union boycott, or organization which will force or bind any of its members, to perform any duties contrary to our conscience, or receive any mark, without our right to affirm or reject same.

However, we regret the false impression created by some groups, or so-called "conscientious objectors," that to obey the Bible is to have a contempt for law or magistrates, to be disloyal to our government and in sympathy with our enemies, or to be unwilling to sacrifice for the preservation of our commonwealth. This attitude would be as contemptible to us as to any patriot. The Word of God commands us to do violence to no man. It also commands us that first of all we are to pray for rulers of our country. We, therefore, exhort our members to freely and willingly respond to the call of our Government, except in the matter of bearing arms. When we say service—we mean service—no matter how hard or dangerous. The true church has no more place for cowards than has the nation. First of all, however, let us earnestly pray that we will with honor be kept out of war.

We believe that we can be consistent in service to our Government in certain noncombatant capacities, but not in the bearing of arms.

PUBLIC SCHOOL ACTIVITIES

We disapprove of school students attending shows, dances, dancing classes, theaters, engaging in school activities against their religious scruples and wearing gymnasium clothes which immodestly expose the body.

Notes: *The Assemblies of the Lord Jesus Christ's articles are derived in part from those of the United Pentecostal Church. Like that body, the Assemblies practice foot washing and disavow participation in secret societies, war, and public school activities considered frivolous (dances) or immodest (gymnasium activities).*

*　　*　　*

ARTICLES OF FAITH (ASSOCIATED BROTHERHOOD OF CHRISTIANS)

PREFACE

Be it understood that this is a Christian Association, based upon brotherly love and Christian principles. Its intentions are to promote Christian fellowship and to encourage unity of the Spirit among all Christians everywhere; not making controversial issues and doctrinal convictions a test of fellowship. We recognize, acknowledge, and appreciate the fact that there are convictions, revelations, and doctrinal truths revealed to some Christians which are not revealed to; nor understood by others. In such cases the A. B. of C. recommends that both parties be considerate of each other, recognizing the fallibility of man; endeavoring to keep the unity of the Spirit in the bonds of peace—until we all come to the unity of the faith. This being, in effect, the general principles of this Association, we, therefore, will follow in our Articles of Faith with only the fundamental truths we deem necessary for our general good.

ARTICLES OF FAITH

A.　THE SCRIPTURES. We believe the Bible to be the inspired Word of God, infallible in its original writings. II Tim. 3:16; II Peter 1:21.

B.　THE GODHEAD. We believe in the one everliving, eternal God, infinite in power, holy in nature, attributes, and purpose; in His absolute diety. That this one true God has revealed Himself as Father, in creation; as Son in redemption; and as the Holy Ghost in this church age. That God was manifest in the flesh (Jesus Christ), justified in the Spirit, seen of angels, preached unto the Gentiles, believed on in the world, received up into glory. I Tim. 3:16. That the fullness of diety was revealed and manifest in the Lord Jesus Christ; and that Jesus is the name of God for this dispensation. I Cor. 8:6; II Cor. 5:19; Matt. 1:21; and Eph. 4:6.

C.　FALLIBILITY OF MAN. We believe in the fallibility of all mankind. Thru the transgression and fall of Adam in the Garden of Eden, all men are declared to be sinners, therefore, in order to be restored to favor with God all must be born again. Jn. 3:3-5.

D.　SUFFERING OF CHRIST. We believe in the vicarious suffering of Jesus Christ the Son of God; that thru His shed blood, atonement for sin has been made for all mankind. Isa. 53:1-12; Matt. 26:28; and Heb. 9:11-28.

E. **THE CRUCIFIXION AND RESURRECTION.** We believe that Jesus Christ was rejected by the world, especially His own nation; was tried and suffered under the hands of Pilate; died on the cross by crucifixion, was buried, rose again the third day; His resurrection being confirmed by many definite proofs. He was seen by many witnesses for about forty days after His resurrection, after which He ascended up on high, and is now seated at the right hand of the throne of God, there to intercede and advocate for all believers. Heb. 12:2.

F. **GRACE.** We believe that our present dispensation is a time of grace, that we are saved by grace thru faith, not of works lest any man should boast. Eph. 2:4-10.

G. **NEW COVENANT.** We believe that God took away the first (covenant) that He might establish the second (Heb. 8:6-10; 10:9) and that under this new covenant in this dispensation none of the statutes of the Mosaic Law are binding. "But now we are delivered from the law, that being dead wherein we were held: that we should serve in newness of Spirit, and not in oldness of the letter" (Rom. 7:6). "For Christ is the end of the law for righteousness to everyone that believeth" (Rom. 10:4). "The law and the prophets were until John: since that time the Kingdom of God is preached" (Luke 16:16).

H. **THE CHURCH.** Jesus said: "Upon this Rock I will build My church." We believe that it is a Spiritual house (church) to offer up Spiritual Sacrifices. (I Peter 2:5). See John 4:23; & Heb. 13:15-16.

I. **CHURCH MEMBERSHIP.**

   a. **REPENTANCE.** We believe in and teach Repentance and faith toward God as the first step for the sinner, as there is but one true entrance into the great Spiritual Church which is the body of Christ (Eph. 1:22-23). God accepts a sinner only when he repents; therefore Repentance and Remission of sins should be preached in Jesus' Name (Luke 24:45-47; Acts 2:37-38).

   b. **BAPTISM.** We believe in Water Baptism by immersion, and that it should be administered in the name of the Lord Jesus, Jesus Christ, or Lord Jesus Christ as practised by the Apostles. See Acts 2:38; 8:16; 10:48; 1 Cor. 1:13; Col. 3:17.

   c. **BAPTISM OF THE HOLY GHOST.** We believe in and teach the baptism of the Holy Ghost for believers, witnessed by the physical sign of speaking in other tongues as the Spirit gives utterance. Acts 2:4; 10:46; 19:6. This procedure is recognized as being the teaching of the Apostles regarding the New Birth and as placing us as members of the New Testament Church. Acts 2:41, 47; 1 Cor. 12:13, 18.

J. **HOLINESS.** Dearly beloved, let us cleanse ourselves from all filthiness of the flesh and spirit perfecting holiness in the fear of God, for God hath not called us unto uncleanliness; but unto holiness. Follow

peace with all men and holiness without which no man shall see the Lord. (II Cor. 7:1; I Thes. 4:7; Heb. 12:14; I Pet. 1:15-16).

K. **DIVINE HEALING.** Deliverance from sickness is provided for in the atonement and is a privilege for believers. As the Lord made our bodies it is not incredible that He should heal them. (Isa. 53:5; Mark 16:15-18; James 5:14).

L. **SPIRITUAL GIFTS.** We believe the nine gifts of the Spirit should be manifested in the church today, and that all Spirit-filled believers should earnestly covet the best gifts for the edification and up-building of the church. (I Cor. 12:8-11; 14:1).

M. **FRUITS OF THE SPIRIT.** We believe the Spirit-filled believers will produce the fruit of the Spirit in their lives and their walk will be according to godliness and holy living. (Gal. 5:22-23; I John 2:6; I Pet. 1:16; Tit. 2:11-13; II Cor. 7:1).

N. **COMMUNION.** Whereas the word Communion expresses Fellowship; we believe in Communion with God through the Spirit as typified in the Shadows of the Old Testament and taught by Jesus and the Apostles in the New Testament. In order to have this Fellowship with God we must be a partaker of the Flesh and Blood of Jesus through the Spirit, as there is no Spiritual Life outside of Him. We believe that the literal emblems of bread and fruit of the vine used at the Passover were shadows of good things to come, and as they were partaking of these emblems Jesus said, This is my body which is broken for you, and This is my blood which is shed for the remission of sins. Matt. 26:17-29; Mark 14:12-25; Luke 22:1-20; I Cor. 11:23-27. That, since Christ, our Passover, is sacrificed for us (I Cor. 5:7), the Passover instituted at the time of the exodus of Israel from Egypt (Ex. 12th chapter) is fulfilled in the Kingdom of God. "The Kingdom of God is not meat and drink; but righteousness, peace and joy in the Holy Ghost." (Rom. 14:17). When we are all baptised into the one body by the Holy Ghost we are made to drink of the one Spirit. (I Cor. 12:13). So then, the cup of Blessing which we bless is the Communion (fellowship) of the Blood of Christ and the bread which we break is the Communion (fellowship) of the Body of Christ. (I Cor. 10:16). For we being many, are one bread, and one body; for we are all partakers of that one bread. (I Cor. 10:17). Hence, we believe in partaking of the flesh and blood of the Lord through the spirit as referred to by the scripture, (Jn. 6:48-63). We hold then, that partaking of natural, or literal elements is not essential to our Salvation, and therefore, refrain from partaking thereof; but with due Christian courtesy we respect those who may hold an opposite view.

O. **FOOT WASHING.** Since Jesus did not wash the disciples' feet in public, in the Temple or Synagogue, and since there is no Scriptural reference to it other than as a common custom, we believe He was giving us an example of Love and Humility. (Luke 22:24-27; John 13:12-15; I Tim. 5:10). Hence: we do not

ARTICLES OF FAITH (ASSOCIATED BROTHERHOOD OF CHRISTIANS) (continued)

support the practice of washing feet in public as a church ordinance.

P. SECOND COMING OF CHRIST. We believe in the second personal coming of the Lord as taught by the Scriptures. (Acts 1:11; I Thes. 4:16; Heb. 9:28).

Q. RESURRECTION. We believe in the Resurrection of the dead (Job 19:26; Isa. 26:19; Dan. 12:2; Rev. 20:11-15).

R. JUDGEMENT. We believe that all will appear before the judgement Seat of Christ to be judged according to the deeds done in the body (Eccl. 12:14; II Cor. 5:10; Rev. 20:11-15).

S. THE SABBATH. We do not hold that our Salvation is contingent upon keeping of certain days, or times. See Romans 14:5-6; Gal. 5:1; Col. 2:16.

T. MARRIAGE AND DIVORCE. We believe that divorce and remarriage is unscriptural and forbidden, except where fornication (as defined by the Scripture) is proven to be the cause of separation. See Matt. 19:3-17; I Cor. 5:1.

U. MORAL STANDARD. We believe in the highest possible standard of moral living, therefore we do not tolerate the Doctrine of Free Love, Spiritual Companionship, Social Purity, or any other kindred teachings that might lead to immoral conduct.

V. BELIEVERS SECURITY. We believe that it is possible for those who have been enlightened, and have tasted of the good Word of God to fall from their steadfastness in Christ (Heb. 3:12-19; II Pet. 3:17). Therefore, the believer is secure from the judgements of God only as he maintains his fellowship with Christ.

W. MEATS AND DRINKS. We believe in total abstinence from all alcoholic drinks. We believe that the eating of meats referred to by Moses under the Law and the drinking of Tea, or Coffee is not obligatory to our Christian experience. However, anyone may refrain from these things at his or her own discretion but must not try to impose such personal opinions upon others.

X. REDEMPTION OF THE BODY. We believe we shall receive our Redeemed Bodies at the Second Appearing of our Lord. (Rom. 8:22-23; I Cor. 5:1-5; 15:43-55; I Thes. 4:16-17).

Y. WAR. We believe that war comes from the enemy of mankind and that it is condemned by the Word of God: That if smitten on one cheek, we as Christians should "turn the other also" (Matt. 5:39; Luke 6:29). Thou shalt not kill (Matt. 5:21). We therefore, desire to be loyal to our Government and above all loyal to God, and since the Scriptures forbids us to kill we recommend that our members accept the provision offered them by the Laws of our Government which gives them the privilege to register as a conscientious objector to War in Any Form, or to register as an objector to Combat Duty where the bearing of Arms is required.

Z. FINALLY. We believe in the seven principles of the doctrine of Christ (Heb. 6:1-2), with all their connections throughout the New Testament as revealed by the Holy Spirit from time to time.

* * *

WHAT WE BELIEVE (BETHEL MINISTERIAL ASSOCIATION)

PREAMBLE

The purpose of the Bethel Temple is to proclaim the gospel of the Lord Jesus Christ as it was taught by the Apostles in the beginning of the Church Age, which we believe to be as follows:

DIVINE INSPIRATION OF THE SCRIPTURE

"For the prophecy came not in old time by the will of man; but holy men of God spake as they were moved by the Holy Ghost" (2 Peter 1:21).

The Bible, being a revelation of the supernatural God, is a supernatural Book—a Book of miracles—not understood by the natural mind (1 Cor. 2:14).

The Bible gives the only plausible explanation of life. The wisest of men, so called, who do not believe the Bible must admit: "Concerning the origin of life, we know little." The Bible reveals God as the source of all life.

The Divine Authorship of the Bible is further proved by the scientific and biological fact that God made all creation with seed in itself able to reproduce after its kind, according to the record in Genesis 1:11, 21, 24, 28. And the Genesis account that man was made from dust (chemical substances in the ground) is corroborated by the fact that man must subsist from that which the ground produces (same chemical substances).

The prophecies of the Bible prove conclusively that the Bible is Divinely inspired. No man could predict 4,000 years ahead concerning future events and describe those events in minute detail, as does the Bible.

Jesus Christ sanctioned all the Writings of the prophets (Matt. 24:37-39; Luke 17:28-32). He sanctioned all the Old Testament Scriptures (Luke 24:27). He sanctioned the Genesis account of the creation of man (Matt. 19:14).

Jesus Christ proved that He was Divine by His resurrection from the dead.

Since Jesus Christ was Divine, and He sanctioned the Scriptures, we must conclude that the Bible is the Divinely inspired Word of God, and the true revelation of God to man.

CHURCH MEMBERSHIP

Bethel's Articles of Incorporation, dated February 17, 1944, state: "This Church will welcome into its membership all who desire to unite in a common effort toward the achievement of its aims and purposes."

We believe God's people are ONE because of Calvary. It is our love and loyalty to Christ which bind us together. Briefly, our position is this:

In things non-essential . . . LIBERTY

In things essential . . . UNITY

In all things . . . CHARITY

CHURCH GOVERNMENT

The Church is governed by the pastor, a Church Board consisting of five members or more, a Board of Trustees consisting of three members or more, a secretary and treasurer, which may be one person or two persons, and any other officers which may be considered necessary. Any business of major importance shall be brought before the entire Church for decision.

The officers of the Church shall be appointed by the pastor, approved by the Church and shall serve until their successors are appointed (a copy of all appointed and elected officers of the church may be obtained by telephoning the church office).

CIVIL GOVERNMENT

Bethel Temple hereby declares its loyalty to our government and to its Chief Executive, and hereby states its fixed purpose to assist our government in every way morally possible, consistent with our faith (Romans 13:1-7).

Bethel Temple believes that nations can and should whenever possible, settle their differences without going to war; however, in the event of war, if a member engages in combatant service, it will not affect his status with the Church. In case a member is called into military service who has conscientious objections to combatant service, Bethel Temple and the Ministers of the Bethel Baptist Assembly will support him in his constitutional rights.

MAN

Man was created in the image and likeness of God (Gen. 1:26). Adam's sin was passed on to the human family (Rom. 5:12-14). For all have sinned and come short of the glory of God (Rom. 3:23). In the last man Adam (1 Cor. 15:45), all are made alive (Rom. 5:15-21).

SALVATION

Salvation is obtained through obedience to the gospel which is the death, burial and resurrection of Jesus Christ (1 Cor. 15:1-4). God's plan of obedience is faith, repentance and baptism in order to receive the Holy Ghost, which is the Spirit of Christ (Acts 2:38, Acts 16:31-33, Acts 10:44-48).

WATER BAPTISM

Baptism is burial with Christ by immersion in water in the Name of the Lord Jesus Christ, and should be administered immediately after one has thoroughly repented of sins and turned from the world (Acts 2:38, Rom. 6:4,5, Acts 16:33).

SPIRIT BAPTISM

Baptism in the Spirit is the new birth which places one in the Body of Christ, which is the Church (1 Cor. 12:13, Gal. 3:27, Col. 1:4). The evidence of the new birth or baptism in the Spirit is the love of God (1 John 3:14). On the day of Pentecost there was a two-fold operation of the Spirit. They were first baptized into the Spirit which formed the Church, the Body of Christ, and they were also immediately filled with the Spirit (Acts 1:5, Acts 2:4).

THE FILLING OF THE SPIRIT

We teach that every Christian who has received the Spirit through the new birth, or baptism into Christ, should yield to the Spirit to be possessed or filled with the Spirit for the operation of all the gifts of the Spirit according to 1 Cor. 12:7-11, Acts 2:4, Acts 10:46, Acts 19:6. To receive the Spirit, and be possessed by or filled with the Spirit are two different experiences in a believer's life. This is the same Spirit but greater possession.

To illustrate: Every sinner has the spirit of the devil but not every sinner is demon possessed, so every Christian has the Spirit of Christ but not every Christian is filled with the Spirit.

THE GODHEAD

There is one God in three manifestations, Father, Son and Holy Spirit. God is an invisible Spirit (John 4:24, Col. 1:15). Jesus Christ is God, the invisible Spirit, manifest in the flesh (1 Tim. 3:16, John 1:14).

THE VIRGIN BIRTH

Jesus was born of a virgin (Matt. 1:23).

TITHING

Tithing is God's financial plan to provide for His work, and has been His only plan since the days of Abraham. It was practiced under Moses' law and Jesus endorsed it (Matt. 23:23). If a Christian gives less than one-tenth of his increase to the work of God, he is robbing God (Mal. 3:10.

THE CHRISTIAN'S CONDUCT

Christians should dress in modest apparel and not follow the extreme, immodest fashions of the world (1 Tim. 2:9, 10). His speech should be as becometh a Christian (Col. 4:6).

TOBACCO AND ALCOHOLIC BEVERAGES

We urge our members to refrain from the use of tobacco and alcoholic beverages in any form (Gal. 5:24, 1 Pet. 2:11, 2 Cor. 7:1).

THE SECOND COMING OF CHRIST

The second coming of Christ is in two stages, the rapture and revelation. In the rapture Jesus will come for His saints before the great tribulation period starts (1 Thess. 4:13-18). In the revelation Jesus will come with His saints (Rev. 19:11-16) to smite the Anti-Christ and set up the millennial kingdom.

ETERNAL SECURITY

The eternal security of the believer depends on his obedience to God's Word (2 John 1:9, 1 John 3:24). God is able to keep us from falling and will keep us if we obey Him (2 Pet. 1:10). When a Christian sins or fails God he should repent, but if he fails to repent and persists in willful disobedience, the ultimate result will be spiritual death and eventually the lake of fire (1 John 5:16, Heb. 10:26, 27, 39).

RESTORATION OF ALL THINGS

The Scriptures teach the restoration of all things that were spoken of by the mouth of the prophets, but the prophets did not include the devil and his angels, nor sinners who reject the Lord Jesus Christ (Acts 3:21).

MARRIAGE AND DIVORCE

It is impossible to deal with the complicated marriage and divorce problems here. Suffice it to say that we advise Christians to marry Christians. To those who are divorced and remarried, and afterwards become saved, it is advisable to live with the companion to whom they are legally married at the time of their conversion.

THE LORD'S SUPPER

The Lord Jesus instituted the Lord's Supper (Matt. 26:26-29). This is an ordinance of the Church and as such is to be taken literally. Self-examination should precede partaking of the Lord's Supper. The Lord's Supper is a memorial service to shew the Lord's death till He comes (1 Cor. 11:26). The order and meaning of the Lord's table is set forth in 1 Cor. 11:23-34.

HEAVEN AND HELL

There is a literal hell for those who reject the Lord Jesus Christ as their personal Saviour (Matt. 10:28, Rev. 20:15). There is a literal heaven for those who accept the Lord Jesus Christ as their personal Saviour and live a life of obedience unto Him (John 14:1, 2, Rev. 7:9).

DIVINE HEALING

God heals in many ways; through medical science, the processes of nature and in answer to prayer. It is the privilege of the Christian today to go to the Lord for the healing of his body (James 5:14, 15).

During the earthly ministry of Jesus, He went about healing all manner of sickness and all manner of disease among the people (Matt. 4:23).

THE CHURCH

The Church had its beginning on the day of Pentecost and consists of all who are truly born of the Spirit, wherever they may be found (Acts 1:5, Gal. 3:27, 1 Cor. 12:13, Eph. 1:22, 23).

DENOMINATIONAL AFFILIATION

Though all the Bethel Churches are sovereign within themselves and emphasize a NON-SECTARIAN POSITION, they are affiliated with the Bethel Baptist Assembly and their ministers are licensed or ordained by the Bethel Baptist Assembly.

The Bethel Temple is incorporated as a non-profit corporation under the laws of the state of Indiana as Bethel Temple of Evansville, Incorporated.

Notes: *The Bethel Ministerial Association holds to several positions not found in the statements of other apostolic pentecostals. While not pacifist, it will support individual conscientious objectors. It teaches that those who have divorced and remarried should stay with their legal marriage partner at the time of their becoming Christians. There is no statement on foot washing.*

ARTICLES OF FAITH (NEW BETHEL CHURCH OF GOD IN CHRIST)

THE ONE TRUE GOD

We believe in the one everliving, eternal God: infinite in power, Holy in nature, attributes and purpose; and possessing absolute, indivisible deity. This one true God has revealed Himself as Father, through His Son, in redemption; and as the Holy Spirit, by emanation. (1 Cor. 8:6; Eph. 4:6; 2 Cor. 5:19; Joel 2:28).

The Scripture does more than attempt to prove the existence of God; it asserts, assumes and declares that the knowledge of God is universal (Romans 1:19, 21, 28, 32; 2:15). God is invisible, incorporeal, without parts, without body, and therefore free from all limitations. He is Spirit (John 4:24), and ". . . a spirit hath not flesh and bones . . . " (Luke 24:39).

". . . The first of all the commandments is, hear, O Israel; the Lord our God is one Lord" (Mark 12:39; Deut. 6:4). "One God and Father of all, who is above all, and through all, and in you all" (Eph. 4:6).

This one true God manifested Himself in the Old Testament in divers ways; in the Son while He walked among men; as the Holy Spirit after the ascension.

THE SON OF GOD

The one true God, the Jehovah of the Old Testament, took upon Himself the form of man, and as the Son of man, was born of the virgin Mary. As Paul says, "and without controversy great is the mystery of Godliness: God was manifest in the flesh, justified in the Spirit, seen of angels, preached unto the Gentiles, believed on in the world, received up into glory" (I Timothy 3:16).

"He came unto His own, and His own received Him not (John 1:11). This one true God was manifest in the flesh, that is, in His Son Jesus Christ. ". . . God was in Christ, reconciling the world unto Himself, not imputing their trespasses unto them. . ." (2 Cor. 5:19).

We believe that, ". . . in Him (Jesus) dwelleth all the fulness of the Godhead bodily" (Col. 2:9). "For it pleased the Father that in Him should all fulness dwell" (Col. 1:19). Therefore, Jesus in His humanity was and is man; in his diety was and is God. His flesh was the lamb, or the sacrifice of God. He is the only mediator between God and man. "For there is one God, and one mediator between God and men, the man Christ Jesus" (1 Timothy 2:5).

Jesus on His Father's side was divine, on His mother's side, human; Thus, He was known as the Son of God and also the Son of man, or the God-man.

"For He hath put all things under His feet. But when He saith all things are put under Him, it is manifest that He is excepted, which did put all things under Him" (1 Cor. 15:27). "And when all things shall be subdued unto Him, then shall the Son also Himself be subject unto Him that put all things under Him, that God may be all in all" (1 Cor. 15:28).

"I am Alpha and Omega, the beginning and the ending, saith the Lord, which is, and which was, and which is to come, the Almighty" (Rev. 1:8).

THE NAME

God used different titles, such as "God Elohim," "God Almighty," "El Shaddai," Jehovah," and especially "Jehovah Lord," the redemptive name in the Old Testament.

". . . unto us a child is born, unto us a son is given; . . . and His name shall be called Wonderful, Counsellor, The Mighty God, The Everlasting Father, The Prince of Peace" (Isaiah 9:6). This prophecy of Isaiah was fulfilled when the Son of God was named, "And she shall bring forth a son, and thou shalt call His name Jesus: for He shall save His people from their sins" (Matt. 1:21).

"Neither is there salvation in any other: for there is none other name under heaven given among men, whereby we must be saved" (Acts 4:12).

CREATION OF MAN AND HIS FALL

In the beginning God created man innocent, pure and holy; but through the sin of disobedience, Adam and Eve, the first of the human race, fell from their holy state, and God banished them from Eden. Hence by one man's disobedience, sin entered into the world. (Gen. 1:27; Rom. 3:23, 5:12).

REPENTANCE AND CONVERSION

Pardon and forgiveness of sins is obtained by genuine repentance, a confessing and forsaking of sins. We are justified by faith in the Lord Jesus Christ (Romans 5:1). John the Baptist preached repentance, Jesus proclaimed it, and the Apostles emphasized it to both Jews and Gentiles. (Acts 2:38; 11:18; 17:30).

The word "repentance" comes from several Greek words which mean, change of views and purpose, change of heart, change of mind, change of life, to transform, etc.

Jesus said, ". . . except ye repent, ye shall all likewise perish" (Luke 13:3).

Luke 24:47 says, "And that repentance and remission of sins should be preached in His name among all nations, beginning at Jerusalem."

WATER BAPTISM

The scripture mode of baptism is immersion, and is only for those who have fully repented, having turned from their sins and a love of the world. It should be administered by a duly authorized minister of the Gospel, in obedience to the word of God, and in the name of our Lord Jesus Christ, according to the Acts of the Apostles 2:38; 8:16; 10:48; 19:5; thus obeying and fulfilling Matthew 28:19.

THE BAPTISM OF THE HOLY SPIRIT

John the Baptist, in Matthew 3:11, said, ". . . He shall baptize you with the Holy Ghost, and with fire."

Jesus, in Acts 1:5, said ". . . ye shall be baptized with the Holy Ghost not many days hence."

Luke tells us in Acts 2:4, ". . . they were all filled with the Holy Ghost, and began to speak with other tongues (languages), as the Spirit gave them utterance."

The terms "baptize with the Holy Ghost and fire," "filled with the Holy Spirit," and the "gift of the Holy Ghost" are synonymous terms used interchangeably in the Bible.

It is scriptural to expect all who receive the gift, filling, or baptism of the Holy Spirit to receive the same physical, initial sign of speaking with other tongues.

The speaking with other tongues, as recorded in Acts 2:4; 10:46, and 19:6, and the gift of tongues, as explained in 1 Corinthians, chapters 12 and 14, are the same in essence but different in use and purpose.

The Lord, through the Prophet Joel, said, ". . . I will pour out my Spirit upon all flesh; . . . (Joel 2:28).

Peter, in explaining this phenomenal experience, said, ". . . having received of the Father the promise of the Holy Ghost, He (Jesus) hath shed forth this which ye now see and hear." (Acts 2:33).

Further, ". . . the promise is unto you, and to your children, and to all that are afar off, even as many as the Lord our God shall call." (Acts 2:39).

FUNDAMENTAL DOCTRINE

The basic and fundamental doctrine of this organization shall be the Bible standard of full salvation, which is repentance, baptism in water by immersion in the name of the Lord Jesus Christ, and the baptism of the Holy Ghost with the initial sign of speaking with other tongues as the Spirit gives utterance.

We shall endeavor to keep the unity of the Spirit until we all come into the unity of the faith, at the same time admonishing all brethren that they shall not contend for their different views to the disunity of the body.

DIVINE HEALING

The first covenant that the Lord (Jehovah) made with the children of Israel after they were brought out of Egypt was a covenant of healing. The Lord said, ". . . if thou wilt diligently hearken to the voice of the Lord (Jehovah-Rapha, the Lord that healeth) thy God, and wilt do that which is right in His sight, and wilt give ear to His commandments, and keep all His statutes, I will put none of these diseases upon thee, which I have brought upon the Egyptians; for I am the Lord that healeth thee." (Exodus 15:26).

Some translations read: "For I am Jehovah, thy physician." He being our physician or doctor, we have the most capable in the whole world. Our Lord Jesus went about Galilee, preaching the Gospel of the Kingdom, and healing all manner of sickness and disease among the people. Matthew 4:23, 24).

"Jesus Christ the same yesterday, and today, and forever." (Hebrews 13:8).

The vicarious suffering of the Lord Jesus Christ paid for the healing of our bodies, the same as for the salvation of our souls, for ". . . with His stripes we are healed" (Isaiah 35:5). Matthew 8:17 reads, ". . . Himself took infirmities, and bare our sickness." (See also 1 Peter 2:24).

We see from this that divine healing for the body is in the atonement. That being true, then it is for all who believe. Jesus said of believers, ". . . they shall lay hands on the sick, and they shall recover." Later, James wrote in his Epistle to all the churches: "Is any sick among you? Let him call for the elders of the church; and let them pray over him, anointing him with oil in the name of the Lord:

and the prayer of faith shall save the sick, and the Lord shall raise him up; and if he have committed sins, they shall be forgiven him. Confess your faults one to another, and pray one for another, that ye may be healed. The effectual fervent prayer of a righteous man availeth much." (James 5:14-16).

All of these promises are for the church today.

SACRAMENT OR COMMUNION

On the night of our Lord's betrayal, He ate the Passover supper with His Apostles, after which He instituted the sacrament. "And He took bread, and gave thanks, and brake it, and gave unto them, saying, this is my body which is given for you: This do in remembrance of me. Likewise also the cup after supper, saying, this cup is the New Testament in my blood, which is shed for you." (Luke 22:19-20).

Paul instructed the church how to observe it (1 Cor. 11:23-34).

Thus was instituted the use of literal bread and the fruit of the vine, which are partaken of, literally, as emblems of His broken body and shed blood. There is also a spiritual significance and blessing in partaking of the sacrament.

FEET-WASHING

When the Passover supper was ended, we read in John 13:4; "He riseth from supper, and laid aside His garments; and took a towel, and girded Himself. After that He poureth water into a basin, and began to wash the disciples' feet, and to wipe them with the towel wherewith He was girded."

Jesus said, "If I then, your Lord and Master, have washed your feet; ye also ought to wash one another's feet. For I have given you an example, that ye should do as I have done to you" (John 13:14-15).

This first example was given by our Lord, and it is a divine institution. It is well to follow His example and wash one another's feet; thus manifesting the spirit of humility.

HOLINESS

Godly living should characterize the life of every child of the Lord, and we should live according to the pattern and example given in the Word of God. "For the grace of God that bringeth salvation hath appeared to all men, teaching us that, denying ungodliness and worldly lusts, we should live soberly, righteously, and Godly, in this present world" (Titus 2:11, 12). "For even hereunto were ye called: because Christ also suffered for us, leaving us an example, that ye should follow His steps: who did no sin, neither was guile found in His mouth: who, when He was reviled, reviled not again; when He suffered, He threatened not; but committed Himself to Him that judgeth righteously" (1 Peter 2:21-23).

"Follow peace with all men, and holiness, without which no man shall see the Lord" (Heb. 12:14).

"But as He which hath called you is holy, so be ye holy in all manner of conversation; because it is written, be ye holy; for I am holy. And if ye call on the Father, who

without respect of persons judgeth according to every man's work, pass the time of your sojourning here in fear: forasmuch as ye know that ye were not redeemed with corruptible things, as silver and gold, from your vain conversation received by tradition from your fathers; but with the precious blood of Christ, as of a lamb without blemish and without spot" (1 Peter 1:15-19).

THE GRACE OF GOD

"For the grace of God that bringeth salvation hath appeared to all men, teaching us that, denying ungodliness and worldly lusts, we should live soberly, righteously, and Godly, in this present world" (Titus 2:11, 12).

"For the law was given by Moses, but grace and truth came by Jesus Christ" (John 1:17).

A Christian, to keep saved, must walk with God and keep himself in the love of God (Jude 21) and in the grace of God. The word "grace" means "favor." When a person transgresses and sins against God, he loses his favor. If he continues to commit sin and does not repent, he will eventually be lost and cast into the lake of fire. (Read John 15:2, 6; 2 Peter 2:20-22). Jude speaks of the backsliders of his day, and their reward. (Also, read Hebrews 6:4-6).

"For by grace are ye saved through faith; and that not of yourselves; it is the gift of God" (Eph. 2:8).

RESTITUTION OF ALL THINGS

We understand the scripture to teach the restitution of all things, which God hath spoken by the mouth of all His holy prophets since the world began. (Acts 3:21). But we cannot find where the devil, his angels, and all sinners are included. (See Rev. 20:10).

CONSCIENTIOUS SCRUPLES

We recognize the institution of human government as being of divine ordination, and, in so doing, affirm unswerving loyalty to our government; however, we take a definite position regarding the bearing of arms or the taking of human life.

As followers of the Lord Jesus Christ, the Prince of Peace, we believe in implicit obedience to His commandments and precepts, which instruct us as follows: ". . . that ye resist not evil. . ." (Matt. 5:39): "Follow peace with all men. . ." (Heb. 12:14). (See also Matt. 26:52; Rom. 12:19; James 5:6; Revelation 13:10). These we believe and interpret to mean Christians shall not shed blood nor take human life.

Therefore, we propose to fulfill all obligations of loyal citizens, but are constrained to declare against participating in combat service in war, armed insurrection, property destruction, aiding or abetting in or the actual destruction of human life.

Furthermore, we cannot conscientiously affiliate with any union, boycott, or organization which will force or bind any of its members to belong to any organization, perform any duties contrary to our conscience or receive any mark, without our right to affirm or reject same. (1930).

However, we regret the false impression created by some groups or so-called "conscientious objectors" that to obey the Bible is to have a contempt for law or magistrates, to be disloyal to our government and in sympathy with our enemies, or to be willing to sacrifice for the preservation of our commonwealth. This attitude would be as contemptible to us as to any patriot. The Word of God commands us to do violence to no man. It also commands us that first of all we are to pray for rulers of our country. We, therefore, exhort our members to freely and willingly respond to the call of our Government except in the matter of bearing arms. When we say service, we mean service—no matter how hard or dangerous. The true church has no more place for cowards than has the nations. First of all, however, let us earnestly pray that we will with honor be kept out of war.

We believe that we can be consistent in serving our Government in certain noncombatant capacities, but not in the bearing of arms. (1940).

SECRET SOCIETIES, ETC.

According to the Word of God, we firmly believe and hold that the people of God should have no connection whatever with secret societies, or any other organization or body wherein there is a fellowship with unbelievers, bound by an oath. (James 5:3-7; 2 Cor. 6:14-18).

TRANSLATION OF SAINTS

We believe that the time is drawing near when our Lord shall appear; then the death in Christ shall arise, and we who are alive and remain shall be caught up with them to meet our Lord in the air. (1 Thess. 4:13-17; 1 Cor. 15:51-54; Phil. 3:20-21).

MARRIAGE AND DIVORCE

"Whosoever shall put away his wife, except it be for fornication, and shall marry another, committeth adultery: (Matt. 19:9), Matt. 5:32). When this sin has been committed, the innocent party may be free to remarry only in the Lord. Our desire being to raise a higher standard for the ministry. We recommend that ministers do not marry again.

Judgment begins at the House of God. See instructions for the ministry under Article VI, Section 6.

TITHING

We believe tithing is God's financial plan to provide for His work, and has been since the days of Abraham. Tithing came with faith under Abraham; Moses' law enjoined it, and Israel practiced it when she was right with God; Jesus endorsed it (Matt. 23:23); and Paul said to lay by in store as God has prospered you. Do not rob God of His portion, viz., tithes and offerings. (Read Mal. 3.)

SECOND COMING OF JESUS

That Jesus is coming again the second time in person, just as He went away, is clearly set forth by the Lord Jesus Himself, and was preached and taught in the early Christian church by the apostles; hence, the children of God today are earnestly, hopefully, looking forward to the glorious event. (Matt. 24; Acts 1:11, 3:19-21; 1 Cor. 11:26; Phil. 3:20-21; 1 Thess. 4:14-17; Titus 2:13, 14.)

THE MILLENNIUM

Moreover, we believe that the distress upon the earth is the "beginning of sorrows" and will become more intense until there "shall be a time of trouble such as there never was since there was a nation even to that same time" (Matt.

24:3-8; Dan. 12:1), and that period of "tribulation" will be followed by the dawn of a better day on earth and that for a thousand years there shall be "peace on earth and good will toward men." (Rev. 20:1-5; Isa. 65:17-25; Matt. 5:5; Dan. 7:27; Mic. 4:1, 2; Heb. 2:14; Rom. 11:25-27.)

FINAL JUDGMENT

When the thousand years are finished, there shall be a resurrection of all the dead, who will be summoned before the great white throne for their final judgment, and all whose names are not found written in the Book of Life shall be cast into the lake of fire, burning with brimstone, which God hath prepared for the Devil and his angels, Satan himself being cast in first. (Matt. 25:41; Rev. 20:7-15; 21:8).

PUBLIC SCHOOL ACTIVITIES

We disapprove of school students attending shows, dancing classes, theatres, engaging in school activities against their religious scruples and wearing gymnasium clothes which immodestly expose the body.

Notes: *Although the New Bethel Church of God in Christ was formed by former members of the Church of God in Christ, its doctrinal statement follows the text and format of the United Pentecostal Church's articles.*

* * *

CREED (PENTECOSTAL ASSEMBLIES OF THE WORLD)

PREAMBLE

In order to foster better cooperation among all churches and saints of the P. A. of W. Inc., and to advance the kingdom of God among ministers and saints of the said churches, we do set forth the following legislation as our Constitution, Fundamental Rules, and Articles of Religion, Organization and Government.

ARTICLE I

Apostolic Doctrine and Fellowship According to the Bible. Our Creed, Discipline, Rules of Order, and Doctrine is the Word of God as taught and revealed by the Holy Ghost. (John 14:26; I Corinthians 2:9-13.)

"All scripture is given by inspiration of God, and is profitable for doctrine, for reproof, for correction, for instruction in righteousness, that the man of God may be perfect, thoroughly furnished unto all good works." (II Timothy 3:16, 17).

ARTICLE II. THE GODHEAD

We fully believe in the mystery of the Godhead. We believe that God has been pleased to manifest Himself as a Father, the Source of all life, as a Son, the Channel and Redeemer of all life, and as the Holy Ghost, the Revealer and Energizer of all life. The Father is the invisible God who is made visible in Jesus, and the Holy Ghost is the invisible counterpart of God. The Father is God in creation, the Son is God in redemption, and the Holy Ghost is God in inspiration. When one manifestation of the Godhead is patent, that is, can be seen, the other two are latent, that is, they can only be seen through the one that is patent. (John 14:6-12). Jesus was both human and

CREED (PENTECOSTAL ASSEMBLIES OF THE
WORLD) (continued)

divine; Mary's son and Mary's God; Creator and Creature; God manifest in the flesh and Eternal Father made visible apart from whom there is no God. We believe that at the final consummation of all things, the one visible God will be our Lord Jesus Christ.

ARTICLE III. NAME OF GOD

We believe that God has changed His name to suit the dispensational needs of His people. His present dispensational name is the Lord Jesus Christ.

ARTICLE IV. MEMBERSHIP—HOW OBTAINED

As members of the Body of Christ, which is the true Church, (Ephesians 1:22, 23,) the Word of God declares but one way of entrance therein and that is, "By one Spirit are we all baptized into one body." This is a baptism of "water and spirit." (I Corinthians 12:12-27; Gal. 3:26-28; Rom. 6:3, 4; John 3:5; Acts 2:38.)

ARTICLE V. REPENTANCE AND REMISSION OF SINS

The only condition on which God will accept a sinner is repentance from the heart for the sins which he has committed—a broken and contrite heart He will not despise. (Psalm 51:17.) John preached repentance, Jesus proclaimed it, and before His Ascension, commanded that repentance and remission of sins should be preached in His Name, beginning at Jerusalem. (Luke 24:47.) Peter fulfilled this command on the Day of Pentecost. (Acts 2:38.)

ARTICLE VI. BAPTISM

We believe that baptism by immersion should be administered "in the name of the Lord Jesus Christ for the remission of sins" only to persons who have reached the age of understanding, and under no condition, do we approve of the baptism of infants. We believe that the initial sign of the Holy Ghost is speaking in tongues. (Acts 2:4; 10:46; 19:6.)

As this rite of baptism is only effectual when one repents of one's sins and believes the Gospel with his heart, prior to its administration, the officiating minister should be careful to examine each candidate as to his belief in the Gospel of Grace which concerns the Person, death, burial, and resurrection of the Lord Jesus Christ for the remission of sins" to persons who have reached the age of understanding and not to infants, under any condition.

FORM OF BAPTISM

The Candidate having entered the water with the Baptizer, shall surrender (himself or herself) to the Baptizer who shall cross the hands of the Candidate. Then a short prayer shall be offered and the following said:

My dearly beloved _____ upon the confession of your faith in the Death, Burial and Resurrection of the Lord Jesus Christ and in the confidence which we have in the Blessed Word of God, I now baptize thee in the name of the Lord Jesus Christ, for the Remission of Sins and ye shall receive the gift of the Holy Ghost. Amen.

ARTICLE VII. RECORD OF MEMBERSHIP

The names of the members are kept on record in heaven. (Luke 10:20.) For it is written, "The Lord shall count, when He writeth up the people, that this man was born there." (Psalms 87:6.) All in this dispensation must be born of "water and spirit," if they desire their names to be written in heaven. (See Hebrews 12:22-23.)

Nevertheless, each church should keep a record of its membership in order to know for whom it is responsible.

ARTICLE VIII. SECOND BIRTH

We believe the second birth to be limited to the human family only, and to be born again is to be born of the water and of the spirit. (John 3:5.)

ARTICLE IX. HOW NAMES ARE BLOTTED OUT

We have nothing whatever to do with the blotting out of names, for thus saith the Lord. "Whosoever hath sinned against me, him will I blot out of my book." (Exodus 32:33.) "He that overcometh—I will not blot out his name out of the book of life." (Rev. 3:5.)

ARTICLE X. GOD'S STANDARD OF SALVATION

We earnestly contend for God's standard of salvation. In the Word of God, we can find nothing short of a holy spirit-filled life with signs following as on the Day of Pentecost. (Mark 16:17-18; Acts 2:4; 8:14-17; 9:17-18; 10:44-48; 19:1-16; Rom. 12:1-21; Heb. 12:14; Matt. 5:48; I Peter 1:15-16.)

ARTICLE XI. THE WHOLLY SANCTIFIED LIFE

We believe that in order to escape the judgment of God and to have the hope of enjoying the glory of life eternal, one must be thoroughly saved from his sins, wholly sanctified unto God, and filled with the Holy Ghost. A wholly sanctified life is the only true standard of a Christian life. (Heb. 12:14; I Peter 1:15-17.)

ARTICLE XII. THE LORD'S SUPPER

Melchisedec, "Priest of the Most High God," gave the first communion consisting of bread and wine to our father Abraham. (Gen. 14:18.) Christ being our "High Priest after the order of Melchisedec," (Heb. 6:20) evidently administered the same. Water and grape juice are modern substitutes that have been introduced by the formal churches of today in which there are many who have never been regenerated and born of the Spirit. (Matt. 26:26-29; I Cor. 11:23-34.)

ARTICLE XIII. FEET WASHING

This ordinance is as much a divine command as any other New Testament ordinance. Jesus gave us an example in order that we should do even as He did. He said that we ought to wash one another's feet. There is scriptural evidence in I Timothy 5:10 that this was practised by the Church in the day of the Apostle Paul. "If ye know these things, happy are ye if ye do them." (See John 13:14-17.)

ARTICLE XIV. HEALING BY FAITH

The Lord is our Healer. (Ex. 15:26; Psalms 103:2-3.) Since the Lord made our bodies, should it be thought incredible that He should be able to heal them? "With his stripes we are healed." (Isa. 53:4-5; Matt. 8:14-17; John 14:12; Mark 16-17-18; James 5:14.)

ARTICLE XV. THE COMING OF JESUS

That Jesus is coming again in person is a doctrine clearly set forth in apostolic times. Jesus taught it, the Apostles preached it, and the saints expected it. (I Thess. 4:14-17. Titus 2:13-14.)

ARTICLE XVI. TRANSLATION OF THE SAINTS

We believe that the time draweth near for the coming of the Lord to make a change in the present order of things. At that time, all the righteous dead shall arise from their graves, and they that are living righteous before God shall be translated or "caught up to meet the Lord in the air." (Matt. 24:36-42; Luke 17:20-37; I Cor. 15:51-54; Phillippians 3:20-21; I Thess. 5:1-10.)

ARTICLE XVII. THE MILLENIUM

Moreover, we believe that the distress upon the earth is the beginning of sorrows and will become more intense until "there shall be a time of trouble such as never was since there was a nation even to that same time." (Matt. 24:3-12; Dan. 12:1.) That period of tribulation will be followed by the dawn of a better day on earth, and for one thousand years thereafter, there shall be peace on earth and good will toward men. (Matt. 5:5; Isa. 65:17-25; Dan. 7:27; Micah 4:1-2; Heb. 2:14; Rom. 11:25-27.)

ARTICLE XVIII. FINAL JUDGMENT

When the thousand years shall have passed, there shall be a resurrection of the dead who shall be summoned before the Great White Throne for their final judgment. All those whose names are not found written in the Book of Life shall be cast into the Lake of Fire, burning with brimstone, which God has prepared for the Devil and his angels. (Rev. 20:10-15.)

ARTICLE XIX. RELATIONSHIP TO CIVIL GOVERNMENT

All civil rulers are ordained of God for peace, safety, and for the welfare of the people. (Rom. 13:1-17.) Therefore, it is our duty to be in obedience to all requirements of the law which are not contrary to the Word of God, or do not force us to the violation of the Sixth Commandment by bearing arms and taking life. It is our duty to honor our rulers, to show respect to them in all requirements of the civil law, and to pay tribute or such taxation as may be required without murmuring. (Matt. 17:24-27; 22:17-21.)

ARTICLE XX. MALTREATMENT

In times of persecution or ill-treatment at the hands of an enemy, we should not avenge ourselves, "but rather give place unto wrath: for it is written, Vengeance is mine; I will repay, saith the Lord." (Rom. 12:19; Deut. 32:33.) Neither should we take up any weapon of destruction to slay another, whether in our own defense or in the defense of others, for it is also written, "Do violence to no man." (Luke 3:14; Matt. 26:52; John 18:10-11, 36.) We should rather suffer wrong than do wrong.

ARTICLE XXI. SECRET SOCIETIES

According to the Word of God, we firmly believe and hold that the people of God should have no connection whatsoever with Secret Societies or any other organization or body wherein there is a fellowship of unbelievers bound by an oath (James 4:4). Members of the Pentecostal Assemblies of the World and its auxiliaries shall not work as pickets or by any other measure bar the way of others to or from their work. This does not abridge their rights to pay dues to the union and work for their families.

Notes: *One of the oldest of pentecostal churches, the Pentecostal Assemblies of the World was also one of the first to adopt the apostolic position. The church practices foot washing.*

* * *

APOSTOLIC DOCTRINE AND FELLOWSHIP ACCORDING TO THE BIBLE [UNITED CHURCH OF JESUS CHRIST (APOSTOLIC)]

The United Church of Jesus Christ (Apostolic) accepts as its Creed, Discipline, Rules of Order and Doctrine the Word of God as taught and revealed by the Holy Ghost. John 14:26; I. Cor. 2:9-13.

"All scriptures are given by the inspiration of God, and is profitable for doctrine, for reproof, for correction, for instruction in righteousness; that the man of God may be perfect, thoroughly furnished unto all good works." II Timothy 3:16-17.

We stand for all Scripture when rightly divided.

THE UNITY OF THE DIVINE BEING

"God is Spirit, and those who worship Him must worship Him in Spirit and truth." John 4:24 RSV. There is but one God, in essence and in person, from whom and in whom there is a divine threefold manifestation and relationship made known as the Father, Son and Holy Ghost. As Father, God is Creator, Source, Origin, and progenitor of all that is, things and souls. He is the self-existent, omniscient, omnipresent, and omnipotent one. As Son, God becomes the perfect Man that He intends all men to be like. Thus, as Son He redeems man from sin, coming into the world and assuming personality through the miracle and mystery of the virgin birth. "In His own body He bore our sins" and wrought redemption through death for all mankind. "For all have sinned and fallen short of the glory of God." As Holy Ghost, God is regenerator and perfector of those who believe, the organizer and baptizer and sustainer of the church, the divine executor of the world. God as Father is Creator and first cause of all existence; as Son He is the Redeemer in time, and as the Holy Spirit He is Regenerator—The Lord Jesus Christ our Saviour, and "this is the true God and eternal life." "And we know that the Son of God has come and has given us understanding, to know Him who is true; and we are in Him who is true, in His son Jesus Christ. This is the true God and eternal life." I John 5:20. Thus we believe that Jesus was both human and divine; God manifest in the flesh, the Eternal Father made visible, apart from whom there is no God.

MEMBERSHIP—HOW OBTAINED

As members of the Body of Christ, which is the true church (Eph. 1:22-23), the Word of God declares that there is one way of entrance therein—"By one spirit are we

APOSTOLIC DOCTRINE AND FELLOWSHIP ACCORDING TO THE BIBLE [UNITED CHURCH OF JESUS CHRIST (APOSTOLIC)] (continued)

all baptized into one body." Believers are added to the church and believers accept His Spirit, His Name and His Nature. Thus they are born of "water and the spirit." I Cor. 12:12-27; Gal. 3:26-28; Romans 6:3-8; John 3:5; Acts 2:38.

GOD'S STANDARD OF SALVATION

We believe in and earnestly contend for God's Standard of Salvation. The Word of God reveals nothing short of a Holy Spirit filled life with signs following as on the day of Pentecost. (Mark 16:16-17; Acts 2:4; 8:14-17; 9:17-18; 10:44-48; 19:1-6; Rom. 12:1-2; Heb. 12:14; Matt. 5:48; I Peter 1:15).

Those admitted to membership must subscribe to God's standard of salvation in full accord with the teaching of the same as set forth in the Bible.

(1) All members shall take as their rule of conduct the Word of God and shall conform outwardly and inwardly in their daily walk and conversation to its teachings.—Gal. 6:16.

(2) God's word commands that we not be unequally yoked together with unbelievers and that we should not have communion or fellowship with the unfruitful works of darkness, such as oath-bound social clubs, etc. (II Cor. 6:14; Eph. 5:11); that we should not conform to this world or the spirit of the age (Rom. 12:2); that we come out from among them, be separate, and turn away from those who have a form of godliness but deny the power thereof. (II Cor. 6:16; II Tim. 3:5); that we should cleanse ourselves from all filthiness of the flesh and Spirit, perfecting holiness in the fear of God (II Cor.7:1), thus we should refrain from the use, growth, or sale of tobacco in any form, and the use of "dope," or intoxicants. We should not use filthy speech, indulge in foolish talking or jesting, and so abstain from all appearance of evil (I Thes. 5:22). As members of the church and of His Body we should not become involved in activities which do not deepen our own spirituality and promote God's glory.

THE LORD'S SUPPER

The Lord's Supper is a sacramental rite instituted by our Lord. It was an act first instituted by the Lord to show forth an example of commemorating His suffering and death. The twelve disciples were witnesses as narrated in Matthew, Mark, and Luke. When Paul wrote the Corinthians concerning it, he said that it was given him by revelation. The Lord's Supper, therefore, is a sacred rite to be carried out by the Christian Church. It cannot be neglected without suffering serious harm and incurring the gravest responsibility.

We believe the "fruit of the vine" and unleavened bread to be the proper elements for this ordinance. As to time, place, and frequency of observation, we have no direct scriptural teaching. Our custom is to observe it once each month, at an evening service. (I Cor. 11:23-32; Luke 22:18; Matt. 26:26-29).

FEET WASHING

We believe that this ordinance is as much a divine command as any other New Testament ordinance. Jesus gave us an example that we should do even as He had done. He said that we ought to wash one another's feet. Again, "If ye know these things, happy are ye if you do them." (John 13:4-17). There is scriptural evidence that feet washing was practiced by the church in the days of Apostle Paul. (I Tim. 5:10).

MALTREATMENT

In times of persecution or ill-treatment at the hands of an enemy, we should not "avenge ourselves," but rather give place to wrath; for it is written, "Vengeance is mine; I will repay, saith the Lord," (Rom. 12:18; Deut. 32:35). Neither shall we take up any weapons to stay another, whether in our own defense or in the defense of others, for it is written, "Do violence to no man." (Luke 3:14; Matt. 26:52; John 18:36; 15:18, 19). We should rather suffer wrong than do wrong. We subscribe to the principle of non-violence. We believe that the shedding of human blood or the taking of human life to be contrary to the teaching of our Lord and Saviour, and as a body we are averse to war in all of its forms. We herewith offer our services to the President for any service that will not conflict with our conscientious scruples in this respect; with love to all, malice toward none, and due respect to all who differ with us in our interpretation of the scriptures.

CIVIL GOVERNMENT

All civil magistrates are ordained of God for peace, safety, and the well-being of all people (Rom. 13:1-10), therefore, it is our duty to be in obedience to all requirements of the laws that are not contrary to the Word of God. It is our duty to honor them, pay tribute, or such taxation as may be required without murmuring (Matt. 17:24-27; 22:17-21), and show respect to them in all lawful requirements of civil government.

BAPTISM

We baptize in the Name of Jesus Christ because it is Apostolic in origin and practice. (Acts 2:38; 8:12-17; 10:47, 48; 19:1-6). Bible students agree that the apostles founded and gave direction to the Church of God, Jesus Christ Himself being the chief cornerstone. Their teachings and doctrines are the fundamental principles upon which the church is built. In the days of His flesh Jesus taught His disciples the plan of salvation. Following His resurrection they saw Him alive and Jesus opened their understanding. The two men en route to Emmaus had their understanding opened up as Jesus said unto them, "Thus it behooved Christ to suffer and to rise from the dead the third day; and that repentance and remission of sins should be preached IN HIS NAME among all nations, beginning at Jerusalem. And ye are witnesses of these things." (Luke 24:46, 47).

According to Acts 2:38, the apostles obeyed the command of Jesus Christ in Luke 24:46, 47. In their obedience to the command of Jesus the apostles became first in the long line of believers to baptize in the Name of Jesus Christ.

Thus baptizing in the Name of Jesus Christ is not only Apostolic in origin, but in practice as well. No other mode of baptism is to be found in the New Testament. For more than one hundred years after Pentecost believers were baptized only in the Name—Jesus Christ, for the remission of sins.

We are exhorted to believe, to obey and follow the teaching of the apostles. (Heb. 2:1-4; Acts 2:38-43; Col. 2:3-9). To reject the teaching of the Apostles is to reject even Jesus Christ. In St. John 17:20 Jesus prayed that we should believe on Him through (the apostles') words.

We do not believe that there is a contradiction between Matt. 28:19, Luke 24:45-48, Mark 16:15-19, and Acts 2:38. We believe that the NAME of the Father and of the Son and of the Holy Ghost in Matt. 28:19, and MY NAME in Mark 16:15-18, and HIS NAME in Luke 24:47, all mean the same name—Jesus Christ. In Matt. 28:19, we have a commission or a command *given*; in Acts 2:38, we have the command *executed*. In the former, the apostles were told *what* to do; in the latter, they *did* it.

We do not baptize infants. We *bless* them or *dedicate* them to the Lord as early as possible after birth. It is the duty and privilege of parents to dedicate their children to God, thereby claiming God's covenant promises to parents and children.

Baptism is administered to all adult persons who show genuine repentance from the heart for sins. Indeed, genuine repentance is the only grounds upon which God will accept a sinner. "A broken and a contrite heart He will not despise." (Psalms 51:17). The time when children and young people come of years of discretion cannot be precisely fixed. A prudent minister should know when the Spirit is moving and when baptism is in order. In questionable cases involving children who appear to be too young, it is better to give an explanation of baptism in childlike language and go on with the baptism.

It should be kept in mind that not only is baptism for remission of sins, it is also an outward and visible sign of the grace of the Lord Jesus Christ. Through it we are initiated into the fellowship of His Holy Church, and become partakers of His righteousness and heirs of His life. In baptism, we "put on Christ," confessing that we believe in His life, His death, His burial, and His resurrection. As St. Paul writes to the Romans, "Know ye not, that so many of us as were baptized into Jesus Christ were baptized into His death? Therefore we are buried with Him by baptism into death: that like as Christ was raised up from the dead by the glory of the Father, even so we also should walk in newness of life." (Rom. 6:3-4).

(At the time of baptism, the candidate, having been examined as to his readiness for the rite, shall be led into the water, and the minister or the baptizer shall say:)

"Beloved Brother or Sister _____ , according to the confession of your faith in the life, death, burial and resurrection of our Lord Jesus Christ from the dead, and by the authority granted to me as minister of the Church of Jesus Christ, I now baptize thee in the Name—Lord Jesus Christ for the remission of sins, and God grant that you shall receive the gift of the Holy Ghost. Amen."

(Then shall the minister or the baptizer immerse the candidate into the water and immediately lift him up again.)

Notes: *While several of the items of the United Church's doctrine derive from the Pentecostal Assemblies of the World (foot washing, civil government), most of it is original to this body.*

*   *   *

ARTICLES OF FAITH (UNITED PENTECOSTAL CHURCH)

PREAMBLE

We believe the Bible to be inspired of God; the infallible Word of God. "All scripture is given by inspiration of God, and is profitable for doctrine, for reproof, for correction, for instruction in righteousness" (2 Timothy 3:16).

The Bible is the only God-given authority which man possesses; therefore, all doctrine, faith, hope, and all instruction for the church must be based upon, and harmonize with, the Bible. It is to be read and studied by all men everywhere, and can only be clearly understood by those who are anointed by the Holy Spirit (1 John 2:27). ". . . no prophecy of the scripture is of any private interpretation. For the prophecy came not in old time by the will of man: but Holy men of God spake as they were moved by the Holy Ghost" (2 Peter 1:20-21).

THE ONE TRUE GOD

We believe in the one everliving, eternal God: infinite in power, Holy in nature, attributes and purpose; and possessing absolute, indivisible deity. This one true God has revealed Himself as Father, through His Son, in redemption; and as the Holy Spirit, by emanation. (1 Cor. 8:6; Eph. 4:6; 2 Cor. 5:19; Joel 2:28).

The Scripture does more than attempt to prove the existence of God; it asserts, assumes and declares that the knowledge of God is universal. (Romans 1:19, 21, 28, 32; 2:15). God is invisible, incorporeal, without parts, without body, and therefore free from all limitations. He is Spirit (John 4:24), and ". . . a spirit hath not flesh and bones. . ." (Luke 24:39).

". . . The first of all the commandments is, hear, O Israel; the Lord our God is one Lord" (Mark 12:29; Deut. 6:4). "One God and Father of all, who is above all, and through all, and in you all" (Eph. 4:6).

This one true God manifested Himself in the Old Testament in divers ways; in the Son while He walked among men; as the Holy Spirit after the ascension.

THE SON OF GOD

The one true God, the Jehovah of the Old Testament, took upon Himself the form of man, and as the Son of man, was born of the virgin Mary. As Paul says, "and without controversy great is the mystery of Godliness: God was manifest in the flesh, justified in the Spirit, seen of angels, preached unto the Gentiles, believed on in the world, received up into glory" (1 Timothy 3:16).

ARTICLES OF FAITH (UNITED PENTECOSTAL CHURCH) (continued)

"He came unto His own, and His own received Him not" (John 1:11). This one true God was manifest in the flesh, that is, in His Son Jesus Christ. ". . . God was in Christ, reconciling the world unto Himself, not imputing their trespasses unto them . . . " (2 Cor. 5:19).

We believe that, ". . . in Him (Jesus) dwelleth all the fulness of the Godhead bodily" (Col. 2:9). "For it pleased the Father that in Him should all fulness dwell" (Col. 1:19). Therefore, Jesus in His humanity was man; in His deity was and is God. His flesh was the lamb, or the sacrifice of God. He is the only mediator between God and man. "For there is one God, and one mediator between God and men, the man Christ Jesus" (1 Timothy 2:5).

Jesus on His Father's side was divine, on His mother's side, human; Thus, He was known as the Son of God and also the Son of man, or the God-man.

"For He hath put all things under His feet. But when He saith all things are put under Him, it is manifest that He is excepted, which did put all things under Him" (1 Cor. 15:27). "And when all things shall be subdued unto Him, then shall the Son also Himself be subject unto Him that put all things under Him, that God may be all in all" (1 Cor. 15:28).

"I am Alpha and Omega, the beginning and the ending, saith the Lord, which is, and which was, and which is to come, the Almighty" (Rev. 1:8).

THE NAME

God used different titles, such as "God Elohim," "God Almighty," "El Shaddai," "Jehovah," and especially "Jehovah Lord," the redemptive name in the Old Testament.

". . . unto us a child is born, unto us a son is given: . . . and His name shall be called Wonderful Counsellor, The Mighty God, The Everlasting Father, The Prince of Peace" (Isaiah 9:6). This prophecy of Isaiah was fulfilled when the Son of God was named, "And she shall bring forth a son, and thou shalt call His name Jesus: for He shall save His people from their sins" (Matt. 1:21).

"Neither is there salvation in any other: for there is none other name under heaven given among men, whereby we must be saved" (Acts 4:12).

CREATION OF MAN AND HIS FALL

In the beginning God created man innocent, pure and holy; but through the sin of disobedience, Adam and Eve, the first of the human race fell from their holy state, and God banished them from Eden. Hence by one man's disobedience, sin entered into the world. (Gen. 1:27; Rom. 3:23; 5:12).

REPENTANCE AND CONVERSION

Pardon and forgiveness of sins is obtained by genuine repentance, a confessing and forsaking of sins. We are justified by faith in the Lord Jesus Christ (Romans 5:1). John the Baptist preached repentance, Jesus proclaimed it, and the Apostles emphasized it to both Jews and Gentiles. (Acts 2:38; 11:18; 17:30).

The word "repentance" comes from several Greek words which mean, change of views and purpose, change of heart, change of mind, change of life, to transform, etc.

Jesus said, ". . . except ye repent, ye shall all likewise perish" (Luke 13:3).

Luke 24:47 says, "And that repentance and remission of sins should be preached in His name among all nations, beginning at Jerusalem."

WATER BAPTISM

The scriptural mode of baptism is immersion, and is only for those who have fully repented, having turned from their sins and a love of the world. It should be administered by a duly authorized minister of the Gospel, in obedience to the Word of God, and in the name of our Lord Jesus Christ, according to the Acts of the Apostles 2:38; 8:16; 10:48; 19:5; thus obeying and fulfilling Matthew 28:19.

THE BAPTISM OF THE HOLY SPIRIT

John the Baptist, in Matthew 3:11, said, ". . . He shall baptize you with the Holy Ghost, and with fire."

Jesus, in Acts 1:5, said, ". . . ye shall be baptized with the Holy Ghost not many days hence."

Luke tells us in Acts 2:4, ". . . they were all filled with the Holy Ghost, and began to speak with other tongues (languages), as the Spirit gave them utterance."

The terms "baptize with the Holy Ghost and fire," "filled with the Holy Spirit," and the "gift of the Holy Ghost" are synonymous terms used interchangeably in the Bible.

It is scriptural to expect all who receive the gift, filling, or baptism of the Holy Spirit to receive the same physical, initial sign of speaking with other tongues.

The speaking with other tongues, as recorded in Acts 2:4; 10:46, and 19:6, and the gift of tongues, as explained in 1 Corinthians, chapters 12 and 14, are the same in essence, but different in use and purpose.

The Lord, through the Prophet Joel, said, ". . . I will pour out my Spirit upon all flesh; . . . " (Joel 2:28).

Peter, in explaining this phenomenal experience, said, ". . . having received of the Father the promise of the Holy Ghost, He (Jesus) hath shed forth this which ye now see and hear." (Acts 2:33).

Further, ". . . the promise is unto you, and to your children, and to all that are afar off, even as many as the Lord our God shall call." (Acts 2:39).

FUNDAMENTAL DOCTRINE

The basic and fundamental doctrine of this organization shall be the Bible standard of full salvation, which is repentance, baptism in water by immersion in the name of the Lord Jesus Christ, and the baptism of the Holy Ghost with the initial sign of speaking with other tongues as the Spirit gives utterance.

We shall endeavor to keep the unity of the Spirit until we all come into the unity of the faith, at the same time admonishing all brethren that they shall not contend for their different views to the disunity of the body.

DIVINE HEALING

The first covenant that the Lord (Jehovah) made with the children of Israel after they were brought out of Egypt was a covenant of healing. The Lord said, ". . . if thou wilt diligently hearken to the voice of the Lord (Jehovah-Rapha, the Lord that healeth) thy God, and wilt do that which is right in His sight, and wilt give ear to His commandments, and keep all His statutes, I will put none of these diseases upon thee, which I have brought upon the Egyptians; for I am the Lord that healeth thee." (Exodus 15:26).

Some translations read: "For I am Jehovah, thy physician." He being our physician or doctor, we have the most capable in the whole world. Our Lord Jesus Christ went about Galilee, preaching the Gospel of the Kingdom, and healing all manner of sickness and disease among the people. (Matthew 4:23, 24).

"Jesus Christ the same yesterday, and today, and forever." (Hebrews 13:8).

The vicarious suffering of the Lord Jesus Christ paid for the healing of our bodies, the same as for the salvation of our souls, for ". . . with His stripes we are healed" (Isaiah 53:5). Matthew 8:17 reads, ". . . Himself took our infirmities, and bare our sicknesses." (See also 1 Peter 2:24.)

We see from this that divine healing for the body is in the atonement. That being true, then it is for all who believe. Jesus said of believers, ". . . they shall lay hands on the sick, and they shall recover." Later, James wrote in his Epistle to all the churches: "Is any sick among you? Let him call for the elders of the church; and let them pray over him, anointing him with oil in the name of the Lord: and the prayer of faith shall save the sick, and the Lord shall raise him up; and if he have committed sins, they shall be forgiven him. Confess your faults one to another, and pray one for another, that ye may be healed. The effectual fervent prayer of a righteous man availeth much." (James 5:14-16).

All of these promises are for the church today.

SACRAMENT OR COMMUNION

On the night of our Lord's betrayal, He ate the Passover supper with His Apostles, after which He instituted the sacrament. "And He took bread, and gave thanks, and brake it, and gave unto them, saying, this is my body which is given for you: This do in remembrance of me. Likewise also the cup after supper, saying, this cup is the New Testament in my blood, which is shed for you." (Luke 22:19-20).

Paul instructed the church how to observe it (1 Cor. 11:23-34).

Thus was instituted the use of literal bread and the fruit of the vine, which are partaken of, literally, as emblems of His broken body and shed blood. There is also a spiritual significance and blessing in partaking of the sacrament.

FOOT-WASHING

When the Passover supper was ended, we read in John 13:4-5, "He riseth from supper, and laid aside His garments; and took a towel, and girded Himself. After that He poureth water into a basin, and began to wash the disciples' feet, and to wipe them with the towel wherewith He was girded."

Jesus said, "If I then, your Lord and Master, have washed your feet; ye also ought to wash one another's feet. For I have given you an example, that ye should do as I have done to you" (John 13:14-15).

This first example was given by our Lord, and it is a divine institution. It is well to follow His example and wash one another's feet; thus manifesting the spirit of humility.

HOLINESS

Godly living should characterize the life of every child of the Lord, and we should live according to the pattern and example given in the Word of God. "For the grace of God that bringeth salvation hath appeared to all men, teaching us that, denying ungodliness and worldly lusts, we should live soberly, righteously, and Godly, in this present world" (Titus 2:11, 12). "For even hereunto were ye called: because Christ also suffered for us, leaving us an example, that ye should follow His steps: who did no sin, neither was guile found in His mouth: who, when He was reviled, reviled not again; when He suffered, He threatened not; but committed Himself to Him that judgeth righteously" (1 Peter 2:21-23).

"Follow peace with all men, and holiness, without which no man shall see the Lord" (Heb. 12:14).

"But as He which hath called you is holy, so be ye holy in all manner of conversation; because it is written, be ye holy; for I am holy. And if ye call on the Father, who without respect of persons judgeth according to every man's work, pass the time of your sojourning here in fear: forasmuch as ye know that ye were not redeemed with corruptible things, as silver and gold, from your vain conversation received by tradition from your fathers; but with the precious blood of Christ, as of a lamb without blemish and without spot" (1 Peter 1:15-19).

We wholeheartedly disapprove of our people indulging in any activities which are not conducive to good Christianity and Godly living, such as theatres, dances, mixed bathing, women cutting their hair, make-up, any apparel that immodestly exposes the body, all worldly sports and amusements, and unwholesome radio programs and music. Furthermore, because of the display of all of these evils on television, we disapprove of any of our people having television sets in their homes. We admonish all of our people to refrain from any of these practices in the interest of spiritual progress and the soon coming of the Lord for His church.

THE GRACE OF GOD

"For the grace of God that bringeth salvation hath appeared to all men, teaching us that, denying ungodliness and worldly lusts, we should live soberly, righteously, and Godly, in this present world" (Titus 2:11, 12).

"For the law was given by Moses, but grace and truth came by Jesus Christ" (John 1:17).

A Christian, to keep saved, must walk with God and keep himself in the love of God (Jude 21) and in the grace of God. The word "grace" means "favor." When a person

ARTICLES OF FAITH (UNITED PENTECOSTAL
   CHURCH) (continued)

transgresses and sins against God, he loses his favor. If he continues to commit sin and does not repent, he will eventually be lost and cast into the lake of fire. (Read John 15:2, 6; 2 Peter 2:20-22.) Jude speaks of the backsliders of his day, and their reward. (Also, read Hebrews 6:4-6).

"For by grace are ye saved through faith; and that not of yourselves; it is the gift of God" (Eph. 2:8).

RESTITUTION OF ALL THINGS

We understand the scripture to teach the restitution of all things, which God hath spoken by the mouth of all His holy prophets since the world began. (Acts 3:21). But we cannot find where the devil, his angels, and all sinners are included. (See Rev. 20:10).

CONSCIENTIOUS SCRUPLES

We recognize the institution of human government as being of divine ordination, and, in so doing, affirm unswerving loyalty to our Government; however, we take a definite position regarding the bearing of arms or the taking of human life.

As followers of the Lord Jesus Christ, the Prince of Peace, we believe in implicit obedience to His commandments and precepts, which instruct us as follows: ". . . that ye resist not evil . . . " (Matt. 5:39): "Follow peace with all men . . . " (Heb. 12:14). (See also Matt. 26:52; Rom. 12:19; James 5:6; Revelation 13:10). These we believe and interpret to mean Christians shall not shed blood nor take human life.

Therefore, we propose to fulfill all the obligations of loyal citizens, but are constrained to declare against participating in combatant service in war, armed insurrection, property destruction, aiding or abetting in or the actual destruction of human life.

Furthermore, we cannot conscientiously affiliate with any union, boycott, or organization which will force or bind any of its members to belong to any organization, perform any duties contrary to our conscience, or receive any mark, without our right to affirm or reject same. (1930).

However, we regret the false impression created by some groups or so-called "conscientious objectors" that to obey the Bible is to have a contempt for law or magistrates, to be disloyal to our Government and in sympathy with our enemies, or to be unwilling to sacrifice for the preservation of our commonwealth. This attitude would be as contemptible to us as to any patriot. The Word of God commands us to do violence to no man. It also commands us that first of all we are to pray for rulers of our country. We, therefore, exhort our members to freely and willingly respond to the call of our Government except in the matter of bearing arms. When we say service, we mean service— no matter how hard or dangerous. The true church has no more place for cowards than has the nation. First of all, however, let us earnestly pray that we will with honor be kept out of war.

We believe that we can be consistent in serving our Government in certain noncombatant capacities, but not in the bearing of arms. (1940).

SECRET SOCIETIES, ETC.

According to the Word of God, we firmly believe and hold that the people of God should have no connection whatever with secret societies, or any other organization or body wherein there is a fellowship with unbelievers, bound by an oath. (James 5:3-7; 2 Cor. 6:14-18).

TRANSLATION OF SAINTS

We believe that the time is drawing near when our Lord shall appear; then the dead in Christ shall arise, and we who are alive and remain shall be caught up with them to meet our Lord in the air. (1 Thess. 4:13-17; 1 Cor. 15:51-54; Phil. 3:20-21).

MARRIAGE AND DIVORCE

"Whosoever shall put away his wife, except it be for fornication, and shall marry another, committeth adultery:" (Matt. 19:9), (Matt. 5:32). When this sin has been committed, the innocent party may be free to remarry only in the Lord. Our desire being to raise a higher standard for the ministry, we recommend that ministers do not marry again.

Judgment begins at the House of God. See instructions for the ministry under Article VI, Section 6.

TITHING

We believe tithing is God's financial plan to provide for His work, and has been since the days of Abraham. Tithing came with faith under Abraham; Moses' law enjoined it, and Israel practiced it when she was right with God; Jesus indorsed it (Matt. 23:23); and Paul said to lay by in store as God has prospered you. Do not rob God of His portion, viz., tithes and offerings. (Read Mal. 3.)

SECOND COMING OF JESUS

That Jesus is coming again the second time in person, just as He went away, is clearly set forth by the Lord Jesus Himself, and was preached and taught in the early Christian church by the apostles; hence, the children of God today are earnestly, hopefully, looking forward to the glorious event. (Matt. 24; Acts 1:11; 3:19-21; 1 Cor. 11:26; Phil. 3:20-21; 1 Thess. 4:14-17; Titus 2:13, 14.)

THE MILLENNIUM

Moreover, we believe that the distress upon the earth is the "beginning of sorrows" and will become more intense until there "shall be a time of trouble such as there never was since there was a nation even to that same time" (Matt. 24:3-8; Dan. 12:1), and that period of "tribulation" will be followed by the dawn of a better day on earth and that for a thousand years there shall be "peace on earth and good will toward men." (Rev. 20:1-5; Isa. 65:17-25; Matt. 5:5; Dan. 7:27; Mic. 4:1-2; Heb. 2:14; Rom. 11:25-27.)

FINAL JUDGMENT

When the thousand years are finished, there shall be a resurrection of all the dead, who will be summoned before the great white throne for their final judgment, and all whose names are not found written in the Book of Life shall be cast into the lake of fire, burning with brimstone, which God hath prepared for the Devil and his angels, Satan himself being cast in first. (Matt. 25:41; Rev. 20:7-15; 21:8.)

PUBLIC SCHOOL ACTIVITIES

We disapprove of school students attending shows, dances, dancing classes, theaters, engaging in school activities against their religious scruples, and wearing gymnasium clothes which immodestly expose the body.

RELIGIOUS HOLIDAY

The annual Conference is declared to be an International Religious Holiday for all members and all members are urged to attend.

Notes: *The articles are related to those of the Pentecostal Assemblies of the World, of which the United Pentecostal Church was once a part. These articles in turn have become the source of statements by the Assemblies of the Lord Jesus Christ and the New Bethel Church of God in Christ.*

*　　*　　*

Black Trinitarian Pentecostal

BASIS OF UNION (AFRICAN UNIVERSAL CHURCH)

SECTION 1. We believe that Jesus Christ shed His blood for the remission of sins. (Romans 3:25) and for the regeneration of penitent sinners, and for salvation from sin and from sinning (1 John 3:5-10: Eph. 2:1-10).

SECTION 2. We believe also that Jesus Christ shed His blood for the complete cleansing of the justified believer from all indwelling sin, and from its pollution subsequent to regeneration.

SECTION 3. We believe, Teach and firmly maintain the scriptural doctrine of justification of faith alone, as taught in Rom. 5:1.

SECTION 4. We believe also that entire sanctification destroys and eradicates sin (Rom. 6:6; Heb. 13:12; 1 John 1:7-9; 1 Thess. 5:23; St. John 17:17; Acts 26:18).

SECTION 5. We believe that entire sanctification is an instantaneous, definite, second work of grace obtainable by faith on the part of the fully consecrated believer.

SECTION 6. We believe that the baptism of the Holy Ghost is obtainable by a definite appropriation of faith on the part of the fully cleansed believer. Acts 1:5; 2:1; 4:38; Luke 11:13; Acts 19).

SECTION 7. We believe also that the baptism with fire is a definite, scriptural experience, obtainable by faith on the part of the spirit filled believer (Matt. 3:11; Luke 3:16; Rev. 15:2; Psa. 104:4; Acts 2:1-4; Heb. 12:29; Ezek. 1:4-14, 10:2-7; Isa. 33:14, 6:1-8.

SECTION 8. We believe also in the divine healing of both soul and body as the atonement (Isa. 5:3; Matt. 8:16-17; Mark 16:14-18; James 5:14-16; Exo. 15:26.)

SECTION 9. We believe in the second coming of Christ according to the revealed light of the scripture (John 3:1-2; Rom. 8:29; 2 Peter 1:4; Psa. 16:11; Matt. 5; John 4:24; John 1:1-10).

SECTION 10. We do not believe that the baptism with fire is an experience independent or disassociated from the Holy Ghost, but we do believe that the divine baptism of Jesus is two fold; Christ Baptism is with the Holy Ghost and with fire. We believe that it is He, the Comforter abiding in the heart of the purified believed who creates an intense longing for the experience of the Baptism of fire and as the executive of the God Head Baptizes those in whom He dwells with fire, and that none can receive the experience of the baptism of fire except those in whom the personal Holy Ghost already abides.

SECTION 11. African Universal Church and Commercial League Corporation do opposed to [sic] all doctrines that are contrary to God's revealed word.

Notes: *Churches serving a predominantly black constituency have played an important part in the whole pentecostal movement. William Seymour, a black holiness preacher, became pastor of a small group of former Baptists at what became the first pentecostal center in Los Angeles, where the famous Azusa Street revival occurred. Early attempts at racial inclusiveness failed within a few years, and black churches were segregated, pushed to the edge of the movement as a whole. The Pentecostal Assemblies of the World, a non-Trinitarian apostolic group, has been the most successful at keeping a limited degree of racial inclusiveness over the years.*

Black churches follow the same division as those whose membership is predominantly white—holiness and two-experience denominations—though most tend to favor the holiness position. The Black Pentecostal churches are treated together because of the very real consequences of racial factors in molding their life and their relationship to the larger Pentecostal movement.

The African Universal Church is a holiness-pentecostal church which has accepted an extreme definition of sanctification as the destruction and eradication of sin.

*　　*　　*

CONFESSION OF FAITH (CHURCH OF GOD IN CHRIST)

1. TRINITY

We believe in the Trinity of the Father, Son and Holy Spirit.

2. THE SON

We believe that Jesus Christ was and is the Son of God, co-equal in wisdom and power and holiness with the Father, and that through His atonement the world is saved from sin and reconciled to God.

3. THE HOLY SPIRIT

We believe in the personality of the Holy Spirit. That He proceedeth from the Father and the Son, and that He is co-equal with the Father and the Son, and that He is the Executive of the Trinity, through which the plan of salvation is carried on in the earth.

4. FALLEN NATURE

We believe that man, by nature is sinful and unholy. Being born in sin he needs to be born again, sanctified and cleansed from all sins by the blood of Jesus.

CONFESSION OF FAITH (CHURCH OF GOD IN CHRIST) (continued)

We believe that man is saved by confessing and forsaking his sins, and believing on the Lord Jesus Christ, and that having become a child of God, by being born again and adopted into the family of God, he may, and should, claim the inheritance of the sons of God, namely, the baptism of the Holy Spirit.

5. BAPTISM OF THE HOLY SPIRIT

We believe in the baptism of the Holy Ghost with the sign and seal of speaking in tongues, as recorded in Acts 2:4; 19:6; 10:46.

We do not believe that we are baptized with the Spirit in order to be saved and become the sons of God, but that we are baptized with the Holy Ghost because we are saved and are the sons of God. (We hold that we are saved by being born of the Spirit, not by being baptized with the Spirit.)

6. THE FATHER

We believe in God, the Father, Almighty, the Author and Creator of all things.

While we do not presume to teach that no one has the Spirit that does not speak in tongues, or that one is not saved that does not speak in tongues, yet we believe that a full baptism of the Holy Ghost as poured out on the day of Pentecost is accompanied by the speaking in tongues. And that the baptism of the Holy Ghost has the same effects and results upon every child of God that receives it the same as the new birth has the same effects and results on every one that is born of the Spirit. And we do not consider anyone Pentecostal who teaches contrary to this doctrine.

7. WATER BAPTISM

We believe that the instructions given us by the Saviour, as recorded in Mt. 28:19, 29 are sufficient for our guide and rule as to the formula of water baptism, namely in the name of the Father and the Son, and of the Holy Ghost.

8. THE SECOND COMING OF CHRIST

We believe in the second coming of our Lord and Saviour Jesus Christ, and that He will reign on the earth in millennial power and glory, and in the rapture of the bride of Christ, when she shall be caught up to meet her bridegroom in the air. We admonish all who have this in them to purify themselves as He is pure.

9. THE SABBATH

We recognize the first day of the week as the Christian Sabbath.

10. GENERAL CHURCH OFFICERS

The Chief Apostle, General Superintendent and State Overseers shall compose the official heads of the church. Said officers are to be elected from among the ordained Elders of the church by the General Assembly, and shall have the care of the work at large. They are empowered to organize and reorganize churches and missions and to ordain Elders and commission Evangelists.

11. ELIGIBILITY OF ELDERS

The certificate of credentials of an Elder are valid only as long as his life adorns the Gospel of Christ, and his teaching are in harmony with the Church of God in Christ. Any Elder, Evangelist or member acting as Pastor of a church, who teaches contrary doctrines, or causes dissensions or in any way proves his inability as a Pastor, may be removed by a State Overseer, or a General Superintendent, and another appointed in his place.

12. CHURCH PROPERTY

All church property must be held in trust for the Church of God in Christ by a legally elected board of trustees, which trustees must be members of said church are subject to removal (sic).

No individual church can change any of the doctrines of the Church of God in Christ. The Chief Apostle, a General Superintendent, or State Overseer, may disorganize a church whose members accept or promulgate doctrine contrary to the Church of God in Christ, and confiscate the property for the general church purpose.

Members of any Church of God in Christ disorganizing or dissolving cannot use or take any property with them, but church property will revert to the State Assembly, for church purposes only, under the supervision of the General Superintendent or State Overseer.

13. POLITICAL GOVERNMENTS

We believe that governments are God-given institutions for the benefit of mankind. We admonish and exhort our members to honor magistrates and the powers that be, to respect and obey civil laws.

We hereby and herewith declare our loyalty to the president and the constitution of the United States, and pledge fidelity to the flag for which the republic stands. But as a God-fearing, peace-loving and law-abiding people, we only claim our inheritance as American citizens, namely: To worship God according to the dictates of our mind.

We believe the shedding of human blood or taking of human life to be contrary to the teaching of our Lord and Saviour, and as a body, we are adverse to war in all its various forms.

We herewith offer our services to the president for any services that will not conflict with our conscientious scruples in this respect, with love to all, with malice toward none, and with due respect to all who differ from us in our interpretation of the Scriptures.

Notes: *Among the oldest of the Pentecostal bodies, the Church of God in Christ began among former Baptists who had accepted holiness doctrines. Its doctrinal position was forged in a split among holiness people who did not follow founder C. H. Mason into the pentecostal movement and in reaction against the Apostolic non-Trinitarian movement. Notice the sophisticated treatment of the relation of salvation, the baptism of the Holy Spirit, and the experience of speaking-in-tongues. The church is also pacifist.*

WHAT WE BELIEVE [CHURCH OF THE LIVING GOD (CHRISTIAN WORKERS FOR FELLOWSHIP)]

What We Believe:

I. ABOUT THE CHURCH:

A. The C.W.F.F. meaning "Christian Workers for Fellowship" is not a part of the name of the Church, but it is only the adopted motto of the Church, which is used in connection with the name "Church of the Living God."

   1. For one to become a member of the Church, he does not join the church, except in the sense that he unites with a local church. To gain entrance into the church one must follow the Plan of Salvation, which will be mentioned later in this writing.

B. We Believe the Church is

   1. The Church is that company of believers called out from the world by the gospel of Jesus Christ and indwelled with the Holy Spirit. These believers are called by His Father's name.

C. We Believe the true scriptural name of the Church is

   1. Church of God or Church of the Living God. Act 20:28; I Cor. 1:1, 2; 10:32; 11:16; 11:22; 15:9; II Cor. 1:1; I Thess. 2:14; II Thess. 1:4; I Tim. 3:5; 3:15

D. The Mission and the purpose of the Church

   1. According to the Scriptures.

      a. The immediate purpose of the Church. Our present concern "Preach the Gospel." Mark 16:15

      b. Make disciples or converts. Matt. 28:19

      c. Teach them to observe all things.

      d. Commit the word to faithful men.

   2. The ultimate purpose.

      a. To gather together in Christ, to praise of His Name.

      b. To perfect the saints; to bring all to the fullness of Christ. Eph. 4:12

      c. To prepare for Christ a glorious Church, without spot or anything. Eph. 5:27

II. ABOUT JESUS CHRIST

A. We believe that Jesus was a man, not a myth, not a phantom, not a mere creation of some fruitful imagination, but a man—a real person, having a human body and soul, and endowed with all the faculties, powers, and susceptibilities of human nature in its primitive state.

We further believe that He was born of a Virgin, lived a holy life, and was crucified, buried, resurrected, and ascended back to His Father with glory and honor. He was both human and divine.

   1. Facts about the Virgin Birth

      a. Matthew and Luke are the only gospel writers who were witness to the Virgin Birth of Christ.

      b. These birth accounts are genuine parts of the gospel narrative which belong to the Apostolic Age.

      c. The virgin birth is never contradicted by other New Testaments writers. Many statements by Mark, John, Paul and Peter are very meaningful in light of the virgin birth.

      d. Isaiah 7:14 is rightly applied to the virgin birth.

   2. Scriptural evidence of a bodily resurrection

      a. The post-resurrection appearances

        (1.) To certain women as they returned from the tomb after seeing an angel. Matt. 28:1-10

        (2.) To Mary Magdalene. Jn. 20:1-18; Mk. 16:12, 13

        (3.) To Peter before the evening of the first day. Lk. 24:13; I Cor. 15:5

        (4.) To two disciples on the way to Emmaeus late the first day. Mk. 16:12, 13; Luke 24

        (5.) To ten apostles and others in the evening. Mk. 16:14-18; Lk. 24:36-40; Jn. 20:19-23

        (6.) To Saul. I Cor. 9:ff; 15:8

        (7.) To John on Patmos. Rev. 1:13

   3. We Believe Jesus Christ to be the eternal Son of God, eternal Word, Creator and Preserver of all things.

III. ABOUT THE BIBLE

A. We Believe the Bible is the inspired Word of God. We accept the revelation of God in the person of Jesus Christ and our only reliable source of information about him is the Bible and Jesus Christ is the central theme in the Holy Scripture.

   1. The Word meets every requirement.

      a. The Bible offers an unchangeable standard as a revelation from God to man. It is ultimate and final.

      b. It provides the power by which man can be led to live up to its high standard. The love of God planted in the Bible is the prime source of power.

      c. It is universally applicable to mankind. It demands that you love and serve your neighbor.

   1. The Unity of the Bible.

This factor is one of the greatest marvels of the Bible. Sixty-six books produced by forty writers in different languages, under many governments and over a period of around fifteen hundred years, yet all brought together to form the Book.

      a. Unity of the Theme

The theme is the plan of redemption. This plan begins in the book of Genesis with the promise concerning woman's seed and continues in the shed blood of the animals whose skin furnished covering for Adam and Eve. It is perpetuated through the Messianic prophecies of the Old

Testament and is typified in animal sacrifices and other types and shadows. John the Baptist pointed that He had come to give His life as a ransom. The Acts and the Epistles further continue the theme, until the last song of the heavenly choir, which is also the song of redemption . . . The Book of Revelation. We take a fundamental view of God's word, that we must live by every word that proceeds out of the mouth of God. We believe that the Bible is perfect from cover to cover. It is our belief that the Scripture is profitable for doctrine, for reproof, or correction and for instruction in righteousness. II Tim. 3:16; II Peter 1:19-21.

IV. ABOUT THE HOLY SPIRIT

We Believe in the Holy Spirit or Holy Ghost. We believe Him to be a person. We believe Him to be the third person in the Godhead. We believe the Holy Spirit is the creative, living, loving and lasting presence of God in the world. There is only one God, but He has three basic roles: Creator, Redeemer and Friend. So we say Father, Son and Holy Spirit.

A. Holy Spirit is like Jesus.

1. He is accessible to all men; as accessible as was Jesus who invited all men to come to him for rest and commanded his disciples to go into all the world and make disciples of all nations. Everybody in the world is included and no one is excluded except he excludes himself.

B. Holy Spirit is understandable like Jesus.

1. The work of the Spirit is full of mystery, but it is not magical. The Holy Spirit makes as much sense as Jesus made. The gift of the Holy Spirit is bestowed upon the repentant and obedient. Luke records in Acts 5:32 "And we are his witnesses in these things and so is also Holy Spirit whom God hath given to them that obey Him." God gives His Spirit to everyone that has fulfilled the steps to salvation.

C. The Holy Spirit is not necessarily an emotional outburst.

1. Speaking in tongues in this age is not an evidence of the Holy Spirit. It is not necessary to go into trance to receive the Spirit but merely obey. We believe that the tongues on Pentecost were languages and not unintelligible utterance. The basic evidence of the Holy Spirit in our lives is the fruit we bear. Gal. 5:22

D. The Holy Spirit has a purpose.

1. The purpose of the Holy Spirit in the life of the Christian is to lead, to guide, sanctify, comfort. We believe the Holy Spirit of God is alive, real and present. He is willing to do exceedingly abundantly above all that we can ask or think. Eph. 3:20-21.

V. ABOUT THE PLAN OF SALVATION

We believe for one to be saved he has to take certain steps to salvation. The commands to be obeyed are: hear, understand, believe, repent, confess, be baptized, partake in the Lord's Supper, and participate in Foot Washing. The commands to be obeyed constitute the Plan of Salvation.

A. Hearing and Understanding

Understanding through preaching by which the facts of the gospel are brought to one's conscious mind for his consideration and action upon them. Hearing consists in giving heed or attention to things presented with the intention of accepting the facts and being obedient to the commands enjoined. Rom. 10:11.

B. Believing (Faith) Heb. 11:6 (acting upon word of another)

1. Means to faith presentation of adequate confirmed evidence. Rom. 10:17

2. Elements of Faith

Faith affects the intellect, fills the heart with powerful emotion, emotion moves the will to act. Hence, we can say that faith is marked by:

a. A change in views and sentiments

b. A change of heart

c. Change of will when faith has its complete work in the life it embraces.

d. A strong conviction of the truth of the gospel as being God's power unto salvation to everyone that believeth.

e. A firm and abiding trust in Christ as the way, the Truth, and the Life. To believe is to be persuaded of an historical fact, but to believe in Christ is not only to assent to His historicity but to place confidence in Him for salvation and justification.

C. Repentance (a change of mind which leads to a change of life)

1. Elements which lead to repentance.

a. Sinner obtains new views of Christ, of sin, and of holiness.

b. He obtains a new view of his condition before God.

c. He feels Godly sorrow for sin and determination to be free.

2. Elements involved in repentance.

a. Intellectual change caused by truth presented.

b. Emotional change caused by truth presented.

c. Change of life resulting from change of will.

3. Results of repentance.

a. Death to sin. Rom. 6:1, 2

b. Hatred for sin. Heb. 1:9; Jude 23

c. Moral impossibility to live longer in sin. Rom. 6:2

d. Position to receive blessings of God which follow repentance. II Corinthians 7:10

D. Confession of Faith (an oral proclamation with the mouth, of the faith within the heart).

1. The importance of the Good Confession

a. To be saved. Rom. 10, 9:10

b. To bear testimony of Christ. I Tim. 6:12

c. Commits us to Christ

d. Signifies to others our own belief

E. Ordinances of the Church

We believe that there are three Sacraments or Rites that are ordained of Christ in the New Convenant namely: Baptism, The Lord's Supper, and the Washing of Feet.

A. Baptism

1. We believe the first Rite of the Church is Baptism. Baptism comes from the Greek word Baptizo—immerse, dip, plunge, submerge. We believe this is the only valid way to be baptized.

2. What Baptism is

(a.) Act of submission and obedience

(b.) An act performed in the manner of a burial, portraying and witnessing to the burial and resurrection.

3. Importance of Baptism

(a.) First public act of Jesus preparatory to beginning of ministry. St. Matt. 3:13-15

(b.) The last public command to his apostles

(c.) The first command given to inquiring sinners

(d.) Mentioned in New Testament at least 117 times

4. Subjects for Christian Baptism

(a.) Those capable of and guilty of committing sin

(b.) Those capable of knowing, reasoning and obeying by their own will the plan of salvation

5. Special consideration showing that infants are not subject to Christian Baptism

(a.) Infants cannot fulfill all or any of the above qualifications

(b.) Not capable of being taught the plan of salvation

(c.) Cannot fulfill the purpose of I Peter 3:21. "Answer of a good conscience."

(d.) Historically infant baptism was not introduced until after the apostles.

B. Lord's Supper

We believe the Lord's Supper or Communion, points backward to the death of Christ and forward to His return.

1. According to the Bible.

(a.) It is a memorial. Luke 22:19; I Cor. 11:28

(b.) It is atonement for sin. Matt. 28:26; Mk. 14:26

(c.) It is communion of the Saint. 1 Cor. 10:16, 17

(d.) The bread is His body. Lk. 22:19. Mk. 14:22. Matt. 26:28

(e.) The cup is His blood. Lk. 22:20. Mk. 14:24. Matt. 26:28

2. Jesus declared Himself to be the Vine.

(a.) Not a grape vine or some other kind

(b.) Old Testament and New. Ps. 80:8; Matt. 2:13; Jn. 15:1

3. Water to be used for the Lord's Supper.

Water is a pure drink.

(a.) Old Testament Scriptures. Gen. 1:2; Ps. 73:10

4. New Testament Scriptures

Matt. 10:42; Mk. 9:41; Lk. 22:20; Jn. 19:34; Rev. 22:1; Rev. 21:6

5. Wine and strong Drinks

We believe that wine and strong drink should not be used by Christians.

(a.) Old Testament Scripture

Gen. 19:38; Lev. 10:8-10; Ps. 75:10; Prov. 20:1; 23:29-30; 23:32; Isa. 5:11; 5:22; 23; Isa. 28:7; Hos. 4:11; 5:22, 23; Isa. 28:7, 8; Hos. 4:11

(b.) New Testament Scriptures. Mk. 15:23; Lk. 1:11-16; 1 Cor. 6:9-10; 9:9.

C. Foot Washing

We Believe if one is to become a member of the Church of the Living God, he must have his feet washed. After he has obtained membership, he must wash the feet of others. The specific purpose of foot washing as an ordinance is closely bound up with the basic reasons underlying the other ordinances of the Church. But why ordinances at all, one might ask? We ought to be willing to obey plain commandments of our Lord, just because He is Lord, whether or not we can discern the reason for such commands.

1. Expressly Commanded

Jesus said, "If I then, your Lord and Master, have washed your feet, Ye also ought to wash one another's feet. For I have given you an example, that ye should do as I have done to you. If ye know these things happy are ye if ye do them" Jn 13:14-15, 17. Some say that this part of the Word does not assert that we must do it but merely that we should or ought. Now the New Testament law of liberty does not consist of "thou shalt" as did the Mosaic law, but is, instead, a law of love, Jesus said, "If a man love me, he will keep my words." (Jn. 14:23) The words ought and should are the strongest words in our language expressing moral obligation or duty.

2. What it symbolizes

As a Rite, foot washing symbolizes the sacredness and holiness of that blessed relationship of God's redeemed saints with each other. Having fellowship with each other.

(a.) Practiced by the Early Church

Paul, writing to Timothy relative to certain conditions under which a widow should be taken under consideration of financial care of the church says "She should be well reported of for good works; if she has brought up children; if she has lodged strangers, if she has washed the Saints feet; if she has relieved the afflicted, if she has diligently followed every good work." I Tim. 5:9-10.

VI. ABOUT PRAYER

We Believe the prayer that Jesus gave to His disciples in the Sermon on the Mount is the prayer to be prayed by all Christians. Matt. 6:9-13; Lk. 11:1-2. This is commonly known as the Lord's Prayer, but it is not the Lord's Prayer but the disciples Prayer. This prayer sustains all of our needs and it contains seven petitions.

Notes: *This statement is reflective of a number of debates within the black religious community, such as the relation of the baptism of the Holy Spirit to trance. It is unique for its position on the Lord's Supper, directing the use of water instead of wine. Foot washing is also practiced.*

* * *

THE FAITH OF THE CHURCH OUTLINED (CHURCH OF THE LIVING GOD, THE PILLAR AND GROUND OF TRUTH)

We believe and really know, according to the word of Christ, that it is necessary to observe and keep the commandment of Christ by washing one another's feet as was His example to do as he did.

We believe it is right and necessary to observe the Lord's supper or passover as He did with His disciples before He was crucified by using unleavened bread as a token of His body and by using pure unadulterated water as a token and agreement of His blood, as nothing except water will agree with His blood.

Read on this subject, the following scripture: Wine forbidden by the word of God: Lev. 10-8, 9, 10; Hosea 4-11; Hosea 9-4; Luke 1:15; Mark 15:23. Water approved of by the word of God: I Cor. 10:1, 2, 3, 4; Exodus 17:6; Matt. 10:42; Mark 9:41; Rev. 22:16-17.

We believe in praying; we believe in fasting; we believe in keeping the Sabbath with the covenant which is God, Christ and the Holy Ghost, instead of with types and

shadows which was fulfilled by the coming of Christ. We believe that to cease from our own works is to cease from sin.

We believe that Christ hath given us rest from sin evil and confusion in our bodies instead of rest from carnal labor which is necessary for the sustenance of our temporal bodies. We believe there is a place of inheritance and joy and happiness beyond expression for those that long for the appearing of the Lord to those that keep His sayings and do His will; and that this place is not a place of carnal rest, for they rest neither day nor night there, but continually give glory to God; and we believe that eyes have not seen, neither have ears heard, what is in store in that city for those that love the Lord, do His will and keep His commandments. We believe that flesh and blood cannot enter there, that sorrow and sighing are not there and that nothing that sin or worketh iniquity, nor any sin has ever been or can ever enter there. This place we believe is eternal into Heaven and is the Heaven of heavens.

We believe also that there is a final Judgment Day in store for all, both the good and for the bad. In it we believe that sinners will be justly judged, condemned and separated from the righteous and turned into the place called the Lake of Fire and Brimstone, prepared for those that do evil for the wicked and for the devil and his angels.

In the Judgment we believe that the righteous shall be changed from this corruptible body and given a body fashioned like the glorious body of the Son of God. For we shall be like Him.

We believe the Church of the Living God, the Pillar and Ground of the Truth is the waiting or preparing bride of Christ and that when she is sufficiently prepared and made glorious without spot or wrinkle Christ will catch His bride away to the marriage supper of the Lamb to live and reign with Him for a period of a thousand years and that in this all the dead in Christ will rise first at the sounding of the first trumpet.

Notes: *This statement covers only those issues above and beyond the basic beliefs on God, Christ, and salvation. Like the Church of the Living God (Christian Workers for Fellowship), the Church of the Living God, the Pillar and Ground of Truth uses water instead of wine for the Lord's Supper.*

* * *

WHAT WE BELIEVE AND TEACH (DELIVERANCE EVANGELICAL CENTERS)

ARTICLE 1. THE BIBLE

The BIBLE is our all-sufficient rule for faith and practice. It is the inspired Word of God, a revelation from GOD to man the INFALLIBLE guide of conduct and faith, the BIBLE is SUPERIOR to conscience and reason, but not contrary to wisdom. 2 Tim. 3:15, 16; I Pet. 2:2; 2 Pet. 1:21. THE WHOLE BIBLE, both the OLD and NEW TESTAMENTS, is the pure Word of God that cannot be changed, added to, nor taken away from its words, without terrific consequences. Rev. 22:18, 19.

ARTICLE 2. GOD

GOD is ONE eternal, omni-present, omniscient, all-powerful God in three persons: namely, the FATHER, the SON, and the HOLY GHOST. God created the whole universe out of nothing in the beginning. Gen. 1:1.

ARTICLE 3. JESUS CHRIST

Jesus Christ, the Son of the Living God, came in the flesh, born of the virgin Mary, begotten by the Holy Spirit and took on Himself the form of man to be able to redeem us from our sins and deliver us from the powers of Satan Matt. 1:18-21; Luke 1:31; John 1:2-14.

For the salvation of man from sin, Jesus Christ suffered under Pontius Pilate, was crucified, died and was buried and rose triumphantly the third day from the dead, ascended into heaven from Mt. Olivet in the presence of many witnesses, and today is sitting on the right hand of the Throne of God interceding for us, from whence He shall come again to raise the dead and judge the world, Matt. 27:6, 28:1-7; Mark 16:19; Luke 24:51; Acts 7:55; Heb. 12:2; John 5:26-29, 11:25; Matt. 25:31-46; I Thess. 4:13-17; I Cor. 15:15-58; Rev. 19:1-10, 20:11-15, 27; Matt. 25:1-13.

There is an eternal punishment for the wicked, and eternal bliss for the righteous. Luke 16:19-31; Matt. 25:41, 46; Rev. 20:11-15, 21:8, 27.

ARTICLE 4. THE HOLY SPIRIT

The Holy Spirit is the third person of the Trinity, sent from the Father to "guide us into all truth", "convict the world of sin, of righteousness and of judgment to come", "to comfort, lead and teach the believers in Jesus Christ . . . to anoint, inspire and empower believers to continue the work Jesus began both to do and teach." Acts 1:1, 8; 2:38, 39; John 14:16, 17, 26; 16:7-15.

The HOLY SPIRIT is the "PROMISE OF THE FATHER"—all believers in Jesus Christ are entitled to receive, and should earnestly seek the Baptism of the HOLY GHOST and fire, according to the command of our Lord. Acts 1:4, 5, 8. THIS is the normal experience of all the early church. With this experience comes power to preach and bestowment of the GIFTS OF THE SPIRIT. Luke 24:19; Acts 1:4, 8; I Cor. 12:1-31. THIS wonderful experience is distinct from and subsequent to the experience of the "NEW BIRTH", Acts 10:44-46; 11:14-16; 15:7-9; Acts 2:38, 39.

THE EVIDENCE OF THE BAPTISM IN THE HOLY SPIRIT

When the believer is filled with the Holy Spirit, there is a physical sign of "speaking in other tongues as the Spirit of God gives the utterance." Acts 2:4. This is accompanied and followed by a burning desire and supernatural power to witness to others of God's salvation and power! Acts 10:44-47.

ARTICLE 5. THE CREATION

1) In the beginning GOD created the heavens and the earth and all things therein by His mighty WORD. Gen. 1:1; John 1.

2) GOD made man in His own image: pure, holy and free from sin—but gave man the free choice of life or death, obedience or disobedience to God's eternal commands and will. Gen. 1:26, 27; 2:17.

ARTICLE 6. THE FALL OF MAN

1) Satan tempted Adam and Eve, who believed his lies, and fell into sin, thus bringing death upon the whole human race. Gen. 2:17, 3:19.

2) Through the fall of Adam and Eve, all children of men are born with sinful natures, and the wages of sin is death—they will be lost throughout eternity if not redeemed from their sins by the grace of God, through Jesus Christ. Romans 5:12; John 3:16.

ARTICLE 7. REDEMPTION OF MAN

In the fulness of time, GOD sent His only begotten Son, Jesus Christ, into this world to pay the penalty for our sins, and redeem us from the power of Satan, sin, sickness, death and hell . . . all of which are the results of Adam's sin and the fall. Matt. 1:21; Luke 1:35.

Man can be saved if he hears the Gospel, believes the provision Christ has made for his salvation, accepts Jesus Christ as the Son of God, to wash away all his sins, and is ready to follow the teachings of Jesus Christ! Romans 10:9-17; Mark 16:15-18.

ARTICLE 8. SALVATION—ETERNAL LIFE

WHAT ONE MUST DO TO RECEIVE SALVATION:

1) REPENT:—this is a genuine sorrow for past sins committed and complete decision and turning FROM all forms of known sin in the life, and from all the appearance of sin. Repentance is accompanied by confession of our personal sins to GOD ALONE, who only can forgive sinners and change their hearts and lives! God is ready to forgive all who confess, and will never remember their sins against them anymore forever. I John 1:9 TRUE repentance makes a man make things right with those he has done wrong to, as far as possible. Luke 3:8; 19:9.

2) When man repents . . . then GOD GIVES SALVATION as a FREE GIFT—we could not earn it by any merits or good works we have done . . . good works cannot cover over the sins of the past . . . it takes GOD to wash away a man's sins and change his sinful nature to one that loves and follows holiness. John 3:16-18; Ephes. 1:13; I John 1:9.

3) EVIDENCES of Salvation: The inward evidence to the believer of his salvation is the direct witness of the SPIRIT of God to one's own spirit. Rom. 8:16. The outward evidence to all men, is a life of righteousness and true holiness. Matt. 5:16.

ARTICLE 9. SANCTIFICATION

Is purification of the nature from sin and filthiness of the flesh. This starts at the moment we are saved and should be a daily experience of "washing by the WORD"—complete dedication daily to God's Will. MAN CAN LIVE ABOVE SIN because our sinful natures have been changed by the "new birth" (John 3:7) and Christ lives in our hearts: I Pet. 1:15, 16; Matt. 5:48; 2 Cor. 7:7.

ARTICLE 10. WATER BAPTISM

Water baptism is administered to those who hear and believe the Gospel and accept Jesus Christ with all their heart. Infants are not baptized, but dedicated to God in prayer, for until a child comes to the age when he knows right from wrong and chooses wrong . . . he is under God's protection—if they die they go to heaven. Water baptism by immersion (in the Name of the FATHER, the SON, and the HOLY GHOST) is an outward testimony that we are as dead to our old sins, but rise to walk in newness of life with Jesus Christ. Water Baptism by immersion is a direct command of Christ to all who are "saved". Matt. 28:19; Mark 16:16; Rom. 6:4, 6: John 3:22, 23; John 4:1.

Notes: *The position of the Deliverance Evangelical Centers is close to that of the Assemblies of God. Baptism is by immersion and is reserved for adult believers.*

* * *

BASIS OF UNION (FIRE-BAPTIZED HOLINESS CHURCH OF GOD OF THE AMERICAS)

Section 1. We believe Jesus Christ shed His blood for the remission of sins that are past (Rom. 3:25) and for the regeneration of penitent sinners and for the salvation from sin and from sinning. (I John 3:5-10; Eph. 2:1-10).

Section 2. We believe, teach and firmly maintain the scriptural doctrine of Justification by faith alone through the blood. (Rom. 5:6-9; Eph. 1:7; Rom. 3:24-25; Col. 1:14).

Section 3. We believe also that Jesus Christ shed His blood for complete cleansing of the justified believer from all indwelling sin and from its pollution subsequent to regeneration. (Rom. 6:6; Heb. 13:12; I John 1:7-9; I Thess. 5:23; John 17:17; Acts. 26:18).

Section 4. We believe also that sanctification is an instantaneous, definite, second work of grace obtainable by faith on the part of the fully justified believer. (Heb. 10:9-14; Exodus 31:13).

Section 5. We believe also that the pentecostal baptism of the Holy Ghost and fire is obtainable by a definite act of appropriating faith on the part of the wholly sanctified believer, and that the initial evidence of the reception of this experience is speaking with other tongues as the spirit gives utterance. (Acts 8:14-17; Acts 1:5; Acts 8:7; Acts 10:44-46 and 19:6).

Section 6. We believe also in divine healing as in the atonement (Isa. 53:4-5; Matt. 8:16-17; Mark 16:14-15; James 5:14-15; Exodus 15:26; Psalms 103:3; Acts 8-7).

Section 7. We believe in the imminent personal premillennial second coming of our Lord Jesus Christ (I Thess. 4:15-18; Titus 2:13; II Peter 3:1-14; Matt. 24:20-44) and we love and wait for His appearing. (II Tim. 4:8).

Section 8. The F.B.H.C. of God of the Americas is utterly opposed to the teachings of the so-called Christian Scientists, Spirtualists, Unitarians, Universalists and Mormons. We deny as false un-Scriptural Seventh Day Adventism, (Col. 2:16-17; Gal. 3:11) annihilation of the wicked, conditional immortality, and antinomianism, absolute perfection, so-called comeoutism, the so-called resurrection life, the so-called redemption or glorification of the body in this life, and the doctrine of the restitution of all things as set forth in millennial dawnism and the false teaching that we are not born of God until we are sanctified wholly. (Matt. 25:26; Rev. 20:10-14; Mark 9:44).

Section 9. The Lord says marriage is honorable in all and the bed undefiled, and the Fire Baptized Holiness Church of God of the Americas FIRMLY HOLDS THAT THERE ARE CERTAIN RELATIONS BETWEEN HUSBAND AND WIFE which are strictly private, according to the word of God, and into this sacred privacy no one has any right to inquire. (Heb. 13:4, I Cor. 7:15).

Section 10. No subsequent General Council shall have authority to change the Basis of Union of the Fire Baptized Holiness Church of God of the Americas without a full representation from the local Churches.

Notes: *The Fire-Baptized Holiness Church of God of the Americas resulted from a division along racial lines of the Fire-Baptized Holiness Church (now a constituent part of the International Pentecostal Holiness Church). This Basis of Union is almost identical with that of the other church sharing similar roots, the Pentecostal Fire-Baptized Church.*

* * *

ARTICLES OF FAITH (UNITED HOLY CHURCH OF AMERICA)

1. We believe in one God, the Father Almighty, Maker of heaven and earth, and all things visible. I Timothy 2:5. And in Jesus Christ, His only Son, our Lord, who is of one substance with the Father, by whom all things were made. Col. 1:15-18. And in the Holy Spirit, the Comforter, who is sent from the Father and Son and who together with the Father and Son is worshipped and glorified. John 14:15-17; Acts 2:4.

2. We believe that man was made in the image of God that he might know, love and obey God, and enjoy Him forever; that our first parents by disobedience fell under the righteous condemnation of God; and that all men are so alienated from God that there is no salvation from the guilt and power of sin, except through God's redeeming grace. Titus 2:11, 12.

3. We believe that God would have all men return to Him; that to this end He has made Himself known, not only through the works of nature, the course of His providence, and the consciences of men, but also through supernatural revelations made especially to a chosen people, and above all when the fulness of time was come, through Jesus Christ, His Son. Gal. 4:4; I Peter 3:9.

4. We believe that the scriptures of the Old and New Testaments are the records of God's revelation of Himself in the work of redemption; that they were written by men under the special guidance of the Holy Spirit; that they are able to make wise unto salvation, and that they constitute the authoritative

standard by which religious teaching and human conduct are to be regulated and judged. II Tim. 3:15; II Peter 1:19-21.

5. We believe that the love of God to sinful men has found its highest expression in the redemptive work of His Son; who became man, uniting His divine nature with our human nature in one person; who was tempted like other men, yet without sin; who by His humiliation, His Holy obedience, His suffering, His death on the cross, and His resurrection, became a perfect Redeemer whose sacrifice of Himself for the sins of the world declares the righteousness of God, and is the sole and sufficient ground of forgiveness, and of reconciliation with Him. Gal. 3:13; Heb. 2:16, 4:15; Phil. 2:8.

6. We believe that Jesus Christ, after He had risen from the dead, ascended into heaven, where, as the one mediator between God and man, He carries forward His work of saving men; that He sends the Holy Spirit to convict them of their sin and to lead them to repentance, and faith; and that those, who through renewing grace turn to righteousness, and trust in Jesus Christ as their Redeemer, receive for His sake the forgiveness of their sins, and are made the children of God. I Tim. 2:5; Eph. 1:7; Gal. 1:14; Heb. 9:24.

7. We believe that justification is an act of God whereby all the sins of past life are forgiven through faith in our Lord Jesus Christ, and comes immediately in connection with true repentance and includes regeneration or being born again. Rom. 5; Titus 3:5; Rom. 3:24, 25.

8. We believe that sanctification is the second act of grace whereby the believer is separated, dedicated and consecrated unto God; body, soul, and spirit. This act of sanctification may be viewed in three aspects: instantaneous, progressive, and entire—

A. Instantaneous sanctification is an act wrought in connection with regeneration. St. John 17:17; Rom. 6:22, 12:1; Heb. 13:12, 13.

B. Progressive sanctification is the process in which the believer continues to grow in grace. II Cor. 3:18; II Peter 3:18; I Peter 1:15, 16; Heb. 2:11, 12:14.

C. Entire sanctification denotes a state of being wholly sanctified, body, soul and spirit. I Thes. 5:23; Heb. 12:14; Jude 24.

9. We believe in the baptism of the Holy Ghost, as the gift of power on the sanctified life. Luke 24:49; Matt. 3:11; John 7:38-39, 14-16, 17-26; Acts 1:5-8, 2:4.

10. We believe in divine healing of the body, through the precious atonement of Jesus, by which sickness and disease are destroyed. Isa. 53:4, 5; Matt. 8:17; Mark 16:18; James 5:14-16.

11. We believe in the observance of Sunday, the first day of the week as a day of holy rest and worship in the ministry of the word.

12. We believe in the ultimate prevalence of the kingdom of Christ over the earth; in the glorious appearing of the Great God and our Saviour Jesus Christ in the resurrection of the dead; and in a final judgment, the issues of which are everlasting life and everlasting punishment. Matt. 25:31-46; Acts 1:11, 17:31; Matt. 13:49; Rev. 1:7.

Notes: *Like the International Pentecostal Holiness Church, the United Holy Church of America accepts the Apostles' Creed as its creed, and has a similarly-worded church covenant. Its articles of faith are unique and include phrases from the Nicene Creed and the Westminster Catechism.*

* * *

THE ORTHODOX HOLY CHRISTIAN SPIRITUAL CREED OF CHRISTIAN SPIRITUAL CHURCH AND BELIEVERS [UNIVERSAL CHRISTIAN SPIRITUAL FAITH AND CHURCHES FOR ALL NATIONS (NATIONAL DAVID SPIRITUAL TEMPLE)]

I BELIEVE:

In God the Holy Father Eloheim Almighty, the Father of Spirits and Creator of heaven and earth; and in Jesus Christ the Holy Word and Emmanuel and only begotten Son of God, our Saviour; Who was conceived by the Holy Ghost, born of the Holy Virgin Saint Mary; He taught and demonstrated spiritual knowledge of His kingdom and church by sermons, teachings, healings, prophesying, mind reading and mastery of mind and matter, flesh and blood, life and death, natural and spiritual forces to the glory of God; He was reviled and persecuted because of His spiritual faith, works and power, as an evil doer; He suffered under the rule and by the hands of Pontius Pilate and spiritually blind sinners; He was tried on false charges by Pontius Pilate, condemned by the Jews, crucified, giving up His life according to the Scriptures of Prophecies for the salvation of sinners, and the sins of the People; He was buried in Saint Joseph's new sepulchre under guard and seal; He descended into Hell (prison of the disembodied souls), and preached to the spirits in prison who perished out of their natural bodies, before, during and after the antediluvian flood; the third day He arose from among the disembodied dead; He was seen forty days upon the earth by His holy Apostles and disciples by personal communion, and by over five hundred spectators at one time; He finally ascended into heaven and sitteth at the right hand of God the Father Almighty; He has become the everlasting spiritual High Priest of His Christian spiritual saints and church; after His ascension His disembodied Spirit (Holy Ghost) has come and set (9) spiritual gifts (spirits) in His New Testament spiritual church (Body) by the Holy Ghost, for the edifying of the spiritual saints in the church (Body), and the spreading of the Gospel of spiritual salvation of souls, and the demonstration of the spiritual mysteries of His Kingdom; that He will return in like manner to gather His elects to himself forever; He is the justifier, sanctifier, and spiritual magnifier of all orthodox Christian spiritual believers in Him; I believe in the Holy Ghost, the Spirit of Promise and

THE ORTHODOX HOLY CHRISTIAN SPIRITUAL CREED OF CHRISTIAN SPIRITUAL CHURCH AND BELIEVERS [UNIVERSAL CHRISTIAN SPIRITUAL FAITH AND CHURCHES FOR ALL NATIONS (NATIONAL DAVID SPIRITUAL TEMPLE)] (continued)

Divine Guide into all the ways of Truth, the Third Person (Power) in the Holy Trinity; I believe in the baptism of the Holy Ghost and the Nine Gifts (Spirits) as demonstrated by the Holy Ghost spirits through the gifted Saints in the orthodox Christian spiritual church of Christ; I believe in the communion of spirits which make known secret mysteries of the past, present and future to the gifted people of all generations, nations and tongues who live in corporeal (natural) bodies upon the earth; I believe that all nations, kindred and tongues should worship God the Holy Father Almighty in spirit and in truth, together in one Lord, one spiritual Faith, and one Baptism, in the body of Christ through the Holy Ghost in the oneness of the Trinity inseparable, whether they be Jews or Gentiles, bond or free, white, red, brown, black or yellow, as saints of our Lord and Saviour Jesus Christ; I believe in the New Testament Scripture's spiritual church doctrines, teachings and practices as examples to be followed by the followers of the Holy Ghost in all genuine churches of the orthodox Christian spiritual faith; I believe in the forgiveness of sin; the resurrection of the quickened body, and life everlasting through the Grace of our Lord and Saviour Jesus Christ. A-men! A-men! A-men Selah!"

Notes: *In 1952 the National David Spiritual Temple merged to become a constituent part of the Universal Christian Spiritual Faith and Churches for All Nations. The statement affirms many orthodox Christian beliefs, the Pentecostal emphases on the gifts of the spirit, and some Spiritualist tenents (in the belief in the communion of spirits). The statement also mentions many items believed by some Christians but almost never included in creedal statements, such as Jesus' trial on "false charges," "Saint Joseph's [of Arimathea] new sepulchre," and the "demonstration of the spiritual mysteries."*

*   *   *

Spanish-Speaking Pentecostal

WE TEACH (DEFENDERS OF THE FAITH)

WE TEACH: The Bible as the inspired Word of God, the revelation of His divine scheme of redemption.

Jesus Christ as God's divinely and only begotten Son.

The gospel as the only power of God unto salvation through the atoning blood of Jesus Christ.

The need of holy living through the power of the Holy Spirit, bringing into the Christian's life the fruits of the Spirit.

Prayer as a power for the unfolding, empowering, and guidance of Christian life, and as a ministry of intercession.

The imminent personal return of Jesus Christ for His saints, and to the earth to set up His kingdom over the nations.

The duty and privilege of all Christians to have some part in the evangelization of the world.

The fact of eternal life through Jesus Christ, and the just punishment of all evil.

Notes: *This statement, not specifically pentecostal, is from the parent organization (a non-church-forming, non-pentecostal organization) of the Defenders of the Faith congregations which emerged in Puerto Rico. In Puerto Rico, members of the Defenders of the Faith became pentecostal, and subsequently migrated to the United States.*

*   *   *

WHAT WE BELIEVE (SOLDIERS OF THE CROSS OF CHRIST)

WE BELIEVE: In the direct calling of the believer to dedicate himself for the cause of God. Jn. 6:65; Jn. 17:2,12; Jn. 18:9; Acts 2:47.

WE BELIEVE: In the complete renunciation of material things to serve the Lord, Lu. 14:33; 1 Kings 19:20,21; Mt. 4:18-22.

WE BELIEVE: In baptism by inmersion as the first step to salvation. Mt. 28:19; Col. 2:12; Ga. 3:27; Acts 22:16.

WE BELIEVE: In the observance, of the commandments of God and Jesus the Son and the Holy Spirit. Ex. 20:1-17; Lu. 4:46; Ga. 3:21; Mt. 5:17.

WE BELIEVE: That the *Sabath*, the seventh day, is the day of rest blessed by God. He. 4: 1-11; Ex. 20:10; Mt. 5:17,18.

WE BELIEVE: In the resurrection of the dead, when Christ will appear in glory; Jn. 5:28; Lu. 14:15; Mr. 12:24; Da. 12:2.

WE BELIEVE: That the ministers ought to practice their life through faith. Jn. 6:27; He. 10:38,39; Ro. 1:17.

WE BELIEVE: In divine healing by means of prayer and anointing. Mt. 10:8; Mk. 6:13; 16: 18.

WE BELIEVE: That all men are equal with the same responsibilities and the same privileges before God. Ga. 3:28; Acts 2:39; 10:34,35; 17:26.

WE BELIEVE: In the baptism of the Holy Spirit. Jl. 2:27,28; Acts 1:5,8; 2:1;14; 1 Co. 14 9-28.

WE BELIEVE: In the prophecy and divine revelation by means of dreams or visions and manifestations of the Holy Spirit. Job 33:14, 15; Jo. 2:28; Nu. 12:6; Mt. 2:12.

WE BELIEVE: In the glory or eternal life for the faithful. Ro. 6:23; 2 Ti. 2:10; He. 11:14-16; Mt. 13:43; 2 Co. 5:1.

WE BELIEVE: In hell, or place of punishment for the unfaithful and unbelievers. Lu. 17:29; Mt. 13:50; Pr. 15:11,24; Ps. 55:15.

WE BELIEVE: That the Bible's healthfulness should be observed by the children of God. That there are clean as well as unclean foods. Ge. 7:2; Le. 11; Acts 10:14; 1 Co. 6:17.

WE BELIEVE: That Christ is the Saviour of mankind and that there is no eternal life by any other means. Acts 4:12; Jn. 10:28,29. 1 Ti. 2:5; Jn. 17:2,3.

WE BELIEVE: In the Bible, as eternal truth and the holy word of God. Jn. 5:39; 20:31; 1 Pe. 1:25.

WE BELIEVE: That the minister should not involve himself in politics. 2 Ti. 2:4; 1 Pe. 4:15; Jn. 18:36.

WE BELIEVE: In the universal message proclaimed by the Lord's church. Mk. 16:15; Mt. 24:14; Mt. 10:7.

WE BELIEVE: In the holy communion, or the Lord's supper, to commemorate his death, not His resurrection. 1 Co. 11:23-32; Jn. 6:48-58.

WE BELIEVE: In the washing of feet as a sign of humility. Lu. 7:44; Jn. 13:2-9.

WE BELIEVE: That we are saved by grace: by faith. Acts 15:11; Ep. 2:5,8; Ro. 4:16.

WE BELIEVE: That fasting and prayer are factors that strengthen the believer. Est. 4:16; Jn. 3:7,8; Mt. 17:21; Mt. 9:15.

WE BELIEVE: In the second coming of Jesus Christ personally that he will descend in clouds of glory and that no one knows the day nor the hour. S. Mt. 25:31; 1 Th. 4:16,17. 2 Pe. 3:10.

Notes: *Formerly known as the Iglesia Bando Evangelico Gedeon/Gilgal Evangelistic International Church, the Soldiers of the Cross of Christ is a two-experience church which also practices sabbatarianism.*

*   *   *

Miscellaneous Pentecostal

STATEMENT OF BELIEF OF THE ALPHA AND OMEGA CHRISTIAN CHURCH AND BIBLE SCHOOL

1. We believe the Bible to be the only inspired, infallible Word of God. II Peter 1:21.

2. We believe the Godhead consists of the Father, the Son, and the Holy Spirit. II Cor. 13:14. Three in One and One in Three.

3. We believe in the Deity of Jesus Christ, in His Virgin birth, in His atoning death, in His bodily resurrection, in His ascension to the right hand of the Father. I Timothy 3:16.

4. We believe in evangelistic and missionary fervor and endeavor. Acts 1:8; Mark 16:15-18.

5. We believe in salvation through the redeeming blood of Christ. Hebrews 9:22.

6. We believe in the keeping power of God. Jude 24.

7. We believe in sanctification and holiness of heart and the overcoming life as Scriptural requirements for the Bride of Christ. Eph. 5:25-27.

8. We believe in the Baptism of the Holy Spirit according to Acts 2:4, 10:46, 19:6, and the present ministry of the Spirit in and through the believer as manifest in the five ministries as they are being restored in end-time revival (Eph. 4:11), the gifts of the Spirit (I Cor. 12:8-11), and the fruit of the Spirit (Gal. 5:22, 23).

9. We believe that divine healing is obtained on the basis of the Atonement. I Peter 2:24.

10. We believe in Christ's imminent personal return in power and great glory, in His millennial reign and in His everlasting dominion. Acts 1:11; Rev. 20:4; Dan. 7:14.

11. We believe in the resurrection of both the saved and the lost; they that are saved unto the resurrection of eternal life and they that are lost unto the resurrection of eternal punishment. John 5:28, 29; Rev. 20:15.

*   *   *

WE BELIEVE (ASSOCIATION OF SEVENTH DAY PENTECOSTAL ASSEMBLIES)

WE BELIEVE:

In the blood of Jesus for the remission of sins, Heb. 9:22; Lev. 17:11.

In Baptism by immersion in water, Rom. 6:4; Col. 2:12; I Peter 2:21; Matt. 28:19; Acts 2:38.

In sanctification by the blood, I John 1:7; Heb. 13:12.

In santification by the Spirit, I Pet. 1:2; II Thess. 2:13; Rom. 15:16.

In sanctification by the Word, John 17:17, 19.

That the Spirit leads us to the Truth, John 16:13, and the Truth makes us free, John 8:31, 32; 6:44, 45.

In the Baptism of the Holy Spirit as rest for the soul, Acts 2:4; Heb. 4:1; Is. 28:12, and endowment of power for service, Acts 1:8.

In keeping the Sabbath as rest for the body, Ex. 20:8-11, Heb. 4:1, 4, 10.

In the millennium as rest for both soul and body.

In the healing of all sickness and disease, Is. 53:5; I Pet. 2:24; Mark 16:18; James 5:14.

That each of the Ten Commandments are equal, and that no one commandment is subordinate of the other, James 2:10; Rom. 7:6.

That Christ has a church which represents His Body, and to have fellowship in said church we must endeavour to keep the unity of the Spirit in the bond of peace, Eph. 4:3.

That we should and will have this unity by obeying God's order of lifting our voices together, and singing together, Is. 52:8, and that we will see eye to eye when He (Christ) brings again Zion, and . . .

That His second coming is personal, imminent, and is the blessed hope of the church, I Thess. 4:16-17.

We believe that Christ is the only one who can help everyone. We preach the whole gospel for the whole man. I Thess. 5:23.

Notes: *As the name implies, this organization is sabbatarian in practice.*

81

THE FUNDAMENTAŁ DOCTRINE OF THE CHURCH (CHURCH OF GOD BY FAITH)

I.   We believe in supporting and observing civil laws that are supported by and in harmony with righteous principles. Rom. 13:1-4.

II. We do not believe in becoming actively involved in armed combat in any capacity. We absolutely do not believe in anyway that the destruction of life is in accord with God's law.

III. We do not believe that a Christian should swear or falsify any statement of any kind, regardless to the situation or condition.

IV. We believe in a total self-committal to one God, who is the sovereign ruler of the universe.

V.   We believe in and support the idea of peace for all men; for God has made all men equal, regardless of race, creed, or color.

VI. We believe in obedience to God as supreme. We believe and support the fact that God is, and should be, recognized as the sovereign ruler of all things.

VII. We believe in obeying God.

We believe that God created the heaven and the earth. Gen. 1:1.

We believe that "God created man." Gen. 1:26-27; Gen. 2:7; Isa. 42:5-6.

Christ has forewarned His people to "fear God." St. Matt. 10:28: Eccl. 12:1; 12-13.

"For I am the Lord and I change not." Mal. 3:6.

Notes: *The Church of God by Faith's brief statement reveals the church to be a holiness-pentecostal body, which is pacifist in practice and believes in racial equality.*

*   *   *

STATEMENT OF FAITH (COMMUNITY CHAPEL AND BIBLE TRAINING CENTER)

We believe in the absolute inspiration of the Bible and hold it to be the inerrant and final authority in all matters of Christian faith and practice (2 Tim. 3:16; Mtt. 5:17-19).

We believe in God the Father, almighty and eternal, Creator of the heavens and the earth and all that dwell therein, contrary to all evolutionary theory (1 Cor. 8:6; 2 Cor. 6:18; 1 Tim. 1:17; Gen. 1:1ff).

We believe in the Lord Jesus Christ, the Son of God, fully God and fully man, who was born of the virgin Mary, suffered and died for our sins on the cross, was buried, rose bodily from the dead on the third day, appeared unto men, ascended into heaven in the sight of many witnesses, and who is coming again with power and great glory (1 Cor. 8:6; Mtt. 16:16; John 20:28; 1 Tim. 2:5; Mtt. 1:23; 1 Cor. 15:3-7; Acts 1:9-11; Mtt. 24:30).

We believe in the Holy Spirit, the Comforter, who inspired the holy apostles and prophets of old; who indwells believers with His presence today as He did in the early church, giving them the ability to speak in languages they have never learned; and who convicts the world concerning sin, righteousness, and judgment (John 14:26; 2 Pe. 1:21; Acts 2:4; John 16:8).

We believe that no one can be saved from sin and judgment and have eternal life without repenting of his sins and personally accepting Jesus Christ as his Lord and Savior, receiving forgiveness through the shed blood of Jesus, the sinless Lamb of God. All who have been born again according to John 3:3-8, we accept as members of the body of Christ, sharing fellowship with them based on our common salvation, not on doctrine, as important as it is (Rom. 6:23; 10:9,10; Luke 13:3; John 1:12; Eph. 1:7; 1 Pe. 1:19; 1 Cor. 12:12; 1 Jn. 1:3).

We believe that water baptism is for the remission of sins (Acts 2:38; 22:16) and should be administered to believers by immersion in keeping with the commission of Jesus in Matthew 28:19 and apostolic practice (Acts 2:38; 19:5).

We believe in participating in the New Covenant communion of the Lord's body, partaking of the emblems which typify the body and blood of Jesus Christ, remembering His death until He comes again. We examine ourselves, confessing our faults and sins, always discerning those in the Lord's body—both locally and universally (1 Cor. 10:16,17; 11:23-33).

We believe that Christians must live in obedience to God's Word, and that those who remain in the faith unto the end shall be saved (2 Tim. 2:19; Luke 8:13; 1 Cor. 15:2; Heb. 3:14; Mtt. 24:13).

We believe that God is a God of order who has established a specific structure of authority within both the church and the family. He has established offices in the church (pastors, elders, and deacons) through which the affairs of the local assembly are to be governed. Members of the assembly are enjoined to obey those who have the rule over them in spiritual matters. God has also ordained that children are to obey their parents, wives are to submit to their husbands, and citizens are to obey their civil governmental authorities. In all the aforementioned cases of submission, exception must be made if obedience would cause one to violate his conscience before God (Rom. 13:1-7; 1 Cor. 12:28; Eph. 4:11-13; 1 Tim. 3:1-13; Heb. 13:17; Eph. 6:1; 5:22; 1 Pe. 2:13, 14; Acts 4:19).

We believe that all New Testament believers should purpose in their hearts to financially support the ministry of their church with at least as much liberality as the tithe and offering which was required to be given to the Lord under the Old Covenant (Lev. 27:30-32; Mal. 3:10; 2 Cor. 9:6,7).

We believe that bodily healing continues to be available to believers today, having been provided by the atonement of Christ on the cross and promised to all who will put their trust in Him (Mark 16:18; Jas. 5:14, 15; 1 Pe. 2:24).

We believe in the exercise of the gifts and ministries of the Holy Spirit within the church body, as described in Romans 12:3-8 and in 1 Corinthians 12 through 14.

We believe that Christians are to endeavor to keep the unity of the Spirit in the bond of peace, so that God may bring the willing and obedient, who truly love Him, unto the unity of the faith before Jesus Christ returns (Eph. 4:1-6, 13-16).

We believe in the out-translation of the bride of Christ, followed by the great tribulation in which the antichrist shall rule over the earth through a world government, world church, and false prophet. Those Christians who fail to make the bride of Christ will, if they are faithful, be martyred in the great tribulation and come into the great wedding feast as guests of the Groom. God will pour out plagues on the earth; the devil will gather all nations against Jerusalem to battle; Christ will return to rule over the earth in the Millennium; all shall stand before God at the great judgment (1 Th. 4:17; Luke 21:27, 28, 36; Rev. 7:14; 2 Th. 2:1-8; Rev. 13:1-18; 17:1-18; 8:7-9:19; 11:15,19; 16:12-14,16; Zec. 14:2-5,9; Rev. 1:7; 20:11-15).

We believe in everlasting life for the believer and everlasting judgment for the unbeliever (John 3:16; Mtt. 25:46; Rev. 20:11-15).

Notes: *This statement strongly affirms the authority of the Bible, adult baptism by immersion, a structure of church authority and government, tithing, divine healing, the gifts of the Spirit, and a pre-millennial eschatology. Though the statement asserts a belief in God the Father; Jesus Christ as the Son of God; and the Holy Spirit, there is no affirmation of the Trinity.*

* * *

DOCTRINE (FULL GOSPEL MINISTER ASSOCIATION)

1. The Bible is the inspired Word of God, and is infallible as to any and all other writings, messages, or man's teachings, II Pet. 1:19-21, and II Tim. 3:16-17.

2. God. There are three persons united and equal in attributes, in the one true and living God, Father, Son and Holy Ghost, I Tim. 2:5, II Cor. 13:14, John 14:26.

3. Man and his fall. Man is a created being, made in the likeness and image of God, Gen. 1:27. Through Adam's disobedience, Gen. 3:1-7 man fell and sin has come into the world, Rom. 5:12, so under the curse of Adam, all men have sinned and have come short of the Glory of God, Rom. 3:23, and Rom. 3:10 none righteous.

4. Man's Redemption is in Jesus Christ, who was God manifested in the flesh, to undo the work of the devil, and He gave His life, shed His Blood, to redeem man back to God, I John 3:8.

5. Born-again is essential to all men in order to enter the Kingdom of God, John 3:3-5.

6. Holy Living is required of man, a life separated from the world, I John 2:15-16.

7. Heaven, the eternal abode of the righteous, I Thess. 1:7-10, Rev. 19:11-16.

8. Hell, the abode of the unrighteous until the day of judgment, Rev. 20:13, and shall be cast into the Lake of Fire together with the unrighteous, Rev. 20:14-15.

9. Ministry, a two-fold purpose is provided and ordained of God in the Bible. The evangelism of the world, and the edifying of the body of Christ, which is the Church, Mark 16:15-20, Eph. 4:11-13, with the confirming of the Word, with signs following and evidence of the power of God, Matt. 11:5.

10. Conscientious Statement, We believe that civil Government is ordained of God, Rom. 3:1-2, and we are thankful for this Government under which we live, for freedom of Worship in spirit and in truth, and that the Bible teaches that man shall not wilfully kill, Exodus 20:13, Romans 13:9, Matt. 5:21. But in time of war or other crisis, we will serve our Government in any capacity consistent with non-combative services.

Notes: *The association has a pacifist orientation.*

* * *

DOCTRINAL STATEMENT (INTERNATIONAL EVANGELISM CRUSADES)

We accept the entire Bible as Truth. There is but ONE GOD, maker and Creater of all things. Jesus Christ as the Son of God who was one with the Father before the foundations of the World. There is personal Salvation through faith in the Son of God, Jesus Christ. There is Divine Healing through Faith in the Bible and in Jesus Christ. The Baptism of the Holy Ghost is for believers (Acts 2:4). There are 9 gifts of the Spirit. The hope of all Christians is the personal return of Jesus Christ. Worldwide Evangelism, Christian Education and Study of the Word, Christian literature and publications, radio and TV, shall be instituted to spread the Truth of the Living God, to fulfill the great God-given Commission (Mark 16:9-20).

Notes: *Designed as a fellowship across traditional denominational lines, the International Evangelism Crusades has a very minimal statement, which allows room for almost the entire doctrinal spectrum within pentecostalism.*

* * *

STATEMENT OF THE BASIC DOCTRINE (JESUS PEOPLE CHURCH)

We believe . . .

The Bible is the inspired and only infallible and authoritative Word of God.

There is one God; God the Father, God the Son, and God the Holy Spirit.

In the Diety of our Lord Jesus Christ, in His virgin birth, in His sinless life, in His miracles, in His atoning death, in His bodily resurrection, in His ascension to the right hand of the Father, and His personal future return to this earth in power and glory to rule for 1,000 years.

In the Blessed Hope, the rapture of the Church, when we shall meet Him in the air.

The only means of being cleansed from sin is through repentance and faith in the blood of Jesus.

Regeneration by the Holy Spirit is essential for personal salvation.

The redemptive work of Jesus Christ on the cross provides healing of the human body in answer to believing prayer.

The baptism of the Holy Spirit, according to Acts 2:4, is given to believers who ask for it.

In the sanctifying power of the Holy Spirit by whose indwelling the Christian is enabled to live a holy life.

In the resurrection of both the saved and the lost, the one to everlasting life, and the other to everlasting damnation.

Notes: *The doctrine of the Jesus People Church is close to the essential position of the Assemblies of God and includes an affirmation of a premillennial eschatology.*

*   *   *

THESE THINGS WE BELIEVE (LIBERTY FELLOWSHIP)

INSPIRATION OF THE SCRIPTURES

We believe in the verbal inspiration of the Bible, both the Old and New Testaments (II Timothy 3:16; Hebrews 4:12; I Peter 1:23-25; II Peter 1:19-21).

GOD

We believe in one God revealed in three Persons: The Father, the Son, and the Holy Ghost (Matthew 3:16,17;28:29; John 17).

MAN

We believe that man, in his natural state, is a sinner, lost, undone, without hope, and without God (Romans 3:19-23; Galatians 3:22; Ephesians 2:1,2,12).

DIVINITY AND HUMANITY OF CHRIST JESUS

We believe that Jesus is God come in the flesh and that He is both divine and human (Luke 1:26-38; John 14:1-3; Acts 2:36; 3:14,15; Philippians 2:5-12; Hebrews 2:9-18).

BLOOD ATONEMENT

We believe in the saving power of the Blood of Jesus and His *imputed righteousness* (Acts 4:12; Romans 4:1-9; 5:1-11; Ephesians 1:3-15).

BODILY RESURRECTION

We believe in the bodily resurrection of Jesus Christ (Luke 24:39-43; John 20:24-29).

ASCENSION

We believe that Christ Jesus ascended to the Father and is presently engaged in building Heaven and interceding for the saints (John 14:1-6; Romans 8:34).

SECOND COMING

We believe in the visible, bodily return of Christ Jesus to this earth to rapture His Church (Bride) and judge the world (Acts 1:10,11; I Thessalonians 4:13-18; II Thessalonians 1:7-10; James 5:8; Revelation 1:7). (It is not necessary that we all believe alike concerning whether He is coming before, during, or after the Great Tribulation.)

SALVATION

We believe that the terms of salvation are repentance toward God for sin, and a personal, heartfelt faith in the Lord Jesus Christ, which results in regeneration of the person. This salvation is entirely by grace of our Lord and not of works. Works are excluded except as FRUIT of salvation (Acts 3:19,20; Romans 4:1-5; 5:1; Ephesians 2:8-10).

LOCAL CHURCH

We believe the Church of the Lord Jesus Christ is a Body of believers who have been baptized in the Name of the Father, Son, and Holy Ghost; who are under recognized, delegated authorities; and who assemble to worship, carry forth the Great Commission, and minister as the Holy Ghost leads (Matthew 16:18; 28:19,20; Acts 2:40-47; 20:28; Ephesians 5:22-32; I Timothy 3:15).

ORDINANCES

We believe that the two ordinances of the Church are Water Baptism and the Lord's Supper.

WATER BAPTISM: Immersion in water in the Name of the Father, Son, and Holy Ghost (Matthew 3:15,16; 28:19,20; Acts 8:38; Romans 6:1-4). A symbol of identification with Jesus Christ in His death, burial, and resurrection.

LORD'S SUPPER: A memorial of the death, resurrection, and Second Coming of our Lord Jesus Christ (Luke 22:13-20).

SEPARATED LIFE

We believe that believers should seek, as the early disciples did, to practice the separated life from the world and unto Christ and to set standards of conduct which shall exalt our Lord and His Church (Romans 12:1-3; II Corinthians 6:17; Galatians 6:14; Ephesians 5:11; Colossians 3:17).

HEAVEN AND HELL

We believe the Scriptures clearly set forth the doctrines of eternal punishment for the lost and eternal bliss and service for the saved—Hell for the unsaved and Heaven for the saved (Matthew 25:34, 41, 46; Luke 16:19-31; John 14:1-3; Revelation 20:11-15).

HOLY SPIRIT

We believe the Holy Spirit to be the third Person of the Trinity whose purpose in the redemption of man is to convict men of sin, regenerate the repentant believer, guide the believer into ALL truth, indwell and give gifts to believers as He wills, that they may minister as Christ would to men. We believe that the manifestations of the Holy Spirit recorded in I Corinthians 12:8-11 shall operate in present-day churches which yield to the Lord Jesus Christ (Luke 11:13; John 7:37-39; 14:16,17; 16:7-14: Acts 2:39-48). We believe that the Baptism in the Holy Spirit, with the evidence of speaking with other tongues as the Spirit gives utterance, is for all believers as promised by John the Baptist (Matthew 3:11) and Jesus (Acts 1:4,5, 8) and Peter (Acts 2:38-41), was witnessed by the early disciples of Christ (Acts 2:4; 10:44-47; 19:1-6), and is evidenced by many present-day disciples of the Lord Jesus Christ.

DIVINE HEALING

We believe that God has used doctors, medicines, and other material means for healing; but divine healing was also provided for in the Atonement (Isaiah 53:5) and may be appropriated by laying on of hands by elders (James 5:14-16), laying on of hands by the believers (Mark 16:18), by the prayer of an anointed person gifted for healing the sick (I Corinthians 12:9), or by a direct act of receiving this provision by faith (Mark 11:23).

PRIESTHOOD OF BELIEVERS

We believe that each believer is a priest of the Lord (Revelation 1:6) and has direct access to the Father through the Lord Jesus Christ. Each person must believe for himself, be baptized for himself, obey for himself, and answer to his Creator for himself.

GOVERNMENT OF THE CHURCH

We believe that the New Testament Church should be apostolic in nature and is governed by delegated authorities. These authorities at Liberty Church are set forth in Article VI of the Liberty Church Charter. When it is deemed best for the life of the church and testimony of the Lord, these authorities may discipline, in the spirit of love, any member who departs from the doctrines set forth in the articles of the Liberty Church Charter or whose conduct is contrary to the spirit and practice of this body.

ORDAINED OFFICERS

The ordained officers of the Church are apostle, prophet, evangelist, pastor, teacher, local (counseling) elders and deacons (Ephesians 4:11; I Timothy 3; Titus 1:5-9). Apostles, prophets, evangelists, pastors, and teachers shall not necessarily all function in one local church. However, it is believed that all of these officers shall function under the covering of a local church and all local (counseling) elders are under the supervision of the five-fold ministry listed in Ephesians 4:11 (Acts 15; I Timothy 5:17-21; Titus 1:5-9).

(All churches in Liberty Fellowship of Churches and Ministers must adopt the same Articles of Faith, but each church sets its own by-laws for local church membership.)

In conclusion, though we believe that the doctrines of the Bible were written by God's men and that they are verbally inspired, it is entirely possible for a person to believe a doctrine and never experience the life set forth in the doctrine. For example, one could believe the new birth without experiencing it; he could believe the Baptism in the Holy Spirit and never experience it; he could give mental assent about the work of the Lord Jesus and never personally know Him. Jesus is not a doctrine—He is a Person. He is not a plan of salvation—He is the Man of salvation. Therefore, it is our desire that those reading these doctrines not only mentally agree with them, but have a witness within themselves that these doctrines are true.

We do not judge those who do not believe as we do, and we have no desire to debate doctrines. It is our commission to proclaim the gospel, not to defend it.

Notes: *The Liberty Fellowship shares the basic Pentecostal affirmations. Its unique feature is the attention given to a hierarchy of authority in the hands of apostles and other church leaders.*

STATEMENT OF FAITH (MARANATHA CHRISTIAN CHURCHES)

We Believe . . .

The Bible to be the inspired, the only infallible, authoritative Word of God.

We believe . . .

There is one eternal, almighty and perfect God; Father, Son and Holy Spirit.

We believe . . .

In the deity of our Lord Jesus Christ, in His virgin birth, in His sinless life, in His miracles, in His vicarious and atoning death through His shed blood, in His bodily resurrection, in His ascension to the right hand of the Father, and in His personal return in power and glory.

We believe . . .

That for the salvation of lost and sinful man regeneration by the Holy Spirit is absolutely essential.

We believe . . .

In the present ministry of the Holy Spirit by whose indwelling the Christian is enabled to live a godly life.

We believe . . .

In the resurrection of both the saved and the lost; they that are saved unto the resurrection of life and they that are lost unto the resurrection of damnation.

We believe . . .

In the spiritual unity of believers in our Lord Jesus Christ.

Notes: *This minimal statement mentions the more controversial aspect of Maranatha's belief and practice (the present ministry of the Holy Spirit) only in the most abstract manner.*

*　　*　　*

STATEMENT OF FAITH (UNITED EVANGELICAL CHURCHES)

ONE IN FAITH

Spiritual unity within U. E. C. rests upon a solid biblical statement of faith.

1. We believe the Bible to be the inspired, infallible, ultimately authoritative Word of God.

2. We believe that there is one God, eternally existent in three Personalities, Father, Son and Holy Spirit.

3. We believe that the Lord Jesus Christ is The Deity, that He was born of a virgin, that He lived a sinless life, performed miracles, that we are redeemed by His atoning death through His shed blood, that He bodily resurrected and ascended to the right hand of the Father, that He will personally return in power and glory.

4. We believe in the total depravity of man.

5. We believe that men are saved through a personal encounter with the Lord Jesus Christ and regeneration by the Holy Spirit.

STATEMENT OF FAITH (UNITED EVANGELICAL CHURCHES) (continued)

6. We believe in the present ministry of the Holy Spirit by Whose indwelling the Christian is enabled to live a victorious life, and the Spirit unites all believers in our Lord Jesus Christ.

7. We believe that every man shall stand before God to give an account of his stewardship of his earthly life.

WE BELIEVE in God the Father, Almighty Creator of the heavens and the earth, and ruler of us all.

WE BELIEVE in Jesus Christ the only begotten Son of God; conceived by the Holy Ghost and born of the virgin Mary, who lived upon this earth and suffered stripes unto Pontius Pilate for our healing.

WE BELIEVE Jesus was crucified, dead and buried; rose again the third day from the dead, ascended unto the heavens and is now sitting on the right hand of God the Father Almighty.

WE BELIEVE that this same Jesus will return to this earth to reign as King of Kings and Lord of Lords.

WE BELIEVE in the Holy Spirit that was given at Pentecost as promised by the Lord Jesus Christ as evidence by miracles, signs and wonders.

WE BELIEVE on the Holy Word of God that gives the highest hope for this world and world to come.

WE BELIEVE the Bible is the inspired Word of God.

WE BELIEVE in the hereafter for all people.

WE BELIEVE in the ultimate triumph of righteousness, resurrection from the dead and life everlasting for the faithful.

WE BELIEVE in being born again by God's Spirit and regeneration into a new life.

WE BELIEVE in forgiveness of sins, sanctification, and baptism of the Holy Spirit. We stand against that which is evil in the sight of God. We stand against drunkeness, brawling, and riotous living.

WE BELIEVE the basic plan of God for man toward others is the golden rule: "Therefore all things whatsoever ye would that men should do to you, do even so to them, for this is the law and the prophets." Matt. 7:12

WE BELIEVE and adhere to the Ten Commandments as given to Moses.

WE BELIEVE in God Eternal, Infinite and unchangeable.

WE BELIEVE both the Old and New Testament to be the Word of God.

WE BELIEVE that the eternal purpose of God is in all things to them that love Him.

WE BELIEVE that God created the Heavens and the earth by his own will.

WE BELIEVE sin violates God's laws whether it be omission or commission and those that break God's law shall be out of favor with Him.

WE BELIEVE that salvation is for all that believe on the name of Jesus.

WE BELIEVE in election, ordination and predestination to God's Word.

WE BELIEVE that the Lord Jesus Christ is the Only redeemer able to forgive sin.

WE BELIEVE in the Holy Ghost and its abode in the hearts of the redeemed.

WE BELIEVE in the justification as given by faith; as received by one upon accepting Christ Jesus as his personal saviour.

WE BELIEVE in all spiritual life imparted by the Holy Ghost, thus helping one to live Christ-like.

WE ACKNOWLEDGE the Church to be the Bride of Christ all born again and baptized believers.

WE BELIEVE in the sacraments; baptism, feet washing and the Lord's Supper.

WE BELIEVE in two states of future existence; heaven the final home of the redeemed; and hell, the final abode of the sinful.

WE BELIEVE that the Lord adds to the church daily such as should be saved.

Notes: *This organization is unique in pentecostalism for its affirmation of belief in total depravity and predestination. The statement is in two parts, a formal statement of faith and a number of additional affirmations.*

Chapter 2

European Free-Church Family

SCHLEITHEIM CONFESSION (1527)

BROTHERLY UNION OF A NUMBER OF CHILDREN OF GOD CONCERNING SEVEN ARTICLES

May joy, peace and mercy from our Father through the atonement of the blood of Christ Jesus, together with the gifts of the Spirit—Who is sent from the Father to all believers for their strength and comfort and for their perseverance in all tribulation until the end, Amen—be to all those who love God, who are the children of light, and who are scattered everywhere as it has been ordained of God our Father, where they are with one mind assembled together in one God and Father of us all: Grace and peace of heart be with you all, Amen.

Beloved brethren and sisters in the Lord: First and supremely we are always concerned for your consolation and the assurance of your conscience (which was previously misled) so that you may not always remain foreigners to us and by right almost completely excluded, but that you may turn again to the true implanted members of Christ, who have been armed through patience and knowledge of themselves, and have therefore again been united with us in the strength of a godly Christian spirit and zeal for God.

It is also apparent with what cunning the devil has turned us aside, so that he might destroy and bring to an end the work of God which in mercy and grace has been partly begun in us. But Christ, the true Shepherd of our souls, Who has begun this in us, will certainly direct the same and teach [us] to His honor and our salvation, Amen.

Dear brethren and sisters, we who have been assembled in the Lord at Schleitheim on the Border, make known in points and articles to all who love God that as concerns us we are of one mind to abide in the Lord as God's obedient children, [His] sons and daughters, we who have been and shall be separated from the world in everything, [and] completely at peace. To God alone be praise and glory without the contradiction of any brethren. In this we have perceived the oneness of the Spirit of our Father and of our common Christ with us. For the Lord is the Lord of peace and not of quarreling, as Paul points out. That you may

understand in what article this has been formulated you should observe and note [the following].

A very great offense has been introduced by certain false brethren among us, so that some have turned aside from the faith, in the way they intend to practice and observe the freedom of the Spirit and of Christ. But such have missed the truth, and to their condemnation are given over to the lasciviousness and self-indulgence of the flesh. They think faith and love may do and permit everything, and nothing will harm them nor condemn them, since they are believers.

Observe, you who are God's members in Christ Jesus, that faith in the Heavenly Father through Jesus Christ does not take such form. It does not produce and result in such things as these false brethren and sisters do and teach. Guard yourselves and be warned of such people, for they do not serve our Father, but their father, the devil.

But you are not that way. For they that are Christ's have crucified the flesh with its passions and lusts. You understand me well and [know] the brethren whom we mean. Separate yourselves from them for they are perverted. Petition the Lord that they may have the knowledge which leads to repentance, and [pray] for us that we may have constancy to persevere in the way which we have espoused, for the honor of God and of Christ, His Son, Amen.

The articles which we discussed and on which we were of one mind are these 1. Baptism; 2. The Ban [excommunication]; 3. Breaking of Bread; 4. Separation from the Abomination; 5. Pastors in the Church; 6. The Sword; and 7. The Oath.

First. Observe concerning baptism: Baptism shall be given to all those who have learned repentance and amendment of life, and who believe truly that their sins are taken away by Christ, and to all those who walk in the resurrection of Jesus Christ, and wish to be buried with Him in death, so that they may be resurrected with him, and to all those who with this significance request it [baptism] of us and demand it for themselves. This excludes all infant baptism, the highest and chief abominations of the pope. In this you have the foundation and testimony of the apostles. Mt. 28,

SCHLEITHEIM CONFESSION (1527) (continued)

Mk. 16, Acts 2, 8, 16, 19. This we wish to hold simply, yet firmly and with assurance.

Second. We agree as follows on the ban: The ban shall be employed with all those who have given themselves to the Lord, to walk in His commandments, and with all those who have been baptized into the one body of Christ and who are called brethren and sisters, and yet who slip sometimes and fall into error and sin, being inadvertently overtaken. The same shall be admonished twice in secret and the third time openly disciplined or banned according to the command of Christ. Mt. 18. But this shall be done according to the regulation of the Spirit (Mt. 5) before the breaking of bread, so that we may break and eat one bread, with one mind and in one love, and may drink of one cup.

Third. In the breaking of bread we are of one mind and are agreed [as follows]: All those who wish to break one bread in remembrance of the broken body of Christ, and all who wish to drink of one drink as a remembrance of the shed blood of Christ, shall be united beforehand by baptism in one body of Christ which is the church of God and whose Head is Christ. For as Paul points out we cannot at the same time be partakers of the Lord's table and the table of devils; we cannot at the same time drink the cup of the Lord and the cup of the devil. That is, all those who have fellowship with the dead works of darkness have no part in the light. Therefore all who follow the devil and the world have no part with those who are called unto God out of the world. All who lie in the evil have no part in the good.

Therefore it is and must be [thus]: Whoever has not been called by one God to one faith, to one baptism, to one Spirit, to one body, with all the children of God's church, cannot be made [into] one bread with them, as indeed must be done if one is truly to break bread according to the command of Christ.

Fourth. We agreed [as follows] on separation: A separation shall be made from the evil and from the wickedness which the devil planted in the world; in this manner, simply that we shall not have fellowship with them [the wicked] and not run with them in the multitude of their abominations. This is the way it is: Since all who do not walk in the obedience of faith, and have not united themselves with God so that they wish to do His will, are a great abomination before God, it is not possible for anything to grow or issue from them except abominable things. For truly all creatures are in but two classes, good and bad, believing and unbelieving, darkness and light, the world and those who [have come] out of the world, God's temple and idols, Christ and Belial; and none can have part with the other.

To us then the command of the Lord is clear when He calls upon us to be separate from the evil and thus He will be our God and we shall be His sons and daughters.

He further admonishes us to withdraw from Babylon and the earthly Egypt that we may not be partakers of the pain and suffering which the Lord will bring upon them.

From all this we should learn that everything which is not united with our God and Christ cannot be other than an abomination which we should shun and flee from. By this is meant all popish and antipopish works and church services, meetings and church attendance, drinking houses, civic affairs, the commitments [made in] unbelief and other things of that kind, which are highly regarded by the world and yet are carried on in flat contradiction to the command of God, in accordance with all the unrighteousness which is in the world. From all these things we shall be separated and have no part with them for they are nothing but an abomination, and they are the cause of our being hated before our Christ Jesus, Who has set us free from the slavery of th flesh and fitted us for the service of God throught the Spirit Whom He has given us.

Therefore there will also unquestionably fall from us the unchristian, devilish weapons of force—such as sword, armor and the like, and all their use [either] for friends or against one's enemies—by virtue of the word of Christ, Resist not [him that is] evil.

Fifth. We are agreed as follows on pastors in the church of God: The pastor in the church of God shall, as Paul has prescribed, be one who out-and-out has a good report of thsoe who are outside the faith. This office shall be to read, to admonish and teach, to warn, to discipline, to ban in the church, to lead out in prayer for the advancement of all the brethren and sister, to lift up the bread when it is to be broken, and in all things to see to the care of the body of Christ, in order that it may be built up and developed, and the mouth of the slanderer be stopped.

This one moreover shall be supported of the church which has chosen him, wherein he may be in need, so that he who serves the Gospel may live of the Gospel as the Lord has ordained. But if a pastor should do something requiring discipline, he shall not be dealt with except [on the testimony of] two or three witnesses. And when they sin they shall be disciplined before all in order that the others may fear.

But should it happen that through the cross this pastor should be banished or led to the Lord [through martyrdom] another shall be ordained in his place in the same hour so that God's little flock and people may not be destroyed.

Sixth. We are agreed as follows concerning the sword: The sword is ordained of God outside the perfection of Christ. It punishes and puts to death the wicked, and guards and protects the good. In the Law the sword was ordained for the punishment of the wicked and for their death, and the same [word] is [now] ordained to be used by the wordly magistrates.

In the perfection of Christ, however, only the ban is used for a warning and for the excommunication of the one who has sinned, without putting the flesh to death,—simply the warning and the command to sin no more.

Now it will be asked by many who do not recognize [this as] the will of Christ for us, whether a Christian may or should employ the sword against the wicked for the defense and protection of the good, or for the sake of love.

Our reply is unanimously as follows: Christ teaches and commands us to learn of Him, for He is meek and lowly in heart and so shall we find rest to our souls. Also Christ says to the heathenish woman who was taken in adultery, not that one should stone her according to the law of His Father (and yet He say, As the Father has commanded me, thus I do), but in mercy and forgiveness and warning, to sin no more, Such [an attitude] we also ought to take completely according to the rule of the ban.

Secondly, it will be asked concerning the sword, whether a Chrisian shall pass sentence in worldly dispute and strife such as unbelievers have with one another. This is our united answer: Christ did not wish to decide or pass judgment between brother and brother in the case of the inheritance, but refused to do so. Therefore we should do likewise.

Thirdly, it will be asked concerning the sword, Shall one be a magistrate if one should be chosen as such? The answer is as follows: They wished to make Christ king, but He fled and did not view it as the arrangement of His Father. Thus shall we do as He did, and follow Him, and so shall we not walk in darkness. For He Himself says, He who wishes to come after me, let him deny himself and take up his cross and follow me. Also, He Himself forbids [the employment of] the force of the sword saying, The worldly princes lord it over them, etc., but not so shall it be with you. Further, Paul says, Whom God did foreknow He also did predestinate to be conformed to the image of His son, etc. Also Peter says, Christ has suffered (not ruled) and left us an example, that ye should follow His steps.

Finally, it will be observed that it is not appropriate for a Christian to serve as a magistrate because of these points: The government magistracy is according to the flesh, but the Christians' is according to the Spirit; their houses and dwelling remain in this world, but the Christians' citizenship is in heaven; the weapons of their conflict and war are carnal and against the flesh only, but the Christians' weapons are spiritual, against the fornication of the devil. The worldlings are armed with steel and iron, but the Christians are armed with the armor of God, with truth, righteousness, peace, faith, salvation and the Word of God. In brief, as is the mind of Christ toward us, so shall the mind of the members of the body of Christ be through Him in all things, that there may be no schism in the body through which it would be destroyed. For every kingdom divided against itself will be destroyed. Now since Christ is as it is written of Him, His members must also be the same, that His body may remain complete and united to its own advancement and upbuilding.

Seventh. We are agreed as follows concerning the oath: The oath is a confirmation among those who are quarreling or making promises. In the Law it is commanded to be performed in God's Name, but only in truth, not falsely. Christ, who teaches the perfection of the Law, prohibits all swearing to His [followers], whether true or false,—neither by heaven, nor by the earth, nor by Jerusalem, nor by our head,—and that for the reason which He shortly thereafter gives, For you are not able to make one hair white or black. So you see it is for this reason that all swearing is forbidden: we cannot fulfill that which we promise when we swear, for we cannot change [even] the very least thing on us.

Now there are some who do not give credence to the simple command of God, but object with this question: Well now, did not God swear to Abraham by Himself (since He was God) when He promised him that He would be with him and that He would be his God if he would keep His commandments,—why then should I not also swear when I promise to someone? Answer: Hear what the Scripture says: God, since He wished more abundantly to show unto the heirs the immutability of His counsel, inserted an oath, that by two immutable things (in which it is impossible for God to lie) we might have a strong consolation. Observe the meaning of this Scripture: What God forbids you to do, He has power to do, for everything is possible for Him. God swore an oath to Abraham, says the Scripture, so that He might show that His counsel is immutable. That is, no one can withstand nor thwart His will; therefore He can keep His oath. But we can do nothing, as is said above by Christ, to keep or perform [our oaths]: therefore we shall not swear at all [nichts schweren].

Then others further say as follows: It is not forbidden of God to swear in the New Testament, when it is actually commanded in the Old, but it is forbidden to swear by heaven, earth, Jerusalem and our head. Answer: Hear the Scripture, He who swears by heaven swears by God's throne and by Him who sitteth thereon. Observe: It is forbidden to swear by heaven, which is only the throne of God: how much more is it forbidden [to swear] by God Himself! Ye fools and blind, which is greater, the throne or Him that sitteth thereon?

Further some say, Because evil is now [in the world, and] because man needs God for [the establishment of] the truth, so did the apostles Peter and Paul also swear. Answer: Peter and Paul only testify of that which God promised to Abraham with the oath. They themselves promise nothing, as the example indicates clearly. Testifying and swearing are two different things. For when a person swears he is in the first place promising future things, as Christ was promised to Abraham Whom we a long time afterwards received. But when a person bears testimony he is testifying about the present, whether it is good or evil, as Simeon spoke to Mary about Christ and testified, Behold this (child) is set for the fall and rising of man in Israel, and for a sign which shall be spoken against.

Christ also taught us along the same line when He said, Let your communication be Yea, yea; Nay, nay; for whatsoever is more than these cometh of evil. He says, Your speech or word shall be yea and nay. (However) when one does not wish to understand, he remains closed to the meaning. Christ is simply Yea and Nay, and all those who seek Him simply will understand His word. Amen.

Dear brethren and sisters in the Lord: These are the articles of certain brethren who had heretofore been in error and who had failed to agree in the true understanding, so that many weaker consciences were perplexed, causing the Name of God to be greatly slandered. Therefore there has been a great need for us to become of one mind in the Lord, which has come to pass. To God be praise and glory!

SCHLEITHEIM CONFESSION (1527) (continued)

Now since you have so well understood the will of God which has been made known by us, it will be necessary for you to achieve perseveringly, without interruption, the known will of God. For you know well what the servant who sinned knowingly heard as his recompense.

Everything which you have unwittingly done and confessed as evil doing is forgiven you through the believing prayer which is offered by us in our meeting for all our shortcomings and guilt. [This state is yours] through the gracious forgiveness of God and through the blood of Jesus Christ. Amen.

Keep watch on all who do not walk according to the simplicity of the divine truth which is stated in this letter from [the decisions of] our meeting, so that everyone among us will be governed by the rule of the ban and henceforth the entry of false brethren and sisters among us may be prevented.

Eliminate from you that which is evil and the Lord will be your God and you will be His sons and daughters.

Dear brethren, keep in mind what Paul admonishes Timothy when he says, The grace of God that bringeth salvation hath appeared to all men, teaching us that, denying ungodliness and worldly lusts, we should live soberly, righteously, and godly, in this present world; looking for that blessed hope, and the glorious appearing of the great God and our Saviour Jesus Christ; Who gave Himself for us, that He might redeem us from all iniquity, and purify unto Himself a people of His own, zealous of good works. Think on this and exercise yourselves therein and the God of peace will be with you.

May the Name of God be hallowed eternally and highly praised, Amen. May the Lord give you His peace, Amen.

The Acts of Schleitheim on the Border [Canton Schaffhausen, Switzerland], on Matthias' [day], Anno MDXXVII.

Notes: *The European Free-Church tradition, especially as it has become manifest in the United States, finds its roots in the Swiss Brethren. The brethren took the Reformation in a much more radical direction than that envisioned by Luther in Germany, or John Calvin or Helmut Zwingli in Switzerland. In 1527, a number of the brethren gathered at Schleitheim to prepare a confession of their faith. Unfortunately, the document served to focus persecution against them, and eventually the movement was destroyed. It survived only through the Mennonite Church. The Schleitheim Confession is no longer used as an official document by any church (in North America), but its historic value as a pioneering statement of free-church faith has earned it a place of respect among free churchmen, and it provided a source for the major Mennonite confession. The text reproduced here is from the translation of J. C. Wenger which appeared in the* Mennonite Quarterly Review *XIX (1974) 247-53.*

German Mennonites/Amish

THE DORDRECHT CONFESSION (1632)

Ariticle I. OF GOD AND THE CREATION OF ALL THINGS

Whereas it is declared, that "without faith it is impossible to please God" (Heb. 11:6), and that "he that cometh to God must believe that He is, and that He is a rewarder of them that diligently seek Him," therefore we confess with the mouth and believe with the heart, together with all the pious, according to the Holy Scriptures, that there is one eternal, almighty, and incomprehensible God, Father, Son, and the Holy Ghost, and none more and none other, before whom no God existed, neither will exist after Him. For from Him, through Him, and in Him are all things. To Him be blessing, praise, and honor, for ever and ever. Gen. 17:1; Deut. 6:4; Isaiah 46:9; I John 5:7.

In this one God, who "worketh all in all," we believe. Him we confess as the Creator of all things, visible and invisible; who in six days created and prepared "heaven and earth, and the sea, and all things that are therein." And we further believe, that this God still governs and preserves the same, together with all His works, through His wisdom, His might, and the "word of His power." Gen. 5:1, 2; Acts 14:15; I Cor. 12:6; Heb. 1:3.

When He had finished His works and, according to His good pleasure, had ordained and prepared each of them, so that they were right and good according to their nature, being, and quality, He created the first man, Adam, the father of all of us, gave him a body formed "of the dust of the ground, and breathed into his nostrils the breath of life," so that he "became a living soul," created by God "in His own image and likeness," in "righteousness and true holiness" unto eternal life. He also gave him a place above all other creatures and endowed him with many high and excellent gifts, put him into the garden of Eden, and gave him a commandment and an interdiction. Thereupon He took a rib from the said Adam, made a woman out of it, brought her to him, and gave her to him as a helpmate and housewife. Consequently He has caused, that from this first man, Adam, all men who "dwell on the face of the earth," have been begotten and have descended. Gen. 1:27; 2:7, 15-17, 22; 5:1; Acts 17:26.

ARTICLE II. OF THE FALL OF MAN

We believe and confess, that, according to the purport of the Holy Scriptures, our first parents, Adam and Eve, did not long remain in the happy state in which they were created; but did, after being seduced by the deceit and subtilty of the serpent, and envy of the devil, violate the high command of God, and became disobedient to their Creator; through which disobedience "sin entered into the world, and death by sin;" so that "death passed upon all men, for that all have sinned," and thereby incurred the wrath of God and condemnation. For which reason our first parents were, by God, driven out of Paradise, to cultivate the earth, to maintain themselves thereon in sorrow, and to "eat their bread in the sweat of their face," until they "returned to the ground, from which they were taken." And that they did, therefore, through this one sin, so far apostatize, depart, and estrange themselves from God, that they could neither help themselves, nor be helped by any of their descendants, nor by angels, nor by any other creature in heaven or on earth, nor be redeemed, or reconciled to God; but would have had to be lost forever, had not God, who pitied His creatures, in mercy, interposed in their behalf and made provision for their restoration. Gen. 3:6, 23; Rom. 5:12-19; Ps. 47:8, 9; Rev. 5:3; John 3:16.

ARTICLE III. OF THE RESTORATION OF MAN THROUGH THE PROMISE OF THE COMING OF CHRIST

Regarding the Restoration of our first parents and their descendants, we believe and confess: That God, not withstanding their fall, transgression and sin, and although they had no power to help themselves, He was nevertheless not willing that they should be cast off entirely, or be eternally lost; but again called them unto Him, comforted them, and showed them that there were yet means with Him for their reconciliation; namely, the immaculate Lamb, the Son of God; who "was fore-ordained" to this purpose "before the foundation of the world," and who was promised to them and all their descendants, while they (our first parents) were yet in paradise, for their comfort, redemption, and salvation; yea, who was given to them thenceforward, through faith, as their own; after which all the pious patriarchs, to whom this promise was often renewed, longed and searched, beholding it through faith at a distance, and expecting its fulfillment—expecting that He (the Son of God), would, at His coming, again redeem and deliver the fallen race of man from their sins, their guilt, and unrighteousness. John 1:29; 11:27; I Pet. 1:18, 19; Gen. 3:15; I John 2:1, 2; 3:8; Gal. 4:4, 5.

ARTICLE IV. OF THE ADVENT OF CHRIST INTO THIS WORLD, AND THE REASON OF HIS COMING

We believe and confess further: That "when the fulness of the time was come," after which all the pious patriarchs so ardently longed, and which they so anxiously awaited—the previously promised Messiah, Redeemer, and Saviour, proceeded from God, being sent by Him, and according to the prediction of the prophets and the testimony of the evangelists, came into the world, yea, into the flesh—, so that the Word itself thus became flesh and man; and that He was conceived by the Virgin Mary (who was espoused to a man named Joseph, of the house of David), and that she bare Him as her first-born son at Bethlehem, "wrapped Him in swaddling clothes, and laid Him in a manger." John 4:25; 16:28; I Tim. 3:16; Matt. 1:21; John 1:14; Luke 2:7.

Further we believe and confess, that this is the same One, "whose goings forth have been from of old, from everlasting;" who has "neither beginning of days, nor end of life." Of whom it is testified, that He is "Alpha and Omega, the beginning and the end, the first and the last." That this is also He—and none other—who was chosen, promised, and sent; who came into the world; and who is God's only, first, and proper Son; who was before John the Baptist, before Abraham, before the world; yea, who was David's Lord, and who was God of the "whole earth," "the first-born of every creature;" who was sent into the world, and Himself delivered up the body prepared for Him, as "an offering and a sacrifice to God for a sweet smelling savour;" yea, for the comfort, redemption, and salvation of all—of the human race. Micah 5:2; Heb. 7:3; Rev. 1:8; John 3:16; Rom. 8:32; Col. 1:15; Heb. 10:5.

But how, or in what manner, this worthy body was prepared, or how the Word became flesh, and He Himself man, we content ourselves with the declaration which the worthy evangelists have given and left in their description thereof; according to which we confess with all the saints, that He is the Son of the living God, in whom exist all our hope, comfort, redemption, and salvation, and which we are to seek in no one else. Luke 1:31-35; John 20:31.

Further, we believe and confess by authority of scripture, that when He had ended His course, and "finished" the work for which He was sent into the world, He was, by the providence of God, delivered into the hands of the unrighteous; suffered under the judge, Pontius Pilate, was crucified, died, was buried, rose again from the dead on the third day, and ascended into heaven, where He now sits at the right hand of the Majesty of God on high; from whence He will come again to judge the living and dead. Luke 23:1, 52, 53; 24:5, 6, 51.

Thus we believe the Son of God died—"tasted death for every man," shed His precious blood, and thereby bruised the head of the serpent, destroyed the works of the devil, "blotted out the hand-writing," and purchased redemption for the whole human race; and thus He became the source of eternal salvation to all who from the time of Adam to the end of the world, shall have believed in Him, and obeyed Him. Gen. 3:15; I John 3:8; Col. 2:14; Rom. 5:18.

Article V. OF THE LAW OF CHRIST, WHICH IS THE HOLY GOSPEL, OR THE NEW TESTAMENT

We also believe and confess, that Christ, before His ascension, established and instituted His New Testament and left it to His followers, to be and remain an everlasting testament, which He confirmed and sealed with His own precious blood; and which He has so highly commended to them, that neither men or angels may change it, neither take therefrom nor add thereto. Jer. 31:31; Heb. 9:15-17; Matt. 26:28; Gal. 1:8; 1 Tim. 6:3-5; Rev. 22:18, 19; Matt. 5:18; Luke 21:33.

And that He has caused this Testament (in which the whole counsel and will of His heavenly Father, so far as these are necessary to the salvation of man, are comprehended), to be proclaimed, in His name, through His beloved apostles, messengers, and servants (whom He chose and sent into all the world for this purpose)—to all nations, people and tongues; these apostles preaching repentance and remission of sins; and that He, in said Testament, caused it to be declared, that all men without distinction, if they are obedient, through faith, follow, fulfill and live according to the precepts of the same, are His children and rightful heirs; having thus excluded none from the precious inheritance of eternal salvation, except the unbelieving and disobedient, the headstrong and unconverted; who despise such salvation; and thus by their own actions incur guilt by refusing the same, and "judge themselves unworthy of everlasting life." Mark 16:15; Luke 24:46, 47; Rom. 8:17; Acts 13:46.

Article VI. OF REPENTANCE AND AMENDMENT OF LIFE

We believe and confess, that, as the "imagination of man's heart is evil from his youth," and consequently inclined to all unrighteousness, sin, and wickedness, that, therefore, the first doctrine of the precious New Testament of the Son of God is, Repentance and amendment of life. Gen. 8:21; Mark 1:15.

Therefore those who have ears to hear, and hearts to understand, must "bring forth fruits meet for repentance," amend their lives, believe the Gospel, "depart from evil and do good," desist from wrong and cease from sinning, "put off the old man with his deeds and put on the new man," which after God is created in "righteousness and true holiness." For neither *Baptism, Supper, nor church-fellowship*, nor any other external ceremony, can, without faith, the new birth, and a change or renewal of life, help, or qualify us, that we may please God, or receive any consolation or promise of salvation from Him. Luke 3:8; Eph. 4:22-24; Col. 3:9, 10.

But on the contrary, we must go to God "with a sincere heart in full assurance of faith," and believe in Jesus Christ, as the Scriptures speak and testify of Him. Through which faith we obtain the pardon of our sins, become sanctified, justified, and children of God; yea, partakers of His mind, nature and image, as we are born again of God through His incorruptible seed from above. Heb. 10:21, 22; John 7:38; II Pet. 1:4.

Article VII. OF HOLY BAPTISM

Regarding baptism, we confess that all penitent believers, who through faith, the new birth and renewal of the Holy Ghost, have become united with God, and whose names are recorded in heaven, must, on such Scriptural confession of their faith, and renewal of life, according to the command and doctrine of Christ, and the example and custom of the apostles, be baptized with water in the ever adorable name of the Father, and of the Son, and of the Holy Ghost, to the burying of their sins, and thus to become incorporated into the communion of the saints; whereupon they must learn to observe all things whatsoever the Son of God taught, left on record, and commanded His followers to do. Matt. 3:15; 28:19, 20; Mark 16:15, 16; Acts 2:38; 8:12, 38; 9:18; 10:47; 16:33; Rom. 6:3, 4; Col. 2:12.

Article VIII. OF THE CHURCH OF CHRIST

We believe in and confess a visible Church of God, consisting of those, who, as before remarked, have truly repented, and rightly believed; who are rightly baptized, united with God in heaven, and incorporated into the communion of the saints on earth. I Cor. 12:13.

And these, we confess, are a "chosen generation, a royal priesthood, an holy nation," who have the testimony that they are the "bride" of Christ; yea, that they are children and heirs of eternal life—a "habitation of God through the Spirit," built on the foundation of the apostles and prophets, of which "Christ Himself is the chief cornerstone"—the foundation on which His church is built. John 3:29; Matt. 16:18; Eph. 2:19-21; Tit. 3:7; I Pet. 1:18, 19; 2:9.

This church of the living God, which He has purchased and redeemed through His own precious blood, and with which He will be—according to His own promise—for her comfort and protection, "always, even unto the end of the world;" yea, will dwell and walk with her, and preserve her, that no "winds" nor "floods," yea, not even the "gates of hell shall prevail against her"—may be known by her evangelical faith, doctrine, love, and godly conversation; also by her pure walk and practice, and her observance of the true ordinances of Christ, which He has strictly enjoined on His followers. Matt. 7:25; 16:18; 28:20; II Cor. 6:16.

Article IX. OF THE ELECTION, AND OFFICES OF TEACHERS, DEACONS, AND DEACONSESSES, IN THE CHURCH

Regarding the offices, and election of persons to the same, in the church, we believe and confess: That, as the church cannot exist and prosper, nor continue in its structure, without offices and regulations, that therefore the Lord Jesus has Himself (as a father in his house), appointed and prescribed His offices and ordinances, and has given commandments concerning the same, as to how each one should walk therein, give heed to His own work and calling, and do it as it becomes Him to do. Eph. 4:11, 12.

For He Himself, as the faithful and great Shepherd, and Bishop of our souls, was sent into the world, not to wound, to break, or destroy the souls of men, but to heal them; to seek that which is lost, and to pull down the hedges and partition wall, so as to make out of many one; thus collecting out of Jews and heathen, yea, out of all nations, a church in His name; for which (so that no one might go astray or be lost) He laid down His own life, and thus procured for them salvation, made them free and redeemed them, to which blessing no one could help them, or be of service in obtaining it. I Pet. 2:25; Matt. 18:11; Eph. 2:13, 14; John 10:9, 11, 15.

And that He, besides this, left His church before His departure, provided with faithful ministers, apostles, evangelists, pastors, and teachers, whom He had chosen by prayer and supplication through the Holy Spirit, so that they might govern the church, feed His flock, watch over, maintain, and care for the same: yea, do all things as He left them an example, taught them, and commanded them to do; and likewise to teach the church to observe all things whatsoever He commanded them. Eph. 4:11, 12; Luke 6:12, 13; 10:1; Matt. 28:20.

Also that the apostles were afterwards, as faithful followers of Christ and leaders of the church, diligent in these matters, namely, in choosing through prayer and supplication to God, brethren who were to provide all the churches in the cities and circuits, with bishops, pastors, and leaders, and to ordain to these offices such men as took "heed unto themselves and unto the doctrine," and also unto the flock; who were sound in the faith, pious in their life and conversation, and who had—as well within the church as "without"—a good reputation and a good report; so that they might be a light and example in all godliness and good works; might worthily administer the Lord's ordinances—baptism and supper—and that they (the brethren sent by the apostles) might also, at all places, where such were to be had, appoint faithful men as elders, who were able to teach others, confirm them in the name of the Lord "with the laying on of hands," and who (the elders) were to take care of all things of which the church stood in need; so that they, as faithful servants, might well "occupy" their Lord's money, gain thereby, and thus "save themselves and those who hear them." I Tim. 3:1; 4:14-16; Acts 1:23, 24; Tit. 1:5; Luke 19:13.

That they should also take good care (particularly each one of the charge over which he had the oversight), that all the circuits should be well provided with deacons, who should have the care and oversight of the poor, and who were to receive gifts and alms, and again faithfully to distribute them among the poor saints who were in need, and this is in all honesty, as is becoming. Acts 6:3-6.

Also that honorable old widows should be chosen as deaconesses, who, besides the deacons are to visit, comfort, and take care of the poor, the weak, afflicted, and the needy, as also to visit, comfort and take care of widows and orphans; and further to assist in taking care of any matters in the church that properly come within their sphere, according to their ability. I Tim. 5:9, 10; Rom. 16:1, 2.

And as it further regards the deacons, that they (particularly if they are fit persons, and chosen and ordained thereto by the church), may also in aid and relief of the bishops, exhort the church (being, as already remarked, chosen thereto), and thus assist in word and doctrine; so that each one may serve the other from love, with the gift which he has received from the Lord; so that through the common service and assistance of each member, according to his ability, the body of Christ may be edified, and the Lord's vineyard and church be preserved in its growth and structure. II Tim. 2:2.

Article X. OF THE LORD'S SUPPER

We also believe in and observe the breaking of bread, or the Lord's Supper, as the Lord Jesus instituted the same (with bread and wine) before His sufferings, and also observed and ate it with the apostles, and also commanded it to be observed to His remembrance, as also the apostles subsequently taught and observed the same in the church, and commmanded it to be observed by believers in commemoration of the death and sufferings of the Lord—the breaking of His worthy body and the shedding of His precious blood—for the whole human race. So is the observance of this sacrament also to remind us of the benefit of the said death and sufferings of Christ, namely, the redemption and eternal salvation which He purchased thereby, and the great love thus shown to sinful man; whereby we are earnestly exhorted also to love one another—to love our neighbor—to forgive and absolve him—even as Christ has done unto us—and also to endeavor to maintain and keep alive the union and communion which we have with God, and amongst one another; which is thus shown and represented to us by the aforesaid breaking of bread. Matt. 26:26; Mark 14:22; Luke 22:19, 20; Acts 2:42, 46; I Cor. 10:16; 11:23-26.

Article XI. OF THE WASHING OF THE SAINTS' FEET

We also confess a washing of the feet of the saints, as the Lord Jesus did not only institute and command the same, but did also Himself wash the feet of the apostles, although He was their Lord and Master; thereby giving an example that they also should wash one another's feet, and thus do to one another as He did to them; which they also afterwards taught believers to observe, and all this is a sign of true humiliation; but yet more particularly as a sign to remind us of the true washing—the washing and purification of the soul in the blood of Christ. John 13:4-17; I Tim. 5:9, 10.

Article XII. OF MATRIMONY

We also confess that there is in the church of God an "honorable" state of matrimony between two believers of the different sexes, as God first instituted the same in paradise between Adam and Eve, and as the Lord Jesus reformed it by removing all abuses which had crept into it, and restoring it to its first order. Gen. 1:27; 2:18, 21-24.

In this manner the Apostle Paul also taught and permitted matrimony in the church, leaving it to each one's own choice to enter into matrimony with any person who would unite with him in such state, provided that it was done "in the Lord," according to the primitive order; the words "in the Lord," to be understood, according to our opinion, that just as the patriarchs had to marry amongst their own kindred or generation, so there is also no other liberty allowed to believers under the New Testament dispensation, than to marry among the "chosen generation," or the spiritual kindred of Christ; that is, to such—and none others—as are already, previous to their marriage, united to the church in heart and soul, have received the same baptism, belong to the same church, are of the same faith and doctrine, and lead the same course of life, with themselves. I Cor. 7:39; 9:5; Gen. 24:4; 28:6, 7; Num. 36:6-9.

Such are then, as already remarked, united by God and the church according to the primitive order, and this is then called, "Marrying in the Lord." I Cor. 7:39.

Article XIII. OF THE OFFICE OF CIVIL GOVERNMENT

We also believe and confess, that God has instituted civil government, for the punishment of the wicked and the protection of the pious; and also further, for the purpose of governing the world, countries and cities; and also to preserve its subjects in good order and under good regulations. Wherefore we are not permitted to despise, revile, or resist the same, but are to acknowledge it as a minister of God and be subject and obedient to it, in all things that do not militate against the law, will, and commandments of God; yea, "to be ready to every good work;" also faithfully to pay it custom, tax, and tribute; thus giving it what is its due; as Jesus Christ taught, did Himself, and commanded His followers to do. That we are also to pray to the Lord earnestly for the government and its welfare, and in behalf of our country, so that we may

THE DORDRECHT CONFESSION (1632) (continued)

live under its protection, maintain ourselves, and "lead a quiet and peaceable life in all godliness and honesty." And further, that the Lord would recompense them (our rulers), here and in eternity, for all the benefits, liberties, and favors which we enjoy under their laudable administration. Rom. 13:1-7; Titus 3:1, 2; I Pet. 2:17; Matt. 17:27; 22:20, 21; I Tim. 2:1, 2.

Article XIV. OF DEFENSE BY FORCE

Regarding revenge, whereby we resist our enemies with the sword, we believe and confess that the Lord Jesus has forbidden His disciples and followers all revenge and resistance, and has thereby commanded them not to "return evil for evil, nor railing for railing;" but to "put up the sword into the sheath," or, as the prophet foretold, "beat them into ploughshares." Matt. 5:39, 44; Rom. 12:14; I Pet. 3:9; Isa. 2:4; Micah 4:3.

From this we see, that, according to the example, life, and doctrine of Christ, we are not to do wrong, or cause offense or vexation to anyone; but to seek the welfare and salvation of all men; also, if necessity should require it, to flee, for the Lord's sake, from one city or country to another, and suffer the "spoiling of our goods," rather than give occasion of offense to anyone; and if we are struck in our "right cheek, rather to turn the other also," than revenge ourselves, or return the blow. Matt. 5:39; 10:23; Rom. 12:19.

And that we are, besides this, also to pray for our enemies, comfort and feed them, when they are hungry or thirsty, and thus by well-doing convince them and overcome the evil with good. Rom. 12:20, 21.

Finally, that we are to do good in all respects, "commending ourselves to every man's conscience in the sight of God," and according to the law of Christ, do nothing to others that we would not wish them to do unto us. II Cor. 4:2; Matt. 7:12; Luke 6:31.

Article XV. OF THE SWEARING OF OATHS

Regarding the swearing of oaths, we believe and confess that the Lord Jesus has dissuaded His followers from and forbidden them the same; that is, that He commanded them to "swear not at all;" but that their "Yea" should be "yea," and their "Nay, nay." From which we understand that all oaths, high and low, are forbidden; and that instead of them we are to confirm all our promises and covenants, declarations and testimonies of all matters, merely with "Yea that is yea," and "Nay that is nay;" and that we are to perform and fulfill at all times, and in all things, to every one, every promise and obligation to which we thus affirm, as faithfully as if we had confirmed it by the most solemn oath. And if we thus do, we have the confidence that no one—not even government itself—will have just cause to require more of us. Matt. 5:34-37; Jas. 5:12; II Cor. 1:17.

Article XVI. OF THE ECCLESIASTICAL BAN OR EXCOMMUNICATION FROM THE CHURCH

We also believe in and acknowledge the ban, or excommunication, a separation or spiritual correction by the church, for the amendment, and not for the destruction, of offenders; so that what is pure may be separated from that which is impure. That is, if a person, after having been enlightened, and received the knowledge of the truth, and has been received into the communion of the saints, does willfully, or out of presumption, sin against God, or commit some other "sin unto death," thereby falling into such unfruitful works of darkness, that he becomes separated from God, and is debarred from His Kingdom—that such an one—when his works are become manifest, and sufficiently known to the church—cannot remain in the "congregation of the righteous;" but must, as an offensive member and open sinner, be excluded from the church, "rebuked before all," and "purged out as a leaven," and thus remain until his amendment, as an example and warning to others, and also that the church may be kept pure from such "spots" and "blemishes;" so that not for the want of this, the name of the Lord be blasphemed, the church dishonored, and a stumblingblock thrown in the way of those "without," and finally, that the offender may not be condemned with the world, but that he may again be convinced of the error of his ways, and brought to repentance and amendment of life. Isa. 59:2; I Cor. 5:5, 6, 12; I Tim. 5:20; II Cor. 13:10.

Regarding the brotherly admonition, as also the instruction of the erring, we are to "give all diligence" to watch over them, and exhort them in all meekness to the amendment of their ways (Jas. 5:19, 20); and in case any should remain obstinate and unconverted, to reprove them as the case may require. In short, the church must "put away from among herself him that is wicked," whether it be in doctrine or life.

Article XVII. OF THE SHUNNING OF THOSE WHO ARE EXPELLED

As regards the withdrawing from, or the shunning of, those who are expelled, we believe and confess, that if any one, whether it be through a wicked life or perverse doctrine—is so far fallen as to be separated from God, and consequently rebuked by, and expelled from, the church, he must also, according to the doctrine of Christ and His apostles, be shunned and avoided by all the members of the church (particularly by those to whom his misdeeds are known), whether it be in eating or drinking, or other such like social matters. In short, that we are to have nothing to do with him; so that we may not become defiled by intercourse with him, and partakers of his sins; but that he may be made ashamed, be affected in his mind, convinced in his conscience, and thereby induced to amend his ways. I Cor. 5:9-11; Rom. 16:17; II Thess. 3:14; Tit. 3:10, 11.

That nevertheless, as well in shunning as in reproving such offender, such moderation and Christian discretion be used, that such shunning and reproof may not be conducive to his ruin, but be serviceable to his amendment. For should he be in need, hungry, thirsty, naked, sick or visited by some other affliction, we are in duty bound, according to the doctrine and practice of Christ and His apostles, to render him aid and assistance, as necessity may require; otherwise the shunning of him might be rather conducive to his ruin than to his amendment. I Thess. 5:14.

Therefore we must not treat such offenders as enemies, but exhort them as brethren, in order thereby to bring them to a knowledge of their sins and to repentance; so that they may again become reconciled to God and the church, and be received and admitted into the same—thus exercising love towards them, as is becoming. II Thess. 3:15.

Article XVIII. OF THE RESURRECTION OF THE DEAD AND THE LAST JUDGMENT

Regarding the resurrection of the dead, we confess with the mouth, and believe with the heart, that according to the Scriptures all men who shall have died or "fallen asleep," will, through the incomprehensible power of God, at the day of judgment, be "raised up" and made alive; and that these, together with all those who then remain alive, and who shall be "changed in a moment, in the twinkling of an eye, at the last trump," shall "appear before the judgment seat of Christ," where the good shall be separated from the evil, and where "every one shall receive the things done in his body, according to that he hath done, whether it be good or bad"; and that the good or pious shall then further, as the blessed of their Father, be received by Christ into eternal life, where they shall receive that joy which "eye hath not seen, nor ear heard, nor hath entered into the heart of man." Yea, where they shall reign and triumph with Christ for ever and ever. Matt. 22:30-32; 25:31; Dan. 12:2; Job 19:25, 26; John 5:28, 29; I Cor. 15:51, 52; I Thess. 4:13.

And that, on the contrary, the wicked or impious, shall, as the accursed of God, be cast into "outer darkness;" yea, into eternal, hellish torments; "where their worm dieth not, and the fire is not quenched;" and where—according to Holy Scripture—they can expect no comfort nor redemption throughout eternity. Isa. 66:24; Matt. 25:46; Mark 9:46; Rev. 14:10. 11.

May the Lord through His grace make us all fit and worthy, that no such calamity may befall any of us; but that we may be diligent, and so take heed to ourselves, that we may be found of Him in peace, without spot, and blameless. Amen.

Notes: *Mennonites in the United States are of two basic varieties—German and Russian. The German Mennonites came to the United States in the seventeenth century at the invitation of William Penn and settled in Pennsylvania. From there they spread south and west. The Russian Mennonites arrived in the late nineteenth century. The Dordrecht Confession predates the division of the Mennonite community.*

Deriving from the radical reformers of the previous century, the Mennonites found haven in relatively tolerant Holland. Gathering at Dordrecht in 1632, they adopted a confession that is still used by the Mennonite Church and has some authority among all Mennonite bodies. It affirms the practices of foot washing, shunning, and pacifism.

In the late seventeenth century, the Amish also adopted the Dordrecht Confession, and it is still accepted by the several Amish bodies currently existing in America.

STATEMENT OF FAITH (CONGREGATIONAL BIBLE CHURCH)

1. We believe in THE HOLY SCRIPTURES: Accepting fully the writings of the Old and New Testaments as the very Word of God, verbally inspired in all parts and therefore wholly without error as originally given of God, altogether sufficient in themselves as our only infallible authority of faith and practice. Psa. 119:89; Matt. 24:35; John 17:17; II Tim. 3:16,17; II Pet. 1:21.

2. We believe in THE ONE TRIUNE GOD: who is personal spirit, and sovereign (Mark 12:29; John 4:24; 14:9; Psa. 135:6); perfect, infinite, and eternal in his being, holiness, love, wisdom, and power (Psa. 18:30; 147:5; Deut. 33:27); absolutely separate and above the world as its Creator, yet everywhere present in the world as the Upholder of all things (Gen. 1:1; Psa. 104); self-existent and self-revealing in three distinct Persons—The Father, the Son, and the Holy Spirit (John 5:26; Matt. 28:19; II Cor. 13:14); each of whom is to be honored and worshipped equally as true God (John 5:23; Acts 5:3,4).

3. We believe in THE LORD JESUS CHRIST: who is the second Person of the Triune God, the Eternal Word and Only Begotten Son, our Great God and Saviour (John 1:1, 3:15; Titus 2:13; Rom. 9:5); that, without any essential change in His divine Person (Heb. 13:8) He became man by the miracle of the virgin birth (John 1:14; Matt. 1:23), thus to continue forever as both true God and true man, one Person with two natures (Col. 2:9; Rev. 22:16); that as man He was in all points tempted like as we are, yet without sin (Heb. 4:15; John 8:46); that as the perfect Lamb of God He gave Himself in death upon the cross, bearing there the sin of the world, and suffering its full penalty of divine wrath in our stead (Isa. 53:5,6; Matt. 20:28; Gal. 3:13; John 1:29); that He rose again from the dead and was glorified in the same body in which He suffered and died (Luke 24:36-43, John 20: 25-28); that as our great High Priest He ascended into heaven there to appear before the face of God as our Advocate and Intercessor (Heb. 4:14; I John 2:1).

4. We believe in THE HOLY SPIRIT: who is the third Person of the Triune God (Matt. 28:19; Acts 5:3,4), the divine Agent in nature, revelation, and redemption (Gen. 1:2; Psa. 104:30; I Cor. 2:10; II Cor. 3:18); that He convicts the world of righteousness, and judgment (John 16:8-11), regenerates those who believe (John 3:5), and baptizes, indwells, seals, empowers, guides, teaches, and sanctifies all who become children of God through Christ (I Cor. 12:13; 6:19; Eph. 4:30; 3:16; Acts 1:8; Rom. 8:14; John 16:13-15; I Cor. 6:11).

5. We believe in THE CREATION AND FALL OF MAN: that he was the direct creation of God, spirit, and soul and body, not in any sense the product of an animal ancestry, but made in the divine image (Gen. 1:26-28; 2:7; 18:24, Matt. 19:4; I Thess. 5:23); that by personal disobedience to the revealed will of God

man became a sinful creature and the progenitor of a fallen race (Gen. 3:1-24; 5:3), all of whom are universally sinful in both nature and practice (Eph. 2:3; Rom. 3:23; 5:12); alienated from the life and family of God (Eph. 4:18; John 8:42-44); under the righteous judgment and wrath of God (Rom. 1:8; 3:19); and has within himself no possible means of recovery or salvation (Mark 7:21-23; Matt. 19:25,26; Rom. 7:18).

6. We believe in SALVATION BY GRACE THROUGH FAITH: that salvation is the free gift of God (Rom. 3:24; 6:23), neither merited nor secured in part or in whole by any virtue or work of man (Titus 3:5; Rom. 4:4,5), but received only by personal faith in the Lord Jesus Christ because of the merit of His shed blood (John 3:16; 6:28,29; Acts 16:30, 31; I Cor. 15:1-4; Heb. 9:22; Eph 2:8,9), in whom all true believers have as a present possession the gift of eternal life, a perfect righteousness, a sonship in the family of God, in which family believers are dealt with as sons, God the Father disciplining and chastening every son whom He receives and are assured deliverance and security from all condemnation, every spiritual resource needed for life and godliness, and divine assurance that they shall never perish (I John 5:13; Rom. 3:22; Gal. 3:26; Heb. 12:5-11; John 5:24; Eph. 1:3; II Pet. 1:3; John 10:27-30); that this salvation includes the whole man, spirit and soul and body (I Thess. 5: 23, 24); and that apart from Christ there is no possible salvation (John 14:6; Acts 4:12).

7. We believe in HOLY LIVING AND GOOD WORKS: not as the procuring cause of salvation in any sense, but as the proper evidence and fruit (I John 3:9-11; 4:19; 5:4; Eph. 2:8-10; Titus 2:14; Matt. 7:16-18; I Cor. 15:10); and therefore as Christians we should keep the Word of our Lord (John 14:23); seek the things which are above (Col. 3:1), walk as He walked (I John 2:6), be careful to maintain good works (Titus 3:8), and ESPECIALLY ACCEPT AS OUR SOLEMN RESPONSIBILITY THE DUTY AND PRIVILEGE OF BEARING THE GOSPEL TO A LOST WORLD IN ORDER THAT WE MAY BEAR MUCH FRUIT (Acts 1:8; II Cor. 5:19; John 15:16); remembering that a victorious and fruitful Christian life is possible only for those who have learned that they are not under law but under grace (Rom. 6:14), and who in gratitude for the infinite and undeserved mercies of God have presented themselves wholly to Him for His service (Rom. 12:1,2).

8. We believe in THE EXISTENCE OF SATAN: who originally was created a holy and perfect being, but through pride and unlawful ambition rebelled against God (Ezek. 28:13-17; Isa. 14:13,14; I Tim. 3:7), thus becoming utterly depraved in character (John 8:44), the great adversary of God and His people (Matt. 4:1-11; Rev. 12:10), leader of all other evil angels and spirits (Matt. 12:24-26, 25:41), the deceiver and god of this present world (Rev. 12:9; II Cor. 4:4), that his powers are supernaturally great, but strictly limited by the permissive will of God who overrules all his wicked devices for good (Job 1:1-22; Luke 22:31,32); that he was defeated and judged at the cross, and therefore his final doom is certain (John 12:31, 32; 16:11; Rev. 20:10); that we are able to resist and overcome him only in the armor of God and by the blood of the lamb (Eph. 6:12-18; Rev. 12:11).

9. We believe in THE SECOND COMING OF CHRIST: that His return from heaven will be personal, visible, and glorious—the blessed hope for which we should constantly watch and pray, the time being unrevealed but always imminent (Acts 1:11; Rev. 1:7; Mark 13:33-37; Titus 2:11-13; Rev. 22:20); that when He comes He will first by resurrection and translation remove from the earth His waiting church (I Thess. 4:16-18), and then pour out the righteous judgments of God upon the unbelieving world (Rev. 6:1-18,24).

10. We believe in FUTURE LIFE, BODILY RESURRECTION, AND ETERNAL JUDGMENT: that the spirits of the saved at death go immediately to be with Christ in heaven (Phil. 1:21-23; II Cor. 5:8), where they abide in joyful fellowship with Him until His second coming, when their bodies shall be raised from the grave and changed into the likeness of His own glorious body (Phil. 3:20,21; I Cor. 15:35-58; I John 3:2), at which time their works shall be brought before the judgment seat of Christ for the determination of rewards, a judgment which may issue in the loss of rewards, but not the loss of the soul (I Cor. 3:8-15; II Cor. 5:10); that the spirits of the unsaved at death descend immediately into Hades where they are kept under punishment until the final day of judgment (Luke 16:19-31; II Pet. 2:9, ARV), at which time their bodies shall be raised from the grave, and they themselves shall be judged according to their works, and cast into the place of final and everlasting punishment (Rev. 20:11-15; 21:8; Mark 9:43-48; Jude 1:13).

11. We believe in THE ONE TRUE CHURCH: the mystical body and bride of the Lord Jesus (Eph. 4:4; 5:25-32), that He began to build on the day of Pentecost (Matt. 16:18; Acts 2:47), and will complete at His second coming (I Thess. 4:16, 17), and into which all true believers of the present age are baptized immediately by the Holy Spirit (I Cor. 12:12-18 with 1:2); that the supreme task of the church is the evangelization of the world (Matt. 28:10,20; Mark 16:15,16; II Cor. 5:18-20); that all the various members of this one spiritual body should gather together in local assemblies for worship, prayer, fellowship, teaching, united testimony, and observance of the ordinaces of our Lord (Heb. 10:25; Acts 2:41-47); among which are the following: the baptism of believers upon their confession of faith in the Lord Jesus Christ as their Saviour (Acts 8:35-38; 10:47,48; I Pet. 3:21), the communion of the

bread and cup as a memorial of the broken body and shed blood of our Lord Jesus Christ, thereby proclaiming the Lord's death until He comes (I Cor. 11:23-26); and in prayer for, and anointing of the sick. (James 5:13-18).

12. We believe in SEPARATION FROM THE WORLD UNTO GOD: that since our Christian citizenship is in heaven, as the children of God we should walk in separation from this present world, having no fellowship with its evil ways (Phil. 3:20, ARV; II Cor. 6:14-18; Rom. 12:2; Eph. 5:11), abstaining from all worldly amusements and unclean habits which defile mind and body (Luke 8:14; I Thess. 5:22; I Tim. 5:6; I Pet. 2:11; Eph. 5:3-11, 18; Col. 3:17; I Cor. 6:19,20), from the sin of divorce and remarriage as forbidden by our Lord (Matt. 19:9, Mark 10:11,12; Luke 16:18), from swearing of any oath (Jas. 5:12), from the use of civil courts for the settlement of disputes between Christians (I Cor. 6:1-8). We believe further that the way of life as lived and taught by Christ implies the fullest exercise of love toward mankind: (Rom. 12:18-21). We believe further that the Christian life will of necessity express itself in conformity to Christ in life and conduct (Col. 3).

We understand that the above articles do not by any means exhaust the content of the believer's creed, which is the whole Word of God, and they are not intended to set a limit beyond which faith cannot go within this Word: but we do believe that in so far as these articles extend they are a true presentation of the sound doctrine taught in the Scriptures, and therefore enjoined upon us as Christian believers.

Notes: *The Congregational Bible Church is a small Mennonite body centered on a single congregation in Pennsylvania.*

*   *   *

WE BELIEVE (MENNONITE CHURCH)

We Believe . . .

In a Triune God—Father, Son, and Holy Ghost (I John 5:7), Creator of all things.—Colossians 1:16.

In Jesus Christ as the Son of God, conceived of the Holy Ghost, born of a virgin.—Matthew 1:20-25.

In the personality and deity of the Holy Spirit.—Acts 1:8, 5:3, 4.

In the plenary and verbal inspiration of the Bible as the Word of God.—Psalm 119:160; II Timothy 3:16.

That man was created pure (Genesis 1:27); that he, by transgression, fell (Genesis 2:17); and that sin, sorrow, and death (natural and spiritual) are results of the Fall.—Romans 5:12.

That the blood of Jesus Christ so atoned for all as to make their salvation possible.—John 3:16.

That innocent children will be saved.—Mark 10:14.

That to be saved, all accountable persons must believe, repent, be "born again," "walk in newness of life."—John 3:3-5; Romans 6:1-7.

That those thus born again are obedient to God and constitute the true Church, of which Christ is the Head.—Romans 6:17; Colossians 1:18.

That self-denial and humility are essential to Christian discipleship.—Luke 9:23; I Peter 5:5, 6.

That Christian baptism is commanded and that pouring is the Scriptural mode.—Matthew 28:19, 20; Acts 1:5, 2:2, 16-18, 41; 10:44-48.

That the bread and cup in communion are symbols of the body and blood of Christ, and show a common union of members.—I Corinthians 10:16-21.

That feet washing as a religious ceremony should be observed literally.—John 13:1-17.

That Christian women should wear the veiling.—I Corinthians 11:2-16.

That the "kiss of charity" should be practiced among believers.—Romans 16:16; I Peter 5:14.

That anointing with oil is for physical restoration of the believer who, in sickness, calls in faith for such anointing.—James 5:14, 15.

That mixed marriages between believers and unbelievers are unscriptural, and marriage with divorced persons with former companions living constitutes adultery.—Nehemiah 13:23-26; Mark 10:2-12.

That it is unscriptural for Christian people to follow wordly fashions, engage in carnal warfare, swear oaths, or hold membership in secret societies.—Romans 12:2; Matthew 5:33-48; II Corinthians 6:14-18; I Peter 3:3, 4; Ephesians 5:11, 12; Jeremiah 49:11.

That obstinate sinners within the Church should be expelled.—I Corinthians 5:13.

That the Church is commanded to evangelize the world.—Matthew 28:19, 20.

In the personal and imminent coming of our Lord Jesus Christ as the blessed hope of the believers.—Acts 1:11; John 14:2, 3; Matthew 24:44; I Thessalonians 4:13-18.

That there will be a bodily resurrection both of the just and of the unjust.—John 5:28, 29.

That the final judgment will be followed by eternal rewards and punishments.—Matthew 25:46; II Corinthians 5:10.

Notes: *This statement is a brief summary of present-day Mennonite faith. Note the affirmation of the "plenary and verbal inspiration of the Bible," a reflection of twentieth-century debates within the North American conservative evangelical community.*

Russian Mennonites

CHURCH COVENANT AND ARTICLES OF FAITH (EVANGELICAL MENNONITE BRETHREN CHURCH)

CHURCH COVENANT

Having been led by the Spirit of God to receive Jesus Christ as my Saviour and Lord and on profession of my faith, having been baptized in the name of the Father, of the Son, and of the Holy Spirit, and accepting the Holy Scriptures as my rule of faith and practice, and recognizing the privilege and duty of uniting myself for Christian fellowship, the enjoyment of Christian ordinances, the public worship of God and this assembly, most solemnly and joyfully enter into covenant and agree to associate myself as a member of this assembly of believers.

I engage, and promise therefore, by the aid of the Holy Spirit to forsake the paths of sin, to walk together in Christian love, to strive for unity and spiritual welfare of this church, to sustain its doctrines, ordinances, worship and discipline; to contribute cheerfully and regularly to its charities, institutions, its local expenses and to the advancement of the Gospel of Christ to all nations.

I also engage and agree to maintain a prayer-life; to seek the salvation of the lost; to walk circumspectly in the world; to be just in my dealings, faithful in my engagements, exemplary in my deportment.

I further engage and promise to watch over another in brotherly love; to pray for another; to aid in sickness and distress; to cultivate Christian sympathy, to be slow to take offense, but always ready for reconciliation; and I shall endeavor at all times and in all places to carry out the spirit of this covenant and the principles of God's Word.

ARTICLES OF FAITH

I. HOLY SCRIPTURE. We believe that all Scripture, the Old and New Testament, is the only inerrant inspired Word of God, written by holy men of God as they were moved by the Holy Spirit (II Tim. 3:16-17; II Peter 1:21). It reveals the will of God to man (I Cor. 2:9-12). It is the truth (John 17:17; I Thess. 2:13; II Tim. 2:15). The Gospel is the power of God unto salvation to every one that believeth (Rom. 1:16; II Tim. 3:15), and all Scripture is profitable for doctrine, for reproof, for correction, and for instruction in righteousness: that the man of God may be prefect, throughly furnished unto all good works (II Tim. 3:16-17). It is the guide to eternal bliss (Titus 3:4-7; Gal. 4:7).

II. GOD. We believe in only one living and true God as the infinite, perfect, and eternal Spirit, in whom all things have their source, support, and end (Isa. 45:21; Eph. 4:6; Gen 1:1; Acts 17:28; Heb. 11:3; Luke 24:39; Col. 1:15; Ps. 90:2; I Tim. 6:16).

We believe in God as omniscient (Heb. 4:13; Acts 15:18); omnipresent (Ps. 139:7; Jer. 23:24; Amos 9:2-3); omnipotent (Jer. 10:12-13; Gen. 35:11; Gen. 1:1, 26); Creator (Gen. 1:1, 26; Jn. 1:1-3); Sustainer (Col.

1:15-17; Ps. 104:27-30; Ps. 75:6-7; Heb. 1:3; Matt. 10:29-30; Gen. 39:21; Gen. 50:20; Dan. 1:9); immutable in His being, holiness, justice, love, and truth (Mal. 3:6; Isa. 6:3; I Jn. 4:8; James 1:17); eternal (Ps. 90:2; Ps. 102:24-27; Heb. 1:12).

Though God is a Spirit (Jn. 4:24), yet Scripture very definitely teaches God as a personality (Ex. 3:14; Gen. 22:13-14; Ps. 23:1; Jn. 17; Acts 14:15; Job 1:12; Gen. 3:8-9, 11, 13, 14; I Thess. 1:9; Ps. 94:9-10; Gen. 6:6; Jn. 3:16; Rev. 3:19f; Gen. 1:1, 26).

III. JESUS CHRIST. We believe in Jesus Christ as the eternal Son of God. The Son is from eternity the only begotten of the Father. Being conceived of the Holy Spirit He was born man of the virgin Mary (Jn. 3:16; Heb. 1:5-10; Luke 1:35; Matt. 1:18-25), in order to fulfill the purpose of God from the foundation of the world to redeem us from eternal curse and bring about our eternal salvation by making full atonement for our sins through His vicarious suffering and death on the cross of Calvary (Jn. 1:14, 29; Mark 10:45; Heb. 10:10-14; I Peter 1:18-29; Isa. 53: 4-6). He took upon Himself the likeness of sinful flesh (Heb. 2:14), thus being true God and also perfect man (I Jn. 3:5; I Tim. 2:5), being made in all things like as we are, yet without sin (Heb. 4:15).

He rose triumphantly from the grave the third day and ascended into heaven, and is now at the right hand of God interceding in our behalf: from whence He shall come again in visible form to judge the living and the dead and to establish His rule as Lord of lords and King of kings (John chapters 20 and 21; Acts 1:9-11; II Tim. 4:1; I Tim. 6:15; John 5:22-29; Matthew 25:31ff).

IV. THE HOLY SPIRIT. We believe that the Holy Spirit is the third person in the Godhead and proceedeth from the Father through the Son, (John 15:26). He took part in the creation of the universe (Gen. 1:2; Job 33:4; Ps. 33:6). He directed God's servants in revealing the will of God to mankind (I Peter 1:10-11). He is the author of the Scriptures, (II Peter 1:20-21; Rev. Ch. 2 and 3). At Pentecost He was poured out upon all man (Acts 2:17-18). In this age of grace He reproves the world of sin, of righteousness, and of judgment (John 16:8-11). He restrains the progress of evil until God's purposes are accomplished (II Thess. 2:7). He regenerates the penitent soul (John 3:3, 5), lives in the body of the believer, which is the temple of the Holy Spirit (I Cor. 3:16; I Cor. 6:19), gives the believer the assurance of salvation (Rom. 8:16), comforts, (John 14:16-17), teaches, and brings to his remembrance the proper Scripture verses in witnessing (John 14:26); and guides the believer into all truth (John 16:13). He will sanctify the believer (II Thess. 2:13), and empower him for life and service (Eph. 3:16; I Cor. 2:1-4), and will quicken his mortal body (Rom. 8:11).

V. TRINITY. We believe, though inscrutable yet not self-contradictory, in the unity of the Godhead, commonly known as the Trinity. This Trinity is made up of three distinct persons; namely, God the Father (Rom. 1:7); God the Son (Heb. 1:18); God the Holy Spirit (Acts 5:3-4). These three, though one in essence, i.e. equal in their divine perfection, yet individual in personality, perform different but harmonious offices in the great plan of redemption (Matt. 28:19; II Cor. 13:14; Eph. 2:18; Jn. 15:26; Jn. 10:30; Jn. 16:14).

God, who is one with respect to His essence, is three with respect to the modes or distinctions of His being.

"The Father is all the fulness of the Godhead invisible (John 1:18); the Son is all the fulness of the Godhead manifested (John 1:14-18); the Spirit is all the fulness of the Godhead acting immediately upon the creature" (I Cor. 2:9-10). Broadman.

VI. SATAN. We believe that Satan is a real supernatural personality, a fallen angel of great power, cunning, and wicked, the enemy of God and of all good, seeking the destruction of Christ and the eternal ruin of every soul (Mark 1:13; John 13:2; Matt. 13:19, 39); but is limited in the scope of his power by God (Job 1:12; Job 2:1-6; Luke 22:31f; I Cor. 10:13).

Satan introduced sin into this world, when he by his subtlety brought about the transgression and fall of our first parents (Gen. 3:1-15). Since then he and the host of fallen angels and evil spirits under his control dominate the present world system deceiving mankind, obstructing the course of the Gospel, blinding the minds of the unbelieving (Eph. 6:11-12; Eph. 2:2; II Cor. 4:4; I John 5:19 R.V.).

Scripture describes his work and character by names such as: "a murderer from the beginning", "a liar and the father of lies", "the accuser of our brethren", "the devil", "the adversary", "the evil one", "the prince of the power of the air", "the god of this world".

His present abode is "in the air", "in the heavenly places" (Eph. 6:12 R.V.); yet the earth is the special field of his awful activity, where he works disguised as an angel of light or roams about as a roaring lion (II Cor. 11:14f; I Peter 5:8).

Christ by His death on the cross defeated and judged Satan and stripped him of his power over death (Col. 2:15; John 12:31; John 16:11; Heb. 2:14; I Cor. 15:54-56) and secured victory for the believer over all the wiles of the devil (I John 4:4; Eph. 6:11-13; I John 5:4-5; I Cor. 15:57; James 4:7).

He is doomed first to be cast from his present abode, then at Christ's second coming to be bound a thousand years, and finally to be cast into the lake of fire where he and his angels shall be tormented forever and ever (Matt. 25:41; Rev. 20:10).

VII. ANGELS. We believe in the existence of a higher order of created, yet spiritual beings between God and man frequently known as ministering spirits, or messengers of God, but more frequently known as angels. These are superior to man but inferior to God

(Matt. 18:10; Mark 13:32; Matt. 13:41; I Pet. 3:22; Heb. 12:22; Col. 1:16; Ps. 104:4; Jn. 5:4; I Cor. 4:9).

Though "spirits", yet they have appeared in visible form as ministers through whom God's power was manifested (Judges 6:11-22; Luke 1:26; John 20:12; Isa. 37:36; Rev. 20:2-10; Gen. 19:1-26; Heb. 1:14).

Angels announced the birth of Jesus (Luke 1:28-35); an angel appeared to the shepherds (Luke 2:9-13); legions of angels were ready to help Jesus (Matt. 26:53); angels ministered to Jesus after His temptation (Matt. 4:11); an angel strengthened Him after the agony in Gethsemane (Luke 22:43); angels were associated with His resurrection (Matt. 28:2-7); attended His ascension (Acts 1:10-11); and will also be associated with His return (I Thess. 4:16; II Thess. 1:7).

Angels assist God in executing judgments upon the earth (Isa. 37:36; Rev. 9:1-5; II Sam. 24:16-17; Gen. 19:13-15; Rev. 19:17).

They are ministering spirits sent forth to minister for them who shall be heirs of salvation (Heb. 1:14); they guard, defend, and deliver God's people (Acts 5:19; II Kings 6:17; Acts 12:7-11; Ps. 34:7); cheer and strengthen them (Acts 5:19, 20); guide the worker to the sinner (Acts 10:3); guard the children, beholding the face of the Father for them (Mt. 18:10); they are eyewitnesses of the church and the believer (I Tim. 5:21; I Cor. 4:9); and receive the departing saints (Luke 16:22).

VIII. ANTHROPOLOGY - MAN

A. HIS CREATION. We believe that by an immediate act of God, man was created in His image (Gen. 1:26-27); possessing righteousness, holiness, and wisdom (Eph. 4:24; Col. 3:10), for the purpose that man should be the object of His love, to praise and glorify Him (Eph. 1:4-6), to replenish the earth with God-fearing people, and to subdue and have dominion over the earth and all animate creatures upon it (Gen. 1:26-28; Gen. 9:1, 2).

B. HIS FALL. We believe that man was subjected to trial in the garden of Eden (Gen. 2:15-17), and voluntarily and consciously transgressed God's command (Gen. 3:1-3, 6), and so fell from his holy estate (Gen. 3:16-19; Gen. 2:16, 17). Thus man became alienated from God (Gen. 3:7-13; Eph. 4:18; Col. 1:21), and became physically, morally, and spiritually depraved (Rom. 1:19-32). As a result of the fall sin was imputed upon the entire human race (Romans 5:12; I Cor. 2:14). Man's heart, being desperately wicked (Jer. 17:9-10), leads to acts of sin in his life and finally to just condemnation (Rom. 5:18).

C. HIS REDEMPTION. We believe that God as the Sovereign Ruler must punish sin (Rom. 6:23). Christ, the Son of God, voluntarily (John 10:17-18) offered Himself on the cross as the perfect sacrifice for sin, the just suffering for the unjust, bearing sin's curse, and tasting death for every

CHURCH COVENANT AND ARTICLES OF FAITH (EVANGELICAL MENNONITE BRETHREN CHURCH) (continued)

man (John 1:29; Heb. 9:11-12; I Tim. 2:5-6; II Cor. 5:21; Gal. 3:13). Nothing prevents the salvation of the greatest sinner on earth but his own stubborn will, his voluntary rejection of Jesus Christ as substitute for penalty (John 3:14-16; John 3:36; Acts 16:31).

D. **HIS RESURRECTION.** Every person will be raised up. The saved unto life everlasting; the unsaved to eternal condemnation (John 5:28, 29).

IX. SOTERIOLOGY—SALVATION

A. **REPENTANCE.** We believe that repentance is a prerequisite to regeneration (Acts 17:30; II Peter 3:9). It manifests itself in the godly sorrow for sin, i.e., in the forsaking of sin and in turning to God (Isa. 55:7; I Thess. 1:9). It is wrought by the convicting power of the Holy Spirit. An illustration of pure repentance is found in the prodigal son (Luke 15:11-24). True repentance, coupled with faith, will result in forgiveness of sins (Acts 3:19).

B. **FAITH.** Faith is fundamental to salvation and Christian conduct (Gen. 15:6). "Faith is the substance of things hoped for, the evidence of things not seen" (Heb. 11:1). Jesus Christ is the author and finisher of our faith (Heb. 12:2). Only faith in Jesus Christ and his work of atonement on the cross saves from eternal condemnation (John 1:12; John 3:16). Faith being both the gift of God and act of man (Eph. 2:8), is based on the Word of God (John 20:30-31), giving assent to the truth, embracing and appropriating Christ as his Lord and Saviour (John 20:25-29), and then worshipping Him (John 4:20-24).

C. **REGENERATION.** Regeneration is the impartation of a new and divine life, a new creation; not the old nature altered or re-invigorated, but a new birth from above (John 3:3-8; Eph. 2:10; II Cor. 5:17). We are made partakers of the divine nature (II Peter 1:4). A new governing power comes into the regenerated man's life, by which he is enabled to become holy in character and conduct: "Old things are passed away; behold, all things are become new", (II Cor. 5:17; I Jn. 5:11-12, 20).

D. **JUSTIFICATION.** As regeneration has to do with the change of the believer's nature, so justification has to do with the change from guilt and condemnation to acquittal and acceptance. We have become justified through the redemption that is in Christ Jesus (Rom. 3:24), and by the faith of Jesus Christ (Gal. 2:16; Rom. 5:1). Therefore, being justified by faith, forgiveness of sin (Eph. 1:7) is imparted to the believer, and he is fully restored to God's favor and receives access to all of God's graces (Rom. 5:1-2).

E. **ADOPTION.** Regeneration begins a new life in the soul; justification deals with the new relation-

ship of that soul to God; and adoption admits that soul into the family of God with filial joy. Adoption deals with the position the soul holds as a child of God. It is the present position of the believer (I John 3:2; Gal. 3:26). The complete revelation of our position as a child of God is future (I John 3:1-3; Col. 3:3-4).

F. **SANCTIFICATION.** Sanctification has to do with our character and conduct in our Christian life. Justification is what God does for us, while sanctification is what God does in us. Sanctification exhibits the fruit of our relationship to God and manifests itself in a cordial love to the brethren and fellowmen (Gal. 5:22-23). Sanctification may be viewed as instantaneous, progressive, and complete. The believer is sanctified at the time of regeneration, that is, he is set aside for the service of God (I Cor. 6:11; Heb. 10:10,14). Then the believer will mortify the deeds of the body (Rom. 8:13; Col. 3:1-9) and "put on the new man which is renewed in the knowledge after the image of Him that created him" (Col. 3:10-17; Eph 4:22-24), and God will sanctify him wholly unto the coming of our Lord Jesus Christ (I Thess. 5:23,24).

G. **PRAYER.** Prayer is the Christian's vital breath. It is the pouring out of the heart to God (Psa. 42:4; Psa. 62:8). It is God's appointed method for man to obtain what He has to bestow (Mt. 7:7-11). It is but the natural way of a child to commune with his father. The possibility to communicate with God, our heavenly Father, was brought about through the sacrificial death of Jesus Christ (Heb. 10:19-22), and with the help of the Holy Spirit (Rom. 8:26) prayer is the means of appropriating the promises of the Bible.

X. ECCLESIOLOGY—THE CHURCH

1. The Church as an organism includes all regenerate believers gathered out of the world between the first and second advents of Christ, while as an organization it includes believers united for the service of Christ in any given assembly.

2. The local visible church is an institution of divine appointment and is composed of professed, baptized believers in Christ: voluntarily joined together and meeting at stated times to worship, to fellowship, to observe ordinances, and when necessary to administer and accept discipline.

XI. ESCHATOLOGY—THE LAST THINGS

A. **SECOND COMING OF CHRIST.** We believe in the personal, visible, imminent, premillenial return of Christ (Acts 1:11; Rev. 1:7; John 14:3; Titus 2:13; Rev. 5:9-10; Rev. 20:4-6). As the first coming covers a period of events, so also His second coming covers a period of events, such as the rapture (I Thess. 4:13-17; I Cor. 15:50-52), the great tribulation (Mt. 24:21; II Thess. 2:3-10), the revelation of Christ at the end of the great tribulation period (Mt. 24:29-31), the Millenium

Age (Rev. 20:1-9), and The Great White Throne judgment (Rev. 20:10-15). The day nor the hour of the beginning of Christ's second coming no one knows (Mt. 24:36-42), but we can know when it is near at hand (I Tim. 4:1-3; II Tim. 3:1-5; James 5:1-9; Mt. 24:24,32; Mt. 24:32-34). This hope of the Second Coming of Christ to receive His own (I Thess. 4:13-17) is a purifying element in the life of the believer (I John 3:3), and a warning to the unbeliever (Matt. 24:42; II Pet. 3:10).

B. THE RESURRECTION. We believe in the bodily resurrection of the just and the unjust (John 5:28-29; I Cor. 15:22) to receive the things done in the body (II Cor. 5:10; Rev. 20:12). The believer's body shall be fashioned like unto His glorious body (Phil. 3:21), but there is no description of the body of the unbeliever.

C. RECOMPENCE OF THE JUST AND THE UNJUST

1. The believer's works will be judged according to his deeds here upon earth (I Cor. 3:11-15; II Cor. 5:10; Rev. 22:12). He will receive rewards or crowns for his service (James 1:12; I Peter 5:4; II Tim. 4:8; I Thess. 2:19; Rev. 4:4; I Cor. 9:25; Rev. 3:11).

2. The unbeliever's wage for sin is death (Rom. 6:23), and in the end will be judged according to his works (Rev. 20:11-15).

D. THE FINAL STATE

1. The wicked after death will be in torment (Luke 16:23) until the final judgment at the Great White Throne when he will be eternally separated from God and cast into the lake of fire or more commonly known as everlasting hell (Matt. 25:41; John 3:36; Rev. 20:14-15).

2. The final state of the believer is far better than this present life in the body (Phil. 1:23; I John 3:2; Rev. 14:13); his final and eternal home is in heaven, the New Jerusalem (Rev. 21-22:5).

ORDINANCES

1. ORDINANCE DEFINED: An ordinance is a symbolic observance which by the specific command of Christ is to be ministered in the church, thereby setting forth the central truths of the Christian faith. It is of a universal and perpetual obligation.

2. BAPTISM:

a. Water baptism expresses the experience of regeneration and union with Christ (Acts 8:36-39); it is a public testimony of the inner experience preceding church membership (Acts 2:38, 41,47; Mark 16:16); it is to be administered to believers only. (Acts 8:37; 16:30-34; 18:8)

b. Water baptism has no saving or cleansing merits, but is rather an act of obedience demonstrating the new relationship with Christ. Infant baptism cannot be recognized as valid according to Scripture. (Mark 16:16; Acts 8:12; Acts 18:8)

c. While the Evangelical Mennonite Brethren churches practice the immersion mode of baptism, other modes are recognized as valid providing salvation preceeded baptism.

3. LORD'S SUPPER:

a. The Lord's Supper is an ordinance, instituted by Christ in the night of betrayal, to be observed frequently (in our Conference at least four times a year) by believers until he returns.

b. The consecrated emblems consist of bread symbolizing Christ's broken body, and the fruit of the vine as a symbol of His shed blood (I Cor. 11:23-29). The observance of this ordinance is to be preceeded by honest self-examination.

c. There is no salvation element in this ordinance; it rather serves as a reminder of Christ's vicarious atonement (I Peter 3:18), and our continued dependence upon Him.

d. The communion table is open to all believers who practice consistent Christian living.

CHURCH PRACTICES

1. HOME AND FAMILY: The Christian home is recognized as the bulwark of the nation in upholding the social, political and spiritual integrity of the country. It behooves the Christian family to observe closely the Biblical teaching regarding the home. Grace at every table, daily family altar, hospitality to friends and strangers, profitable leisure time and reasonable working hours, and regular church attendance should be the unfluctuating standard of every Christian home.

2. MARRIAGE:

a. We believe that marriage is a sacred institution, ordained of God, and is an indissoluble union of one husband and one wife to be entered into with an attitude of godly reverence and wisdom, love and purity. (Gen. 1:27; 2:18, 24; Prov. 18:22; Matt. 19:4-6)

b. We believe that it is unscriptural for a believer to unite with an unbeliever in the bond of matrimony (Deut. 7:2-4; Neh. 13:25-27). Consequently, social friendships with unbelievers inclined to lead toward courtship and marriage should be discouraged.

c. Ministers are forbidden to officiate at the marriage of a believer with an unbeliever, and cautioned against officiating at marriages of questionable social, moral or mixed relationships.

d. Weddings, and all activities connected therewith, shall be planned and proceed in a demonstration of simplicity and dignity without ceremonial display or worldly formality.

3. DIVORCE AND REMARRIAGE:

a. Since we believe in the indissoluble union of husband and wife, a divorce should not as much as be anticipated among believers (Gen. 2:18, 21-23; Matt. 19:3-9); neither divorced party should marry another as long as both live. (Mark 10:11-

CHURCH COVENANT AND ARTICLES OF FAITH
(EVANGELICAL MENNONITE BRETHREN
CHURCH) (continued)

12; 5:32; I Cor. 6:16) Note: Evangelical Christianity is not united on the question of divorce and remarriage. There are those who would grant a divorce on the ground of fornication or adultery as based upon Matthew 5:31-32; 19:9, and would not stand in the way of remarriage while both divorcees live. Our Conference has not found liberty to yield to this interpretation.

b. Separation without divorce is recognized but deprecated in Scriptures. (I Cor. 7:10-16)

c. Remarriage after death of either husband or wife has Biblical sanction. (I Cor. 7:30; Rom. 7:2-3)

4. THE LORD'S DAY: We believe that the first day of the week is of divine origin, commonly called the Lord's Day, and is to be held sacred in commemoration of Christ's resurrection from the dead (Acts 20:7; John 20:19; Mark 2:27-28; I Cor. 16:1-2), as a day of worship, Christian service, and rest from all secular labor and abstinence from active participation in organized sport.

5. GENERAL CHRISTIAN WALK: We believe that man is created in the image and similitude of God (James 3:9; Eph. 2:24; Gen. 1:26). A Christian, therefore, should be willing to walk in all simplicity and humility, love and unity, honesty and purity. Discretion should be used in regards to appearance and dress. Believers should glorify God in all things. (Rom. 12:1-2; I Tim. 2:8-10; I Peter 3:1-16; I Tim. 4:12; Col. 3:1-14; Eph. 4:1-7; Rom. 12:9-12; I Cor. 11:1-16; Deut. 22:5)

6. CHRISTIAN STEWARDSHIP: We believe and teach that God is the possessor and sustainer of everything (Hag. 2:8; Ps. 24:1; Col. 1:16-17). The Bible clearly teaches systematic and proportionate giving (I Cor. 16:1-2; II Cor. 9:7-8). To give the tithe and beyond the tithe has the promise of God's blessing (Mal. 3:10; Luke 6:38; II Cor. 9:6, 10). The Christian is also steward over that which he retains as well as his time and talents (Matt. 35:14-30; Eph. 5:16; Col. 4:5).

7. DEDICATION OF CHILDREN: We believe that it is scriptural to dedicate children to the Lord (I Sam. 1:28; Matt. 19:13-16; Luke 18:15-17) by the setting apart and prayer at a public meeting where parents make voluntary declaration of their willingness to submit their children to the Lord for whatever ministry He would choose for them.

8. DIVINE HEALING: We believe that divine healing of the body can be realized by God's children on conditions as set forth in Scripture (James 5:13-16). The Believer is admonished to preserve life and health. (Ex. 20:13; Phil. 4:5,11; I Cor. 9:27; 10:31; I John 4:1-6; II Cor. 11:13-15) In light of these passages we caution against the obvious abuse of the spectacular in the modern day phenomena of mass "faith healing".

9. TONGUES: We believe the New Testament use of "tongues" was an Apostolic sign gift to proclaim the "mighty works of God to Jews out of every nation under heaven" in their own language. (I Cor. 14:20-22; Acts 2:5-21; Joel 2:26-32) The Holy Spirit's purpose in causing tongues was to authenticate those specially appointed representatives of Christ, that is, the Apostles. Tongues speaking was a sign of His presence and ministry for the purpose of validating the Apostolic message before it was inscripturated. The purpose of Biblical tongues limits them to the Apostolic age. In light of historical and grammatical interpretation of Scripture, we believe the gift of tongues as emphasized by the present day charismatic movement is not a valid gift for the church today and should not be tolerated in the church. (I Cor. 13:8-10; Eph. 2:19-20)

10. CIVIL GOVERNMENT: We believe that civil government is ordained of God for the punishment of evil doers, for the protection of the good, and to justly direct the interaction of society. (Rom. 13:1-7; Ex. 18:21-23) We, therefore, consider it our duty to pray for our rulers and magistrates (I Tim. 2:1-3), and to be submissive and obedient to their authority except in things which militate against the supreme law and will of our Lord Jesus Christ. (Titus 3:1; I Peter 3:13-14; Acts 4:19; 5:29; Matt. 23:10; Rev. 19:16; Rom. 14:9-13)

11. EDUCATION: Educational provision is recommended in the Bible. Throughout the years educational opportunities have advanced through improved facilities and teaching qualities. While Christianity has enjoyed its freedom in the separation of church and state, there are increasingly strong indication that the school will become grafted wholly in the state trunk. Our children and youth are a God-given heritage which must be preserved at any cost. The quality of our school rests largely upon the parents and teachers. As long as these will remain true to Scriptural principles and are willing to stand on guard for our rights and privileges, we need not fear the future.

12. OATHS AND PROFANITY: We believe that the Scriptures strictly forbid the swearing of oaths (Matt. 5:33-37, James 5:12), and that everything beyond an affirmation which is as binding as though we confirmed it by an oath, is violating the command of our Lord Jesus Christ. The Scripture also teaches that it is a sin to use the name of the Lord irreverently. (Ex. 21:7)

13. SECRET SOCIETIES: We believe that all secret orders are contrary to the teaching of the Scriptures. There is nothing belonging to Christianity of which the followers of Christ need to be ashamed or want to conceal to men. Therefore, under no circumstances should members be allowed to hold membership in any secret organization. (John 3:18-20; Eph. 5:11-12; II Cor. 6:14-18), neither shall any such person be received into church membership.

14. GOING TO LAW: The Scriptures teach to "Follow peace with all men" (Heb. 12:14), to be inoffensive (Eph. 4:3; Rom. 12:8), not to seek revenge or recompense evil for evil of those who do us evil (Rom. 12:17-21), and particularly forbids going to law with a believer before unbelievers. (I Cor. 6:1-8; Matt. 5:25)

15. CARNAL WARFARE:

a. We believe that God has called us to live peaceably with all men, to overcome evil with good, and to walk worthy of our vocation. (II Cor. 10:3-4; I Thess. 5:15; I Peter 2:21-23; John 15:12; Gal. 5:3-15; I Peter 3:8-9; I John 3:15,23)

b. The Historic position of the Evangelical Mennonite Brethren Church has been to oppose the bearing of arms in warfare and the development of strife between nations, classes, groups, or individuals.

c. Our churches, however, respect the right of individual conviction and recognize that various positions will be taken on war and military service. Our churches support our Christian youth who because of faith and conscience accept the exemptions or alternatives to combat service. In any event, our churches give spiritual aid to all of our youth in service by encouraging them to exert a positive testimony for Christ.

d. We believe that the proper expression of Christian love and discipleship is by a daily manifestation of a meek spirit. We believe that it is necessary in daily living to return evil with good and not evil for evil. The position of non-resistance is as important in daily contacts with people as it is in any national or international crisis.

e. We also believe that the taking of a non-resistant position, and the registering of the same with our government, shall be a matter of personal conscience and conviction.

Notes: *These documents are taken from the church's constitution. The Articles of Faith are unique primarily for their affirmations concerning angels. The constitution covers the ordinances (baptism and the Lord's Supper) and a variety of practices in a separate section.*

* * *

ARTICLES OF FAITH (EVANGELICAL MENNONITE CHURCH)

I. THE SCRIPTURES

We believe that the Old and New Testament Scriptures were given by holy men of God, who were divinely inspired, who wrote in obedience to the divine command, and were kept from error whether the truths were familiar or unknown. God is the author, salvation the objective, and by its principles all will be judged. (II Tim. 3:16-17, II Pet. 1:21, Acts 3:21, Rom. 2:1-16). The scripture is not to be broken. (Jno. 10:35). It is the supreme standard by which all human conduct, creeds, and opinions shall be tried. (Psa. 119:105, Acts 17:2, II Tim. 3:16-17). It is the

revelation of God Himself, speaking to man, revealing man's state by nature, and presenting the only means of his salvation. (Rom. 3:10-12, Acts 4:12).

II. GOD

We believe there is only one living and true God, Perfect, Infinite and Eternal. (Isa. 45:21-22, Eph. 4:6, I Cor. 8:6, I Kings 8:27, Psa. 90:2, 102:24-27, I Tim. 6:16). God is omniscient, (Heb. 4:13, Acts 15:18), omnipresent, (Psa. 139:7-10, Jer. 23:24, Amos 9:2-3,) omnipotent, (Jer. 10:12-13, Gen. 35:11) and is unchangeable in His being, holiness, justice, love and truth. (Mal. 3:6, Isa. 6:3, Psa. 19:9, Jas. 1:17). He is the Creator, Preserver and Ruler of the Universe. (Gen. 1:1, Heb. 11:3, Psa. 103:19, Acts 17:28). He exists in three persons, namely: Father, Son and Holy Spirit, who are equal in their divine perfection though distinct in personality and execute distinct but harmonious offices in the great work of redemption. (Matt. 28:19, Jno. 15:26, I Cor. 2:10, Jno. 10:30, Eph. 2:18, II Cor. 13:14).

III. JESUS CHRIST

We believe the Son was made in the likeness of men, being born of the Virgin Mary, thus uniting organically and indissolubly the divine and human natures in their completeness in the one unique person of Jesus Christ. (Phil. 2:6-11, Matt. 1:18-25, Jno. 1:14, I Tim. 3:16, Heb. 2:14). The purpose of the incarnation was redemption. He took upon Himself the likeness of sinful flesh (Phil. 2:6-7, II Cor. 5:21) and by His death made full atonement for our sins. (Isa. 53:4-5, Matt. 20:28. Heb. 10:9-10, I Jno. 4:10). And having risen from the dead He ascended into heaven, and is now at the right hand of God (I Pet. 3:22, Heb. 8:1, Col. 3:1) interceding in our behalf. (I Jno. 2:1, Rom. 8:34).

IV. THE HOLY SPIRIT

We believe the Holy Spirit, the third person of the Trinity, proceedeth from the Father and the Son. (Jno. 15:26). His principal ministry, since His advent at Pentecost is to reprove or convict the world of sin, of righteousness, and of judgment, (Jno. 16:8-11 see R.V.) to restrain the progress of evil until God's purposes are accomplished, (II Thess. 2:7) to bear witness to the truth preached, (Jno. 15:26, Acts 5:30-32) to regenerate those who repent of their sins and exercise faith in Christ, (Jno. 3:5-8, Titus 3:5) to instruct, comfort and guide God's children, (Jno. 14:16-18, Jno. 16-13, Rom. 8:26) to sanctify them, (II Thess. 2:13, I Pet. 1:2) to empower them for life and service, (Acts 1:8, Eph. 3:16, I Cor. 2:1-4, I Thess. 1:5) and to quicken their mortal bodies. (Rom. 8:11).

V. MAN

A. HIS CREATION. We believe that man was created by an immediate act of God, that he was created in the image and likeness of God, possessing personality and holiness and that the purpose of his creation was to glorify God. (Gen. 2:7, Gen. 1:27, Eph. 4:24, Col. 3:10, Eph. 1:5-6, 12).

B. HIS FALL. We believe that man was subjected to trial in the Garden of Eden in order to test his loyalty to his Creator. (Gen. 2:15-17). By voluntarily transgressing God's positive command and yielding to the enticement of Satan, man lost his holy state, was alienated from God, and became physically,

ARTICLES OF FAITH (EVANGELICAL MENNONITE
CHURCH) (continued)

morally, and spiritually depraved. In consequence of
this act of disobedience, the entire human race
became involved in sin so that in every heart there is
by nature that evil disposition which eventually leads
to responsible acts of sin and just condemnation.
(Gen. 3:1-6, Rom. 5:12, 18, Rom. 3:10-12, Rom.
1:19-32, I Jno. 1:8-10, I Cor. 2:14, Isa. 53:6, Jer.
17:9).

C. HIS REDEMPTION. We believe that God as the
Sovereign Ruler must punish sin. Christ, the son of
God, voluntarily offered Himself on the cross as the
perfect sacrifice for sin, the just suffering for the
unjust, bearing sin's curse, and tasting death for
every man. Nothing prevents the salvation of the
greatest sinner on earth, but his own stubborn will,
and voluntary rejection of Jesus Christ as substitute
for penalty. (Matt. 20:28, Heb. 9:11, 12, I Pet. 3:18, I
Pet. 1:18-21, Gal. 3:13, Heb. 2:9, Titus 3:4-7, I Tim.
2:5-6, II Cor. 5:21).

VI. SALVATION

A. REPENTANCE. We believe that the scriptures
teach that repentance precedes regeneration, and is
manifested in genuine Godly sorrow for sin, and a
consequent turning therefrom unto God, that it
involves a heart confession wrought by the convicting power of the Holy Spirit. (Isa. 55:7, Mk. 1:15,
Acts 11:18, Acts 3:19).

FAITH. We believe that faith is essential to salvation. It is that persuasion by which the Word of God
is received as true (Heb. 11:1). It is both the gift of
God and the act of the creature (Rom. 10:9, 10, 17;
Eph. 2:8; Col. 2:12). It is a reasonable confidence
based upon good evidence (John 20:30, 31; 10: 37,
38). Salvation by faith supersedes mental assent by
laying hold of moral powers and relying upon them
(Rom. 10:10; 3:25). It not only believes that the
death of Christ is the sacrifice for sin but is a trust in
its efficacy.

B. REGENERATION AND JUSTIFICATION. We
believe that salvation is wholly of grace and free to
all, (Isa. 55:1, Rev. 22:17, Eph. 2:8) but is condi-
tioned solely on repentance toward God and acceptance of Christ by faith. (Eph. 2:8-9, Titus 3:5, Acts
4:12, 16:31, 20:21, II Cor. 7:10). When the sinner has
met these requirements, God justifies and regenerates him. Justification is a judicial declaration
absolving from punishment and restoring to divine
favor. (Rom. 5:1-9, Gal. 3:11, Acts 13:39). Regeneration is the impartation of Divine life. By the
operation of the Holy Spirit through the word he is
given a disposition to obey God (Jno. 3:3-5, 1:12-13,
II Cor. 5:17, I Pet. 1:23, Phil. 2:13). This experience
is witnessed to by the Holy Spirit. Proper evidence
appears in the holy fruits of repentance and faith,
and a personal knowledge of forgiveness of sin,
perfect peace to the soul and newness of life. (Gal.
5:22-23, I Jno. 5:4, Eph. 5:9).

C. SANCTIFICATION AND BAPTISM OF THE
SPIRIT. We believe that the Scriptures teach that
sanctification is both instantaneous and progressive
and is made possible by the vicarious death of Jesus
Christ. (Heb. 10:10, I Cor. 1:30). It is a work of the
Holy Spirit, separating and keeping the believer
separated from sin unto God. (Psa. 4:3). This He
does by indwelling, filling and controlling. It involves
a voluntary separation from sin, a yielding to God,
and a putting off of the old man by the power of the
Holy Spirit. (Rom. 6:13, 19, Eph. 4:22-24, Col. 3:9-
10). It is the call of God. (I Thess. 4:7). It is the will
and work of God. (Jno. 17:17, I Thess. 4:3). It is
provided for in the atonement. (Heb. 13:11-12). It is
experienced by the individual through faith and
dedication. (Acts 15:9, 26:18, Gal. 2:20, Rom. 12:1).
The word and the blood are the means used to
accomplish it. (Jno. 17:17, Eph. 5:25-27, Heb. 9:14).

We believe that the baptism with the Holy Spirit is a
distinct experience of the believer subsequent to
regeneration. (Luke 11:13, Jno. 14:16, 17, Acts 1:4-5,
8:12-18, 19:1-6, Gal. 4:6). It is variously designated
and referred to in the scriptures. (Luke 24:49, Acts
1:4, 5, 8, 2:4, 8:15-17, 10:44, 11:15-16, Eph. 1:13). It
is necessary for holiness and fruitfulness of life and
enduement with power for service, (I Cor. 12:4-13,
Gal. 5:22-23, Luke 24:49, Acts 1:8, 4:31), and is
experienced on conditions of complete obedience to
God. (Acts 5:32). It involves separation, sacrifice,
self denial and death to self, (Rom. 6:11-13, 12:1,
Matt. 16:24), is received by prayer, (Luke 11:13) and
appropriating faith. (Gal. 3:2). We must trust the
Holy Spirit's leadership unreservedly and let him
work unhindered. (Eph. 4:30-32, Rom. 8:13-14, Gal.
5:16, Isa. 59:19).

VII. THE CHURCH

We believe that the church, invisible and universal, is
composed of all true regenerated believers of whatever
name, race or nation, who are separated from sin and
vitally united by faith to Christ, the living Head and Ruler.
(Jno. 10:1-5, 15:1-8, I Pet. 2:9-10, Eph. 1:22-23, 4:15-16, I
Cor. 12:12-27). Jesus Christ Himself being the chief
cornerstone. (Eph. 2:19-22). The church local and visible is
an organization made up of a company of professed
believers in Christ, voluntarily joined together and meeting
at stated times to worship and fellowship, to observe
ordinances and when necessary to administer discipline.
(Acts 2:46-47, 20:7, I Cor. 16:2, Matt. 18:15-17, I Cor. 5:1-
4, Acts 6:1-6, 14:23). It is the duty of the church to give
the Gospel as a witness to all men, (Matt. 28:18-20, Acts
1:8) to build itself up in the most holy faith, (Jude 20-21,
Eph. 4:11-16, Acts 20:32, II Pet. 3:18) and to glorify God.
(Eph. 1. 1:5-6, 3:21, I Pet. 4:11).

VIII. THE LORD'S DAY

We believe that the first day of the week is of Divine origin
commonly called the Lord's Day or Christian Sabbath,
(Acts 20:7, Jno. 20:19, Mark 2:27-28, I Cor. 16:1-2) and is
to be kept sacred for religious purposes (Exod. 20:8, Rev.
1:10, Psa. 118:24) in commemoration of the resurrection of

our Lord from the dead (Jno. 20:19, 26), by resting from all secular labor except works of mercy and necessity.

IX. ORDINANCES

A. BAPTISM. We believe that water baptism symbolizes the experience of regeneration and union with Christ, (Acts 8:36-39) is a public confession of the same and initiates the believer into the visible church, (Acts 2:38, 41, 47, Mark 16:16) is to be administered to believers only, (Acts 8:37, 16:30-34) in the name of the Father and of the Son and of the Holy Ghost. (Matt. 28:19). Water baptism has no saving or cleansing efficacy. (Rom. 10:9-10, Jno. 1:12). We cannot recognize infant baptism as valid according to Scripture.

B. FEET WASHING. The washing of the saint's feet was instituted by our Lord who also Himself washed the disciple's feet. (Jno. 13:4-17). This practice is encouraged in our churches where it can be used effectively as a means of growth in Grace.

C. LORD'S SUPPER. The Lord's supper is an ordinance, instituted by Christ in the night of betrayal, to be observed by His children until He returns. It consists in partaking of the consecrated emblems of bread and the fruit of the vine which symbolizes the death of Christ for the remission of our sins and our continual dependence upon Him for our sustenance. Its observance is to be preceded by faithful self-examination. The communion table shall be open to all believers who are living consistent Christian lives, regardless of denomination. (Matt. 26:26-30, Luke 22:19-20, I Cor. 10:16, 11:23-29).

D. DEDICATION OF CHILDREN. The Scriptures give instances where children were publicly dedicated. (I Sam. 1:28, Luke 2:22-24, Matt. 19:13-16, Luke 18:15-17). We therefore encourage parents to dedicate their children to the Lord by prayer and the laying on of hands of the ministers.

X. ESCHATOLOGY

A. SECOND ADVENT OF CHRIST. We believe in the personal, visible, pre-millenial and imminent return of Christ. (Jno. 14:1-3, Acts 1:10-11, Mark 13:22-37). This will be accomplished in two stages. First Christ will descend into mid-air to catch away His waiting bride the church. (I Thess. 4:16-17). Then after the tribulation judgments are visited upon the apostate and rebellious world. (I Tim. 4:1-3, II Tim. 4:1-4, Matt. 24:21, II Thess. 1:3-10). He will descend with His saints (Jude 14, Rom. 8:16-19, Col. 3:4, Rev. 19:7, 8, 19) to establish the long promised kingdom and to reign upon the earth for a thousand years. (Dan. 7:13-14, Luke 1:32-33, Rev. 5:9, 10, 20:4-6).

B. JUDGMENTS. We believe that the believer's works will be judged for rewards at the judgment seat of Christ at the time of His coming. (I Cor. 3:8-15, 4:5, 5:10, II Tim. 4:8). We believe that the impenitent wicked will appear before God for judgment at the Great White Throne after the millenium, and that they will be consigned to the lake of fire, there to suffer torment forever and ever together with the devil and his angels according as their works deserve. (Eccl. 12:14, Mark 9:43-48, Rom. 2:8-9, Heb. 9:27, Rev. 20:10-15).

C. ETERNAL STATE. We believe that after all God's enemies are consigned to their place of punishment, the present order of things will be dissolved and the new heaven and the new earth, wherein dwelleth righteousness, shall be brought in as the final state in which the righteous shall dwell forever. (Isa. 65.17, 66:22, II Pet. 3:13, Rev. 21:1-7, 22:3-7).

XI. DIVINE HEALING

We believe that healing for the body has been provided in the atonement of Christ, (Isa. 53:4-5, Matt. 8:16-17) and it can be realized by God's children on conditions as set forth in Mark 6:13, Jas. 5:13-16.

XII. GENERAL PRINCIPLES

A. MARRIAGE. We believe that marriage is a sacred institution, ordained of God, and is an indissoluble union of one husband and one wife, to be entered into in the fear of God and according to the teachings of the Holy Scriptures. (Gen. 1:27, 2:18, 24, Matt. 19:4-6, I Cor. 7:39).

We believe that it is unscriptural for believers to unite with unbelievers in the bond of matrimony, (Duet. 7:2-4, Neh. 13:25-27, II Cor. 6:14-15) and therefore such unions should be discouraged by our churches and our ministers are forbidden to officiate at the marriage of an unbeliever with a believer. We definitely discourage a Protestant-Catholic courtship or courtship with a follower of any of the various cults.

B. DIVORCE. We believe that the Scriptures forbid divorce except on the grounds of adultery, and that neither divorced party should marry another as long as both live. (Matt. 5:31-32, 19:3-12, I Cor. 6:16, Mark 10:11-12). If the offender fully repents and both agree, there may be a remarriage except in a case described in Duet. 24:1-4. Separation without divorce is recognized but deprecated in the Scriptures. In the case of an unbeliever who is dissatisfied to live with a believer, the former shall not be forbidden to depart. (I Cor. 7:12-15).

C. CIVIL GOVERNMENT. We believe that civil government is ordained of God for the punishment of evil doers, for the protection of the good, and to justly direct the interaction of society. (Rom. 13:1-7, Exod. 18:21-23). We, therefore consider it our duty to pray for our rulers and magistrates (I Tim. 2:1-3) and to be submissive and obedient to their authority except in things which militate against the supreme law and will of our Lord Jesus Christ. (Titus 3:1, I Pet. 2:13, 14, Acts 4:19, 5:29, Matt. 23:10, Rev. 19:16, Rom. 14:9-13).

D. OATHS. We believe that the Scriptures strictly forbid the swearing of oaths, (Matt. 5:33-37, Jas. 5:12) and that everything beyond an affirmation which is as binding as though we confirmed it by an oath, is violating the command of our Lord Jesus Christ.

E.   NON-RESISTANCE.

1.   GOING TO LAW. The Scriptures teach to "Follow peace with all men," (Heb. 12:14), to be inoffensive (Eph. 4:3, Rom. 12:8), and it is forbidden for a disciple of Christ to seek revenge, or recompense evil for evil, of those who do us evil (Rom. 12:17-21) and particularly is it forbidden to go to law with a believer before unbelievers (I Cor. 6:1-8, Matt. 5:25).

2.   CARNAL WARFARE. We believe it is contrary to the teachings of Christ and the New Testament for Christians to take up arms in wars of aggression, revenge, and self defense. (Matt. 5:44, 26:51-52, Rom. 12:17-21, II Cor. 10:3-4, I Thess. 5:15, I Pet. 2:21-23, Jno. 15:12, Gal. 5:13-15, I Pet. 3:8-9, I Jno. 3:15, 23).

F.   SECRET SOCIETIES. We believe that all secret orders are contrary to the teaching of the Scriptures. There is nothing belonging to Christianity of which the followers of Christ need to be ashamed or to conceal from men. Therefore, under no circumstances should members be allowed to hold membership in any secret organization (Jno. 3:19, 18:20, Eph. 5:11-12, II Cor. 6:14-18), neither shall any such person be received into church membership.

G.   TITHING. God is the owner of everything. (Hag. 2:8; Psa. 24:1). He has a system whereby the Christian ministry is financed. Abraham practiced it (Gen. 14:18-20); Jacob continued it (Gen. 28:20-22); Moses confirmed it (Lev. 27:30; Malachi commanded it (Mal. 3:10); and the Lord Jesus Christ commended it (Mt. 23:23). The Scriptures teach systematic giving. (I. Cor. 16:2). A blessing is promised to the liberal giver. (Lu. 6:38; Mal. 3:10-12).

Notes: *The Evangelical Mennonite Church has adopted the major belief of the Holiness movement, which identifies the baptism of the Holy Spirit with sanctification. Sanctification is seen as a second work of the Holy Spirit in the believer, separating the believer from sin. Otherwise, Mennonite distinctives such as pacifism are maintained, and foot washing is practiced.*

*   *   *

OUR COMMON CONFESSION (GENERAL CONFERENCE MENNONITE CHURCH)

A.   BASIC FAITH. The General Conference believes in the divine inspiration and the infallibility of the Bible as the Word of God and the only trustworthy guide of faith and life; in Jesus Christ as the only Savior and Lord. For no other foundation can any one lay than that which is laid, which is Jesus Christ" (1 Cor. 3:11).

In the matter of faith it is, therefore, required of the congregations which unite with the conference that, accepting the above confession, they hold fast to the doctrine of salvation by grace through faith in the Lord Jesus Christ (Eph. 2:8, 9; Tit. 3:5), baptism on confession of faith (Mk. 16:16; Acts 2:38), the avoidance of oaths (Mt. 5:34-37; Jas. 5:12), the biblical doctrine of nonresistance (Mt. 5:39-48; Rom. 12:9-21), nonconformity to the world (Rom. 12:1, 2; Eph. 4:22-24), and the practice of a scriptural church discipline (Mt. 18:15-17; Gal. 6:1).

At no time shall any rules be made or resolutions adopted which in any way contradict the historical principles of faith as laid down in this Constitution.

B.   SEPARATED LIFE.

1.   The General Conference believes that membership in oathbound secret societies, military organization, or other groups which tend to compromise the loyalty of the Christian to the Lord and to the church is contrary to such apostolic admonitions as: "Do not be mismated with unbelievers" (2 Cor. 6:14, 15, and that the church "should be holy and without blemish" (Eph. 5:27).

2.   Further, regarding "the works of the flesh" (Gal. 5:19-21), the conference believes "that those who do such things shall not inherit the kingdom of God."

Therefore, every congregation should seriously strive to remain free from these evils.

Much rather, "If we live by the Spirit, let us also walk by the Spirit" (Gal. 5:25).

(ADOPTED IN 1941)

Accepting the full Bible and the Apostolic Creed:

1.   We believe in one God, eternally existing and manifest as Father, Son and Holy Spirit.

2.   We believe in the deity of Jesus Christ, the only begotten of the Father, full of grace and truth, born of the virgin Mary, in His perfect humanity, His atoning death, His bodily resurrection from the dead, and His personal triumphant return.

3.   We believe in the immortality of the soul, the resurrection of the dead, and a future state determined by divine judgment.

4.   We believe in the divine inspiration and the infallibility of the Bible as the Word of God and the only trustworthy guide of faith and life.

5.   We believe a Christian is one saved by grace, whose life is transformed into the likeness of Christ by His atoning death and the power of His resurrection.

6.   We believe that Christ lived and taught the way of life as recorded in the Scriptures, which is God's plan for individuals and the race; and that it becomes disciples of Christ to live in this way, thus manifesting in their personal and social life and relationship the love and holiness of God. And we believe that this way of life also implies nonresistance to evil by carnal means, the fullest exercise of love, and the resolute abandonment of the use of violence, includ-

ing warfare. We believe further that the Christian life will of necessity express itself in nonconformity to the world in life and conduct.

7. We believe in prayer as fellowship with God, a desire to be in His will, and in its divine power.

8. We believe that the Christian Church consists of believers who have repented from their sins, have accepted Christ by faith and are born again, and sincerely endeavor by the grace of God to live the Christian life.

9. We believe in the brotherhood of the redeemed under the fatherhood of God in Christ.

Notes: *The first brief statement, taken from the church's constitution, covers only the most essential beliefs. A lengthier statement of doctrine was adopted at the General Conference session in 1941.*

* * *

Brethren

WE BELIEVE (ASSOCIATION OF FUNDAMENTAL GOSPEL CHURCHES)

WE BELIEVE:

1. In the Diety-God in Trinity—Father, Son, and Holy Ghost.

2. In the Virgin Birth, Crucifixion, Death and Resurrection; Ascension and Second Coming of Christ.

3. The Blood of Jesus Christ was shed for the remission of sins.

4. In the Resurrection of the dead.

5. In the return of Jesus Christ for His Bride (The Church).

6. In a literal Heaven as the future abode for the righteous.

7. In a literal Hell as the future abode for the wicked.

8. It is the responsibility of every individual to work out his own soul's salvation.

9. The Church (The Body of Christ) to be the accepted believer of all ages.

WE BELIEVE, PRACTICE, AND TEACH:

1. Faith in our Lord Jesus Christ.

2. Repentence.

3. Baptism by immersion and the application of the Blood of Jesus Christ for the remission of sins.

4. Laying on of Hands for the Gift of the Holy Ghost.

5. The new Birth, a life dedicated and consecrated to God.

6. Feet washing.

7. Lord's Supper.

8. Holy Communion.

9. Kiss of Charity.

10. Anointing with oil of the sick.

11. The Sisters cover, the Brethren uncover their heads in worship.

12. Going to war, taking an oath, divorce, going to law, ornamental adorning to be unscriptural.

OUR PURPOSE:

Believing salvation is the responsibility of each individual, our purpose is to:

Establish a church where man can worship God, find access to God, and be taught of God. Lay claim to every attribute of God available to us. Use every means at our command to bring lost and dying humanity to a saving knowledge of our Lord and Saviour Jesus Christ.

Notes: *Originating as an independent fellowship in Germany, the Brethren came to America and settled in Lancaster County, Pennsylvania, from whence they spread across the United States. Like the Amish they wore plain clothes until recent decades when they experienced splinters along a conservative-liberal spectrum concerning such issues as wearing apparel, behavior, and doctrine. Brethren have traditionally practiced foot washing. Also, the Lord's Supper among the Brethren refers to a meal (love feast) which is eaten concurrently with the taking of the traditional communion elements, bread and wine.*

The Association of Fundamental Gospel Churches is one of the more conservative bodies in the Brethren tradition.

* * *

AFFIRMATION OF FAITH [ASHLAND THEOLOGICAL SEMINARY—BRETHREN CHURCH (ASHLAND, OHIO)]

Acknowledging the absolute supremacy and Lordship of Jesus Christ, and believing that His Word and Will must be final in all matters to those who claim to be Christian, on His authority we affirm the following truths as the basic faith and teaching of this institution.

1. The Holy Scriptures of the Old and New Testaments, as originally given of God, are the infallible record of the perfect, final and authoritative revelation of His work and will, together sufficient in themselves as the rule of faith and practice.

2. The One True God, perfect and infinite in His being, holiness, love, wisdom and power; transcendent above the world as its Creator, yet immanent in the world as the Preserver of all things; self-existent and self-revealing in three divine Persons, the Father, the Son, and the Holy Spirit, who are equal in power and glory.

3. Jesus Christ the Eternal Son, Revealer of the invisible God, Who became incarnate by virgin birth, lived the perfect human life upon earth, gave Himself in death upon the Cross as the Lamb of God bearing sin and its penalty in our stead, was raised and glorified in the body in which He suffered and died, ascended as our only Saviour and Lord into Heaven, from whence He will come again personally and visibly to raise and translate His waiting Church,

establish His Kingdom fully over all the nations, and
at last be the Raiser and Judge of the Dead.

4. The Holy Spirit, third person of the Godhead, the
divine Lifegiver and Artist in creation, history and
redemption; Who indwells, seals, empowers, guides,
teaches and perfects all them who become children of
God through Christ.

5. That Man was the direct creation of God, made in
the divine image, not in any sense the offspring of an
animal ancestry; and that by transgression man
became a fallen creature, alienated from the life of
God, universally sinful by nature and practice, and
having within himself no means of recovery.

6. That Salvation is the free gift of God's grace,
received through personal faith in the Lord Jesus
Christ, in Whom all those who believe have eternal
life, a perfect righteousness, sonship in the family of
God, and even spiritual blessing needed for life and
godliness; but those who reject the gift of grace in
Christ shall be forever under the abiding wrath of
God.

7. That Christian Character and Conduct are the
outgrowth and evidence of salvation in Christ; and
therefore the Christian is bound to honor His Word,
to walk as He walked, to keep His commandments
and ordinances, and thus bear the fruit of the Spirit
which is love, joy, peace, long-suffering, kindness,
goodness, faithfulness, meekness, and self-control,
against which there is no law; and that the teachings
of the Bible on such matters as marriage, divorce and
the family are of permanent value and obligation to
the Church and society.

Notes: *The Brethren Church, a liberal church on issues of
dress and behavior in the nineteenth century, absorbed a
theological perspective in the twentieth century close to that
of conservative evangelicalism. The church is a member of
the National Association of Evangelicals. It has refused, as a
body, to adopt any statement of faith or creed, taking the
whole Bible as its standard of faith and teaching. The
seminary of the church has, however, published a statement
which generally represents the church's beliefs. It has also
published the "Message of the Brethren Ministry," a
statement adopted in 1921 by the National Brethren
Ministry Association.*

*The church has remained open on the question of premille-
nialism in its eschatology.*

* * *

DOCTRINAL STATEMENT OF THE BRETHREN IN CHRIST CHURCH

ARTICLE I. THE HOLY SCRIPTURES

The Holy Bible, Old and New Testaments, is the Word of
God. This Word, given by divine inspiration, completes
the revelation of God partially disclosed through nature,

providence and the voice of conscience. The Holy Scriptures are necessary for the understanding of God and His
character, attributes and purposes for men.

The Bible as the written Word of God reaches its climax in
revelation in the incarnation of Jesus Christ as the living
Word of God. Through Christ, the living Word, and the
Bible, the written Word, are unfolded God's purpose,
provision and plan for the salvation of men.

The Holy Scriptures as the revelation of God and His will
constitute an authoritative standard of truth, a basis for
faith and the supreme guide for life and conduct. The
illumination of the Holy Spirit is necessary to the proper
understanding of the Scriptures. The best source of
interpretation of the Scripture is the Scriptures themselves.

II Timothy 3:16; Psalms 19:14; Romans 2:14, 15; John 1:1,
14; John 6:45; I Corinthians 2:9, 10, 12; Matthew 22:29,
31.

ARTICLE II. GOD—THE HOLY TRINITY

There is but one living and true God, infinite, eternal,
almighty, omniscient, omnipresent, righteous, loving and
merciful. The Scriptures reveal that the God-head is a
Trinity of three eternal, divine persons: God the Father,
God the Son, and God the Holy Spirit. These three are
one.

Intimations of the Trinity are found in the Old Testament,
where God is revealed as the Creator and Sustainer of the
universe, as providing the standard for man's holiness, and
the sole object of his worship. The Spirit of God is revealed
as associated in the work of creation, and as representing
the God-head in personal relationships with men. The Son
and His work as the world's Redeemer are prophetically
revealed.

In the New Testament the work of the three Persons of the
Trinity and Their oneness in the God-head are more fully
brought into view. Here is revealed the active participation
of the Son with the Father in the work of creation. Here
the functions of the Trinity find their highest expression in
relation to the plan of redemption. This plan was conceived through the love of God, the Father; it was
provided through the death of God, the Son; and it
becomes operative through the work of God, the Holy
Spirit.

Thus from eternity to eternity the three Persons of the
Trinity through Their separate yet complementary functions accomplish the divine purposes of the triune Godhead.

Jno. 14:26; I Pet. 1:2; Jno. 1:1, 2; I Jno. 5:7; Gen. 1; Neh.
9:6; Lev. 11:45; 20:26; Ex. 20:3; Deut. 6:4, 5; Gen. 1:2;
Gen. 6:3; Ex. 31:3; Isa. 9:6, 7; Isa. 63; Matt. 3:16, 17; II
Cor. 13:14; Jno. 1:3; Heb. 1; Jno. 3:16; I Cor. 15:3; Jno.
14:16, 17; 16:8.

ARTICLE III. SIN

The Holy Scriptures teach that man was created by God,
in His own image and likeness. He was righteous and holy
in character and enjoyed fellowship with God.

The Word also teaches that by sin, through the transgression of our first parents, man's original righteousness and
communion with God were lost and the image of God

marred and defaced. Thus the human family became dead in sin, unholy, and incapable of doing right according to the divine standard. By this original sin man by nature is inclined to evil, and actual transgressions of the law of God inevitably result.

Controlled by Satan through the inherited depravity of man's fallen nature, guilty by sins both of commission and omission, man by nature stands condemned under the dominion of spiritual, physical, and eternal death. Moreover, man by his own effort cannot change his inherent preference for sin to love for God, nor even make an approach to such a change without the aid of the Holy Spirit.

Gen. 2:17; Rom. 5:12; Eph. 4:18; Rom. 6:23a; II Thess. 1:9; Jno. 1:13; 6:44.

ARTICLE IV. REDEMPTION

Scripture reveals the fact that the plan of redemption was included in the eternal counsel of God. Its purpose is to deliver all men from the dominion of Satan and restore them to divine favor and fellowship with God. To accomplish this, God, in infinite love and grace, gave His only begotten Son to be Mediator between God and men.

When the fulness of time was come, Christ as the Son of God was born of the Virgin Mary. Thus, He took upon Himself the likeness of men, yet without sin.

This divine-human Saviour, anointed by the Spirit, revealed God and taught by His life how man should live. He atoned for the sins of man by shedding His blood on Calvary's cross. His resurrection witnessed to His glorious triumph over death and Satan. He ascended to the Father by Whom the Holy Spirit was poured out upon His Church. Christ now sits at the right hand of God to make intercession for us.

Eph. 1:4; II Thess. 2:13; II Pet. 3:9; I Tim. 2:5, 6; Phil. 2:7; Gal. 4:4; Heb. 10:5, 7; 9:26; II Tim. 1:10; Heb. 7:25; I Jno. 2:1.

ARTICLE V. FREE WILL

God created man in His own image, a moral being with free will, obligated to exercise personal choice and responsibility to his Creator with respect to his conduct relative to right and wrong.

Through the fall of Adam, man became so depraved that he cannot prepare himself by his own works to merit or receive God's favor. However, God through Jesus Christ, freely extends His grace by mercy to all men, enabling all who will to turn from sin to righteousness, thus preparing them to do works pleasing unto Him.

The believer's relationship of life in Christ remains secure as he exercises his own voluntary will unto yieldedness and obedience to the known will of God. To willfully disregard God's will and commandments will result in his being eternally lost.

Gen. 2:16, 17; Eph. 2:8, 9; Jno. 1:11, 12; Phil. 2:13; Rom. 12:1, 2; Rom. 6:16; II Pet. 1:10; II Pet. 2:20-22; Rev. 3:5.

ARTICLE VI. JUSTIFICATION

Justification and condemnation are the only two possibilities existing in man's relationship to God. A man is either condemned to pay the penalty of his wickedness, or he is justified (acquitted) of all guilt and set free.

Universal guilt has been charged against every member of the human race. God, the Judge, holds all men to be sinners and He must deal with mankind as such, unless some provision for his salvation is found. Such provision has been made through the redemptive work of Christ on the cross of Calvary, where He became the substitute for all men. He assumes all man's guilt, bears all his penalty and he is adjudged free from all his sins. This is the glorious realization of all repentant sinners who appropriate the offer of redemptive love and atoning blood.

Judicially, justification accounts man as guiltless with regard to all his past sins and as the recipient of the imputed righteousness of Christ. Experientially, justification implies a spiritual birth and a new life. The Holy Spirit witnesses to this divine relationship and gives peace with God. The believer maintains this vital relationship with God, even unto eternal life, subject to his obedience to the revealed will of God.

Rom. 5:12; Rom. 3:23; 3:10; II Cor. 5:21; I Pet. 2:24; Rom. 3:25; II Cor. 5:21; Jno. 3:3; II Cor. 5:17; Rom. 8:16; Rom. 5:1; I Jno. 2:24, 25.

ARTICLE VII. SANCTIFICATION

Sanctification throughout the Word of God is used with various meanings: to declare holy, to set apart, and to cleanse.

As a Christian experience, sanctification embodies the setting apart of the believer in entire consecration, and the cleansing of the believer's heart from carnality, accompanied by the baptism of the Holy Spirit.

The sanctification of the believer is required by God, provided for by Christ in His atonement, and divinely wrought by the Holy Spirit.

When the believer led by the Spirit becomes aware of an inner conflict of flesh and Spirit, loathes his condition, confesses his state and need; makes an unreserved consecration, and exercises a living faith in the work of Christ on Calvary, he is definitely cleansed from the carnal mind. Thus the work of holiness which was begun in regeneration is perfected, and the believer is "sanctified wholly."

This experience for believers is obtained instantaneously and subsequent to the new birth. The scriptural terms used to describe the cleansing of the believer's heart imply the same: purifying the heart; crucifixion of the old man; body of sin destroyed; circumcision of the heart; deliverance; creation.

Even though it is possible for a sanctified believer to fall into sin, the Scriptures reveal that by giving heed to the Word, being devoted in prayer, and by rendering loving and obedient service to Christ he is kept from willful transgression by the power of God.

Although sanctification perfects the motives and desires of the heart, the expression of these in terms of accomplishment is a progressive growth in grace until the close of this life.

Gen. 2:3; Ex. 29:43, 44; Ex. 13:2; Jno. 17:19; Ex. 19:10; Eph. 5:26, 27; Rom. 12:1, 2; Jno. 17:17; Acts 15:8, 9; Eph.

DOCTRINAL STATEMENT OF THE BRETHREN IN CHRIST
  CHURCH (continued)

5:26; Matt. 3:11; Acts 2:1-10; Rom. 8:5-8; Heb. 12:14;
Heb. 10:10; Heb. 13:12; Heb. 10:14, 15; Acts 15:8, 9; Gal.
5:17; Rom. 7:14-24; Rom. 6:13-16; Rom. 12:1; II Cor. 7:1;
I Thess. 5:23; Acts 8:14-17; Jas. 4:8; Acts 15:8, 9; Rom.
6:6; Rom. 6:6; Col. 2:11; Rom. 7:24; Psa. 51:10; Jno. 15:6;
II Pet. 2:20-22; I Tim. 4:15, 16; Heb. 4:15, 16; Rom. 6:16;
Jude 20-24; II Tim. 3:16, 17; II Pet. 3:18.

ARTICLE VIII. THE CHURCH

The Church is composed of all those of every nation who
through saving faith in Christ have entered into spiritual
union with Him.

This body of believers is characterized by having been
cleansed from sin, possessing the Holy Spirit, having the
hope of glory, holding joint heirship with Christ and
having fellowship with one another. Her eternal foundation is secured in the sonship, atonement, and resurrection
of her living Head, the Christ.

The Church came into being through the operation of the
Holy Spirit on the day of Pentecost. Through election of
grace she stands actively performing the functions of
ambassador and evangel, light of the world, and salt of the
earth.

Her perfection is attained through the mediums of her
experiences, gifts, growth, fruitage, doctrine, and ordinances. Ultimately as the bride of Christ she will become
the glorious church triumphant.

Acts 10:34, 35; Rom. 1:14-16; Eph. 5:26; Eph. 1:13; Col.
1:27; Rom. 8:17; Acts 2:42; Jno. 3:16; Eph. 1:4; Rom. 5:10;
Acts 2; Eph. 2:8; Matt. 28:19, 20; II Cor. 5:20; Matt. 5:14;
Phil. 2:15; Matt. 5:13; Eph. 4:11-16; I Cor. 11:2; Rev. 19:7-
9; Eph. 5:27.

ARTICLE IX. WATER BAPTISM

Water baptism, an inclusion in the Great Commission, is a
rite of public profession, indicating that one has now come
into the family of God the Father, into the mystical body
of Christ, the Son, and into the communion of the Holy
Spirit, which relationships are symbolized in the observance of this ordinance by triune immersion. Baptism is to
be accompanied by a teaching ministry that guides the
believer into the observance of all things, "whatsoever I
have commanded you."

The necessity of water baptism is established by the
command and example of Jesus and the practice of the
New Testament Church. Those who have sincerely repented of sin, who have by the exercise of their own personal
faith received the Lord Jesus Christ as Saviour and have
been "born again" by the Holy Spirit, are eligible for the
observance of this ordinance.

Baptism has no saving merit in and of itself. It is an
outward sign or symbol by which the believer testifies to
the inner change of heart and redirection of life. Christian
experience is illustrated by the figure of a spiritual baptism
which suggests the death and burial of the old life and the
resurrection to a new life in Christ. Baptism by immersion
typifies and witnesses to such a burial and the coming
forth to walk in newness of life.

Matt. 28:19; Matt. 28:20; Jno. 15:12-17; Matt. 3:13-17;
Acts 2:38-41; I Pet. 3:21; Rom. 6:4; Col. 2:12.

ARTICLE X. THE LORD'S SUPPER

In connection with His last observance of the Passover
feast Jesus instituted the sacred ordinance of the Lord's
Supper, through the use of the broken bread and the cup.
On this occasion He consecrated the bread, which represents His broken body; and the fruit of the vine, which
represents His shed blood, as symbols of His redemptive
sacrifice.

The Lord's Supper thus commemorates with renewed and
tender meaning the sufferings and death of our crucified
Lord; it beautifully portrays through the sharing of the
sacred emblems the unity of the body of Christ; and it also
points forward with hope and expectancy to the time
when, according to His promise, Christ will again fellowship in person with His followers.

This ordinance is observed by those, who having been
saved by faith in Christ, and who having examined
themselves as to their present fellowship with Him, esteem
it a blessed privilege to partake of the sacred emblems in
remembrance of their Lord.

As often as the church observes the Lord's Supper, she
witnesses to the world concerning the death of Christ, and
the promise of His coming again.

I Cor. 11:24; Jno. 6:48-51; Lu. 22:20; I Cor. 11:25; Heb.
10:12; Jno. 19; Phil. 2:7, 8; Rom. 12:5; I Cor. 10:17; Matt.
26:29; Lu. 22:19; I Cor. 11:28; I Cor. 11:26.

Notes: *This statement of belief is noteworthy for its position
on sanctification, which shows the influence of the Holiness
movement. The church is a member of the Christian
Holiness Association. The statement on the Lord's Supper
differentiates the Brethren in Christ from many other
Brethren churches which partake of a full meal at the time
of receiving the communion; however, triune immersion is
practiced as a baptismal form.*

*The Brethren in Christ also use the Apostles' Creed. The
Lutheran text, which includes both the phrase "He descend-
ed into hell" and the affirmation of the "holy Christian
Church," has been adopted.*

*   *   *

A DECLARATION OF FAITH (CHURCH OF THE BRETHREN)

1. We believe that the Holy Scriptures of the Old and
    the New Testament have their authority from God
    and are a sufficient standard of faith and practice.

2. We believe there is one true and living God, infinite,
    self-existent, omnipresent, omniscient, omnipotent,
    good, wise, just, and merciful; that he is the Creator,
    Preserver, and Sovereign of the universe; that in the
    Godhead there are three persons—the Father, the
    Son, and the Holy Ghost.

3. We believe in Jesus Christ, the Son of God, the
    Redeemer and Savior of men.

4. We believe in the Holy Spirit, one with the Father
    and the Son in will and purpose.

5. We believe that man was created in holiness, but through temptation and voluntary transgression fell under condemnation and needs salvation.

6. We believe that the salvation of sinners can be obtained alone through the merits of the Son of God, who by his death made a full atonement for our sins.

7. We believe that in his death he conquered, rose triumphant from the grave, and ascended to the right hand of the Father; that he will come again to judge the world in righteousness.

8. We believe that repentance and faith are absolutely essential, enabling us to receive holy baptism, confessing the Lord Jesus Christ as an all-sufficient Savior.

9. We believe that Christian baptism is the immersion in water of a believer by a triune immersion.

10. We believe that justification is an act of God, on the condition of faith in and obedience to the truth as revealed in the Scriptures.

11. We believe that the visible church of Christ is a body of baptized believers, associated by covenant in faith and fellowship of the gospel, observing all the ordinances of Christ governed by all his laws, and exercising the gifts, rights, and privileges invested in them by his Word.

12. We believe that it is our duty to keep all the ordinances "as they were delivered to us by our Lord Jesus Christ":

   a. That feet-washing is an ordinance, instituted by our Lord.

   b. That the Lord's Supper is a sacred meal, in connection with the communion.

   c. That the communion is the partaking of bread and wine as emblems of the broken body and the shed blood of our Lord and Savior Jesus Christ, a memorial of his suffering and death.

   d. That the anointing of the sick for healing is appointed by the Lord, to be perpetuated in his church.

13. We believe that the first day of the week is the true Christian Sabbath.

14. We believe that civil government is ordained of God for the care and protection of the good and for the punishment of those who do evil.

15. We believe that the principle of nonresistance is clearly taught in the Scriptures and therefore has been accepted as a doctrine of the church.

16. We believe it wrong to swear or to take the civil oath.

17. We believe temperance to be a moderate use of the things that are essential and useful, and total abstinence from such things as are harmful or lead to evil.

18. We believe it to be wrong to conform to the vain fashions, maxims, and customs of the world.

Notes: *There is no official statement of faith for the Church of the Brethren. However, several attempts at statements have been made and published by the church in its* Manual. *The statement reproduced here was written by H. B. Brumbaugh and first published in 1916.*

* * *

A STATEMENT OF BELIEF AND PURPOSE (CHURCH OF THE BRETHREN)

I. We believe that Jesus Christ is the expression of God's love for all men.

   Therefore, we pledge our loyalty to him and his way of life.

II. We accept the New Testament as the guidebook to abundant Christian living.

   Therefore, we pledge ourselves to study its message for our day and to follow the light we discover.

III. We believe that communion with God and fellowship with Christ are essential to daily living and spiritual growth.

   Therefore, we will devote time regularly to private devotions, family worship, and group meditation.

IV. We believe that God is our Father and all men are our brothers.

   Therefore, as we attempt to live Christ's way of reconciling love, we can consider no man our enemy, we dare not hate, we cannot kill.

V. We believe that spiritual values are more important than material possessions.

   Therefore, we will live modestly, dress simply, and eat temperately in order to place God's kingdom first.

Notes: *This statement was written and adopted by the National Youth Cabinet of the Church of the Brethren in 1948. It is much more confessional than the church's declaration of faith.*

* * *

BIBLE TEACHINGS (DUNKARD BRETHREN)

From a careful study of God's Word we conclude:

1. That there is only one true, almighty, everliving God, the Creator and Sustainer of all things visible and invisible, the Ruler of heaven and earth.—Gen. 1:1; 2:7; Psa. 97:9; Isa. 45:5-7; 64:8; 66:1,2.

2. That Jesus Christ is the Son of the living God; that He was born of Virgin Mary, lived in the flesh, and died on the cross, the Redeemer and Saviour of man; that He was buried, rose from the dead the third day, ascended to heaven the fortieth day, where He now "liveth to make intercession"—Matt. 3:17; Luke 2:7; John 3:16; 19:40-42; Acts 1:9-11; Heb. 4:15; 7:25.

3. That the Holy Ghost is the Spirit of the living God, sent forth by the Father and the Son; that He is the Reprover of the wicked, and the Guide and abiding Comforter of God's elect.—John 14:16, 26; 16:7-11, 13; Acts 2:4.

BIBLE TEACHINGS (DUNKARD BRETHREN) (continued)

4. That man was created pure and spotless, in the image of his Maker.—Gen. 1:26, 27, 31; Eccl. 7:29.

5. That the human family became alienated from God as a result of the transgression of our first parents in the Garden of Eden; that sin, sorrow, depravity and death (natural and spiritual) are results of the fall.—Gen. 3:22-24; Rom. 3:10, 23; 5:12; Eph. 2:12.

6. That man was again reconciled through the atonement of Christ on the cross.—Rom. 5:11, 19; Heb. 10:14.

7. That there is no salvation but by Jesus Christ.—John 14:6; Acts 4:12.

8. That salvation is offered as a free gift to all them that believe.—Rom. 5:18; 6:23; Eph. 2:8.

9. That a faith which does not take hold of the individual and bind him to a life of obedience, made manifest in works, has no Bible recognition.—Jas. 2:14-20.

10. That every one who is converted to God will manifest by a holy life that he has been saved from his sins.—Jas. 2:14-20; Tit. 3:3-8.

11. That a sinful, disobedient life is an evidence that the soul is not converted, and that the heart is not right with God.—Matt. 7:16; I John 3:8.

12. That self-denial is an essential feature in Christian living and the gratification of carnal lusts is an abomination in the sight of God.—Matt. 10:38; Luke 9:23; Eccl. 11:9; Gal. 5:19-24; Tit. 2:12.

13. That every child of God should be sober, serious, industrious, spiritually-minded and obedient to the will of God as revealed in His Word.—Tit. 2:12; I Tim. 5:8; I John 2:3-5; Col. 1:8.

14. That the Word of God and the Spirit of God never conflict; that there is no such thing, therefore, as the Spirit leading any one to do differently from what the Bible teaches; and that all our impressions of right and wrong should be diligently compared with God's Word.—John 14:26; 16:13, 14; I John 4:1.

15. That God has on earth a church, instituted by Himself, designed as the earthly home of His people, in which they may labor together for the edification and spiritual growth of the saved and the salvation of the unsaved.—Eph. 4:11-24.

16. That the visible church should be composed of converted souls; that applicants should give evidence of conversion before being received into the church; that the church should exercise a vigilant care over the spiritual welfare of its individual members; and that whenever it becomes clearly apparent that any of them are wedded to sin rather than righteousness (and all available means to effect a reformation have proved fruitless) they should be no longer fellowshipped as members.—Matt. 3:7,8; 18:15-18; Luke 13:6-9; I Cor. 5:7-13; 10:20; II Cor. 6:14, 15.

17. That all believers are to be baptized for the remission of sins. Acts 2:38. Baptism in mode, is immersion. In form it is triune, and consists of an immersion into the name of the Father, and of the Son, and of the Holy Ghost. Matt. 28:19; Mark 1:8; Matt. 3:6; Acts 8:38, 39; Baptism a necessity. John 3:3-5; Mark 16:16. The door to the church. Rom. 6:3; I Cor. 12:13. A new birth. John 3:3-5; I Peter 1:23.

18. That the washing of the saints' feet as an ordinance instituted by our Saviour, and enjoined upon His disciples, should be literally observed by all believers. John 13:1-17; I Tim. 5:10.

19. That the Lord's Supper as instituted by Christ in the night of His betrayal is a full meal to be kept among His people until His return. Matt. 26:20-23; Luke 22:20; John 13:1-17, 30.

20. That the Communion as instituted by Christ consists in partaking of the bread and the cup in a worthy manner at the close of the day, in connection with, but following feet washing and the Lord's Supper. (1) The bread and the cup representing the broken body and the shed blood of Jesus; (2) a common union of communicants. Mark 14:22-24; I Cor. 10:16; 11:21-26.

21. That the believing woman should wear a modest, appropriate head-covering in time of prayer, gospel teaching or other seasons of devotion.—I Cor. 11:2-16.

22. That the salutation of the kiss of brotherhood, "holy kiss," or "kiss of charity," should be practiced by believers.—Rom. 16:16; I Pet. 5:14.

23. That the anointing with oil for the sick is divinely recommended.—Jas. 5:14.

24. That marriage is an institution ordained of God for the purity of humanity and the perpetuation of the race; that believers should marry "only in the Lord"; that man and wife once united remain so until death separates them.—Matt. 19:3-9; I Cor. 7:1-11, 39; II Cor. 6:14.

25. That the Bible specifies a line of demarcation between the Church and the world in every department of life, which if adhered to by the church, so completely separates the two bodies that no one need ever mistake a child of God for a worldling if we know their "manner of life."—Rom. 12:2; Eph. 2:3; 4:16; Tit. 2:14; Jas. 1:27.

26. That it is wrong for Christians to dress according to the fashion of the world; that they should adorn themselves as men and women professing godliness, in modest apparel; that costly array and jewelry and superfluities of all kinds should be scrupulously avoided.—Rom. 12:2; Isa 3:16-24; I Tim. 2:9, 10; I Pet. 3:3,4.

27. That no Christian should ever engage in any business, occupation, recreation or amusement in which he cannot conscientiously ask God to bless him in what he is doing.—I Cor. 10:31; Col. 3:17, 23; Tit. 2:12; I Pet. 3:3,4.

28. That carnal warfare is contrary to the spirit of the Gospel; that it is inconsistent, therefore, for Chris-

tians to manifest a quarrelsome disposition in the home, in the church, in society, or in business; that it is unscriptural to take vegeance upon enemies, or to grasp carnal weapons to inflict injury upon or take the life of our fellow men on the field of battle, or under any circumstances whatsoever.—Matt. 5:38-40; Luke 2:14; John 18:36; Rom. 12:17-21; II Cor. 10:4.

29. That Christians should at all times be law-abiding citizens, subject to the powers that be, obedient to all laws which do not conflict with the higher laws of God, in which case "we ought to obey God rather than men."—Rom. 13:1, 2; Luke 20:25; Acts 4:19; 5:29; Tit. 3:1.

30. That swearing of oaths, both profane and judicial, under any and all circumstances, is wrong.—Matt. 5:33-37; Jas. 5:12.

31. That law-suits are contrary to the spirit of the Gospel, and should be avoided,—Matt. 5:40; Acts 4:19; I Cor. 6:1-8.

32. That it is contrary to the teaching of the Gospel to hold membership in secret organizations.—Matt. 5:15; John 3:19; 18:20; II Cor. 6:14-17; Eph. 5:11-13.

33. That the Christian, as a child of God, put his entire trust in his heavenly Father for support and keeping in this life; as well as glorification in the life to come; that he must therefore consider life-insurance contrary to the spirit of the Gospel.—Jer. 49:11; Psa. 37:25; 118:8; Matt. 6:19, 20, 27-34; Heb. 13:5.

34. That obedience to God's commandments is one of the foremost requirements of God's Word, and that the truly converted child of God has only to know the will of God in any matter and he is ready to obey.—I Sam. 15:22,23; Eccl. 12:13; John 14:15; 15:14.

35. That the Christian's aim should be to get all the light that he can, and live up to all the light that he has.—John 5:39; Acts 17:11; II Tim. 2:15.

36. That God hears and answers prayer; that in answer to prayer He lightens life's burdens, arms us against the power of temptation, gives us His Holy Spirit and whatsoever things we need.—Luke 11:9, 10, 13; 22:42, 43, 46; I John 5:14, 15; Jas. 1:5.

37. That the great mission of the Christian Church is to teach "all nations" to observe "all things" which our Saviour taught His disciples to keep; that it is the duty of the church to Christianize the world.—Matt. 10:8; 28:19, 20; Luke 24: 47.

38. That Christ will come again with power and great glory to gather to Himself the elect of the earth and to bring the world to judgment; that there will be a coming forth of all the dead, who shall appear before the judgment bar of God to be rewarded according to their deeds done in the body.—Matt. 24:30, 31; 25:31-46; John 5:28, 29; II Cor. 5:10; Rev. 1:7; 20: 12, 13.

39. That the eternal abode of the wicked is the place prepared for the devil and his angels—the horrible,

bottomless pit, where the smoke of their torment ascendeth for ever and for ever.—Psa. 9:17; Matt. 25:41; Rev. 14:9-11; 21:8.

40. That the righteous, saved and redeemed through Christ, will be received into glory, where in the presence of God they will sing the new song and enjoy the loveliness, holiness and bliss of heaven in eternity.—Matt. 25:34; II Tim. 4:8; Rev. 21:3, 4; 22:3-5.

Notes: *This statement of teachings identifies the Dunkard Brethren as the strict and conservative group within the Brethren tradition. It includes strong statements on baptism by triune immersion, foot washing, the Lord's Supper, communion, and the holy kiss.*

* * *

STATEMENT OF BELIEF (EMMANUEL'S FELLOWSHIP)

We believe that the Bible teaches authority and discipline in the church, and to be exercised by the church, to help to maintain order and unity of purpose among the members. Titus 2:15, 1 Tim. 5:20, 2nd Thessalonians 3:6-15, 1 Cor. 11:1, 1 Tim. 4:12.

We believe in one God, the Father, Almighty Creator of heaven and earth. And in Jesus Christ, His only begotten son, our Lord. Who was conceived of the Holy Ghost, and born of the virgin Mary. Who suffered under Pontius Pilate, was crucified, died and was buried. Rose again from the dead on the third day, ascended into heaven, and sitteth at the right hand of God, the Almighty Father. From whence He will come to judge the quick and the dead. We believe in the Holy Ghost, in the holy general Christian Church, the communion of saints. We believe in forgiveness of sins, resurrection of the body, and in eternal life.

1. We believe the law of Christ is the supreme law of love. Teaching us to love one another as He has loved us. His love was to seek and to save that which was lost. Luke 19:10, John 13:34, 35.

2. We believe that all men are guilty before God, need to repent, confess and forsake their sin, and to believe and obey God's word. Rom. 3:23, Acts 2:38, Rom. 10:9.

3. We believe in water baptism (as a sign that we have received the Spirit baptism, which gives a regenerated mind to walk in newness of life) upon confession of faith in Christ. One must meet this requirement in order to be baptized. Rom. 6:3-4; Acts 10:47, 1 Peter 3:21, Matt. 3:15, 17.

4. Those admitted to membership are to show evidence of the new birth by their way of life and personal testimony, and are to agree with and be willing to uphold these regulations to the glory of God and for a testimony to the world, living victoriously over sin, walking by faith in the son of God, rightly dividing the word of the truth. Eph. 7:19, 21, 1 Cor. 15:57, 1 John 4:4.

5. We believe that new applicants for membership should serve 6 mo. probationary period in order to become better acquainted with the brotherhood and to prove their testimony.

6. We believe that if one has been taken into the church and fallen away from the truth; and when the church has prayed, fasted, admonished, and exhorted such a person, without acknowledgement, that such a person should be excommunicated from the church. Matt. 18:17 to 19, 1 Cor. 5:11, 2nd Thes. 3:14, 15, Titus 3:10.

7. We believe in the practice of nonresistance in life, in words, and in whatsoever things we do. Whether in Church matters, school problems, paying taxes, occupations or taking up arms, etc. Jer. 17:5, Matt. 5:44, 22:21.

8. We believe in nonconformity, in not being conformed to the things of this world. Members shall not be unequally yoked with unbelievers in business and in other phases of life. They shall abstain from politics, secret societies, labor unions, life insurance, etc. We disapprove of accepting unearned government handouts. 2 Cor. 6:14, 1 John 2:15.

9. We believe in the Lord's Supper as a memorial of His suffering instituted with bread and fruit of the vine for those of like faith and Christian Standards. All who partake must have (a) peace with God, (b) victory over lusts of the flesh, (c) as much as possible peace with their fellow man. Luke 22:19, 1 Cor. 10:21, 11:28, Gal. 5:19.

10. We believe in the Christian ordinances, such as baptism, communion, feet washing, marriage, women's head covering, holy kiss, annointing with oil, etc. 1 Cor. 11:2.

11. We believe that we are called with an high and holy calling to live lives of victory, obedience, and holiness. 1 Pet. 1:15, 16, Acts 5:32, 1 Cor. 16:57.

PRACTICES OF THE CHURCH

1. Our bodies are the temples of God and all that we do or say should be done to His honor and glory. Worldly practices and fleshly lusts, such as strong drink, tobacco, dope, card playing, radios, television, movies, musical instruments, carnivals, circuses, fairs, auto and horse races, public ball games, skating rinks, foolish talk and filthy jokes, games that steal precious time from the Lord, all gatherings that are not edifying, membership in lodges, boys' clubs, etc. are not permitted. Rom. 32, 6:16, 13:13, 1 Cor. 3:16, 6:16-17, Eph. 2:3, 5:3-11, 2nd Tim. 3:4.

2. We believe in the Christian home, the standards of which include regular family worship, and in bringing children up in nurture and admonition of the Lord. Unclean literature is not permitted. Gen. 18:19, Eph. 6:4, 1 John 2:15.

3. Good Stewardship of earthly possessions is encouraged so we can help the poor and extend the kingdom of God with our means. We believe in mission work. Expect each member to participate.

4. Automobiles are to be plain models and black in color, and moderately priced. White sidewalls tires, radio aerials and all unnecessary equipment such as extra chrome etc. are not acceptable.

5. The Bible teaches that the Lord's Day is set aside for special worship, and testimony, and that we must not desecrate it in unnecessary labor, pleasure seeking, joy riding and other unnecessary driving.

6. We believe in purity in courtship. Courtship not recommended before age of 18, and not permitted before age of 17. Also not to be practiced too frequently. Courtship with non-Christians, in dark rooms, autos, on beaches, petting, late hours, and other impure actions are not permitted. Weddings to be simple, with spiritual emphasis.

7. Sisters are to wear the devotional covering made with opaque material corners and strings, we encourage a plain bonnet, consistent in size; not to be mistaken for a hat. Sisters also to wear a cape dress with sufficient length halfway between knee and sole, sleeves to be full length in public, necklines to be full height at all times. No flashy or loud colors, no thin or transparent materials are allowed. No anklets. Black hose not less than service weight and shoes with low heel to be worn. 1 Pet. 3:3, 1 Tim. 2:9, 1 John 2:15-17.

8. Brethern to wear plain suits. Short and rolled up sleeves not permitted in church services. Dress hats are to be plain and black except straw hats. Hair to be parted in middle, not shingled or combed straight back, and to have definite hair line in back. Brethern to wear full beard.

9. Wrist watches not permitted except where duty calls, such as nurses, etc. Jewelery of all descriptions not permitted, including wedding bands.

10. Guidelines for childrens dress, girls hair should not be cut or curled, modestly dressed skirt length below the knees, no anklets. No jewelery permitted. Boys no flat tops, crew cuts or any sort of ridiculous hair cuts. No neckties permitted.

11. These regulations are of a general nature and any member who feels to go beyond these requirements should feel free to do so.

Notes: *Emmanuel's Fellowship is a small conservative Brethren group.*

*   *   *

THE MESSAGE OF THE BRETHREN MINISTRY (FELLOWSHIP OF GRACE BRETHREN CHURCHES)

THE MESSAGE

The message which Brethren ministers accept as a Divine Entrustment to be heralded to a lost world, finds its sole source and authority in the Bible. This message is one of hope for a lost world and speaks with finality and authority. Fidelity to the apostolic injunction to preach the Word demands our utmost endeavor of mind and heart. We, the members of the National Ministerial Association of the Brethren Church, hold that the essential and constituent elements of our message shall continue to be the following declarations:

1. Our Motto: The Bible, the whole Bible and nothing but the Bible.

2. The Authority and Integrity of the Holy Scriptures. The ministry of the Brethren Church desires to bear testimony to the belief that God's supreme revelation has been made through Jesus Christ, a complete and authentic record of which revelation is the New Testament; and, to the belief that the Holy Scripture of the Old and New Testaments, as originally given, is the infallible record of the perfect, final and authoritative revelation of God's will, altogether sufficient in themselves as a rule of faith and practice.

3. We understand the Basic Content of our Doctrinal Preaching and Teaching to Be:

   (1) The Pre-existence, Deity and Incarnation by Virgin Birth of Jesus Christ, the Son of God;

   (2) The Fall of Man, his consequent spiritual death and utter sinfulness, and the necessity of his New Birth;

   (3) The Vicarious Atonement of the Lord Jesus Christ through the shedding of His own Blood;

   (4) The Resurrection of the Lord Jesus Christ in the body in which He suffered and died and His subsequent Glorification at the Right Hand of God;

   (5) Justification by personal faith in the Lord Jesus Christ, of which obedience to the will of God and works of righteousness are the evidence and result; the resurrection of the dead; the judgment of the world, and the life everlasting of the just;

   (6) The Personality and Deity of the Holy Spirit Who indwells the Christian and is his Comforter and Guide;

   (7) The Personal and Visible Return of our Lord Jesus Christ from Heaven as King of Kings and Lord of Lords; the glorious goal for which we are taught to watch, wait and pray;

   (8) The Christian should "be not conformed to this world, but be transformed by the renewing of the mind," should not engage in carnal strife and should "swear not at all";

   (9) The Christian should observe, as his duty and privilege, the ordinances of our Lord Jesus Christ, among which are (a) baptism of believers by Triune Immersion; (b) confirmation; (c) The Lord's Supper; (d) The Communion of the Bread and Wine; (e) the washing of the saints' feet; and (f) the anointing of the sick with oil.

STATEMENT OF BIBLICAL TRUTHS

The National Fellowship of Brethren Churches, standing firmly on the historic slogan of The Brethren Church, "The Bible, the whole Bible, and nothing but the Bible," and feeling our responsibility to make known its divine truths, hereby presents the following articles as a Statement in part of those Biblical truths essential to our Christian faith and practice:

1. The verbal inspiration and infallibility of the Bible as the written Word of God.

2. The One Triune God; existing eternally in three persons—the Father, the Son, and the Holy Spirit.

3. The Lord Jesus Christ: His deity, incarnation, virgin birth, sinless life, substitutionary death, bodily resurrection, and heavenly ascension.

4. The Holy Spirit: His personality, deity, and work in creation, preservation, revelation, and redemption.

5. The divine creation of man as a holy being, his subsequent fall into sin, and the hopeless condition of all men apart from Jesus Christ.

6. A complete and eternal salvation by God's grace alone, apart from works of law, received through personal faith in the Lord Jesus Christ and His finished work.

7. The existence and personality of Satan, the great adversary of God: his judgment and final doom.

8. The personal, visible, and premillennial second coming of our Lord Jesus Christ; the time being unrevealed but always imminent.

9. The conscious existence of the dead, the resurrection of the body, final judgment, eternal life of the saved, and everlasting punishment of the lost.

10. The one true Church which is the body and bride of Christ, composed of all true believers of the present age; and the organization of its members in local churches, self-supporting and self-governing, each supreme in its own affairs, but cooperating in fellowship and work.

11. A Christian life of righteousness, good works, and separation unto God from the world and its ways, such as unclean amusements and habits, divorce and remarriage, the swearing of oaths, the use of civil courts to settle disputes between members of our churches, and the taking of human life in carnal strife.

12. The solemn obligations of a worldwide gospel witness; the baptism of believers by triune immersion with the laying on of hands; the training of an evangelistic and Bible-teaching ministry; sacrificial proportionate giving by every believer; a family altar in every home; and prayer with anointing for the sick.

13. The Threefold Communion Service, symbolical of the threefold ministry of our Lord Jesus Christ; consisting of the Washing of the Saints' Feet as a symbol of His present ministry of cleansing, the Lord's Supper as a symbol of His future ministry at His coming, and the Bread and Cup as a symbol of His past ministry.

We want all to know that we take the Bible literally from Genesis to Revelation. The National Fellowship of Breth-

THE MESSAGE OF THE BRETHREN MINISTRY
  (FELLOWSHIP OF GRACE BRETHREN
  CHURCHES) (continued)

ren Churches is strictly a Bible church. The Word of God as the Holy Spirit reveals it is our *supreme rule and authority for faith and practice.*

We believe that these are days of apostasy. Churchmen and whole denominations are departing from the truth of God's Word (Jude 3-4). As a result the church has become largely powerless. Often it has degenerated into a purely social agency.

Therefore, it is supremely important that we understand at the outset the uncompromising position of the NFBC on the whole Word of God (II Tim. 4:1-5), and that continued membership in the church is dependent upon the pastors and churches maintaining this Biblical doctrinal position.

Notes: *The refusal of the Brethren Church (Ashland, Ohio) to adopt The Message of the Brethren Ministry (originally adopted by the National Brethren Ministerial Association in 1921) was one of several factors leading to the formation of the Fellowship of Grace Brethren Churches. In more recent years, the fellowship adopted an additional expanded statement that is specifically premillennial in its eschatology.*

* * *

DOCTRINAL STATEMENT OF THE OLD GERMAN BAPTIST BRETHREN

The Dunkers accept the ancient belief in:

JEHOVAH the God of Abraham, Isaac, and Jacob, and in the Messiah, Jehovah's only Son,

JESUS CHRIST, miraculously born of the Virgin, who saved us from the penalty of sin by willingly shedding His blood as an atonement for sins, and who is now our Resurrected Lord and Master; who strengthens us by His Spirit, the Spirit of Truth, the

HOLY SPIRIT who enables us to overcome the world, the flesh and Satan. We believe that the

BIBLE is the verbally inspired Word of God, and that the

CHURCH is built by Christ; He is her only head, therefore she cannot be overthrown. She stands as a refuge or haven from the sin-engulfing storms of Satan. Her duties involve the faithful preaching of the Gospel, practical obedience to the commands of our Lord, the administration of God's means of grace, and the application of Christian principles in the life and conduct of her membership, thereby presenting an unfailing witness to the world.

We believe

FAITH is simply nothing else but believing the Word of God, taking God at His word, believing without seeing, or even to obey without fully understanding. Faith, without which it is impossible to please God, follows the hearing of the Gospel, is the product of the Word of God in the heart, and prompts to action. The Faith endorsed by the Word of God is never "belief alone," being invariably accompanied

by the duties for which faith calls, taking in all that has been enjoined by Christ and the Apostles. With Faith as the "conception" of the "new life,"

REPENTANCE is the heart's response to the divinely wrought sense of conviction in the soul, the result of the Holy Spirit's work condemning the conscience or heart of the guilt of sin, and is the first step fallen humanity can take back toward the bosom of the Father. This is a work each must do for himself, and unless this "first work" is done, everything else seemingly good is useless and worthless. True repentance reclines on the mercy of God for help, cannot do one thing in overcoming the flesh without it. The sinner now sees that through the work of saving grace, he may turn from the desire to sin and be filled with the love for holiness. With Faith as the "conception" and with Repentance as the "prenatal growth" of the new life,

CONFESSION makes known the desire for birth; but neither of these can be said to be birth itself. Not until the body is brought forth has birth transpired; therefore water

BAPTISM is the initatory rite into the church, is for believers only, and is a covenant between God and man. On the part of man it is a seal of faith in Christ and His Word, a renunciation of Satan and sin, and a dedication or complete surrender to the holy life of Christ; on the part of God it is the seal to man of the remission of sins and of the gift of the Holy Ghost. It signifies the burial of the carnal nature and the birth of the new creature by putting on of Christ by being baptized into Him. Children, dying in innocence without baptism, are saved by the virtue of Christ's atonement "for of such is the kingdom of God."

After confessing before God and many witnesses that Jesus is indeed the Christ, the Son of God, and that He brought the Gospel of Salvation from Heaven; and after promising to live a faithful Christian life devoted to Jesus till death or until His coming; after willingly renouncing Satan with all his pernicious ways and all the sinful pleasures of this world; we are then, upon this confession, thrice dipped forward, submersed once into each name of the Godhead, "into the name of the Father, and of the Son, and of the Holy Ghost." This, we believe, is the pattern of the first Christians.

These are the first principles that lead to right standing with God, and they are binding upon all who know them and have it within their power to observe them.

The sinner has his heart changed by faith, his conduct by repentance, and his relation by baptism, but the pardoning act itself takes place in heaven. In "going on unto perfection" we find that true

CONVERSION involves a change of mind, a change of heart, and a change of life and service from selfish and worldly goals to serve the living God. The appearance is changed; speech, conduct, associates—all combine to make manifest the new creature in Christ. He will bear criticism, rebuke, and persecution for Christ's sake and do it without wavering or complaint. He will show love and kindness toward all. If there be any lasting or eternal benefit,

OBEDIENCE must spring from a willing heart. Jesus makes it plain that love of the truth is the only motive which makes obedience acceptable. True obedience is the measure of our faith, and alone can be used as the basis for

SELF EXAMINATION which judgment of self is a lifetime work and not just of passing moment. Especially important before partaking of the communion emblems of His body and blood that we enter not into condemnation, "self judgment" precedes the literal observance of

FEET-WASHING, a command and ordinance in which is exemplified the virtues of faith, love, obedience, humility, service, and sacrifice. As we are "washed" in baptism, so feet-washing symbolizes our need of an additional "washing" or "after cleansing" by the Lord. The

LORD'S SUPPER is a common meal taken at night as did the early Christians and beautifully shows forth the mutual fellowship of love and union that should characterize the people of God in this world of strife and division. Also, the Supper, being a "type," looks forward in anticipation to the "marriage supper of the Lamb," which is the "Lord's Supper" being "fulfilled in the Kingdom of God." After supper we take the

COMMUNION, unleavened bread and fermented wine, which are set apart as emblematical of the broken body and the shed blood of our Lord and Saviour, Jesus Christ. There can be no real communion (a common union) without unity, and fellowship, and purpose. We believe in

CLOSE COMMUNION because there is "common union" only where there exists sufficient union, harmony, and oneness to worship, work, and keep the rest of the ordinances together. We believe in the mystery of the

TRINITY, the Father, Son, and Holy Spirit being equally divine, and also personally distinct from each other. The spiritual baptism of the

HOLY SPIRIT wherein the Spirit dwells within and directs the life of the believer is plainly revealed in God's Word. In this the Spirit comforts the saints and reproves the world of sin. We preach both Faith and

WORKS, believing that man cannot adopt the promises of God without heeding the requirements of Grace. The witness of God's Spirit with man's spirit establishes a reciprocatory relation between the Father and His children. Our simple

WORSHIP consists of reading the Scriptures, preaching, praying, and singing. Musical instruments are not used in worship and the singing is congregational, thus encouraging worship appealing to the understanding and avoiding purely emotional methods. Our favorite position in

PRAYER is kneeling, and as commanded through the Apostle Paul, the sisters always have their heads veiled when praying or prophesying, and the brethren's heads are uncovered in worship. We advocate closet religion in the home; also prayer, singing, family worship and the parental duties of training the children to reverence and love God. The love of God shed abroad in the hearts of His adopted children overflows, and they delight to give expression to that holy love by observing the

HOLY KISS, as oft commanded in the Scriptures, not only on various special occasions, but when greeting one another privately. Thus, the brethren greet the brethren and the sisters the sisters, and between the sexes we greet with a handclasp. Brethren labor for

NONCONFORMITY to the world in all its vain and wicked customs. The church is a light and a life-saving station to men dwelling in darkness and sin. The Scriptures and the spirit of the life of Christ are the guide, "bringing into captivity every thought to the obedience of Christ." Dunkers are willingly subject to every

CIVIL LAW wherein that law does not conflict with the spirit of Christ and demand of us those "things belonging to God." Since God has "made of one blood all nations" we hold that all human life is equally sacred, and therefore we do not join in

WARFARE. Consistency demands that we refrain from supporting the cause of war in any way, also refusing to join or support any peacetime organization which may use violent means. As did our Lord Jesus, we choose to suffer, rather than retaliate, and we refuse all violent methods of self-defense. In short, we believe that the Sermon on the Mount can be lived today, and that it has always been the rule of His Church. True Christians are "peace makers" not "peace breakers." True

CONSCIENTIOUS OBJECTION to war is not found only in literally obeying a few Scriptures but springs from a life in which the Spirit of Jesus has subdued those passions that make violence possible, a "new life" lived on a plane above the causes and occasions of war.

CHURCH DISCIPLINE has for its object, restoration through the principle of correction administered in love. That the Church as a body is held responsible for the condition of the body is clearly defined in the book of Revelation. Dunkers follow "democratic" form of church

GOVERNMENT, for to be scriptural it must be applied with equal respect to every member of the body. Matters of general import for which an answer is not clearly defined in the Scriptures are brought up at an Annual Meeting and those decisions based upon the Spirit and tenor of the Scriptures we consider no less binding than did those Gentiles who received the decision of the Jerusalem council. The sick receive the

ANOINTING with oil (at their request) for the forgiveness of sins and the restoring of health according to the will of God. Brethren generally regard the advances of medical science as an aid to natural healing. This is doing what man has been enjoined to do in taking care of the body, as the temple of the Holy Spirit. All healing, whether in nature or by a special act of His will, is by the power of God. We do not give

OATHS but simply affirm or deny. Oath-taking implies a double standard of honesty, but a follower of Jesus desires to be consistently truthful. Brethren believe that the marriage covenant is irrevocable, that the Scriptures permit separation only on the grounds of fornication, but forbid

DIVORCE. We believe that mixed marriages between believers and unbelievers is unscriptural, and marriage with divorced persons with former companions living constitutes adultery. Thus, it is imperative that in this we maintain a standard above reproach, seeing that no

DOCTRINAL STATEMENT OF THE OLD GERMAN BAPTIST BRETHREN (continued)

institution in nature can be more holy, and none should be more highly respected than that which "God hath joined together." We firmly believe in the imminent, literal

SECOND COMING of Jesus, and that we should each be in a constant state of readiness to meet our Lord should He make His appearance at any hour to receive His Bride, the Church. The way of natural death, for the saints, leads to life. The truth of the

RESURRECTION assures us that death is but the portal to eternity. The Scriptures intimately and inseparably connect the fact of the resurrection of Christ, and that of the resurrection of the saints. The hour of death and the call to

JUDGMENT are universally given to all mankind. "For if we would judge ourselves, we should not be judged." If we repent, confess our sins, and are baptized, we are promised forgiveness for all our sins. The additional Gospel means of self-judgment are given to separate the faithful from a life of sin for the rest of life's journey.

Notes: *The separatism of the Old German Baptist Brethren is best shown in its position on the Lord's Supper, communion, and closed communion.*

* * *

Quakers (Friends)

STATEMENT OF FAITH (EVANGELICAL FRIENDS ALLIANCE)

The Holy Bible:

We believe that the Holy Scriptures were given by the inspiration of God; that there can be no appeal from them to any other authority whatsoever; that they are fully sufficient to make one wise unto salvation through faith which is in Jesus Christ; that the Holy Spirit who inspired the scriptures must ever be its true interpreter as He works through the disciplined and dedicated minds of those within His Church; that any professed guidance which is contrary to these scriptures must be counted as a delusion.

God:

We believe in one God, revealed through the Holy Bible in the person of Jesus Christ; that He is both the Creator and Preserver of all things visible and invisible; that He alone is worthy of worship—honor, glory, dominion, praise, and thanksgiving—both now and forevermore; and that in the unity of the Godhead there exists three persons, Father, Son, and Holy Spirit, inseparable in divinity, power, glory, and eternity.

Jesus Christ:

We believe Jesus Christ to be the only begotten Son of God; that He was conceived by the Holy Spirit and born of the virgin Mary; that He is the express image of the invisible God; and that He combines within Himself both the nature of God and the nature of man in one perfect indivisible personality—the God-man.

We believe that He was crucified as an atonement for the sins of the whole world, making provision whereby man could find the forgiveness of sins, the power for a new life, and be brought back into a perfect relationship with the Father.

We believe that He arose from the dead, ascended to the right hand of God, making intercession for us, and that He will come to earth again to receive His Church unto Himself and to judge the world in righteousness.

Holy Spirit:

We believe the Holy Spirit to be the third person of the Godhead, proceeding from both Father and Son, but equal with them in authority, power, and glory; that He convicts the world of sin, imparts life to the penitent believer, sanctifies the child of God, and enables one by His indwelling presence to love God supremely.

Man:

We believe that God created man in His own image; that he enjoyed unbroken fellowship with his maker; and that his whole life centered in the person of God. We believe that man fell from this original state by an act of transgression; that in this fall man suffered the immediate loss of his perfect relationship to God, making self the center of his life; and that in this act he suffered immediate spiritual death. In this disposition to sin all men are born. We own no principle inherent naturally in man by which he may be saved, except by the grace of our Lord Jesus Christ as a provision for all mankind.

Salvation:

We believe that by the grace of our Lord Jesus Christ, and by the direct and immediate agency of the Holy Spirit, man may be recovered from his fallen state through divine enlightenment, forgiveness of sin, regeneration and sanctification of his affections, and the final glorification of his body; that in this life man may love God with all his heart, soul, mind, and strength; that he may live in victory over sin, and enjoy unbroken fellowship with his Father; and that once more his whole life may center in and revolve around his Creator and Father.

We believe that the experience of sanctification is the work of God's grace by which the affections of men are purified and exalted to a supreme love to God; and the believer is empowered to witness to the living Christ. This is accomplished by the baptism with the Holy Spirit in the life of a dedicated and believing child of God; that this is both an act in which the heart is cleansed from an imperfect relationship and state, and a process in which the life is continuously disciplined into paths of holiness.

The Church:

We believe that all those persons who repent of their sins, and believe in Jesus Christ as their Savior are born again into His kingdom by the Holy Spirit, and that these constitute the church universal of Jesus Christ. This church we believe to be spiritual in nature, universal in scope, holy in character, and redemptive in her life and purpose.

We believe that wherever two or three are gathered together in the name of Christ, He is truly present in the person of the Holy Spirit, and that such an assembly is a local church, the visible expression of His body, and the church universal.

We believe that every believer must relate himself to the local and visible body of Christ being fitly framed together with others into a holy temple in the Lord and builded together for a habitation of His Spirit.

Spiritual Realities:

We believe that both Christian baptism and communion are spiritual realities beyond the mere physical and outward ordinances; that baptism is an inward receiving of the Holy Spirit in which He becomes Lord over all— guiding, cleansing, empowering, and in general representing God to us in immediate experience; that communion is the daily receiving and realization of Jesus Christ as Savior and Lord; that this communion is dependent not only upon the condition of the believer walking daily in the light of Christ, but in the historic act of Christ on Calvary as His body was broken and blood shed once and for all for us; that Christ thus becomes a daily personal spiritual reality known immediately in Christian experience; and that through Him and His baptism God and divine realities are known experientially and immediately.

Christian Work:

We believe that in the church, the believer is committed to both the worship and the work of God; that this work involves not only personal righteousness as the fruit of a new life, but the ministry of evangelism and teaching; that in this commission of Christ every believer is involved in the stewardship of the Kingdom, and that it is fulfilled only by faithful service in and through the fellowship of His Church; and that this work is continuous until Christ comes again calling the Church unto Himself. We believe that all Christians are called upon to witness by word and by deed within a sinful world, not returning evil for evil, but in Christlikeness demonstrating love, forgiveness, and the way of peace.

We believe that in the fellowship of His body, the Holy Spirit gives to every member a gift to be exercised for the mutual advantage of every member in the body, and for the influence of the church upon those outside; that the ministry is such a gift given to certain ones whom God calls and ordains for a special service of leadership in His church; that this service may be that of pastoring, teaching, evangelizing, or administration.

Liberty:

We believe in the doctrine of Christian liberty, and that this liberty is to be granted in all areas that are not essential to one's final salvation. While we recognize that among God's children there are differences of faith and practice, due to our imperfection, we must look forward to the time when we shall all come into a greater unity of the faith. Until then we believe that in essentials there must be unity, that in non-essentials there must be liberty, but in all things there must be charity.

Resurrection and Judgment:

We believe in the second coming of Christ: that at His coming the dead shall be resurrected some to everlasting glory and others to everlasting shame; that we shall all stand before the judgment seat of Christ to receive recompense for the things done in the flesh; that the judgment of the blessed shall be unto heaven, and the judgment of the lost unto hell; that the punishment of the wicked and the blessedness of the righteous shall be everlasting; that this judgment is in the hands of our compassionate Redeemer, who doeth all things after the counsel of His wisdom, love and holiness.

Notes: *The Friends, usually thought of as a noncreedal fellowship, have nevertheless produced a number of statements of belief, especially among those groups in America which were most influenced by Wesleyan evangelicalism in the nineteenth century.*

The basic organizational unit for Friends is the annual meeting, composed of congregations in a given area (in the United States, often a state). Each yearly meeting usually publishes a manual containing doctrinal statements or documents. Yearly meetings may combine nationally into loosely organized associations. The Evangelical Friends Alliance has several conservative evangelical yearly meetings as members, including the Evangelical Friends Church, Eastern Division, the Mid-America Yearly Meeting, and the Rocky Mountain Yearly Meeting.

The Evangelical Friends Alliance is a member of the National Association of Evangelicals. Although the alliance is also a member of the Christian Holiness Association, its statements of belief (and those of its member yearly meetings) do not contain a specific statement of the distinctive holiness doctrine of sanctification as a second definite work of grace in the life of the Christian.

* * *

STATEMENT OF FAITH (EVANGELICAL FRIENDS CHURCH, EASTERN REGION)

GOD

We believe in one eternal, omnipresent, unchanging, personal God; perfect in holiness, wisdom, love, power and justice; without preceding cause or beginning; creator and preserver of all things, visible and invisible.

He exists as one divine being and yet as a trinity of three distinct persons, identical, inseparable, and equal in divinity, power and eternity: God the Father, God the Son, and God the Holy Spirit.

God revealed Himself in the past in many and various ways, though supremely in the person of Jesus Christ. He continues to reveal Himself today through His creation, the Holy Scriptures and the workings of the Holy Spirit in the hearts of men.

He alone is worthy of our worship, honor, praise and thanksgiving, now and forevermore.

JESUS CHRIST

We believe that Jesus Christ, the Word who was with God and was God, is the only begotten Son of God. He was conceived by the Holy Spirit and born of the virgin Mary; and is the express image of the invisible God. He combines within Himself both the nature of God and the nature of man in one perfect indivisible personality—the God-man.

STATEMENT OF FAITH (EVANGELICAL FRIENDS CHURCH, EASTERN REGION) (continued)

He lived and suffered in the world to show the Way of Life. He was crucified and died as the atonement for the sin of the whole world, making the only provision whereby man can find forgiveness of sins and cleansing from all unrighteousness.

He died in our place and rose again the third day for our justification; He ascended into heaven and sits at the right hand of God, ever living as our only mediator and High Priest making intercession for us, and from there will return again to receive His church unto Himself and to judge the world in righteousness.

THE HOLY SPIRIT

We believe in the Holy Spirit, not as an impersonal principle or influence, but as a divine person, and though distinct from the Father and Son, proceeding from both, with whom He is equal in authority, power, glory, and titles.

He is the divine agent in conviction of sin, regeneration, sanctification and the believers' assurance.

He is given as an indwelling Presence to every believer to be a teacher, guide, and source of comfort. He purifies the heart of the believer and imparts at His own choosing spiritual gifts for service and the building up of the Body of Christ. He produces in believers the fruit of the Spirit so that they may conform to the image of Christ.

HOLY SCRIPTURE

With early Friends, we believe that all Scripture both of the Old and New Testaments is given by inspiration of God, without error in all that it affirms and is the only infallible rule of faith and practice. It is fully authoritative and trustworthy, fully sufficient to all believers now and always, and profitable for teaching, reproof, correction, and training in righteousness.

Thus, the declarations contained in it rest on the authority of God Himself, and there can be no appeal from them to any other authority whatever. They are the only divinely authorized record of the doctrines which we are bound as Christians to believe, and of the moral principles which are to regulate our behavior. Only such doctrines as are contained in the Scripture can be regarded as Articles of Faith. The Holy Spirit, who inspired the Scripture, must ever be its true interpreter. Whatsoever any man says or does which is contrary to the Scripture, though under profession of the guidance of the Spirit, must be reckoned and accounted a delusion.

The Scripture demands of believers complete obedience and is made increasingly open to those who study and obey it.

CREATION

We believe creation to be that free act of the triune God, the Father, Son, and Holy Spirit, by which in the beginning and for His own glory God made, without the use of pre-existing material, the whole visible and invisible universe.

SATAN

We believe in the existence of the Evil One, "that old serpent which is the Devil, and Satan", the old deceiver who by his own choice rebelled against God and became evil, who tempted our first parents to sin, and who through their disobedience brought about the fall of the human race; with all its attendant degeneracy, unhappiness and misery.

Satan has demonstrated his evil character and purpose in his perpetual opposition to Christ by the temptation in the wilderness, and to His people and to His kingdom. But his power is limited, and in God's own time he will be chained and finally cast into the lake of fire.

While Satan is active in this world the Christian, through the power of the Holy Spirit dwelling in him, is able to resist Satan's temptation and have victory over him.

MAN

HIS CREATION: We believe that by a definite act God created man in His own image, holy and capable of knowing and obeying God's will, so that he might glorify God and enjoy His fellowship forever.

HIS FALL: We believe that man fell from this original state by a voluntary act of disobedience. In this fall man suffered the immediate loss of his perfect relationship to God, making self the center of his life. By this act, he suffered spiritual death, and sin entered the world and death by sin, so that death passed upon all.

We further believe that as a consequence of the fall mankind are all born with a nature which is thoroughly sinful and not subject to the law of God, so that only through the operation of the grace of God can they repent and call upon Him. However, by God's grace infants are not under condemnation but are heirs of salvation.

SALVATION

We believe that by the grace of our Lord Jesus Christ, through the direct and immediate agency of the Holy Spirit, man may be reconciled to God and recovered from his fallen state through justification, regeneration, sanctification and ultimately the resurrection of his body.

JUSTIFICATION: In response to sinners' repentance, surrender of themselves, and sincere faith in the power and sufficiency of Jesus' atoning death and shed blood, God pardons them from past sins and declares them righteous, not for anything they have done but because of the obedience and atoning death of Christ.

REGENERATION: In response to sinners' repentance, surrender of themselves, and sincere faith in the power and sufficiency of Jesus' atoning death and shed blood, God also by His gracious power makes them new creatures. By the Holy Spirit they are born again into the family of God to a new life of love to God and to men. Their minds are enlightened to understand His truth, and their wills are renewed to do His will, as He begins to conform them to His image. The evidence of this regeneration of the believer is the fruit of the Spirit.

SANCTIFICATION: We believe that children of God at the moment of their conversion do receive the Holy Spirit. As they trust in Him and obey His will, they manifest more and more of the fruit of the Spirit and conform more and more to the likeness of God and thus are being continously sanctified.

It is also the will of God that believers receive the fullness of the Spirit which He will graciously grant in response to their full consecration to His will and their faith in Christ's promises and in His atoning death. Sanctification is thus a process in which the Holy Spirit continuously disciplines the believer into paths of holiness and an act in which He cleanses the heart from an imperfect relationship and state.

We further believe that the fullness of the Holy Spirit does not make believers incapable of choosing to sin, nor even from completely falling away from God, yet it so cleanses and empowers them as to enable them to have victory over sin, to endeavor fully to love God and man, and to witness to the living Christ.

THE CHURCH

We believe that the church is made up of all those from the apostles until now, both the triumphant dead and the living, who through response to God's gracious offer of salvation by repentance of their sins and faith in the Lord Jesus Christ as their Saviour have been born again as new creatures in Christ. This church is spiritual in nature, universal in scope, holy in character, and redemptive in its life and purpose.

Its purposes are to make disciples of all nations by its witness to the grace and love of God and to live as a loving brotherhood who build up one another in the grace and knowledge of God.

The church accomplishes these purposes by its existence as particular local congregations gathered out of the world and as associations of congregations in larger organizations under the leadership and service of those called and gifted to such service. It worships in prayer, thanksgiving and song; diligently studies the Word of God; witnesses to and proclaims the gospel of God's Son; exercises the gifts of the Spirit; administers discipline; and performs works of blessing and service both physical and spiritual to its members and to all men in need.

LAST THINGS

We believe that upon death the bodies of men will return to the dust from which they came. The spirits of the righteous will experience joy and life in the presence of God, but the unrighteous will be separated from His presence in the darkness and torment of their evil.

We believe in the literal and personal return of the Lord Jesus Christ to this earth at a time not revealed. At His return the righteous dead will be raised and the righteous living will be changed to their glorification in bodies like their Lord's glorious resurrected body—bodies which they possessed in earthly life but now with glorified, heavenly qualities. The unrighteous will also be resurrected for the final judgment.

We believe that Christ will consummate His kingdom over men and nations by His final triumph over Satan.

We believe that the Lord Jesus Christ will finally judge all mankind for their belief in Him as demonstrated by commitment of their lives to the way of the cross, the lost to everlasting punishment, the redeemed to eternal blessing and life.

Notes: *The Evangelical Friends Church, Eastern Region is a member of the Evangelical Friends Alliance, which in turn is a member of the National Association of Evangelicals as well as the Christian Holiness Association. In the original text of the church's statement of faith, each sentence is footnoted with Biblical references. These references have been deleted here.*

*　　*　　*

DECLARATION OF FAITH [FRIENDS UNITED MEETING—WESTERN YEARLY MEETING (1881)]

We believe in God, the Father Almighty, (I Cor. viii. 6.) Maker of Heaven and earth, (Gen.i.I.) and of all things visible and invisible; and in Jesus Christ, His only son, (John iii. 16.) our Lord, by whom he created all things; (Heb. I. 2.) and in the Holy Spirit, who proceedeth from the Father and the Son; (John XV. 26.) and that these three, the Father, and the Son, and the Holy Spirit, are one in the Eternal Godhead. (John x. 30; Acts v. 3, 4.)

OUR LORD JESUS CHRIST

We believe that Jesus of Nazareth was conceived of the Holy Spirit, (Luke i. 35.) and born of the Virgin Mary, (Matt. i. 18, 25.) and that He is the beloved and only begotten Son of God, in whom the Father is well pleased. (Matt. xvii. 5.) We believe that the eternal Word, who was with God, and was God, was made flesh and dwelt among men in the person of Him, our Lord and Saviour Jesus Christ. (John i. 14,) "In Him dwelleth all the fullness of the Godhead bodily." (Colos. ii. 9.) He is the one perfect man, who hath fulfilled all righteousness, and who was in all points tempted like as we are, yet without sin. (Heb. iv. 15.)

We believe that He died for our sins, (I Cor. xv. 3.) that He was buried, and rose again the third day, (I Cor. xv. 4) that He ascended into Heaven, (Luke xxiv. 51.) and is on the right hand of God, angels and authorities and powers being made subject unto Him. (I Peter iii. 22.) He is the one Mediator between God and man, (I Tim. ii. 5.) our Advocate with the Father, (I John ii. I.) our High-Priest forever, (Heb. vi. 20.) who is able to save them to the uttermost that come unto God by Him, seeing He ever liveth to make intercession for them. (Heb. vii. 25.) He baptizes with the Holy Spirit. (Matt. iii. II.) He is the Shepherd and Bishop of souls, (I Peter ii. 25.) the Head over all things to the Church, (Ephes. i. 22.) the King who reigns in righteousness, the Prince of Peace. (Isaiah ix. 6, 7.) By Him the world shall be judged in righteousness, for the Father judgeth no man, but hath committed all judgment unto the Son, that all men should honor the Son, even as they honor the Father. [John v. 22, 23.] We believe in the Deity and manhood of our Lord Jesus Christ, [Heb. i. 8; ii. 16, 17.] and that His willing sacrifice [John x. 17, 18.] upon the cross was the one propitiation and atonement for the sins of the whole world, wherein God hath declared his righteousness, that He might be just, and the justifier of him that believeth in Jesus. [Rom. iii. 24, 25, 26.] He is the Lamb of God, without blemish and without spot, with whose precious blood we are redeemed. [I Peter i. 18, 19.] The remission of sins which any partake of is only in and by virtue of that most satisfactory sacrifice. [Acts iv. 12; Heb. ix. 22.] We sincerely confess and believe in Jesus Christ, both as He is the true God and perfect man. We confess that Divine Honor and worship are due to Him, and that He is in true faith to be prayed unto, and the name of the Lord Jesus Christ be called upon, as the primitive Christians did, because of the glorious union, or oneness, of the Father and the Son, and that we can not acceptably offer up prayers or praises to God, nor receive a gracious answer or blessing from Him, but in and through his dear Son, Christ. 1693.

THE HOLY SPIRIT

We believe that the Holy Spirit is, in the unity of the Eternal Godhead, one with the Father and the Son; [Acts v. 3, 4.] that He is the promise of the Father [Acts i. 4, 5.] whom Christ declared He would send in His name: [John xiv. 26.] that He is come and convicts the world of sin; that he leads to repentance towards God, [Rom. ii. 4.] and, as the Gospel is known, to faith in the Lord Jesus Christ. Coming in the name [John xiv. 26.] and in the authority of the risen and ascended Saviour, the Holy Spirit is the most precious pledge of his continued love and care. He glorifies the Saviour and takes of the things of Christ and gives them as a realized possession to the believing soul. He dwells in the hearts of believers according to the promise of the Saviour; "I will pray the Father, and He shall give you another Comforter, [John xvi. 7-15.] that He may abide with you forever." He opens to them the truths of the Gospel as set forth in Holy Scripture, and as they exercise faith, guides, sanctifies, comforts and supports them. [John xiv. 16, 17.]

His light must ever be distinguished, both from the conscience he illumines, and from the natural faculty of reason, which, when unsubjected to His holy influences, is, in the things of God, very foolishness. [I Cor. ii. 14.]

We believe that the qualification for the Lord's service in the enduement of power for His work is bestowed on His children through the reception and baptism of the Holy Ghost. [Acts ii. 16-18.]

The Holy Spirit is the seal of reconciliation to the humble believer in Jesus, the earnest and the foretaste of the full communion and perfect joy which are reserved for them that endure unto the end. [Ephes. i, 13, 14.]

THE HOLY SCRIPTURES

It is the belief of the Society of Friends, that the Holy Scriptures of the Old and New Testament were given by inspiration of God; [2 Tim. iii. 15-17.] that, therefore, the declarations contained in them rest on the authority of

God Himself, and that there can be no appeal from them to any other authority whatsoever; that they are able to make wise unto salvation, through faith which is in Christ Jesus. "These are written that ye might believe that Jesus is the Christ, the Son of God; and that believing ye might have life through his name." [John xx. 31.] The Scriptures are the only divinely authorized record of the doctrines which we are bound as Christians to accept, and of the moral principles which are to regulate our actions. No one can be required to believe as an article of faith any doctrine which is not contained in them; [Isaiah viii. 20.] and whatsoever any one says or does contrary to the Scriptures, though under profession of the immediate guidance of the Holy Spirit, must be reckoned and accounted a delusion of the Devil. [Rev. xxii. 18, 19; Gal. i. 8-12.]

MAN'S CREATION AND FALL

It pleased God in His wisdom and goodness, to create man out of the dust of the earth, and to breathe into his nostrils the breath of life, so that man became a "living soul," [Gen. ii. 7.] formed after the image and likeness of God, capable of fulfilling the divine law, and of holding communion with his Maker. Being free to obey or to disobey, under the temptation of Satan, through unbelief, he fell into transgression, [Gen. iii. 6.] and thereby lost that spiritual life of righteousness in which he was created; and so death passed upon him as the inevitable consequence of his sin. [Rom. v. 12.] As the children of fallen Adam, all mankind bear his image, [Gen. v. 3.] and partake of his nature: and until created anew in Christ Jesus by the regenerating power of the Holy Spirit they are fallen, degenerated, and dead to the divine life. [I Cor. xv. 21, 22.]

But while we hold these views of the lost condition of man in the fall, we rejoice to believe that sin is not imputed to any until they transgress the divine law after sufficient capacity has been given to understand it, and that infants, though inheriting this fallen nature, are saved, in the infinite mercy of God, through the redemption, which is in Christ Jesus. [Mark x. 14.]

JUSTIFICATION AND SANCTIFICATION

"God so loved the world that He gave His only begotten Son, that whosoever believeth in Him should not perish, but have everlasting life." [John iii. 16.]

We believe that justification is of God's free grace [Rom. iii. 24, 25.] through which, upon repentance and faith, He pardons our sins and accepts us as righteous in His sight for the sake of the Lord Jesus Christ; [Rom. v. I.] that it is received, not because of our works, but of our acceptance of God's mercy in Christ Jesus; [Titus. iii. 5.] that through faith in Him and His atoning blood, the guilt of sin is taken away, and we stand reconciled to God. [Colos. i. 19, 20.]

We believe that in connection with Justification is Regeneration; that being reconciled to God by the death of His Son, we are saved by His life, [Rom. v. 10.] a new heart is given and new desires, old things are passed away, and we become children of God through faith in Christ Jesus. [Ezek. xxxvi. 25-27.] Sanctification, or being made holy, is experienced in connection with justification, in so far that every pardoned sinner, on account of faith in Christ, is clothed with a measure of His righteousness and receives the promised Holy Spirit. [I Cor. vi. II.] The provisions of God's grace are sufficient to deliver from the power of evil, [John xvii. 15,] as well as from the guilt of sin, and to enable His believing children always to triumph in Christ. [2 Cor. ii. 14.] This is to be experienced by faith: "according to your faith be it unto you." [Matt. ix. 29.] Whoever submits himself wholly to God, believing His promises, and exercises faith in Christ Jesus, will have his heart continually cleansed from all sin by His precious blood, [I John i.-7.] and through the renewing, refining power of the Holy Spirit be brought into perfect conformity to the will of God, [Rom. xii. 2.] love him with all his heart, mind, soul and strength, and be able to say with the Apostle Paul: "The law of the spirit of life in Christ Jesus hath made me free from the law of sin and death." [Rom. viii. 2.] "This is the will of God, even your sanctification," and if any fall short of this experience, it is because they frustrate the grace of God. [Ephes. v. 25-27.]

RESURRECTION OF THE DEAD AND THE FINAL JUDGMENT

Concerning the resurrection of the dead, and the great day of judgment yet to come, beyond the grave, or after death, and Christ's coming without us, to judge the quick and the dead: (as divers questions are put in such terms,) what the Holy Scriptures plainly declare and testify in these matters, we have been always ready to embrace.

1.   For the doctrine of the resurrection; if, in this life only, we have hope in Christ, we are of all men most miserable. [I Cor. x. v. 19.] We sincerely believe, not only a resurrection in Christ from the fallen sinful state here, but a rising and ascending into glory with him hereafter: that when he at last appears, we may appear with him in glory. [Col. iii. 4; I John iii. 2.]

But that all the wicked who live in rebellion against the light of grace, and die finally impenitent, shall come forth to the resurrection of condemnation.

"For our conversation is in heaven, from whence also we look for the Savior, the Lord Jesus Christ, who shall change our vile body, that it may be fashioned like unto his glorious body according to the working whereby he is able even to subdue all things unto himself." [Phill. iii. 20-21.]

And that the soul or spirit of every man and woman shall be reserved in its own distinct and proper being, and every seed (yea every soul) shall have its proper body, as God is pleased to give it. [I Cor. xv.]

It is sown a natural body; it is raised a spiritual body. There is a natural body, and there is a spiritual body. That being first which is natural, and afterward that which is spiritual. And though it is said, this corruptible shall put on incorruption, and this mortal shall put on immortality; the change shall be such as flesh and blood cannot inherit the kingdom of God, neither doth corruption inherit incorruption. (I Cor. xv.) We shall be raised out of all corruption and corruptibility, out of all mortality; and the children of God and of the resurrection shall be equal to the Angels of God in heaven. And as the celestial bodies do far excel terrestrial, so we expect our spiritual bodies in the resurrection shall far excel what our bodies now are.

2.   For the doctrine of eternal judgment; God hath committed all judgment unto his Son Jesus Christ; and he is Judge both of quick and dead, and of the states and ends of all mankind. [John v. 22, 27; Acts x, 42; 2 Timothy iv, I; I Peter iv, 5.]

That there shall be hereafter a greater harvest, which is the end of the world, a great day of judgment, and concerning the judgment of that great day, the Holy Scripture is clear. [Matt. xiii. 39, 40, 41; ch. x. 15, and xi. 24; Jude. 6.]"When the Son of Man cometh in His glory, and all the holy angels with him, then shall he sit upon the throne of his glory, and before him shall be gathered all nations," &c. [Matt. xxv. 31, 32, to the end, compared with ch. xxii, 31; Mark viii, 38, Luke ix, 26, and I Cor. xv, 52; 2 Thess, i, 7, 8, to the end, and I Thess. iv, 16; Rev. xx, 12, 13, 14, 15: John v, 24-29.]

THE EVIL SPIRIT

We believe in the existence of an evil being, distinct from man, who tempted our first parents to sin, and through their disobedience wrought the fall of our race, whom the Saviour met and resisted when tempted in the wilderness.

In the degeneracy of man, and all its consequent woes; in the crucifixion of the Son of God; and in all his mighty opposition to the Messiah's reign in all ages, Satan has developed, and still continues to develop, the malignity of his character and purposes. His power is limited, and in God's own time he will be chained, and finally "cast into the lake of fire." [John xii. 31; Eph. ii, 2; 2 Cor. iv. 4; Rev. xx. 2; I John v. 18; I Peter v. 8; John viii, 44; Matt. xii, 24; 2 Cor. vi. 15; Rev. xii. 10, &c.]

CONCERNING THE SABBATH,

which, since the time of Christ, is observed on the First day of the week.

The observance of a day of worship and rest is traced back to the time of the creation, when, it is said, "And on the seventh day God ended His work, which He had made; and He rested on the seventh day from all His works which He had made; And God blessed the seventh day, and sanctified it." We feel ourselves religiously bound to observe the spirit of the Fourth Commandment, and to regard one day in seven, as a day of rest and devotion. And since, in accordance with the practice of the apostles and early church, Christians by common consent, have set apart for religious services the day of the week upon which our Saviour rose from the dead, it is the judgment of the Yearly Meeting that Friends, and others in their employ, should lay aside all avocations of a temporal nature in which they are engaged, and devote the time to the important duties of the day, in accordance with its sacred associations. This observance is of so much importance to the preservation of piety and virtue, and the neglect of it so evidently marked with irreligion, and frequently with immorality, that every reasonable consideration recommends a faithful maintenance of this duty, as affording an opportunity which many could not otherwise obtain of receiving religious instruction and improvement, and of publicly worshiping our Heavenly Father. We therefore earnestly advise all our members to avoid unprofitably passing their time on this day of the week, either in listless idleness, or in indulging in mere social pastime, but rather devoting themselves to such reading, conversation and meditation, as will most advance their spiritual welfare.

BAPTISM

"One Lord, one Faith, one Baptism." (Ephes. iv. 5.) "John answered, saying unto them all, I indeed baptize you with water; but one mightier than I cometh, the latchet of whose shoes I am not worthy to unloose; he shall baptize you with the Holy Ghost, and with fire." (Luke iii. 16.)

We believe the one and saving baptism of the Gospel dispensation is that of Christ, who baptizes his people with the Holy Ghost. The ordinances instituted by God under the law were typical. When Christ the great antitype came and fulfilled the law, he took away the handwriting of ordinances, "nailing it to His cross," (Col. ii. 14,) and since He opened the new and living way, which He hath consecrated for us, through the Vail, that is to say, His flesh, we have access by faith, and enter into the holiest by the blood of Jesus, without the intervention of priest, or ordinance, or any mediation, but that of Him, the one Mediator. (Heb. x. 19, 22.)

We believe that he established no new rite or ordinance, and that the "one baptism," which now saveth, and which is essential to living membership in His church, is that which He himself administers as the glorious Minister of the sanctuary—the baptism of the Holy Spirit—as saith the apostle, "by one spirit are ye all baptized into one body." (I Cor. xii. 13.)

THE SUPPER OF THE LORD

We believe that the true supper of the Lord is the Communion which His believeing children are enabled to hold with Him, through the realization of the presence of the Lord Jesus Christ in their hearts, who has cleansed them from all sin, through the offering of His body, and the shedding of His blood upon the cross.

This communion is described by Him in the words: "Behold, I stand at the door and knock; if any man hear my voice, and open the door, I will come into him, and sup with him, and he with me." [Rev. iii. 20.]

We believe this experience to be essential to the life of the Christian. It is only in the strength of this communion that he can pursue his heavenward journey, or bring forth fruit unto holiness; for, saith our blessed Lord, "Except ye eat the flesh of the son of man and drink His blood, ye have no life in you." [John vi. 53-63.]

PUBLIC WORSHIP

God is a Spirit, and they that worship Him, must worship Him in Spirit, and in truth. [John iv. 24.] We recognize worship as the adoring response of the heart and mind to the influence of the Spirit of God, whether in silent or vocal prayer, preaching the word, reading the Holy Scriptures, or in singing His praise. The preparation of the heart and the answer of the tongue are of the Lord.

Having become His children through faith in the Lord Jesus Christ, it is our privilege to meet together and unite in the worship of Almighty God; to wait upon Him for the renewal of our strength, [Isaiah x. 31,] for communion with Him and with one another, for the edification of believers in the exercise of spiritual gifts, and for the declaration of the glad tidings of salvation to the unconverted who may gather with us. [I Cor. xiv. 26.]

By the immediate operations of the Holy Spirit, the Head of the Church alone selects and qualifies those who are to present His messages, or to engage in other service for Him, and hence we cannot admit of a formal arrangement of exercises, or commit them to any individual. [I Cor. xii. 3-6.]

The worship of any heart or assembly most glorifies God, which most perfectly responds to the promptings of His Spirit, whether it be in vocal service or in silent adoration.

THE MINISTRY

We believe the preaching of the Gospel is one of the means divinely appointed for the spreading of glad tidings of life and salvation through our crucified Redeemer, for the awakening and conversion of sinners, and for the comfort and edification of believers. [Matt. xxviii. 19,20.]

As it is prerogative of the great Head of the Church alone, to select and call the ministers of his Gospel, so we believe both the gift and the qualification to exercise it must be derived immediately from Him, and that, as in the primitive church, so now also, he confers them on women as well as men, agreeably to the prophecy recited by the Apostle Peter: "It shall come to pass in the last days, saith God, I will pour out of my Spirit upon all flesh; and your sons and your daughters shall prophesy;" [Acts ii. 16, 18,] respecting which the apostle declares, "the promises is unto you and to your children, and to all that are afar off, even as many as the Lord our God shall call." As this gift is freely received, so it is to be freely exercised, in simple obedience to the will of God.

The Apostle Paul in speaking of his ministry declares, "I neither received it of man, neither was I taught it, but by the revelation of Jesus Christ; [Gal. i. 12,] that the exercise of it was not in the words which man's wisdom teacheth, but which the Holy Ghost teacheth; and that his speech and his preaching was not with enticing words of man's wisdom, but in demonstration of the Spirit and of power; that the faith of his hearers might not stand in the wisdom of men, but in the power of God. [I Cor. ii. 4, 5.] Nothing but power from on high, renewedly furnished, can enable men to preach the Gospel. A clear apprehension of Scripture doctrine, or a heart enlarged in love to others, is not sufficient for this work. Whatever may be the talents or Scriptural knowledge of any, unless there be a distinct call to the ministry our Society cannot acknowledge it.

While the Church cannot confer Spiritual gifts, it is its duty to recognize and foster them, and to promote their efficiency by all the means in its power. And while on the one hand the Gospel should never be preached for money, [Matt. x. 8,] on the other it is the duty of the Church to make such provision that it shall never be hindered for want of it. [I Cor. ix. 13, 14.]

PRAYER

We have ever believed in the obligation of prayer, both silent and vocal. We should cultivate the habit of frequently turning the mind to God in prayer and praise, breathing our secret desires and aspirations unto Him. This should be done, not only when we are apart from others, but also in the midst of our ordinary engagements. Prayer is the result of a feeling of need and dependence upon God. The condition of heart and mind which cries, in substance, "God be merciful to me a sinner," [Luke xviii. 13,] must precede pardon and remission of sins. At every stage, prayer is essential to Christian life. [Phil. iv. 6.]

Prayer and praise are indispensable to a growth in grace, and for a qualification for those duties which devolve upon every Christian; that without these, any religious experience which may have been gained will finally be lost.

Without prayer there can be no acceptable worship. It is therefore incumbent upon all Christians, in their meetings especially, to seek after Divine help to offer spiritual sacrifices, acceptable to God by Jesus Christ. [I Peter ii. 5.] Vocal prayer, uttered in response to the promptings of the Holy Spirit, is an important part of public worship; and whenever God's people meet together in his name, they should reverently seek unto Him in united prayer. [I Tim. ii. I—3.]

We would encourage parents and heads of families to be faithful in the exercise of this privilege before their children or households, and instruct and admonish them to faithfulness in this exercise. The qualification for such services may differ in degree from that which should be looked for on more public occasions. The sense of need, of parental responsibility, of the priceless value of the souls entrusted to our care, not only warrant, but require, such acts of dedication, whilst our countless blessings claim the tribute of praise from thankful hearts.

The spirit of prayer and thanksgiving will be bestowed upon us if we duly ask for it; and thus to ask is a prayer which may be safely regarded as always in accordance with the Divine will. "If ye, then, being evil, know how to give good gifts unto your children, how much more shall your Heavenly Father give the Holy Spirit to them that ask Him." [Luke xi. 13.]

"I will therefore that men pray everywhere, lifting up holy hands, without wrath and doubting." [I Tim. ii. 8.]

WAR

"From whence come wars and fightings among you? Come they not hence even of your lusts that war in your members?" [James iv. I.]

War, and keeping about our persons weapons for self-defense, conflict with and are a violation of the principles, precepts, and injunctions of the Gospel, which brings peace on earth and good will toward men. War is entirely incompatible with the commands of our holy Redeemer, "I say unto you that ye resist not evil," "Love your enemies, bless them that curse you, do good to them that hate you, and pray for them which despitefully use you and persecute you; that ye may be the children of your Father which is in Heaven; for He maketh His sun to rise on the evil and the good, and sendeth rain on the just and on the unjust. [Matt. v. 39. 44. 45.]

The emphatic prayer of our Lord, "Forgive us our debts, as we forgive our debtors," [Matt. vi. 12,] and His declaration, "If ye forgive not men their trespasses, neither will your Father forgive your trespasses," [Matt. vi. 15.] continue of binding force. No Divine injunction or command that is binding upon individuals, under the Christian dispensation, can be rendered void by any number of individuals in a collective capacity, as nations or otherwise. The prophecy which foretold the coming of the Messiah declared him to be the Prince of Peace; [Isaiah ix. 6,] and his birth was announced by the Heavenly anthem, "Glory to God in the highest, and on earth peace, goodwill toward men." [Luke ii. 14.]

CAPITAL PUNISHMENT

The fundamental moral law has ever been, "Thou shalt not kill." We accept that Christ, in the New Testament, has abrogated the law of retribution in the Old Testament, requiring men to inflict by Divine authority the death penalty; and now, "Vengeance is mine; I will repay," saith the Lord. To neither men as citizens, or as rulers, is given the right to inflict the death penalty upon their fellow-men.

OATHS

Our Lord evidently forbade a kind of swearing which had been allowed before: "Ye have heard that it hath been said by them of old time, thou shalt not forswear thyself, but shalt perform unto the Lord thine oaths; but I say unto you, swear not at all, neither by Heaven, for it is God's throne, nor the earth, for it is His footstool; neither by Jerusalem, for it is the city of the Great King; neither shalt thou swear by thy head, because thou canst not make one hair white or black; but let your communication be yea, yea, nay, nay; for whatsoever is more than these cometh of evil." [Matt. v. 33-37.] And the Apostle James declared, "But above all things, my brethren, swear not, neither by heaven, neither by the earth, neither by any other oath; but let your yea be yea, your nay, nay, lest ye fall into condemnation." [James v. 12.]

We therefore consider the prohibition to include judicial oaths, and refuse, for conscience sake, either to administer or take an oath. In courts of law and in the authentication of documents, instead of taking an oath we make affirmation to the truth of that which we assert.

DECLARATION OF FAITH, AS STATED IN THE EPISTLE OF GEORGE FOX, TO THE GOVERNOR OF BARBADOS, 1671

We own and believe in the only wise, omnipotent, and everlasting God, the Creator of all things in Heaven and in Earth, and the Preserver of all that He hath made; who is God over all, blessed forever; to whom be all honor, glory, dominion, praise, and thanksgiving, both now and forevermore! And we own and believe in Jesus Christ, His beloved and only begotten Son, in whom He is well pleased; who was conceived by the Holy Ghost and born of the Virgin Mary; in whom we have redemption through His blood, even the forgiveness of sins; who is the express image of the invisible God, the first born of every creature, by

DECLARATION OF FAITH [FRIENDS UNITED MEETING—
WESTERN YEARLY MEETING (1881)] (continued)

whom were all things created that are in heaven and in
earth, visible and invisible, whether they be thrones,
dominions, principalities or powers; all things were created
by Him. And we own and believe that He was made a
sacrifice for sin, who knew no sin, neither was guile found
in His mouth; that He was crucified for us in the flesh
without the gates of Jerusalem; and that he was buried and
rose again the third day by the power of His Father for our
justification; and that He ascended up into heaven, and
now sitteth at the right hand of God. This Jesus, who was
the foundation of the holy prophets and apostles, is our
foundation, and we believe there is no other foundation to
be laid but that which is laid, even Christ Jesus; who tasted
death for every man, shed His blood for all men, is the
propitiation for our sins, and not for ours only, but also for
the sins of the whole world; according as John the Baptist
testified of Him, when he said: "Behold the Lamb of God
which taketh away the sin of the world," [John i. 29.] We
believe that He alone is our Redeemer and Saviour, the
Captain of our salvation (who saves us from sin, as well as
from hell and from the wrath to come, and destroys the
devil and his works). He is the seed of the woman that
bruiseth the serpent's head, to wit, Christ Jesus, the Alpha
and Omega, the First and the Last; He is, as the Scriptures
of truth say of Him, our wisdom, righteousness, sanctification, and redemption; neither is there salvation in any
other, for there is no other name under heaven given
among men, whereby we must be saved. He alone is the
Shepherd and Bishop of our souls; He is our Prophet
whom Moses long since testified of, saying, "A Prophet
shall the Lord your God raise up unto you of your
brethren, like unto me; Him shall ye hear in all things,
whatsoever He shall say unto you: and it shall come to
pass, that every soul which will not hear that Prophet shall
be destroyed from among the people." [Acts ii. 22, 23.] He
it is that has now come, "and hath given us an understanding, that we know Him that is true." He rules in our hearts
by His law of love and of life, and makes us free from the
law of sin and death. We have no life but by Him, for He is
the quickening Spirit, the second Adam, the Lord from
heaven by whose blood we are cleansed, and our consciences sprinkled from dead works to serve the living
God. He is our Mediator that makes peace and reconciliation between God offended and us offending; He being the
Oath of God, the new covenant of light, life, grace, and
peace, the author and finisher of our faith. This Lord Jesus
Christ, the heavenly man, the Emmanuel, God with us, we
all own and believe in; He whom the high-priest raged
against, and said he had spoken blasphemy; whom the
priests and elders of the Jews took counsel together
against, and put to death; the same whom Judas betrayed
for thirty pieces of silver, which the priests gave him as a
reward for his treason; who also gave large money to the
soldiers to broach an horrible lie, namely, "That His
disciples came and stole Him away by night whilst they
slept." After He was risen from the dead, the history of the
Acts of the Apostles sets forth how the chief priests and
elders persecuted the disciples of this Jesus for preaching

Christ and His resurrection. This, we say, is that Lord
Jesus Christ, whom we own to be our life and salvation.

Concerning the Holy Scriptures, we believe that they were
given forth by the Holy Spirit of God, through the holy
men of God, who, as the Scripture itself declares (2 Peter i.
21), spake as they were moved by the Holy Ghost. We
believe they are to be read, believed, and fulfilled—he that
fulfills them is Christ—and they are "profitable for
doctrine, for reproof, for correction, for instruction in
righteousness, that the man of God may be perfect,
thoroughly furnished unto all good works," (2 Tim. iii. 16,
17); and are able to make wise unto salvation, "through
faith which is in Christ Jesus."

We believe the Holy Scriptures are the words of God, for it
is said in Exodus xx. I; "God spake all these words,
saying," etc., meaning the ten commandments given forth
upon Mount Sinai; and in Revelation xxii. 18, 19, saith
John, "I testify unto every man that heareth the words of
the prophecy of this book. If any man shall add unto these
things." "And if any man shall take away from the words
of the book of this prophecy" (not the word). So in Luke i,
20: "Because thou believest not my words;" and in John v.
47; xv. 7; xiv. 23; xii. 47. So that we call the Holy
Scriptures, as Christ, the Apostles, and holy men of God
called them—the words of God.

We declare that we esteem it a duty incumbent on us to
pray with and for, to teach, instruct, and admonish those
in and belonging to our families. This being a command of
the Lord, disobedience thereunto will provoke His displeasure, as may be seen in Jeremiah x. 25: "Pour out Thy fury
upon the heathen that know Thee not, and upon the
families that call not upon Thy name." Now Negroes,
Tawnies, and Indians make up a very great part of the
families in this island, for whom an account will be
required by Him who comes to judge both quick and dead,
at the great day of judgment, when every one shall be
rewarded according to the deeds done in the body, whether
they be evil—at that day, we say, of the resurrection both
of the good and of the bad, of the just and of the unjust,
"when the Lord Jesus shall be revealed from heaven with
His mighty angels in flaming fire, taking vengeance on
them that know not God and obey not the Gospel of our
Lord Jesus Christ; who shall be punished with everlasting
destruction from the presence of the Lord, and from the
glory of His power; when He shall come to be glorified in
His Saints, and to be admired in all them that believe, in
that day." (2 Thess, i. 7, 10; 2 Peter iii. 3, 7.)

Notes: *This older statement of the Western Yearly Meeting
is typical of those nineteenth-century meetings which
eventually combined to create the Friends' Five Years
Meeting (now the Friends United Meeting). This statement
was in effect until 1887, when a new statement was written
at the first of the conferences held to pursue union with
other yearly meetings. It includes a letter from George Fox,
founder of the Quakers, to the Governor of Barbados.*

ESSENTIAL TRUTHS AND GENERAL DOCTRINAL STATEMENTS (FRIENDS UNITED MEETING—WESTERN YEARLY MEETING)

ESSENTIAL TRUTHS

The vital principle of the Christian faith is the truth that man's salvation and higher life are personal matters between the individual soul and God.

Salvation is deliverance from sin and possession of spiritual life. This comes through a personal faith in Jesus Christ as the Saviour, Who, through His love and sacrifice draws us to Him.

Conviction for sin is awakened by the operation of the Holy Spirit causing the soul to feel its need of reconciliation with God. When Christ is seen as the only hope of salvation, and a man yields to Him, he is brought into newness of life, and realizes that his sonship to God has become an actual reality. This transformation is wrought without the necessary agency of any human priest, or ordinance, or ceremony whatsoever. A changed nature and life bear witness to this new relation to Him.

The whole spiritual life grows out of the soul's relation to God and its co-operation with Him, not from any outward or traditional observances.

Christ Himself baptizes the surrendered soul with the Holy Spirit, enduing it with power, bestowing gifts for service. This is an efficient baptism, a direct incoming of divine power for the transformation and control of the whole man. Christ Himself is the Spiritual bread which nourishes the soul, and He thus enters into and becomes a part of the being of those who partake of Him. This participation with Christ and apprehension of Him become the goal of life for the Christian. Those who thus enter into oneness with Him become also joined in living union with each other as members of one body.

Both worship and Christian fellowship spring out of this immediate relation of believing souls with their Lord.

The Holy Scriptures were given by inspiration of God and are the divinely authorized record of the doctrines which Christians are bound to accept, and of the moral principles which are to regulate their lives and actions. In them, as interpreted and unfolded by the Holy Spirit, is an ever fresh and unfailing source of spiritual truth for the proper guidance of life and practice.

The doctrines of the apostolic days are held by the Friends as essentials of Christianity. The Fatherhood of God, the Deity and humanity of the Son; the gift of the Holy Spirit; the atonement through Jesus Christ by which men are reconciled to God; the Resurrection; the High-priesthood of Christ, and the individual priesthood of believers, are most precious truths, to be held not as traditional dogmas, but as vital, life giving realities.

The sinful condition of man and his proneness to yield to temptation, the world's absolute need of a Saviour, and the cleansing from sin in forgiveness and sanctification through the blood of Jesus Christ, are unceasing incentives to all who believe to become laborers together with God in extending His kingdom. By this high calling the Friends are pledged to the proclamation of the truth wherever the Spirit leads, both in home and in foreign fields.

The indwelling Spirit guides and controls the surrendered life, and the Christian's constant and supreme business is obedience to Him. But while the importance of individual guidance and obedience is thus emphasized this fact gives no ground for license; the sanctified conclusions of the Church are above the judgment of a single individual.

The Friends find no scriptural evidence or authority for any form or degree of sacerdotalism in the Christian Church, or for the establishment of any ordinance or ceremonial rite for perpetual observance. The teachings of Jesus Christ concerning the spiritual nature of religion, the impossibility of promoting the spiritual life by the ceremonial application of material things, the fact that faith in Jesus Christ Himself is all-sufficient, the purpose of His life, death, resurrection and ascension, and His presence in the believer's heart, virtually destroys every ceremonial system and points the soul to the only satisfying source of spiritual life and power.

With faith in the wisdom of Almighty God, the Father, the Son and the Holy Spirit, and believing that it is His purpose to make His Church on earth a power for righteousness and truth, the Friends labor for the alleviation of human suffering; for the intellectual, moral and spiritual elevation of mankind; and for purified and exalted citizenship. The Friends believe war to be incompatible with Christianity, and seek to promote peaceful methods for the settlement of all the differences between nations and between men.

It is an essential part of the faith that a man should be in truth what he professes in word, and the underlying principle of life and action for individuals, and also for society, is transformation through the power of God, and implicit obedience to His revealed will.

For more explicit and extended statements of belief, reference is made to those officially put forth at various times, especially to the letter of George Fox to the Governor of Barbados in 1671, and to the Declaration of Faith issued by the Richmond Conference in 1887.

GENERAL DOCTRINAL STATEMENTS

EXTRACT FROM GEORGE FOX'S LETTER TO THE GOVERNOR OF BARBADOS, 1671

We do own and believe in God, the only wise, omnipotent, and evelasting God, the Creator of all things both in heaven and in earth, and the Preserver of all that He hath made; who is God over all, blessed forever; to whom be all honor and glory, dominion, praise and thanksgiving, both now and forevermore.

And we own and believe in Jesus Christ, His beloved and only-begotten Son, in whom He is well pleased; who was conceived by the Holy Ghost, and born of the Virgin Mary; in whom we have redemption through His blood, even the forgiveness of sins; who is the express image of the invisible God, the first-born of every creature, by whom were all things created that are in heaven and that are in earth, visible and invisible, whether they be thrones or dominions, principalities, or powers; all things were created by Him. And we do own and believe that He was made a sacrifice for sin, who knew no sin, neither was guile found in His mouth; that He was crucified for us in the flesh, without the gates of Jerusalem; and that He was buried, and rose again the third day by the power of His Father, for our justification; and that He ascended up into heaven, and now sitteth at the right hand of God. This Jesus, who was the foundation of the holy prophets and apostles, is our foundation; and we believe that there is no other foundation to be laid than that which is laid, even Christ Jesus; who tasted death for every man, shed His blood for all men and is the propitiation for our sins, and not for ours only, but also for the sins of the whole world according as John the Baptist testified of Him, when he said, "Behold the Lamb of God, that taketh away the sin of the world!" (John 1:29.) We believe that He alone is our Redeemer and Saviour, even the captain of our salvation, who saves us from sin, as well as from hell and the wrath to come, and destroys the devil and his works. He is the Seed of the woman that bruises the serpent's head, to wit, Jesus Christ, the Alpha and Omega, the First and the Last. He is (as the Scriptures of truth say of Him) our wisdom and righteousness, justification, and redemption; neither is there salvation in any other, for there is no other name under heaven given among men, whereby we may be saved. It is He alone who is the Shepherd and Bishop of our souls: He is our Prophet, whom Moses long since testified of, saying, "A prophet shall the Lord your God raise up unto you of your brethren, like unto me; him shall ye hear in all things whatsoever he shall say unto you; and it shall come to pass, that every soul that will not hear that prophet shall be destroyed from among the people." (Acts 3:22, 23.)

He it is that is now come, "and hath given us an understanding, that we may know him that is true." He rules in our hearts by His law of love and of life, and makes us free from the law of sin and death. We have no life, but of Him; for He is the quickening Spirit, the second Adam, the Lord from heaven, by whose blood we are cleansed, and our consciences sprinkled from dead works, to serve the living God. He is our Mediator, that makes peace and reconciliation between God offended and us offending; He being the Oath of God, the new covenant of light, life, grace and peace; the author and finisher of our faith. This Lord Jesus Christ, the heavenly man, the Emmanuel, God with us, we all own and believe in; He whom the high-priest raged against and said, He had spoken blasphemy; whom the priests and elders of the Jews took counsel together against and put to death; the same whom Judas betrayed for thirty pieces of silver, which the priests gave him as a reward for his treason; who also gave large money to the soldiers to broach a horrible lie, namely, "That his disciples came and stole him away by night whilst they slept." After He was arisen from the dead, the history of the acts of the apostles sets forth how the chief priests and elders persecuted the disciples of this Jesus, for preaching Christ and His resurrection. This, we say, is that Lord Jesus Christ, Whom we own to be our life and salvation.

Concerning the Holy Scriptures, we do believe that they were given forth by the Holy Spirit of God, through the holy men of God, who, as the Scripture itself declares, (2 Pet. 1:21) spake as they were moved by the Holy Ghost. We believe they are to be read, believed, and fulfilled; (He that fulfills them is Christ), and they are "profitable for doctrine, for reproof, for correction, and for instruction in righteousness, that the man of God may be perfect, throughly furnished unto all good works," (2 Tim. 3:16, 17); and are able to make wise unto salvation. "through faith in Christ Jesus."

DECLARATION OF FAITH ISSUED BY THE RICHMOND CONFERENCE IN 1887

(N. B. It should be understood that the quotations from Scripture are made from the Authorized Version unless stated to be from the Revised Version.)

It is under a deep sense of what we owe to Him who has loved us that we feel called upon to offer a declaration of those fundamental doctrines of Christian truth that have always been professed by our branch of the Church of Christ.

OF GOD

We believe in one holy, (Isa. 6:3, 57:15.) almighty, (Gen. 17:1.) all-wise, (Rom. 11:33, 16:27.) and everlasting (Ps. 90:1, 2.) God, the Father, (Matt. 11:25-27.) the Creator (Gen. 1:1.) and Preserver (Job 7:20.) of all things; and in Jesus Christ, His only Son, our Lord, by whom all things were made, (John 1:3.) and by whom all things consist; (Col. 1:17.) and in one Holy Spirit, proceeding from the Father and the Son, (John 15:26, 16:7.) the Reprover (John 16:8.) of the world, the Witness for Christ, (John 15:26.) and the Teacher, (John 14:26.) Guide, (John 16:13.) and Sanctifier (2 Thes. 2:13.) of the people of God; and that these three are one in the eternal Godhead; (Matt. 28:19, John 10:30, 17:21) to whom be honor, praise, and thanksgiving, now and forever. Amen.

THE LORD JESUS CHRIST

It is with reverence and thanksgiving that we profess our unwavering allegiance to our Lord and Saviour, Jesus Christ. No man hath seen God at any time; the only begotten Son, who is in the bosom of the Father, He hath declared Him (John 1:18.). In Him was life; and the life was the light of men (John 1:4.). He is the true Light which lighteth every man that cometh into the world (John 1:9.); through whom the light of truth in all ages has proceeded from the Father of lights (James 1:17.). He is the eternal Word (John 1:1.) who was with God and was God, revealing Himself in infinite wisdom and love, both as man's Creator and Redeemer; for by Him were all things created that are in heaven and that are on earth, visible and invisible (Col. 1:13-16). Conceived of the Holy Ghost (Matt. 1:20.) born of the virgin Mary, (Matt. 1:23-25, Luke 1:35.) the word was made flesh, and dwelt amongst men (John 1:14.). He came in the fullness (Gal. 4:4.) of the appointed time, being verily foreordained before the foundation of the world (I Peter 1:20.) that He might fulfill (Isa. 11:1-5, Isa. 52:13-15.) the eternal counsel of the righteousness and love of God for the redemption of man (Isa. 53.). In Him dwelleth all the fullness of the Godhead bodily (Col. 2:9.). Though He was rich, yet, for our sakes, He became poor, veiling in the form of a servant (Phil. 2:7.) the brightness of His glory, that, through Him the kindness and love of God (Titus 3:4.) toward man might appear in a manner every way suited to our wants and finite capacities. He went about doing good (Acts 10:38.); for us He endured (Isa. 53:4, Luke 12:50, Luke 19:41, 22:44.) sorrow, hunger, thirst, weariness, (John 4:6.) pain, unutterable anguish (Luke 22:43, 44.) of body and of soul, being in all points tempted like as we are, yet without sin (Heb. 4:15.). Thus humbling Himself that we might be exalted, He emphatically recognized the duties and the sufferings of humanity as among the means whereby, through the obedience of faith, we are to be disciplined for heaven, sanctifying them to us, by Himself performing and enduring them, leaving us the one perfect example (1 Peter 2:21.) of all righteousness (Matt. 3:15.) in self-sacrificing love.

But not only in these blessed relations must the Lord Jesus be ever precious to His people. In Him is revealed as true God and perfect man, (Eph. 4:13.) a Redeemer, at once able to suffer and almighty to save. He became obedient (Phil. 2:8.) unto death, even the death of the cross, and is the propitiation for our sins, and not for ours only, but also for the sins of the whole world (1 John 2:2.); in whom we have redemption through His blood, (Eph. 1:7.) the forgiveness of sins according to the riches of His grace. It is our joy to confess that the remission of sins which any partake of is only in and by virtue of His most satisfactory sacrifice and not otherwise. (Barclay's Apology, Propos. v. and vi. par. 15, p. 141.) He was buried and rose again the third day (1 Cor. 15:4.) according to the Scriptures, becoming the first fruits (1 Cor. 15:23.) of them that sleep, and having shown Himself alive after His passion, by many infallible proofs (Acts 1:3.), He ascended into heaven, and hath sat down at the right hand of the Majesty on high, now to appear in the presence of God for us (Heb. 1:3, 9:24.). With the apostles who beheld His ascension, we rest in the assurance of the angelic messengers, "This same Jesus, which is taken up from you into heaven shall so come in like manner as ye have seen him go into heaven." (Acts 1:11, and see v. 7.). With the Apostle John, we would desire to unite in the words "Amen; even so, come, Lord Jesus." (Rev. 22:20.). And now, whilst thus watching and waiting, we rejoice to believe that He is our King and Saviour. He is the one Mediator of the new and everlasting covenant, (1 Tim. 2:5, Heb. 9:15.); Who makes peace and reconciliation between God offended and man offending (George Fox's Epistle to the Governor of Barbados.); the great High Priest whose priesthood is unchangeable (Heb. 4:14, 7:24.). He is able to save them to the uttermost that come unto God by Him, seeing He ever liveth to make intercession for them (Heb. 7:25.). All power is given unto Him in heaven and in earth (Matt. 28:18.). By Him the world shall be judged in righteousness (Acts 17:31.); for the Father judgeth no man, but hath committed all judgment unto the Son, that all men should honor the Son even as they honor the Father (John 5:22, 23.). All that are

in the graves shall hear His voice, and shall come forth, they that have done good unto the resurrection of judgment (John 5:28, 29 R. V.).

We reverently confess and believe that divine honor and worship are due to the Son of God, and that He is in true faith to be prayed unto, and His name to be called upon, as the Primitive Christians did because of the glorious oneness of the Father and the Son; and that we cannot acceptably offer prayers and praises to God, nor receive from Him a gracious answer or blessing, but in and through His dear Son (Declaration of 1693, in Sewell's Hist., vol. II, 379.).

We would, with humble thanksgiving, bear an especial testimony to our Lord's perpetual dominion and power in His church. Through Him the redeemed in all generations have derived their light, their forgiveness, and their joy. All are members of this church, by whatsoever name they may be called among men, who have been baptized by the one Spirit into the one body; who are builded as living stones upon Christ, the Eternal Foundation, and are united in faith and love in that fellowship which is with the Father and with the Son. Of this church the Lord Jesus Christ is the alone Head (Eph. 1:22.). All its true members are made one in Him. They have washed their robes and made them white in His precious blood (Rev. 7:14.), and He has made them priests unto God and His Father (Rev. 1:6.). He dwells in their hearts by faith, and gives them of His peace. His will is their law, and in Him they enjoy the true liberty, a freedom from the bondage of sin.

THE HOLY SPIRIT

We believe that the Holy Spirit is, in the unity of the eternal Godhead, one with the Father and with the Son (Matt. 28:19; 2 Cor. 13:14.). He is the Comforter "Whom," saith Christ, "the Father will send in my name" (John 14:26.). He convinces the world of sin, of righteousness, and of judgment (John 16:8.). He testifies of and glorifies Jesus (John 16:14.). It is the Holy Spirit Who makes the evil manifest. He quickens them that are dead in trespasses and sins, and opens the inward eye to behold the Lamb of God that taketh away the sin of the world (Eph. 2:1.). Coming in the name and with the authority of the risen and ascended Saviour, He is the precious pledge of the continued love and care of our exalted King. He takes of the things of Christ and shows them, as a realized possession, to the believing soul (John 16:14.). Dwelling in the hearts of believers (John 16:17.), He opens their understandings that they may understand the Scriptures, and becomes, to the humbled and surrendered heart, the Guide, Comforter, Support, and Sanctifier.

We believe that the essential qualifications for the Lord's service is bestowed upon His children through the reception and baptism of the Holy Ghost. This Holy Spirit is the seal of reconciliation to the believer in Jesus (Eph. 1: 13, 14), the witness to His adoption into the family of the redeemed (Rom. 8:15, 16.); the earnest and the foretaste of the full communion and perfect joy which are reserved for them that endure unto the end.

We own no principle of spiritual light, life of holiness, inherent by nature in the mind or heart of man. We believe in no principle of spiritual light, life or holiness, but the influence of the Holy Spirit of God, bestowed on mankind, in various measures and degrees, through Jesus Christ our Lord. It is the capacity to recieve this blessed influence, which, in an especial manner, gives man preeminence above the beasts that perish; which distinguishes him, in every nation and in every clime, as an object of the redeeming love of God; as a being not only intelligent but responsible; for whom the message of salvation through our crucified Redeemer is, under all possible circumstances, designed to be a joyful sound. The Holy Spirit must ever be distinguished, both from the conscience which He enlightens, and from the natural faculty of reason, which when unsubjected to His Holy influence, is, in the things of God, very foolishness. As the eye is to the body, so is the conscience to our inner being, the organ by which we see; and, as both light and life are essential to the eye, so conscience, as the inward eye, cannot see aright, without the quickening and illumination of the Spirit of God. One with the Father and the Son, the Holy Spirit can never disown or dishonor our once crucified and now risen and glorified Redeemer. We disavow all professed illumination or spirituality that is divorced from faith in Jesus Christ of Nazareth, crucified for us without the gates of Jerusalem.

THE HOLY SCRIPTURES

It has ever been, and still is, the belief of the Society of Friends that the Holy Scriptures of the Old and New Testaments were given by inspiration of God; that, therefore, there can be no appeal from them to any other authority whatsoever; that they are able to make wise unto salvation, through faith which is in Jesus Christ. "These are written that ye might believe that Jesus is the Christ the Son of God; and that believing ye might have life through His name" (John 20:31.) The Scriptures are the only divinely authorized record of the doctrines which we are bound, as Christians, to accept, and of the moral principles which are to regulate our actions. No one can be required to believe, as an article of faith, any doctrine which is not contained in them; and whatsoever any one says or does, contrary to the Scriptures, though under profession of the immediate guidance of the Holy Spirit, must be reckoned and accounted a mere delusion. To the Christian, the Old Testament comes with the solemn and repeated attestation of his Lord. It is to be read in the light and completeness of the New; thus will its meaning be unveiled, and the humble disciple will be taught to discern the unity and mutual adaptation of the whole, and the many-sidedness and harmony of its testimony to Christ. The great Inspirer of Scripture is ever its true Interpreter. He performs this office in condescending love, not by superseding our understandings, but by renewing and enlightening them. Where Christ presides, idle speculation is hushed; His doctrine is learned in the doing of His will, and all knowledge ripens into a deeper and richer experience of His truth and love.

MAN'S CREATION AND FALL

It pleased God, in His wisdom and goodness, to create man out of the dust of the earth, and to breathe into his nostrils the breath of life, so that man became a living soul; formed after the image and likeness of God, capable of fulfilling the divine law, and of holding communion with his Maker (Gen. 2:7; 1:26, 27.). Being free to obey, or to disobey, he fell into transgression, through unbelief, under the temptation of Satan (Gen. 3:1-7.), and, thereby, lost that spiritual life of righteousness, in which he was created; and, so, death passed upon him, as the inevitable consequence of his sin (Rom. 5:12.). As the children of fallen Adam, all mankind bear his image. They partake of his nature, and are involved in the consequences of his fall. To every member of every successive generation, the words of the Redeemer are alike applicable, "Ye must be born again" (John 3:7.). But while we hold these views of the lost condition of man in the fall, we rejoice to believe that sin is not imputed to any, until they transgress the divine law, after sufficient capacity has been given to understand it; and that infants, though inheriting this fallen nature, are saved in the infinite mercy of God through the redemption which is in Christ Jesus.

JUSTIFICATION AND SANCTIFICATION

"God so loved the world that He gave His only begotten Son, that whosoever believeth in Him should not perish, but have everlasting life" (John 3:16.). We believe that justification is of God's free grace, through which, upon repentance and faith, He pardons our sins, and imparts to us a new life. It is received, not for any works of righteousness that we have done (Titus 3:5.), but in the unmerited mercy of God in Christ Jesus. Through faith in Him, and the shedding of His precious blood, the guilt of sin is taken away, and we stand reconciled to God. The offering up of Christ as the propitiation for the sins of the whole world, is the appointed manifestation both of the righteousness and of the love of God. In this propitiation the pardon of sin involves no abrogation or relaxation of the law of holiness. It is the vindication and establishment of that law (Rom. 3:31.), in virtue of the free and righteous submission of the Son of God Himself to all its requirements. He, the unchangeably just, proclaims Himself the justifier of him that believeth in Jesus (Rom. 3:26.). From age to age, the sufferings and death of Christ have been a hidden mystery, and a rock of offense to the unbelief and pride of man's fallen nature; yet, to the humble penitent whose heart is broken under the convicting power of the Spirit, life is revealed in that death. As he looks upon Him who was wounded for our transgressions (Isa. 53:5.), and upon whom the Lord was pleased to lay the iniquity of us all (Isa. 53:6.), his eye is more and more opened to see, and his heart to understand, the exceeding sinfulness of sin for which the Saviour died; whilst, in the sense of pardoning grace, he will joy in God through our Lord Jesus Christ, by whom we have now received the atonement (Rom. 5:11.).

We believe that in connection with Justification is Regeneration: that they who come to this experience know that they are not their own (1 Cor. 6:19.), that being reconciled to God by the death of His Son, we are saved by His life

(Rom. 5:10.); a new heart is given and new desires; old things are passed away, and we become new creatures (2 Cor. 5:17.), through faith in Christ Jesus; our wills being surrendered to His holy will, grace reigns through righteousness, unto eternal life, by Jesus Christ our Lord (Rom. 5:21.).

Sanctification is experienced in the acceptance of Christ in living faith for justification, in so far as the pardoned sinner, through faith in Christ, is clothed with a measure of His righteousness and receives the Spirit of promise; for, as saith the Apostle, "Ye are washed, ye are sanctified, ye are justified, in the name of the Lord Jesus, and by the Spirit of our God" (1 Cor. 6:11.). We rejoice to believe that the provisions of God's grace are sufficient to deliver from the power, as well as from the guilt, of sin, and to enable His believing children always to triumph in Christ (2 Cor. 2:14.). How full of encouragement is the declaration, "According to your faith be it unto you" (Matt. 9:29.). Whosoever submits himself wholly to God, believing and appropriating His promises, and exercising faith in Christ Jesus, will have his heart continually cleansed from all sin, by His precious blood, and, through the renewing, refining power of the Holy Spirit, be kept in conformity to the will of God, will love Him with all his heart, mind, soul and strength, and be able to say, with the Apostle Paul, "The law of the Spirit of life in Christ Jesus hath made me free from the law of sin and death" (Rom. 8:2.). Thus, in its full experience, Sanctification is deliverance from the pollution, nature, and love of sin. To this we are every one called, that we may serve the Lord without fear, in holiness and righteousness before Him, all the days of our life (Luke 1:74, 75.). It was the prayer of the apostle for the believers, "The very God of peace sanctify you wholly; and I pray God your whole spirit and soul and body be preserved blameless unto the coming of our Lord Jesus Christ. Faithful is He that calleth you who also will do it" (1 Thes. 5:23, 24). Yet the most holy Christian is still liable to temptation, is exposed to the subtle assaults of Satan, and can only continue to follow holiness as he humbly watches unto prayer, and is kept in constant dependence upon his Saviour, walking in the light (1 John 1:7), in the loving obedience of faith.

THE RESURRECTION AND FINAL JUDGMENT

We believe, according to the Scriptures, that there shall be a resurrection from the dead, both of the just and of the unjust (Acts 24:15.), and that God hath appointed a day in which He will judge the world in righteousness, by Jesus Christ whom He hath ordained (Acts 17:31.). For, as saith the apostle, "We must all appear before the judgment seat of Christ, that every one may receive the things done in his body, according to that he hath done, whether it be good or bad" (2 Cor. 5:10.).

We sincerely believe, not only a resurrection in Christ from the fallen and sinful state here, but a rising and ascending into glory with Him hereafter; that when He at last appears we may appear with Him in glory. But that all the wicked, who live in rebellion against the light of grace, and die finally impenitent, shall come forth to the resurrection of condemnation. And that the soul of every man and woman shall be reserved, in its own distinct and proper being, and shall have its proper body as God is pleased to give it. It is sown a natural body, it is raised a spiritual body (1 Cor. 15:44.); that being first which is natural, and afterward that which is spiritual. And though it is said, "this corruptible shall put on incorruption, and this mortal shall put on immortality" (1 Cor. 15:53.), the change shall be such as will accord with the declaration, "Flesh and blood cannot inherit the Kingdom of God, neither doth corruption inherit incorruption" (1 Cor. 15:50.). We shall be raised out of all corruption and corruptibility, out of all mortality, and shall be the children of God, being the children of resurrection (Luke 20:36.). (See also Declaration of 1693, Sewell's History, vol. II, 383-384.)

"Our citizenship is in heaven" (R. V.), from whence also we look for the Saviour the Lord Jesus Christ, who shall change our vile body that it may be fashioned like unto His glorious body, according to the working whereby He is able even to subdue all things unto Himself (Phil. 3:20, 21.).

We believe that the punishment of the wicked and the blessedness of the righteous shall be everlasting; according to the declaration of our compassionate Redeemer, to whom the judgment is committed, "These shall go away into eternal punishment, but the righteous into eternal life" (R. V., Matt. 25:46.).

BAPTISM

We would express our continued conviction that our Lord appointed no outward rite or ceremony for observance in His church. We accept every command of our Lord in what we believe to be its genuine import, as absolutely conclusive. The question of the use of outward ordinances is with us a question, not as to the authority of Christ, but as to His real meaning. We reverently believe that, as there is one Lord and one faith, so there is, under the Christian dispensation, but one baptism (Eph. 4:4, 5.), even that whereby all believers are baptized in the one Spirit into the one body (1 Cor. 12:13, R.V.). This is not an outward baptism with water, but a spiritual experience; not the putting away of the filth of the flesh (1 Pet. 3:21.), but that inward work which, by transforming the heart and settling the soul upon Christ, brings forth the answer of a good conscience towards God, by the resurrection of Jesus Christ, in the experience of His love and power, as the risen and ascended Saviour. No baptism in outward water can satisfy the description of the apostle, of being buried with Christ by baptism unto death (Rom. 6:4). It is with the Spirit alone that any can thus be baptized. In this experience the announcement of the Forerunner of our Lord is fulfilled, "He shall baptize you with the Holy Ghost and with fire" (Matt. 3:11.). In this view we accept the commission of our blessed Lord as given in Matthew 28:18, 19 and 20th verses: "And Jesus came to them and spake unto them saying. All authority hath been given unto me in heaven and on earth. Go ye, therefore, and make disciples of all the nations, baptizing them into the name of the Father and of the Son and of the Holy Ghost; teaching them to observe all things whatsoever I commanded you, and, lo, I am with you always, even unto the end of the world" (R. V.). This commission, as we believe, was not designed to set up a new ritual under the new covenant, or to connect the initiation into a membership, in its nature essentially spiritual, with a mere ceremony of a typical character. Otherwise it was not possible for the Apostle Paul, who was not a whit behind the very chiefest apostle (2 Cor. 11:5.), to have disclaimed that which would, in that case, have been of the essence of his commission when he wrote, "Christ sent me not to baptize, but to preach the Gospel" (1 Cor. 1:17.). Whenever an external ceremony is commanded, the particulars, the mode and incidents of that ceremony, become of its essence. There is an utter absence of these particulars in the text before us, which confirms our persuasion that the commission must be construed in connection with the spiritual power which the risen Lord promised should attend the witness of His apostles and of the church to Him, and which, after Pentecost, so mightily accompanied their ministry of the word and prayer, that those to whom they were sent were introduced into an experience wherein they had a saving knowledge of, and living fellowship with, the Father and the Son and the Holy Spirit.

THE SUPPER OF THE LORD

Intimately connected with the conviction already expressed is the view that we have ever maintained as to the true supper of the Lord. We are well aware that our Lord was pleased to make use of a variety of symbolical utterances, but He often gently upbraided His disciples for accepting literally what He had intended only in its spiritual meaning. His teaching, as in His parables or in the command to wash one another's feet, was often in symbols, and ought ever to be received in the light of His own emphatic declaration, "The words that I speak unto you they are spirit and they are life" (John 6:63.). The old covenant was full of ceremonial symbols; the new covenant, to which our Saviour alluded at the last supper, is expressly declared by the prophet to be "not according to the old" (Jer. 31:32; Heb. 8:9.). We cannot believe that in setting up this new covenant the Lord Jesus intended an institution out of harmony with the spirit of this prophecy. The eating of His body and the drinking of His blood cannot be an outward act. They truly partake of them who habitually rest upon the sufferings and death of their Lord as their only hope, and to whom the indwelling Spirit gives to drink of the fullness that is in Christ. It is this inward and spiritual partaking that is the true supper of the Lord.

The presence of Christ with His church is not designed to be by symbol or representation, but in the real communication of His own Spirit. "I will pray the Father and He shall give you another Comforter, who shall abide with you forever" (John 14:16.) convincing of sin, testifying of Jesus, taking of the things of Christ, this blessed Comforter communicates to the believer and to the church, in a gracious, abiding manifestation, the REAL PRESENCE of the Lord. As the great remembrancer, through whom the promise is fulfilled, He needs no ritual or priestly intervention in bringing to the experience of the true

commemoration and communion. "Behold," saith the risen Redeemer, "I stand at the door and knock. If any man hear my voice and open the door, I will come in and sup with him and he with me" (Rev. 3:20.). In an especial manner, when assembled for congregational worship, are believers invited to the festival of the Saviour's peace, and, in a united act of faith and love, unfettered by any outward rite or ceremonial, to partake together of the body that was broken and of the blood that was shed for them, without the gates of Jerusalem. In such a worship they are enabled to understand the words of the apostle as expressive of a sweet and most real experience: "The cup of blessing which we bless, is it not the communion of the blood of Christ? The bread that we break, is it not the communion of the body of Christ? For we being many are one bread, and one body; for we are all partakers of that one bread" (1 Cor. 10:16, 17.).

PUBLIC WORSHIP

Worship is the adoring response of the heart and mind to the influence of the Spirit of God. It stands neither in forms nor in the formal disuse of forms: it may be without words as well as with them, but it must be in spirit and in truth (John 4:24.). We recognize the value of silence, not as an end, but as a means toward the attainment of the end; a silence, not of listlessness or of vacant musing, but of holy expectation before the Lord. Having become His adopted children through faith in the Lord Jesus Christ, it is our privilege to meet together and unite in the worship of Almighty God, to wait upon Him for the renewal of our strength, for communion one with another, for the edification of believers in the exercise of various spiritual gifts, and for the declaration of glad tidings of salvation to the unconverted who may gather with us. This worship depends not upon numbers. Where two or three are gathered together in the name of Christ there is a church, and Christ, the living Head, in the midst of them. Through His mediation without the necessity for any inferior instrumentality, is the Father to be approached and reverently worshiped. The Lord Jesus has forever fulfilled and ended the typical and sacrificial worship under the law, by the offering up of Himself upon the cross for us, once for all. He has opened the door of access into the inner sanctuary, and graciously provided spiritual offerings for the service of His temple, suited to the several conditions of all who worship in spirit and in truth. The broken and the contrite heart, the confession of the soul prostrate before God, the prayer of the afflicted when he is overwhelmed, the earnest wrestling of the spirit, the outpouring of humble thanksgiving, the spiritual song and melody of the heart (Eph. 5:19.), the simple exercise of faith, the self denying service of love, these are among the sacrifices which He, our merciful and faithful High Priest, is pleased to prepare, by His Spirit, in the hearts of them that receive Him, and to present with acceptance unto God.

By the immediate operations of the Holy Spirit, He as the Head of the church, alone selects and qualifies those who are to present His messages or engage in other service for Him; and, hence, we cannot commit any formal arrangement to any one in our regular meetings for worship. We are well aware that the Lord has provided a diversity of gifts (1 Cor. 12:4-6.) for the needs both of the church and of the world, and we desire that the church may feel her responsibility, under the government of her Great Head, in doing her part to foster these gifts, and in making arrangements for their proper exercise.

It is not for individual exaltation, but for mutual profit, that the gifts are bestowed (1 Cor. 12:7.); and every living church, abiding under the government of Christ is humbly and thankfully to receive and exercise them, in subjection to her Holy Head. The church that quenches the Spirit and lives to itself alone must die.

We believe the preaching of the Gospel to be one of the chief means, divinely appointed, for the spreading of the glad tidings of life and salvation through our crucified Redeemer, for the awakening and conversion of sinners, and for the comfort and edification of believers. As it is the prerogative of the Great Head of the church alone to select and call the ministers of His Gospel, so we believe that both the gift and the qualification to exercise it must be derived immediately from Him; and that, as in the primitive church, so now also, He confers spiritual gifts upon women as well as upon men, agreeably to the prophecy recited by the Apostle Peter, "It shall come to pass in the last days, saith God, I will pour out my Spirit upon all flesh; and your sons and your daughters shall prophesy" (Acts 2:17.). Respecting which the apostle declares, "the promise is unto you, and to your children, and to all that are afar off, even as many as the Lord our God shall call" (Acts 2:39.). As the gift is freely received so it is to be freely exercised (Matt. 10:8. See also Acts 20:33-35.), in simple obedience to the will of God.

Spiritual gifts, precious as they are, must not be mistaken for grace; they add to our responsibility, but do not raise the minister above his brethren or sisters. They must be exercised in continued dependence upon our Lord and blessed is that ministry in which man is humbled, and Christ and His grace exalted. "He that is greatest among you," said our Lord and Master, "let him be as the younger; and he that is chief as he that doth serve. I am among you as he that serveth" (Luke 22:26, 27.).

While the church cannot confer spiritual gifts, it is its duty to recognize and foster them, and to promote their efficiency by all the means in its power. And while, on the one hand, the Gospel should never be preached for money (Acts 8:20; 20:33-35.), on the other, it is the duty of the church to make such provisions that it shall never be hindered for want of it.

The church, if true to her allegiance, cannot forget her part in the command, "Go ye into all the world, and preach the Gospel to every creature" (Mark 16:15.). Knowing that it is the Spirit of God that can alone prepare and qualify the instruments who fulfill this command, the true disciple will be found still sitting at the feet of Jesus, listening that he may learn, and learning that he may obey. He humbly places himself at his Lord's disposal, and, when he hears the call, "Whom shall I send, and who will go for us?" is prepared to respond, in childlike reverence and love, "Here am I, send me" (Isaiah 6:8.).

PRAYER AND PRAISE

Prayer is the outcome of our sense of need, and of our continual dependence upon God. He who uttered the invitation, "Ask and it shall be given you" (Matt. 7:7.), is Himself the Mediator and High Priest who, by His Spirit, prompts the petition, and who presents it with the acceptance before God. With such an invitation, prayer becomes the duty and the privilege of all who are called by His name. Prayer is, in the awakened soul, the utterance of the cry, "God be merciful to me a sinner" (Luke 18:13.), and, at every stage of the believer's course, prayer is essential to his spiritual life. A life without prayer is a life practically without God. The Christian's life is a continual asking. The thirst that prompts the petition produces, as it is satisfied, still deeper longings, which prepare for yet more bounteous supplies, from Him who delights to bless. Prayer is not confined to the closet. When uttered in response to the promptings of the Holy Spirit, it becomes an important part of public worship, and, whenever the Lord's people meet together in His name, it is their privilege to wait upon Him for the spirit of grace and supplications (Zech. 12:10.). A life of prayer cannot be other than a life of praise. As the peace of Christ reigns in the church, her living members accept all that they receive, as from His pure bounty, and each day brings them fresh pledges of their Father's love. Satisfied with the goodness of His house, whether as individuals, in families, or in congregations, they will be still praising Him (Psalm 84:4.), heart answering to heart, "Bless the Lord, O my soul: and all that is within me, bless His holy name" (Ps. 103:1.).

LIBERTY OF CONSCIENCE IN ITS RELATION TO CIVIL GOVERNMENT

That conscience should be free, and that in matters of religious doctrine and worship man is accountable only to God, are truths which are plainly declared in the New Testament; and which are confirmed by the whole scope of the Gospel, and by the example of our Lord and His disciples. To rule over the conscience, and to command the spiritual allegiance of his creature man, is the high and sacred prerogative of God alone. In religion every act ought to be free. A forced worship is plainly a contradiction in terms, under that dispensation in which the worship of the Father must be in spirit and in truth (John 4:24.).

We have ever maintained that it is the duty of Christians to obey the enactments of civil government, except those which interfere with our allegiance to God. We owe much to its blessings. Through it we enjoy liberty and protection, in connection with law and order. Civil government is a divine ordinance (Rom. 13:1; I Pet. 2:13-16.), instituted to promote the best welfare of man, hence magistrates are to be regarded as God's ministers who should be a terror to evil doers and a praise to them that do well. Therefore, it is with us a matter of conscience to render them respect and obedience in the exercise of their proper functions.

MARRIAGE

Marriage is an institution graciously ordained by the Creator Himself, for the help and continuance of the human family. It is not a mere civil contract, and ought

never to be entered upon without a reference to the
sanction and blessing of Him who ordained it. It is a
solemn engagement for the term of life (Matt. 19:5, 6.),
designed for the mutual assistance and comfort of both
sexes, that they may be helpmeets to each other in things
temporal and spiritual. To this end it should imply
concurrence in spiritual as well as temporal concerns, and
should be entered upon discreetly, soberly, and in the fear
of the Lord.

PEACE

We feel bound explicitly to avow our unshaken persuasion
that all war is utterly incompatible with the plain precepts
of our divine Lord and Law-giver, and the whole spirit of
His Gospel, and that no plea of necessity or policy,
however urgent or peculiar, can avail to release either
individuals or nations from the paramount allegiance
which they owe to Him who hath said, "Love your
enemies" (Matt. 5:44; Luke 6:27). In enjoining this love,
and the forgiveness of injuries, He who has bought us to
Himself has not prescribed for man precepts which are
incapable of being carried into practice, or of which the
practice is to be postponed until all shall be persuaded to
act upon them. We cannot doubt that they are incumbent
now, and that we have in the prophetic Scriptures the
distinct intimation of their direct application not only to
individuals, but to nations also (Isaiah 2:4; Micah 4:1.).
When nations conform their laws to this divine teaching,
wars must necessarily cease.

We would, in humility, but in faithfulness to our Lord,
express our firm persuasion that all the exigencies of civil
government and social order may be met under the banner
of the Prince of Peace, in strict conformity with His
commands.

OATHS

We hold it to be the inalienable privilege of the disciple of
the Lord Jesus that his statements concerning matters of
fact within his knowledge should be accepted, under all
circumstances, as expressing his belief as to the fact
asserted. We rest upon the plain command of our Lord
and Master, "Swear not at all" (Matt. 5:34.); and we
believe any departure from this standard to be prejudicial
to the cause of truth and to that confidence between man
and man, the maintenance of which is indispensable to our
mutual well being. This command, in our persuasion,
applies not to profane swearing only, but to judicial oaths
also. It abrogates any previous permission to the contrary,
and is, for the Christian, absolutely conclusive.

THE FIRST DAY OF THE WEEK

Whilst the remembrance of our Creator ought to be at all
times present with the Christian, we would express our
thankfulness to our Heavenly Father that He has been
pleased to honor the setting apart of one day in seven for
the purposes of holy rest, religious duties, and public
worship; and we desire that all under our name may avail
themselves of this great privilege as those who are called to
be risen with Christ, and to seek those things that are

above where He sitteth at the right hand of God (Coloss.
3:1.). May the release thus granted from other occupations
be diligently improved. On this day of the week especially
ought the households of Friends to be assembled for the
reading of the Scriptures and for waiting upon the Lord;
and we trust that, in a Christianly wise economy of our
time and strength, the engagements of the day may be so
ordered as not to frustrate the gracious provision thus
made for us by our Heavenly Father, or to shut out the
opportunity either for public worship or for private
retirement and devotional reading.

In presenting this declaration of our Christian faith, we
desire that all our members may be afresh encouraged, in
humility and devotedness, to renewed faithfulness in
fulfilling their part in the great mission of the Church, and
through the Church to the world around us, in the name of
our Crucified Redeemer. Life from Christ, life in Christ,
must ever be the basis of life for Christ. For this we have
been created and redeemed, and, by this alone, can the
longings of our immortal souls be satisfied.

THE EXPANDING APPRECIATION OF TRUTH

Human understanding of truth is always subject to growth.
This basic principle also underlies the development of the
organizations and institutions through which the spirit of
Christianity is made operative in life. While fundamental
principles are eternal, expressions of truth and methods of
Christian activity should develop in harmony with the
needs of the times. God, who spoke through the prophets,
and supremely in Jesus Christ, still speaks through men
and women who have become new creatures in Christ,
being transformed by the renewing of their minds and,
therefore, able and willing to receive fresh revelations of
truth.

Frequently, however, men see "through a glass darkly,"
and may misinterpret or make incorrect applications.
Therefore, as the stream of life flows on, bringing new
conceptions, insights, and situations, it is necessary to
strive constantly for a clearer comprehension of divine
truth that will enter vitally into personal experience and
become a creative factor for the redemption of human
character and the remolding of society on the Christian
pattern. "A religion based on truth must be progressive.
Truth being so much greater than our conception of it, we
should ever be making fresh discoveries."

ORIGIN AND DEVELOPMENT OF THE
DISCIPLINE

The term "discipline" is used by Friends to designate those
arrangements which they have instituted for their civil and
religious nurture and guidance as a Christian group. For
almost a decade following the beginning of the ministry of
George Fox, the founder of the Society of Friends, his
followers were without organization, but as they grew in
unity and in numbers there arose responsibilities to
admonish, encourage, and help one another both in
spiritual and in temporal affairs. They found it necessary
to make certain provisions for the preservation of order in
their fellowship and for the care of the poor and those who
suffered for conscience sake.

There was also need for the supervision of the exercise of spiritual gifts and of the work of publishing truth. The rules and advices pertaining to such ministrations were finally incorporated in the discipline. The earliest Quaker advice on Christian practice was issued by the famous gathering of Friends at Balby in Yorkshire in 1656, a statement that well describes the spirit which should characterize all books of discipline: "Dearly beloved friends, these things we do not lay upon you as a rule or form to walk by, but that all with the measure of light which is pure and holy may be guided, and so in the light walking and abiding these may be fulfilled in the spirit, not from the letter; for the letter killeth, but the spirit giveth life."

An important step in the development of the discipline was the drafting by George Fox in 1668 of a body of advices and regulations to which his opponents gave the name of "Canons and Institutions." This served for a long time as the discpline of the Society, although the name was formally disclaimed by Friends in 1675. It formed the basis for the Discipline of London Yearly Meeting and for all later books of discipline. As the various Yearly meetings were established in America, each prepared and adopted its own book of discipline, but there was much similarity because of the common use of material from older editions. These disciplines were revised from time to time as the rules and advices which they contained became inadequate and inappropriate. Thus, as the conscience of Friends became aware of the evils involved in human slavery or in the use of intoxicating drinks, these convictions were expressed in their disciplines.

ADOPTION OF THE UNIFORM DISCIPLINE

Many diverse factors during the latter half of the nineteenth century had affected the outlook, activities, and relationships of members of the Society of Friends. As these cross currents were faced in the conferences of Yearly Meetings held in 1887, 1892, and 1897, sentiment developed for a closer union of the Yearly Meetings to be accomplished partly by a general representative meeting and partly by the adoption of a uniform discipline. A committee of two representatives from each of the Yearly Meetings taking part in the conferences of 1897 was appointed to formulate a plan of union and to prepare the proposed discipline. "The Constitution and Discipline for the American Yearly Meetings of Friends," was the official name of the discipline which was written to serve the needs of the new organization, to be known as the Five Years Meeting of Friends in America. It was adopted by the Yearly Meetings of New England, Wilmington, Indiana, and Kansas in 1900; California, New York, Western, and Baltimore in 1901; Oregon, North Carolina, and Iowa in 1902; Nebraska, when it was established in 1908. Canada Yearly Meeting, when received into the Five Years Meeting in 1907, was given the privilege of adapting the Discipline to its own needs.

THE BOOK OF FAITH AND PRACTICE

The Uniform Discipline met quite acceptable the needs of the Yearly Meetings which adopted it. But the revolutionary changes in life and thought experienced in the twentieth century brought to Friends the realization that the statements of faith and practice as set forth by the Discipline should be re-examined and revised that they might more adequately meet the needs of the Yearly Meetings. This concern found expression in numerous proposals by Yearly Meetings for amendments to the Discipline. Eventually in 1940, the Executive Committee of the Five Years Meeting recommended to that body that steps be taken for a revision. The Five Years Meeting of 1940, acting upon a recommendation of its Executive Committee that steps be taken for a revision, adopted a method of procedure providing for the appointment of a committee which was instructed to prepare a revised draft of the Discipline for the consideration of the Five Years Meeting and its constituent Yearly Meetings.

Notes: *The largest of the Quaker bodies in North America can be traced to a meeting at Richmond, Indiana in 1887. It was officially formed as the Five Years Meeting in 1902, and later adopted its present name. The Western Yearly Meeting includes in its statement of faith the confession agreed upon in 1887 and a shortened version of a letter from George Fox, founder of the Quakers, to the Governor of Barbados.*

* * *

THE CHURCH AND ITS ESSENTIAL DOCTRINES [MID-AMERICA (FORMERLY KANSAS) YEARLY MEETING]

CHAPTER I. THE CHURCH AS A DENOMINATION

Section 1. *Christ's Members.* The Church of Jesus Christ is composed of those persons who, through repentance of their sins and faith in the Lord Jesus Christ as their Saviour, have been born into His kingdom by the Holy Spirit. By the revelation of the Holy Spirit they look to Christ as their Prophet, Priest, and King; and, by the baptism with the Holy Spirit they are enabled to resist temptation and to live in obedience to God's Holy will.

Section 2. *Friends as a Denomination.* A Christian denomination is an organization composed of those who hold similar views of the teachings of the Holy Scriptures, maintain certain practices based upon these teachings, and voluntarily associate themselves for joint participation in worship, for fellowship and mutual help, and for united effort in the promotion of truth and righteousness. The denomination of Friends is such a Christian body.

Each denominational body has its own system of government and rules for the transaction of its business and for individual observance by its members.

CHAPTER II. ESSENTIAL TRUTHS

Section 1. *God's Dealings with Man.* The vital principle of the Christian faith is the truth that man's salvation and higher life are personal matters between the individual soul and God. Salvation is deliverance from sin and the possession of spiritual life. This comes through a personal faith in Jesus Christ as the Saviour, who through His love and sacrifice draws us to Him.

THE CHURCH AND ITS ESSENTIAL DOCTRINES [MID-
AMERICA (FORMERLY KANSAS) YEARLY
MEETING] (continued)

The whole spiritual life grows out of the soul's relation to God and its co-operation with Him, not from any outward or traditional observances.

Christ Himself baptizes the surrendered soul with the Holy Spirit, enduing it with power, bestowing gifts for service. This is an efficient baptism, a direct incoming of divine power for the transformation and control of the whole man. Christ Himself is the Spiritual bread which nourishes the soul, and He thus enters into and becomes a part of the being of those who partake of Him. This participation with Christ and apprehension of Him become the goal of life for the Christian. Those who thus enter into oneness with Him become also joined in living union with each other as members of one body. Both worship and Christian fellowship spring out of this immediate relation of believing souls with their Lord.

Section 2. *The Scriptures.* The Holy Scriptures were given by inspiration of God and are the divinely authorized record of the doctrines which Christians are bound to accept, and of the moral principles which are to regulate their lives and actions. In them, as interpreted and unfolded by the Holy Spirit, is an ever fresh and unfailing source of spiritual truth for the proper guidance of life and practice.

Section 3. *Fundamental Doctrines.* The doctrines of the apostolic days are held by the Friends as essentials of Christianity. The Fatherhood of God, the deity and humanity of the Son, the gift of the Holy Spirit, the atonement through Jesus Christ by which men are reconciled to God, the resurrection of our Lord which gives us assurance of the resurrection of of all true believers, the high-priesthood of Christ, by whom we have access to the Father in the forgiveness of our sins, the individual priesthood of believers—these are all most precious truths, to be held as vital, life-giving realities.

Section 4. *The Spirituality of Religious Experience.* The sinful condition of man, his proneness to yield to temptation, the world's absolute need of a Saviour, and the cleansing from sin in the work of forgiveness and sanctification through the blood of Jesus are clearly set forth in the gospel of salvation. The possession of spiritual life is thus assured man through a personal faith in Jesus Christ as the Saviour who through His love and sacrifice draws us to Him. The teachings of Jesus Christ concerning the spiritual nature of religion, the impossibility of promoting the spiritual life by the ceremonial application of material things, the fact that faith in Jesus Christ Himself is all-sufficient, and His presence in the believer's heart—these virtually make unnecessary every priestly system and point the soul to the only satisfying source of spiritual life and power. Friends accord to every man the right of equality with every other.

Section 5. *The Work of the Holy Spirit.* The indwelling Spirit guides and controls the surrendered life, and the Christian's constant and supreme business is obedience to Him. But while the importance of individual guidance and obedience is thus emphasized, this fact gives no ground for license; the sanctified conclusions of the church are above the judgment of a single individual. Conviction for sin is awakened by the operation of the Holy Spirit, Who causes the soul to feel its need of reconciliation with God. The Holy Spirit testifies of Christ as the only hope of salvation; as man yields to Him, he is brought into newness of life through the regenerating power of the Spirit, and has a true realization of citizenship in the kingdom of God. The Holy Spirit witnesses further to the fact of a saved man's adoption into the family of God and of a consequent sonship through Christ. A changed nature and life give evidence of this new relation. Thus established in grace, man is able to bring forth the fruit of the Spirit, which gives further confirmation of a renewed state in grace.

Section 6. *The Baptism with the Holy Spirit.* The newly converted child of God soon realizes that, although his Christian experience is well begun, he is not yet been met. As he seeks for further light, he is but a babe in Christ. He senses a soul need that has a longing for a greater triumph over the sin in his nature that so constantly besets him. At this point Friends call his attention to the purifying and empowering baptism with the Holy Spirit with which Christ baptizes the earnest believer. Through it the Spirit is poured out upon him, and a complete separation takes place in his life, in that sin and holiness are clearly seen as antipodes which cannot coexist if complete victory is to be experienced. The soul is thus sanctified wholly, or made pure from the defilement of sin within. Thus a complete triumph over sin in the nature is provided for and growth in grace is greatly accelerated.

Section 7. *The Bestowment of Gifts.* The spiritual gifts are bestowed by the Holy Spirit, and by His incoming in cleansing baptism the essential power for their most efficient employment is given. It is thus that the Head of the Church has been pleased to make use of human instrumentalities in the accomplishment of His purposes. To this end He bestows special gifts upon certain members of the body for the propagation of the Gospel, for the perfecting of believers, and for the edifying and strengthening of the whole body in faith and life and power. The exercise of these gifts is a potent means by which the Church brings the truth to the individual consciousness, interprets and proclaims its message, and reveals its scope and purpose. There are varieties of gifts in the ministry, and in a properly organized body provision is made for the exercise and development of them all. It is not easy to draw a sharp distinction between the different types of ministry; frequently they are united in one person, who is thus peculiarly qualified for helpful service.

There is a gift for the ministry of instruction and of exposition, or of teaching the truth. Those who possess this gift are enabled to contribute in different degrees to the establishment of the membership, and to the expansion of the conception of divine things. This ministry of teaching requires a balanced, trained and well-stored mind, and the consecration of that mind to the service of Him who is the Truth.

There is a gift of speaking to states and needs of individuals, and of congregations. This prophetic ministry is characterized by the spiritual vision, the self-evidence of its message, and its fitness for the situation. It is a gift of seeing truth immediately and of effectively teaching it to others.

There is a gift for exhortation, which is an ability for making an appeal to the hearts of men, and for stirring them to a sense of God's love and of His purposes for men—the power of moving and convincing souls. Those who possess this gift are peculiarly fitted for evangelistic work.

There is also the pastoral gift, which consists especially in ability to do personal work with individuals or with families. This gift fits the possessor of it to comfort those who mourn, to lead the members into a closer religious life, to arouse in the young an interest in the things of the Spirit, and to impress others with a sense of the scope and reality of the spiritual life. It is the gift of shepherding and feeding the flock.

A gift of the Spirit is given to "every man to profit withal." There are many gifts set forth in the Scriptures in addition to those for the ministry of the Word. All should prayerfully await and receive the divine leading, to be open to the movings of the Spirit on any line that He may bring as a concern for special service. He who calls will empower, will equip, and will lead into avenues of blessed usefulness.

Section 8. *Worship.* The counsel of Hebrews 10:25 is timely: "Not forsaking the assembling of ourselves together, as the manner of some is; but exhorting one another; and so much the more, as ye see the day approaching." It is the duty and the privilege of believers to meet together for the public worship of God. In doing this they each time make a public profession to the world of their faith in Christ, and avail themselves of opportunities for spiritual blessings and mutual helpfulness not otherwise offered.

Worship is the highest act of which the human faculties are capable, and it can be truly performed only as it is in response to the influence of the Spirit of God. Public worship in the Christian church is in accordance with the declaration of our Lord, that "where two or three are met together in My name, there am I in the midst of them." The congregation is thus "the congregation of the Lord," and the meeting is primarily with Him. He touches the spiritual consciousness of believers, and thus, through Him, their High Priest and Intercessor, they are enabled to worship the Father in spirit and in truth. Worship stands neither in forms nor in the formal disuse of forms; it may be without words as well as with them. Both silence and vocal exercises are recognized and valued, not as ends but as means toward the attainment of an end, which is the divine blessing upon the individual and the congregation.

As Master of the Assembly, the Lord directs and leads the profitable exercises of His congregation. He calls and qualifies whom He will to be the bearer of His message, and the individual believer should hold himself in obedient submission to His will. The occasions of public worship are divinely appointed for the edification of believers in the truth and for the proclamation of fresh and vital messages of salvation to the world.

Section 9. *Christianity in Action.* With faith in the wisdom of Almighty God, the Father, the Son, and the Holy Spirit, and believing that it is His purpose to make His Church on earth a power for righteousness and truth, the Friends labor for the alleviation of human suffering; for the intellectual, moral, and spiritual elevation of mankind; and for purified and exalted citizenship. The Friends believe war to be incompatible with Christianity, and seek to promote peaceful methods for the settlement of all the differences between men and between nations.

It is an essential part of the faith that a man should be in truth what he professes in word; and the underlying principle of life and action for individuals, and also for society, is transformation through the power of God and implicit obedience to His revealed will.

Section 10. *The Lord's Return.* The grand consummation of the divine purpose in regard to His people is seen in the prophetic utterances found in the Scriptures concerning the return of the Lord. He will come as King of kings and Lords of lords to reign over all His universe and thus bring to an end the operations of Satan and his minions. The saints are comforted, as they view the devastations caused by sin in the world, in the assurance that the Lord will come in power and great glory for the punishment of evil doers and the eternal deliverance of His people from the evils of the world. The Lord declares in Revelation 22:20, "Surely I come quickly": and the church responds. "Even so, come, Lord Jesus." Friends should ever keep this great truth in mind, and thus not be misled by the arguments and reasoning of unbelievers.

For explicit and more extended statement of belief, the reader is referred to those officially put forth at various times by the Friends, especially to the letter of George Fox to the Governor of Barbados in 1671, and to the Declaration of Faith issued by the Richmond Conference in 1887. See pages 17-45.

CHAPTER III. EXTRACT FROM GEORGE FOX'S LETTER TO THE GOVERNOR OF BARBADOS, 1671

We do own and believe in God, the only wise, omnipotent, and everlasting God, the Creator of all things both in heaven and in earth, and the Preserver of all that He hath made; who is God over all, blessed forever; to whom be all honor and glory, dominion, praise, and thanksgiving, both now and forevermore.

And we own and believe in Jesus Christ, His beloved and only-begotten Son, in whom He is well pleased; who was conceived by the Holy Ghost and born of the Virgin Mary; in whom we have redemption through His blood, even the forgiveness of sins; who is the express image of the invisible God, the first-born of every creature, by whom were all things created that are in heaven and that are in earth, visible and invisible, whether they be thrones or dominions, principalities, or powers; all things were created by Him. And we do own and believe that He was made a sacrifice for sin, who knew no sin, neither was guile found in His mouth; that He was crucified for us in the flesh, without the gates of Jerusalem; and that He was buried, and rose again the third day by the power of His Father, for our justification; and that He ascended up into heaven, and now sitteth at the right hand of God. This Jesus, who was the foundation of the holy prophets and apostles, is our foundation; and we believe that there is no other foundation to be laid than that which is laid, even Christ Jesus; who tasted death for every man, shed His blood for all men and is the propitiation for our sins, and not for ours only, but also for the sins of the whole world according as John the Baptist testified of Him, when he said, "Behold the Lamb of God, that taketh away the sin of the world!" (John 1:29). We believe that He alone is our Redeemer and Saviour, even the captain of our salvation, who saves us from sin, as well as from hell and the wrath to come, and destroys the devil and his works; he is the Seed of the woman that bruises the serpent's head, to wit, Jesus Christ, the Alpha and Omega, the First and the Last. He is (as the Scriptures of truth say of Him) our wisdom and righteousness, justification, and redemption; neither is there salvation in any other, for there is no other name under heaven given among men whereby we may be saved. It is He alone who is the Shepherd and Bishop of our souls. He is our Prophet, whom Moses long since testified of saying, "A prophet shall the Lord your God raise up unto you of your brethren, like unto me; him shall ye hear in all things whatsoever he shall say unto you; and it shall come to pass, that every soul that will not hear that prophet shall be destroyed from among the people." (Acts 3:22, 23.)

He it is that is now come, "and hath given us an understanding, that we may know him that is true." He rules in our hearts by His law of love and of life, and makes us free from the law of sin and death. We have no life, but of Him; for He is the quickening Spirit, the second Adam, the Lord from heaven, by whose blood we are cleansed, and our consciences sprinkled from dead works, to serve the living God. He is our Mediator, that makes peace and reconciliation between God offended and us offending; He being the Oath of God, the new covenant of light, life, grace, and peace; the author and finisher of our faith. This Lord Jesus Christ, the heavenly man, the Emmanuel, God with us, we all own and believe in; He whom the high-priest raged against and said, He had spoken blasphemy; whom the priests and elders of the Jews took counsel together against and put to death; the same whom Judas betrayed for thirty pieces of silver, which the priests gave him as a reward for his treason; who also gave large money to the soldiers to broach a horrible lie, namely, "That his disciples came and stole him away by night whilst they slept." After He was arisen from the dead, the history of the acts of the apostles sets forth how the chief priests and elders persecuted the disciples of this Jesus, for preaching Christ and His resurrection. This, we say, is that Lord Jesus Christ, whom we own to be our life and salvation.

Concerning the Holy Scriptures we do believe that they were given forth by the Holy Spirit of God, through the holy men of God, who, as the Scripture itself declares, spake as they were moved by the Holy Ghost. (II Peter 1:21) We believe they are to be read, believed, and fulfilled

(He that fulfills them is Christ); and they are "profitable for doctrine, for reproof, for correction, and for instruction in righteousness that the man of God may be perfect, throughly furnished unto all good works," (II Tim. 3:15); and are able to make wise unto salvation, "through faith in Christ Jesus."

CHAPTER IV. DECLARATION OF FAITH ISSUED BY THE RICHMOND CONFERENCE IN 1887

(N.B. It should be understood that the quotations from Scripture are made from the Authorized Version unless stated to be from the American Standard Version—R.V.)

It is under a deep sense of what we owe to Him who has loved us that we feel called upon to offer a declaration of those fundamental doctrines of Christian truth that have always been professed by our branch of the Church of Christ.

OF GOD

We believe in one holy, almighty, all-wise, and everlasting God the Father, the Creator and Preserver of all things; and in Jesus Christ, His only Son, our Lord, by whom all things are made, and by whom all things consist; and in one Holy Spirit, proceeding from the Father and the Son, the Reprover of the world, the Witness for Christ, and the Teacher, Guide, and Sanctifier of the people of God; and that these three are one in the eternal Godhead; to whom be honor, praise, and thanksgiving, now and forever. Amen.

(Taken from these verses: Isa. 6:3; Isa. 57:15; Gen. 17:1; Rom. 11:33; Rom. 16:27; Psa. 90:1, 2; Matt. 11:25-27; Gen. 1:1; Job 7:20; John 1:3; Col. 1:17; John 15:26; John 16:7; John 16:8; John 15:26; John 14:26; John 16:13; II Thess. 2:13; Matt. 28:19; John 10:30; John 17:21.)

THE LORD JESUS CHRIST

It is with reverence and thanksgiving that we profess our unwavering allegiance to our Lord and Saviour, Jesus Christ. No man hath seen God at any time; the only begotten Son, who is in the bosom of the Father, He hath declared Him. In Him was life, and the life was the light of men. He is the true Light which lighteth every man that cometh into the world; through whom the light of truth in all ages has proceeded from the Father of lights. He is the eternal Word who was with God and was God, revealing Himself in infinite wisdom and love, both as man's Creator and Redeemer; for by Him were all things created that are in heaven and that are on earth, visible and invisible. Conceived of the Holy Ghost, born of the virgin Mary, the Word was made flesh and dwelt amongst men. He came in the fulness of the appointed time, being verily foreordained before the foundation of the world, that He might fulfill the eternal counsel of the righteousness and love of God for the redemption of man. In Him dwelleth all the fullness of the Godhead bodily. Though He was rich, yet for our sakes He became poor, veiling in the form of a servant the brightness of His glory, that through Him the kindness and love of God toward man might appear in a manner every way suited to our wants and finite capacities. He went about doing good; for us He endured sorrow, hunger, thirst, weariness, pain, unutterable anguish of body and of soul, being in all points tempted like as we are, yet without sin. Thus humbling Himself that we might be exalted, He emphatically recognized the duties and the sufferings of humanity as among the means whereby, through the obedience of faith, we are to be disciplined for heaven, sanctifying them to us, by Himself performing and enduring them, leaving us the one perfect example of all righteousness in self-sacrificing love.

But not only in these blessed relations must the Lord Jesus be ever precious to His people. In Him is revealed, as true God and perfect man, a Redeemer, at once able to suffer and almighty to save. He became obedient unto death, even the death of the cross, and is the propitiation for our sins, and not for ours only, but also for the sins of the whole world; in whom we have redemption through His blood for the forgiveness of sins according to the riches of His grace. It is our joy to confess that the remission of sins which any partake of is only in and by virtue of His most satisfactory sacrifice and not otherwise. He was buried and rose again the third day according to the Scriptures, becoming the first fruits of them that sleep, and having shown Himself alive after His passion, by many infallible proofs. He ascended into heaven, and hath sat down at the right hand of the Majesty on high, now to appear in the presence of God for us. With the apostles who beheld His ascension, we rest in the assurance of the angelic messengers, "This same Jesus, which is taken up from you into heaven shall so come in like manner as ye have seen him go into heaven." With the apostle John, we would desire to unite in the words "Amen; even so, come, Lord Jesus." And now, whilst thus watching and waiting, we rejoice to believe that He is our King and Saviour. He is the one Mediator of the new and everlasting covenant, who makes peace and reconciliation between God offended and man offending; the great High Priest whose priesthood is unchangeable. He is able to save them to the uttermost that come unto God by Him, seeing He ever liveth to make intercession for them. All power is given unto Him in heaven and in earth. By Him the world shall be judged in righteousness; for the Father judgeth no man, but hath committed all judgment unto the Son, that all men should honor the Son even as they honor the Father. All that are in the tombs shall hear his voice, and shall come forth, they that have done good unto the resurrection of life, and they that have done evil unto the resurrection of judgment. (John 5:28, 29 R.V.)

We reverently confess and believe that divine honor and worship are due to the Son of God, and that He is in true faith to be prayed unto, and His name to be called upon, as the primitive Christians did, because of the glorious oneness of the Father and the Son; and that we cannot acceptably offer prayers and praises to God, nor receive from Him a gracious answer or blessing, but in and through his dear Son.

We would, with humble thanksgiving, bear an especial testimony to our Lord's perpetual dominion and power in His church. Through Him the redeemed in all generations have derived their light, their forgiveness, and their joy. All are members of this church, by whatsoever name they may be called among men, who have been baptized by the one Spirit into the one body; who are builded as living stones upon Christ, the Eternal Foundation, and are united in faith and love in that fellowship which is with the Father and with the Son. Of this church the Lord Jesus Christ is the alone Head. All its true members are made one in Him. They have washed their robes and made them white in His precious blood, and He has made them priests unto God and His Father. He dwells in their hearts by faith, and gives them of his peace. His will is their law, and in Him they enjoy the true liberty, a freedom from the bondage of sin.

(Taken from these verses: Paragraph 1—John 1:18; John 1:4, 9; James 1:17; John 1:1; Col. 1:13-16; Matt. 1:20, 23-25; Luke 1:35; John 1:14; Gal. 4:4; I Peter 1:20; Isa. 11:1-5; Isa. 52:13-15; Isa. 53; Col. 2:9; Phil. 2:7; Titus 3:4; Acts 10:38; Isa. 53:4; Luke 12:50; 19:41; 22:44; John 4:6; Luke 22:43, 44; Heb. 4:15; I Peter 2:21; Matt. 3:15. Paragraph 2—Eph. 4:13; Phil. 2:8; I John 2:2; Eph. 1:7; I Cor. 15:4, 23; Acts 1:3; Heb. 1:3; 9:24; Acts 1:11, 7; Rev. 22:20; I Tim. 2:5; Heb. 9:15; 4:14; 7:24, 25; Matt. 28:18; Acts 17:31; John 5:22, 23. Paragraph 4—Eph. 1:22; Rev. 7:14; 1:6.)

THE HOLY SPIRIT

We believe that the Holy Spirit is, in the unity of the eternal Godhead, one with the Father and with the Son. He is the Comforter "Whom," saith Christ, "the Father will send in my name." He convinces the world of sin, of righteousness, and of judgment. He testifies of and glorifies Jesus. It is the Holy Spirit who makes the evil manifest. He quickens them that are dead in trespasses and sins, and opens the inward eye to behold the Lamb of God that taketh away the sin of the world. Coming in the name and with the authority of the risen and ascended Saviour, He is the precious pledge of the continued love and care of our exalted King. He takes of the things of Christ and shows them, as a realized possession, to the believing soul. Dwelling in the hearts of believers, He opens their understandings that they may understand the Scriptures, and becomes, to the humbled and surrendered heart, the Guide, Comforter, Support, and Sanctifier.

We believe that the essential qualification for the Lord's service is bestowed upon His children through the reception and baptism of the Holy Ghost. This Holy Spirit is the seal of reconciliation to the believer in Jesus, the witness to his adoption into the family of the redeemed; the earnest and the foretaste of the full communion and perfect joy which are reserved for them that endure unto the end.

We own no principle of spiritual light, life, or holiness inherent by nature in the mind or heart of man. We believe in no principle of spiritual light, life, or holiness but the influence of the Holy Spirit of God bestowed on mankind in various measures and degrees, through Jesus Christ our Lord. It is the capacity to receive this blessed influence, which, in an especial manner, gives man pre-eminence above the beasts that perish; which distinguishes him, in every nation and in every clime, as an object of the redeeming love of God, as a being not only intelligent but responsible, for whom the message of salvation through our crucified Redeemer is, under all possible circumstances, designed to be a joyful sound. The Holy Spirit must ever be distinguished both from the conscience which

He enlightens and from the natural faculty of reason, which when unsubjected to His holy influence, is, in the things of God, very foolishness. As the eye is to the body, so is the conscience to our inner being, the organ by which we see; and as both light and life are essential to the eye, so conscience, as the inward eye, cannot see aright without the quickening and illumination of the Spirit of God. One with the Father and the Son, the Holy Spirit can never disown or dishonor our once crucified and now risen and glorified Redeemer. We disavow all professed illumination or spirituality that is divorced from faith in Jesus Christ of Nazareth, crucified for us without the gates of Jerusalem.

(Taken from these verses: Matt. 28:19; II Cor. 13:14; John 16:26, 8, 14; John 14:17; Eph. 2:1; 1:13, 14; Rom. 8:15, 16.)

THE HOLY SCRIPTURES

It has ever been, and still is, the belief of the Society of Friends that the Holy Scriptures of the Old and New Testament were given by inspiration of God; that, therefore, there can be no appeal from them to any other authority whatsoever; that they are able to make wise unto salvation, through faith which is in Jesus Christ. "These are written that ye might believe that Jesus is the Christ, the Son of God; and that believing ye might have life through His name." (John 20:31.) The Scriptures are the only divinely authorized record of the doctrines which we are bound as Christians to accept and of the moral principles which are to regulate our actions. No one can be required to believe, as an article of faith, any doctrine which is not contained in them; and whatsoever any one says or does, contrary to the Scriptures, though under profession of the immediate guidance of the Holy Spirit, must be reckoned and accounted a mere delusion. To the Christian the Old Testament comes with the solemn and repeated attestation of his Lord. It is to be read in the light and completeness of the New; thus will its meaning be unveiled, and the humble disciple will be taught to discern the unity and mutual adaptation of the whole and the many-sidedness and harmony of its testimony to Christ. The great Inspirer of Scripture is ever its true Interpreter. He performs this office in condescending love, not by superseding our understandings, but by renewing and enlightening them. Where Christ presides, idle speculation is hushed; His doctrine is learned in the doing of His will, and all knowledge ripens into a deeper and richer experience of His truth and love.

MAN'S CREATION AND FALL

It pleased God, in His wisdom and goodness, to create man out of the dust of the earth, and to breathe into his nostrils the breath of life, so that man became a living soul; formed after the image and likeness of God, capable of fulfilling the divine law, and of holding communion with his Maker. Being free to obey or to disobey, he fell into transgression, through unbelief, under the temptation of Satan and thereby lost that spiritual life of righteousness in which he was created; and so death passed upon him as the inevitable consequence of his sin. As the children of fallen Adam, all mankind bear his image. They partake of his nature and are involved in the consequences of his fall. To every member of every successive generation, the words of the Redeemer are alike applicable, "Ye must be born again." But while we hold these views of the lost condition of man in the fall, we rejoice to believe that sin is not imputed to any until they transgress the divine law after sufficient capacity has been given to understand it; and that infants, though inheriting this fallen nature, are saved in the infinite mercy of God through the redemption which is in Christ Jesus.

(Scripture verses quoted are Gen. 2:7; 1:26, 27; 3:1-7; Rom. 5:12; John 3:7.)

JUSTIFICATION AND SANCTIFICATION

"God so loved the world that He gave His only begotten Son, that whosoever believeth in Him should not perish, but have everlasting life." We believe that justification is of God's free grace, through which, upon repentance and faith, He pardons our sins and imparts to us a new life. It is received, not for any works of righteousness that we have done, but in the unmerited mercy of God in Christ Jesus. Through faith in Him and the shedding of His precious blood, the guilt of sin is taken away, and we stand reconciled to God. The offering up of Christ as the propitiation for the sins of the whole world is the appointed manifestation both of the righteousness and of the love of God. In this propitiation the pardon of sin involves no abrogation or relaxation of the law of holiness. It is the vindication and establishment of that law, in virtue of the free and righteous submission of the Son of God Himself to all its requirements. He, the unchangeably just, proclaims Himself the justifier of him that believeth in Jesus. From age to age, the sufferings and death of Christ have been a hidden mystery and a rock of offense to the unbelief and pride of man's fallen nature; yet, to the humble penitent whose heart is broken under the convicting power of the Spirit, life is revealed in that death. As he looks upon Him who was wounded for our transgressions, and upon whom the Lord was pleased to lay the iniquity of us all, his eye is more and more opened to see, and his heart to understand, the exceeding sinfulness of sin for which the Saviour died; whilst, in the sense of pardoning grace, he will joy in God through our Lord Jesus Christ, by Whom we have now received the atonement.

We believe that in connection with justification is regeneration: that they who come to this experience know that they are not their own; that being reconciled to God by the death of His Son, we are saved by His life; a new heart is given and new desires; old things are passed away, and we become new creatures through faith in Christ Jesus. Our wills being surrendered to His holy will, grace reigns through righteousness unto eternal life by Jesus Christ our Lord.

Sanctification is experienced in the acceptance of Christ in living faith for justification, in so far as the pardoned sinner, through faith in Christ, is clothed with a measure of His righteousness and receives the Spirit of promise; for, as saith the Apostle, "Ye are washed, ye are sanctified, ye are justified, in the name of the Lord Jesus, and by the Spirit of our God." We rejoice to believe that the provisions of God's grace are sufficient to deliver from the power, as well as from the guilt, of sin and to enable His believing children always to triumph in Christ. How full of encouragement is the declaration, "According to your faith be it unto you." Whosoever submits himself wholly to God, believing and appropriating His promises and exercising faith in Christ Jesus, will have his heart continually cleansed from all sin by His precious blood and, through the renewing, refining power of the Holy Spirit, be kept in conformity to the will of God, will love Him with all his heart, mind, soul, and strength, and be able to say with the Apostle Paul, "The law of the Spirit of life in Christ Jesus hath made me free from the law of sin and death." Thus, in its full experience sanctification is deliverance from the pollution, nature, and love of sin. To this we are every one called that we may serve the Lord without fear, in holiness and righteousness before Him all the days of our life. It was the prayer of the apostle for the believers, "The very God of peace sanctify you wholly; and I pray God your whole spirit and soul and body be preserved blameless unto the coming of our Lord Jesus Christ. Faithful is he that calleth you who also will do it." Yet the most holy Christian is still liable to temptation, is exposed to the subtle assaults of Satan, and can only continue to follow holiness as he humbly watches unto prayer and is kept in constant dependence upon his Saviour, walking in the light in the loving obedience of faith.

(Taken from these verses: Paragraph 1—John 3:16; Titus 3:5; I John 2:2; Rom. 3:31, 26; Isa. 53:5, 6; Rom. 5:11. Paragraph 2—I Cor. 6:19; Rom. 5:10; II Cor. 5:17; Rom. 5:21. Paragraph 3—I Cor. 6:11; II Cor. 2:14; Matt. 9:29; Rom. 8:2; Luke 1:74, 75; I Thess. 5:23, 24; I John 1:7.)

THE RESURRECTION AND FINAL JUDGMENT

We believe, according to the Scriptures, that there shall be a resurrection from the dead, both of the just and of the unjust, and that God hath appointed a day in which He will judge the world in righteousness, by Jesus Christ whom he hath ordained. For, as saith the apostle, "We must all appear before the judgment seat of Christ, that every one may receive the things done in his body according to that he hath done, whether it be good or bad."

We sincerely believe not only a resurrection in Christ from the fallen and sinful state here but a rising and ascending into glory with Him hereafter; that when He at last appears we may appear with Him in glory, but that all the wicked, who live in rebellion against the light of grace and die finally impenitent, shall come forth to the resurrection of condemnation. The soul of every man and woman shall be reserved in its own distinct and proper being and shall have its proper body as God is pleased to give it. It is sown a natural body, it is raised a spiritual body; that being first which is natural, and afterward that which is spiritual. And though it is said, "this corruptible shall put on incorruption, and this mortal shall put on immortality," the change shall be such as will accord with the declaration, "Flesh and blood cannot inherit the Kingdom of God, neither doth corruption inherit incorruption." We shall be raised out of all corruption and corruptibility, out of all mortality, and shall be the children of God, being the children of resurrection.

"Our citizenship is in heaven" (R.V.), from whence also we look for the Savior the Lord Jesus Christ, who shall change our vile body that it may be fashioned like unto His glorious body, according to the working whereby He is able even to subdue all things unto Himself.

We believe that the punishment of the wicked and the blessedness of the righteous shall be everlasting; according to the declaration of our compassionate Redeemer, to whom the judgment is committed, "These shall go away into eternal punishment but the righteous into eternal life." (R. V., Matt. 25:46.)

(Verses quoted are: Paragraph 1—Acts 24:15; 17:31; II Cor. 5:10. Paragraph 2—I Cor. 15:44, 53, 50; Luke 20:36. Paragraph 3—Phil. 3:20, 21.)

BAPTISM

We would express our continued conviction that our Lord appointed no outward rite or ceremony for observance in His church. We accept every command of our Lord, in what we believe to be its genuine import, as absolutely conclusive. The question of the use of outward ordinances is with us a question, not as to the authority of Christ but as to his real meaning. We reverently believe that, as there is one Lord and one faith, so there is under the Christian dispensation but one baptism, even that whereby all believers are baptized in one Spirit into one body. (I Cor. 12;13. R. V.) This is not an outward baptism with water, but a spiritual experience; not the putting away of the filth of the flesh, but that inward work which, by transforming the heart and settling the soul upon Christ, brings forth the answer of a good conscience towards God by the resurrection of Jesus Christ in the experience of His love and power as the risen and ascended Saviour. No baptism in outward water can satisfy the description of the apostle of being buried with Christ by baptism unto death. It is with the Spirit alone that any can thus be baptized. In this experience the announcement of the forerunner of our Lord is fulfilled, "He shall baptize you with the Holy Ghost and with fire." In this view we accept the commission of our blessed Lord as given in Matthew 28:18-20 R.V.: "And Jesus came to them and spake unto them saying, All authority hath been given unto me in heaven and on earth. Go ye, therefore, and make disciples of all the nations, baptizing them into the name of the Father and of the Son and of the Holy Spirit: teaching them to observe all things whatsoever I commanded you; and lo, I am with you always, even unto the end of the world." This commission, as we believe, was not designed to set up a new ritual under the new covenant, or to connect the initiation into a membership—in its nature essentially spiritual—with a mere ceremony of a typical character. Otherwise it was not possible for the Apostle Paul, who was not a whit behind the very chiefest apostle, to have disclaimed that which would in that case have been of the essence of his commission when he wrote, "Christ sent me not to baptize, but to preach the Gospel." Whenever an external ceremony is commanded, the particulars, the mode, and incidents of that ceremony become of its essence. There is an utter absence of these particulars in the text before us which confirms our persuasion that the commission must be construed in

connection with the spiritual power which the risen Lord
promised should attend the witness of his apostles and of
the church to Him and which, after Pentecost, so mightily
accompanied their ministry of the word and prayer, that
those to whom they were sent were introduced into an
experience wherein they had a saving knowledge of, and
living fellowship with, the Father and the Son and the
Holy Spirit.

(Taken from these verses: Eph. 4:4, 5; I Peter 3:21;
Romans 6:4; Matt. 3:11; II Cor. 11:5; I Cor. 1:17.)

THE SUPPER OF THE LORD

Intimately connected with the conviction already expressed is the view that we have ever maintained as to the
true supper of the Lord. We are well aware that our Lord
was pleased to make use of a variety of symbolical
utterances, but He often gently upbraided His disciples for
accepting literally what He had intended only in its
spiritual meaning. His teaching, as in His parables or in
the command to wash one another's feet, was often in
symbols, and ought ever to be received in the light of His
own emphatic declaration, "The words that I speak unto
you, they are spirit and they are life." The old covenant
was full of ceremonial symbols; the new covenant, to
which our Saviour alluded at the last supper, is expressly
declared by the prophet to be "not according to the old."
We cannot believe that in setting up this new covenant the
Lord Jesus intended an institution out of harmony with
the spirit of this prophecy. The eating of His body and the
drinking of His blood cannot be an outward act. They
truly partake of them who habitually rest upon the
sufferings and death of their Lord as their only hope, and
to whom the indwelling Spirit gives to drink of the fullness
that is in Christ. It is this inward and spiritual partaking
that is the true supper of the Lord.

The presence of Christ with His church is not designed to
be by symbol or representation, but in the real communication of His own Spirit. "I will pray the Father, and He
shall give you another Comforter, that he may abide with
you forever." Convincing of sin, testifying of Jesus, taking
of the things of Christ, this blessed Comforter communicates to the believer and to the church in a gracious,
abiding manifestation the REAL PRESENCE of the Lord.
As the great remembrancer through whom the promise is
fulfilled, He needs no ritual or priestly intervention in
bringing to the experience of the true commemoration and
communion. "Behold," saith the risen Redeemer, "I stand
at the door and knock. If any man hear my voice and open
the door, I will come in and sup with him and he with
me." In an especial manner, when assembled for congregational worship, are believers invited to the festival of the
Saviour's peace and, in a united act of faith and love,
unfettered by any outward rite or ceremonial, to partake
together of the body that was broken and of the blood that
was shed for them without the gates of Jerusalem. In such
a worship they are enabled to understand the words of the
apostle as expressive of a sweet and most real experience:
"The cup of blessing which we bless, is it not the

communion of the blood of Christ? The bread that we
break, is it not the communion of the body of Christ? For
we being many are one bread and one body; for we are all
partakers of that one bread."

(Taken from these verses: John 6:63; Jer. 31:32; Heb. 8:9;
John 14:16; Rev. 3:20; I Cor. 10:16, 17.)

PUBLIC WORSHIP

Worship is the adoring response of the heart and mind to
the influence of the Spirit of God. It stands neither in
forms nor in the formal disuse of forms: it may be without
words as well as with them, but it must be in spirit and in
truth. We recognize the value of silence, not as an end but
as a means toward the attainment of the end; a silence, not
of listlessness or of vacant musing but of holy expectation
before the Lord. Having become His adopted children
through faith in the Lord Jesus Christ, it is our privilege to
meet together and unite in the worship of Almighty God
and to wait upon Him for the renewal of our strength, for
communion one with another, for the edification of
believers in the exercise of various spiritual gifts, and for
the declaration of the glad tidings of salvation to the
unconverted who may gather with us. This worship
depends not upon numbers. Where two or three are
gathered together in the name of Christ there is a church,
and Christ, the living Head, in the midst of them. Through
His mediation, without the necessity for any inferior
instrumentality, is the Father to be approached and
reverently worshipped. The Lord Jesus has forever fulfilled
and ended the typical and sacrificial worship under the law
by offering up of Himself upon the cross for us, once for
all. He has opened the door of access into the inner
sanctuary and graciously provided spiritual offerings for
the service of His temple, suited to the several conditions
of all who worship in spirit and in truth. The broken and
the contrite heart, the confession of the soul prostrate
before God, the prayer of the afflicted when he is
overwhelmed, the earnest wrestling of the spirit, the
outpouring of humble thanksgiving, the spiritual song and
melody of the heart, the simple exercise of faith, the self-
denying service of love—these are among the sacrifices
which He, our merciful and faithful High Priest, is pleased
to prepare by His Spirit in the hearts of them that receive
Him and to present with acceptance unto God.

By the immediate operations of the Holy Spirit, He, as the
Head of the church, alone selects and qualifies those who
are to present His messages or engage in other service for
Him; and hence, we cannot commit any formal arrangement to any one in our regular meetings for worship. We
are well aware that the Lord has provided a diversity of
gifts for the needs both of the church and of the world, and
we desire that the church may feel her responsibility,
under the government of her Great Head, in doing her part
to foster these gifts and in making arrangements for their
proper exercise.

It is not for individual exaltation, but for mutual profit,
that the gifts are bestowed; and every living church,
abiding under the government of Christ, is humbly and
thankfully to receive and exercise them in subjection to her
Holy Head. The church that quenches the Spirit and lives
to itself alone must die.

We believe the preaching of the Gospel to be one of the chief means, divinely appointed, for the spreading of the glad tidings of life and salvation through our crucified Redeemer, for the awakening and conversion of sinners, and for the comfort and edification of believers. As it is the prerogative of the Great Head of the church alone to select and call the ministers of His Gospel, so we believe that both the gift and the qualification to exercise it must be derived immediately from Him; and that, as in the primitive church so now also, He confers spiritual gifts upon women as well as upon men, agreeably to the prophecy recited by the apostle Peter, "It shall come to pass in that the last days saith God, I will pour out of my Spirit upon all flesh; and your sons and your daughters shall prophesy." Respecting which the apostle declares, "The promise is unto you, and to your children, and to all that are afar off, even as many as the Lord our God shall call." As the gift is freely received, so it is to be freely exercised in simple obedience to the will of God.

Spiritual gifts, precious as they are, must not be mistaken for grace; they add to our responsibility, but do not raise the minister above his brethren or sisters. They must be exercised in continued dependence upon our Lord, and blessed is that ministry in which man is humbled, and Christ and His grace exalted. "He that is greatest among you," said our Lord and Master, "let him be as the younger; and he that is chief as he that doth serve. I am among you as he that serveth."

While the church cannot confer spiritual gifts, it is its duty to recognize and foster them and to promote their efficiency by all means in its power. And while, on the one hand, the Gospel should never be preached for money, on the other, it is the duty of the church to make such provision that it shall never be hindered for want of it.

The church, if true to her allegiance, cannot forget her part in the command, "Go ye into all the world, and preach the Gospel to every creature." Knowing that it is the Spirit of God that can alone prepare and qualify the instruments who fulfill this command, the true disciple will be found still sitting at the feet of Jesus, listening that he may learn and learning that he may obey. He humbly places himself at his Lord's disposal, and when he hears the call, "Whom shall I send, and who will go for us?" is prepared to respond, in childlike reverence and love. "Here am I, send me."

(Taken from these verses: Paragraph 1—John 4:24; Eph. 5:19; Paragraph 2—I Cor. 12:4-6. Paragraph 3—I Cor. 12:7. Paragraph 4—Acts 2:17, 39; Matt. 10:8; Acts 20:33-35. Paragraph 5—Luke 22:26, 27. Paragraph 6—Acts 8:20; 20:33-35. Paragraph 7—Mark 16:15; Isa. 6:8.)

PRAYER AND PRAISE

Prayer is the outcome of our sense of need and of our continual dependence upon God. He who uttered the invitation, "Ask and it shall be given you," is Himself the Mediator and High Priest who, by His Spirit, prompts the petition and presents it with acceptance before God. With such an invitation, prayer becomes the duty and the privilege of all who are called by His name. Prayer is, in the awakened soul, the utterance of the cry, "God be merciful to me a sinner," and at every stage of the

believer's course prayer is essential to his spiritual life. A life without prayer is a life practically without God. The Christian's life is a continual asking. The thirst that prompts the petition produces, as it is satisfied, still deeper longings, which prepare for yet more bounteous supplies from Him who delights to bless. Prayer is not confined to the closet. When uttered in response to the promptings of the Holy Spirit, it becomes an important part of public worship, and whenever the Lord's people meet together in His name, it is their privilege to wait upon Him for the spirit of grace and supplications. A life of prayer cannot be other than a life of praise. As the peace of Christ reigns in the church, her living members accept all that they receive as from His pure bounty, and each day brings them fresh pledges of their Father's love. Satisfied with the goodness of His house, whether as individuals, in families, or in congregations, they will be still praising Him, heart answering to heart, "Bless the Lord, O my soul: and all that is within me, bless His holy name."

(Scripture verses quoted are: Matt. 7:7; Luke 18:13; Zech. 12:10; Psa. 84:4; 103:1.)

LIBERTY OF CONSCIENCE IN ITS RELATION TO CIVIL GOVERNMENT

That conscience should be free and that in matters of religious doctrine and worship man is accountable only to God are truths which are plainly declared in the New Testament, and which are confirmed by the whole scope of the Gospel and by the example of our Lord and His disciples. To rule over the conscience and to command the spiritual allegiance of his creature man are the high and sacred prerogatives of God alone. In religion every act ought to be free. A forced worship is plainly a contradiction in terms, under that dispensation in which the worship of the Father must be in spirit and in truth.

We have ever maintained that it is the duty of Christians to obey the enactments of civil government, except those which interfere with our allegiance to God. We owe much to its blessings. Through it we enjoy liberty and protection in connection with law and order. Civil government is a divine ordinance, instituted to promote the best welfare of man; hence magistrates are to be regarded as God's ministers who should be a terror to evil doers and a praise to them that do well. Therefore, it is with us a matter of conscience to render them respect and obedience in the exercise of their proper functions.

(Taken from these verses: John 4:24; Rom. 13:1; I Peter 2:13-16.)

MARRIAGE

Marriage is an institution graciously ordained by the Creator Himself for the help and continuance of the human family. It is not a mere civil contract and ought never to be entered upon without a reference to the sanction and blessing of Him who ordained it. It is a solemn engagement for the term of life, (Matt. 19:5, 6), designed for the mutual assistance and comfort of both sexes, that they may be helpmates to each other in things temporal and spiritual. To this end it should imply concurrence in spiritual as well as temporal concerns and

THE CHURCH AND ITS ESSENTIAL DOCTRINES [MID-AMERICA (FORMERLY KANSAS) YEARLY MEETING] (continued)

should be entered upon discreetly, soberly, and in the fear of the Lord.

(Scripture verses quoted are: Matt. 5:44; Luke 6:27; Isaiah 2:4; Micah 4:1.)

PEACE

We feel bound explicitly to avow our unshaken persuasion that all war is utterly incompatible with the plain percepts of our divine Lord and Law-giver and the whole spirit of His Gospel, and that no plea of necessity or policy, however urgent or peculiar, can avail to release either individuals or nations from the paramount allegiance which they owe to Him who hath said, "Love your enemies." In enjoining this love and the forgiveness of injuries, He who has bought us to Himself has not prescribed for man precepts which are incapable of being carried into practice, or of which the practice is to be postponed until all shall be persuaded to act upon them. We cannot doubt that they are incumbent now, and that we have in the prophetic Scriptures the distinct intimation of their direct application not only to individuals, but to nations also. When nations conform their laws to this divine teaching, wars must necessarily cease.

We would, in humility but in faithfulness to our Lord, express our firm persuasion that all the exigencies of civil government and social order may be met under the banner of the Prince of Peace in strict conformity with His command.

OATHS

We hold it to be the inalienable privilege of the disciple of the Lord Jesus that his statements concerning matters of fact within his knowledge should be accepted, under all circumstances, as expressing his belief as to the fact asserted. We rest upon the plain command of our Lord and Master, "Swear not at all" (Matt. 5:34); and we believe any departure from this standard to be prejudicial to the cause of truth and to that confidence between man and man, the maintenance of which is indispensable to our mutual well being. This command, in our persuasion, applies not to profane swearing only but to judicial oaths also. It abrogates any previous permission to the contrary, and is, for the Christian, absolutely conclusive.

THE FIRST DAY OF THE WEEK

Whilst the remembrance of our Creator ought to be at all times present with the Christian, we would express our thankfulness to our Heavenly Father that He has been pleased to honor the setting apart of one day in seven for the purpose of holy rest, religious duties, and public worship; and we desire that all under our name may avail themselves of this great privilege as those who are called to be risen with Christ and to seek those things that are above where He sitteth at the right hand of God. (Coloss. 3:1.) May the release thus granted from other occupations be diligently improved. On this day of the week especially ought the households of Friends to be assembled for the reading of the Scriptures and for waiting upon the Lord; and we trust that, in a Christianly wise economy of our

time and strength, the engagements of the day may be so ordered as not to frustrate the gracious provision thus made for us by our Heavenly Father, or to shut out the opportunity either for public worship or for private retirement and devotional reading.

In presenting this declaration of our Christian faith, we desire that all our members may be afresh encouraged, in humility and devotedness, to renewed faithfulness in fulfiling their part in the great mission of the Church, and through the Church to the world around us in the name of our Crucified Redeemer. Life *from* Christ, life *in* Christ, must ever be the basis of life *for* Christ. For this we have been created and redeemed, and by this alone can the longings of our immortal souls be satisfied.

Notes: *The Kansas Yearly Meeting has recently changed its name to the Mid-America Yearly Meeting. It is a member of the Evangelical Friends Alliance, which is a member of the National Association of Evangelicals as well as the Christian Holines Association.*

*   *   *

QUAKER FAITH AND PRACTICE (PACIFIC YEARLY MEETING)

Friends from the first have stressed the interdependence of faith and practice. They refrain from fixing their faith in a formal set of words because they feel the divine lies deeper than words: it must be lived and demonstrated throughout the whole of life. They value greatly the record of God's dealing with men in the Judeo-Christian scriptures and feel these are to be interpreted in the Spirit which inspired them and which continues to reveal Truth to men. Friends have used various expressions—the Light Within, the Light or Spirit of Christ, living God, Word, that of God, Truth, Power, Seed, and many more—in trying to describe their experience of the divine Life at the heart of the universe. They have emphasized that by living and walking in this Light, which was revealed in the life of Jesus on earth and which enlightens every man, they may answer to the same Light, or that of God, in other persons. Friends thus approach faith less as a matter of profession than of experience. The Quaker interpretation of Christianity keeps in creative tension its particular and universal character, its Christ-centered and God-centered orientation, its mystical and practical demands.

The religious practices of Friends follow from the conviction that the divine Light is accessible to all; yet it is one Light; therefore men are to wait in the Light for agreement in their common affairs. This is the key to the Quaker Meeting, whether for worship or for business. Quaker worship has been described as "group mysticism." Meetings for business and for action on social concerns are thought of as worship translated into action. Through agreement in a "sense of the Meeting," Quaker practice seeks to reconcile the demands both of freedom and order, individual inspiration and corporate wisdom. (In its early days, the Quaker movement specifically rejected so-called "Ranterism," the view that religious activities ought to be left entirely to individual inspiration, with no accepted common order of any kind.) The Quaker movement has found coherence and continuity in a system of Monthly, Quarterly, and Yearly Meetings, with certain more general gatherings for larger associations of Friends.

Notes: *The Pacific Yearly Meeting includes congregations stretched from Canada to Mexico. It emphasizes the experience of the inner light and the freedom of belief of its members.*

*   *   *

BASIC BELIEFS (ROCKY MOUNTAIN YEARLY MEETING)

Friends believe that apostolic (New Testament) doctrines are essentials of Christianity. Fundamental truths considered as vital and life-giving are: the Fatherhood of God; the deity and humanity of Jesus the Son, the ministry of the Holy Spirit; Christ's atonement which reconciles men to God; the resurrection of Jesus Christ which assures true believers of life after death; the high priesthood of Christ who gives access to the Father by forgiving men's sins; and the individual priesthood of believers who may approach God directly without human intervention.

While Friends do not stress a formal written creed, they do state the primary principles of their faith in order to make their doctrinal position clear. Not wishing to be dogmatic, they record certain beliefs which are held as basic to their faith. The statement of faith of Friends may be summarized as follows:

The Bible is the inspired rule of faith and subject to the Holy Spirit's interpretation.

God is sovereign.

Jesus Christ offers vicarious atonement through His death and resurrection.

The Holy Spirit brings men to experience salvation.

Man is sinful, but redeemable.

Salvation comprises both forgiveness and sanctification.

The Church is the visible expression of Christ; it will be fulfilled in the final resurrection and judgment.

Inner communion and the baptism with the Holy Spirit are spiritual realities beyond outward symbols.

Christian witness is given through word and deed both in general and specific ministries.

The following pages amplify the subjects mentioned above; for more complete statements on fundamental doctrines, refer to the historical documents which appear in the Appendix.

1. THE BIBLE. The Holy Bible was given to men by the direct inspiration of God. It is sufficient to inform men of salvation through faith in Jesus Christ. God's Holy Spirit, who inspired the Scriptures, also interprets them, working through those yielded to Him within His Church. The Bible is the final authority by which all guidance should be measured for truth. Genuine guidance from God is in accord with the Holy Scriptures.

2. GOD. There is one sovereign God who is revealed through the Bible in the person of His Son, Jesus Christ. God is the Maker and Preserver of all things; He alone is worthy of worship. In the unity of the Godhead exist three equal and distinct, yet inseparable, persons: the Father, the Son Jesus Christ, and the Holy Spirit.

3. JESUS CHRIST. Jesus Christ, the only begotten Son of God, is God's revelation of Himself to man. He was divine and yet human, being conceived by God's Spirit and born of a virgin. Through the blood He shed dying on the cross, Jesus Christ became the atonement for man's sin, thus providing direct access to God by His priesthood. Upon His resurrection from the dead, He ascended again to the right hand of His Father, assuming the role of Intercessor and drawing men to God by His Spirit. When Jesus Christ returns to earth, He will receive His Church and judge the world.

4. THE HOLY SPIRIT. The Holy Spirit proceeds from the Father and the Son and is equal with them. He convinces men of their sin, gives life to penitent believers, and sanctifies the child of God. He enables one to love God supremely and to give evidence of the Spirit's presence in his life. The Holy Spirit works through individual lives as well as in corporate groups of the church, enabling men to serve in various ways as He chooses.

5. MAN. Created in the image of God, at first man enjoyed unbroken fellowship with His Maker. By his disobedience, he incurred the displeasure of God and the penalty of spiritual death. Consequently, since Adam sinned, all men are born in a sinful state; there is no inherent principle which naturally leads man to salvation outside the atoning provision of Jesus Christ for all mankind. While man is sinful by nature, he can be redeemed from sin's penalty, which is eternal death, because Christ paid this penalty in full.

Through His sacrificial death, Jesus Christ destroyed the wall separating man from God. By the individual priesthood of believers, all men stand equal before God and may approach Him directly.

6. SALVATION. Salvation is a personal matter between man and his Maker. It consists of forgiveness for sin as well as sanctification or the cleansing of man's sinful nature. Man can be redeemed because of the atoning death of Jesus Christ and the direct work of the Spirit. The Holy Spirit restores man to fellowship with God the Father and enables man to love Him wholeheartedly. Salvation does not depend on outward ceremonies or symbols.

Sanctification is the work of God which is accomplished through baptism with the Holy Spirit in the life of a believer who yields himself totally to God. He is thus empowered to witness to the living Christ. Sanctification is both an act in which one's heart is cleansed and a process in which life is continuously disciplined to God's holy standards.

BASIC BELIEFS (ROCKY MOUNTAIN YEARLY
MEETING) (continued)

7. BAPTISM AND COMMUNION. Both Christian baptism and communion are spiritual realities beyond the mere physical, outward ordinances. Therefore Friends believe so strongly in these spiritual realities that most do not practice the ceremonies. True baptism is the inward receiving of God's Spirit by asking in faith for Him to become the Lord of one's life. Communion is the continuing fellowship with Jesus Christ as Saviour and Lord; it is often practiced in worship and may be exercised in a period of quiet waiting before the Lord, in verbal witness, through prayer, sharing of the Holy Spirit's witness in one's life, or in the expression of needs or concerns. Although it is rooted in the historical act of Christ's body being broken and His blood shed, communion depends upon obedience to Him.

8. THE CHURCH. Those who repent of their sins and trust in Jesus Christ as their personal Saviour are born again into His kingdom by His Spirit. These persons make up the true Church of Jesus Christ which is spiritual in nature and universal in scope. By His Spirit, Christ is present wherever two or three meet together in His name. Such a meeting is a local church which is a visible manifestation of the Church universal. Every believer should be related to a local visible part of Christ's universal body in order to worship, witness and work more effectively for the glory of God. Every believer is committed to be involved in the stewardship of God's Kingdom through the Church until the Lord returns.

9. CHRISTIAN WORSHIP AND WORK. Christians should meet together for public worship; it is both a duty and a privilege. By doing so, they testify to others of their faith in Christ and also receive mutual benefit. Worship may be silent or vocal, taking various forms; it does not depend on certain ceremonies or traditions. Worship is a natural outgrowth of union with Christ and should be directed by His Spirit. Friends emphasize that Christ may be known experientially through His Holy Spirit and hold that He is present to lead His people Himself. Though Friends worship has been noted for its silence, in reality it is not a worship of silence but a worship on the basis of obedience to God.

The emphasis is on the ministry of each individual in the body of Christ and the importance of each one ministering to the spiritual needs of others according to the direction of the Holy Spirit.

It is extremely important that as one attends meetings among Friends that he come not as an observer but as a participant in an exciting adventure which is unpredictable for the precise reason that we are seeking to do God's will rather than our own. He should come not primarily to hear a sermon or to repeat ready made phrases but with fellow Christians to sense the presence of the living Christ and to be led by Him.

Every meeting should be an adventure in which God speaks to individuals through His Spirit. In addition to public worship, Friends encourage daily private and family worship.

Believers are committed to the work of God, not only to manifest personal righteousness as the fruit of a new life, but also to share their faith. All Christians are called upon to witness by word and deed, in Christlikeness demonstrating love, forgiveness, and the way of peace. Certain ones are called and ordained by God for a special service of leadership in His Church; this service may be that of teaching, evangelizing, pastoring or administration. The church should recognize such special gifts among its members and encourage their use.

10. FRUIT AND GIFTS OF THE SPIRIT. The Holy Spirit is the indwelling agent of leadership for each Christian. He always leads in harmony with Holy Scriptures. Growth and maturity come as the Spirit is allowed to control the individual life, producing love, joy, peace, patience, kindness, goodness, faithfulness, gentleness, and self-control. Gifts, or abilities, are also given by the Spirit to be used to encourage and strengthen each other. While each gift is Spirit-given, Friends prefer to emphasize seeking the Giver more than the gifts.

As believers receive gifts, love will provide the motivation for the best use of each one. Speaking in other tongues does not constitute the essential sign of the baptism with the Holy Spirit. The evidence of the fullness of the Holy Spirit is the fruit of the Spirit, and especially *agape* love emanating from a truly transformed life.

11. THE LORD'S RETURN. At His second coming, Jesus Christ will return in power as King of kings to consummate His rule over men and nations by the final triumph over Satan. The dead shall be resurrected, some to eternal life, others to everlasting punishment. All shall be judged by God and receive just recompence for their deeds. The blessed ones shall live forever in heaven, but the lost suffer eternally in hell.

12. LIBERTY. Christian liberty is to be granted in all areas not essential to one's final salvation. Due to human imperfection, there are differences of faith and practice among God's children, but we anticipate a time of greater unity in the faith. Until that time, there must be unity in essentials but liberty in nonessentials, with love in all things.

Notes: *The Rocky Mountain Yearly Meeting is a member of the Evangelical Friends Alliance, which is a member of the National Association of Evangelicals as well as the Christian Holiness Association.*

Miscellaneous European Free

THE COMMON VIEWS [CHRISTIAN COMMUNITY OF UNIVERSAL BROTHERHOOD (DOUKHOBORS)]

1. The members of the Community honour and love God, as the source of all being.

2. They respect the merit and worth of mankind, both of themselves, and likewise of other [persons].

3. The members of the Community regard all that is, lovingly and with delight. They try to inspire their growing ones with this line [of thought].

4. By the word 'God', the members of the Community understand the power of love, the power of life, which is the source of all being.

5. The world is based upon going forward; all things strive for perfection, and through this process seek to rejoin their source, as seeds yield ripe fruit.

6. In all that is in our world we see changing steps toward perfection, as, for example, beginning with stones, it passes on to plants, then beasts, of which the very last one can count is man—in the sense of life, in the sense of a thinking creature.

7. To do away with, to destroy, that which lives, the members of the Community count blameworthy. In every single being there is life, hence [there is] God, and above all in man. To rob the life from a person is not, in whatever case, [to be] allowed.

8. The members of the Community in their beliefs allow utter freedom to all that is, including the life of man. Every organization, founded upon violence, is counted unlawful.

9. The chief base of the life of man—thought, reason serves as [that]. For material food this serves: air, water, fruits and vegetables.

10. It is held that the life of mankind is communal, upheld through the strength of moral law, for which [this] rule serves: 'Whatever I do not want for myself, that I should not wish for others.'

Notes: *This statement, originally written in Russian, dates to December 1896, appearing in a letter written by Doukhobor leader Peter Vasilievich Verigin. It served as the ideological manifesto of the community until it was replaced in 1934 by the Declaration of the Society of Named Doukhobors (now the Union of Spiritual Communities of Christ).*

* * *

FUNDAMENTAL PRINCIPLES (SCHWENKFELDER CHURCH)

1. Every person desiring to be a member of this Church should concern himself about a proper and approved ideal upon which the members are to be established in all things, and in accordance with which they are to form their union.

2. All those who would be in this religious association should place this foundation and ideal before their eyes as an aim set before them for which they are to strive with becoming zeal and energy.

3. In God's nature one beholds love primarily as that excellent outflowing virture which binds together God and man. All those who wish to take sure steps for the realization of said ideal must, first of all, form and maintain their unity by this bond of perfection among themselves.

4. Built on this fundamental principle of the divine nature—namely, love—their single, immovable aim must and will be to glorify God and promote the general welfare of each member.

5. In compliance with such object, their first care in their common affairs must be directed to a proper arrangement of public worship flowing from said foundation and agreeing with said ideal.

6. The gospel or word of God is the treasure which the Lord Jesus gave his apostles, and by which, as He commanded, the nations were to be called to faith and gathered, to be nurtured and ruled. It is the chief element in public worship and the rule of all its exercises.

7. It follows that they not only ought to possess this treasure, but they must also, with care, see to it that the gospel and the word of God are preserved and practiced by them in purity and simplicity, without which they cannot be nor remain a Christian people.

8. It follows, also, that they must have persons among themselves who know, live and teach the doctrine: otherwise it would be a dead letter, and could not bring about the good referred to in 6; hence proper plans must be devised in this respect.

9. There follow also the unceasing effort and care for the instruction of youth, both in what may be learned in schools as also in what should be taught in the study of the word of God or Christian doctrine, without which their aim referred to in 4 cannot be maintained nor the doctrine be upheld.

10. The repeated voluntary gathering for public worship with appointment of time and place for the same belongs also to the common care and concern.

11. Besides the appointment of public worship and the practice of God's word, a religious society, if it would at all attain its object, must strive to uphold a proper discipline among themselves, in order that through the same a guard and restraint may be set against the attacks and hindrances of the evil one, and that his work may be destroyed where it has taken root; that a good and useful deportment may be maintained in intercourse and conduct; that the hand of mutual help may be offered under all occurrences, and that virtue and good morals may be promoted.

12. They must have fixed rules and regulations among themselves by which they may know who belong to their society or not; they must also use diligence to keep correct records of all that is enacted by them

FUNDAMENTAL PRINCIPLES (SCHWENKFELDER
CHURCH) (continued)

and upon which they have mutually agreed in
matters relating to discipline, in order that no one
may take ignorance as an excuse, but that all may
conform thereto.

13. Since good rules are necessary in the exercise of
commendable discipline, the revealed will of God
contained in the Ten Commandments in their full
and perfect sense will be to them the best and most
adequate rule for the promotion of good conduct or
morals, for defense against the evil, for discriminat-
ing between the good and the evil.

14. In conformity to their aim and rules, they will,
besides this, also consider useful and proper regulations, so that commendable decorum may be preserved under the diverse circumstances, as marriage,
training of children, family life, death, burials and
the like.

15. The practice and maintenance of such discipline and
regulations will always have their temptations, since
we all carry these by nature in our own bosoms; it
will, therefore, likewise be necessary to have faithful
persons who will see to it that discipline and good
order are not neglected, but maintained and promoted by each member.

16. In order, however, that such service may not be
made too difficult, but be possible and endurable for
such persons, each and every member, by proper
regulations, must take part in said exercises and
supervision, whereby at the first notice of the
outbreak of an offence its progress may at once be
checked, and the deacon not be troubled by it.

17. Certain conferences should also be appointed as time
may occasion or the circumstances of the general
welfare may demand, at which the condition of the
Church, for weal or woe, may be considered,
doubtful or questionable matters decided, and the
general welfare and useful arrangements and institutions in general may be cared for.

Notes: *The Schwenkfelder Church has grown out of the
mystical Christianity of its founder, Casper Schwenkfeld.
The Fundamental Principles were adopted in 1782.*

* * *

DECLARATION! (UNION OF SPIRITUAL COMMUNITIES OF CHRIST)

1. We, "The Union of Spiritual Communities of
Christ," have been, are and will be members of
Christ's Church, confirmed by the Lord and Saviour
Jesus Christ Himself and assembled by His Apostles.

2. Members of "The Union of Spiritual Communities of
Christ" essentially are of the law of God and of the
faith of Jesus. The law of God is expounded in the
Ten Commandments and the faith is professed thus:
We believe in and profess—Jesus Christ the Son of
God—Who came in the flesh and was crucified. He

is our sole—Leader, Saviour and only Hope. There is
none and could not be any other name under the
heavens—through which man ought to be saved. We
have faith and hope through His name to attain the
highest blessings. There is no higher blessing than
"eternal life in unutterable joy." This is the hope and
reward in Christ Jesus and the principle aim of "The
Union of Spiritual Communities of Christ." Following in the footsteps of our Divine Teacher, we, "The
Union of Spiritual Communities of Christ" proclaim
as did He: we have come into this world not to
transgress the law of God, but to fulfill it, and
therefore all idolatry and desecration we strongly
renounce and acknowledge only the law and supreme
authority of God. We, "The Union of Spiritual
Communities of Christ," having acknowledged and
submitted ourselves to the law and authority of God
by this have liberated ourselves from the guardian-
ship and power established by men, because: "we
cannot serve two masters" and members of "The
Union of Spiritual Communities of Christ" cannot be
slaves of men—having been redeemed by the precious
blood of Jesus Christ. Members of "The Union of
Spiritual Communities of Christ" are not slaves of
corruption, but are Sons of the Free Spirit of Christ
and declare: we ought to submit more to God than to
man. We triumphantly declare that we do not allow
any force whatever by man over man and even more
so the allowance of killing of man or of men by a
man or men under no circumstances, causes or
arguments whatsoever. Every individual, group of
individuals, parties or governments of men, and
anyone whoever they may be proclaiming their
struggle against war and its non-allowance but at the
same time agreeing and allowing to kill every one
individual for the sake of any interests whatsoever.—
is a lie and a hypocrisy and nothing but a "leaven of
the Pharisees." The life of one individual is of equal
value to the lives of many individuals. The commandment of God states: "Thou shalt not kill."
Christ explains and warns: "No murderer shall
inherit Eternal Life." War—mass slaughter is an
item compiled, where the killing of one individual is
allowed there the allowance of mass murder is
inevitably admitted—which is war.

3. The modern world—mankind, has scattered and
divided itself into countless numbers of groups—
following the watch-words and programmes of the
various political parties. Every political party strug-
gles against each other not for the good and benefit
of the people but for dominance over them—with all
the consequences as a "diabolical incitement." Members of "The Union of Spiritual Communities of
Christ" have never recognized and do not recognize
any political party. They have never entered nor will
they ever enter into the ranks of any political party.
They have never given nor will they ever give their
votes during elections, thereby, are free from any
responsibility before God or man for the acts of any
government established by men. Members of "The
Union of Spiritual Communities of Christ" essential-

ly are above party politics—they not only gave their votes but their bodies, blood and souls to the One and Unreplaceable—Guardian of the hearts and souls of men—the Lord and Saviour Jesus Christ, thereby we have attained perfect freedom by egressing from the slavery of corruption into the freedom of glory to the children of God. We emphatically declare unto all: KNOW THE TRUTH AND THE TRUTH SHALL SET YOU FREE.

4. Members of "The Union of Spiritual Communities of Christ accepted and are fulfilling the command of Jesus Christ: 'Render therefore unto Caesar the things which are Caesar's (meaning the governments of men); and unto God the things that are God's.'" Residing in whatever state or country in this world, we triumphantly declare: going under of the banner of "Toil and Peaceful Life"—everything demanded of us which is not contradictory to the law of God and to the faith of Jesus, we will accept, fulfill and execute, not through fear but by conscientious guidance.

Notes: *This declaration, originally issued by the Society of Named Doukhobors, still serves as the ideological manifesto of the largest segment of the Doukhobor community. The statement covers many of the Christian beliefs neglected in the earlier and briefer statement by leader Peter Verigin, The Common Views. While the declaration affirms many common Christian doctrines, its emphasis is upon the free life under Christ. Submission to human authority ultimately leads to war and killing. Taking a pacifist stance, the Doukhobors affirm the ultimate worth of each life.*

Chapter 3

Baptist Family

NEW HAMPSHIRE CONFESSION OF FAITH (1830)

I. THE SCRIPTURES.

We believe that the Holy Bible was written by men divinely inspired, and is a perfect treasure of heavenly instruction; that it has God for its author, salvation for its end, and truth without any mixture of error for its matter; that it reveals the principles by which God will judge us, and therefore is, and shall remain to the end of the world, the true center of Christian union, and the supreme standard by which all human conduct, creeds, and opinions shall be tried.

2 Timothy 3:16, 17; Romans 1:16; Proverbs 30:5; Romans 2:12; Philippians 3:16.

II. THE TRUE GOD.

We believe the Scriptures teach that there is one, and only one, living and true God, an infinite, intelligent Spirit, whose name is Jehovah, the Maker and Supreme Ruler of heaven and earth; inexpressibly glorious in holiness, and worthy of all possible honor, confidence and love; that in the unity of the Godhead there are three persons, the Father, the Son, and the Holy Ghost; equal in every divine perfection, and executing distinct but harmonious offices in the great work of redemption.

John 4:24; 10:30; Psalm 147:5; Exodus 15:11; Mark 12:30.

III. THE FALL OF MAN.

We believe the Scriptures teach that Man was created in holiness, under the law of his Maker; but by voluntary transgressions fell from that holy and happy state; in consequence of which all mankind are now sinners, not by constraint but choice; being by nature utterly void of that holiness required by the law of God, positively inclined to evil; and therefore under just condemnation to eternal ruin, without defense or excuse.

Genesis 1:27; Romans 5:12, 19; Ephesians 2:1-3.

IV. THE WAY OF SALVATION.

We believe that the Scriptures teach that the salvation of sinners is wholly of grace; through the mediatorial offices of the Son of God; who by the appointment of the Father, freely took upon him our nature, yet without sin; honored the divine law by his personal obedience, and by his death made a full atonement for our sins; that having risen from the dead, he is now enthroned in heaven; and uniting in his wonderful person the tenderest sympathies with divine perfections, he is in every way qualified to be a suitable, a compassionate, and an all-sufficient Saviour.

Ephesians 2:8; John 3:16; Philippians 2:6, 7; Isaiah 42:21; 53:4, 5; Hebrews 7:25.

V. JUSTIFICATION.

We believe the Scriptures teach that the great Gospel blessing which Christ secures to such as believe in him is justification; that justification includes the pardon of sin, and the promise of eternal life on principles of righteousness; that it is bestowed, not in consideration of any works of righteousness which we have done, but solely through faith in the Redeemer's blood; by virtue of which faith his perfect righteousness is freely imputed to us of God; that it brings us into a state of most blessed peace and favor with God, and secures every other blessing needful for time and eternity.

John 1:16; Acts 13:39; Romans 5:17; 4:4, 5.

VI. THE FREENESS OF SALVATION.

We believe that the Scriptures teach that the blessings of salvation are made free to all by the Gospel; that it is the immediate duty of all to accept them by cordial, penitent and obedient faith; and that nothing prevents the salvation of the greatest sinner on earth, but his own determined depravity and voluntary rejection of the Gospel; which rejection involves him in an aggravated condemnation.

Isaiah 55:1; Revelation 22:17; Romans 16:25, 26; John 5:40; John 3:16, 19.

VII. REGENERATION.

We believe that the Scriptures teach that in order to be saved, sinners must be regenerated, or born again; that regeneration consists in giving a holy disposition to the mind that it is effected in a manner above our comprehension by the power of the Holy Spirit in connection with divine truth, so as to secure our voluntary obedience to the Gospel; and that its proper evidence appears in the holy fruits of repentance and faith, and newness of life.

NEW HAMPSHIRE CONFESSION OF FAITH (1830) (continued)

John 3:3; 2 Corinthians 5:17; John 3:8; 1 Peter 1:22-25; Ephesians 5:9.

VIII. REPENTANCE AND FAITH.

We believe the Scriptures teach that repentance and faith are sacred duties, and also inseparable graces, wrought in our souls by the regenerating Spirit of God; whereby being deeply convinced of our guilt, danger and helplessness and of the way of salvation by Christ, we turn to God with unfeigned contrition, confession, and supplication for mercy; at the same time heartily receiving the Lord Jesus Christ as our prophet, priest and king, and relying on him alone as the only and all-sufficient Saviour.

Mark 1:15; Romans 10:9; John 16:8; Luke 18:13.

IX. GOD'S PURPOSE OF GRACE.

We believe the Scriptures teach that election is the eternal purpose of God, according to which he graciously regenerates, sanctifies and saves sinners; that being perfectly consistent with the free agency of man, it comprehends all the means in connection with the end; that it is a most glorious display of God's sovereign goodness, being infinitely free, wise, holy and unchangeable; that it utterly excludes boasting and promotes humility, love, prayer, praise, trust in God, and active imitation of his free mercy; that it encourages the use of means in the highest degree; that it may be ascertained by its effects in all who truly believe the Gospel; that it is the foundation of Christian assurance; and that to ascertain it with regard to ourselves demands and deserves the utmost diligence.

2 Timothy 1:8; Exodus 33:18, 19; 1 Corinthians 4:7; 2 Timothy 2:10; 2 Thessalonians 2:13-14.

X. SANCTIFICATION.

We believe the Scriptures teach that Sanctification is the process by which, according to the will of God, we are made partakers of his holiness; that it is a progressive work; that it is begun in regeneration; and that it is carried on in the hearts of believers by the presence and power of the Holy Spirit, the Sealer and Comforter, in the continual use of the appointed means especially the word of God, self-examination, self-denial, watchfulness, and prayer.

1 Thessalonians 4:3; 1 John 2:29; Philippians 2:12, 13.

XI. PERSERVERANCE OF SAINTS.

We believe the Scriptures teach that such only are real believers as endure to the end; that their persevering attachment to Christ is the grand mark which distinguishes them from superficial professors; that a special Providence watches over their welfare; and they are kept by the power of God through faith unto salvation.

John 8:31; 1 John 2:19; Romans 8:28; Philippians 1:6.

XII. THE LAW AND GOSPEL.

We believe the Scriptures teach that the Law of God is the eternal and unchangeable rule of his moral government; that it is holy, just and good; and that the inability which the Scriptures ascribe to fallen men to fulfill its precepts, arise entirely from their love of sin; to deliver them from which, and to restore them through a Mediator to unfeigned obedience to the Holy Law, it is one great end of the Gospel, and of the Means of Grace connected with the establishment of the visible church.

Romans 3:31; 7:12; 8:7, 8; 8:2-4.

XIII. A GOSPEL CHURCH.

We believe the Scriptures teach that a visible church of Christ is a congregation of baptized believers, associated by covenant in the faith and fellowship of the Gospel; observing the ordinances of Christ; governed by his laws; and exercising the gifts, rights, and privileges invested in them by His Word; that its only scriptural officers are Bishops or Pastors, and Deacons whose Qualifications, claims and duties are defined in the Epistles to Timothy and Titus.

1 Corinthians 1:1-13; Acts 2:41, 42; 1 Corinthians 11:2; Matthew 28:20.

XIV. BAPTISM AND THE LORD'S SUPPER.

We believe the Scriptures teach that Christian baptism is the immersion in water of a believer, in the name of the Father, and Son, and Holy Ghost; to show forth in a solemn and beautiful emblem, our faith in the crucified, buried, and risen Saviour, with its effect, in our death to sin and resurrection to a new life; that it is prerequisite to the privileges of a church relation; and to the Lord's Supper, in which the members of the church, by the sacred use of bread and wine, are to commemorate together the dying love of Christ; preceded always by solemn self-examination.

Acts 8:36-39; Matthew 28:20; Acts 2:41, 42; 1 Corinthians 11:26, 28.

XV. THE CHRISTIAN SABBATH.

We believe the Scriptures teach that the first day of the week is the Lord's Day, or Christian Sabbath, and is to be kept sacred to religious purposes, by abstaining from all secular labor and sinful recreations, by the devout observance of all the means of grace, both private and public, and by preparation for that rest that remaineth for the people of God.

Acts 20:7; Exodus 20:8; Isaiah 58:13, 14; Hebrew 10:24, 25.

XVI. CIVIL GOVERNMENT.

We believe the Scriptures teach that civil government is of divine appointment, for the interest and good order of human society; and that magistrates are to be prayed for, conscientiously honored and obeyed; except only in things opposed to the will of our Lord Jesus Christ, who is the only Lord of the conscience, and the Prince of the Kings of the earth.

Romans 13:1-7; Matthew 22:21; Acts 5:29; Matthew 23:10.

XVII. RIGHTEOUS AND WICKED.

We believe the Scriptures teach that there is a radical and essential difference between the righteous and the wicked; that such only as through faith are justified in the name of the Lord Jesus, and sanctified by the Spirit of our God, are truly righteous in his esteem; while all such as continue in impenitence and unbelief are in his sight wicked, and under the curse; and this distinction holds among men both in and after death.

Malachi 3:18; Romans 1:17; 1 John 5:19; Proverbs 14:32.

XVIII. THE WORLD TO COME.

We believe the Scriptures teach that the end of the world is approaching; that at the last day, Christ will descend from heaven, and raise the dead from the grave for final retribution; that a solemn separation will then take place; that the wicked will be adjudged to endless punishment, and the righteous to endless joy; and that this judgment will fix forever the final state of men in heaven or hell, on principles of righteousness.

1 Peter 4:7; Acts 1:11, 24:15; Matthew 25:31-46; 13:49.

Notes: *Baptist confessions of faith really begin with the London Confession of 1644, though some authors see precursors in the prior Continental Free Church confessions such as Schleitheim or Dordrecht, or in those of the British Separatists. The Second London Confession (1677), based upon the Westminster Confession, became the basis of the first American confessions, especially the Philadelphia Confession of Faith (1742). The most influential confession of faith for American Baptists, however, has been the New Hampshire Confession. It is still used by the great majority of Baptists, in spite of numerous twentieth-century doctrinal statements.*

During the first decades of the nineteenth century, the growing Baptist community was torn between old line Calvinists, who followed the perspective of the Westminster Confession on such issues as predestination, and Free Will Baptists, who followed a more Arminian position which emphasized free will and free grace. The mainstream of the Baptist movement gravitated toward a more moderate Calvinist position, which was articulated in the New Hampshire Confession. This position is most clearly presented in Article VI, "The Freeness of Salvation."

The New Hampshire Confession remains the accepted doctrine of the several National Baptist Conventions and the American Baptist Association, among others. It was the basis of the Articles of Faith of the General Association of Regular Baptist Churches, and of new statements issued in 1925 and 1960 by the Southern Baptist Convention. The Black Baptist conventions have either formally adopted or informally adhere to the New Hampshire Confession. The text presented here is the version published by the National Baptist Convention of America to which scriptural references (not in the original) have been added.

* * *

Calvinist Missionary Baptist

DOCTRINAL STATEMENT (AMERICAN BAPTIST ASSOCIATION)

DOCTRINAL STATUS

This Association shall recognize the freedom of speech as essential to the highest achievements in its work. It shall stand or fall upon its own conformity of truth. It shall exercise no ecclesiastical authority but it shall by every precaution recognize the sovereignty of every individual church. It shall encourage on the part of the churches and messengers that greatest possible freedom of expression in discussing matters pertaining to its work, and in the pre-eminence of missions and evangelism in the work of the churches.

DOCTRINAL STATEMENT

1. We believe in the infallible verbal inspiration of the whole Bible, II Tim. 3:16.

2. The Triune God, Matt. 28:19.

3. The Genesis Account of Creation.

4. The Virgin Birth of Jesus Christ, Matt. 1:20.

5. The Deity of Jesus Christ.

6. His crucifixion and suffering as vicarious substitutionary.

7. The bodily resurrection and ascension of Christ and the bodily resurrection of His saints, I Cor. 15th chapter.

8. The second coming of Christ, personal and bodily as the crowning event of this Gentile age, Acts 1:11.

9. The Bible doctrine of eternal punishment of the finally impenitent, Matt. 25.48.

10. We also hold in common what real Baptists have ever held: That the great commission was given to the churches only. That in kingdom activities the church is the unit and only unit that the churches have, and should exercise equal authority, and responsibility should be met by them according to their several abilities.

11. That all co-operating bodies, such as Association, Conventions and the Board of Committees, etc., are and properly should be the servants of the churches.

12. We believe that the great commission teaches that there has been a succession of Missionary Baptist Churches from the days of Christ to this day.

13. We believe that Baptism, to be valid, must be administered by a Scriptural Baptist Church.

Notes: *The New Hampshire Confession does not address the great debates which split the Baptists in the early nineteenth century—the organization of missionary societies, Sunday schools, and national associations and conventions which seemed to claim powers and authority rightfully belonging to the local church. It also could not predict the heated debate about the Bible and the nature of its authority, and the premillennial dispensational theology that would arrive from England and become so popular among Baptists in the early twentieth century. Since 1830, newer Baptist bodies have thus felt the need to define their position on local church autonomy, the nature of scripture, and eschatology.*

The American Baptist Association (ABA) grew out of the "Old Landmarks" controversy in the Southern Baptist Convention (SBC). Adherents to the Old Landmark position believed in the sovereignty of the local church and opposed the growing centralization of authority in the SBC. Forming as a separate association of churches in 1905, the ABA adopted the New Hampshire Confession, to which it added a number of statements, including those on scriptural authority and the local church.

* * *

ARTICLES OF FAITH (BAPTIST BIBLE FELLOWSHIP)

A Bible Baptist is one who believes in a supernatural Bible, which tells of a supernatural Christ, Who had a supernatural birth, Who spoke supernatural words, Who performed supernatural miracles, Who lived a supernatural life, Who died a supernatural death, Who rose in supernatural splendor, Who intercedes as a supernatural priest and Who will one day return in supernatural glory to establish a supernatural kingdom on the earth.

I. OF THE SCRIPTURES

We believe that the Holy Bible was written by men supernaturally inspired; that it has truth without any admixture of error for its matter; and therefore is, and shall remain to the end of the age, the only complete and final revelation of the will of God to man; the true center of Christian union and the supreme standard by which all human conduct, creeds, and opinions should be tried.

1. By "The Holy Bible" we mean that collection of sixty-six books, from Genesis to Revelation, which as orignally written does not only contain and convey the Word of God, but IS the very Word of God.

2. By "inspiration" we mean that the books of the Bible were written by holy men of old, as they were moved by the Holy Spirit, in such a definite way that their writings were supernaturally and verbally inspired and free from error, as no other writings have ever been or ever will be inspired.

II Tim. 3:16-17; II Pet. 1:19-21; Acts 1:16; Acts 28:25; Psa. 119:160; Psa. 119:105; Psa. 119: 130; Luke 24:25-27; John 17:17; Luke 24:44-45; Psa. 119:89; Prov. 30:5-6; Rom. 3:4; I Pet. 1: 23; Rev. 22:19; John 12:48; Isa. 8:20; Eph. 6:17; Rom. 15:4; Luke 16:31; Psa. 19:7-11; John 5: 45-47; John 5:39.

II. OF THE TRUE GOD

We believe that there is one, and only one, living and true God, and infinite, intelligent Spirit, the maker and supreme ruler of heaven and earth; inexpressibly glorious in holiness and worthy of all possible honor, confidence and love; that in the unity of the Godhead there are three persons, the Father, the Son and the Holy Ghost, equal in every divine perfection, and executing distinct but harmonious offices in the great work of redemption.

Ex. 20:2-3; Gen. 17:1; I Cor. 8:6; Eph. 4:6; John 4:24; Psa. 147:5; Psa. 83:18; Psa. 90:2; Jer. 10:10; Ex. 15:11; Rev. 4:11; I Tim. 1:17; Rom. 11:33; Mark 12:30; Matt. 28:19; John 15: 26; I Cor. 12:4-6; I John 5:7; John 10:30; John 17:5; Acts 5:3-4; I Cor. 2:10-11; Phil. 2:5-6; Eph. 2:18; II Cor. 13:14.

III. OF THE HOLY SPIRIT

That the Holy Spirit is a divine person; equal with God the Father and God the Son and of the same nature; that He was active in the creation; that in His relation to the unbelieving world He restrains the Evil one until God's purpose is fulfilled; that He convicts of sin, of judgment and of righteousness; that He bears witness to the Truth of the Gospel in preaching and testimony; that He is the agent in the New Birth: that He seals, endues, guides, teaches, witnesses, sanctifies and helps the believer.

John 14:16-17; Matt. 28:19; Heb. 9:14; John 14: 26; Luke 1:35; Gen. 1:1-3; II Thess. 2:7; John 16: 8-11; John 15:26-27; Acts 5:30-32; John 3:5-6; Eph. 1:13-14; Matt. 3:11; Mark 1:8; Luke 3:16; John 1:33; Acts 11:16; Luke 24:49; John 16:13; John 14:26; Rom. 8:14; Rom. 8:16; II Thess. 2: 13; I Pet. 1:2; Rom. 8:26-27.

IV. OF THE DEVIL, OR SATAN

We believe that Satan was once holy, and enjoyed heavenly honors; but through pride and ambition to be as the Almighty, fell and drew after him a host of angels; that he is now the malignant prince of the power of the air, and the unholy god of this world. We hold him to be man's great tempter, the enemy of God and His Christ, the accuser of the saints, the author of all false religions, the chief power back of the present apostasy; the lord of the antichrist, and the author of all the powers of darkness—destined however to final defeat at the hands of God's own Son, and to the judgment of an eternal justice in hell, a place prepared for him and his angels.

Isa. 14:12-15; Ezek. 28:14-17; Rev. 12:9; Jude 6; II Pet. 2:4; Eph. 2:2; John 14:30; I Thess. 3:5; Matt. 4:1-3; I Pet. 5:8; I John 3:8; Matt. 13:25; 37:39; Luke 22:3-4; Rev. 12:10; II Cor. 11:13-15; Mark 13:21-22; I John 4:3; II John 7; I John 2:22; Rev. 13:13-14; II Thess. 2:8-11; Rev. 19:11, 16, 20; Rev. 12:7-9; Rev. 20:1-3; Rev. 20:10; Matt. 25:41.

V. OF CREATION

We believe in the Genesis account of creation, and that it is to be accepted literally, and not allegorically or figuratively; that man was created directly in God's own image and after His own likeness; that man's creation was not a matter of evolution or evolutionary change of species, or development through interminable periods of time from lower to higher forms; that all animal and vegetable life was made directly and God's established law was that they should bring forth only "after their kind."

Gen. 1:1; Ex. 20:11; Acts 4:24; Col. 1:16-17; Heb. 11:3; John 1:3; Rev. 10:6; Rom. 1:20; Acts 17:23-26; Jer. 10:12; Neh. 9:6; Gen. 1:26-27; Gen. 2:21-23; Gen. 1:11; Gen. 1:24.

VI. OF THE FALL OF MAN

We believe that man was created in innocence under the law of his Maker, but by voluntary transgression fell from his sinless and happy state, in consequence of which all mankind are now sinners, not by constraint, but of choice; and therefore under just condemnation without defense or excuse.

Gen. 3:1-6, 24; Rom. 5:12; Rom. 5:19; Rom. 3: 10-19; Eph. 2:1, 3; Rom. 1:18; Ezek. 18:19-20; Rom. 1:32; Rom. 1:20; Rom. 1:28; Gal. 3:22.

VII. OF THE VIRGIN BIRTH

We believe that Jesus Christ was begotten of the Holy Ghost, in a miraculous manner; born of Mary, a virgin, as no other man was ever born or can ever be born of woman, and that He is both the Son of God, and God, the Son.

Gen. 3:15; Isa. 7:14; Matt. 1:18-25; Luke 1:35; Mark 1:1; John 1:14; Psa. 2:7; Gal. 4:4; I John 5:20; I Cor. 15:47.

VIII. OF THE ATONEMENT FOR SIN

We believe that the salvation of sinners is wholly of grace; through the mediatorial offices of the Son of God, who by appointment of the Father, freely took upon Him our nature, yet without sin, honored the divine law by His personal obedience, and by His death made a full and vicarious atonement for our sins; that His atonement consisted not in setting us an example by His death as a martyr, but was the voluntary substitution of Himself in the sinner's place, the Just dying for the unjust, Christ, the Lord, bearing our sins in His own body on the tree; that, having risen from the dead, He is now enthroned in heaven and uniting in His wonderful person the tenderest sympathies with divine perfection, He is every way qualified to be a suitable, a compassionate and an all-sufficient Saviour.

Eph. 2:8; Acts 15:11; Rom. 3:24; John 3:16; Matt. 18:11; Phil. 2:7; Heb. 2:14; Isa. 53:4-7; Rom. 3:25; I John 4:10; I Cor. 15:3; II Cor. 5:21; John 10:18; Phil. 2:8; Gal. 1:4; I Pet. 2:24; I Pet. 3:18; Isa. 53:11; Heb. 12:2; I Cor. 15:20; Isa. 53:12; Heb. 9:12-15; Heb. 7:25; I John 2:2.

IX. OF GRACE IN THE NEW CREATION

We believe that in order to be saved, sinners must be born again; that the new birth is a new creation in Christ Jesus; that it is instantaneous and not a process; that in the new birth the one dead in trespasses and in sins is made a partaker of the divine nature and receives eternal life, the free gift of God; that the new creation is brought about in a manner above our comprehension, not by culture, not by character, nor by the will of man, but wholly and solely by the power of the Holy Spirit in connection with divine truth, so as to secure our voluntary obedience to the gospel; that its proper evidence appears in the holy fruits of repentance and faith and newness of life.

John 3:3; II Cor. 5:17; Luke 5:27; I John 5:1; John 3:6-7; Acts 2:41; II Pet. 1:4; Rom. 6:23; Eph. 2:1; II Cor. 5:19; Col. 2:13; John 1:12-13; Gal. 5:22; Eph. 5:9.

X. OF THE FREENESS OF SALVATION

We believe in God's electing grace; that the blessings of salvation are made free to all by the gospel; that it is the immediate duty of all to accept them by a cordial, penitent and an obedient faith; and that nothing prevents the salvation of the greatest sinner on earth but his own inherent depravity and voluntary rejection of the gospel; which rejection involves him in an aggravated condemnation.

I Thess. 1:4; Col. 3:12; I Pet. 1:2; Titus 1:1; Rom. 8:29-30; Matt. 11:28; Isa. 55:1; Rev. 22:17; Rom. 10:13; John 6:37; Isa. 55:6; Acts 2:38; Isa. 55:7; John 3:15-16; I Tim. 1:15; I Cor. 15:10; Eph. 2:4-5; John 5:40; John 3:18; John 3:36.

XI. OF JUSTIFICATION

We believe that the great gospel blessing which Christ secures to such as believe in Him is Justification; that Justification includes the pardon of sin, and the gift of eternal life on principles of righteousness; that it is bestowed not in consideration of any works of righteousness which we have done; but solely through faith in the Redeemer's blood, His righteousness is imputed unto us.

Acts 13:39; Isa. 53:11; Zech. 13:1; Rom. 8:1; Rom. 5:9; Rom. 5:1; Tit. 3:5-7; Rom. 1:17; Hab. 2:4; Gal. 3:11; Rom. 4:1-8; Heb. 10:38.

XII. OF REPENTANCE AND FAITH

We believe that Repentance and Faith are solemn obligations, and also inseparable graces, wrought in our souls by the quickening Spirit of God; thereby, being deeply convicted of our guilt, danger and helplessness, and of the way of salvation by Christ, we turn to God with unfeigned contrition, confession and supplication for mercy; at the same time heartily receiving the Lord Jesus Christ and openly confessing Him as our only and all-sufficient Saviour.

Acts 20:21; Mark 1:15; Acts 2:37-38; Luke 18:13; Rom. 10:13; Psa. 51:1-4; Psa. 51:7; Isa. 55: 6-7; Luke 12:8; Rom. 10:9-11.

XIII. OF THE CHURCH

We believe that a Baptist Church is a congregation of baptized believers associated by a covenant of faith and fellowship of the gospel, said church being understood to be the citadel and propagator of the Divine and Eternal Grace; observing the ordinances of Christ; governed by His laws; exercising the gifts, rights, and privileges invested in them by His Word; that its officers of ordination are pastors or elders whose qualifications, claims, and duties are clearly defined in the scriptures; we believe the true mission of the church is found in the Great Commission: First, to make individual disciples; Second, to build up the church; Third, to teach and instruct as He has commanded. We do not believe in the reversal of this order; we hold that the local church has the absolute right of self government, free from the interference of any hierarchy of individuals or organizations; and that the one and only superintendent is Christ through the Holy Spirit; that it is scriptural for true churches to cooperate with each other in contending for the faith and for the furtherance of the Gospel; that every church is the sole and only judge of the measure and method of its cooperation; on all matters of membership, of policy, of government, of discipline, of benevolence, the will of the local church is final.

Acts 2:41; Acts 2:42; I Cor. 11:2; Eph. 1:22-23; Eph. 4:11; I Cor. 12:4, 8-11; Acts 14:23; Acts 6:5-6; Acts 15:23; Acts 20:17-28; I Tim. 3:1-13; Matt. 28:19-20; Col. 1:18; Eph. 5:23-24; I Pet. 5:1-4; Acts 15:22; Jude 3,4; II Cor. 8:23-24; I Cor. 16:1; Mal. 3:10; Lev. 27:32; I Cor. 16:2; I Cor. 6:1-3; I Cor. 5:11-13.

XIV. OF BAPTISM AND THE LORD'S SUPPER

We believe that Christian baptism is the immersion in water of a believer; in the name of the Father, of the Son, and of the Holy Ghost, with the authority of the local church, to show forth in a solemn and beautiful emblem our faith in the crucified, buried and risen Saviour, with its effect in our death to sin and resurrection to a new life; that it is pre-requisite to the privileges of a church relation and to the Lord's supper; in which the members of the church, by the sacred use of bread and the fruit of the vine are to commemorate together the dying love of Christ; preceded always by solemn self-examination.

Acts 8:36-39; Matt. 3:6; John 3:23, Rom. 6:4-5; Matt. 3:16; Matt. 28:19; Rom. 6:3-5; Col. 2:12; Acts 2:41-42; Matt. 28:1, 9-20; I Cor. 11:23-28.

XV. OF THE PERSEVERANCE OF THE SAINTS

We believe that such only are real believers as endure unto the end; that their persevering attachment to Christ is the grand mark which distinguishes them from superficial professors; that a special Providence watches over their welfare; and that they are kept by the power of God through faith unto eternal salvation.

John 8:31-32; Col. 1:21-23; I John 2:19; Matt. 13:19-21; Rom. 8:28; Matt. 6:20; Psa. 121:3; Heb. 1:14; I Pet. 1:5; Phil. 1:6; John 10:28, 29; John 16:8; Rom. 8:35-39.

XVI. OF THE RIGHTEOUS AND THE WICKED

We believe that there is a radical and essential difference between the righteous and the wicked; that such only as through faith are justified in the name of the Lord Jesus, and sanctified by the Spirit of our God, are truly righteous in His esteem; while all such as continue in impenitence and unbelief are in His sight wicked, and under the curse, and this distinction holds among men both in and after death, in the everlasting felicity of the saved and the everlasting conscious suffering of the lost.

Mal. 3:18; Gen. 18:23; Rom. 6:17-18; Prov. 11:31; I Pet. 1:18; Rom. 1:17; I Cor. 15:22; Acts 10: 34-35; I John 2:29; I John 2:7; Rom. 6:16; I John 5:19; Gal. 3:10; Rom. 7:6; Rom. 6:23; Prov. 14: 32; Luke 16:25; Matt. 25:34, 41; John 8:21; Luke 9:26; John 12:25; Matt. 7:13-14.

XVII. OF CIVIL GOVERNMENT

We believe that civil government is of divine appointment, for the interests and good order of human society; that magistrates are to be prayed for, conscientiously honored and obeyed; except only in things opposed to the will of our Lord Jesus Christ; who is the only Lord of the conscience, and the coming Prince of the kings of the earth.

Rom. 13:7; II Sam. 23:3; Ex. 18:21-22; Acts 23:5; Matt. 22:21; Tit. 3:1; I Pet. 2:13, 14; I Pet. 2:17; Acts 4:19-20; Dan. 3:17-18; Matt. 10:28; Matt. 23:10; Phil. 2:10-11; Psa. 72:11.

XVIII. OF THE RESURRECTION AND RETURN OF CHRIST AND RELATED EVENTS

We believe in and accept the sacred Scriptures upon these subjects at their face and full value. Of the Resurrection, we believe that Christ rose bodily "the third day according to the Scriptures;" that He alone is our "merciful and faithful high priest in things pertaining to God;" "that this

same Jesus which is taken up from you into heaven shall so come in like manner as ye have seen Him go into heaven"—bodily, personally and visible; that the "dead in Christ shall rise first," that the living saints "shall all be changed in a moment, in the twinkling of an eye, at the last trump;" "that the Lord God shall give unto Him the throne of His Father David;" and that "Christ shall reign a thousand years in righteousness until He hath put all enemies under His feet."

Matt. 28:6-7; Luke 24:39; John 20:27; I Cor. 15: 4; Mark 16:6; Luke 24:2, 4-6; Acts 1:9, 11; Luke 24:51; Mark 16:19; Rev. 3:21; Heb. 8:1; Heb. 12: 2; Heb. 8:6; I Tim. 2:5; I John 2:1; Heb. 2:17; Heb. 5:9-10; John 14:3; I Thess. 4:16; Matt. 24: 27; Matt. 24:42; Heb. 9:28; I Cor. 15:42-44, 51-53; I Thess. 4:17; Phil. 4:20-21; Luke 1:32; I Cor. 15:25; Isa. 11:4-5; Psa. 72:8; Rev. 20:1-4; Rev. 20:6.

XIX. OF MISSIONS

The command to give the gospel to the world is clear and unmistakable and this Commission was given to the churches.

Matt. 28:18-20, "And Jesus came and spake unto them saying, All power is given unto me in heaven and in earth. Go ye therefore, and teach all nations, baptizing them in the name of the Father, and of the Son, and of the Holy Ghost: Teaching them to observe all things whatsoever I have commanded you and, lo I am with you alway, even unto the end of the world. Amen."

Mark 16:15, "And he said unto them, Go ye into all the world, and preach the gospel to every creature."

John 20:21, "Then said Jesus to them again, Peace be unto you: as my Father hath sent me, even so send I you."

Rom. 10:13-15, "For whosoever shall call upon the name of the Lord shall be saved. How then shall they call on him in whom they have not believed? And how shall they believe in him of whom they have not heard? And how shall they hear without a preacher? And how shall they preach except they be sent? As it is written, How beautiful are the feet of them that preach the gospel of peace, and bring glad tidings of good things!"

XX. OF THE GRACE OF GIVING

Scriptural giving is one of the fundamentals of the faith.

II Cor. 8:7, "Therefore as ye abound in everything, in faith, and utterance, and knowledge, and in all diligence, and in your love to us, see that ye abound in this grace also."

We are commanded to bring our gifts into the storehouse (common treasury of the church) upon the first day of the week.

I Cor. 16:2, "Upon the first day of the week let every one of you lay by him in store, as God hath prospered him, that there be no gatherings when I come."

Under Grace we give, and do not pay, the tithe—"Abraham GAVE the tenth of the spoils"—Hebrews 7:2, 4—and this was four hundred years before the law, and is confirmed in the New Testament; Jesus said concerning the tithe, "These ye ought to have done"—Matt. 23:23.

We are commanded to bring the tithe into the common treasury of the church.

Lev. 27:30, "The tithe . . . is the Lord's."

Mal. 3:10, "Bring ye all the tithes into the storehouse, that there may be meat in mine house, and prove me now herewith, saith the Lord of hosts, if I will not open you the windows of heaven, and pour you out a blessing, that there shall not be room enough to receive it."

In the New Testament it was the common treasury of the church.

Acts 4:34, 35, 37, "And brought the prices of the things that were sold and laid them down at the apostles' feet . . . Having land, sold it, and brought the money, and laid it AT THE APOSTLES' FEET."

Notes: *The statement of the Baptist Bible Fellowship, one of the largest of the contemporary fundamentalist churches, is the epitome of the fundamentalist position. Notice its affirmation of supernaturalism, biblical authority, creation, and the virgin birth. Otherwise, it follows the mild Calvinism of the New Hampshire Confession.*

* * *

A CONFESSION (BAPTIST CONVENTION OF ONTARIO AND QUEBEC)

The regular Baptist Denomination, whereby is intended Regular Baptist churches exclusively composed of persons who have been baptised in a personal profession of their faith in Christ holding and maintaining *substantially* the following doctrines that is to say

The Divine Inspiration of the Scriptures of the Old and New Testaments and their absolute supremacy and sufficiency in matters of faith and practice,

The existence of one living and true God sustaining the personal relations of Father, Son and Holy Spirit, the same in essence and equal in attributes

The total and universal depravity of mankind

The election and effectual calling of all God's people

The atoning efficacy of the death of Christ

The free justification of believers in Him by His imputed righteousness

The preservation unto eternal life of the Saints

The necessity and efficacy of the Spirit in regeneration and sanctification

The resurrection of the dead both just and unjust

The general judgment

The everlasting happiness of the righteous and the everlasting misery of the wicked

Immersion in the name of the Father, the Son and the Holy Spirit, *the only* gospel baptism

That parties so baptised are alone entitled to communion at the Lord's Table

and that a Gospel Church is a Body of baptised believers voluntarily associated together for the service of God.

Notes: *The loosely constructed Canadian Baptist Federation is a noncreedal body, as are the several conventions of which it is composed. However, one of these conventions, the Baptist Convention of Ontario and Quebec, did adopt a*

confessional statement in 1925 during the height of the fundamentalist controversy. The statement was not published as a binding document of the convention's member churches; rather it appeared as a statement of those who were supporting McMaster University in Toronto. The school had become an issue when fundamentalists accused it of deviations in doctrine. In this document, the convention affirmed its allegiance to those traditional Baptist beliefs under question and asserted that its member churches substantially hold and teach these beliefs.

* * *

DOCTRINAL STATEMENT (BAPTIST MISSIONARY ASSOCIATION)

1. The Trinity of God.
2. The infallible and plenary verbal inspiration of the Scriptures.
3. The Biblical account of creation.
4. The personality of Satan.
5. Hereditary and total depravity of man in his natural state involving his fall in Adam.
6. The virgin birth and deity of Jesus Christ.
7. Christ's blood atonement for fallen man.
8. His bodily resurrection and ascension back to His Father.
9. The person and work of the Holy Spirit.
10. Justification before God by faith without any admixture of works.
11. Separation of God's children from the world.
12. Water baptism (immersion) to be administered to believers only and by Divine authority as given to Missionary Baptist churches.
13. The Lord's Supper, a church ordinance to be administered to baptized believers only and in Scriptural church capacity.
14. Eternal security of the believer.
15. The establishment of a visible church by Christ himself during His personal ministry on earth.
16. World-wide missions according to the Great Commission which Christ gave His Church. (Matthew 28:19, 20.)
17. The perpetuity of Missionary Baptist churches from Christ's day on earth until His second coming.
18. The right of scriptural churches to be held as equal units in their associated capacities, with equal right and privileges for all.
19. The subjection of all scriptural associational assemblies and their committees to the will of the churches, so that they shall forever remain as servants of the churches originating them.
20. The separation of the Lord's Church from all so-called churches or church alliances which advocate, practice, or uphold heresies and other human innovations which are not in harmony with the word of God. Open communion, alien baptism, pulpit affilia-

tion with heretical churches, Modernism, and all kindred evils arising from these practices are unscriptural.

21. The only valid baptism is that administered by the authority of a scriptural Missionary Baptist Church. Any so-called Baptist Church which knowingly receives alien baptism, habitually practices this or other evils as those listed in statement 20 cannot be a scriptural Baptist Church, nor can its ordinances remain valid.

22. The personal, bodily and imminent return of Christ to earth.

23. The bodily resurrection of the dead.

24. The reality of heaven, involving Divine assurance of eternal happiness for the redeemed of God.

25. The reality of Hell, involving everlasting punishment of the incorrigible wicked.

26. We believe in absolute separation of church and state.

NOTE: The following statements are not binding upon the churches already affiliated with this association nor require adoption by churches petitioning this body for privileges of cooperation, nor are to be a test of fellowship between brethren or churches. However, they do express the preponderance of opinion among the churches of the Baptist Missionary Association of America:

1. We believe in the premillennial return of Christ to earth after which He shall literally reign in peace upon the earth for a thousand years. (Rev. 20:4-6.)

2. We believe the Scriptures to teach two resurrections: the first of the righteous at Christ's coming; the second of the wicked dead at the close of the thousand-year reign. (I Thes. 4:13-17; Rev. 20:4-6, 12-15.)

It is easy for the fellowshipping churches of one Baptist group to think of themselves as being sound in the faith and of all others as being unsound or loose in their principles and practices. However, the real test is that of how well a church or denominational group measures up to the Bible requirements for a New Testament church.

Churches of the B.M.A. of America have the assurance from the Holy Scriptures that their doctrinal beliefs and practices are the same as those taught by the Lord Jesus, believed and preached by the Apostles, and practiced by the first century churches.

(With a few alterations the following is a summary of things believed, of things not believed, of the characteristics of truly New Testament Baptist churches, and of the composition of associations as prepared by W. J. Burgess, who for eighteen years served as General Secretary of Missions for the B.M.A. of America—J.W.D.).

SOME THINGS WE BELIEVE

1. We believe in salvation solely by grace through faith.

2. We believe in the doctrines and Scriptural order of repentance and faith.

3. We believe one must be born again to enter Heaven.

4. We believe in "heartfelt" salvation that can be known.

5. We believe in absolute equality among local churches.

6. We believe that churches may cooperate together without losing their sovereignty or independency.

7. We believe that women have a place in public worship and service, but not as ordained Ministers.

8. We believe that the Gospel is the power of God unto salvation to believers only.

9. We believe that true worship is worship in Spirit and in truth.

10. We believe that all of our preaching and teaching should be Christ-Centered.

11. We believe in living a separate life from the world.

12. We believe that church associations must ever be the servants of the churches composing them.

SOME THINGS WE DO NOT BELIEVE

1. We do not believe in being Modernists (Liberals) in any sense of the word.

2. We do not believe in pulpit affiliation with heretical groups.

3. We do not believe in alien (non-Baptist) immersion.

4. We do not believe in the invisible, universal church theory.

5. We do not believe in pastor dictatorship.

6. We do not believe in deacon dictatorship.

7. We do not believe in one church dictatorship over other churches.

8. We do not believe in dictatorship (overlordship) of any kind.

9. We do not believe in showing respect of persons, a "Big I and little you" sort of philosophy.

10. We do not believe that the Gospel is merely a social formula.

11. We do not believe in the now-popular "Universal Fatherhood of God—Brotherhood of Men" idea, except in the sense of creation.

12. We do not believe in the modern ecumenical church movement.

Notes: *Formed in 1950, the Baptist Missionary Association grew out of the American Baptist Association. Its statement is based upon, but enlarges, that of its parent body. New articles, such as those on alien baptism and the reality of heaven and hell, were added. Notice the final declaration concerning the relation of the Doctrinal Statement to churches and members affiliated with the association.*

CONSERVATIVE BAPTIST MANIFESTO AND DECLARATION OF FAITH (CONSERVATIVE BAPTIST ASSOCIATION OF AMERICA)

CONSERVATIVE BAPTIST MANIFESTO

Whereas, on this happy and historic celebration of Conservative Baptist advance, which gives us occasion to reflect upon God's gracious blessing in the formation and ongoing of various Conservative Baptist agencies, we desire to give a real assurance to Bible-believing Baptists everywhere of our position and direction:

Therefore, be it resolved, that we re-affirm our unchanging confidence in the trustworthiness of the Scriptures and in those foundational truths as expressed in the Confession of Faith and Constitution of our various Conservative Baptist organizations; and

Be it further resolved, that we re-affirm our unswerving opposition to the practice of the Inclusive Policy, that policy which is inclusive of belief and unbelief alike, and results in division and conflicting testimony at home and abroad, and that we acknowledge that the Conservative Board movement logically thereby continues to be separatist in spirit and objective; and

Be it further resolved, that it is our conviction that Conservative Baptist board members and officers be men who have openly declared themselves to stand with Conservative Baptists on the principles set forth in this declaration, to be in sympathy with the purposes of the Conservative Baptist movement, and to be in opposition to the Inclusive Policy as shown by their personal non-co-operation with the inclusive program.

Finally, that a committee be authorized to study the problems inherent in our growing Conservative Baptist movement, the interrelations of the Boards, the role of the Regional and National Conferences, and other related problems; that this committee be composed of two representatives from each of the four Boards, one representative from each of the two Seminaries, plus two members elected from each of the Regional Conferences; and that this committee report at the 1954 Annual Meeting.

THE REPORT OF THE MANIFESTO COMMITTEE

The Manifesto Committee, authorized at the annual meeting in Portland in 1953, held two meetings in the city of Chicago. Attendance on the part of many members of the committee entailed very heavy expenses, borne either by the individuals, or their churches, or the institutions they represented. The Committee meetings were irenical and amicable in spirit. We present our report with great optimism for the future of our Conservative Baptist movement and our societies and organizations.

We have sought to more clearly define and delineate our ideology and objectives. We have sought to deal thoroughly and faithfully with all points of difference or of potential difference. Our report consists of three parts: (1) our findings relative to the intent and purpose of the Manifesto, (2) a statement of the ideology of our movement, and (3) recommendations for the consideration of the boards of the organizations concerned.

THE INTENT AND PURPOSE OF THE MANIFESTO

The Intent and Nature of the Manifesto:

A. It is only an expressional instrument from messengers of churches and from Board members of our four Societies assembled in Annual Meeting in Portland, Oregon, in June, 1953.

B. The Manifesto is not binding upon any church or any Society represented in this expression.

C. The Manifesto is a purely voluntary, democratic and positive expression of a working and workable ideal to serve as a common denominator for each of our four organizations in particular and for the whole Conservative Baptist Movement in general.

D. The Manifesto as a working and workable ideal, in its very language in at least two places, makes this Manifesto self-interpreting:

  1. "Unswerving opposition to the practice of the inclusive policy;"

    a. Theological form of the inclusive policy which is an admixture of belief and unbelief.

    b. Ecclesiastical form of inclusive policy which is churches and individuals being associated with unsound bodies.

    c. Financial form of inclusive policy which is giving financial support to unsound bodies, individuals, or objectives and enterprises.

    d. Practical form of the inclusive policy which is giving one's vote, voice or volitional influence to unsoundness as expressed in the inclusive policy in its theological, ecclesiastical or financial form, without protest.

  2. "Separatist in spirit and objective"

    a. Separatist in spirit means: the sincere heart attitudes, motives, impulses, desires, expressions, prayers and actions of the individual, or individuals comprising a church or organization to give with protest the least possible cooperation to all forms of the inclusive policy as named above which will be determined in degree of cooperation by the particular circumstances that prevail.

    b. Separatist in objective means: the individual, church, or organization desires as soon as possible to arrive at the place where

      (1) All disbelief can be disfellowshipped.

      (2) All unsound associations can be disassociated.

      (3) All unsound objectives can be met with non-support.

      (4) All participation with unbelief, unsound organizations, and financial objectives can be discontinued.

IDEOLOGY OF THE CONSERVATIVE BAPTIST MOVEMENT

AS CONSERVATIVE BAPTISTS:

1. We hold the New Testament pattern of the interdependence of autonomous local churches in which messengers gather from local churches in association meetings for the purpose of inspiration and business, rejecting the concept of a convention as we have come to know it in the form of an ecclesiastical hierarchy with delegates, a convention and an incorporation.

2. We hold that severance resolutions from other bodies are not to be regarded as a pre-requisite to affiliation with our Conservative Baptist agencies. We hold that the ethical problem of affiliations, and severance resolutions is the problem of the local autonomous Baptist church.

   While it is not our province to regulate affiliations, we do declare that cooperation with inclusivism in any form does militate against the best interests of both the local churches and their agencies.

3. We hold that no form of coercion on local churches should be employed by any of our agencies in order to enlist them in fellowship and cooperation.

4. Recognizing that the relationship of our C. B. movement to outside groups must be guided by our own need of preserving our distinctives as Conservative Baptists, let us agree that in these relationships we:

   Will not support affiliations with apostate ecumenical organizations (that is, organizations that would combine the professed Christian communions of the world into one universal church) knowing that God's blessing in such affiliations would not be upon us.

DECLARATION OF FAITH

ONE. We believe that the Bible is God's Word, that it was written by men Divinely inspired and that it is the supreme infallible authority in all matters of faith and conduct.

TWO. We believe in God the Father, perfect in holiness, infinite in wisdom, measureless in power. We rejoice that He concerns Himself mercifully in the affairs of men, that He hears and answers prayer, and that He saves from sin and death all that come to Him through Jesus Christ.

THREE. We believe in Jesus Christ, the eternal and only begotten Son of God, conceived of the Holy Spirit, of virgin birth, sinless in His life, making atonement for the sins of the world by His death. We believe in His bodily resurrection, His ascension and visible, pre-millennial return to the world according to His promise.

FOUR. We believe in the Holy Spirit who came forth from God to convince the world of sin, or righteousness and of judgment, and to regenerate, sanctify and comfort those who believe in Jesus Christ.

FIVE. We believe that all men by nature and by choice are sinners but that "God so loved the world that He gave His only begotten Son that whosoever believeth in Him should not perish but have everlasting life;" we believe, therefore, that those who accept Christ as Lord and Saviour will rejoice forever in God's presence and those who refuse to accept Christ as Lord and Saviour will be forever separated from God.

SIX. We believe in the Church—a living spiritual body of which Christ is the head and of which all regenerated people are members. We believe that a local church is a company of believers in Jesus Christ, immersed on a credible confession of faith, and associated for worship, work and fellowship. We believe that to these local churches were committed, for perpetual observance, the ordinances of baptism and the Lord's supper, and that God has laid upon these churches the task of proclaiming to a lost world the acceptance of Jesus Christ as Saviour, and the enthroning of Him as Lord and Master. We believe that all human betterment and social improvements are the inevitable by-products of such a Gospel.

SEVEN. We believe that every human being is responsible to God alone in all matters of faith; that each church is independent and autonomous and must be free from interference by any ecclesiastical or political authority; that therefore Church and State must be kept separate as having different functions, each fulfilling its duties free from the dictation or patronage of the other.

Notes: *The Conservative Baptist Manifesto was adopted in 1953 and provides an overall perspective on the conservative Baptist position.*

The Declaration of Faith is taken from the constitution of the Conservative Baptist Association. It is derived from the original statement of the Fundamental Fellowship, but differs in wording. Most importantly, it adds specific references to the virgin birth and premillennialism.

* * *

ARTICLES OF FAITH (DUCK RIVER AND KINDRED ASSOCIATIONS OF BAPTISTS)

1. We believe in only one true and living God. Father, Word and Holy Ghost and these three are one.

2. We believe that by one man sin entered into the world, and death by sin, and so death passed upon all men, for that all have sinned and are by nature the children of wrath.

3. We believe that the scriptures of the Old and New Testaments are *the words of God,* and the only rules of faith and practice.

4. We believe that Jesus Christ, by the grace of God, tasted death for every man, and through his meritorious death, the way of salvation is made possible for God to have mercy upon all who come unto him upon Gospel terms.

5. We believe that sinners are justified in the sight of God only by the righteousness of God imputed unto them through faith in the Lord Jesus Christ.

6. We believe that the saints will persevere in grace, and that not one of them will be finally lost.

7. We believe that there will be a resurrection of the dead, both of the just and of the unjust, and a general judgment, and that the happiness of the righteous and the punishment of the wicked will be eternal.

8. We believe that the visible church of Christ is a congregation of faithful men and women, who have given themselves to the Lord, and have obtained fellowship with each other, and have agreed to keep a godly discipline according to the rules of the Gospel.

9. We believe in revealed religion by the operation of the Spirit, agreeable to the word of God, and that Jesus Christ is the great head of the Church, and that the government thereof is with the body.

10. We believe that water baptism, the Lord's supper and the washing of the saints' feet are ordinances of the Gospel, to be continued until the second coming of the Lord Jesus Christ, and that true believers are the only fit subjects for baptism and immersion the only true Gospel mode.

11. We believe that none but the regularly baptized members have a right to commune at the Lord's table, and that no person has the right to administer the ordinance of the Gospel, except that he is legally called and qualified.

12. We believe that the Lord's day ought to be observed and set apart for the worship of God, and that no work or worldly business should be transacted thereon—works of piety and mercy and necessity excepted.

Notes: *Several of the issues which led to the formation of both the Duck River and Kindred Associations of Baptists (such as support for missions) are not mentioned in the Articles of Faith, but others (such as general atonement) are. Association members also practice foot washing.*

* * *

DOCTRINAL STATEMENT (FUNDAMENTAL BAPTIST FELLOWSHIP)

1. We believe that the Bible is God's Word, that it was written by men divinely inspired, and that it has supreme authority in all matters of faith and conduct.

2. We believe in God the Father, perfect in holiness, infinite in wisdom, measureless in power. We rejoice that He concerns Himself mercifully in the affairs of men, that He hears and answers prayer, and that He saves from sin and death all who come to Him through Jesus Christ.

3. We believe in Jesus Christ, God's only begotten Son, miraculous in His birth, sinless in His life, making atonement for the sins of the world by His death. We believe in His bodily resurrection, His ascension into Heaven, His perpetual intercession for His people and His personal visible return to the world according to His promise.

4. We believe in the Holy Spirit who came forth from God to convince the world of sin, of righteousness, and of judgment, and to regenerate, sanctify and comfort those who believe in Jesus Christ.

5. We believe that all men by nature and by choice are sinners, but that "God so loved the world that He gave His only begotten Son that whosoever believeth in Him should not perish but have everlasting life;" we believe therefore that those who accept Christ as Lord and Saviour will rejoice forever in God's presence, and those who refuse to accept Christ as Lord and Saviour will be forever separated from God.

6. We believe in the Church—a living spiritual body of which Christ is the head and of which all regenerated people are members. We believe that a visible church is a company of believers in Jesus Christ, baptized on a credible confession of faith, and associated for worship, work and fellowship. We believe that to these visible churches were committed, for perpetual observance, the ordinances of baptism and the Lord's Supper, and that God has laid upon these churches the task of persuading a lost world to accept Jesus Christ as Saviour, and to enthrone Him as the Lord and Master. We believe that all human betterment and social improvements are the inevitable byproduct of such a Gospel.

7. We believe that every human being has direct relations with God, and is responsible to God alone in all matters of faith; that each church is independent and autonomous and must be free from interference by any ecclesiastical or political authority; that therefore Church and State must be kept separate as having different functions, each fulfilling its duties free from the dictation or patronage of the other.

8. We believe in our Lord's return—a personal, visible, imminent, pre-tribulation rapture, and subsequent millennial enthronement, in fulfillment of His promise.

Notes: *The doctrinal statement of the Fundamental Baptist Fellowship is derived from the original statement of the Fundamental Fellowship, differing in its addition of a new statement on premillennial eschatology which commits the fellowship to specific refinement within the larger premillennial eschatological picture. The fellowship believes that those who have saving faith in Christ will be "raptured," or taken from earth to be with Jesus, prior to the time of tribulation preceeding His second coming and the millennium.*

* * *

A CONFESSION OF FAITH (FUNDAMENTAL FELLOWSHIP)

1. We believe that the Bible is God's Word, that it was written by men divinely and uniquely inspired, that it is absolutely trustworthy and has supreme authority in all matters of faith and conduct.

A CONFESSION OF FAITH (FUNDAMENTAL FELLOWSHIP) (continued)

2. We believe in God the Father, creator of heaven and earth, perfect in holiness, infinite in wisdom, measureless in power. We rejoice that He concerns Himself mercifully in the affairs of men, that He hears and answers prayer and that He saves from sin and death all who comes to Him through Jesus Christ.

3. We believe in Jesus Christ, God's only begotten Son, conceived of the Holy Spirit, born of the Virgin Mary, sinless in His life, making atonement for the sin of the world by His death on the cross. We believe in His bodily resurrection, His Ascension into heaven, His high priestly intercession for His people and His personal, visible return to the world according to His promise.

4. We believe in the Holy Spirit, who came forth from God to convince the world of sin, of righteousness and of judgment, and to regenerate, sanctify and comfort those who believe in Jesus Christ.

5. We believe that all men by nature and by choice are sinners, but that "God so loved the world that He gave His only begotten Son, that whosoever believeth in Him should not perish, but have everlasting life." We believe, therefore, that those who accept Christ as their Lord and Saviour will rejoice forever in God's presence and those who refuse to accept Christ as Lord and Saviour will be forever separated from God.

6. We believe in the Church—a living, spiritual body of which Christ is the Head and of which all regenerated people are members. We believe that a visible church is a company of believers in Jesus Christ, buried with Him in baptism and associated for worship, work and fellowship. We believe that to these visible churches were committed for observance "till He come," the ordinances of baptism and the Lord's Supper; and that God has laid upon these churches the task of persuading a lost world to accept Jesus Christ as Saviour and to enthrone Him as Lord and Master. We believe that human betterment and social improvement are essential products of the Gospel.

7. We believe that every human being is responsible to God alone in all matters of faith.

8. We believe that each church is independent and autonomous, and must be free from interference by any ecclesiastical or political authority; that, therefore, Church and State must be kept separate as having different functions, each fulfilling its duties free from the dictation or patronage of the other.

Notes: *The Fundamental Fellowship was the original organization formed by conservative members of the Northern Baptist Convention (now the American Baptist Churches in the U.S.A.). This confession, written by Frank M. Goodchild, was adopted by the fellowship at a meeting preceeding the 1921 gathering of the Northern Baptist Convention. Members of the fellowship tried, unsuccessful-*

ly, to get the entire convention to adopt it. The confession became the basis of the present statements of the Conservative Baptist Association of America and the Fundamental Baptist Fellowship.

* * *

ARTICLES OF FAITH (GENERAL ASSOCIATION OF REGULAR BAPTIST CHURCHES)

I. OF THE SCRIPTURES

We believe that the Holy Bible as originally written was verbally inspired and the product of Spirit-controlled men, and therefore, has truth without any admixture of error for its matter. We believe the Bible to be the true center of Christian union and the supreme standard by which all human conduct, creeds, and opinions shall be tried.

2 Tim. 3:16, 17; 2 Pet. 1:19-21.

II. OF THE TRUE GOD

We believe there is one and only one living and true God, an infinite Spirit, the Maker and supreme Ruler of heaven and earth; inexpressibly glorious in holiness, and worthy of all possible honor, confidence and love; that in the unity of the Godhead there are three persons, the Father, the Son and the Holy Ghost, equal in every divine perfection, and executing distinct but harmonious offices in the great work of redemption.

Exod. 20:2, 3: I Cor. 8:6; Rev. 4:11.

III. OF THE HOLY SPIRIT

We believe that the Holy Spirit is a divine person, equal with God the Father and God the Son and of the same nature; that He was active in the creation; that in His relation to the unbelieving world He restrains the evil one until God's purpose is fulfilled; that He convicts of sin, of righteousness and of judgment; that He bears witness to the truth of the Gospel in preaching and testimony; that He is the Agent in the new birth; that He seals, endues, guides, teaches, witnesses, sanctifies and helps the believer.

John 14;16, 17; Matt. 28:19; Heb. 9:14; John 14:26; Luke 1:35; Gen. 1:1-3; John 16:8-11; Acts 5:30-32; John 3:5,6; Eph. 1:13, 14; Mark 1:8; John 1:33; Act 11:16; Luke 24:49; Rom. 8:14, 16, 26, 27.

IV. OF THE DEVIL, OR SATAN

We believe in the personality of Satan, that he is the unholy god of this age, and the author of all the powers of darkness, and is destined to the judgment of an eternal justice in the lake of fire.

Matt. 4:1-3; 2 Cor. 4:4; Rev. 20:10.

V. OF CREATION

We accept the Genesis account of creation and believe that man came by direct creation of God and not by evolution.

Gen. 1 and 2; Col. 1:16, 17; John 1:3.

VI. OF THE FALL OF MAN

We believe that man was created in innocence under the law of his Maker, but by voluntary transgression fell from his sinless and happy state in consequence of which all mankind are now sinners, not only by constraint, but of choice; and therefore under just condemnation without defense or excuse.

Gen 3:1-6, 24; Rom. 3:10-19; Rom. 1:18, 32.

VII. OF THE VIRGIN BIRTH

We believe that Jesus was begotten of the Holy Ghost in a miraculous manner, born of Mary, a virgin, as no other man was ever born or can be born of woman, and that He is both the Son of God and God, the Son.

Gen. 3:15; Isa. 7:14; Matt. 1:18-25; Luke 1:35; John 1:14.

VIII. OF THE ATONEMENT FOR SIN

We believe that the salvation of sinners is wholly of grace; through the mediatorial offices of the Son of God, Who by the appointment of the Father, freely took upon Him our nature, yet without sin, honored the divine law by His personal obedience, and by His death made a full and vicarious atonement for our sins; that His atonement consisted not in setting us an example by His death as a martyr, but was a voluntary substitution of Himself in the sinner's place, the Just dying for the unjust; Christ, the Lord, bearing our sin in His own body on the tree; that having risen from the dead, He is now enthroned in Heaven, and uniting in His wonderful person the tenderest sympathies with divine perfection, He is in every way qualified to be a suitable, a compassionate and an all-sufficient Savior.

Eph. 2:8; Acts 15:11; Rom. 3:24; John 3:16; Matt. 18:11; Phil. 2:7; Heb. 2:14; Isa. 53:4-7; Rom 3:25; I John 4:10; I Cor. 15:3; 2 Cor. 5:21.

IX. OF GRACE IN THE NEW CREATION

We believe that in order to be saved, sinners must be born again; that the new birth is a new creation in Christ Jesus; that it is instantaneous and not a process; that in the new birth the one dead in trespasses and in sins is made a partaker of the divine nature and receives eternal life, the free gift of God; that the new creation is brought about in a manner above our comprehension, solely by the power of the Holy Spirit in connection with divine truth, so as to secure our voluntary obedience to the gospel; that its proper evidence appears in the holy fruits of repentance and faith and newness of life.

John 3:3; 2 Cor. 5:17; I John 5:1; John 3:6, 7; Acts 16:30-33; 2 Pet. 1:4; Rom. 6:23; Eph. 2:1, 5; 2 Cor. 5:19; Col. 2:13; John 3:8.

X. OF JUSTIFICATION

We believe that the great gospel blessing which Christ secures to such as believe in Him is Justification;

(a) That Justification includes the pardon of sin, and the gift of eternal life, on principles of righteousness;

(b) That it is bestowed not in consideration of any works of righteousness which we have done; but solely through faith in the Redeemer's blood, His righteousness is imputed to us.

Acts 13:39; Isa. 53:11; Zech. 13:1; Rom. 8:1; Rom. 5:1, 9.

XI. OF FAITH AND SALVATION

We believe that faith in the Lord Jesus Christ is the only condition of salvation.

Acts 16:31.

XII. OF THE LOCAL CHURCH

We believe that a local church is a congregation of immersed believers, associated by covenant of faith and fellowship of the Gospel; observing the ordinances of Christ; governed by His laws; and exercising the gifts, rights, and privileges invested in them by His Word; that its officers are pastors and deacons, whose qualifications, claims, and duties are clearly defined in the Scriptures. We believe the true mission of the church is the faithful witnessing of Christ to all men as we have opportunity. We hold that the local church has the absolute right of self-government free from the interference of any hierarchy of individuals or organizations; and that the one and only Superintendent is Christ through the Holy Spirit; that it is scriptural for true churches to cooperate with each other in contending for the faith and for the furtherance of the Gospel; that each local church is the sole judge of the measure and method of its cooperation; on all matters of membership, of polity, of government, of discipline, of benevolence, the will of the local church is final.

Acts 2:41, 42; 1 Cor. 11:2; Eph. 1:22, 23; Eph. 4:11; Acts 20:17-28; 1 Tim. 3:1-7; Col. 1:18; Eph. 5:23, 24; Acts 15:13-18.

XIII. OF BAPTISM AND THE LORD'S SUPPER

We believe that Christian baptism is the immersion of a believer in water to show forth in a solemn and beautiful emblem our faith in the crucified, buried and risen Savior, with its effect in our death to sin and resurrection to a new life; that it is prerequisite to the privileges of a church relation. We believe that the Lord's Supper is the commemoration of His death until He come, and should be preceded always by solemn self-examination.

Acts 8:36, 38, 39; John 3:23; Rom. 6:3-5; Matt. 3:16; Col. 2:12; 1 Cor. 11:23-28.

XIV. OF THE SECURITY OF THE SAINTS

We believe that all who are truly born again are kept by God the Father for Jesus Christ.

Phil. 1:6; John 10:28, 29; Rom. 8:35-39; Jude 1 (A.S.V.).

XV. OF THE RIGHTEOUS AND THE WICKED

We believe that there is a radical and essential difference between the righteous and the wicked; that such only as though faith are justified in the name of the Lord Jesus Christ, and sanctified by the Spirit of our God, are truly righteous in His esteem; while all such as continue in impenitence and unbelief are in His sight wicked, and under the curse; and this distinction holds among men both in and after death, in the everlasting felicity of the saved and the everlasting conscious suffering of the lost.

Mal. 3:18; Gen. 18:23; Rom. 6:17, 18; 1 John 5:19; Rom. 7:6; Rom. 6:23; Prov. 14:32; Luke 16:25; Matt. 25:34-41; John 8:21.

XVI. OF CIVIL GOVERNMENT

We believe that civil government is of divine appointment for the interests and good order of human society; that magistrates are to be prayed for, conscientiously honored, and obeyed; except in things opposed to the will of our

Lord Jesus Christ Who is the only Lord of the conscience, and the coming Prince of the kings of the earth.

Rom. 13:1-7; 2 Sam. 23:3; Exod. 18:21, 22; Acts 23:5; Matt. 22:21; Acts 5:29; Acts 4:19, 20; Dan. 3:17, 18.

XVII. OF THE RESURRECTION, PERSONAL, VISIBLE, PREMILLENNIAL RETURN OF CHRIST, AND RELATED EVENTS

(a) We believe in the Bodily Resurrection.

Matt. 28:6, 7; Luke 24:39;, John 20:27; I Cor. 15:4; Mark 16:6; Luke 24:2-6.

(b) The Ascension.

Acts 1:19-11; Luke 24:51; Rev. 3:21; Heb. 12:2.

(c) The High Priesthood.

Heb. 8:6; I Tim. 2:5; I John 2:1; Heb. 2:17; Heb. 5:9, 10.

(d) The Second Coming.

John 14:3; Acts 1:11; I Thess. 4:16; James 5:8; Heb. 9:28.

(e) The Resurrection of the Righteous Dead.

I Thess. 4:13-18; I Cor. 15:42-44, 51-54.

(f) The Change of the Living in Christ.

I Cor. 15:51-53; I Thess. 4:13-18; Phil. 3:20, 21.

(g) The Throne of David.

Luke 1:32; Isa. 9:6, 7; Acts 2:29, 30.

(h) The Millennial Reign.

I Cor. 15:25; Isa. 32:1; Isa. 11:4, 5; Psa. 72:8; Rev. 20:1-4, 6.

Notes: *Using the New Hampshire Confession as a basis, the General Association of Regular Baptist Churches has added references to the verbal inspiration of scripture, the personality of Satan, the virgin birth, and premillennialism.*

*   *   *

CONFESSION OF FAITH (MINNESOTA BAPTIST ASSOCIATION)

CONCERNING THE SCRIPTURES

We believe that the Holy Bible was written inerrant in its original languages by men divinely inspired, and is a perfect treasure of heavenly instruction;[1] that is has God for its Author, salvation for its end,[2] and truth without any mixture of error, for its matter;[3] that it reveals the principles by which God will judge us;[4] and therefore is, and shall remain to the end of the age, the true center of Christian union,[5] and the supreme standard by which all human conduct, creeds, and opinions should be tried.[6]

Places in the Bible Where Taught. [1] 2 Tim. 3:16, 17. (Also 2 Peter 1:21; 2 Sam. 23:2; Acts 1:16; 3:21; John 10:35; Luke 16:29, 31; Ps. 119:111; Rom. 3:1, 2). [2] 2 Tim. 3:15. (Also I Peter 1:10-12; Acts 11:14; Rom. 1:16; Mark 16:16; John 5:38, 39). [3] Prov. 30:5, 6. (Also John 17:17; Rev. 22:18, 19; Rom. 3:4). [4] Rom. 2:12. (Also I Cor. 4:3, 4; Luke 10:10-16; 12:47, 48). [5] Phil. 3:16. (Also Eph. 4:3-6; Phil. 2:1, 2; I Cor.

1:10; I Peter 4:11). [6] I John 4:1, (Also Acts 17:11; I John 4:6; Jude 3; Eph. 6:17; Ps. 119:59, 60; Phil. 1:9-11).

CONCERNING THE TRUE GOD

We believe that there is one, and only one, living and true God, an infinite, intelligent, perfect Spirit and personal Being, the Creator, Preserver, and Supreme Ruler of the universe,[1] inexpressibly glorious in holiness[2] and all other perfections, and worthy of all possible honor, confidence and love;[3] that in the unity of the Godhead there are three persons, the Father, the Son, and the Holy Ghost;[4] equal in every divine perfection,[5] and executing distinct but harmonious offices in the great work of redemption.[6]

Places in the Bible Where Taught. [1] I John 4:24. (Also Heb. 3:4; Rom. 1:20; Jer. 10:10). [2] Exod. 15:11. (Isa. 6:3; I Peter 1:15, 16; Rev. 4:6-8). [3] Mark 12:30. (Matt. 10:37; Jer. 2:12, 13). [4] Matt. 28:19. (I Cor. 12:4-6; I John 5:7). [5] John 10:30. (John 5:17; 14:23; 17:5, 10; Acts 5:3, 4; I Cor. 2:10, 11; Phil. 2:5, 6). [6] Eph. 2:18. (Rev. 1:4, 5; comp. ch, 2:7).

CONCERNING THE FALL OF MAN

We believe that man was created by the special act of God, as recorded in Genesis. "So God created man in His own image, in the image of God created He him; male and female created He them" (Gen. 1:27).[1] "And the Lord God formed man of the dust of the ground, and breathed into his nostrils the breath of life; and man became a living soul". (Gen. 2:7).[2]

We believe that man was created in a state of holiness, under the law of his Maker,[3] but through the temptation of Satan he voluntarily transgressed and fell from this holy state;[4] in consequence of which all mankind are now sinners,[5] not by constraint, but choice,[6] being by nature utterly void of that holiness required by law of God, positively inclined to evil, and therefore under just condemnation to eternal ruin,[7] without defense or excuse.[8]

Places in the Bible Where Taught. [1] Gen. 1:27. [2] Gen. 2:7. [3] Gen. 1:27. (Eccl. 7:29; Acts 17:26-29; Gen. 2:16, 17). [4] Gen. 3:6-24. (Rom. 5:12). [5] Rom. 5:19. (John 3:6; Ps. 51:5; Rom. 5:15-19; 8:7). [6] Isa. 53:6. (Gen. 6:12; Rom. 3:9-18). [7] Eph. 2:13. (Rom. 1:32; 2:1-16; Gal. 3:10; Matt. 20:15). [8] Ezek. 18:19, 20. (Gal.3:22).

CONCERNING THE WAY OF SALVATION

We believe that the salvation of sinners is wholly of grace;[1] through the mediatorial offices of the Son of God;[2] Who pre-existed,[3] and Who by the appointment of the Father, and Who by the Holy Spirit was conceived, and born of the virgin Mary, freely took upon Him man's nature, yet without sin;[4] honored the divine law by His perfect obedience,[5] and after a miraculous ministry, by His death made a full atonement for our sins;[6] that having risen from the dead bodily He is now enthroned in heaven[7] to reign in eternal sovereignty and uniting in His wonderful person the tenderest sympathies with divine perfections, He is in every way qualified to be a suitable, a compassionate and all-sufficient Savior and Lord.[8]

Places in the Bible Where Taught. [1] Eph. 2:8. (Matt. 18:11; I John 4:10; I Cor. 3:5, 7; Acts 15:11). [2] John 3:16. (John 1:1-14; Heb. 4-14; 12:24). [3] John 8:58. [4] Phil. 2:6, 7. (Heb. 2:9, 14; 2 Cor. 5:21). [5] Heb. 5:8, 9. (Phil. 2:8; Gal. 4:4, 5; Rom. 3:21). [6] Isa. 53:4, 5. (Matt. 20:28; Rom. 4:25; 3:21-26;

1 John 4:10; 2:2; 1 Cor. 15:1-3; Heb. 9:13-15). [7]Heb. 1:8. (Heb. 1:3; 8:1; Col. 3:1-4). [8]Heb. 7:25. (Heb. 7:26; Ps. 89:19; Ps. 34).

CONCERNING JUSTIFICATION

We believe that the great Gospel blessing which Christ[1] secures to such as believe in Him is Justification;[2] that Justification includes the pardon of sin,[3] and the promise of eternal life on principles of righteousness;[4] that it is bestowed, not in consideration of any works of righteousness which we have done, but solely through faith in the Redeemer's blood;[5] by virtue of which faith His perfect righteousness is freely imputed to us of God;[6] that it brings us into a state of most blessed peace and favor with God, and secures every other blessing needful for time and eternity.[7]

Places in the Bible Where Taught. [1]John 1:16. (Eph. 3:8). [2]Acts 13:39. (Isa. 53:11, 12; Rom. 8:1). [3]Rom. 5:9. (Zech. 13:1; Matt. 9:6; Acts 10:43). [4]Rom. 5:17. (Titus 3:5-7; 1 Peter 3:7; 1 John 2:25; Rom. 5:21). [5]Rom. 4:4, 5. (Rom. 5:21; 6:23; Phil. 3:7-9). [6]Rom. 5:19. (Rom. 3:24-26; 4:23-25; 1 John 2:12). [7]Rom. 5:1, 2. (I Cor. 1:30, 31; Matt, 6:33; I Tim. 4:8).

CONCERNING THE FREENESS OF SALVATION

We believe that the blessings of salvation are made free to all by the Gospel;[1] that it is the immediate duty of all to accept them by a cordial, penitent, and obedient faith;[2] and that nothing prevents the salvation of the greatest sinner on earth but his own inherent depravity and voluntary rejection of the Gospel;[3] which rejection involves him in an aggravated condemnation.[4]

Places in the Bible Where Taught. [1]Isa. 55:1. (Luke 14:17). [2]Rom. 16:25, 26. (Mark 1:15; Rom. 1:15-17). [3]John 5:40. (Matt. 23:37; Rom. 9:32; Prov. 1:24; Acts 13:46). [4]John 3:19. (Matt. 11:20; Luke 19:27; 2 Thess. 1:8).

CONCERNING GRACE IN REGENERATION

We believe that, in order to be saved, sinners must be regenerated or born again,[1] that regeneration consists in giving a holy disposition to the soul;[2] that it is effected, in a manner above our comprehension, by the power of the Holy Spirit in connection with divine truth,[3] so as to secure our voluntary obedience to the Gospel;[4] and that its proper evidence appears in the holy fruits of repentance and faith and newness of life.[5]

Places in the Bible Where Taught. [1]John 3:3. (John 3:6, 7; 1 Cor. 2:14; Rev. 14:3; 21:27). [2]Cor. 5:17. (Ezek. 36:26; Deut. 30:6; Rom. 2:28, 29; 5:5; 1 John 4:7). [3]John 3:8. (1 Cor. 1:30; Phil. 2:13). [4]1 Peter 1:22-25. (Eph. 4:20-24; Col. 3:9-11). [5]Eph. 5:9. (Rom. 8:9; Gal. 5:16-23; Eph. 2:14-21; Matt. 3:8-10; 7:20; 1 John 5:4, 18).

CONCERNING REPENTANCE AND FAITH

We believe that Repentance and Faith are sacred duties, and also inseparable graces, wrought in our souls by the regenerating Spirit of God;[1] whereby, being deeply convinced of our guilt, danger, and helplessness, and of the way of salvation by Christ,[2] we turn to God with unfeigned contrition, confession, and supplication for mercy;[3] at the same time heartily receiving the Lord Jesus Christ as the only and all-sufficient Savior.[4]

Places in the Bible Where Taught. [1]Mark 1:15. [2]John 16:8. (Acts 16:30, 31). [3]Luke 18:13. (Luke 15:18-21; James 4:7-10; 2 Cor. 7:11; Rom. 10:12, 13; Psalm 51). [4]Rom. 10:9-11. (Acts 3:22, 23; Heb. 4:14; Ps. 2:6; Heb. 1:8; 7:25; 2 Tim. 1:12).

CONCERNING GOD'S PURPOSE OF GRACE

We believe that Election is the eternal purpose of God, according to which He graciously regenerates, sanctifies, and saves sinners;[1] that it being perfectly consistent with the free agency of man, it comprehends as wells as embraces all the means in connection with the end;[2] that it is a most glorious display of God's soverign goodness, being infinitely free, wise, holy and unchangeable;[3] that it utterly excludes boasting, and promotes humility, love, prayer, praise, trust in God, and active imitation of His free mercy;[4] that it encourages the use of means in the highest degree;[5] that it may be ascertained by its effects in all who truly believe the Gospel;[6] that it is the foundation of Christian assurance;[7] and that to ascertain it with regard to ourselves demands and deserves the utmost diligence.[8]

Places in the Bible Where Taught. [1]Tim. 1:8, 9. (Eph. 1:3-14; 1 Peter 1:1, 2; Rom. 11:5, 6; John 15:16; 1 John 4:19). [2]2 Thess. 2:13, 14. (Acts 13:48; John 10:16; Matt. 20:16; Acts 15:14). [3]Exod. 33:18, 19. (Eph. 1:11; Rom. 9:23, 24; Jer. 31:3; Rom. 11:28, 29; James 1:17, 18; 2 Tim. 1:9; Rom. 11:32-36). [4]1 Cor. 4:7. (1 Cor. 1:26-31; Rom. 3:27; 4-16; Col. 3:12; 1 Cor. 15:10; 1 Peter 5:10; 1 Thess. 2:12, 13; 1 Peter 2:9; Luke 18:7). [5]Tim. 2:10. (John 6:37-40; 2 Peter 1:10). [6]1 Thess. 1:4-10. [7]Rom. 8:28-31. (Isa. 42:16; Rom. 11:29). [8]2 Peter 1:10, 11. (Phil. 3:12; Heb. 6:11).

CONCERNING SANCTIFICATION

We believe that Sanctification is the process by which, according to the will of God, we are made partakers of His holiness;[1] that it is a progressive work;[2] that it is begun in regeneration;[3] and that it it is carried on in the hearts of believers through out their earthly life, by the presence and power of the Holy Spirit, the Sealer and Comforter, in the continual use of the appointed means, especially the Word of God, self-examination, self-denial, watchfulness, and prayer.[4]

Places in the Bible Where Taught. [1]Thess. 4:3. (2 Cor. 7:1; 13:9; Eph. 1:4). [2]Prov. 4:18. (Heb. 6:1; 2 Peter 1:5-8; Phil. 3:12-16). [3]1 John 2:29. (John 3:6; Phil. 1:9-11). [4]Phil. 2:12, 13. (Eph. 4:11, 12, 30; 6:18; 1 Peter 2:2; 2 Peter 3:18; 2 Cor. 13:5; Luke 9:23; 11:35; Matt. 26:41).

CONCERNING THE PERSEVERANCE OF THE SAINTS

We believe that all real believers endure unto the end,[1] that their persevering attachment to Christ is the grand mark which distinguishes them from superficial professors;[2] that a special Providence watches over their welfare;[3] and they are kept by the power of God through faith unto salvation.[4]

Places in the Bible Where Taught. [1]John 8:31. (1 John 2:27, 28; 3:9; 5:18). [2]I John 2:19. (John 13:18; Matt. 13:20, 21; John 6:66-69). [3]Rom. 8:28. (Matt. 6:30-33; Jer. 32:40; Ps. 121:2; 91:11, 12). [4]Phil. 1:6. (Phil 2:12, 13; Jude 24, 25; Heb. 1:14; 13:5; 1 John 4:4).

CONERNING THE HARMONY OF THE LAW AND THE GOSPEL

We believe that the Law of God is the eternal and unchangeable rule of His moral government;[1] that it is holy, just and good;[2] and that the inability which the Scriptures ascribe to fallen men to fulfil its precepts arises entirely from their love of sin;[3] to deliver them from which, and to restore them through a Mediator to unfeigned obedience to the holy Law, is one great end of the Gospel, and of the means of grace connected with the establishment of the visible church.[4]

Places in the Bible Where Taught. [1]Rom. 3:31. (Matt. 5:17; Luke 16:17; Rom. 3:20; 4:15). [2]Rom. 7:12. (Rom. 7:7, 14, 22; Gal. 3:21; Ps. 119). [3]Rom. 8:7, 8. (Josh. 24:19; Jer. 13:23; John 6:44; 5:44). [4] Rom. 8:2-4. (Rom. 10:4; Heb. 8:10; 12:14; Jude 20, 21).

CONCERNING A GOSPEL CHURCH

We believe that a visible church of Christ is a congregation of baptized believers,[1] associated by convenant in the faith and fellowship of the Gospel;[2] observing the ordinances of Christ;[3] governed by His Laws;[4] and exercising the gifts, rights, and privileges invested in them by His Word;[5] seeking to extend the Gospel to the ends of the earth;[6] that its only Scriptural officers are Bishops, or Pastors, and Deacons,[7] whose qualifications, claims, and duties are defined in the epistles to Timothy and Titus.

Places in the Bible Where Taught. [1]1 Cor. 1:1-13 (Matt. 18:17; Acts. 5:11; 8:1; 11:21-23; 1 Cor. 4:17; 14:23; 3 John 9). [2]Acts 2:41, 42. (Acts 2:47; 1 Cor. 5:12; 13). [3]1 Cor. 11:2. (2 Thess. 3:6; Rom. 16:17-20; 1 Cor. 4:17). [4]Matt. 28:20. (John 14:15; 15:12; 1 John 4:21; John 14:21; 1 Thess. 4:2; 2 John 6; Gal. 6:2; all the Epistles). [5]Eph. 4:7. [6]Matt. 28:20. [7]Phil. 1:1. (Acts 14:23; 15:22; 1 Tim. 3; Titus 1).

CONCERNING A GOSPEL CHURCH IN ITS INDEPENDENCE AND RELATIONSHIPS

We believe that the local visible church of Christ is a voluntary and independent autonomous group of baptized believers;[1] that it is a pure democracy, which organically can join nothing;[2] and that it has the power and right within itself to confess its own faith in accordance with the New Testament;[3] and that each congregation recognizes its own democratic self-containing government as its highest authority for carrying out the will of the Lord Jesus Christ.[4]

Places in the Bible Where Taught. [1]Matt. 18:15-18. (Matt. 23:8-10; 1 Peter 5:3). [2]Rom. 12:16. (1 Cor. 1:10; Eph. 4:3; Phil. 1:27). [3] Tim. 3:15. (Jude 3; Rev. 2 and 3). [4]Matt. 18:15-18. (Acts 1:23-26; 6:3-5; 1 Cor. 5:4, 5, 13).

CONCERNING BAPTISM AND THE LORD'S SUPPER

We believe that both Christian baptism and the Lord's Supper are each a memorial, a symbol and a prophecy.[1] We believe that Christian baptism is the immersion in water of a believer;[2] into the name of the Father, the Son, and the Holy Ghost;[3] to show forth, in a solemn and beautiful emblem, our faith in the crucified, buried, and risen Savior, with its effect in our death to sin and resurrection to a new life;[4] that it is prerequisite to the privileges of a church relation; and a commendable prerequisite to the Lord's Supper;[5] in which the members of the Church, by the sacred use of bread and fruit of the vine to commemorate together the dying love of Christ;[6] preceded always by solemn self-examination.[7]

Places in the Bible Where Taught. [1]Rom. 6:3. (Mark 10:38; Rom. 6:4; Gal. 3:27; 1 Peter 3:21; Eph. 4:5; 1 Cor. 12:13; 1 Cor. 15:12, 22). [2]Acts 8:36-39. (Matt. 3:5, 6; John 3:22, 23; 4:1, 2; Matt. 28:19; Mark 16:16; Acts 2:38; 8:12; 16:32-34; 18:8). [3]Matt. 28:19. (Acts 10:47, 48; Gal. 3:27, 28). [4]Rom. 6:4. (Col. 2:12; 1 Peter 3:20, 21; Acts 22:16). [5]Acts 2:41, 42. (Matt. 28:19, 20; Acts and Epistles). [6]1 Cor. 11:26. (Matt. 26:26-29; Mark 14:22-25; Luke 22:14-20). [7]1 Cor. 11:28. (1 Cor. 5:1, 8; 10:3-32; 11:17-32; John 6:26-71).

CONCERNING THE LORD'S DAY

We believe that the first day of the week is the Lord's Day, and is a Christian institution,[1] it is to be kept sacred to spiritual purposes,[2] by abstaining from all unnecessary secular labor and sinful recreations,[3] for it commemorates the resurrection of the Lord Jesus Christ from the dead;[4] by the devout observance of all the means of grace, both private,[5] and public,[6] and by preparation for the rest that remaineth for the people of God.[7]

Places in the Bible Where Taught. [1]Acts 20:7. (Gen. 2:3; Col. 2:16, 17; Mark 2:27; John 20:19; 1 Cor. 16:1, 2). [2]Exod. 20:8. [3]Isa. 58.13, 14. [4]Acts 20:7. (Mark 16:9; John 20:19). [5]Ps. 118:15. [6]Heb. 10:24, 25. [7]Heb. 4:3-11.

CONCERNING CIVIL GOVERNMENT AND RELIGIOUS LIBERTY

We believe that civil government is of divine appointment, for the interests and good order of human society;[1] and that magistrates are to be prayed for, conscientiously honored and obeyed;[2] except only in things opposed to the will of our Lord Jesus Christ,[3] Who, is the only Lord of the conscience, and the Prince of the kings of the earth;[4] and that church and state should be separated, the state owing the church protection and full freedom;[5] no ecclesiastical group or denomination should be preferred above another by the state;[6] the state should not impose taxes for the support of any form of religion; a free church in a free state is the Christian ideal.[7]

Places in the Bible Where Taught. [1]Rom. 13:1-7. (Deut. 16:18; 2 Sam. 23:3; Exod. 18:21-23; Jer. 30-21). [2]Matt. 22:21. (Titus 3:1; 1 Peter 2:13; 1 Tim. 2:1-3). [3]Acts 5:29. (Dan. 3:15-18; 6:7-10; Acts 4:18-20). [4]Matt. 23:10. (Ps. 72:11; Ps. 2; Rom. 14:9-13). [5]1 Tim. 2:1, 2. (2 Pet. 2:18-21). [6]James 4:12. [7]1 Cor. 3:5. (Matt. 22:21; Mark 12:17).

CONCERNING THE STATE OF THE RIGHTEOUS AND THE WICKED

We believe that there is a radical and essential difference between the righteous and the wicked,[1] that such only as through faith are justified in the name of the Lord Jesus, and sanctified by the Spirit of our God, are truly righteous in His sight;[2] while all such as continue in impenitence and unbelief are in His sight wicked, and under the curse,[3] and this distinction holds among men both in and after death.[4]

Places in the Bible Where Taught. [1]Mal. 3:18. (Prov. 12:26; Isa. 5:20; Gen. 18:23; Acts 10:34, 35; Rom. 6:16). [2]Rom. 1:17. (1 John 3:7; Rom. 6:18, 22; 1 Cor. 11:32; Prov. 11:31; 1 Peter 4:17, 18). [3]1 John 5:19. (John 3:36; Isa. 57:21; Ps. 10:4; Isa. 55:6, 7). [4]Prov. 14:32. (John 8:21-24; Luke 12:4, 5; 9:23-26; John 12:25, 26; Eccl. 3:17; Matt. 7:13, 14).

CONCERNING THE RESURRECTION

We believe the Scriptures clearly teach that Jesus rose from the dead bodily, His grave was emptied of its contents;[1] that He appeared to the disciples after His resurrection in many convincing manifestations;[2] that He now exists in His glorified body at God's right hand;[3] and that there will be a resurrection of the righteous and a resurrection, of the wicked, separated in time;[4] that the bodies of the righteous will conform to the glorious spiritual body of the Lord Jesus Christ.[5]

Places in the Bible Where Taught. [1]Matt. 28:1-8. (1 Cor. 15:1-58; 2 Cor. 5:1-8). [2]Matt. 28:6. (John 20:9, 20; Acts 1:3; 10:39-41). [3]Peter 3:22; Heb. 4:14. [4]John 5:28, 29; Acts 24:15. [5]Phil. 3.21.

CONCERNING THE RETURN OF THE LORD

We believe that the end of the age is approaching;[1] "For the Lord Himself shall descend from heaven with a shout, with the voice of the archangel, and with the trump of God: and the dead in Christ shall rise first: Then we which are alive and remain shall be caught up together with them in the clouds, to meet the Lord in the air; and so shall we ever be with the Lord. Wherefore comfort one another with these words."[2] "Marvel not at this: for the hour is coming, in the which all that are in the graves shall hear His voice, And shall come forth; they that have done good, unto the resurrection of life; and they that have done evil, unto the resurrection of damnation."[3] "But the rest of the dead lived not again until the thousand years were finished, This is the first resurrection. Blessed and holy is he that hath part in the first resurrection; on such the second death hath no power, but they shall be priests of God and of Christ, and shall reign with Him a thousand years. And when the thousand years are expired, Satan shall be loosed out of his prison . . .";[4] that a solemn separation will then take place;[5] that the wicked will be adjudged to endless punishment, and the righteous to endless joy;[6] and that this judgment will fix forever the final state of men in heaven and hell, on principles of righteousness.

Places in the Bible Where Taught. [1]Peter 4:7. (1 Cor. 7:29-31; Heb. 1:10, 12; Matt. 25:31; 28:20; 13:39-43; 1 John 2:17; 2 Peter 3:3-13; Acts 1:11). [2]1 Thess. 4:16-18. [3]John 5:28, 29. [4]Rev. 20:5-7. [5]Matt. 13:49. (Matt. 13:37-43; 24:30, 31; 25:31-33). [6]Matt. 25:31-46. (1 Cor. 6:9, 10; Mark 9:43-48; 2 Peter 2:9; Jude 7; Phil. 3:19; Romans 6:23; 2 Cor. 5:10, 11; John 4:36; 2 Cor. 4:18). [7]Rom. 3:5, 6. (Heb. 6:1, 2; 1 Cor. 4:5; Acts 17:31; Rom. 2:2-16; Rev. 20:11, 12; 1 John 2:28, 4:17).

CONCERNING CHRISTIAN EDUCATION

We believe that Christianity is the religion of enlightenment and intelligence; that in Jesus Christ are hidden all the treasures of wisdom and knowledge;[1] and that all sound learning is therefore a part of our Christian heritage;[2] that the new birth opens all human faculties and creates a thirst for knowledge; that an adequate system of school is necessary to a complete spiritual program for Christ's church; and that the cause of education among New Testament churches is coordinate with the causes of evangelism, missions and general benevolence, and should receive along with these the liberal support of the churches.[3]

Places in the Bible Where Taught. [1]Matt. 28:20; Col. 2:3. [2]Deut. 4:1, 5, 9, 13, 14; 6:1, 7-10; Ps. 19:7, 8; Prov. 8:1-7; 4:1-10; Neh 8:1-4. [3]Matt. 28:20.

CONCERNING SOCIAL SERVICE

We believe that every Christian is under obligation to seek to make the will of Christ regnant in his own life and in human society;[1] to oppose in the spirit of Christ every form of greed, selfishness, and vice; to provide for the orphaned, the aged, the helpless, and the sick; to support everything that is good and righteous in industry, government and society as a whole for the benefit of men so that all men may live spiritually and righteously before God;[2] and that all means and methods used in social service for the amelioration of society and the establishment of righteousness among men must finally depend on the regeneration of the individual by the saving grace of God in Christ Jesus.[3]

Places in the Bible Where Taught. [1]Luke 10:25-27; Ex. 22:10, 14. [2]Lev. 6:2, Deut. 20:10; 4:42; Deut. 15:2; 27:17; Ps. 101:5. [3]Heb. 2:15; Zech. 8:16; Ex. 20:16; James 2:8; Rom. 12:14; Col. 3:12-17.

Notes: *In 1951, at the direction of the Minnesota Baptist Convention (now the Minnesota Baptist Association), George J. Carlson, Richard V. Clearwaters, and William H. Murk were appointed to prepare a statement of faith. Beginning with the New Hampshire Confession and the Baptist Faith and Message (adopted by the Southern Baptist Convention in 1925), they added items which drew from contemporary fundamentalist concerns. The result of their efforts was unanimously adopted in 1952. The confession includes an item which commits the association to a belief in a pretribulation rapture of the saints and a premillennial return of Christ.*

* * *

CONFESSION OF FAITH (NEW TESTAMENT ASSOCIATION OF INDEPENDENT BAPTIST CHURCHES)

I. CONCERNING THE SCRIPTURES

We believe that the Bible, sixty-six books in the Old and New Testaments, is without error in its original writing;[1] its author was God[2] using Spirit-guided men,[3] being thereby verbally and plenarily inspired;[4] it is the sole authority for faith and practice.[5]

Some places where taught: [1]Prov. 30:5, 6; John 17:17; Rev, 22:18, 19. [2]II Pet. 1:19-21; Acts 3:21; Jude 3; Heb. 1:1-3. [3]II Pet. 1:19-21; II Sam. 23:2; Acts 1:16; I Cor. 2:13, 14. [4]II Tim. 3:16; Matt. 5:18; Gal. 3:16. [5]II Tim. 3:15; Rom. 1:16; I Cor. 10:6-12; Eph. 6:17; I Tim 5:18; II Tim 3:17; II Pet. 3:15, 16; John 10:35; Acts 17:11; I John 4:1.

CONFESSION OF FAITH (NEW TESTAMENT ASSOCIATION
OF INDEPENDENT BAPTIST CHURCHES) (continued)

II. CONCERNING THE TRUE GOD

We believe that there is one, and only one living and true God,[1] an infinite, eternal, self-existing, perfect Spirit;[2] He is a personal Being, the creator and upholder of the universe;[3] in the unity of the Godhead there are three persons, the Father, and Son, and the Holy Spirit,[4] equal in essence and in every divine perfection[5] but having distinct work.[6]

Some places where taught: [1]Deut. 6:4, 5; Jer. 10:10. [2]John 4:24; James 1:17; Hab. 1:12. [3]Heb. 3:4; Ps. 139:1-16. [4]Matt. 28:19; Matt. 3:16, 17; II Cor. 13:14; Ps. 2:2; Isa. 48:16 (ASV); Isa. 63:10. [5]John 10:30; John 17:5; Phil. 2:5, 6; I Cor. 8:6. [6]John 3:16; John 15:26.

III. CONCERNING CREATION

We believe in the Genesis account of Creation and that it is to be accepted literally and not figuratively;[1] that the six days of creation in Genesis chapter one were solar, that is twenty-four hour, days;[2] that all animal and vegetable life was made directly and God's established law is that they bring forth only "after their kind",[3] that man was created directly in God's own image and after His own likeness and did not evolve from any lower form of life.[4]

Some places where taught: [1]Gen. 1:1-2:25; Heb. 11:3; John 1:3: Col. 1:16-17: Ps. 33:6-9; Neh. 9:6; Rev. 4:11. [2]Ex. 20:11; 31:17. [3]Gen. 1:11, 12, 21, 24, 25. [4]Gen. 1:26.

VIII. CONCERNING THE LOCAL CHURCH

We believe that a local, visible church[1] is a congregation of baptized believers[2] associated together by a common faith and fellowship in the Gospel; observing the ordinances of Christ[3] and governed by His Word;[4] seeking to extend the Gospel to the ends of the earth; that its only Scriptural officers are bishops (or pastors) and deacons, whose qualifications, claims and duties are defined in the Epistles to Timothy and Titus.[5]

Some places where taught: [1]Matt. 18:17; Acts 5:11; Acts 8:1. [2]Acts 2:41, 42. [3]Matt. 28:19, 20; I Cor. 11:23, 24; Heb. 10:25. [4]II Tim. 3:15, 16. [5]I Tim. 3:1-16; Titus 1:5-9.

IX. CONCERNING A GOSPEL CHURCH IN ITS INDEPENDENCE AND RELATIONSHIPS

We believe that the local visible church of Christ is a voluntary and independent autonomous group of baptized believers;[1] that it is a pure democracy, which organically can join nothing, and that it has the power and right within itself to confess its own faith in accordance with the New Testament;[2] and that each congregation recognizes its own democratic self-containing government as its highest authority for carrying out the will of the Lord Jesus Christ.[3]

Some places where taught: [1]Matt. 18:15-18; I Cor. 5:4, 5, 13. [2]I Tim. 3:15; Jude 3; Rev. 2 and 3. [3]Matt. 18:15-18; Acts 6:3-5; I Cor. 5:4, 5, 13; I Tim. 3:15.

X. CONCERNING BAPTISM AND THE LORD'S SUPPER

We believe that both Christian baptism and the Lord's Supper are each a memorial, a symbol and a prophecy.[1] We believe that Christian baptism is the immersion in

water of a believer,[2] in the name of the Father, the Son, and the Holy Ghost;[3] to show forth, in a solemn and beautiful figure, our faith in the crucified, buried, and risen Savior, with its effect in our death to sin and resurrection to a new life;[4] that it is prerequisite to the privileges of church membership; and a prerequisite to the Lord's Supper;[5] in which the members of the Church by the use of bread and fruit of the vine commemorate together the death of Christ;[6] preceded always by solemn self-examination.[7]

Some places where taught: [1]Rom 6:3, 4; I Pet. 3:21. [2]Acts 8:36-39; John 3:22, 23; 4:1, Matt 28:19; Mark 16:16; Acts 2:38; 8:12; 16:32-34; 18:8. [3]Matt. 28:19. [4]Rom. 6:4; Col. 2:12; I Pet. 3:20, 21; Acts 22:16. [5]Acts 2:41, 42; Matt. 28:19, 20. [6]I Cor. 11:26; Matt. 26:26-29. [7]I Cor. 11:28; 5:1, 8; 11:17-32.

XI. CONCERNING THE LORD'S DAY

We believe that the first day of the week in the Lord's Day, and is a Christian institution;[1] it is to be kept sacred to spiritual purposes by abstaining from all unnecessary secular labor and recreation, for it commemorates the resurrection of the Lord Jesus Christ from the dead;[2] by the devout, observance of all the means of growing in grace, both private and public[3] and by predicting the rest that remaineth for the people of God.[4]

Some places where taught: [1]Acts 20:7; Col. 2:16, 17; John 20:19; I Cor. 16:1, 2. [2]Acts 20:7; Mark 16:9; John 20:19. [3]Heb. 10:24, 25. [4]Heb. 4:3-11.

XII. CONCERNING CIVIL GOVERNMENT AND RELIGIOUS LIBERTY

We believe that civil government is of divine appointment, for the interests and good order of human society;[1] and that civil authorities are to be prayed for, conscientiously honored and obeyed;[2] except only in the things opposed by the Word of God, which reveals the will of our Lord Jesus Christ,[3] Who is the only Lord of the conscience, and the Prince of the kings of the earth;[4] and that church and state should be separate, the state owing the church protection and full freedom; no ecclesiastical group or denomination should be preferred above another by the state;[6] the state should not impose taxes for the support of any form of religion; a free church in a free state is the Christian ideal.[7]

Some places where taught: [1]Rom. 13:1-7. [2]Matt. 22:21; Titus 3:1; I Pet. 2:13, 14; I Tim. 2:1-3. [3]Acts 5:29; Acts 4:18-20. [4]Matt. 23:10; Ps. 72:11; Ps. 2; Rom. 14:9-13. [5]I Tim. 2:1.2. [6]James 4:12. [7]Matt 22:21.

XIII. CONCERNING THE STATE OF THE RIGHTEOUS AND THE WICKED

We believe that there is a radical and essential difference between the righteous and the wicked;[1] that such only as through faith are justified in the name of the Lord Jesus, and sanctified by the Spirit of our God, are truly righteous in His sight;[2] while all such as continue in impenitence and unbelief are in His sight wicked,[3] and under condemnation, and that there will be a resurrection of the righteous and a resurrection of the unrighteous.

Some places where taught: [1]Mal. 3:18. [2]Rom. 1:17. [3]John 3:18. [4]Dan. 12:2; Matt. 7:13, 14; Luke 9:23-26.

XIV. CONCERNING FUTURE EVENTS

We believe the Scriptures teach that at death the spirit and soul of the believer pass instantly into the presence of Christ and remain in conscious joy until the resurrection of the body when Christ[1] comes for His own[2] the blessed hope of the believer is the imminent, personal, pre-tribulational, premillennial appearance of Christ to rapture the church,[3] His bride; His righteous judgments will then be poured out on an unbelieving world during the Tribulation (the seventieth week of Daniel), the last half of which is the Great Tribulation;[4] the climax of this fearful era will be the physical return of Jesus Christ to the earth in great glory to introduce the Davidic kingdom;[5] Israel will be saved and restored as a nation;[6] Satan will be bound and the curse will be lifted from the physical creation;[7] following the Millennium, the Great White Throne judgment will occur, at which time the bodies and souls of the wicked shall be reunited and cast into the Lake of Fire.[8]

Some places where taught: [1]II Cor. 5:8. [2]I Cor. 15:51-57. [3]Titus 2:13; I Thess. 4:14-17. [4]Matt 24:21. [5]Rev. 19:11-16. [6]Rom. 11:26, 27. [7]Rev. 20:2, 3. [8]Rev. 20:11-15.

XV. CONCERNING HERESY AND APOSTASY

We believe in total and complete separation as taught in the Word of God from all forms of heresy and ecclesiastical apostasy. We believe the Scripture teaches that we are to: 1. Try them.[1] 2. Mark them.[2] 3. Rebuke them.[3] 4. Have no fellowship.[4] 5. Withdraw ourselves.[5] 6. Receive them not.[6] 7. Have no company with him.[7] 8. Reject them.[8] 9. Separate ourselves.[9]

Some places where taught: [1]I John 4:1. [2]Rom. 16:17. [3]Titus 1:13. [4]Eph. 5:11. [5]II Thess. 3:6. [6]II John 10, 11. [7]II Thess. 3:14. [8]Titus 3:10. [9]II Cor. 6:17.

Notes: *Adopted in 1966 as part of the association's constitution, this confession emphasizes the verbal plenary inspiration of scripture, the literalism of the creation account in the book of Genesis, the pretribulation rapture of the saints, premillennialism, and separation from those considered apostate Christians.*

*   *   *

PREAMBLE (TO THE CONSTITUTION OF THE NORTH AMERICAN BAPTIST CONFERENCE)

We, as New Testament Baptists, affirm our faith in the Lord Jesus Christ for our salvation and believe in those great distinctive principles for which Baptists have lived and died, such as:

1. Soul liberty;
2. The inspired authority of the Scriptures in matters of faith and conduct;
3. The separation of Church and State;
4. The Revelation of God through Jesus Christ as only Savior and Lord;
5. Regenerated church membership;
6. Believer's baptism by immersion;
7. The congregational form of church government; and

8. The proclamation of the Gospel throughout all the world, and we do hereby set forth and declare the following as our Constitution and By-Laws.

Notes: *This brief statement emphasizes a few Baptist distinctives.*

*   *   *

ARTICLES OF FAITH (UNION ASSOCIATION OF REGULAR BAPTIST CHURCHES)

1. We believe in one true and living God, Father, Son, and Holy Ghost and these three are one.
2. We believe that the Old and New Testaments Scriptures are the written word of God, and the only rule of faith and practice.
3. We believe in the doctrine of election by grace.
4. We believe in the doctrine of original sin, and man's impotency to rescue himself from the fallen state he is in by nature by his own free will ability.
5. We believe that sinners are called, converted, regenerated and sanctified by the Holy Spirit and all are so regenerated and born again by the Spirit of God shall never fall finally away.
6. We believe sinners are justified in the sight of God only by the imputed righteousness of Jesus Christ.
7. We believe that baptism, the Lord's Supper and feet washing are ordinances of Jesus Christ and that true believers are the only proper subjects of these ordinances and we believe the only true mode of baptism is by immersion.
8. We believe in the resurrection of the dead and a general judgment and that the joys of the righteous and the punishment of the wicked will be eternal.
9. We believe no minister has the right to administer the ordinances of the Gospel, except such as are regularly called, and come under the imposition of hands by a presbytery of the church.

Notes: *Regular Baptists follow a Calvinist doctrine of election and perseverance of the saints. They practice foot washing.*

*   *   *

BAPTIST FAITH AND MESSAGE (1925) (SOUTHERN BAPTIST CONVENTION)

REPORT OF COMMITTEE ON BAPTIST FAITH AND MESSAGE

Your committee beg leave to report as follows:

Your committee recognize that they were appointed "to consider the advisability of issuing another statement of the Baptist Faith and Message, and to report at the next Convention."

In pursuance of the instructions of the Convention, and in consideration of the general denominational situation, your committee have decided to recommend the New Hampshire Confession of Faith, revised at certain points, and with some additional articles growing out of present

BAPTIST FAITH AND MESSAGE (1925) (SOUTHERN
BAPTIST CONVENTION) (continued)

needs, for approval by the Convention, in the event a
statement of the Baptist faith and message is deemed
necessary at this time.

The present occasion for a reaffirmation of Christian
fundamentals is the prevalence of naturalism in the
modern teaching and preaching of religion. Christianity is
supernatural in its origin and history. We repudiate every
theory of religion which denies the supernatural elements
in our faith.

As introductory to the doctrinal articles, we recommend
the adoption by the Convention of the following statement
of the historic Baptist conception of the nature and
function of confessions of faith in our religious and
denominational life, believing that some such statement
will clarify the atmosphere and remove some causes of
misunderstanding, friction, and apprehension. Baptists
approve and circulate confessions of faith with the
following understandings, namely:

(1) That they constitute a consensus of opinion of some
Baptist body, large or small, for the general instruction and guidance of our own people and others
concerning those articles of the Christian faith which
are most surely held among us. They are not
intended to add anything to the simple conditions of
salvation revealed in the New Testament, viz.,
repentance towards God and faith in Jesus Christ as
Saviour and Lord.

(2) That we do not regard them as complete statements
of our faith, having any quality of finality or
infallibility. As in the past so in the future Baptists
should hold themselves free to revise their statements
of faith as may seem to them wise and expedient at
any time.

(3) That any group of Baptists, large or small, have the
inherent right to draw up for themselves and publish
to the world a confession of their faith whenever they
may think it advisable to do so.

(4) That the sole authority for faith and practice among
Baptists is the Scriptures of the Old and New
Testaments. Confessions are only guides in interpre-
tation, having no authority over the conscience.

(5) That they are statements of religious convictions,
drawn from the Scriptures, and are not to be used to
hamper freedom of thought or investigation in other
realms of life.

THE SCRIPTURES

1. We believe that the Holy Bible was written by men
divinely inspired, and is a perfect treasure of heavenly instruction; that it has God for its author,
salvation for its end, and truth, without any mixture
of error, for its matter; that it reveals the principles
by which God will judge us; and therefore is, and
will remain to the end of the world, the true center of
Christian union, and the supreme standard by which
all human conduct, creeds and religious opinions
should be tried.

GOD

2. There is one and only one living and true God, an
intelligent, spiritual and personal Being, the Creator,
Preserver and Ruler of the universe, infinite in
holiness and all other perfections, to whom we owe
the highest love, reverence and obedience. He is
revealed to us as Father, Son and Holy Spirit, each
with distinct personal attributes, but without division
of nature, essence or being.

THE FALL OF MAN

3. Man was created by the special act of God, as
recorded in Genesis. "So God created man in his
own image, in the image of God created he him;
male and female created he them." (Gen. 1:27).
"And the Lord God formed man of the dust of the
ground, and breathed into his nostrils the breath of
life; and man became a living soul." (Gen. 2:7.) He
was created in a state of holiness under the law of his
maker, but, through the temptation of Satan he
transgressed the command of God and fell from his
original holiness and righteousnss; whereby his
posterity inherit a nature corrupt and in bondage to
sin, are under condemnation, and as soon as they are
capable of moral action, become actual transgressors.

THE WAY OF SALVATION

4. The salvation of sinners is wholly of grace, through
the mediatorial office of the Son of God, who by the
Holy Spirit was born of the Virgin Mary and took
upon him our nature, yet without sin; honored the
divine law by his personal obedience, and made
atonement for our sins by his death. Being risen from
the dead, he is now enthroned in heaven, and,
uniting in his person the tenderest sympathies with
divine perfections, he is in every way qualified to be a
compassionate and all-sufficient Saviour.

JUSTIFICATION

5. Justification is God's gracious and full acquittal
upon principles of righteousness of all sinners who
believe in Christ. This blessing is bestowed, not in
consideration of any works of righteousness which
we have done, but through the redemption that is
and through Jesus Christ. It brings us into a state of
most blessed peace and favor with God, and secures
every other needed blessing.

THE FREENESS OF SALVATION

6. The blessings of salvation are made free to all by the
Gospel. It is the duty of all to accept them by
penitent and obedient faith. Nothing prevents the
salvation of the greatest sinner except his own
voluntary refusal to accept Jesus Christ as teacher,
Saviour and Lord.

REGENERATION

7. Regeneration or the new birth is a change of heart
wrought by the Holy Spirit, whereby we become
partakers of the divine nature and a holy disposition
is given, leading to the love and practice of righteousness. It is a work of God's free grace condi-

tioned upon faith in Christ and made manifest by the fruit which we bring forth to the glory of God.

REPENTANCE OF FAITH

8. We believe that repentance and faith are sacred duties, and also inseparable graces, wrought in our souls by the regenerating Spirit of God; whereby being deeply convinced of our guilt, danger, and helplessness, and of the way of salvation by Christ, we turn to God with unfeigned contrition, confession, and supplication for mercy; at the same time heartily receiving the Lord Jesus Christ as our Prophet, Priest and King, and relying on him alone as the only and all-sufficient Saviour.

GOD'S PURPOSE OF GRACE

9. Election is the gracious purpose of God, according to which he regenerates, sanctifies and saves sinners. It is perfectly consistent with the free agency of man, and comprehends all the means in connection with the end. It is a most glorious display of God's sovereign goodness, and is infinitely wise, holy and unchangeable. It excludes boasting and promotes humility. It encourages the use of means in the highest degree.

SANCTIFICATION

10. Sanctification is the process by which the regenerate gradually attain to moral and spiritual perfection through the presence and power of the Holy Spirit dwelling in their hearts. It continues throughout the earthly life, and is accomplished by the use of all the ordinary means of grace, and particularly by the Word of God.

PERSEVERANCE

11. All real believers endure to the end. Their continuance in well-doing is the mark which distinguishes them from mere professors. A special Providence cares for them, and they are kept by the power of God through faith unto salvation.

A GOSPEL CHURCH

12. A church of Christ is a congregation of baptized believers, associated by covenant in the faith and fellowship of the gospel; observing the ordinances of Christ, governed by his law, and exercising the gifts, rights and privileges invested in them by his word, and seeking to extend the Gospel to the ends of the earth. Its Scriptural officers are bishops or elders and deacons.

BAPTISM AND THE LORD'S SUPPER

13. Christian baptism is the immersion of a believer in water in the name of the Father, the Son and the Holy Spirit. The act is a symbol of our faith in a crucified, buried and risen Saviour. It is prerequisite to the privileges of a church relation and to the Lord's Supper, in which the members of the church, by the use of bread and wine, commemorate the dying love of Christ.

THE LORD'S DAY

14. The first day of the week is the Lord's day. It is a Christian institution for regular observance. It commemorates the resurrection of Christ from the dead, and should be employed in exercises of worship and spirtual devotion, both public and private, and by refraining from worldly amusements, and resting from secular employments, works of necessity and mercy only excepted.

THE RIGHTEOUS AND THE WICKED

15. There is a radical and essential difference between the righteous and wicked. Those only who are justified through the name of the Lord Jesus Christ and sanctified by the Holy Spirit are truly righteous in his sight. Those who continue in impenitence and unbelief are in his sight wicked and are under condemnation. This distinction between the righteous and the wicked holds in and after death, and will be made manifest at the judgment when final and everlasting awards are made to all men.

THE RESURRECTION

16. The Scriptures clearly teach that Jesus rose from the dead. His grave was emptied of its contents. He appeared to the disciples after his resurrection in many convincing manifestations. He now exists in his glorified body at God's right hand. There will be a resurrection of the righteous and the wicked. The bodies of the righteous will conform to the glorious spiritual body of Jesus.

THE RETURN OF THE LORD

17. The New Testament teaches in many places the visible and personal return of Jesus to this earth. "This same Jesus which is taken up from you into Heaven, shall so come in like manner as ye have seen him go into Heaven." The time of his coming is not revealed. "Of that day and hour knoweth no one, no, not the angels in heaven, but my Father only." (Matt. 24:36). It is the duty of all believers to live in readiness for his coming and by diligence in good works to make manifest to all men the reality and power of their hope in Christ.

RELIGIOUS LIBERTY

18. God alone is Lord of the conscience, and he has left it free from the doctrines and commandments of men which are contrary to his word or not contained in it. Church and state should be separate. The state owes to the church protection and full freedom in the pursuit of its spiritual ends. In providing for such freedom no ecclesiastical group or denomination should be favored by the state more than others. Civil government being ordained of God, it is the duty of Christians to render loyal obedience thereto in all things not contrary to the revealed will of God. The church should not resort to the civil power to carry on its work. The Gospel of Christ contemplates spiritual means alone for the pursuit of its ends. The state has no right to impose penalties for religious opinions of any kind. The state has no right to impose taxes for the support of any form of religion. A free church in a free state is the Christian ideal, and this implies the right of free and unhindered access to God on the part of all men, and the right to

form and propagate opinions in the sphere of religion without interference by the civil power.

PEACE AND WAR

19. It is the duty of Christians to seek peace with all men on principles of righteousness. In accordance with the spirit and teachings of Christ they should do all in their power to put an end to war.

    The true remedy for the war spirit is the pure gospel of our Lord. The supreme need of the world is the acceptance of his teachings in all the affairs of men and nations, and the practical application of his law of love.

    We urge Christian people throughout the world to pray for the reign of the Prince of Peace, and to oppose everything to provoke war.

EDUCATION

20. Christianity is the religion of enlightenment and intelligence. In Jesus Christ are hidden all the treasures of wisdom and knowledge. All sound learning is therefore a part of our Christian heritage. The new birth opens all human faculties and creates a thirst for knowledge. An adequate system of schools is necessary to a complete spiritual program for Christ's people. The cause of education in the Kingdom of Christ is co-ordinate with the causes of missions and general benevolence, and should receive along with these the liberal support of the churches.

SOCIAL SERVICE

21. Every Christian is under obligation to seek to make the will of Christ regnant in his own life and in human society; to oppose in the spirit of Christ every form of greed, selfishness and vice; to provide for the orphaned, the aged, the helpless, and the sick; to seek to bring industry, government and society as a whole under the sway of the principles of righteousness, truth and brotherly love; to promote these ends Christians should be ready to work with all men of good will in any good cause, always being careful to act in the spirit of love without compromising their loyalty to Christ and his truth. All means and methods used in social service for the amelioration of society and the establishment of righteousness among men must finally depend on the regeneration of the individual by the saving grace of God in Christ Jesus.

CO-OPERATION

22. Christ's people should, as occasion requires, organize such associations and conventions as may best secure co-operation for the great objects of the Kingdom of God. Such organizations have no authority over each other or over the churches. They are voluntary and advisory bodies designed to elicit, combine and direct the energies of our people in the most effective manner. Individual members of New Testament churches should co-operate with each other, and the churches themselves should co-operate with each other, in carrying forward the missionary, educational and benevolent program for the extension of Christ's Kingdom. Christian unity in the New Testament sense is spiritual harmony and voluntary co-operation for common ends by various Christian denominations, when the end to be attained is itself justified, and when such co-operation involves no violation by conscience or compromise of loyalty to Christ and his Word as revealed in the New Testament.

EVANGELISM AND MISSIONS

23. It is the duty of every Christian man and woman, and the duty of every church of Christ, to seek to extend the gospel to the ends of the earth. The new birth of man's spirit of God's Holy Spirit means the birth of love for others. Missionary effort on the part of all rests thus upon a spiritual necessity of the regenerate life. It is also expressly and repeatedly commanded in the teachings of Christ. It is the duty of every child of God to seek constantly to win the lost to Christ by personal effort and by all other methods sanctioned by the Gospel of Christ.

STEWARDSHIP

24. God is the source of all blessings, temporal and spiritual; all that we have and are we owe to him. We have a spiritual debtorship to the whole world, a holy trusteeship in the Gospel, and a binding stewardship in our possessions. We are therefore under obligation to serve him with our time, talents and material possessions; and should recognize all these as entrusted to us to use for the glory of God and helping others. Christians should cheerfully, regularly, systematically, proportionately, and liberally contribute of their means to advancing the Redeemer's cause on earth.

THE KINGDOM

25. The Kingdom of God is the reign of God in the heart and life of the individual in every human relationship, and in every form and institution of organized human society. The chief means for promoting the Kingdom of God on earth are preaching the Gospel of Christ, and teaching the principles of righteousness contained therein. The Kingdom of God will be complete when every thought and will of man shall be brought into captivity to the will of Christ. And it is the duty of all Christ's people to pray and labor continually that his Kingdom may come and his will be done on earth as it is in heaven.

Since matters of science have no proper place in a religious confession of faith, and since it is desirable that our attitude towards science be clearly understood, your committee deem it proper to submit the following statement on the relation between science and religion, adopted in 1923 by this Convention at Kansas City, and request that it be published in the minutes of the Convention.

SCIENCE AND RELIGION

1. We recognize the greatness and value of the service which modern science is rendering to the cause of truth in uncovering the facts of the natural and the

Christian religion. We have no interest or desire in covering up any fact in any realm of research. But we do protest against certain unwarranted procedures on the part of some so-called scientists. First, in making discoveries, or alleged discoveries, in physical nature, a convenient weapon of attack upon the facts of religion; second, using the particular sciences, such as psychology, biology, geology, and various others, as if they necessarily contained knowledge pertaining to the realm of the Christian religion, setting aside the supernatural; third, teaching as facts what are merely hypotheses. The evolution doctrine has long been a working hypothesis of science, and will probably continue to be, because of its apparent simplicity in explaining the universe. But its best exponents freely admit that the causes of the origin of species have not been traced, nor has any proof been forthcoming that man is not the direct creation of God as recorded in Genesis. We protest against the imposition of this theory upon the minds of our children in denominational, or public schools, as if it were a definite and established truth of science. We insist that this and all other theories be dealt with in a truly scientific way, that is, in careful conformity to establish facts.

2. We record again our unwavering adherence to the supernatural elements in the Christian religion. The Bible is God's revelation of himself through men moved by the Holy Spirit, and is our sufficient, certain and authoritative guide in religion. Jesus Christ was born of the Virgin Mary, through the power of the Holy Spirit. He was the divine and eternal Son of God. He wrought miracles, healing the sick, casting out demons, raising the dead. He died as the vicarious, atoning Saviour of the world, and was buried. He arose again from the dead. The tomb was emptied of its contents. In his risen body he appeared many times to his disciples. He ascended to the right hand of the Father. He will come again in person, the same Jesus who ascended from the Mount of Olives.

3. We believe that adherence to the above truths and facts is a necessary condition of service of teachers in our Baptist schools. These facts of Christianity in no way conflict with any fact of science. We do not sit in judgment upon the scientific views of teachers of science. We grant them the same freedom of research in their realm that we claim for ourselves in the religious realm. But we do insist upon a positive content of faith in accordance with the preceding statement as a qualification for acceptable service in Baptist schools. The supreme issue today is between naturalism and super-naturalism. We stand unalterably for the supernatural in Christianity. Teachers in our schools should be careful to free themselves from any suspicion of disloyalty on this point. In the present period of agitation and unrest they are obligated to make their position clear. We pledge our support to all schools and teachers who are thus loyal to the facts of Christianity as revealed in the Scriptures.

Signed by the Committee,

E. Y. MULLINS, Chairman;

S. M. BROWN,

W. J. McGLOTHLIN,

E. C. DARGAN,

L. R. SCARBOROUGH.

Notes: *The preamble of this statement, derived in part from the New Hampshire Confession, establishes the limited context for the statement's use. The statement should be compared with its revision adopted in 1963. The paragraphs on science are of particular importance. They constitute a significant appraisal of the creation-evolution controversy of the 1920s and were adopted by the convention meeting in Memphis, Tennessee, during the height of the debate on the Bible's account of the natural world.*

* * *

BAPTIST FAITH AND MESSAGE (1963) (SOUTHERN BAPTIST CONVENTION)

COMMITTEE ON BAPTIST FAITH AND MESSAGE

The 1962 session of the Southern Baptist Convention, meeting in San Francisco, California, adopted the following motion:

"Since the report of the Committee on Statement of Baptist Faith and Message was adopted in 1925, there have been various statements from time to time which have been made, but no overall statement which might be helpful at this time as suggested in Section 2 of that report, or introductory statement which might be used as an interpretation of the 1925 Statement.

"We recommend, therefore, that the president of this Convention be requested to call a meeting of the men now serving as presidents of the various state conventions that would qualify as a member of the Southern Baptist Convention committee under Bylaw 18 to present to the Convention in Kansas City some similar statement which shall serve as information to the churches, and which may serve as guidelines to the various agencies of the Southern Baptist Conventions. It is understood that any group or individual may approach this committee to be of service. The expenses of this committee shall be borne by the Convention Operating Budget."

Your committee thus constituted begs leave to present its report as follows:

Throughout its work your committee has been conscious of the contribution made by the statement of "The Baptist Faith and Message" adopted by the Southern Baptist Convention in 1925. It quotes with approval its affirmation that "Christianity is supernatural in its origin and history. We repudiate every theory of religion which denies the supernatural elements in our faith."

Furthermore, it concurs in the introductory "statement of the historic Baptist conception of the nature and function of confessions of faith in our religious and denominational life. . . . " It is, therefore, quoted in full as a part of this report to the Convention:

"(1) That they constitute a consensus of opinion of some Baptist body, large or small, for the general instruction and guidance of our own people and others concerning those articles of the Christian faith, which are most surely held among us. They are not intended to add anything to the simple conditions of salvation revealed in the New Testament, viz., repentance towards God and faith in Jesus Christ as Saviour and Lord.

"(2) That we do not regard them as complete statements of our faith, having any quality of finality or infallibility. As in the past so in the future, Baptists should hold themselves free to revise their statements of faith as may seem to them wise and expedient at any time.

"(3) That any group of Baptists, large or small, have the inherent right to draw up for themselves and publish to the world a confession of their faith whenever they may think it advisable to do so.

"(4) That the sole authority for faith and practice among Baptists is the Scriptures of the Old and New Testaments. Confessions are only guides in interpretation, having no authority over the conscience.

"(5) That they are statements of religious convictions, drawn from the Scriptures, and are not to be used to hamper freedom of thought or investigation in the other realms of life."

The 1925 Statement recommended "the New Hampshire Confession of Faith, revised at certain points, and with some additional articles growing out of certain needs . . . " Your present committee has adopted the same pattern. It has sought to build upon the structure of the 1925 Statement, keeping in mind the "certain needs" of our generation. At times it has reproduced sections of that statement without change. In other instances it has substituted words for clarity or added sentences for emphasis. At certain points it has combined articles, with minor changes in wording, to endeavor to relate certain doctrines to each other. In still others—e.g., "God" and "Salvation"—it has sought to bring together certain truths contained throughout the 1925 Statement in order to relate them more clearly and concisely. In no case has it sought to delete from or to add to the basic contents of the 1925 Statement.

Baptists are a people who profess a living faith. This faith is rooted and grounded in Jesus Christ who is "the same yesterday, and to-day, and for ever." Therefore, the sole authority for faith and practice among Baptists is Jesus Christ whose will is revealed in the Holy Scriptures.

A living faith must experience a growing understanding of truth and must be continually interpreted and related to the needs of each new generation. Throughout their history Baptist bodies, both large and small, have issued statements of faith which comprise a consensus of their beliefs. Such statements have never been regarded as complete, infallible statements of faith, nor as official creeds carrying mandatory authority. Thus this generation of Southern Baptists is in historic succession of intent and purpose as it endeavors to state for its time and theological climate those articles of the Christian faith which are most surely held among us.

Baptists emphasize the soul's competency before God, freedom of religion, and the priesthood of the believer. However, this emphasis should not be interpreted to mean that there is an absence of certain definite doctrines that Baptists believe, cherish, and with which they have been and are now closely identified.

It is the purpose of this statement of faith and message to set forth certain teachings which we believe.

I. THE SCRIPTURES

The Holy Bible was written by men divinely inspired and is the record of God's revelation of Himself to man. It is a perfect treasure of divine instruction. It has God for its author, salvation for its end, and truth, without any mixture of error, for its matter. It reveals the principles by which God judges us; and therefore is, and will remain to the end of the world, the true center of Christian union, and the supreme standard by which all human conduct, creeds, and religious opinions should be tried. The criterion by which the Bible is to be interpreted is Jesus Christ.

II. GOD

There is one and only one living and true God. He is an intelligent, spiritual, and personal Being, the Creator, Redeemer, Preserver, and Ruler of the universe. God is infinite in holiness and all other perfections. To him we owe the highest love, reverence, and obedience. The eternal God reveals Himself to us as Father, Son, and Holy Spirit, with distinct personal attributes, but without division of nature, essence, or being.

1. GOD THE FATHER. God as Father reigns with providential care over His universe, His creatures, and the flow of the stream of human history according to the purpose of His grace. He is all powerful, all loving, and all wise. God is Father in truth to those who become children of God through faith in Jesus Christ. He is fatherly in his attitude toward all men.

2. GOD THE SON. Christ is the eternal Son of God. In His incarnation as Jesus Christ He was conceived of the Holy Spirit and born of the virgin Mary. Jesus perfectly revealed and did the will of God, taking upon Himself the demands and necessities of human nature and identifying Himself completely with mankind yet without sin. He honored the divine law by His personal obedience, and in His death on the cross He made provision for the redemption of men from sin. He was raised from the dead with a glorified body and appeared to His disciples as the person who was with them before His crucifixion. He ascended into heaven and is now exalted at the right hand of God where He is the One Mediator, partaking of the nature of God and of man, and in whose Person is effected the reconciliation between

God and man. He will return in power and glory to judge the world and to consummate His redemptive mission. He now dwells in all believers as the living and ever present Lord.

3. GOD THE HOLY SPIRIT. The Holy Spirit is the Spirit of God. He inspired holy men of old to write the Scriptures. Through illumination He enables men to understand truth. He exalts Christ. He convicts of sin, of righteousness and of judgment. He calls men to the Saviour, and effects regeneration. He cultivates Christian character, comforts believers and bestows the spiritual gifts by which they serve God through His church. He seals the believer unto the day of final redemption. His presence in the Christian is the assurance of God to bring the believer into the fulness of the stature of Christ. He enlightens and empowers the believer and the church in worship, evangelism, and service.

III. MAN

Man was created by the special act of God, in His own image, and is the crowning work of His creation. In the beginning man was innocent of sin and was endowed by His Creator with freedom of choice. By his free choice man sinned against God and brought sin into the human race. Through the temptation of Satan man transgressed the command of God, and fell from his original innocence; whereby his posterity inherit a nature and an environment inclined toward sin, and as they are capable of moral action become transgressors and are under condemnation. Only the grace of God can bring man into His holy fellowship and enable man to fulfil the creative purpose of God. The sacredness of human personality is evident in that God created man in His own image, and in that Christ died for man; therefore every man possesses dignity and is worthy of respect and Christian love.

IV. SALVATION

Salvation involves the redemption of the whole man, and is offered freely to all who accept Jesus Christ as Lord and Saviour, who by His own blood obtained eternal redemption for the believer. In its broadest sense salvation includes regeneration, sanctification, and glorification.

1. Regeneration, or the new birth, is a work of God's grace whereby believers become new creatures in Christ Jesus. It is a change of heart wrought by the Holy Spirit through conviction of sin, to which the sinner responds in repentance toward God and faith in the Lord Jesus Christ.

   Repentance and faith are inseparable experiences of grace. Repentance is a genuine turning from sin toward God. Faith is the acceptance of Jesus Christ and commitment of the entire personality to Him as Lord and Saviour. Justification is God's gracious and full acquittal upon principles of his righteousness of all sinners who repent and believe in Christ. Justification brings the believer into a relationship of peace and favor with God.

2. Sanctification is the experience, beginning in regeneration, by which the believer is set apart to God's purposes, and is enabled to progress toward moral and spiritual perfection through the presence and power of the Holy Spirit dwelling in him. Growth in grace should continue throughout the regenerate person's life.

3. Glorification is the culmination of salvation and is the final blessed and abiding state of the redeemed.

V. GOD'S PURPOSE OF GRACE

Election is the gracious purpose of God, according to which He regenerates, sanctifies, and glorifies sinners. It is consistent with the free agency of man and comprehends all the means in connection with the end. It is a glorious display of God's sovereign goodness, and is infinitely wise, holy, and unchangeable. It excludes boasting and promotes humility.

All true believers endure to the end. Those whom God has accepted in Christ, and sanctified by His Spirit, will never fall away from the state of grace, but shall persevere to the end. Believers may fall into sin through neglect and temptation, where by they grieve the Spirit, impair their graces and comforts, bring reproach on the cause of Christ, and temporal judgments on themselves, yet they shall be kept by the power of God through faith unto salvation.

VI. THE CHURCH

A New Testament church of the Lord Jesus Christ is a local body of baptized believers who are associated by covenant in the faith and fellowship of the gospel, observing the two ordinances of Christ, committed to His teachings, exercising the gifts, rights, and privileges invested in them by His Word, and seeking to extend the gospel to the ends of the earth.

The church is an autonomous body, operating through democratic processes under the Lordship of Jesus Christ. In such a congregation, members are equally responsible. Its Scriptural officers are pastors and deacons.

The New Testament speaks also of the church as the body of Christ which includes all the redeemed of all the ages.

VII. BAPTISM AND THE LORD'S SUPPER

Christian baptism is the immersion of a believer in water in the name of the Father, the Son, and the Holy Spirit. It is an act of obedience symbolizing the believer's faith in a crucified, buried, and risen Saviour, the believer's death to sin, the burial of the old life, and the resurrection to walk in newness of life in Christ Jesus. It is a testimony to his faith in the final resurrection of the dead. Being a church ordinance, it is prerequisite to the privileges of church membership and to the Lord's Supper.

The Lord's Supper is a symbolic act of obedience whereby members of the church, through partaking of the bread and the fruit of the vine, memorialize the death of the Redeemer and anticipate His second coming.

VIII. THE LORD'S DAY

The first day of the week is the Lord's Day. It is a Christian institution for regular observance. It commemorates the resurrection of Christ from the dead and should be employed in exercises of worship and spiritual devotion, both public and private, and by refraining from worldly amusements, and resting from secular employments, work of necessity and mercy only being excepted.

IX. THE KINGDOM

The kingdom of God includes both His general sovereignty over the universe and His particular kingship over men who willfully acknowledge Him as King. Particularly the kingdom is the realm of salvation into which men enter by trustful, childlike commitment to Jesus Christ. Christians ought to pray and to labor that the kingdom may come and God's will be done on earth. The full consummation of the kingdom awaits the return of Jesus Christ and the end of this age.

X. LAST THINGS

God, in His own time and in His own way, will bring the world to its appropriate end. Acording to His promise, Jesus Christ will return personally and visibly in glory to the earth; the dead will be raised; and Christ will judge all men in righteousness. The unrighteous will be consigned to hell, the place of everlasting punishment. The righteous in their resurrected and glorified bodies will receive their reward and will dwell forever in heaven with the Lord.

XI. EVANGELISM AND MISSIONS

It is the duty and privilege of every follower of Christ and of every church of the Lord Jesus Christ to endeavor to make disciples of all nations. The new birth of man's spirit by God's Holy Spirit means the birth of love for others. Missionary effort on the part of all rests thus upon a spiritual necessity of the regenerate life, and is expressly and repeatedly commanded in the teachings of Christ. It is the duty of every child of God to seek constantly to win the lost of God to Christ by personal effort and by all other methods in harmony with the gospel of Christ.

XII. EDUCATION

The cause of education in the kingdom of Christ is co-ordinate with the causes of missions and general benevolence and should receive along with these the liberal support of the churches. An adequate system of Christian schools is necessary to a complete spiritual program for Christ's people.

In Christian education there should be a proper balance between academic freedom and academic responsibility. Freedom in any orderly relationship of human life is always limited and never absolute. The freedom of a teacher in a Christian school, college, or seminary is limited by the preeminence of Jesus Christ, by the authoritative nature of the Scriptures, and by the distinct purpose for which the school exists.

XIII. STEWARDSHIP

God is the source of all blessings, temporal and spiritual; all that we have and are we owe to Him. Christians have a spiritual debtorship to the whole world, a holy trusteeship in the gospel, and a binding stewardship in their possessions. They are therefore under obligation to serve Him with their time, talents, and material possessions; and should recognize all these as entrusted to them to use for the glory of God and for helping others. According to the

Scriptures, Christians should contribute of their means cheerfully, regularly, systematically, proportionately, and liberally for the advancement of the Redeemer's cause on earth.

XIV. CO-OPERATION

Christ's people should, as occasion requires, organize such associations and conventions as may best secure co-operation for the great objects of the kingdom of God. Such organizations have no authority over one another or over the churches. They are voluntary and advisory bodies designed to elicit, combine, and direct the energies of our people in the most effective manner. Members of New Testament churches should co-operate with one another in carrying forward the missionary, educational, and benevolent ministries for the extension of Christ's kingdom. Christian unity in the New Testament sense is spiritual harmony and voluntary co-operation for common ends by various groups of Christ's people. Co-operation is desirable between the various Christian denominations, when the end to be attained is itself justified, and when such co-operation involves no violation of conscience or compromise of loyalty to Christ and his Word as revealed in the New Testament.

XV. THE CHRISTIAN AND THE SOCIAL ORDER

Every Christian is under obligation to make the will of Christ supreme in his own life and human society. Means and methods used for the improvement of society and the establishment of righteousness among men can be truly and permanently helpful only when they are rooted in the regeneration of the individual by the saving grace of God in Christ Jesus. The Christian should oppose in the spirit of Christ every form of greed, selfishness, and vice. He should work to provide for the orphaned, the needy, the aged, the helpless, and the sick. Every Christian should seek to bring industry, government, and society as a whole under the sway of the principles of righteousness, truth, and brotherly love. In order to promote these ends Christians should be ready to work with all men of good will in any good cause, always being careful to act in the spirit of love without compromising their loyalty to Christ and his truth.

XVI. PEACE AND WAR

It is the duty of Christians to seek peace with all men on principles of righteousness. In accordance with the spirit and teachings of Christ they should do all in their power to put an end to war.

The true remedy for the war spirit is the gospel of our Lord. The supreme need of the world is the acceptance of His teachings in all the affairs of man and nations, and the practical application of His law of love.

XVII. RELIGIOUS LIBERTY

God alone is Lord of the conscience, and He has left it free from the doctrines and commandments of men which are contrary to His Word or not contained in it. Church and state should be separate. The state owes to every church protection and full freedom in the pursuit of its spiritual ends. In providing for such freedom no ecclesiastical group or denomination should be favored by the state more than others. Civil government being ordained of God, it is the duty of Christians to render loyal obedience thereto in all things not contrary to the revealed will of God. The church should not resort to the civil power to carry on its work. The gospel of Christ contemplates spiritual means alone for the pursuit of its ends. The state has no right to impose penalties for religious opinions of any kind. The state has no right to impose taxes for the support of any form of religion. A free church in a free state is the Christian ideal, and this implies the right of free and unhindered access to God on the part of all men and the right to form and propagate opinions in the sphere of religion without interference by the civil power.

Notes: *In 1963 the Southern Baptist Convention adopted a revised form of the statement originally adopted in 1925. The lengthy item on science was dropped, and a more positive item on "The Christian and the Social Order" replaced the item "Social Service."*

*　　*　　*

STATEMENT OF FAITH (SOUTHWIDE BAPTIST FELLOWSHIP)

We believe in the verbal inspiration of the 66 books of the Bible in its original writings and that it is without error and is the sole authority in all matters of faith and practice.

We believe there is only one true God, existing in three Persons, Father, Son and Holy Spirit. These three are co-eternal and co-equal from all eternity, each with distinct personalities but of one essence.

We believe that Adam was created without sin but fell by disobedience and thus the whole race fell and is by nature spiritually dead and lost.

We believe that Jesus Christ is the Son of God, co-existent with the Father and the Holy Spirit, and that He came to the world, born of a virgin, shed His blood on Calvary as a vicarious substitute for all sin, that He was buried and rose again bodily and ascended to the right hand of the Father.

We believe in the Person work of the Holy Spirit which includes conviction of sin, regeneration of sinners, and indwelling believers.

We believe that a soul is saved when Christ is accepted as personal Saviour and Lord and the Holy Spirit imparts eternal life.

We believe that it is the plan of God for each believer to walk after the spirit and not fulfill the lusts of the flesh.

We believe in the eternal preservation and therefore the eternal perseverance of the saints.

We believe in the immersion of the believer in water to signify His death, burial, and resurrection and the believer's identification with Him.

We believe that a New Testament Church is a local group of baptized believers united for His purpose and the knowledge and spread of the Word including worldwide missions. We believe that it is completely self-determining and responsible only to Christ, the Head of the church. We believe it to be completely independent with no other

person, group, or body having any authority, right or intervention, or control in any form whatsoever over or within a local church. The Lord's Supper constitutes the other of the only two ordinances of the church.

We believe in the Premillennial Second Coming of the Lord, in the bodily resurrection of the righteous dead at His coming, and in an endless Heaven for all the redeemed and an endless punishment for the lost.

We believe the Revised Standard Version of the Bible is a perverted translation of the original languages, and that collaboration or participation with all forms of modernism, whether in the Nation Council of Churches or otherwise is wrong, and demands separation on our part.

Notes: *The Southwide Baptist Fellowship is among the most theologically conservative of Baptist bodies. It is premillennial in its eschatology and opposes the use of the Revised Standard Version of the Bible.*

*　　*　　*

Primitive Baptist

ABSTRACTS OF PRINCIPLES [*BANNER HERALD* (PROGRESSIVE)]

The editors of the Banner Herald subscribe to the following scriptural principles which have identified the cause of Bible truth in every generation, and pledge the purpose of this publication to be to the upholding and declaration of these Bible truths.

We believe in the only true and living God, and that there are three persons in the Godhead, Father, Son, and Holy Ghost, and that these agree in one, are co-equal, co-eternal, and co-existent.

We believe in the total depravity of the entire human family, and that man is unable to recover himself from his lost and ruined estate.

We believe Jesus Christ to be the Son of God, the only Saviour and Redeemer, and that salvation is by His grace and that alone.

We believe in particular, eternal and unconditional election, the effectual calling of the elect, and the final preservation of the saints.

We believe the scriptures of the Old and New Testaments to be the word of God, inspired and inerrant, and only rule of faith and practice.

We believe that Baptism and the Lord's Supper are ordinances of the Church of Jesus Christ, and that washing of the Saint's feet is an example to be kept, and that true believers, born of the Holy Spirit, are the only fit subjects of these ordinances. And that the only water baptism taught and recognized in the Bible is immersion or dipping.

We believe that no minister has the right to administer the ordinances of Baptism and the Lord's Supper but such as are regularly called by the God of Heaven and come under the imposition of hands by a presbytery.

ABSTRACTS OF PRINCIPLES [*BANNER HERALD* (PROGRESSIVE)] (continued)

We believe in the resurrection of the just and the unjust, that the just shall be raised, changed and fashioned like unto the glorious body of the Son of God, and dwell in heaven forever, soul and body reunited, and that the unjust shall be raised and consigned to eternal punishment.

Notes: *Doctrinally, the Primitive Baptists represent the assertion of a Calvinist theological perspective against both the general (Arminian) or free-will theological position and the mild Calvinism of the early Philadelphia and New Hampshire Confessions. Primitive Baptists emerged in the 1830s as a distinctive set of Baptist associations who rejected the new missionary societies, which did not have their base in the local church.*

Progressive Primitive Baptists are those associations which, in recent decades, have been most open to innovation in organization activities (and in particular, cooperative endeavors). Their theology remains very close to that of the "regulars," those Primitive Baptists holding a more lax position on predestination. This theology is evident in the statement of the Banner Herald, *the most prominent Progressive periodical.*

* * *

ARTICLES OF FAITH (COVENANTED BAPTIST CHURCH OF CANADA)

We believe that there is but one only true God, and that there is none other than He.—John xvii. 3; Deuteronomy vi. 4.

We believe that this God is Almighty, Eternal, Invisible, Incomprehensible.—1 Timothy i. 17.

We believe that this God is unspeakably perfect in all His attributes of Power, Wisdom, Truth, Holiness, Justice, Mercy and Love.

We believe that in the Godhead there are three Persons, the Father, the Word and the Holy Ghost, and these three are one.—1 John i. 5, 7.

We believe there will be a resurrection of the dead, both of the Just and of the Unjust.—John v. 25, 29.

We believe that because God in His own nature is holy and just, even so He is good and merciful; therefore all having sinned, none can be saved without the means of a Redeemer.—Job xxxiii. 24; Hebrews ix. 15.

We believe that Jesus Christ Himself is Lord and Redeemer.—1 Peter i. 18, 19.

We believe the great reason why the Lord did clothe Himself with our flesh and blood was that He might be capable of obtaining the Redemption, which before the world was ordained for us.—Hebrews ii. 15, 16; ix. 15; Ephesians ii. 10.

We believe that the time when He clothed Himself with our flesh was in the days of the reign of Caesar Augustus. Then, and not till then, was the Word made flesh.—Luke ii. 1, 2.

We believe therefore that this very child, as afore is testified, is both God and man, the Christ of the living God.—Luke i. 26-34.

We believe therefore the righteousness and redemption by which we that believe stand just before God, as saved from the curse of the law, is the righteousness and redemption that consists in the permanent acts and performances of this child Jesus, this God-man, the Lord's Christ; it consists in fulfilling the law for us to the utmost requirements of the justice of God.—Matthew i. 21; Daniel ix. 24; 1 Corinthians i. 30.

We believe that for the completing of this work He was always sinless, did always the things that pleased God's justice; that every one of His acts, both of doing and suffering and rising again from the dead, was really and infinitely perfect, being done by Him as God-man; the Godhead, which gave virtue to all the acts of the human nature, was then in perfect union with it when He hanged upon the cross for the sins of His people.—Romans iii. 22; Hebrews x. 14.

We believe that the righteousness that saveth the sinner from the wrath to come is properly and personally Christ's, and ours but as we have union with Him, God by grace imputing it to us.—1 Corinthians i. 30; Philippians iii. 8. 9.

HOW CHRIST IS MADE OURS.

We believe that being sinful creatures in ourselves, no good thing done by us can procure of God the imputation of the righteousness of Jesus Christ, but that the imputation thereof is an act of grace, a free gift, without our deserving.—Romans iii. 24-27; 2 Timothy i. 9.

We believe also that the power of imputing righteousness resteth in God only by Jesus Christ.—Romans iv. 6-8.

PREDESTINATION AND ELECTION.

We believe that God has freely ordained all things that come to pass, which doctrine is called Absolute Predestination.—Isaiah xlvi. 9, 10; Acts iv. 27, 28; ii. 22, 23.

We believe that election is free and permanent, being founded in grace and the unchangeable will of God.—Romans ix. 11; xi, 5, 7; Ephesians i, 4, 5.

We believe that the decree of election is so far from making works in us foreseen the ground or cause of the choice, that it containeth in the bowels of it not only the persons, but also the graces that accompany salvation.—Ephesians ii. 5, 10; 2 Timothy i. 10.

We believe that Christ is He in whom the elect are always considered, and that without Him there is neither election, grace nor salvation.—Ephesians i. 5-10; Acts iv. 12.

We believe there is not any impediment attending the elect of God that can hinder their conversion of eternal salvation.—Romans viii. 30-33; xi. 7.

We believe no man can know his election but by his calling.—Romans ix. 21-23; 2 Peter i. 10.

OF THE SCRIPTURES.

We believe that the Holy Scriptures of themselves, without the addition of human inventions, are able to make the man of God perfect in all things, and thoroughly to furnish him unto all good works.—2 Timothy iii. 16, 17.

We believe that they cannot be broken, but will certainly be fulfilled in all the prophecies, threatenings, promises, either to the salvation or damnation of men.—Acts xiii. 41; Matthew v. 17; Psalm ix. 8.

We believe that God made the world and all things that are therein.—Genesis i. 31; ii. 2; Colossians i. 16.

OF PREACHING.

We do not believe that sinners dead in trespasses and sins should be urged to believe savingly in the Lord Jesus Christ; but we hold it right to preach to such their lost and ruined condition, and point out the only way of escape from the wrath of God, which is through the finished work of the Savior.

We do not therefore believe that the general call or use of general invitations and exhortations is preaching the gospel.

OF BAPTISM.

We believe that believers are the only fit subjects of baptism.—Mark xvi. 16; Acts ii. 41; viii. 37.

We believe that immersion is the only scriptural mode of administering the holy ordinance of baptism.—Matthew iii. 15, 16; Acts viii. 37-40.

We believe that baptism and the Lord's Supper are to be administered by lawfully ordained Elders only.—1 Corinthians xi. 23, 26; Titus i. 5; Acts xiv. 23.

We believe that baptized believers only are fit communicants.—Acts ii. 42, 43.

We believe that converts ought to relate their religious experience before the church only.—Psalm lxvi. 16; Matthew vii. 6.

We believe in close communion.—Song iv. 12; Acts vi. 14-16.

We believe that all matters of importance ought to be settled, conducted, transacted, only before the church.—1 Corinthians vi. 1-8; Acts vi. 6; xv. 6, 7, 12, 19, 22, 23.

We believe that the children of God ought not to frequent meetings, nor associate with any sect professing religion, who maintains error either in doctrine or principle.—2 John 10.

We believe that the first day of the week is proper to be observed as a day of worship, and that no work or worldly business ought to be transacted thereon.

We believe that brethren ought not to go to law with each other before the unbelievers.—1 Corinthians vi. 1-7.

Notes: *The Covenanted Baptist Church of Canada is a small absolute predestinarian Primitive Baptist church that fellowships with the various predestinarian Baptist associations in the United States. Soon after its formation, it adopted a lengthy statement of its belief. These articles of faith are important for their statements of beliefs commonly held among predestinarians but rarely stated, concerning preaching and personal witnessing to non-Christians.*

ARTICLES OF FAITH [FORKED DEER ASSOCIATION (REGULAR)]

1. We believe in one true and living God, the Father, Son and Holy Spirit, and that these three are one.

2. We believe that the Scriptures of the Old and New Testaments are the inspired word of God, and they furnish us all we ought to know, or practice religiously.

3. We believe in the doctrine of unconditional election, that is upon the sinner's part, but according to the foreknowledge and predestination of God.

4. We believe in the doctrine of original or inherited sin.

5. We believe that man is wholly unable to expedite himself from the fallen state he is in by reason of sin and transgression.

6. We believe poor sinners are justified by the imputed righteousness of Jesus Christ.

7. We believe in the final security or surety of all the heirs of promise.

8. We believe that baptism, and the Lord's Supper, and washing the saints' feet are ordinances of the church, given by Jesus Christ, its head and lawgiver, and that true believers are the only subjects for baptism: that immersion the only true mode of baptism.

9. We believe that regular ordained ministers of the gospel, having been baptized by the authority of the church, and having come under the hands of a presbytery, are the only ones authorized to administer the ordinances of baptism.

10. We believe Christ, while suffering on the cross, made a complete atonement for the elect only.

11. We believe in the resurrection of the dead bodies; and that the joys of the righteous will be eternal and the punishment of the wicked everlasting.

Notes: *Those Primitive Baptists holding the less strict position on predestination or "single-edged" predestination, are designated "Regulars." Each association has its own individual articles of faith, but those of the Forked Deer (Tennessee) Association are typical. Items 3 and 10 are the crucial and central statements representative of the association's theological stance.*

* * *

ARTICLES OF FAITH [KEHUKEE (NORTH CAROLINA) ASSOCIATION (PREDESTINARIAN)]

1. We believe in the being of God as almighty, eternal, unchangeable, of infinite wisdom, power, justice, holiness, goodness, mercy, and truth; and that this God has revealed Himself in His word under the characteristics of Father, Son and Holy Ghost.

2. We believe that Almighty God has made known His mind and will to the children of men in His word which word we believe to be of divine authority, and contains all things necessary to be known for the salvation of men and women. The same is compre-

hended or contained in the Books of the Old and
New Testaments as are commonly received.

3. We believe that God, before the foundation of the
world, for a purpose of His own glory, did elect a
certain number of men and angels to eternal life and
that His election is particular, eternal and unconditional on the creature's part.

4. We believe that, when God made man first, he was
perfect, holy and upright, able to keep the law, but
liable to fall and that he stood as a federal head, or
representative, of all his natural offspring or exposed
to the misery which sprang from his disobedience.

5. We believe that Adam fell from his state of moral
rectitude, and that he involved himself and all his
natural offspring in a state of death; and, for that
original transgression, we are both guilty and filthy
in the sight of our holy God.

6. We believe that it is utterly out of the power of men,
as fallen creatures, to keep the law of God perfectly,
repent of their sins truly, or believe in Jesus Christ,
except they be drawn by the Holy Ghost.

7. We believe that in God's appointed time and way (by
means which He has ordained) the elect shall be
called, justified, pardoned and sanctified, and that it
is impossible they can utterly refuse the call, but
shall be made willing by divine grace to receive the
offers of mercy.

8. We believe that justification in the sight of God is
only by the imputed righteousness of Jesus Christ,
received and applied by faith alone.

9. We believe, in like manner, that God's elect shall not
only be called, and justified, but that they shall be
converted, born again, and changed by the effectual
workings of God's holy spirit.

10. We believe that such as are converted, justified and
called by His grace, shall persevere in holiness, and
never fall finally away.

11. We believe it to be duty incumbent on all God's
people to walk religiously in good works; not in the
Old Covenant way of seeking life and favor of the
Lord by it, but only as a duty from a principle of
love.

12. We believe baptism and the Lord's Supper are gospel
ordinances, both belonging to the converted or true
believers: and that persons who are sprinkled or
dipped while in unbelief were not regularly baptised
according to God's word, and that such ought to be
baptised after they are savingly converted into the
faith of Christ.

13. We believe that every church is independent in
matters of discipline; and that Associations, Councils
and Conferences of several ministers, or churches,
are not to impose on the churches the keeping,
holding or maintaining of any principle or practice.

14. We believe in the resurrection of the dead, both of
the just and unjust and a general judgment.

15. We believe the punishment of the wicked is everlasting and the joys of the righteous are eternal.

16. We believe that no minister has a right to administration of the ordinances, only such as are regularly
called and come under the imposition of hands by
the presbytery.

17. Lastly, we believe that, for the mutual comfort,
union and satisfaction of the several churches of the
aforesaid faith and order, we ought to meet in an
Association way, wherein each church ought to
represent their case by their delegates and attend as
often as is necessary to advise with the several
churches in conference and that the decision of
matters in such associations are not to be imposed, or
in any wise binding, on the churches, without their
consent, but only to sit and act as an advisory
council.

Notes: *Many Primitive Baptists look to the Kehukee as the
first of the Baptist associations to formally adopt the Old
School, or Primitive, position in the face of rising support for
missionary societies. The association legislated against such
support in 1927. However, its position on missionary
societies was not addressed in its doctrinal statement. The
association would later become identified with the absolute
predestinarian stance about which Primitive Baptist disagree among themselves. As with missionary societies, the
association's opinion on predestination was not added to its
statement of faith.*

* * *

ARTICLES OF FAITH [KETOCTON (NORTH CAROLINA) ASSOCIATION (REGULARS)]

1. We believe there is one living and true God; that He
is self-existent and independent, in whom all power,
wisdom, holiness, justice, godliness and truth center;
who is omniscient and omnipotent—the almighty
Creator of all things that do exist, visible and
invisible, who upholds and governs all things by His
providential hand, according to the council of His
own will.

2. That in the divine essence there are (according to the
scripture) three persons or subsistences, distinguished by the relative names of Father, Son, and
Holy Ghost; and that each subsistence possesses
proper Deity; that the work of creation is ascribed to
them; divine worhip is addressed to each of them;
each one of them is called by divine names and in the
name of Three in One, the New Testament ordinances are to be administered.

3. That the Holy Scriptures of the Old and New
Testaments are the word of God; that they were
given by divine inspiration, and that this system of
revelation comprehends everything necessary for us
to know concerning God, and the direction of our
obedience to Him. By this divine book, God hath
made revelation of His gracious design in saving
poor sinners, and pointing out the way through the
mediation of the Lord Jesus; that the instrumentality

of this sacred word, stubborn and obstinate sinners are brought into the ordinances of faith, and the incorrigible left without excuse; and that by this word of the Lord all men shall be judged in the last day.

4. That man was created upright, free from sin, and possessed with holiness of nature; that he fell from that innocent state in which he was created, by transgressing God's command, by which he became morally dead, and subjected himself to bodily and eternal death, and as a public head involved his unborn progeny in like ruin, for all descending from him by ordinary generation are born in a state of pollution, and under the dominion of sin, and guilty before God.

5. That in eternity, God, out of His own good pleasure, chose a certain number of Adams's progeny to eternal life, and that He did not leave the accomplishment of His decrees to accident or chance; but decreed all the means to bring about the event; therefore they are chosen to salvation, through sanctification of the Spirit unto obedience and sprinkling of the blood of Jesus Christ. Their calling was decreed to the purpose of election. It is said, when called, they are called according to His purpose and grace given us in Christ Jesus before the world began; and all in order to manifest the glory of His grace.

6. That the covenant of redemption was between the Father and the Son, that the elect were given by the Father to the Son, to be by Him redeemed and finally saved; and that the Son, as Head and representative of His people, engaged to perform everything necessary or requisite to carry their complete salvation into effect. It is called in scripture, a well ordered covenant in all things, and sure.

7. That in the fulness of time, the Son of God was manifested, by taking human nature into union with His divine person, in which capacity He wrought out a righteousness for the justification of His people, yielding a perfect and spotless obedience to all the requirements of the divine law, and submitted Himself to the shameful and ignominious death on the cross, as an atonement for their sins, and reconciliation of their souls to God.

8. That those that are redeemed by Christ, are in due time called to a saving knowledge of the Lord Jesus—embracing Him as the only way to God and Savior of poor sinners. This effectual calling is accomplished by the agency of the Holy Ghost operating in a free, irresistible and unfrustrable manner, by which the understanding is enlightened and the will subjected to Christ. Hence the scriptures testify that they are made willing in the day of His power. This eternal change or new birth in the souls is wholly ascribed to the power of God; for it is said of the regenerate, they are begotten of God, quickened of God, born of God—all expressive that it is the Lord's work, and He is entitled to the praise.

9. All that are effectually called by efficacious grace, are fully justified of God. This perfect obedience, or in other words, the righteousness of Christ being imputed to them, their sins are pardoned, and their persons accepted in God's beloved Son. Such are taken under the care of the great Shepherd of souls, and rest on the infallible promises and power of God, which has engaged to protect them under all their trials; to succor them when tempted; to supply all their wants, and withhold no good thing from them; to continue the good work of grace begun in them, and crown the end of their faith in the complete salvation of their souls.

10. That being bought with the precious blood of Christ, and called by rich grace, it becomes a bounden duty to walk in all the commandments and ordinances of the Lord; although justified by grace, to which our works can add nothing, yet by good works the declarative glory of God is manifested, and the genuineness of faith proved, which while others behold, they may be led to glorify God who is in heaven.

11. And lastly, that God will judge men and angels in the last day, by Jesus Christ. That when Christ appears in the clouds of heaven with the sound of the trumpet, the dead saints shall be raised incorruptible and reunited to their soul; then shall they, together with the living saints, be caught up to meet the Lord in the air; and so shall they be forever with the Lord. The wicked will be raised likewise in that sinful state in which they died; and never having been regenerated and qualified by grace for the kingdom of heaven, will be sentenced to unspeakable torments, for ever and ever, form which there will be no recovery, to endless duration.

These Articles, or Principles of Faith, were supported and defended by such ministers as Elders Jeremiah Moore, James Ireland, William and Daniel Fristoe, David Thomas, John Alderson; and more recently by Elders John Clark, W. S. Athey, Dr. C. Waters, T. N. Alderton, T. S. Dalton, Thomas W. Alderton, J. E. L. Alderton, and many others.

Notes: *The Ketocton Association was formed in 1766, making it one of the oldest Baptist associations in the United States. Its articles of faith were adopted at its organizational session and formally reaffirmed in 1927 in the midst of the missionary society controversy.*

* * *

ARTICLES OF FAITH (NATIONAL PRIMITIVE BAPTIST CONVENTION)

ARTICLE I—WE BELIEVE in only one true and living God and the trinity of persons in the God-head, Father, Son, and Holy Ghost, and yet there are not three, but one God. Reference: Deuteronomy 6:4, Matthew 3:16, 17; 28:19; John 1:1, 14, 16; II Corinthians 13:14; I Peter 1:2; I John 5:7.

ARTICLES OF FAITH (NATIONAL PRIMITIVE BAPTIST CONVENTION) (continued)

ARTICLE II—WE BELIEVE the Scriptures of the Old and New Testaments are the Word of God, and the only rule of faith and practice. Reference: Isaiah 8:20; II Peter 1:21; II Timothy 3:16-17; Romans 1:19-21.

ARTICLE III—WE BELIEVE in the doctrine of eternal and particular election of a definite number of the human race and chosen in Christ before the foundation of the world, that they should be holy and without blame before Him in love. Reference: John 6:7; 13:18-19; Acts 13:48; Romans 11:5; I Thessalonians 5:9; II Timothy 1:9; I Corinthians 7:9; Ephesians 1:1-4; Revelations 20:15.

ARTICLE IV—WE BELIEVE in a covenant redemption between God the Father, and God the Son. Reference: Genesis 3:15; Psalms 51:5; Romans 5:12; I Corinthians 15:22.

ARTICLE V—WE BELIEVE in the fall of man and the communication of Adam's sinful nature to his posterity by ordinary generation and their impotency to recover themselves from the fallen state they are in by nature by their own free will and ability. Reference: Jeremiah 13:23; John 6:44; Ephesians 2:8; Romans 3:23; I Thessalonians 1:10.

ARTICLE VI—WE BELIEVE that all chosen in Christ shall hear the voice of the Son of God, and be effectually called, regenerated and born again. Reference: Psalms 37:28; John 10:28; Acts 2:39; Colossians 3:3; Jude 1; II Timothy 1:8, 9; Romans 8:29, 30.

ARTICLE VII—WE BELIEVE that those born again are justified in the sight of God alone by the righteousness of Jesus Christ imputed to them by faith. Reference: Jeremiah 33:6; II Corinthians 5:21.

ARTICLE VIII—WE BELIEVE that faith is the gift of God, and good works the fruit of faith, and justify us in the sight of men and angels as evidences of our gracious state. Reference: Acts 13:37; Romans 3:20-24; 5:1; 8:1; James 2:18, 19, 22; Hebrews 13:20, 21; I John 2:3, 5.

ARTICLE IX—WE BELIEVE that all the Saints of God justified by the righteousness of Christ shall preserve in grace, and none of them finally fall away so as to be lost. Reference: Deuteronomy 32:6; Psalms 12:5; John 10:27-29; Romans 3:24-25; I Peter 1:5; Phil. 1:6 II Timothy 2:19; I John 2:19.

ARTICLE X—WE BELIEVE in the general judgment, both of the just and the unjust, and that joys of the righteous shall be eternal and the punishment of the wicked shall be everlasting. Reference: Ecclesiastes 12:14; Psalms 16:9; Isaiah 26:19; John 5:28 and Revelations 20:12.

ARTICLE XI—WE BELIEVE that the visible Church of Christ is a congregation of Baptized Believers in Christ adhering to a special covenant, which recognizes Christ as their only lawgiver and ruler, and His word their exclusive guide in all religious matters. It is complete in itself and independent under Christ of every other church organization. It is alone a religious assembly, selected and called out of the world by the doctrine of the Gospel to worship the true God according to His Word. Reference: Acts 2:41,

42; I Corinthians 1:13; Ephesians 4:7; 5:23, 27, 32; Colossians 1:18; Revelations 2:7.

ARTICLE XII—WE BELIEVE that the Scriptural officers of the church are: Pastor and Deacon, whose, qualifications and duties are defined in the Epistles of 1st Timothy 3rd chapter and Titus 1st chapter. Reference: Phil. 1:1; Acts 20:17, 21; Hebrews 13:17.

ARTICLE XIII—WE BELIEVE that Baptism is the immersion of a believer in water by a proper administrator in the name of the Father, Son, and Holy Ghost. Reference: Matthew 28:19; Mark 16:12-16; Acts 8:36; Acts 8:36, 39; Romans 6:3, 4; Colossians 2:12.

ARTICLE XIV—WE BELIEVE that no Minister has a right to administer the ordinances of the gospel only such as have been regularly baptized, called and come under the imposition of a Presbytery by the majority of the Church of Christ. Reference: Matthew 28:18; Ephesians 4:11-14; Acts 9:15; 13:1, 2; Titus; Acts 14:23.

ARTICLE XV—WE BELIEVE that none but regularly baptized and orderly Church Members have a right to communion at the Lord's Table. Reference: Matthew 26: Mark 14; Luke 22; I Corinthians 14:24, 25, 26.

ARTICLE XVI—WE BELIEVE in washing the Saints' Feet in a Church capacity immediately after the Lord's Supper. Reference: John 13.

THE NAMES OF THE CANONICAL BOOKS OF THE BIBLE

Genesis, Exodus, Leviticus, Numbers, Deuteronomy, Joshua, Judges, Ruth, The 1st Book of Samuel, 2nd Book of Samuel, The 1st Book of Kings, 2nd Book of Kings, The 1st Book of Chronicles, 2nd Book of Chronicles, The Book of Ezra, The Book of Nehemiah, The Book of Esther, The Book of Job, The Psalms, The Proverbs, Ecclesiastes or the Preacher, Canticle or Songs of Solomon, Four Prophets the Greater, Twelve Prophets the Lesser. All the books of the New Testament, as they are commonly received, we do receive and account canonical.

Notes: *Some Primitive Baptist associations composed predominantly of black members have organized into a national convention, which has in turn adopted a statement of faith for the participating associations. The statement reflects the Regular (less strict) position on predestination.*

*　　　*　　　*

ARTICLES OF FAITH [SUCARNOCHEE RIVER (MISSISSIPPI) ASSOCIATION (BLACK)]

1. We believe in one true and living God the Father, the Word and the Holy Ghost—St. John 1:1; 1 Tim. 2:5.

2. We believe that the scriptures of the Old and New Testaments are the word of God, and the only rule of faith and practice—2 Tim. 8:16; St. John 5:39.

3. We believe in the doctrine of election by grace and that God chose His people in Christ before the foundation of the world—Eph. 1:4; 2 Thess. 2:13.

4. We believe in the doctrine of originalism—Psa. 58:3, 1 Jn. 5:16.

5. We believe in man's impotency to recover himself from the fallen state he is in by nature, by his own will and ability—Eph. 2:1-5; Prov. 20:9; Eccl. 8:8.

6. We believe that sinners are justified in the sight of God only by imputed righteousness of Christ—Rom. 3:4; 5:16.

7. We believe that the saints shall persevere in grace and never fall finally away—1 Pet. 1:5; Psa. 7:10.

8. We believe that baptism and the Lord's Supper and the washing of the saint's feet are ordinances of Jesus Christ and that true believers are the only subjects and the only mode of baptism is by burial in water—Matt. 3:13-17; St. John 13:14, 15.

9. We believe in the resurrection of the dead and that the joys of the righteous and the punishment of the wicked will be eternal—I Cor. 15:12-23: Matt. 25:46.

10. We believe that no minister has the right to administer the ordinances of the gospel only such as are baptised, called and come under the imposition of hands by a presbytery.—Rom. 10:15; 1 Tim. 3:17.

11. We believe that none but regularly baptised members have a right to commune at the Lord's table—2 Epistle of Jn. 1:10; Acts 19:1-5.

Notes: *Those Primitive Baptists in predominantly black associations who did not affiliate with the national convention continued a more loosely affiliated fellowship. There are no significant doctrinal differences between the two groups.*

*   *   *

ARTICLES OF FAITH AND EXPOSITION OF THE DOCTRINE [UPPER COUNTRY LINE (NORTH CAROLINA) ASSOCIATION (PREDESTINARIAN)]

ARTICLES OF FAITH

We, the messengers of the several churches composing the Upper Country Line Association, agree, for the satisfaction of our brethren and friends, to publish an abstract of principles upon which we unite and will endeavor with the help of the Lord to maintain.

1. We believe in the being of God, as Almighty, eternal, unchangeable, of infinite wisdom, power, justice, holiness, goodness, mercy and truth, and that this God has revealed Himself in His word under the character of Father, Son and Holy Ghost.

2. We believe Almighty God has made known His mind and will to the children of men in His word, which word we believe to be divine authority, and contains all things necessary to be known for the salvation of men. The same is comprehended or contained in the books of the Old and New Testaments.

3. We believe that God before the foundation of the world, for a purpose of His own glory, did elect a certain number of men and angels to eternal life, and that this election is particular, eternal and unconditional on the creature's part.

4. We believe that when God made man he was good and upright, but by his own transgression he fell from that good and upright state, and being the head representative of the whole human race, they being his natural offspring, he involved all of them in the same ruined state with himself, and they were partakers of, the exposed to the miseries which sprang from his disobedience.

5. We believe that it is utterly out of the power of man as a fallen creature to keep the law of God perfectly, or to truly repent of his sins, or believe in Christ, except, he be drawn by the Holy Spirit.

6. We believe in God's own appointed time and way the elect will be called, justified, pardoned, and sanctified, and that it is impossible that they can utterly refuse the call; but shall be willing by divine grace to receive mercy.

7. We believe that justification to the sight of God is only by the imputed righteousness of Jesus Christ received and applied by faith.

8. We believe that God's elect will be converted and born again by the effectual work of the Holy Spirit.

9. We believe that those who are called by grace and born again shall persevere in holiness and never fall finally away.

10. We believe it to be a duty incumbent on all God's people to walk religiously in all good works, not in the old covenant way of seeking life and favor of the Lord by it, but only as a duty from a principle of love.

11. We believe baptism by immersion and the Lord's Supper are gospel ordinances, both belonging to the converted or true believer.

12. We believe that every church is independent in matters of discipline, and that Associations, councils and conferences of ministers or churches, are not to impose on the church the keeping, holding or maintaining of any principle or practice contrary to the church's judgment.

13. We believe in the general resurrection of the dead, both of the just and the unjust, and final judgment.

14. We believe the punishment of the wicked is everlasting and the joys of the righteous eternal.

15. We believe that no minister has a right to administer the ordinances unless called and comes under the imposition of hands by the Presbytery.

EXPOSITION OF THE DOCTRINE

An exposition of the doctrine relating to God's Decree, His Purpose, Predestination, Providence, Good Works, and Obedience, as approved by a majority of our churches in the Upper Country Line Association in their conferences in 1932, and now authorized, forms or constitutes a part of the Articles of Faith of this Association, as follows, to-wit:

Our position and contention on certain controverted questions of doctrine disturbing our people at this time is as follows: London Confession, Chapter III, of God's Decree, Section 1: God hath (Isa. 46:10; Eph. 1:11; Heb.

ARTICLES OF FAITH AND EXPOSITION OF THE
DOCTRINE [UPPER COUNTRY LINE (NORTH
CAROLINA) ASSOCIATION
(PREDESTINARIAN)] (continued)

6:17; Rom. 9:15, 18) decreed in Himself from all eternity,
by the most wise and holy counsel of His will freely and
unchangeably all things whatsoever come to pass; yet so as
thereby is God neither the author of sin (Jas. 1:15; 1 Jn.
1:5), nor hath fellowship with any therein; nor is violence
offered to the will of the creature, nor is the liberty or
contingency of second causes taken away, but rather (Acts
4:27, 28; Jn. 19:11) established, in which appears His
wisdom in disposing all things and power and faithfulness
(Num. 23:19; Eph. 1:3-5) in accomplishing His decree; Sec.
2: Although God knoweth whatsoever may or can come to
pass upon all (Acts 15:18) supposed conditions, yet hath
He not decreed anything (Rom. 9:11, 13, 16, 18) because
He foresaw it as future, or as that which would come to
pass upon such conditions;" Chapter V: Divine Providence, Sec. 1: God, the Creator of all things, in His infinite
power and wisdom, doth (Heb. 1:3; Job 38:11; Isa. 46:10,
11; Psa. 13:5, 6) uphold, direct, dispose and govern all
creatures and things, from the greatest event to the (Matt.
10:26, 30, 31) least, by His most holy providence, to the
end for which they were created, according unto His
infallible foreknowledge and the free and immutable
counsel of His (Eph. 1:11) own will; to the praise of the
glory of His wisdom, power, justice, infinite goodness and
mercy; 2nd. Although in relation to the foreknowledge and
decree of God, the first cause, all things come to pass (Acts
2:28) immutably, and infallibly, so that there is not
anything befalls any (Prov. 16:23) by chance or without
His providence; yet by the same providence He ordereth
them to fall out according to the nature of second causes,
either (Gen. 8:22) necessarily, freely or contingently;
thirdly, God in His ordinary providence (Acts 27:31, 44;
Isa. 55:10, 11) maketh use of means; yet is free (Hosea 1:7)
to work without (Rom. 4:19, 21), above the (Dan. 3:27)
against them at His pleasure; fourthly, The Almighty
power, unsearchable wisdom and infinite goodness of God
so far manifest themselves in His providence, that His
determinate counsel (Rom. 11:32-34; 2 Sam. 24:1; 1
Chron. 2:11) extendeth itself even to the first fall, and all
other sinful actions both of angels and men (and that not
by a bare permission); which also He most wisely and
powerfully (2 Kings 19:28; Psa. 76:10) boundeth, and
otherwise ordereth and governeth, in a manifold dispensation to His most holy (Gen. 1:20; Isa. 10:6, 7:12) ends; yet
so as the sinfulness of their acts proceedeth only from the
creatures, and not from God, who being most holy and
righteous, neither is, nor can be the author or (Psa. 11:21;
Jn. 2:16) approver of sin . . . Of Good Works, Chapter
16, Sec. 1: Good works are only such as God hath (Micah
6:8; Heb. 13:21) commanded in His holy word, and not
such as without the warrant thereof are devised by man,
out of blind zeal (Matt. 15:9; Isa. 19:13), or upon any
pretense of good intentions.

N. B. We believe that God has wrought all the works of
His children in them (Isa. 26:12), and they as His
workmanship, are created in Christ Jesus unto good
works, which God hath before ordained that they should

walk in them (Eph. 2:10), and that their ability to do good
works is not of themselves, but wholly of the Spirit, and
according as God works in them both to will and to do of
His own good pleasure (Phil 2:13), and that as the
branches are in the vine, so are His children in Him, and
have their fruits unto holiness and the end everlasting life
(Rom. 6:22); and that it is of God that His children are in
Christ, who, of God are made unto them, wisdom,
righteousness, sanctification and redemption, and hence
God not only puts them in this Way, which is Christ, but
they are kept by the power of God through faith unto
salvation ready to be revealed in the last time (1 Pet. 1:5),
and that the preservation of the saints depends not upon
their own free will, but upon the immutability of the
decree of (Rom. 8:30; 9:11, 16) election, flowing from the
free and unchangeable love of God the Father, upon the
efficacy of the merit and intercession of Jesus Christ (Rom.
5:9, 19; Jn. 14:19) and union with Him, the (Heb. 6:17, 18)
oath of God, the abiding of His spirit and the (1 Jn. 3:9)
seed of God within them and the nature of the (Jer. 22:40)
covenant of grace, from all which ariseth also the certainty
and infallibility thereof;" and in our conclusion, join with
Elder Hassell in saying that "While the sinner has
destroyed himself, all his salvation, from first to last, is of
the pure, unmerited, almighty grace of God." (Hassell's
History, page 942).

Now upon the subject of obedience, our faith lays hold on
Christ Jesus, the Savior of sinners—the Obedient One, for
strength and every necessary help in time of need,
confessing that of myself I can do nothing, but all things
through Christ that strengtheth me. When God works the
will, He also works the strength, and, obedience always
follows. David said unto the Lord, When thou saidst, Seek
ye My face, my heart said unto thee, Thy face, Lord will I
seek (Psa. 27:8), and again, Paul declares, having received
grace and apostleship, for obedience to the faith among all
nations (Rom. 1:5) his obedience, saying, "So as much as
in me is, I am ready to preach the gospel to you that are at
Rome also (Rom. 1:15), and we believe as God has said,
My word shall not return unto me void, but it shall
accomplish that which I please, and it shall prosper in the
thing whereunto I send it (Isa. 55:11); and when Jesus was
exceeding sorrowful, even unto death, we hear His words,
O My Father, if it be possible, let this cup pass from me;
nevertheless, not as I will, but as thou wilt (Matt. 26:39);
hence, concerning His people (the children of obedience)
He says, Thy people shall be willing in the day of thy
power (Psa. 110:3), and all the promises of God in Him are
yea, and in Him Amen, unto the glory of God by us (2
Cor. 1:26). All obedience is based on love—God's love
toward us, which causes our love toward Him, and with
His mind in us, His will and pleasure becomes our will and
pleasure—acquiescence—obedience.

Submitted by Elder J. W. Gilliam

N. B.—The above expression of the doctrine was adopted
by the churches of our Association in 1982, and ordered
inserted as part of our Articles of Faith.

Notes: *Predestinarian Primitive Baptists are generally
differentiated from the Regulars by their acceptance of what
is termed "double-edged," or absolute, predestination.*

Associations' positions on predestination are rarely spelled out in their statements of faith, most having been composed before the issue between Absolute Predestinarians and the Regulars arose. The Upper Country Line Association, however, has adopted an additional statement to its Articles of Religion which spelled out the predestinarian position in some detail.

*   *   *

General Baptist

AN AFFIRMATION OF OUR FAITH (BAPTIST GENERAL CONFERENCE)

1. THE WORD OF GOD

We believe that the Bible is the Word of God, fully inspired and without error in the original manuscript, written under the inspiration of the Holy Spirit, and that it has supreme authority in all matters of faith and conduct.

2. THE TRINITY

We believe that there is one living and true God, eternally existing in three persons; that these are equal in every divine perfection, and that they execute distinct, but harmonious offices in the work of creation, providence and redemption.

3. GOD THE FATHER

We believe in God, the Father, an infinite, personal spirit, perfect in holiness, wisdom, power and love. We believe that He concerns Himself mercifully in the affairs of men, that He hears and answers prayer, and that He saves from sin and death all who come to Him through Jesus Christ.

4. JESUS CHRIST

We believe in Jesus Christ, God's only begotten Son, conceived by the Holy Spirit. We believe in His virgin birth, sinless life, miracles and teachings. We believe in His substitutionary atoning death, bodily resurrection, ascension into heaven, perpetual intercession for His people, and personal visible return to earth.

5. THE HOLY SPIRIT

We believe in the Holy Spirit who came forth from the Father and Son to convict the world of sin, righteousness, and judgment, and to regenerate, sanctify, and empower all who believe in Jesus Christ. We believe that the Holy Spirit indwells every believer in Christ, and that He is an abiding helper, teacher and guide.

6. REGENERATION

We believe that all men are sinners by nature and by choice and are, therefore, under condemnation. We believe that those who repent of their sins and trust in Jesus Christ as Savior are regenerated by the Holy Spirit.

7. THE CHURCH

We believe in the universal church, a living spiritual body of which Christ is the head and all regenerated persons are members. We believe in the local church, consisting of a company of believers in Jesus Christ, baptized on a credible profession of faith, and associated for worship, work and fellowship. We believe that God has laid upon the members of the local church the primary task of giving the Gospel of Jesus Christ to a lost world.

8. CHRISTIAN CONDUCT

We believe that a Christian should live for the glory of God and the well being of his fellowmen; that his conduct should be blameless before the world; that he should be a faithful steward of his possessions; and that he should seek to realize for himself and others the full statute of maturity in Christ.

9. THE ORDINANCES

We believe that the Lord Jesus Christ has committed two ordinances to the local church, baptism and the Lord's Supper. We believe that Christian baptism is the immersion of a believer in water into the name of the triune God. We believe that the Lord's Supper was instituted by Christ for commemoration of His death. We believe that these two ordinances should be observed and administered until the return of the Lord Jesus Christ.

10. RELIGIOUS LIBERTY

We believe that every human being has direct relations with God, and is responsible to God alone in all matters of faith; that each church is independent and must be free from interference by an ecclesiastical or political authority; that therefore Church and State must be kept separate as having different functions, each fulfilling its duties free from dictation or patronage of the other.

11. CHURCH COOPERATION

We believe that local churches can best promote the cause of Jesus Christ by cooperating with one another in a denominational organization. Such an organization, whether a regional or district conference, exists and functions by the will of the churches. Cooperation in a conference is voluntary and may be terminated at any time. Churches may likewise cooperate with inter-denominational fellowships on a voluntary independent basis.

12. THE LAST THINGS

We believe in the personal and visible return of the Lord Jesus Christ to earth and the establishment of His kingdom. We believe in the resurrection of the body, the final judgment, the eternal felicity of the righteous, and the endless suffering of the wicked.

Notes: *The General Baptists differ from the Calvinist Baptists in their adoption of an Arminian theological position, which emphasizes God's free grace and humanity's free will (as opposed to predestination). The differences represented by the general Baptist perspective are but another example of the controversy which led to the production of the Canons of Dort in response to Arminianism. Among items about which General (free-will) Baptists disagree is the inclusion of foot washing as a third ordinance.*

The affirmation reflects the larger concerns of conservative evangelical controversy concerning scriptural authority. There is no mention of foot washing. The statement on "Church Cooperation" is rare among Baptists, but not incompatible with the usual statements on the authority of the local church.

STATEMENT OF FAITH (GENERAL ASSOCIATION OF GENERAL BAPTISTS)

I. GOD

We believe that there is only one true, living, and eternal God and that the Godhead is revealed as Father, Son, and Holy Spirit.

A. One true and eternal God: Deut. 6:4; 33:27; Jer. 10:10; Matt. 3:15-16; 28:19; Mk. 12:29; Jn. 14:9-11; 10:30; Rom. 8:9-11; I Cor. 8:4-6; II Cor. 3:17; I Thess. 1:9; I Timothy 1:17; 2:5; 6:17; Hebrews 1:1-13; 3:12

B. The Godhead:

1. God as Father: Gen. 1:1; Matt. 6:9; Eph. 4:6

2. God as Son: Isa. 9:6; Matt. 16:16; Jn. 1:1; 3:14, 16; 14:28; I Cor. 15:28; Heb. 1:8

   Virgin Birth of Jesus: Matt. 1:18-25; Luke 1:26-38

3. God as Holy Spirit: Jn. 14:16, 26; Acts 1:5, 8; 2:1-4; Rom. 8:16

II. THE BIBLE

We believe that the Holy Scriptures are the Old and New Testaments; the inspired and infallible Word of God and therein is found the only reliable guide of Christian faith and conduct.

A. The Inspired Revelation: Lk. 24:44-46; Rom. 16: 25-26; II Tim. 3:15-17; Heb. 1:1-2; II Pet. 1:20-21

B. The Infallible Word: Isa. 40:8; Lk. 21:33; Jn. 17: 17; Titus 1:2; I Pet. 1:25

C. The Reliable Guide: Deut. 6:6-9; Ps. 19:7-10; 119:105, 140; Jn. 5:39; Acts 17:11-12; Rom. 10:14-15; 15:4; II Tim. 3:16-17

III. MAN

We believe that God created man in his own image to bring Him honor through obedience, and that when man disobeyed, he became a fallen and sinful creature, unable to save himself. We believe that infants are in the covenant of God's grace and that all all persons become accountable to God when they reach a state of moral responsibility.

A. Man's Origin: Gen. 1:26-27; 2:7; Ps. 8:5

B. Man's Purpose: Gen. 1:28-31; 2:15-25; Isa. 43:7

C. Man's Sin: Gen. 3:1-24; Ps. 51:5; Jer. 13:23; Rom. 1:18—3:23; 5:12-21; 7:1-25

D. Man's Accountability: Matt. 19:13-15; Rom. 4:15; 5:13; 6:16; Heb. 11:24-26.

IV. SALVATION

We believe that Salvation (regeneration, sanctification, justification and redemption) has been provided for all mankind through the redemptive work (life, death, resurrection, ascension, and intercession) of Jesus Christ, and that this Salvation can be received only through repentance toward God and faith toward our Lord Jesus Christ.

Salvation: Heb. 5:9; I Thess. 5:9; I Pet. 1:9; Heb. 7:25

Regeneration: Jn. 3:3-8; 1:11-13; I Pet. 1:23; Eph. 2:1-10; II Cor. 5:17; II Pet. 1:4; Titus 3:5

Sanctification: I Cor. 1:30; Eph. 5:26; Heb. 10:9-10, 29; II Tim. 2:21; Heb. 13:12; Rom. 12:1-2; I Pet. 1:2

Justification: Rom. 3:20-24; 5:1-2, 18; 8:30-33; Acts 13:38-39; I Cor 6:11; II Cor. 5:21

Redemption: Matt. 20:28; Isa. 53:6; Col. 1:14; Titus 2:14; I Pet. 1:18-19; Rev. 5:9

Christ's Redemptive Work: Jn. 3:16; Rom. 5:8; Heb. 2:9; Rev. 22:17; II Pet. 3:9; Jn. 14:6; Acts 4:12; Rom. 6:23; Eph. 2:8-9

Life and Death: Rom. 5:10; Heb. 9:12-15; Jn. 10:11; I Jn. 3:16

Resurrection: Rom. 4:25; I Pet. 1:3; I Cor. 15:14, 17

Ascension: Heb. 4:14-16, 19-20; 9:24; 10:11-12

Intercession: Rom. 8:34; Heb. 9:15; Isa. 53:12; I Tim. 2:5

Repentance: Isa. 55:6-7; Luke 24:47; Luke 13:3-5; Acts 2:38; I Thess. 1:9-10

Faith: Jn 3:16-18; Heb. 11:1, 6; I Pet. 1:5

V. ASSURANCE AND ENDURANCE

We believe that those who abide in Christ have the assurance of salvation. However, we believe that the Christian retains his freedom of choice; therefore, it is possible for him to turn away from God and be finally lost.

A. Assurance: Matt. 28:20; I Cor. 10:13; Heb. 5:9

B. Endurance: Matt. 10:22; Lk. 9:62; Col. 1:23; Rev. 2:10-11; 3:3-5

C. Warnings: Jn. 15:6; Rom. 11:20-23; Gal. 5:4; Heb. 3:12; 10:26-29; II Pet. 2:20-21

D. Finally lost: Jn. 15:6; I Cor. 9:27; Heb. 6:4-6

VI. CHRISTIAN DUTIES

We believe that Christians should live faithfully by serving in and through the local church, praying diligently, witnessing earnestly, practicing tolerance, showing loving kindness, giving as God prospers, and conducting themselves in such a way as to bring glory to God.

A. Faithful service: I Chron. 16:11; Ps. 101:6; Matt. 28:18-20; Jn. 15:7-14; Rom. 12:14; I Cor. 13; II Cor. 8, 9; Eph. 4, 6; Heb. 12:1

B. Prayer: II Chron. 7:14; Dan. 6:10; Matt. 6:1-13; 26:41; Lk. 18:1; I Thess. 5:17

C. Witnessing: Matt. 28:19-20; Acts 1:8

D. Tolerance: Matt. 18:15-17; Lk. 10:27; Gal. 5:22- 23; II Pet. 1:5-9

E. Loving Kindness: Jn. 13:35; I Jn. 3:11; 4:7, 11-12

F. Financial Stewardship: Matt. 23:23; I Cor. 16:2; II Cor. 9:6-7

VII. THE CHURCH

We believe that the Church Universal is the body of Christ, the fellowship of all believers, and that its members have been called out from the world to come under the dominion and authority of Christ, its head. We believe that a local church is a fellowship of Christians, a part of the Body of Christ, voluntarily banded together for worship, nurture, and service.

A. The Church Universal: Matt. 16:18; Jn. 10:10; I Cor. 3:16; 12:12-14, 27; Eph. 1:22-23; Col. 1:18, 24; Heb. 12:23

B. The Local Church: Matt. 18:17; Acts 2:38-47; 11: 19-30; Rev. 1:4; 3:22

1. Worship and Service: Rom. 12:1; I Cor. 14:12, 23:25; Heb. 10:25; Ja. 1:26-27

2. Nurture: Eph. 4; II Pet. 1:2-8; 3:18

VIII. ORDINANCES

We believe that baptism and the Lord's Supper are ordinances instituted by Christ to be observed by Christians only. We also believe that the Biblical mode of baptism is immersion and that participation in the Lord's Supper should be open to all Christians.

(NOTE: Several associations and local churches recognize foot washing as an ordinance. We believe that this should be left to the individual, and that neither the practice nor the non-practice of it should be any bar to fellowship, either in the church, the local association, the Presbytery, or the General Association. Jn. 13; I Tim. 5:10.)

A. Baptism

1. Instituted: Matt. 3:13-15; 28:19

2. Subjects: Acts 2:41; 8:12, 37-38; 10:47-48; 16:30-33; 19:5

3. Biblical Mode: Rom. 6:3-5; Col. 2:12

4. Purpose: Matt. 3:14; I Pet. 3:21

B. Communion

1. Instituted: Matt. 26:26-29; Mk. 14:22-25; Lk. 22:19-20; I Cor. 11:23-25

2. Subjects: I Cor. 11:27-29

3. Purpose: I Cor. 11:26

IX. THE LORD'S DAY

We believe in the Sanctify of the Lord's Day, the first day of the week, and that this day ought to be observed by worshipping God, witnessing for Christ, and ministering to the needs of humanity. We believe that secular work on Sunday should be limited to cases of necessity or mercy.

A. Sanctity: Ex. 20:8; Isa. 58:13-14

B. Observance: Mk. 2:27-28; Lk. 4:16; 14:1-6; Acts 20:7; I Cor. 16:2; Rev. 1:10

X. LAST THINGS

We believe in the personal return of Jesus Christ, and in the bodily resurrection of the dead. We believe that God will judge all mankind by Jesus Christ; that He will reward the righteous with eternal life in heaven, and that He will banish the unrighteous to everlasting punishment in hell.

A. Return: Matt. 24, 25; Lk. 12:40; Jn. 14:3; Acts 1: 11; I Jn. 3:2; Rev. 1:7

B. Resurrection: Jn. 5:25, 28-29; 6:40; 11:24-25; Rom. 8:11; I Cor. 15; Phil. 3:21; I Thess. 4:16-17; Rev. 20:4-6

C. Judgment and Reward: Matt. 25:21; Mk. 9:43- 48; Jn. 5:27; Acts 17:31; Rom. 2:16; 14:12; II Cor. 5:1, 10; Col. 3:24; II Thess. 1:7-10; Heb. 9: 27; II Pet. 3:8-13; Jude 21; Rev. 2:7; 14:13; 20: 10-15; 22:12

Notes: *This brief statement is in contrast to the very detailed statement of the National Association of Free-Will Baptists.*

* * *

THE FAITH OF FREE-WILL BAPTISTS (NATIONAL ASSOCIATION OF FREE-WILL BAPTISTS)

CHAPTER I. THE HOLY SCRIPTURES

These are the Old and the New Testaments: they were written by holy men, inspired by the Holy spirit, and are God's revealed word to man. They are a sufficient and infallible rule and guide to salvation and all Christian worship and service.

Since the Bible is the Word of God, it is without error in all matters upon which it speaks, whether history, geography, matters relating to science or any other subject.

CHAPTER II. BEING AND ATTRIBUTES OF GOD

The Scriptures teach that there is only one true and living God, who is Spirit, self-existent, eternal, immutable, omnipresent, omniscient, omnipotent, independent, good, wise, holy, just, and merciful, the . . . Creator, Preserver, and Governor of the Universe; the Redeemer, Saviour, Sanctifier, and Judge of men; and the only proper object of worship.

The mode of His existence, however, is a subject far above the understanding of man—finite beings cannot comprehend Him. There is nothing in the universe that can justly represent Him, for there is none like Him. He is the fountain of all perfection and happiness. He is glorified by the whole creation, and is worthy to be loved and served by all intelligence.

CHAPTER III. DIVINE GOVERNMENT AND PROVIDENCE

1. God exercises a providential care and superintendence over all His creatures, and governs the world in wisdom and mercy, according to the testimony of His Word.

2. God has endowed man with power of free choice, and governs him by moral laws and motives; and this power of free choice is the exact measure of man's responsibility.

3. All events are present with God from everlasting to everlasting; but His knowledge of them does not in any sense cause them, nor does He decree all events which He knows will occur.

CHAPTER IV. CREATION, PRIMITIVE STATE OF MAN, AND HIS FALL

SECTION I. CREATION

1. OF THE WORLD. God created the world, and all things that it contains, for His own pleasure and glory and the enjoyment of His creatures.

2. OF THE ANGELS. The angels were created by God to glorify Him and obey His commandments. Those who have kept their first estate He employs

in ministering blessings to the heirs of salvation and in executing His judgements upon the world.

3. OF MAN. God created man, consisting of a material body and a thinking, rational soul. He was made in the image of God, to glorify his Maker.

SECTION II. PRIMITIVE MAN, AND HIS FALL

Our first parents, in their original state, were upright. They naturally preferred and desired to obey their Creator, and had no preference or desire to transgress His will until they were influenced and inclined by the tempter to disobey God's commands. Previous to this, the only tendency of their nature was to do righteousness. In consequence of the first trangression, the state under which the posterity of Adam came into the world is so different from that of Adam that they have not that righteousness and purity which Adam had before the fall; they are not willing to obey God, but are inclined to evil. Hence, none, by virtue of any natural goodness and mere work of their own, can become the children of God, but they are all dependent for salvation upon the redemption effected through the blood of Christ, and upon being created anew unto obedience through the operation of the Spirit; both of which are freely provided for every descendant of Adam.

CHAPTER V. OF CHRIST

SECTION I. HIS DIVINITY

Jesus Christ, the Son of God, possesses all divine perfections. As He and the Father are one, He in His divine nature, filled all the offices and performed the works of God to His creatures that have been the subjects of revelation to us. As man, He performed all the duties toward God that we are required to perform, repentance of sin excepted.

His divinity is proved from His titles, His attributes, and His works.

A. HIS TITLES. The Bible ascribes to Christ the titles of Saviour, Jehovah, Lord of hosts, the first and the last, God, true God, great God, God over all, mighty God, and the everlasting Father.

B. HIS ATTRIBUTES. He is eternal, unchangeable, omnipresent, omniscient, omnipotent, holy, and to be worshipped.

C. HIS WORKS. By Christ the world was created. He preserves and governs it; He has provided redemption for all men and He will be their final Judge.

SECTION II. THE INCARNATION OF CHRIST

The Word, which in the beginning was with God and which was God, by whom all things were made, condescended to a state of humiliation in being united with human nature and becoming like us, pollution and sin excepted. In this state, as a subject of the law, He was liable to the infirmities of our nature, was tempted as we are, but lived our example, perfect obedience to the divine requirements. As Christ was made of the seed of David, according to the flesh, He is "Son of man," and as the divine existence is the fountain from which He proceeded, and was the only agency by which He was begotten, He is "the Son of God," being the only begotten of the Father, and the only incarnation of the Divine Being.

CHAPTER VI. THE ATONEMENT AND MEDIATION OF CHRIST

1. THE ATONEMENT. As sin cannot be pardoned without a sacrifice, and the blood of beasts could never wash away sin, Christ gave Himself a sacrifice for the sins of the world, and thus made salvation possible for all men. He did for us, suffering in our stead, to make known the righteousness of God, that he might be just in justifying sinners who believe in His Son. Through the redemption effected by Christ, salvation is actually enjoyed in his world, and will be enjoyed in the next by all who do not in this life refuse obedience to the known requirements of God. The atonement for sin was necessary. For present and future obedience can no more blot out our past sins than past obedience can remove the guilt of present and future sins. If God pardoned the sins of men without satisfaction for the violation of His law, it would follow that transgression might go on with impunity; government would be abrogated, and the obligation of obedience to God would be, in effect, removed.

2. MEDIATION OF CHRIST. Our Lord not only died for our sins, but He arose for our justification, and ascended up to heaven, where, as the only mediator between God and man, He makes intercession for us until He comes again.

3. We believe that all children dying in infancy, having not actually transgressed against the law of God in their own persons, are only subject to the first death, which was brought on by the fall of the first Adam, and not that any one of them dying in that state shall suffer punishment in hell by the guilt of Adam's sin for of such is the Kingdom of God.

CHAPTER VII. THE HOLY SPIRIT

1. The Scriptures ascribe to the Holy Spirit the acts and attributes of an intelligent being. He guides, knows, moves, gives information, commands, forbids, sends forth, reproves, and can be sinned against.

2. The attributes of God are ascribed to the Holy Spirit.

3. The works of God are ascribed to the Holy Spirit: creation, inspiration, giving of life, and sanctification.

4. The apostles assert that the Holy Spirit is Lord of God.

From the foregoing the conclusion is that the Holy Spirit is in reality God and one with the Father in all divine perfections. It has also been shown that Jesus Christ is God—one with the Father. Then these three—the Father, Son, and Holy Spirit—are one God.

The truth of this doctrine is also proved from the fact that the Father, the Son and the Holy Ghost are united in the authority by which believers are baptized; and in the benedictions pronounced by the apostles, which are acts of the highest religious worship.

CHAPTER VIII. THE GOSPEL CALL

The call of the Gospel is co-extensive with the atonement to all men, both by the word and strivings of the Spirit, so that salvation is rendered equally possible to all; and if any fail of eternal life, the fault is wholly his own.

CHAPTER IX. REPENTANCE

The repentance which the Gospel requires includes a deep conviction, a penitential sorrow, an open confession, a decided hatred, and an entire forsaking of all sin. This repentance God has enjoined on all men; and without it in this life the sinner must perish eternally.

CHAPTER X. FAITH

Saving faith is an assent of the mind to the fundamental truths of revelation, an acceptance of the Gospel, through the influence of the Holy Spirit, and a firm confidence and trust in Christ. The fruit of faith is obedience to the Gospel. The power to believe is the gift of God, but believing is an act of the creature, which is required as a condition of pardon, and without which the sinner cannot obtain salvation. All men are required to believe in Christ, and those who yield obedience to this requirement become the children of God by faith.

CHAPTER XI. REGENERATION

As man is a fallen and sinful being, he must be regenerated in order to obtain salvation. This change is an instantaneous renewal of the heart by the Holy Spirit, whereby the penitent sinner receives new life, becomes a child of God, and is disposed to serve him. This is called in Scripture being born again, born of the Spirit, being quickened, passing from death unto life, and a partaking of the divine nature.

CHAPTER XII. JUSTIFICATION AND SANCTIFICATION

1. JUSTIFICATION. Personal justification implies that the person justified has been guilty before God; and, in consideration of the atonement of Christ, accepted by faith, the sinner is pardoned and absolved from the guilt of sin, and restored to the divine favor. Christ's atonement is the foundation of the sinner's redemption, yet, without repentance and faith, it can never give him justification and peace with God.

2. SANCTIFICATION is the continuing of God's grace by which the Christian may constantly grow in grace and in the knowledge of our Lord Jesus Christ.

CHAPTER XIII. PERSEVERANCE OF THE SAINTS

There are strong grounds to hope that the truly regenerate will persevere unto the end, and be saved, through the power of divine grace which is pledged for their support;

but their future obedience *and final salvation are neither determined nor certain,* since through infirmity and manifold temptations they are in *danger of falling;* and they ought, therefore, to watch and pray lest they make *shipwreck* of their faith and be lost.

CHAPTER XIV. THE LORD'S DAY

This is one day in seven, which from the creation of the world God has set apart for sacred rest and holy service. Under the former dispensation, the seventh day of the week, as commemorative of the work of creation, was set apart for the Lord's Day. Under the Gospel, the first day of the week, in commemoration of the resurrection of Christ, and by authority of Christ and the Apostles, is observed as the Christian Sabbath. On this day all men are required to refrain from secular labor and devote themselves to the worship and service of God.

CHAPTER XV. THE CHURCH

A *Christian Church* is an organized body of believers in Christ who stately assemble to worship God, and who sustain the ordinances of the Gospel according to the Scriptures. Believers in Christ are admitted to this church on giving evidence of faith in Christ, obtaining consent of the body, being baptized, and receiving the right hand of fellowship.

The church of God, or members of the body of Christ, is the whole body of Christians throughout the whole world, and none but the regenerate are its members.

CHAPTER XVI. TITHING

Both the Old and New Scriptures teach tithing as God's financial plan for the support of His work.

CHAPTER XVII. THE GOSPEL MINISTRY

1. QUALIFICATION OF MINISTERS. They must possess good, natural and acquired abilities, deep and ardent piety, be especially called of God to the work, and ordained by prayer and the laying on of hands.

2. DUTIES OF MINISTERS. These are to preach the Word, administer the ordinances of the Gospel, visit their people, and otherwise perform the work of faithful ministers.

CHAPTER XVIII. ORDINANCES OF THE GOSPEL

1. CHRISTIAN BAPTISM. This is the immersion of believers in water, in the name of the Father, the Son, and the Holy Spirit, in which are represented the burial and resurrection of Christ, the death of Christians to the world, the washing of their souls from the pollution of sin, their rising to newness of life, their engagement to serve God, and their resurrection at the last day.

2. THE LORD'S SUPPER. This is a commemoration of the death of Christ for our sins in the use of *bread* which He made the emblem of His broken body, and the *cup,* the emblem of His shed blood, and by it the believer expresses his love for Christ, his faith and hope in Him, and pledges to Him perpetual fidelity.

It is the privilege and duty of all who have spiritual union with Christ to commemorate His death, and no man has a right to forbid these tokens to the least of His disciples.

3. WASHING THE SAINTS' FEET. This is a sacred ordinance, which teaches humility and reminds the believer of the necessity of a daily cleansing from all sin. It was instituted by the Lord Jesus Christ, and called an "example" on the night of His betrayal, and in connection with the institution of the Lord's Supper. It is the duty and happy prerogative of every believer to observe this sacred ordinance.

CHAPTER XIX. DEATH

As a result of sin, all mankind is subject to the death of the body. The soul does not die with the body, but immediately after death enters into a conscious state of happiness or misery, according to the character here possessed.

CHAPTER XX. SECOND COMING OF CHRIST

The Lord Jesus, who ascended on high and sits at the right hand of God, will come again to close the Gospel dispensation, glorify His saints, and judge the world.

CHAPTER XXI. THE RESURRECTION

The Scriptures teach the resurrection of the bodies of all men, each in its own order; they that have done good will come forth to the resurrection of life, and they that have done evil to the resurrection of damnation.

CHAPTER XXII. THE JUDGMENT AND RETRIBUTION

1. THE JUDGMENT. There will be a judgment, when time and man's probation will close forever. Then all men will be judged according to their works.

2. RETRIBUTION. Immediately after the judgment, the righteous will enter into eternal life, and the wicked will go into a state of endless punishment.

APPENDIX TO CHAPTER XIII. ADOPTED JULY, 1969

1. We believe that salvation is a present possession by faith in the Lord Jesus Christ as Savior and that a person's eternal destiny depends on whether he has this possession. This we hold in distinction from those who teach that salvation depends on human works or merit.

2. We believe that a saved individual may, in freedom of will, cease to trust in Christ for salvation and once again be lost. This we hold in distinction from those who teach that a believer may not again be lost.

3. We believe that any individual living in the practice of sin (whether he be called "backslider" or "sinner") must be judged by that evidence to be lost should he so die in his sins. This we hold in distinction from those who suggest that pernicious doctrine that a man may live in sin as he pleases and still claim Heaven as his eternal home.

4. We believe that any regenerate person who has sinned (again, whether he be called "backslider" or "sinner") and in whose heart a desire arises to repent may do so and be restored to favor and fellowship with God. This we hold in distinction from those who teach that when a Christian sins he can not repent and be restored to favor and fellowship with God.

APPENDIX TO CHAPTER I. ADOPTED JULY, 1979

Free Will Baptist believe in the plenary, verbal inspiration of the Bible. By *plenary* we mean "full and complete." We hold that all parts of the Bible are inspired and that inspiration extends to all its subjects. By verbal we mean that inspiration extends to the very words of the Scriptures, not just to the thoughts and ideas expressed by human authors.

We believe the Scriptures are infallible and inerrant. The Bible is without error and trustworthy in all its teachings, including cosmogony, geology, astronomy, anthropology, history, chronology, etc. as well as in matters of faith and practice. Being the very word of God, it is God's final revelation and our absolute authority.

APPENDIX TO CHAPTER VII. ADOPTED JULY, 1979

Free Will Baptists understand the Bible teaches the following facts: On the Day of Pentecost believers spoke in distinct foreign languages which were readily understood by the nationalities present.

Tongues were given as a special gift to the early church as only one sign which confirms the witness of the Gospel to unbelievers.

While tongues were bestowed by the sovereign will of God on some believers, all did not speak with tongues. When this gift was abused, it became a source of disturbance in the congregational meetings. To eliminate confusion and correct the error, Paul set particular guidelines for the Christian church to follow. The gift of tongues was neither an evidence of the baptism of the Holy Spirit, nor does it bring about sanctification.

We believe that speaking in tongues as a visible sign of the baptism of the Holy Spirit is an erroneous doctrine to be rejected. Any implication of a "second work of grace" has never been tolerated in our fellowship of churches, and will not be permitted.

We teach and preach the fulness of the Holy Spirit and heed the scriptural admonition. "Be filled with the Spirit; Speaking to yourselves in psalms and hymns and spiritual songs, singing and making melody in your heart to the Lord; Giving thanks always for all things unto God and the Father in the name of our Lord Jesus Christ."

Notes: *Approaching the length and thoroughness of the reformation confessions, this document is the most definitive statement of the General Baptist position. The text has undergone periodic revision, the latest in 1981. In 1979, the statement on biblical authority (chapter 1) was modified to make explicit the church's position on matters in the forefront of contemporary evangelical theological debate. An appendix to chapter 1 was also adopted. The church practices foot washing. A pentecostal variant of this document was adopted by the Free Will Baptist Church of the Pentecostal Faith.*

ARTICLES OF FAITH (NATIONAL ASSOCIATION OF FREE-WILL BAPTISTS)

1. THE BIBLE. The Scriptures of the Old and New Testaments were given by inspiration of God, and are our infallible rule of faith and practice.

2. GOD. There is one living and true God, revealed in nature as the Creator, Preserver, and Righteous Governor of the universe; and in the Scriptures as Father, Son, and Holy Ghost; yet as one God, infintely wise and good, whom all intelligent creatures are supremely to love, adore, and obey.

3. CHRIST. Christ is God manifest in the flesh; in His divine nature truly God, in His human nature truly man. The mediator between God and man, once crucified, He is now risen and glorified, and is our ever present Saviour and Lord.

4. THE HOLY SPIRIT. The Scriptures assign to the Holy Spirit all the attributes of God.

5. THE GOVERNMENT OF GOD. God exercises a wise and benevolent providence over all beings and all things by maintaining the constitution and laws of nature. He also performs special acts, not otherwise provided for, as the highest welfare of men requires.

6. THE SINFULNESS OF MAN. Man was created innocent, but by disobedience fell into a state of sin and condemnation. His posterity, therefore, inherit a fallen nature of such tendencies that all who come to years of accountability, sin and become guilty before God.

7. THE WORK OF CHRIST. The Son of God by His incarnation, life, sufferings, death, and resurrection effected for all a redemption from sin that is full and free, and is the ground of salvation by faith.

8. THE TERMS OF SALVATION. The conditions of salvation are: 1. Repentance or sincere sorrow for sin and hearty renunciation of it. 2. Faith or the unreserved committal of one's self to Christ as Saviour and Lord with purpose to love and obey Him in all things. In the exercise of saving faith, the soul is renewed by the Holy Spirit, freed from the dominion of sin, and becomes a child of God. 3. Continuance in faith and obedience until death.

9. ELECTION. God determined from the beginning to save all who should comply with the conditions of Salvation. Hence by faith in Christ men become His elect.

10. FREEDOM OF THE WILL. The human will is free and self-controlled, having power to yield to the influence of the truth and the Spirit, or to resist them and perish.

11. SALVATION FREE. God desires the salvation of all, the Gospel invites all, the Holy Spirit strives with all, and whosoever will may come and take of the water of life freely.

12. PERSEVERANCE. All believers in Christ, who through grace persevere in holiness to the end of life, have promise of eternal salvation.

13. GOSPEL ORDINANCES. BAPTISM, or the immersion of believers in water, and the LORD'S SUPPER, are ordinances to be perpetuated under the Gospel. FEET WASHING, an ordinance teaching humility, is of universal obligation, and is to be ministered to all true believers.

14. TITHING. God commanded tithes and offerings in the Old Testament; Jesus Christ endorsed it in the Gospel (Matt. 23:23), and the apostle Paul said, "Upon the first day of the week let every one of you lay by him in store, as God hath prospered him" (I Cor. 16:2a).

15. THE CHRISTIAN SABBATH. The divine law requires that one day in seven be set apart from secular employments and amusements, for rest, worship, holy works, and activities, and for personal communion with God.

16. RESURRECTION, JUDGMENT, AND FINAL RETRIBUTION. The Scriptures teach the resurrection of all men at the last day. They that have done good will come forth to the resurrection of life, and they that have done evil unto the resurrection of damnation; then the wicked will "go away into eternal punishment, but the righteous into eternal life."

Notes: *This document is a very condensed summary of The Faith of Free Will Baptists.*

*   *   *

AGREED UPON BELIEFS OF THE GREEN RIVER (KENTUCKY) ASSOCIATION OF UNITED BAPTISTS

1. The scriptures of the old and new Testaments are the infallible word of God, and the only true rule of faith and practice.

2. There is only one true God, and in the Godhead or divine essence, there are the Father, the Son and the Holy Ghost.

3. By nature we are depraved and fallen creatures.

4. Salvation, regeneration, santification and justification are by the life, death, resurrection and ascension of Jesus Christ.

5. The saints will finally persevere through grace to glory.

6. Believer's baptism by immersion are necessary to receive the Lord's Supper.

7. The salvation of the righteous and the punishment of the wicked will be eternal.

8. It is our duty to tender affection to each other, and study the happiness of the children of God; in general, to to be engaged singly to promote the honor of God.

9. The preaching, "Christ tasted death for every man, shall be no bar to communion."

Notes: *One of several associations formed by the union of Regular and Separate Baptists in the 1790s, the Green River*

AGREED UPON BELIEFS OF THE GREEN RIVER
(KENTUCKY) ASSOCIATION OF UNITED
BAPTISTS (continued)

Association of United Baptists, like other United Baptists, embraces beliefs that are Arminian in perspective. However, the association's unnamed statement is mildly Calvinist in its affirmation of human depravity (item 3) and the perseverance of the saints (item 5). There is no mention of election or predestination, and the last item allows some freedom on the issue of limited (Christ died for the elect) versus unlimited (Christ died for every person) atonement.

*   *   *

Seventh-Day Baptist

STATEMENT OF BELIEF OF SEVENTH-DAY BAPTISTS (SEVENTH-DAY BAPTIST GENERAL CONFERENCE)

1. GENERAL STATEMENT

Seventh Day Baptists cherish liberty of thought as an essential condition for the guidance of the Holy Spirit. Therefore they have no binding creed to which members must subscribe. They hold however, that certain beliefs and practices, having the support of Scripture and adhered to by followers of Christ through the centuries, are binding upon all Christians. Among these are the following which they hold to be fundamental.

These statements approved by Conference are passed on to the churches for such action as the Holy Spirit shall lead them to take. It is believed they will be helpful in training the children in religion, in establishing the young people in the fundamentals of Christian faith, in deepening the work of God's grace in all our people, and in making these essential Christian truths known to others.

2. POLITY

The Seventh Day Baptist denomination is historically, like other Baptists, congregational in polity, and desires that its churches and its members shall continue to enjoy freedom of conscience in all matters of religion. Therefore, the Statement of Belief here set forth is simply an exhibition of the views generally held by Seventh Day Baptists and is not adopted as having binding force in itself.

3. ARTICLES OF BELIEF

I.   GOD. We believe in God, the one personal, perfect, and eternal Spirit, Creator, and Sustainer of the universe, our Father, who manifests a holy, redeeming love toward all men.

II.   JESUS CHRIST. We believe in Jesus Christ, God manifest in the flesh, our Saviour, Teacher, and Guide, who draws to himself all men who will come to him in love and trustful obedience.

III. THE HOLY SPIRIT. We believe in the Holy Spirit, the indwelling God, the Inspirer of Scripture, the Comforter, active in the hearts and minds and lives of men, who reproves of sin, instructs in righteousness, and empowers for witnessing and service.

IV.   THE BIBLE. We believe that the Bible is the inspired record of God's will for man, of which Jesus Christ is the supreme interpreter; and that it is our final authority in matters of faith and conduct.

V.   MAN. We believe that man was made in the image of God in his spiritual nature and personality, and is therefore the noblest work of creation; that he has moral responsibility, and was created for divine sonship and human fellowship, but because of disobedience he is in need of a Savior.

VI.   SIN AND SALVATION. We believe that sin is any want of conformity to the character and will of God, and that salvation from sin and death, through repentance and faith in Christ our Savior, is the gift of God by redeeming love, centered in the atoning death of Christ on the cross.

VII. ETERNAL LIFE. We believe that Jesus rose from the dead and lives eternally with the Father, and that he will come in heavenly glory; and that because he lives, eternal life with spiritual and glorified bodies, is the gift of God to the redeemed.

VIII. THE CHURCH. We believe that the Church of god is the whole company of redeemed people gathered by the Holy Spirit into one body of which Christ is the head: and that the local church is a community of Christ's followers organized for fellowship and service, practicing and proclaiming common convictions.

IX.   THE SACRAMENTS. We believe that baptism of believers by immersion is a witness to the acceptance of Jesus Christ as Savior and Lord, and is a symbol of death to sin, a pledge to a new life in Christ. We believe that the Lord's Supper commemorates the suffering and death of the world's Redeemer, "Til he come," and is a symbol of Christian fellowship and a pledge of renewed allegiance to our risen Lord.

X.   THE SABBATH. We believe that the Sabbath of the Bible, the seventh day of the week, is sacred time, antedating Moses and having the sanction of Jesus; that it should be faithfully kept by all Christians as a day of rest and worship, a symbol of God's presence in time, a pledge of eternal Sabbath rest.

XI.   EVANGELISM. We believe that Jesus Christ by his life and ministry and his final command to the disciples, commissions us to promote evangelism, missions, and religious education, and that it is through these agencies that the church must promote Christianity throughout the whole world and in all human relationships.

SOME SCRIPTURE REFERENCES

POLITY

Matthew 18: 15-20; 23: 8-10; Luke 22: 24-27; Acts 6: 1-6; 2: 44, 45; Colossians 3: 15-17; I Peter 5: 1-5.

I. GOD

Genesis 1: 1; Isaiah 25: 1-9; Psalms 90: 1, 2; 91: 2; John 4: 24; I Timothy 1: 17; John 3: 16; I John 3: 1; Ephesians 4: 6.

II. JESUS CHRIST

John 1: 14-18; 12: 32; Romans 1: 3-5; Galatians 4: 4-6; Ephesians 1: 18-23; I John 3: 16; 2: 2.

III. THE HOLY SPIRIT

John 14: 26; 16: 7-14; Acts 1: 8; Romans 5: 5; II Peter 1: 21.

IV. THE BIBLE

II Timothy 3: 14-17; Hebrews 1: 1, 2; II Peter 1: 19, 20; John 20: 30, 31.

V. MAN

Genesis 1: 26, 27; Micah 6: 8; Psalms 8: 4, 5; II Corinthians 4: 15, 16; Ephesians 2: 4-10.

VI. SIN AND SALVATION

John 1: 29; 3: 5; I John 3: 4; Romans 3: 23-27; Acts 2: 37-39; I Peter 2: 21-25; Ephesians 2:8.

VII. ETERNAL LIFE

John 3: 14, 15; 17: 1-3; I Corinthians 15: 20-22, 42-44; I John 5: 11, 12; Matthew 25: 31-34; Colossians 3: 1-4.

VIII. THE CHURCH

Matthew 16: 16-19; Colossians 1: 18; I Corinthians 12: 13, 14; Ephesians 1: 22, 23; 2: 19-22; Acts 14: 23.

IX. THE SACRAMENTS

Matthew 3: 13-17; Acts 2: 37-39; Romans 6: 3, 4; Mark 16: 16; Matthew 26: 26-28; I Corinthians 10: 16, 17; 11: 23-29.

X. THE SABBATH

Genesis 2: 2, 3; Exodus 20: 8-11; Isaiah 58: 13, 14; Ezekiel 20: 20; Luke 4: 16; Mark 2: 27, 28; Acts 13: 42-44; Matthew 5: 17-19.

XI. EVANGELISM

Deuteronomy 6: 6, 7; Matthew 28: 18-20; 4: 19, 23; Acts 5: 42; 20: 28-32; I Corinthians 4: 17; I Thessalonians 5: 12-22.

Notes: *The sabbatarian Baptists differ primarily on their keeping of Saturday, rather than Sunday, as a day of rest and worship. The statement follows a General Baptist theological perspective.*

* * *

Christian Church

A DECLARATION OF THE TRUTH REVEALED IN THE BIBLE AS DISTINGUISHABLE FROM THE THEOLOGY OF CHRISTENDOM (AMENDED CHRISTADELPHIANS)

THE BIBLE

1. The Bible is a revelation of God's purpose given through chosen men who were guided by His Spirit. It is therefore an infallible and authoritative expression of His will for man.

God, who at sundry times and in divers manners spake in time past unto the fathers by the prophets, hath in these last days spoken unto us by his Son, whom he hath appointed heir of all things, by whom also he made the worlds (Heb.1:1,2).

Now these be the last words of David. David the son of Jesse said, and the man who was raised up on high, the annointed of the God of Jacob, and the sweet psalmist of Israel, said, The Spirit of the Lord spake by me, and his word was in my tongue. The God of Israel said, the Rock of Israel spake to me. He that ruleth over men must be just, ruling in the fear of God (2 Sam. 23:1-3).

Yet many years didst thou forbear them, and testifiedst against them by thy spirit in thy prophets : yet would they not give ear : therefore gavest thou them into the hand of the people of the lands (Neb. 9:30).

For David himself said by the Holy Spirit, The Lord said to my Lord, Sit thou on my right hand, till I make thine enemies thy footstool (Mark 12:36).

All scripture is given by inspiration of God, and is profitable for doctrine, for reproof, for correction, for instruction in righteousness : that the man of God may be perfect, thoroughly furnished unto all good works (2 Tim. 3:16,17).

I will raise them up a Prophet from among their brethren, like unto thee, and will put my words in his mouth ; and he shall speak unto them all that I shall command him (Deut. 18:18,19).

For the prophecy came not in old time by the will of man : but holy men of God spake as they were moved by the Holy Spirit (2 Peter 1:21.)

See also Ezek. 1:3; Micah 1:1; Zeph. 1:1; Jer. 1:1-9.

GOD

2. The Bible reveals God to be the Creator and Sustainer of all things. He dwells in the heavens in unapproachable light. He is all powerful, all wise, a God of love, mercy, holiness, righteousness and truth. God is a unity.

In the beginning God created the heaven and the earth (Gen. 1:1).

The blessed and only potentate, the King of kings, and Lord of lords, who only hath immortality, dwelling in the light which no man can approach unto (1 Tim. 6:15).

And this is life eternal, that they might know thee, the only true God, and Jesus Christ, whom thou hast sent (John 17:3).

He made known his ways unto Moses, his acts unto the children of Israel. The Lord is merciful and gracious, slow to anger, and plenteous in mercy. He will not always chide: neither will he keep his anger for ever. He hath not dealt with us after our sins: nor rewarded us according to our iniquities. For as the heaven is high above the earth, so great is his mercy toward them that fear him (Psa. 103:8-11).

Hear, O Israel, the Lord our God is one lord (Deut. 6:4).

But to us there is but one God, the Father, of whom are all things, and we in him; and one Lord Jesus Christ, by whom are all things, and we by him (1 Cor. 8:6).

For there is one God, and one mediator between God and men, the man Christ Jesus (1 Tim. 2:5).

A DECLARATION OF THE TRUTH REVEALED IN THE
BIBLE AS DISTINGUISHABLE FROM THE THEOLOGY
OF CHRISTENDOM (AMENDED
CHRISTADELPHIANS) (continued)

See also Isa. 45:12; Psa. 11:4; Psa. 33: 104:30; Mark 12:29;
Eph. 4:6.

THE SPIRIT OF GOD

3.   The Spirit of God is His power by which He sustains
     creation, is everywhere present, and reveals and
     fulfils His will.

And the Spirit of God moved upon the face of the waters
(Gen. 1:2).

Thou knowest my downsitting and mine uprising; thou
understandest my thoughts afar off. Thou compassest my
path and my lying down, and art acquainted with all my
ways. For there is not a word on my tongue, but lo, Lord,
thou knowest it altogether. Thou hast beset me behind and
before, and laid thine hand upon me. Such knowledge is
too wonderful for me; it is high, I cannot attain unto it.
Whither shall I go from thy Spirit, or whither, shall I flee
from thy presence? If I ascend up into heaven thou art
there: if I make my bed in hell (*sheol,* the grave), behold,
thou art there . . . The darkness hideth not from thee,
but the night shineth as the day: the darkness and the light
are both alike to thee (Psa. 139:2-12).

The Spirit of God hath made me, and the breath of the
Almighty hath given me life (Job 26:13).

Yet many years didst thou forbear them, and testifiedst
against them by thy Spirit in thy prophets (Neh. 9:30).

See also Psa. 10:30; Micah 3:8.

4.   The Holy Spirit is the same power of God directed to
     fulfil any special purpose, as in His redeeming work.
     Thus by the Holy Spirit God's revelation was made
     through the prophets: by the Holy Spirit Jesus was
     begotten and enabled to do his mighty works and
     speak the Father's words: by it the apostles were
     guided into all truth and were able to attest their
     message by wonderful works. Special gifts of the
     Holy Spirit were granted in the early church, and by
     the Holy Spirit God dwelt among the believers.

For the prophecy came not in old time by the will of man:
but holy men of God spake as they were moved by the
Holy Spirit (2 Peter 1:21).

And the angel answered and said unto her, The Holy Spirit
shall come upon thee, and the power of the Highest shall
overshadow thee; therefore also that holy thing that shall
be born of thee shall be called the Son of God (Luke 1:35).

And John bare record, saying, I saw the Spirit descending
from heaven like a dove, and it abode upon him. And I
knew him not: but he that sent me to baptize with water,
the same said unto me, Upon whom thou shalt see the
Spirit descending, and remaining on him, the same is he
which baptizeth with the Holy Spirit (John 1:32, 33).

God anointed Jesus of Nazareth with the Holy Spirit and
with power; who went about doing good, and healing all
that were oppressed of the devil, for God was with him
(Acts 10:38).

The Spirit of the Lord is upon me, because he hath
anointed me to preach the gospel to the poor; he hath sent
me to heal the brokenhearted, to preach deliverance to the
captives, and recovering of sight to the blind, to set at
liberty them that are bruised, to preach the acceptable year
of the Lord. And he closed the book, and he gave it again
to the minister, and sat down. And the eyes of all them
that were in the synagogue were fastened on him. And he
began to say unto them. This day is this scripture fulfilled
in your ears (Luke 4:18-21).

The Comforter, which is the Holy Spirit whom the Father
will send in my name, he shall teach you all things, and
bring all things to your remembrance, whatsoever I have
said unto you (John 14:26).

John truly baptized with water, but ye shall be baptized
with the Holy Spirit not many days hence . . . Ye shall
receive power after the Holy Spirit is come upon you (Acts
1:5-8).

And suddenly there came a sound from heaven as of a
rushing mighty wind, and it filled all the house where they
were sitting, and they were all filled with the Holy Spirit
(Acts 2:2-4).

And as I began to speak, the Holy Spirit fell on them as on
us at the beginning. Then remembered I the word of the
Lord how that he said, John indeed baptized with water,
but ye shall be baptized with the Holy Spirit (Acts 11:15-
16).

Then laid they their hands on them, and they received the
Holy Spirit; and when Simon saw that through the laying
on of the apostles' hands the Holy Spirit was given, he
offered them money, saying, Give me also this power (Acts
8:17-19).

Now there are diversities of gifts, but the same Spirit. And
there are differences of administrations, but the same
Lord. And there are diversities of operations, but it is the
same God which worketh all in all. But the manifestation
of the Spirit is given to every man to profit withal. For to
one is given by the Spirit the word of wisdom; to another
the word of knowledge by the same Spirit; to another faith
by the same Spirit; to another the gifts of healing by the
same Spirit; to another the working of miracles; to another
prophecy; to another discerning of spirits; to another
divers kinds of tongues; to another the interpretation of
tongues; but all these worketh that one and the selfsame
Spirit, dividing to every man severally as he will (1 Cor.
12:4-11).

Know ye not that your body is the temple of the Holy
Spirit, which is in you, which ye have of God, and ye are
not your own? (1 Cor. 6:19).

JESUS CHRIST

5.   Jesus Christ, the only begotten Son of God, was born
     of the virgin Mary. He was raised up a last Adam,
     born of our nature, tempted as we are, yet without
     sin, to remove by his obedience, death and resurrec-
     tion, all the evils resulting from the disobedience of
     the first Adam.

But while he thought on these things, behold, the angel of
the Lord appeared unto him in a dream, saying, Joseph,
thou son of David, fear not to take unto thee Mary thy

wife: for that which is conceived in her is of the Holy Spirit. And she shall bring forth a son, and thou shalt call his name JESUS: for he shall save his people from their sins (Matt. 1:20, 21).

And the angel answered and said unto her, The Holy Spirit shall come upon thee, and the power of the Highest shall overshadow thee: therefore also that holy thing which shall be born of thee shall be called the Son of God (Luke 1:35).

But when the fulness of the time was come, God sent forth his Son, made of a woman, made under the law (Gal. 4:4).

Who in the days of his flesh, when he had offered up prayers and supplications with strong crying and tears upon him that was able to save him from death, and was heard in that he feared: though he were a Son, yet learned he obedience by the things which he suffered (Heb. 5:7, 8).

For verily he took not on him the nature of angels; but he took on him the seed of Abraham. Wherefore in all things it behoved him to be made like unto his brethren, that he might be a merciful and faithful high priest in things pertaining to God, to make reconciliation for the sins of the people. For in that he himself hath suffered being tempted, he is able to succour them that are tempted (Heb. 2:16-18).

For since by man came death, by man came also the resurrection of the dead. For as in Adam all die, even so in Christ shall all be made alive . . . And so it is written, The first man Adam was made a living soul; the last Adam was made a quickening spirit. Howbeit that was not first which is spiritual, but that which is natural; and afterward that which is spiritual. The first man is of the earth, earthy: the second man is the Lord from heaven. As is the earthy, such are they also that are earthy: and as is the heavenly, such are they also that are heavenly. And as we have borne the image of the earthy, we shall also bear the image of the heavenly (1 Cor. 15:21, 22, 45, 49).

For there is one God, and one mediator between God and men, the man Christ Jesus (1 Tim. 2:5).

6. Death which sin brought into the world could only be conquered by the conquest of sin itself. This, man himself could not achieve. The death of Jesus was an act of loving obedience to God by which we may have forgiveness of our sins and be reconciled to God, the sinless life of Jesus making him conqueror over sin, an effective offering for sin, and ensuring his triumph over death by resurrection. God revealed His love is providing him as a saviour.

For God so loved the world, that he gave his only begotten Son, that whosoever believeth in him should not perish, but have everlasting life (John 3:16).

The next day John seeth Jesus coming unto him, and saith, Behold the Lamb of God, which taketh away the sin of the world (John 1:29).

Whom God hath set forth to be a propitiation through faith in his blood, to declare his righteousness for the remission of sincs that are past, through the forbearance of God (Rom. 3:25).

But God commendeth his love toward us, in that, while we were yet sinners, Christ died for us (Rom. 5:8).

In whom we have redemption through his blood, the forgiveness of sins, according to the riches of his grace (Eph. 1:7).

Who hath delivered us from the power of darkness, and hath translated us into the kingdom of his dear Son: in whom we have redemption through his blood, even the forgiveness of sins (Col. 1:13, 14).

Who gave himself for our sins, that he might deliver us from the present evil world, according to the will of God and our Father (Gal. 1:4).

Who gave himself for us, that he might redeem us from all iniquity, and purify unto himself a peculiar people, zealous of good works (Titus 2:14).

For he hath made him to be sin for us, who knew no sin; that we might be made the righteouess of God in him (2 Cor. 5:21).

But he was wounded for our transgressions, he was bruised for our iniquities: the chastisement of our peace was upon him; and with his stripes we are healed . . . He shall see of the travail of his soul, and shall be satisifed: by his knowledge shall my righteous servant justify many; for he shall bear their iniquities (Isa. 53:5 and 11).

7. Jesus was raised from death on the third day, bringing life and immortality to light. Exalted to his Father's right hand he is alive for evermore, and pleads the cause of his people as their High Priest and Mediator.

Whom God hath raised up, having loosed the pains of death: because it was not possible that he should be holden of it (Acts 2:24).

Him God raised up the third day, and shewed him openly (Acts 10:40).

Concerning his Son Jesus Christ our Lord, which was made of the seed of David according to the flesh; and declared to be the Son of God with power, according to the spirit of holiness, by the resurrection from the dead (Rom. 1:3, 4).

Knowing that Christ being raised from the dead dieth no more; death hath no more dominion over him (Rom. 6:9).

Which he wrought in Christ, when he raised him from the dead, and set him at his own right hand in the heavenly places, far above all principality, and power, and might, and dominion, and every name that is named, not only in this world, but also in that which is to come (Eph. 1:20, 21).

Wherefore, holy brethren, partakers of the heavenly calling, consider the Apostle and High Priest of our profession, Christ Jesus (Heb. 3:1).

Wherefore he is able to save them to the uttermost that come unto God by him, seeing he ever liveth to make intercession for them (Heb. 7:25).

For there is one God, and one mediator between God and men, the man Christ Jesus (1 Tim. 2:5).

8. At the time appointed God is to send His Son to the earth again in power and great glory, to judge the living and the dead, and to establish upon earth a universal and abiding Kingdom.

And when he had spoken these things, while they beheld, he was taken up; and a cloud received him out of their sight. And while they looked stedfastly toward heaven as he went up, behold, two men stood by them in white apparel; which also said, Ye men of Galilee, why stand ye gazing up into heaven? this same Jesus, which is taken up from you into heaven, shall so come in like manner as ye have seen him go into heaven (Acts 1:9-11).

And he shall send Jesus Christ, which before was preached unto you: whom the heaven must receive until the times of restitution of all things, which God hath spoken by the mouth of all his holy prophets since the world began (Acts 3:20, 21).

For the Son of man shall come in the glory of his Father with his angels; and then shall he reward every man according to his works (Matt. 16:27).

For this we say unto you by the word of the Lord, that we which are alive and remain unto the coming of the Lord shall not prevent them which are asleep. For the Lord himself shall descend from heaven with a shout, with the voice of the archangel, and with the trump of God: and the dead in Christ shall rise first: then we which are alive and remain shall be caught up together with them in the clouds to meet the Lord in the air: and so shall we ever be with the Lord (1 Thess. 4:15-17).

For our conversation is in heaven; from whence also we look for the Saviour, the Lord Jesus Christ (Phil. 3:21).

I charge thee therefore before God, and the Lord Jesus Christ, who shall judge the quick and the dead at his appearing and his kingdom (2 Tim. 4:1).

And the seventh angel sounded; and there were great voices in heaven, saying, The kingdoms of this world are become the kingdoms of our Lord, and of his Christ; and he shall reign for ever and ever (Rev. 11:15).

For he must reign, till he hath put all enemies under his feet (1 Cor. 15:25).

MAN

9. A creature of dust, man is mortal: that is, subject to death or dissolution of being, in consequence of the disobedience of Adam which brought death as the penalty of sin. In the death state a man is a body deprived of life, and is as utterly unconscious as if he had never existed. His dead body corruption will presently destroy.

And the Lord God formed man of the dust of the ground, and breathed into his nostrils the breath of life; and man became a living soul (Gen. 2:7).

In the sweat of thy face shalt thou eat bread, till thou return unto the ground; for out of it wast thou taken: for dust thou art, and unto dust shalt thou return (Gen. 3:19).

For he knoweth our frame; he remembereth that we are dust (Psa. 103:14).

Wherefore, as by one man sin entered into the world, and death by sin; and so death passed upon all men, for that all have sinned (Rom. 5:12).

For in death there is no remembrance of thee: in the grave who shall give thee thanks? (Psa. 6:5).

Thou hidest thy face, they are troubled: thou takest away their breath, they die, and return to their dust (Psa. 104:29).

Put not your trust in princes, nor in the son of man, in whom there is no help. His breath goeth forth, he returneth to his earth; in that very day his thoughts perish (Psa. 146:3, 4).

For the living know that they shall die: but the dead know not anything, neither have they any more a reward; for the memory of them is forgotten. Also their love, and their hatred, and their envy, is now perished: neither have they any more a portion for ever in any thing that is done under the sun . . . Whatsoever thy hand findeth to do, do it with thy might; for there is no work nor device, nor knowledge, nor wisdom, in the grave, whither thou goest (Eccl. 9:5, 6 and 10).

For the grave cannot praise thee, death cannot celebrate thee: they that go down into the pit cannot hope for thy truth. The living, the living, he shall praise thee, as I do this day: the father to the children shall make known thy truth (Isa. 38:18, 19).

10. "Soul" in the Bible means, primarily, creature; but it is also used of the various aspects in which a living creature—man or beast—can be contemplated, such as person, body, life, breath, mind. It never expresses the idea of immortality.

And God said, Let the waters bring forth abundantly the moving creature that hath life, (margin-soul) and fowl that may fly above the earth in the open firmament of heaven . . . And God said, Let the earth bring forth the living creature afater his kind, cattle, and creeping thing, and beast of the earth after his kind (Gen. 1:20, 24).

It shall even be as when an hungry man dreameth, and, behold, he eateth; but he awaketh, and his soul is empty: or as when a thirsty man dreameth, and, behold, he drinketh; but he awaketh, and, behold he is faint, and his soul hath appeite: so shall the multitude of all nations be, that fight against mount Zion (Isa. 29:8).

And in the first day there shall be an holy convocation, and in the seventh day there shall be an holy convocation to you: no manner of work shall be done in them, save that which every man (margin—soul) must eat (Exod. 12:16).

Men do not despise a thief, if he steal to satisfy his soul when he is hungry (Prov. 6:30).

Behold, for peace I had great bitterness: but thou hast in love to my soul delivered it from the pit of corruption: for thou hast cast all my sins behind thy back (Isa. 38:17).

And levy a tribute unto the Lord of the men of war which went out to battle: one soul of five hundred, both of the persons, and of the beeves, and of the asses, and of the sheep (Num. 31:28).

And Samson said, Let me (margin—my soul) die with the Philistines. And he bowed himself with all his might; and the house fell upon the lords, and upon all the people that were therein. So the dead which he slew at his death were more than they which he slew in his life (Judges 16:30).

Behold, all souls are mine; as the soul of the father, so also the soul of the son is mine: the soul that sinneth, it shall die . . . The soul that sinneth, it shall die (Ezek. 18:4, 20).

Yea, a sword shall pierce through thy own soul also (Luke 2:35).

And it shall come to pass that every soul, which will not hear that prophet, shall be destroyed from among the people (Acts 3:23).

Let every soul be subject unto the higher powers. For there is no power but of God: the powers that be are ordained of God (Rome 13:1).

And the second angel poured out his vial upon the sea; and it became as the blood of a dead man: and every living soul died in the sea (Rev. 16:3).

11. "Spirit" in the Scripture, as applied to man, is no more expressive of the notion of an immortal soul than is "soul", but signifies breath, life, energy, disposition, mind, conscience, as attributes of man while alive.

And it came to pass in the morning that his spirit was troubled; and he sent and called for all the magicians of Egypt, and all the wise men thereof: and Pharaoh told them his dream; but there was none that could interpret them unto Pharaoh (Gen. 41:8).

And they told him all the words of Joseph, which he had said unto them: and when he saw the wagons which Joseph had sent to carry them, the spirit of Jacob their father received (Gen. 45:27).

And Moses spake so unto the children of Israel: but they hearkened not unto Moses for anguish of spirit, and for cruel bondage (Exod. 6:9).

And Hannah answered and said, No, my lord, I am a woman of sorrowful spirit: I have drunk neither wine nor strong drink, but have poured out my soul before the Lord (1 Sam. 1:15).

And when the queen of Sheba had seen the wisdom of Solomon . . . and the attendance of his ministers, and their apparel; his cup bearers also, and their apparel; and his ascent by which he went up into the house of the Lord; there was no more spirit in her (2 Chron. 9:4).

I remembered God, and was troubled: I complained, and my spirit was overwhelmed . . . I call to remembrance my song in the night: I commune with mine own heart: and my spirit made diligent search (Psa. 77:3 and 6).

A merry heart maketh a cheerful countenance: but by sorrow of the heart the spirit is broken (Prov. 15:13).

Blessed are the poor in spirit: for theirs is the kingdom of heaven (Matt. 5:3).

When Jesus had thus said, he was troubled in spirit, and testified, and said, Verify, verify, I say unto you, that one of you shall betray me (John 13:21).

Now while Paul waited for them at Athens, his spirit was stirred in him, when he saw the city wholly given to idolatry (Acts 17:16).

Not slothful in business; fervent in spirit; serving the Lord (Rom. 12:11).

And he renewed in the spirit of your mind (Eph. 4:23).

12. Immortality is not inherent in man, but is the gift of God, made available through the work of Jesus Christ His Son, to all who truly believe and follow his example.

For God so loved the world, that he gave his only begotten Son, that whosoever believeth in him should not perish, but have everlasting life (John 3:16).

And I give unto them eternal life; and they shall never perish, neither shall any man pluck them out of my hand (John 10:28).

As thou hast given him power over all flesh, that he should give eternal life to as many as thou hast given him (John 17:2).

For the wages of sin is death; but the gift of God is eternal life through Jesus Christ our Lord (Rom. 6:23).

But is now made manifest by the appearing of our Saviour Jesus Christ, who hath abolished death, and hath brought life and immortality to light through the gospel (2 Tim. 1:10).

And this is the record, that God hath given to us eternal life, and this life is in his Son. He that hath the Son hath life; and he that hath not the Son of God hath not life (1 John 5:11, 12).

And Jesus answered and said, Verify, I say unto you. There is no man that hath left house, or brethren, or sisters, or father, or mother, or wife, or children, or lands, for my sake, and the gospel's, but he shall receive an hundredfold now in this time, houses, and brethren, and sisters, and mothers, and children, and lands, with persecutions; and in the world to come eternal life (Mark 10:29, 30).

13. Immortality is not possessed now but will be bestowed at the resurrection and judgment at the advent of the Lord Jesus.

For I know that my redeemer liveth, and that he shall stand at the latter day upon the earth: and though after my skin worms destroy this body, yet in my flesh shall I see God: whom I shall see for myself, and mine eyes shall behold, and not another: though my reins be consumed within me (Job 19:25-27).

And many of them that sleep in the dust of the earth shall awake, some to everlasting life, and some to shame and everlasting contempt (Dan. 12:2).

And this is the Father's will which hath sent me, that of all which he hath given me I should lose nothing, but should raise it up again at the last day. And this is the will of him that sent me, that every one which seeth the Son, and believeth on him, may have everlasting life: and I will raise him up at the last day . . . No man can come to me, except the Father which hath sent me draw him: and I will raise him up at the last day (John 6:39, 40 and 44).

A DECLARATION OF THE TRUTH REVEALED IN THE BIBLE AS DISTINGUISHABLE FROM THE THEOLOGY OF CHRISTENDOM (AMENDED CHRISTADELPHIANS) (continued)

But I would not have you to be ignorant, brethren, concerning them which are asleep, that ye sorrow not even as others which have no hope. For if we believe that Jesus died and rose again, even so them also which sleep in Jesus will God bring with him. For this we say unto you by the word of the Lord, that we which are alive and remain unto the coming of the Lord shall not prevent them which are alseep. For the Lord himself shall descent from heaven with a shout, with the voice of the archangel, and with the trump of God: and the dead in Christ shall rise first: then we which are alive and remain shall be caught up together with them in the clouds, to meet the Lord in the air; and so shall we ever be with the Lord. Wherefore comfort one another with these words (1 Thess. 4:13-18).

But if there be no resurrection of the dead, then is Christ not risen: and if Christ be not risen, then is our preaching vain, and your faith is also vain (1 Cor. 15:13, 14).

Now this I say, brethren, that flesh and blood cannot inherit the kingdom of God; neither doth corruption inherit incorruption. Behold, I shew you a mystery: we shall not all sleep, but we shall all be changed, in a moment, in the twinkling of an eye, at the last trump: for the trumpet shall sound, and the dead shall be raised incorruptible, and we shall be changed. For this corruptible must put on incorruption, and this mortal must put on immortality. So when this corruptible shall have put on incorruption, and this mortal shall have put on immortality, then shall be brought to pass the saying that is written, Death is swallowed up in victory (1 Cor. 15:50-54).

But they which shall be accounted worthy to obtain that world, and the resurrection from the dead, neither marry nor are given in marriage: neither can they die any more: for they are equal unto the angels, and are children of God, being the children of the resurrection (Luke 20:35, 36).

14. The earth is the destined sphere of the activity of God's people, when made immortal.

For evildoers shall be cut off: but those that wait upon the Lord, they shall inherit the earth. For yet a little while, and the wicked shall not be: yea, thou shalt diligently consider his place, and it shall not be. But the meek shall inherit the earth; and shall delight themselves in the abundance of peace . . . For such as be blessed of him shall inherit the earth: and they that be cursed of him shall be cut off (Psa. 37:9-11 and 22).

And the kingdom and dominion, and the greatness of the kingdom under the whole heaven, shall be given to the people of the saints of the most High, whose kingdom is an everlasting kingdom, and all dominions shall serve and obey him (Dan. 7:27).

Blessed are the meek: for they shall inherit the earth (Matt. 5:5).

And Jesus said unto them, Verily I say unto you, That ye which have followed me, in the regeneration when the Son of Man shall sit in the throne of his glory, ye also shall sit upon twelve thrones, judging the twelve tribes of Israel (Matt. 19:28).

For the promise, that he should be the heir of the world, was not to Abraham, or to his seed, through the law, but through the righteousness of faith (Rom. 4:13).

And he that overcometh, and keepeth my works unto the end, to him will I give power over the nations: and he shall rule them with a rod of iron; as the vessels of the potter shall they be broken to shivers: even as I received of my Father (Rev. 2:26, 27).

And they sung a new song, saying, Thou art worthy to take the book, and to open the seals thereof: for thou wast slain, and hast redeemed us to God by thy blood, out of every kindred, and tongue, and people, and nation; and hast made us unto our God kings and priests: and we shall reign on the earth (Rev. 5:9, 10).

15. It follows also of necessity that the once popular theory of hell as a place of eternal torments, is untrue. The original, unspoilt meaning of "hell" was an unseen or covered place. "Hell" in the Bible often means the grave. (In the Old Testament, the original Hebrew word SHEOL occurs 65 times, being translated 31 times "hell", 31 times "the grave" and three times "pit". In the New Testament the original Greek word HADES occurs 11 times, being translated 10 times "hell" and once "the grave".)

Let me not be ashamed, O Lord: for I have called upon thee: let the wicked be ashamed, and let them be silent in the grave (Psa. 31:17).

For great is thy mercy toward me: and thou hast delivered my soul from the lowest hell (Psa. 86:13).

Then Jonah prayed unto the Lord his God out of the fish's belly, and said, I cried by reason of mine affliction unto the Lord, and he heard me; out of the belly of hell cried I, and thou heardest my voice. For thou hadst cast me into the deep, in the midst of the seas; and the floods compassed me about: all thy billows and thy waves passed over me (Jonah 2:1-3).

And if ye take this also from me, and mischief befall him, ye shall bring down my gray hairs with sorrow to the grave. Now therefore when I come to thy servant my father, and the lad be not with us; seeing that his life is bound up in the lad's life; it shall come to pass, when he seeth that the lad is not with us, that he will die: and thy servants shall bring down the gray hairs of thy servant our father with sorrow to the grave (Gen. 44:29-31).

For in death there is no remembrance of thee: in the grave who shall give thee thanks? (Psa. 6:5).

Whatsoever thy hand findeth to do, do with thy might: for there is no work, nor device, nor knowledge, nor wisdom, in the grave, whither thou goest (Eccl. 9:10).

I said in the cutting of my days, I shall go to the gates of the grave: I am deprived of the residue of my years . . . For the grave cannot praise thee, death cannot celebrate thee: they that go down into the pit cannot hope for thy truth (Isa. 38:10 and 18).

I will ransom them from the power of the grave; I will redeem them from death: O death, I will be thy plagues: O grave, I will by thy destruction: repentance shall be hid from mine eyes (Hosea 13:14).

And thou, Capernaum, which art exalted unto heaven, shalt be brought down to hell: for if the mighty works, which have been done in thee, had been done in Sodom, it would have remained until this day (Matt. 11:23).

Because thou wilt not leave my soul in hell, neither wilt thou suffer thine Holy One to see corruption. Thou hast made known to me the ways of life: thou shalt make me full of joy with thy countenance. Men and brethren, let me freely speak unto you of the patriach David, that he is both dead and buried, and his sepulchre is with us unto this day. Therefore being a prophet, and knowing that God had sworn with an oath to him, that of the fruit of his loins, according to the flesh, he would raise up Christ to sit on his throne; he seeing this before spake of the resurrection of Christ, that his soul was not left in hell, neither his flesh did see corruption (Acts 2:27-31).

I am he that liveth, and was dead: and, behold, I am alive for evermore, Amen; and have the keys of hell and of death (Rev. 1:18).

O death, where is thy sting? O grave, where is thy victory? (1 Cor. 15:55).

16. Sometimes in the New Testament the original word for hell is GETHENNA, a term associated with the valley of Hinnom, a place near Jerusalem once the scene of idolatrous burnings and consequently so abhorred by the Jews of later Bible times that it was used as a place for the destruction of refuse and the dead bodies of animals and criminals, fires being continually kept burning for this purpose. It is therefore fittingly used to describe the future judgment.

And if thy hand offend thee, cut it off: it is better for thee to enter into life maimed, than having two hands to go into hell, into the fire that never shall be quenched (Mark 9:43).

But I say unto you, That whosoever is angry with his brother without a cause shall be in danger of the judgment: and whosoever shall say to his brother, Raca, shall be in danger of the council: but whosoever shall say, Thou fool, shall be in danger of hell fire (Matt. 5:22).

And fear not them which kill the body, but are not able to kill the soul; but rather fear him which is able to destroy both soul and body in hell (Matt. 10:28).

17. The true Bible doctrine of reward and punishment is that at his return in power and glory Jesus Christ will judge all those who are made responsible to him by knowledge of God's will; these will include some living at the time, and those whom he will raise from the dead, both righteous and unrighteous. He will invest the righteous with immortality in his kingdom, but will commit the wicked to destruction.

And at that time shall Michael stand up, the great prince which standeth for the children of thy people: and there shall be a time of trouble, such as never was since there was a nation even to that same time: and at that time thy people shall be delivered, every one that shall be found written in the book. And many of them that sleep in the dust of the earth shall awake, some to everlasting life, and some to shame and everlasting contempt (Dan. 12:1, 2).

For God so loved the world, that he gave his only begotten Son, that whosoever believeth in him should not perish, but have everlasting life. For God sent not his Son into the world to condemn the world; but that the world through him might be saved. He that believeth on him is not condemned: but he that believeth not is condemned already, because he hath not believed in the name of the only begotten Son of god. And that is the condemnation, that light is come into the world, and men loved darkness rather than light, because their deeds were evil (John 3:16-19).

Marvel not at this: for the hour is coming, in the which all that are in the graves shall hear his voice, and shall come forth; they that have done good, unto the resurrection of life; and they that have done evil unto the resurrection of damnation (John 5:28.29).

He that rejecteth me, and receiveth not my words, hath on that judgeth him: the word that I have spoken, the same shall judge him in the last day (John 12:48).

Who then is a faithful and wise servant, whom his lord hath made ruler over his household, to give them meat in due season? Blessed is that servant, whom his lord when he cometh shall find so doing. Verily I say unto you, That he shall make him ruler over all his goods. But and if that evil servant shall say in his heart, My lord delayeth his coming; and shall begin to smite his fellowservants, and to eat and drink with the drunken: the lord of that servant shall come in a day when he looketh not for him, and in an hour that he is not aware of, and shall cut him asunder, and appoint him his portion with the hypocrites: there shall be weeping and gnashing of teeth (Matt. 24:44-51).

And he commanded us to preach unto the people, and to testify that it is he which was ordained of God to be the Judge of quick and dead. To him give all the prophets witness, that through his name whosoever believeth in him shall receive remission of sins (Acts 10:42, 43).

And have hope toward God, which they themselves also allow, that there shall be a resurrection of the dead, both of the just and unjust (Acts 24:15).

For we must all appear before the judgment seat of Christ; that every one may receive the things done in his body, according to that he hath done, whether it be good or bad (2 Cor. 5:10).

The Lord Jesus shall be revealed from heaven, in flaming fire taking vengeance on them that know not God, and that obey not the gospel of our Lord Jesus Christ: who shall be punished with everlasting destruction from the presence of the Lord, and from the glory of his power (2 Thess. 1:8, 9).

I charge thee therefore before God and the Lord Jesus Christ, who shall judge the quick and the dead at his appearing and his kingdom (2 Tim. 4:1).

And the nations were angry, and thy wrath is come, and the time of the dead, that they should be judged, and that thou shouldest give reward unto thy servants the prophets, and to the saints, and them that fear thy name, small and

A DECLARATION OF THE TRUTH REVEALED IN THE BIBLE AS DISTINGUISHABLE FROM THE THEOLOGY OF CHRISTENDOM (AMENDED CHRISTADELPHIANS) (continued)

great; and shouldest destroy them which destroy the earth (Rev. 11:18).

See also Matt. 25:31, 46; Luke 13:24-30; Rom. 2:1-16.

18. Without the knowledge of the saving gospel men have no hope of life; but neither are they responsible to judgment; their death will be an endless sleep.

For God so loved the world, that he gave his only begotten Son, that whosoever believeth in him should not perish, but have everlasting life (John 3:16).

Wherefore remember, that ye being in time past Gentiles in the flesh, . . . that at that time ye were without Christ, being aliens from the commonwealth of Israel, and strangers from the covenants of promise, having no hope, and without God in the world (Eph. 2:11, 12).

This I say therefore, and testify in the Lord, that ye henceforth walk not as other Gentiles walk, in the vanity of their mind, having the understanding darkened, being alienated from the life of God through the ignorance that is in them, because of the blindness of their heart (Eph. 4:17, 18).

But I would not have you to be ignorant, brethren, concerning them which are asleep, that ye sorrow not, even as others which have no hope (1 Thess. 4:13).

He that hath the Son hath life; and he that hath not the Son of God hath not life (1 John 5:12).

Man that is in honour, and understandeth not, is like the beasts that perish (Psa. 49:20).

O Lord our god, other lords beside thee have had dominion over us: but by thee only will we make mention of thy name. They are dead, they shall not live; they are deceased, they shall not rise; therefore hast thou visited and destroyed them, and made all their memory to perish (Isa. 26:13, 14).

They shall . . . sleep a perpetual sleep, and not wake, saith the Lord (Jer. 51:39).

The man that wandereth out of the way of understanding shall remain in the congregation of the dead (Prov. 21:16).

THE DEVIL

19. Since Jesus was manifested expressly for the purpose of destroying the Devil and his works (1 John 3:8; Heb. 2:14) the Lord's mission is imperfectly understood when the nature of the Bible Devil is not comprehended. The Devil is not a supernatural person but a personification of sin in its various manifestations—individual, social and political.

Jesus answered them, Have not I chosen you twelve, and one of you is a devil? (John 6:70).

Ye are of your father the devil, and the lusts of your father ye will do. He was a murderer from the beginning, and abode not in the truth, because there is not truth in him. When he speaketh a lie, he speaketh of his own: for he is a liar, and the father of it (John 8:44).

God anointed Jesus of Nazareth with the Holy Spirit and with power: who went about doing good and healing all that were oppressed of the devil; for God was with him (Acts 10:38).

Be sober, be vigilant; because your adversary the devil, as a roaring lion, walketh about, seeking whom he may devour (1 Peter 5:8).

Fear none of those things which thou shalt suffer: behold, the devil shall cast some of you into prison, that ye may be tried; and ye shall have tribulation ten days: be thou faithful unto death, and I will give thee a crown of life (Rev. 2:10).

The following parallels illustrate Scripture usage of the word "devil":

Sin bringeth forth death (Jas. 1:15). Parallel with the devil hath the power of death (Heb. 2:14).

He put away sin by the sacrifice of himself (Heb. 9:26). Parallel with That through death he might destroy the devil (Heb. 2:14).

Why hast thou conceived this in thine heart? (Acts 5:4). Parallel with Why hath Satan filled thine heart? (Acts 5:3).

According to the course of this world (Eph. 2:2). Parallel with According to the prince of the power of the air (Eph. 2:2).

The desires of the flesh and of the mind (Eph. 2:3). Parallel with The spirit that now worketh in the children of disobedience (Eph. 2:2).

Every man tempted is drawn away of his own lust, and enticed (Jas. 1:14). Parallel with Taken captive by the devil at his will (2 Tim. 2:26).

The children of disobedience (Eph. 2:2). Parallel with The children of the devil (1 John 3:10).

Put off the old man, which is corrupt according to the deceitful lusts (Eph. 4:22). Parallel with Stand against the wiles of the devil (Eph. 6:11).

Loved this present world (2 Tim. 4:10). Parallel with The god of this world hath blinded their minds (2 Cor. 4:4).

Deliver us from this present evil world (Gal. 1:4). Parallel with Deliver us from the evil one (Revised Version) (Matt. 6:13).

The children of this world (Luke 20:34). Parallel with The children of the wicked one (Matt. 13:38).

Overcome the world (1 John 5:5). Parallel with Overcome the wicked one (1 John 2:14).

Keep himself unspotted from the world (Jas. 1:27). Parallel with Keep them from the evil one (Revised Version) (John 17:15).

The lamb shall overcome them (the ten kings) (rev. 17:14). Parallel with He laid hold on the dragon, that old serpent, which is the Devil, and Satan (Rev. 20:2).

20. The Bible term Satan means simply "adversary" and is used of human beings.

And the princes of the Philistines were wroth with him; and the princes of the Philistines said unto him, Make this fellow return, that he may go again to his place which thou hast appointed him, and let him not go down with us to battle, lest in the battle he be an adversary to us (1 Sam. 29:4).

And the Lord stirred up an adversary unto Solomon, Hadad the Edomite: he was of the king's seed in Edom . . . And God stirred him up another adversary, Rezon the son of Eliadah . . . And he was an adversary to Israel all the days of Solomon, beside the mischief that Hadad did: and he abhorred Israel, and reigned over Syria (1 Kings 11:14, 23, 25).

For my love they are my adversaries: but I give myself unto prayer . . . Let this be the reward of mine adversaries from the Lord, and of them that speak evil against my soul . . . Let mine adversaries be clothed with shame, and let them cover themselves with their own confusion, as with a mantle (Psa. 109: 4, 20 and 29).

But he turned, and said unto Peter, Get thee behind me, Satan: thou art an offence unto me: for thou savourest not the things that be of God, but those that be of men (Matt. 16:23).

Later it came to mean much the same as Devil, *i.e.* a personification of the influence of sin or evil, individual or political.

And ought not this woman, being a daughter of Abraham, whom Satan hath bound, lo, these eighteeen years, be loosed from this bond on the sabbath day? (Luke 13:16).

Then entered Satan into Judas surnamed Iscariot, being of the number of the twelve (Luke 22:3). And the Lord said, Simon, Simon, behold, Satan hath desired to have you, that he may sift you as wheat (Luke 22:31).

To open their eyes, and to turn them from darkness to light, and from the power of Satan unto God, that they may receive forgiveness of sins, and inheritance among them which are sanctified by faith that is in me (Acts 26:18).

And the God of peace shall bruise Satan under your feet shortly (Rom. 16:20).

Defraud ye not one the other, except it be with consent for a time, that ye may give yourselves to fasting and prayer; and come together again, that Satan tempt you not for your incontinency (1 Cor. 7:5).

Fear none of those things which thou shalt suffer: behold, the devil shall cast some of you into prison, that ye may be tried; and ye shall have tribulation ten days: be thou faithful unto death, and I will give thee a crown of life . . . I know thy works, and where thou dwellest, even where Satan's seat is: and thou holdest fast my name, and hast not denied my faith, even in those days wherein Antipas was my faithful martyr, who was slain among you, where Satan dwelleth (Rev. 2:10, 13).

Sometimes the personification of the Devil or Satan is on a dramatic scale.

Job 1 and 2; Matt. 4; Luke 4; Luke 10:18; Jude 9.

THE PURPOSE AND PROMISES OF GOD

21. God has unfolded His purpose in the past by promises made at certain stages in human history. Peter calls them "exceeding great and precious promises" by which we might become partakers of the divine nature.

According as his divine power hath given unto us all things that pertain unto life and godliness, through the knowledge of him that hat called us to glory and virtue: whereby are given unto us exceeding great and precious promises: that by these ye might be partakers of the divine nature, having escaped the corruption that is in the world through lust (2 Peter 1:3, 4).

(a) The first promise was made when Adam had transgressed God's law in Eden, and revealed that one would be born in whom sin would be overcome and through whom all the evil that resulted from sin would be abolished.

And I will put enmity between thee and the woman, and between thy seed and her seed: it shall bruise thy head, and thou shalt bruise his heel (Gen. 3:15).

(b) An important unfolding of God's purpose arose when He called Abram to leave Ur of the Chaldees and to go to Palestine. It was revealed to Abram that his descendants should be God's people, that Abram and his seed should have the land for an eternal inheritance, and that all nations should be blessed in him. This great promise is called the Gospel in the New Testament, for it involves Abraham's greatest seed, Jesus Christ, the resurrection fro the dead of Abraham and all in his faithful line, and the eternal blessing of the world when Jesus establishes the Kingdom of Heaven upon earth.

Now the Lord had said unto Abram, Get thee out of thy country, and from thy kindred, and from thy father's house, unto a land that I will show thee: and I will make of thee a great nation, and I will bless thee, and make thy name great; and thou shalt be a blessing: and I will bless them that bless thee, and curse him that curseth thee: and in thee shall all families of the earth be blessed (Gen. 12:1-3).

And the Lord said unto Abram, after that Lot was separated from him, Lift up now thine eyes, and look from the place where thou art northward and southward, and eastward, and westward: for all the land which thou seest, to thee will I give it, and to thy seed for ever. And I will make thy seed as the dust of the earth: so that if a man can number the dust of the earth, then shall thy seed also be numbered. Arise, walk through the land in the length of it and in the breadth of it; for I will give it unto thee (Gen. 13:14-17).

And the scripture, foreseeing that God would justify the heathen through faith, preached before the gospel unto Abraham saying, In thee shall all nations be blessed . . . Now to Abraham and his seed were the promises made. He saith not, And to seeds as of many; but as of one, And to thy seed, which is Christ . . . And if ye be Christ's, then are ye Abraham's seed, and heirs according to the promise (Gal. 3:8, 16, 29).

Your father Abraham rejoiced to see my day: and he saw it, and was glad (John 8:56).

A DECLARATION OF THE TRUTH REVEALED IN THE
BIBLE AS DISTINGUISHABLE FROM THE THEOLOGY
OF CHRISTENDOM (AMENDED
CHRISTADELPHIANS) (continued)

And Jesus answering said unto them. The children of
this world marry, and are given in marriage: but they
which shall be accounted worthy to obtain that
world, and the resurrection from the dead, neither
marry, nor are given in marriage: neither can they
die any more: for they are equal unto the angels; and
are the children of God, being the children of the
resurrection. Now that the dead are raised, even
Moses showed at the bush, when he calleth the Lord
the God of Abraham and the God of Isaac, and the
God of Jacob. For he is not a God of the dead but of
the living: for all live unto him (Luke 20:34-38).

And I say unto you, That many shall come from the
east and west, and shall sit down with Abraham, and
Isaac, and Jacob, in the kingdom of heaven (Matt.
8:11).

Ye are the children of the prophets, and of the
covenant which God made with our fathers, saying
unto Abraham. And in thy seed shall all the kindreds
of the earth be blessed (Acts 3:25).

The word that Isaiah the son of Amoz saw concerning Judah and Jerusalem. And it shall come to pass
in the last days, that the mountain of the Lord's
house shall be established in the top of the mountains, and shall be exalted above the hills; and all
nations shall flow unto it. And many people shall go
and say, Come ye, and let us go up to the mountain
of the Lord, to the house of the god of Jacob; and he
will teach us of his ways, and we will walk in his
paths: for out of Zion shall go forth the law, and the
word of the Lord from Jerusalem. And he shall judge
among the nations, and shall rebuke many people:
and they shall beat their swords into plowshares, and
their spears into pruninghooks: nation shall not lift
up sword against nation, neither shall they learn war
any more (Isa. 2:1-4).

Say to them that are of a fearful heart. Be strong,
fear not: behold, your God will come with vengeance, even God with a recompence; he will come
and save you. Then the eyes of the blind shall be
opened, and the ears of the deaf shall be unstopped.
Then shall the lame man leap as an hart, and the
tongue of the dumb sing: for in the wilderness shall
waters break out, and streams in the desert . . .
And the ransomed of the Lord shall return and come
to Zion with songs and everlasting joy upon their
heads: they shall obtain joy and gladness, and sorrow
and sighing shall flee away (Isa. 35:4-10).

Rejoice greatly, O daughter of Zion: shout, O
daughter of Jerusalem: behold thy King cometh unto
thee: he is just, and having salvation: lowly, and
riding upon an ass, and upon a colt the foal of an ass.
And I will cut off the chariot from Ephraim, and the
horse from Jerusalem, and the battle bow shall be cut
off: and he shall speak peace unto the heathen: and

his dominion shall be from sea even to sea, and from
the river even to the ends of the earth (Zech. 9:9, 10).

And the Lord shall be king over all the earth: in that
day shall there be one Lord, and his name one (Zech.
14:9).

See also Heb. 11:8-16.

(c)　The promises were renewed to Isaac and Jacob,
who are henceforth associated with Abraham in
Scriptures of promise.

And the Lord appeared unto him, and said, Go not
down into Egypt; dwell in the land which I shall tell
thee of: sojourn in this land, and I will be with thee,
and will bless thee: for unto thee, and unto thy seed,
I will give all these countries, and I will perform the
oath which I sware unto Abraham thy father: and I
will make thy seed to multiply as the stars of heaven,
and will give unto thy seed all these countries; and in
thy seed shall all nations of the earth be
blessed . . . And the man waxed great, and went
forward, and grew until he became very great: for he
had possession of flocks, and possession of herds, and
great store of servants, and the Philistines envied him
(Gen. 26:3-4, 13, 14).

Thou wilt perform the truth to Jacob, and the mercy
to Abraham, which thou hast sworn into our fathers
from the days of old (Miah 7:20).

There shall be weeping and gnashing of teeth, when
ye shall see Abraham, and Isaac, and Jacob, and all
the prophets, in the kingdom of God, and you
yourselves thrust out (Luke 13:28).

(d)　The promises received a partial fulfilment in
Israel's occupation of Palestine (Neh. 9:7, 8), but
their ultimate, perfect and lasting fulfilment,
especially in their personal application to Abraham and all his faithful line, is associated with
Christ and his Kingdom.

And he gave him none inheritance in it (the land),
no, not so much as to set his foot on: yet he promised
that he would give it to him for a possession, and to
his seed after him, when as yet he had no child (Acts
7:5).

These all died in faith, not having received the
promises, but having seen them afar off, and were
persuaded of them, and embraced them, and confessed that they were strangers and pilgrims on the
earth . . . And these all, having obtained a good
report through faith, received not the promise: God
having provided some better thing for us, that they
without us should not be made perfect (Heb. 11:13,
39, 40).

Blessed be the Lord God of Israel; for he hath visited
and redeemed his people, and hath raised up an horn
of salvation for us in the house of his servant David:
as he spake by the mouth of his holy prophets, which
have been since the world began: that we should be
saved from our enemies, and from the hand of all
that hate us; to perform the mercy promised to our
fathers, and to remember his holy covenant; the oath

which he sware to our father Abraham (Luke 1:68-73).

And I say unto you, That many shall come from the east and west, and shall sit down with Abraham, and Isaac, and Jacob, in the kingdom of heaven (Matt. 8:11).

Now I say that Jesus Christ was a minister of the circumcision for the truth of God, to confirm the promises made unto the fathers; and that the Gentiles might glorify God for his mercy; as it is written, For this cause I will confess to thee among the Gentiles, and sing unto thy name. And again he saith, Rejoice, ye Gentiles, with his people. And again, Praise the Lord, all ye Gentiles; and laud him, all ye people. And again, Esaias saith, There shall be a root of Jesse, and he that shall rise to reign over the Gentiles; in him shall the Gentiles trust (Rom. 15:8-12).

(e) When Abraham's descendants had become fully established as God's Kingdom in the land of Palestine and David ruled over them, God revealed His purpose concerning the future of mankind. A descendant of David who would also be the Son of God should reign on David's restored and glorified throne forever.

The heir to David's throne is Jesus Christ.

(The significance of the first verse of the New Testament should be noted in connection with God's promises to Abraham and David.)

And when thy days be fulfilled, and thou shalt sleep with thy fathers, I will set up they seed after thee, which shall proceed out of thy bowels, and I will establish his kingdom. He shall build an house for my name, and I will establish the throne of his kingdom forever. I will be his father, and he shall be my son. If he commit iniquity, I will chasten him with the rod of men, and with the stripes of the children of men: but my mercy shall not depart away from him, as I took it from Saul, whom I put away before thee. And thine house and thy kingdom shall be established for ever before thee: thy throne shall be established for ever (2 Sam. 7:12-16).

The Lord hath sworn in truth unto David; he will not turn from it; Of the fruit of thy body will I set upon thy throne (Psa. 132:11).

And the angel said unto her, Fear not, Mary: for thou has found favour with God. And behold, thou shalt conceive in thy womb, and bring forth a son, and shalt call his name JESUS. He shall be great, and shall be called the Son of the Highest: and the Lord God shall give unto him the throne of his father David: and he shall reign over the house of Jacob for ever; and of his kingdom there shall be no end (Luke 1:30-33).

God had sworn with an oath to him (David) that of the fruit of his loins, according to the flesh, he would raise up Christ to sit on his throne (Acts 2:30).

Now these be the last words of David. David the son of Jesse said, and the man who was raised up on high, the anointed of the God of Jacob, and the sweet psalmist of Israel, said, The Spirit of the Lord spake by me, and his word was in my tongue. The God of Israel said, the Rock of Israel spake to me, He that ruleth over men must be just, ruling in the fear of God . . . Although my house be not so with God; yet he hath made with me an everlasting covenant, ordered in all things, and sure: for this is all my salvation, and all my desire, although he make it not to grow (2 Sam. 23:1-3,5).

For unto us a child is born, unto us a son is given: and the government shall be upon his shoulder: and his name shall be called Wonderful, Counsellor, The mighty God, The everlasting Father, The Prince of Peace. Of the increase of his government and peace there shall be no end, upon the throne of David, and upon his kingdom, to order it, and to establish it with judgment and with justice from henceforth even for ever. The zeal of the Lord of hosts will perform this (Isa. 9:6, 7).

See also Isaiah 11:1-10

(f) The unique character of the Kingdom of God was further revealed through the ministry of the prophets.

The word that Isaiah to son of Amoz saw concerning Judah and Jerusalem. And it shall come to pass in the last days, that the mountain of the Lord's house shall be established in the top of the mountains, and shall be exalted above the hills; and all nations shall flow unto it. And many people shall go and say, Come ye, and let us go up to the mountain of the Lord, to the house of the God of Jacob; and he will teach us of his ways, and we will walk in his paths: for out of Zion shall go forth the law, and the word of the Lord from Jerusalem. And he shall judge among the nations, and shall rebuke many people: and they shall beat their swords into plowshares, and their spears into pruning hooks: nation shall not lift up sword against nation, neither shall they learn war any more (Isa. 2:1-4).

And in this mountain shall the Lord of hosts make unto all people a feast of fat things, a feast of wines on the lees, of fat things full of marrow, of wines on the lees well refined. And he will destroy in this mountain the face of the covering cast over all people, and the vail that is spread over all nations. He will swallow up death in victory; and the Lord God will wipe away tears from off all faces; and the rebuke of his people shall he take away from off all the earth; for the Lord hath spoken it. And it shall be said in that day, Lo, this is our God; we have waited for him, and he will save us: this is the Lord; we have waited for him, we will be glad and rejoice in his salvation (Isa. 25:6-9).

Then the eyes of the blind shall be opened, and the ears of the deaf shall be unstopped. Then shall the lame man leap as an hart, and the tongue of the dumb sing: for in the wilderness shall waters break out, and streams in the desert . . . And an highway shall be there, and a way, and it shall be called

The way of holiness; the unclean shall not pass over
it; but it shall be for those: the wayfaring men,
though fools, shall not err therein . . . And the
ransomed of the Lord shall return, and come to Zion
with songs and everlasting joy upon their heads: they
shall obtain joy and gladness, and sorrow and sighing
shall flee away (Isa. 35:5, 6, 8, 10).

For the nation and kingdom that will not serve thee
shall perish; yea, those nations shall be utterly
wasted . . . Violence shall no more be heard in thy
land, wasting nor destruction within thy borders; but
thou shalt call thy walls Salvation, and thy gates
Praise . . . Thy people also shall be all righteous:
they shall inherit the land for ever, the branch of my
planting, the work of my hands, that I may be
glorified (Isa. 60:12, 18, 21).

For, behold, I create new heavens and a new earth:
and the former shall not be remembered, nor come
into mind. But be ye glad and rejoice for ever in that
which I create: for, behold, I create Jerusalem a
rejoicing, and her people a joy. And I will rejoice in
Jerusalem, and joy in my people: and the voice of
weeping shall be no more heard in her, nor the voice
of crying. There shall be no more thence an infant of
days, nor an old man that hath not filled his days: for
the child shall die an hundred years old; but the
sinner being an hundred years old shall be accursed
(Isa. 65:17-20).

Behold, the days come, saith the Lord, that I will
perform that good thing which I have promised unto
the house of Israel and to the house of Judah. In
those days, and at that time, will I cause the Branch
of righteousness to grow up into David; and he shall
execute judgment and righteousness in the land. In
those days shall Judah be saved, and Jerusalem shall
dwell safely: and this is the name wherewith she shall
be called. The Lord our righteousness (Jer. 33:14-
16).

Thus speaketh the Lord of hosts, saying, Behold the
man whose name is The BRANCH; and he shall
grow up out of his place, and he shall build the
temple of the Lord: even he shall build the temple of
the Lord; and he shall bear the glory, and shall sit
and rule upon his throne; and he shall be a priest
upon his throne: and the counsel of peace shall be
between them both (Zech. 6:12, 13).

And the Lord shall be king over all the earth: in that
day shall there be one Lord, and his name one . . .
And it shall come to pass, that every one that is left
of all the nations which came against Jerusalem shall
even go up from year to year to worship the King,
the Lord of hosts, and to keep the feast of tabernacles . . . In that day shall there be upon the bells of
the horses, HOLINESS UNTO THE LORD; and
the pots in the Lord's house shall be like the bowls
before the alter. Yea, every pot in Jerusalem and in

Judah shall be holiness unto the Lord of hosts; and
all they that sacrifice shall come and take of them,
and seethe therein: and in that day there shall be no
more the Canaanite in the house of the Lord of hosts
(Zech. 14:9, 16, 20, 21).

Behold, I will send my messenger, and he shall
prepare the way before me: and the Lord, whom ye
seek, shall suddenly come to his temple, even the
messenger of the covenant, whom ye delight in:
behold, he shall come, saith the Lord of hosts. But
who may abide the day of his coming? and who shall
stand when he appeareth? for he is like a refiner's
fire, and like fullers' soap: and he shall sit as a refiner
and purifier of silver: and he shall purify the sons of
Levi, and purge them as gold and silver, that they
may offer unto the Lord an offering in righteousness.
Then shall the offering of Judah and Jerusalem be
pleasant unto the Lord, as in the days of old, and as
in former years (Mal. 3:1-4).

And he shall send Jesus Christ, which before was
preached unto you: whom the heaven must receive
until the times of restitution of all things, which God
hath spoken by the mouth of all his holy prophets
since the world began (Acts 3:20, 21).

THE KINGDOM OF ISRAEL

22. "Salvation is of the Jews", Jesus said. The Kingdom
to be established is so far rooted in God's dealings
with the Jews in the past that it is described as the
Kingdom of Israel restored, enlarged and perfected.

(a) The kingdom of Israel, as divinely constituted at
Sinai and established in the land of Palestine was
the kingdom of God.

And of all my sons (for the Lord hath given me
many sons), he hath chosen Solomon my son to sit
upon the throne of the kingdom of the Lord over
Israel (1 Chron. 28:5).

Then Solomon sat on the throne of the Lord as king
instead of David his father, and prospered; and all
Israel obeyed him (1 Chron. 29:23).

And now ye think to withstand the kingdom of the
Lord in the hand of the sons of David (2 chron.
13:8).

(b) It was divinely overturned on account of the
iniquity of its rulers and people.

For he rent Israel from the house of David; and they
made Jeroboam the son of Nebat king: and Jeroboam
drave Israel from following the Lord, and made
them sin a great sin. For the children of Israel
walked in all the sins of Jeroboam which he did; they
departed not from them; until the Lord removed
Israel out of his sight, as he had said by all his
servants the prophets. So was Israel carried away out
of their own land to Assyria unto this day (2 Kings
17:21-23).

And thou, profane wicked prince of Israel, whose
day is come, when iniquity shall have an end, Thus,
saith the Lord God; Remove the diadem, and take
off the crown: this shall not be the same: exalt him

that is low, and abase him that is high. I will overturn, overturn, overturn, it: and it shall be no more, until he come whose right it is: and I will give it him (Ezek. 21:25-27).

For the children of Israel shall abide many days without a king, and without a prince, and without a sacrifice, and without an image, and without an ephod, and without teraphim (Hosea 3:4).

And they shall fall by the edge of the sword, and shall be led away captive into all nations: and Jerusalem shall be trodden down of the Gentiles, until the times of the Gentiles be fulfilled (Luke 21:24).

I have sent also unto you all my servants the prophets, rising up early and sending them, saying, Return ye now every man from his evil way, and amend your doing, and go not after other gods to serve them, and ye shall dwell in the land which I have given to you and to your fathers: but ye have not inclined your ear, nor hearkened unto me . . . Therefore thus saith the Lord God of hosts, the God of Israel; Behold I will bring upon Judah and upon all the inhabitants of Jerusalem all the evil that I have pronounced against them: because I have spoken unto them, but they have not heard; and I have called unto them, but they have not answered (Jer. 35:15 and 17).

(c)   It is to be re-established in glory.

In that day will I raise up the tabernacle of David that is fallen, and close up the breaches thereof; and I will raise up his ruins, and I will build it as in the days of old (Amos 9:11).

Lift up thine eyes round about, and see: all they gather themselves together, they come to thee: thy sons shall come from far, and thy daughters shall be nursed at thy side (Isa. 60:4).

And the Lord shall inherit Judah his portion in the holy land, and shall choose Jerusalem again (Zech. 2:12).

But upon mount Zion shall be deliverance, and there shall be holiness; and the house of Jacob shall possess their possessions . . . And the captivity of this host of the children of Israel shall possess that of the Canaanites . . . And saviours shall come up on mount Zion to judge the mount of Esau; and the kingdom shall be the Lord's (Obadiah 17, 20, 21).

But in the last days it shall come to pass that the mountain of the house of the Lord shall be established in the top of the mountains, and it shall be exalted above the hills; and people shall flow unto it. And many nations shall come, and say. Come, and let us go up to the mountain of the Lord, and to the house of the God of Jacob; and he will teach us of his ways, and we will walk in his paths: for the law shall go forth of Zion, and the word of the Lord from Jerusalem. And he shall judge among many people, and rebuke strong nations afar off; and they shall beat their swords into plowshares, and their spears into pruninghooks: nation shall not lift up a sword against nation, neither shall they learn war any more. But they shall sit every man under his vine and under his fig tree; and none shall make them afraid: for the mouth of the Lord of hosts hath spoken it. For all people will walk every one in the name of his god, and we will walk in the name of the Lord our God for ever and ever. In that day, saith the Lord, will I assemble her that halteth, and I will gather her that is driven out, and her that I have afflicted; and I will make her that halted a remnant, and her that was cast far off a strong nation: and the Lord shall reign over them in mount Zion from henceforth, even for ever. And thou, O tower of the flock, the strong hold of the daughter of Zion, unto thee shall it come, even the first dominion: the kingdom shall come to the daughter of Jerusalem (Micah 4:1-8).

When they therefore were come together, they asked of him, saying, Lord, wilt thou at this time restore again the kingdom to Israel? And he said unto them, It is not for you to know the times or the seasons, which the Father hath put in his own power (Acts 1:6, 7).

23.   The establishment of the Kingdom of God will thus involve the regathering of the Jews to the land of Palestine which will be restored to its former fertility, and made wondrously beautiful.

And it shall come to pass in that day, that the Lord shall set his hand again the second time to recover the remnant of his people, which shall be left, from Assyria, and from Egypt, and from Pathros, and from Cush, and from Elam, and from Shinar, and from Hamath, and from the islands of the sea. And he shall set up an ensign for the nations, and shall assemble the outcasts of Israel, and gather together the dispersed of Judah from the four corners of the earth (Isa. 11:11, 12).

For the Lord shall comfort Zion: he will comfort all her waste places; and he will make her wilderness like Eden, and her desert like the garden of the Lord; joy and gladness shall be found therein, thanksgiving and the voice of melody (Isa. 51:3).

Whereas thou hast been forsaken and hated, so that no man went through thee, I will make thee an eternal excellency, a joy of many generations (Isa. 60:15).

Hear the word of the Lord, O ye nations, and declare it in the isles afar off, and say, He that scattered Israel will gather him, and keep him, as a shepherd doth his flock . . . Behold, the days come, said the Lord, that I will sow the house of Israel and the house of Judah with the seed of man, and with the seed of beast. And it shall come to pass, that like as I have watched over them, to pluck up, and to break down, and to throw down, and to destroy, and to afflict; so will I watch over them, to build, and to plant, saith the Lord (Jer. 31:10, 27, 28).

And all the nations shall call you blessed: for ye shall be a delightsome land, said the Lord of hosts (Mal. 3:12).

Therefore say unto the house of Israel, Thus saith the Lord God; I do not this for your sakes, O house of Israel, but for mine holy name's sake, which ye have profaned among the heathen, whither ye went. And I will sanctify my great

A DECLARATION OF THE TRUTH REVEALED IN THE
BIBLE AS DISTINGUISHABLE FROM THE THEOLOGY
OF CHRISTENDOM (AMENDED
CHRISTADELPHIANS) (continued)

name, which was profaned among the heathen, which ye
have profaned in the midst of them; and the heathen shall
know that I am the Lord, saith the Lord God, when I shall
be sanctified in you before their eyes. For I will take you
from among the heathen, and gather you out of all
countries, and will bring you into your own land (Ezek.
36:22-24).

And the desolate land shall be tilled, whereas it lay
desolate in the sight of all that passed by. And they shall
say, This land that was desolate is become like the garden
of Eden; and the waste and desolate and ruined cities are
become fenced, and are inhabited (Ezek. 37:34-36).

Thus saith the Lord God; Behold, I will take the children
of Israel from among the heathen, whither they be gone,
and will gather them on every side, and bring them into
their own land: and I will make them one nation in the
land upon the mountains of Israel: and one king shall be
king to them all: and they shall be no more two nations,
neither shall they be divided into two kingdoms any more
at all (Ezek. 37:218 22).

Thus saith the Lord of hosts; Behold, I will save my people
from the east country, and from the west country. And I
will bring them, and they shall dwell in the midst of
Jerusalem: and they shall be my people, and I will be their
God, in truth and in righteousness (Zech. 8:7, 8).

And all the nations shall call you blessed: for ye shall be a
delightsome land, saith the Lord of hosts (Mal. 3:12).

24. Jerusalem, rebuilt and glorified, will become the
     metropolis of God's Kingdom which will embrace all
     nations.

Beautiful for situation, the joy of the whole earth, is Mount
Zion, on the sides of the north, the city of the great King
(Psa. 48:2).

Then the moon shall be confounded, and the sun ashamed,
when the Lord of hosts shall reign in mount Zion, and in
Jerusalem, and before his ancients gloriously (Isa. 25:23).

Awake, awake; put on thy strength, O Zion; put on thy
beautiful garments, O Jerusalem, the holy city; for
henceforth there shall no more come into thee the
uncircumcised and the unclean (Isa. 52:1).

The sons also of them that afflicted thee shall come
bending unto thee; and all they that despised thee shall
bow themselves down at the soles of thy feet; and they
shall call thee, The city of the Lord, The Zion of the Holy
One of Israel (Isa. 60:14).

At that time they shall call Jerusalem the throne of the
Lord; and all the nations shall be gathered unto it, to the
name of the Lord, to Jerusalem: neither shall they walk
any more after the imagination of their evil heart (Jer.
3:17).

And many nations shall come, and say, Come, and let us
go up to the mountain of the Lord, and to the house of the
God of Jacob; and he will teach us of his ways, and we will
walk in his paths: for the law shall go forth of Zion, and

the word of the Lord from Jerusalem . . . And I will
make her that halted a remnant, and her that was cast far
off a strong nation: and the Lord shall reign over them in
mount Zion from henceforth, even for ever. And thou, O
tower of the flock, the strong hold of the daughter of Zion,
unto thee shall it come, even the first dominion; the
kingdom shall come to the daughter of Jerusalem (Micah
4:2, 7, 8).

And it shall come to pass, that every one that is left of all
the nations which came against Jerusalem shall even go up
from year to year to worship the King, the Lord of Hosts,
and to keep the feast of tabernacles (Zech. 14:16).

But I say unto you, Swear not at all; neither by heaven; for
it is God's throne; nor by the earth; for it is his footstool:
neither by Jerusalem: for it is the city of the great King
(Matt. 5:34, 35).

25. The Kingdom of God will be a visible, irresistible
     and everlasting dominion to be established on earth
     in the place of all existing kingdoms for the purpose
     of subjecting, blessing and perfecting the world.

And in the days of these kings shall the God of heaven set
up a kingdom, which shall never be destroyed: and the
kingdom shall not be left for other people, but it shall
break in pieces and consume all these kingdoms, and it
shall stand forever (Dan. 2:44).

I saw in the night visions, and, behold, one like the Son of
Man came with the clouds of heaven, and came to the
Ancient of days, and they brought him near before him.
And there was given him dominion, and glory, and a
kingdom, that all people, nations and languages, should
serve him: his dominion is an everlasting dominion, which
shall not pass away, and his kingdom that which shall not
be destroyed . . . And the kingdom and dominion, and
the greatness of the kingdom under the whole heaven, shall
be given to the people of the saints of the most High,
whose kingdom is an everlasting kingdom, and all dominions shall serve and obey him (Dan. 7:13, 14, 27).

And the Lord shall be king over all the earth: in that day
shall there be one Lord, and his name one (Zech. 14:9).

Ask of me, and I shall give thee for heathen for thine
inheritance, and the uttermost parts of the earth for thy
possession. Thou shalt break them with a rod of iron; thou
shalt dash them in pieces like a potter's vessel (Psa. 2:8, 9).

And the seventh angel sounded: and there were great
voices in heaven, saying. The kingdoms of this world are
become the kingdoms of our Lord, and of his Christ: and
he shall reign for ever and ever (Rev. 11:15).

And I saw heaven opened, and behold a white horse; and
he that sat upon him was called Faithful and True, and in
righteousness he doth judge and make war. His eyes were
as a flame of fire, and on his head were many crowns; and
he had a name written, that no man knew, but he himself.
And he was clothed with a vesture dipped in blood: and his
name is called The Word of God. And the armies which
were in heaven followed him upon white horses, clothed in
fine linen, white and clean. And out of his mouth goeth a
sharp sword, that with it he should smite the nations: and
he shall rule them with a rod of iron: and he treadeth the

winepress of the fierceness and wrath of Almighty God (Rev. 19:11-16).

26. Christ and his saints will reign a thousand years, until all that is evil, including finally death itself, is abolished.

And I saw an angel come down from heaven, having the key of the bottomless pit and a great chain in his hand. And he laid hold on the dragon, that old serpent, which is the Devil, and Satan, and bound him a thousand years, and cast him into the bottomless pit, and shut him up, and set a seal upon him, that he should deceive the nations no more till the thousand years should be fulfilled: and after that he must be loosed a little season. And I saw thrones, and they sat upon them, and judgment was given unto them: and I saw the souls of them that were beheaded for the witness of Jesus, and for the word of God, and which had not worshipped the beast, neither his image, neither had received his mark upon their foreheads, or in their hands; and they lived and reigned with Christ a thousand years. But the rest of the dead lived not again until the thousand years were finished. This is the first resurrection. Blessed and holy is he that hath part in the first resurrection: on such the second death hath no power, but they shall be priests of God and of Christ, and shall reign with him a thousand years. And when the thousand years are expired, Satan shall be loosed out of his prison, and shall go out to deceive the nations which are in the four quarters of the earth, Gog and Magog, to gather them together to battle: the number of whom is as the sand of the sea. And they went up on the breadth of the earth, and compassed the camp of the saints about, and the beloved city: and fire came down from God out of heaven, and devoured them . . . And I saw the dead, small and great, stand before God, and the books were opened: and another book was opened, which is the book of life: and the dead were judged out of those things which were written in the books, according to their works. And the sea gave up the dead which were in it; and death and hell delivered up the dead which were in them: and they were judged every man according to their works. And death and hell were cast into the lake of fire. This is the second death. And whosoever was not found written in the book of life was cast into the lake of fire (Rev. 20:1-9, 12-15).

There shall be no more thence an infant of days, nor an old man that hath not filled his days: for the child shall die an hundred years old; but the sinner being an hundred years old shall be accursed (Isa. 65:20).

Then cometh the end, when he shall have delivered up the kingdom to God, even the Father; when he shall have put down all rule and all authority and power. For he must reign, till he hath put all enemies under his feet. The last enemy that shall be destroyed is death. For he hath put all things are put under him, it is manifest that he is excepted, which did put all things under him. And when all things shall be subdued unto him, then shall the Son also himself be subject unto him that put all things under him, that God may be all in all (1 Cor. 15:24-28).

27. The Gospel preached by Jesus and the apostles concerns the Kingdom of God.

And Jesus went about all Galilee, teaching in the synagogues, and preaching the gospel of the kingdom, and healing all manner of sickness and all manner of disease among the people (Matt. 4:23).

Now after that John was put in prison, Jesus came into Galilee, preaching the gospel of the kingdom of God (Mark 1:14).

And it came to pass afterward, that he went throughout every city and village, preaching and showing the glad tidings of the kingdom of God (Luke 8:1).

But when they believed Philip preaching the things concerning the kingdom of God, and the name of Jesus Christ, they were baptized, both men and women (Acts 8:12).

And he went into the synagogue, and spake boldly for the space of three months, disputing and persuading the things concerning the kingdom of God (Acts 19:8).

And now, behold, I know that ye all among whom I have gone preaching the kingdom of God, shall see my face no more (Acts 20:25).

Preaching the kingdom of God and teaching those things which concern the Lord Jesus Christ, with all confidence, no man forbidding him (Acts 28:31).

God by the Gospel invites men to participate in this Kingdom and share with Christ in the glory.

Then shall the King say unto them on his right hand, Come, ye blessed of my Father, inherit the kingdom prepared for you from the foundation of the world (Matt. 25:34).

Fear not, little flock; for it is your Father's good pleasure to give you the kingdom (Luke 12:32).

That ye would walk worthy of God, who hath called you unto his kingdom and glory (1 Thess. 2:12).

Hath not God chosen the poor of this world, rich in faith, and heirs of the kingdom which he hath promised to them that love him? (James 2:5).

Wherefore the rather, brethren, give diligence to make your calling and election sure: for if ye do these things, ye shall never fall; for so an entrance shall be ministered unto you abundantly into the everlasting kingdom of our Lord and Saviour Jesus Christ (2 Peter 1:10, 11).

And he that overcometh, and keepeth my works unto the end, to him will I give power over the nations: and he shall rule them with a rod of iron; as the vessels of a potter shall they be broken to shivers: even as I received of my Father (Rev. 2:26, 27).

I charge thee therefore before God, and the Lord Jesus Christ, who shall judge the quick and the dead at his appearing and his kingdom . . . Henceforth there is laid up for me a crown of righteousness, which the Lord, the righteous judge, shall give me at that day: and not to me only, but unto all them also that love his appearing (2 Tim. 4:1 and 8).

28. The Way to God's Kingdom and eternal life is by accepting God's gracious invitation, believing His word, and obeying His will. This involves;

A DECLARATION OF THE TRUTH REVEALED IN THE BIBLE AS DISTINGUISHABLE FROM THE THEOLOGY OF CHRISTENDOM (AMENDED CHRISTADELPHIANS) (continued)

(a)   Belief in His Son as Saviour and Lord.

For God so loved the world, that he gave his only begotten Son, that whosoever believeth in him should not perish, but have everlasting life . . . He that believeth on the Son hath everlasting life: and he that believeth not the Son shall not see life; but the wrath of God abideth on him (John 3:16, 36).

And this is the will of him that sent me, that every one which seeth the Son, and believeth on him, may have everlasting life: and I will raise him up at the last day (John 6:40).

Jesus saith unto him, Thomas, because thou hast seen me, thou hast believed: blessed are they that have not seen, and yet have believed . . . But these are written, that ye might believe that Jesus is the Christ, the Son of God; and that believing ye might have life through his name (John 20:29, 31).

And they said, Believe on the Lord Jesus Christ, and thou shalt be saved, and thy house (Acts 16:31).

If thou shalt confess with thy mouth the Lord Jesus, and shalt believe in thine heart that God hath raised him from the dead, thou shalt be saved (Rom. 10:9).

(b)   Repentance from past sin, error or indifference.

From that time Jesus began to preach, and to say, Repent: for the kingdom of heaven is at hand (Matt. 4:17).

The time is fulfilled, and the kingdom of God is at hand: repent ye: and believe the gospel (Mark 1:15).

There were present at that season some that told him of the Galilaeans, whose blood Pilate had mingled with their sacrifices. And Jesus answering said unto them, Suppose ye that these Galilaeans were sinners above all the Galilaeans, because they suffered such things? I tell you, Nay: but, except ye repent, ye shall all likewise perish. Or those eighteen, upon whom the tower in Siloam fell, and slew them, think ye that they were sinners above all men that dwelt in Jerusalem? I tell you. Nay: but, except ye repent ye shall all likewise perish (Luke 13:1-5).

Repent ye therefore, and be converted, that your sins may be blotted out, when the times of refreshing shall come from the presence of the Lord (Acts 3:19).

And the times of this ignorance God winked at; but now commandeth all men every where to repent (Acts 17:30).

The Lord is not slack concerning his promise, as some men count slackness; but is longsuffering to us-ward, not willing that any should perish, but that all should come to repentance (2 Peter 3:9).

(c)   Baptism for the remission of sins.

Go ye therefore, and teach all nations, baptizing them in the name of the Father, and of the Son, and of the Holy Spirit: teaching them to observe all things whatsoever I have commanded you: and lo, I am with you alway, even unto the end of the world (Matt. 28:19, 20).

He that believeth and is baptized shall be saved; but he that believeth not shall be damned (Mark 16:16).

Jesus answered, Verily, verily, I say unto thee, Except a man be born of water and of the Spirit, he cannot enter into the kingdom of God (John 3:5).

The Peter said unto them, Repent, and be baptized every one of you in the name of Jesus Christ for the remission of sins, and ye shall receive the gift of the Holy Spirit (Acts 2:38).

But when they believed Philip preaching the things concerning the kingdom of God, and the name of Jesus Christ, they were batized, both men and women. Then Simon himself believed also: and when he was baptized, he continued with Philip, and wondered, beholding the miracles and signs which were done . . . And as they went on their way, they came upon a certain water: and the eunuch said, See, here is water; what doth hinder me to be baptized. And Philip said, If thou believest with all thine heart, thou mayest. And he answered and said, I believe that Jesus Christ is the Son of God. And he commanded the chariot to stand still: and they went down both into the water, both Philip and the eunuch; and he baptized him. And when they were come up out of the water, the Spirit of the Lord caught away Philip, that the eunuch saw him no more: and he went on his way rejoicing (Acts 8:12, 13, 36-39).

And immediately there fell from his eyes as it had been scales: and he received sight forthwith, and arose, and was baptized (Acts 9:18).

For they heard them speak with tongues, and magnify God. Then answered Peter, Can any man forbid water, that these should not be baptized, which have received the Holy Spirit as well as we? And he commanded them to be baptized in the name of the Lord. Then prayed they him to tarry certain days (Acts 10:46-48).

And when she was baptized, and her household, she besought us, saying, If ye have judged me to be faithful to the Lord, come into my house, and abide there . . . And he took them the same hour of the night, and washed their stripes and was baptized, he and all his, straightway (Acts 16:15, 35).

The like figure whereunto even baptism doth also now save us (not the putting away of the filth of the flesh, but the answer of a good conscience toward God) by the resurrection of Jesus Christ (1 Peter 3:21).

(d)   This baptism as an act of faith unites the believer with Jesus Christ, the Saviour. Through a symbolic burial by immersion in water he is identified with Christ's death and resurrection. Baptism marks the end of the old undedicated life. It indicates, with the forgiveness of past sins, the rising to a new life in Christ, with the privilege of being a son or daughter of God: and confers heirship to eternal life in the Lord's Kingdom at his advent.

What shall we say then? Shall we continue in sin, that grace may abound? God forbid. How shall we, that are dead to sin, live any longer therein? Know ye not, that so many of us as were baptized into Jesus Christ were baptized into his death? Therefore we are buried with him by baptism into death: that like as Christ was raised up from the dead by the glory of the Father, even so we also should walk in newness of life. For if we have been planted together in the likeness of his death, we shall be also in the likeness of his resurrection: knowing this, that our old man is crucified with him, that the body of sin might be destroyed, that henceforth we should not serve sin. For he that is dead is freed from sin. Now if we be dead with Christ, we believe that we shall also live with him (Rom. 6:1-8).

And such were some of you: but ye are washed, but ye are sanctified, but ye are justified in the name of the Lord Jesus, and by the Spirit of our God (1 Cor. 6:11).

That he might sanctify and cleanse it with the washing of water by the word (Eph. 5:26).

Jesus answered and said unto him, Verily, verily, I say unto thee, Except a man be born again, he cannot see the kingdom of God (John 3:5).

For ye are all the children of God by faith in Christ Jesus. For as many of you as have been baptized into Christ have put on Christ. There is neither Jew nor Greek, there is neither bond nor free, there is neither male nor female: for ye are all one in Christ Jesus. And if ye be Christ's, then are ye Abraham's seed, and heirs according to the promise (Gal. 3:26-29).

Not by works of righteousness which we have done, but according to his mercy he saved us, by the washing of regeneration, and renewing of the Holy Spirit (Titus 3:5).

(e)   Union with Christ involves a life devoted to God's service in love to Him and to one's neighbour, characterized by the regular, thoughtful reading of God's Word, prayer to God through Jesus for forgiveness, strength and guidance; the first-day remembrance of the Lord's saving death and resurrection in the breaking of bread with those of like precious fatih; the letting of the light of the Gospel shine in word and deed; the patient waiting for the Lord's advent; the forsaking of sin, the separation from all that is evil in the world, and the doing of good to all, especially to the household of faith.

Jesus said unto him, Thou shalt love the Lord thy God with all thy heart, and with all thy soul, and with all thy mind. This is the first and great commandment. And the second is like unto it, Thou shalt love thy neighbour as thyself. On these two commandments hang all the law and the prophets (Matt. 22:37-40).

If we say that we have fellowship with him, and walk in darkness, we lie, and do not the truth: but if we walk in the light, as he is in the light, we have fellowship one with another, and the blood of Jesus Christ his Son cleanseth us from all sin. If we say that we have no sin, we deceive ourselves, and the truth is not in us. If we confess our sins, he is faithful and just to forgive us our sins, and to cleanse us from all unrighteousness (1 John 1:6-9).

But continue thou in the things which thou hast learned and hast been assured of, knowing of whom thou hast learned them; and that from a child thou hast known the holy scriptures, which are able to make thee wise unto salvation through faith which is in Christ Jesus. All scripture is given by inspiration of God, and is profitable for doctrine, for reproof, for correction, for doctrine, for reproof, for correction, for instruction in righteousness: that the man of God may be perfect, thoroughly furnished unto all good works (2 Tim. 3:14-17).

Pray without ceasing (1 Thess. 5:17).

And it came to pass, that, as he was praying in a certain place, when he ceased, one of his disciples said unto him, Lord, teach us to pray, as John also taught his disciples. And he said unto them, when ye pray, say, Our Father which art in heaven, hollowed by thy name. They kingdom come. Thy will be done, as in heaven, so in earth. Give us day by day our daily bread. And forgive us our sins; for we also forgive every one that is indebted to us. And lead us not into temptation: but deliver us from evil (Luke 11:1-4).

But of that day and that hour knoweth no man, no, not the angels which are in heaven, neither the Son, but the Father. Take ye heed, watch and pray: for ye know not when the time is. For the Son of man is as a man taking a far journey, who left his house, and gave authority to his servants, and to every man his work, and commanded the porter to watch. Watch ye therefore: for ye know not when the master of the house cometh, at even, or at midnight, or at the cockcrowing, or in the morning: lest coming suddenly he find you sleeping. And what I say unto you I say unto all, Watch (Mark 13:32-37).

And as they did eat, Jesus took bread, and blessed, and brake it, and gave to them, and said, Take, eat: this is my body. And he took the cup, and when he had given thanks, he gave it to them: and they all drank of it. And he said unto them, This is my blood of the new testament, which is shed for many. Verily I say unto you, I will drink no more of the fruit of the vine, until that day that I drink it new in the kingdom of God (Mark 14:22-25).

And he took bread, and gave thanks, and brake it, and gave unto them, saying This is my body, which is given for you: this do in remembrance of me. Likewise also the cup after supper, saying, This cup is the new testament in my blood, which is shed for you (Luke 22:19, 20).

For I have received of the Lord that which also I delivered unto you, That the Lord Jesus the same night in which he was betrayed took bread: and when he had given thanks, he brake it, and said, Take, eat: this is my body, which is broken for you: this do in remembrance of me. After the same manner also he took the cup, when he had supped, saying, This cup is the new testament in my blood: this do ye, as oft as ye drink it, in remembrance of me. For as often as ye eat this bread, and drink this cup, ye do show the Lord's death till he come. Wherefore whosoever shall eat this bread, and drink this cup of the Lord, unworthily, shall be guilty of the body and blood of the Lord. But let a man examine himself, and so let him eat of that bread, and drink of that cup (1 Cor. 11:23-28).

Not forsaking the assembling of ourselves together, as the manner of some is; but exhorting one another: and so much the more, as ye see the day approaching (Heb. 10:25).

Preach the word; be instant in season, out of season, reprove, rebuke, exhort with all longsuffering and doctrine (2 Tim. 4:2).

Blessed are they which do hunger and thirst after righteousness: for they shall be filled. Blessed are the merciful: for they shall obtain mercy (Matt. 5:6, 7).

And to wait for his Son from heaven, whom he raised from the dead, even Jesus which delivered us from the wrath to come (1 Thess. 1:10).

Love not the world, neither the things that are in the world. If any man love the world, the love of the Father is not in him. For all that is in the world, the lust of the flesh, and the lust of the eyes, and the pride of life, is not of the Father, but is of the world. And the world passeth away, and the lust thereof; but he that doeth the will of God abideth forever (1 John 2; 15-17).

I beseech you therefore, brethren, by the mercies of God, that ye present your bodies a living sacrifice, holy, acceptable unto God, which is your reasonable service. And be not conformed to this world: but be ye transformed by the renewing of your mind, that ye may prove what is that good, and acceptable, and perfect, will of God (Rom. 12:1, 2).

As we have therefore opportunity, let us do good unto all men, especially unto them who are of the household of faith (Gal. 6:10).

Be careful for nothing; but in every thing by prayer and supplication with thanksgiving let your requests be made known unto God. And the peace of God, which passeth all understanding, shall keep your hearts and minds through Christ Jesus. Finally, brethren, whatsoever things are true, whatsoever things are honest, whatsoever things are just, whatsoever things are pure, whatsoever things are of good report; if there be any virtue, and if there by any praise, think on these things (Phil. 4:6-8).

Read also Psa. 119; Col. 3; Eph. 4:17-32 and very many other Scriptures.

AN APPENDIX

THE CALL TO SEPARATION. Some are at first disturbed to find that the true teaching of Scripture is very different from much popular religious belief, and wonder how so many can be wrong. The answer is that from the earliest times men were drawn away by false philosophy and eventually the apostles' forecasts of apostasy were fulfilled. The proof is fourfold:

1. The contrast between Scripture truth as set out in the preceding pages and current views, which may be briefly indicated as follows:

BIBLE TEACHING	CURRENT RELIGIOUS VIEWS
THE BIBLE	
A fully authoritative expression of God's unfolding purpose with the earth and His will for men.	Though unique, not thoroughly reliable.
GOD	
Is One.	Is three Persons in unity, often involving tritheism.
JESUS	
Son of God, subordinate to the Father: born of the virgin Mary, raised from the dead.	God the Son, co-equal with the Father. Some leading churchmen reject his virgin birth and resurrection.
MAN	
Mortal because of sin.	Possesses an immortal soul.
FINAL RECOMPENSE	
On earth, after resurrection, in the Kingdom of God to be established at Christ's return.	In heaven at death.
BAPTISM	
The act of faith and obedience ordained by God's grace for entry in a new life in Christ. A "burial" by immersion in water.	Baptism by immersion is unnecessary.

2. The witness of Scripture, foretelling departure from the truth, and calling men and women who believe to be separate, "in the world" but "not of the world".

There shall come in the last days scoffers, walking after their own lust, and saying. Where is the promise of his coming? For since the fathers fell asleep, all things continue as they were from the beginning of the creation (2 Peter 3:3, 4).

The time will come when they will not endure sound doctrine; but after their own lusts shall they heap to themselves teachers, having itching ears. And they shall turn away their ears from the truth, and shall be turned unto fables (2 Tim. 4:3, 4).

For I know this, that after my departing shall grievous wolves enter in among you not sparing the flock. Also of your own selves shall men arise, speaking perverse things, to draw away disciples after them (Acts 20:29, 30).

For, behold, the darkness shall cover the earth, and gross darkness the people (Isa. 60:2).

As the days of Noah were, so also shall the coming of the Son of Man be. For as in the days that were before the flood they were eating and drinking, marrying, and giving in marriage, until the day Noah entered into the ark, and knew not until the flood came and took them all away; so shall also the coming of the Son of Man be (Matt. 24:27-39).

Wherefore come out from among them, and be ye separate, saith the Lord, and touch not the unclean *thing*; and I will receive you, and will be a Father unto you, and ye shall be my sons and daughteres, saith the Lord Almighty (2 Cor. 6:17-18).

3. The Scriptures reveal that it is God's purpose at the present time to take out a people for His Name, and not to convert the world. Relatively few respond today.

Notes: *The Christadelphians originated with John Thomas, an early close associate of Alexander Campbell, one of the founders of the Christian Church (Disciples of Christ). Thomas left the Christian Church over a number of doctrinal points. Christadelphians do not believe in the Trinity (see item 2), humanity's natural immortality (see items 9, 10, and 13), and hell as a place of eternal torment (see items 15-17). They do believe in the necessity of baptism by immersion for salvation (see item 28c). In the 1890s the Christadelphians were split, at least in part, over a disagreement on eschatology. One group affirmed that only those who die "in Christ" (i.e., Christians) will be resurrected to face the judgment of Christ. The group amended the beliefs of the Christadelphians in accordance with those teachings and thus became know as Amended Christadelphians. This crucial doctrine, which continues to divide Christadelphians after almost a century, is presented in item 17. The statement reproduced here is circulated by the office of* The Christadelphian, *the leading Amended Christadelphian periodical, which is published in Birmingham, England.*

*   *   *

PREAMBLE TO A DESIGN FOR THE CHRISTIAN CHURCH (DISCIPLES OF CHRIST)

As members of the Christian Church,
We confess that Jesus is the Christ,
    the Son of the living God,
    and proclaim him Lord and Savior of the world.
In Christ's name and by his grace

we accept our mission of witness
    and service to all people.
We rejoice in God,
    maker of heaven and earth,
    and in the covenant of love
    which binds us to God and one another.
Through baptism into Christ
    we enter into newness of life
    and are made one with the whole people of God.
In the communion of the Holy Spirit
    we are joined together in discipleship
    and in obedience to Christ.
At the table of the Lord
    we celebrate with thanksgiving
    the saving acts and presence of Christ.
Within the universal church
    we receive the gift of ministry
    and the light of scripture.
In the bonds of Christian faith
    we yield ourselves to God
    that we may serve the One
    whose kingdom has no end.
Blessing, glory and honor
    be to God forever. Amen.

Notes: *The church bodies that have grown out of the work of such men as Alexander Campbell, Barton Stone, and James O'Kelley generally follow the theology and practice of the Baptists, out of which many of the early leaders and members of the Christian Churches had come. Baptism by immersion is almost universally accepted. An extreme congregational polity is followed, an outgrowth of the original committment to a "nondenominational" approach to church life.*

The Christian Churches as a whole are noncreedal and take the Bible as their standard of faith and practice. They have been reluctant to codify doctrinal affirmations into summary articles of belief and highly critical of individuals making the attempt. The Disciples of Christ has only recently produced a confessional statement.

During the 1960s the Christian Church (Disciples of Christ) involved itself in an intensive self-study which culminated in a denominational restructuring. A Design for the Christian Church (Disciples of Christ) *has served as the constituting document for the restructured body. Adopted in 1968, it contains a preamble offering a broad doctrinal perspective, which allows a wide variety of theological opinions.*

*   *   *

A DECLARATION OF THE TRUTH REVEALED IN THE BIBLE, THE SUBLIME AND SIMPLE THEOLOGY OF THE PRIMITIVE CHRISTIANS (UNAMENDED CHRISTADELPHIANS)

THE THINGS CONCERNING THE KINGDOM OF GOD

I. The gospel preached by Jesus when upon the earth had reference to THE KINGDOM OF GOD.

A DECLARATION OF THE TRUTH REVEALED IN THE
BIBLE, THE SUBLIME AND SIMPLE THEOLOGY OF
THE PRIMITIVE CHRISTIANS (UNAMENDED
CHRISTADELPHIANS) (continued)

Now after that John was put in prison, Jesus came into
Galilee preaching the gospel of the KINGDOM OF GOD
(Mark 1:14).

And Jesus went about all Galilee teaching in their
synagogues, and preaching the gosepl of THE KING-
DOM (Matt. 4:17, 23).

And he said unto them, I must preach the KINGDOM
OF GOD to other cities also; for therefore am I sent (Luke
4:43).

And it came to pass afterwards that he went throughout
every city and village, preaching and shewing the glad
tidings of THE KINGDOM OF GOD, and the twelve
were with him (Luke 8:1).

ADDITIONAL TESTIMONIES (Matt. 9:35; 6:33; 13:19;
Luke 9:11; 13:28).

II.   The gospel preached by the Apostles had reference to
      the same thing—that is, THE KINGDOM OF
      GOD.

When they believed Philip, preaching THE THINGS
CONCERNING THE KINGDOM OF GOD and the
name of Jesus Christ they were baptized, both men and
women (Acts 8: 12, 25).

And he (Paul) went into the synagogue and spake boldly
for the space of three months, disputing and persuading
THE THINGS CONCERNING THE KINGDOM OF
GOD (Acts 19:8).

And now, behold, I know that ye all, among whom I
(Paul) have gone preaching THE KINGDOM OF GOD,
shall see my face no more (Acts 20:25).

Paul dwelt in his own hired house . . . preaching THE
KINGDOM OF GOD, and teaching those things which
concern the Lord Jesus Christ with all confidence, no man
forbidding him (Acts 28:30, 31).

III. What is this Kingdom? It is a DIVINE POLITICAL
      DOMINION to be *established* on the earth, on the
      ruins of all existing governments, for the purpose of
      blessing and bringing the world into subjection of
      God.

And in the days of these kings shall the God of heaven
SET UP A KINGDOM which shall never be destroyed,
and the kingdom shall not be left to other people, but it
shall break in pieces and consume all these kingdoms, and
it shall stand for ever (Dan. 2:44; see also Dan. 7:13, 14,
18, 22, 27).

And *I will overthrow* the throne of kingdoms, and *I will
destroy* the strength of the kingdoms of the heathen (Heb.
nations).—(Hag. 2:22).

And the seventh angel sounded: and there were great
voices in heaven, saying, THE KINGDOMS OF THIS
WORLD ARE BECOME THE KINGDOMS OF OUR
LORD AND OF HIS CHRIST, and he shall reign for
ever and ever (Rev. 11:15).

And the Lord *shall be king* OVER ALL THE EARTH; *in
that day* shall there be one Lord, and his name one (Zech.
14:9).

Ask of me, and I shall give thee the heathen (*i.e. nations*)
for thine inheritance and the UTTERMOST PARTS OF
THE EARTH *for* thy possession. Thou shalt break them
with a rod of iron; thou shalt dash them in pieces like a
potter's vessel (Psalm 2: 8, 9).

And I saw heaven opened, and behold, a white horse; and
he that sat upon him was called Faithful and True, and in
righteousness he doth *judge* and make *war* . . . Out of
his mouth goeth a sharp sword, that with it he should
smite the nations; and *he shall rule them* with a rod of iron
and he treadeth the winepress of the fierceness and wrath
of Almighty God. And he hath on his vesture and on his
thigh a name written KING OF KINGS and LORD OF
LORDS (Rev. 19:11, 13, 15, 16).

For he *must reign* till he hath put ALL ENEMIES under
his feet (I Cor. 15:25).

IV.   This purpose of God to establish a universal king-
      dom on earth, with Christ at its head, *has a
      connection with God's past dealings with the nation of
      Israel.* This connection must be perceived before the
      bearing of God's purpose can be clearly understood.
      To assist in the attainment of this understanding,
      consider the following facts:

a.   The kingdom of Israel, as divinely constituted
      under the hand of Moses, and existent in the land
      of Palestine 3,000 years ago, was the kingdom of
      God.

And of all my sons (for the Lord hath given me
many sons), he hath chosen Solomon my son to sit
upon the throne of THE KINGDOM OF THE
LORD over Israel (1 Chron. 28:5; see also 29:23).

And now ye think to withstand the KINGDOM OF
THE LORD in the hand of the sons of David (2
Chron. 13:8).

b.   It was divinely overturned and scattered to the
      winds on account of iniquity.

Return for thy servant's sake, the tribes of thine
inheritance. The people of thy holiness have possessed it but a little while: our adversaries have
trodden down thy sanctuary. We are thine: thou
never barest rule over them (the nations); they were
not called by thy name (Isa. 63:17-19).

And thou, profane wicked prince of Israel, whose
day is come, when iniquity shall have an end, thus
saith the Lord God: Remove the diadem and take off
the crown; this shall not be the same: exalt him that
is low, and abase him that is high. *I will overturn,
overturn, overturn* it: and *it shall be no more,* UNTIL
HE COME WHOSE RIGHT IT IS; AND I WILL
GIVE IT HIM (Ezek. 21: 25-27).

*For the children of Israel shall abide many days
without a king,* and without a prince, and without a
sacrifice, and without an image, and without an
ephod, and without teraphim. Afterwards shall the
children of Israel return and seek the Lord their

God, and David (HEB. "beloved") their king; and shall fear the Lord and his goodness *in the latter days* (Hos. 3:4-5).

And they shall fall by the edge of the sword, and *shall be led away captive into all nations:* and Jerusalem shall be trodden down of the Gentiles, UNTIL the times of the Gentiles *be fulfilled* (Luke 21: 24; Matt. 23: 36-39).

c. It is to be re-established.

Thou shalt arise, and have mercy upon Zion: FOR THE TIME to favour her, yea, THE SET TIME is come (Psa. 102;13).

And they shall BUILD the old wastes, they shall RAISE UP the former desolations, and they shall REPAIR *the waste cities, the desolation of* MANY GENERATIONS (Isa. 61: 4; 33: 20, 21).

In that day will I *raise up the Tabernacle of David that is fallen,* and close up the breaches thereof; and I will raise up his ruins, and I WILL BUILD IT AS IN THE DAYS OF OLD (Amos 9:11).

Cry yet, saying, Thus saith the Lord of Hosts: My cities through prosperity shall yet be spread abroad; *and the Lord shall* YET *comfort Zion,* and shall YET *choose Jerusalem* (Zech. 1: 16, 17).

The Lord shall inherit Judah, his portion in the holy land, and *shall choose Jerusalem* AGAIN (Zech. 2:12).

The Lord God shall give unto him (Jesus) *the throne of his father David,* and he shall reign over the house of Jacob for ever and of his KINGDOM there shall be no end (Luke 1:32, 33).

Lord, wilt thou at this time *restore again* THE KINGDOM *to Israel?* (Acts 1:6).

And to this agree the words of the prophets; as it is written. After this I will return, and will build again *the tabernacle of David, which is fallen down;* and I *will build again* the ruins thereof, and I will set it up (Acts 14:16; see also Amos 9:11, above).

V. The Kindgom of God to be set up on the earth will be the ancient Kingdom of Israel restored.

In that day, saith the Lord, *will I assemble her* that halteth, and *I will gather her* that is driven out and her that I have afflicted. And I will make her that halted a remnant, and her that was cast far off *a strong nation;* and the LORD SHALL REIGN over them in Mount Zion from henceforth even for ever. And thou, O tower of the flock, the stronghold of the daughter of Zion, *unto thee shall it come, even* THE FIRST DOMINION; THE KINGDOM *shall come to the daughter of Jerusalem* (Micah 4:6-8).

But upon Mount Zion shall be deliverance, and there shall be holiness; and the house of Jacob shall possess their possessions . . . And the captivity of this host of the children of Israel shall possess that of the Canaanites, even unto Zarephath; and the captivity of Jerusalem, which *is in Sepharad, shall possess the cities of the* south. And saviours shall come up on Mount Zion to judge the mount of Esau; AND THE KINGDOM SHALL BE THE LORD'S (Obad. 17, 20, 21).

VI. The establishment of the Kingdom of God by the restoration of the Kingdom of Israel, will involve the gathering of the Jews from their present dispersion among the nations of the earth.

He shall *assemble the outcasts of Israel,* and *gather together the dispersed of Judah,* from the four corners of the earth (Isa. 11:12).

Hear the word of the Lord, O ye nations, and declare it in the isles afar off, and say, *He that scattered Israel* WILL GATHER HIM, *and keep him as a* shepherd doth his flock (Jer. 31:10).

Behold, I will *save my people from the east country, and from the west country:* and I will bring them, *and they shall dwell in the midst of Jerusalem;* and they shall be my people, and I will be their God in truth and in righteousness (Zech. 8:7, 8).

Behold the days come, saith the LORD, that I will sow *the house of Israel, and the house of Judah* with the seed of man, and with the seed of beast. And it shall come to pass, that like as I have watched over them, to pluck up, and to break down, and to throw down, and to destroy, and to afflict: *so will I watch over them, to build and to plant,* saith the Lord (Jer. 31:27, 28).

Behold the days come, saith the LORD, that *I will perform* THAT GOOD THING WHICH I HAVE PROMISED UNTO THE HOUSE OF ISRAEL, AND TO THE HOUSE OF JUDAH. *In those days, and at that time, will I cause the Branch of Righteousness to grow up unto David,* and he shall execute judgment and righteousness.—*In those days shall Judah be saved, and Jerusalem shall dwell safely,* and this is the name whereby she shall be called, THE LORD OUR RIGHTEOUSNESS (Jer. 33: 14-16).

I do not this for your sakes, O house of Israel, but for mine holy name's sake, which ye have profaned among the heathen, whither ye went. *For I will take you from among the heathen, and gather you out of all countries, and will bring you into your own land (Ezek. 36: 22-24).*

And say unto them, Thus saith the Lord God: Behold, *I will take the children of Israel from among the heathen,* whither they be gone, and will gather them on every side, and bring them into their own land: AND I WILL MAKE THEM ONE NATION *in the land upon the mountains of Israel;* and ONE KING SHALL be king to them all: and they shall be *no more* two nations, neither shall they be divided into two kingdoms *any more* at all (Ezek. 37: 21, 22).

And I will make her that halted a remnant, and *her that was cast far off a* strong nation; and the LORD shall reign *over them* in MOUNT ZION from henceforth, even for ever (Micah 4:7).

Thus saith the Lord of hosts; In those days shall it come to pass, that ten men shall take hold, out of all languages of the nations, even shall take hold of the skirt of him that is a Jew, saying, We will go with you; for we have heard that God is with you (Zech. 8:23).

And all nations shall call you blessed: for ye shall be a delightsome land, saith the Lord of hosts (Mal. 3:12).

A DECLARATION OF THE TRUTH REVEALED IN THE
BIBLE, THE SUBLIME AND SIMPLE THEOLOGY OF
THE PRIMITIVE CHRISTIANS (UNAMENDED
CHRISTADELPHIANS) (continued)

VII.   The city Jerusalem will then become the residence of
the Lord Jesus, the headquarters and metropolis of
the Kingdom of God, whose dominion will stretch to
the utmost bounds of the earth.

Then the moon shall be confounded, and the sun ashamed,
when the *Lord of Hosts shall reign* IN MOUNT ZION,
and IN JERUSALEM, and before his ancients gloriously
(Isa. 24:23).

Awake, awake, put on thy strength, O Zion; put on thy
beautiful garments, O Jerusalem, THE HOLY CITY: for
henceforth there shall *no more* come into thee the
uncircumcised and the unclean (Isa. 52:1).

And they shall call thee, THE CITY OF THE LORD,
THE ZION OF THE HOLY ONE OF ISRAEL (Isa.
60:14).

For behold, I create new heavens and a new earth; and the
former shall not be remembered, nor come into mind. But
be ye glad and rejoice for ever in that which I create: for
behold, *I create Jerusalem a rejoicing, and her people a joy*
(Isa. 65: 17, 18).

At that time they shall call *Jerusalem* THE THRONE OF
THE LORD; and all the nations shall be gathered unto it,
to the name of the LORD to *Jerusalem;* neither shall they
walk any more after the imagination of their evil heart
(Jer. 3:17).

Thus saith the Lord of hosts, the God of Israel: As yet they
shall use this speech in the land of Judah and in the cities
thereof when I shall bring againg their captivity; The Lord
bless, O HABITATION OF JUSTICE, *and* MOUNTAIN
OF HOLINESS (Jer. 31:23).

Beautiful for situation, *the joy of the whole earth,* is Mount
Zion, on the sides of the north, *the city of the great King*
(Psa. 48:2).

The Lord shall reign over them in MOUNT ZION . . .
THE KINGDOM SHALL COME TO THE DAUGH-
TER OF JERUSALEM (Micah 4:7, 8).

So shall ye know that I *am the* Lord your God, *dwelling in
Zion, my holy mountain;* THEN SHALL JERUSALEM
BE HOLY, *and there shall no strangers pass through her
any more* (Joel 3:17).

And it shall come to pass, that every one that is left of all
the nations which came against Jerusalem shall even *go up
from year to year to worship the King,* the Lord of hosts,
and to keep the feast of tabernacles (Zech. 14:16).

But I say unto you, Swear not at all . . . neither by
Jerusalem, *for it is the city of the great King* (Matt. 5:34,
35).

VIII. The Supreme Ruler in this glorious order of things
will be Jesus of Nazareth. It is important to put this
in a more specific form, by calling attention to THE
COVENANT MADE WITH DAVID, in which
God promised him a SON, under whom his kingdom
should be established for ever.

And when thy days be fulfilled, and thou shalt sleep with
thy fathers, I will set up thy seed after thee, which shall
proceed out of thy bowels, and I will establish his
kingdom. He shall build a house for my name, and *I will
establish the throne of his kingdom for ever.* If he commit
iniquity, I will chasten him with the rod of men, and with
the stripes of the children of men (2 Sam. 7:12-14).

The Lord HATH SWORN IN TRUTH UNTO DAVID;
He will not turn from it; *Of the fruit of thy body will I set
upon thy throne* (Psa. 132:11).

These be the last words of David . . . He that ruleth
over men must be just, ruling in the fear of God. And HE
SHALL BE AS THE LIGHT OF THE MORNING,
when the sun riseth, even a morning without clouds; as the
tender grass springing out of the earth by clear shining
after rain. Although my house be not so with God: yet HE
HATH MADE WITH ME AN EVERLASTING CO-
VENANT, ordered in all things and sure: for this is all my
salvation, and all my desire, although he make it not to
grow. (2 Sam. 23:1, 3-5).

IX.   The Son promised to David is Jesus Christ, who will
sit on David's throne, when it is restored in the era of
his re-appearing on the earth.

(David) being a prophet and knowing that God had sworn
with an oath to him that of the fruit of his loins, according
to the flesh, he would RAISE UP CHRIST TO SIT ON
HIS THRONE (Acts 2:30).

And, behold, thou shalt conceive in thy womb, and bring
forth a son, and shalt call his name JESUS. He shall be
great, and shall be called the Son of the Highest; *and the
Lord God shall give unto him* THE THRONE OF HIS
FATHER DAVID. And he shall reign over the House of
Jacob for ever; And of HIS KINGDOM there shall be no
end (Luke 1:30-33).

And Pilate asked him, Art thou the King of the Jews? and
he answering said unto him, Thou sayest it (Mark 15:2).

And Jesus said unto them, Verily I say unto you, That ye
which have followed me, in the regeneration when THE
SON OF MAN SHALL SIT IN THE THRONE OF HIS
GLORY, ye also shall sit upon twelve thrones, judging the
twelve tribes of Israel (Matt. 19:28).

Of the increase of his government and peace there shall be
no end, UPON THE THRONE OF DAVID, AND
UPON HIS KINGDOM, to order it, and to establish it
with judgment and with justice from henceforth even for
ever. The zeal of the Lord of hosts will perform this (Isa.
9:7).

In those days, and at that time, will I cause the BRANCH
OF RIGHTEOUSNESS to *grow up unto David:* and he
shall execute judgment and righteousness in the land (Jer.
33:15). Behold the man whose name is the Branch; and he
shall grow up out of his place, and he *shall build the
temple* of the Lord. Even he shall build the temple of the
Lord . . . HE SHALL SIT AND RULE UPON HIS
THRONE; and he shall be a priest upon his throne, and
the counsel of peace shall be between them both (Zech. 6:
12, 13).

X.   The reward in store for those whom Christ shall
acknowledge in the day of his glory, is A PARTICI-

PATION IN THE "GLORY, HONOUR, AND POWER" OF THE KINGDOM in the sense of being his associates and coadjutors (as kings and priests) in the work of ruling the world in righteousness.

THY KINGDOM COME. *Thy will be done on earth as it is in heaven* (Matt. 6:10).

Blessed are the meek: for they shall inherit the earth (Matt. 5:5; Psa. 37:11).

Therefore I say unto you, THE KINGDOM OF GOD shall be taken from you (Scribes and Pharisees) and given to a nation bringing forth the fruits thereof (viz., the saints, see 1 Peter 2:9).—Matt. 21:43).

Fear not, little flock, for it is your Father's good pleasure to GIVE YOU THE KINGDOM . . . and be yourselves like unto men that wait for their Lord, when he will return from the wedding (Luke 12:32, 36).

And I appoint unto you a KINGDOM, as my Father hath appointed unto me; that ye may eat and drink at my table in my kingdom, and *sit on thrones judging the twelves tribes of Israel* (Luke 22:29, 30).

I charge thee therefore before God, and the Lord Jesus Christ, who shall judge the quick and the dead at his appearing and HIS KINGDOM (2 Tim. 4:1).

Henceforth there is laid up for me a crown of righteousness, which the Lord, the righteous judge, shall give me at that day: *and not to me only,* BUT UNTO ALL THEM ALSO THAT LOVE HIS APPEARING (2 Tim. 4:8).

There shall be weeping and gnashing of teeth, when ye shall see Abraham, and Isaac, and Jacob, and all the prophets in the KINDGOM OF GOD, and ye yourselves thrust out. And they shall come from the east, and from the west, and from the north, and from the south, and SHALL SIT DOWN IN THE KINGDOM OF GOD (Luke 13:28, 29).

If we suffer, we shall also REIGN WITH HIM; if we deny him, he also will deny us (2 Tim. 2:12).

And hast made us unto our God KINGS AND PRIESTS; *and we shall reign* ON THE EARTH (Rev. 5:10).

But the saints of the Most High shall take THE KINGDOM, and possess the kingdom for ever, even for ever and ever . . . And the kingdom and dominion, and the greatness of the kingdom UNDER THE WHOLE HEAVEN, shall be given to the people of the saints of the Most High, whose kingdom is an everlasting kingdom, and all dominions shall serve and obey him (Dan. 7:18, 27).

And he that overcometh, and keepeth my works unto the end, to him will I give POWER OVER THE NATIONS: *and he shall rule them with a rod of iron,* as the vessels of a potter shall they be broken to shivers: even as I received of my father (Rev. 2:26, 27).

To him that overcometh will I grant to SIT WITH ME IN MY THRONE, even as I also overcame, and am set down with my Father in his throne (Rev. 3:21).

XI.   The state of blessedness developed among the nations of the earth when they are thus ruled by Jesus and his brethren, has been the subject of promise from

the earliest dealings of Jehovah with mankind, and will be the realization of the purpose enunciated from the beginning. The reader will perceive this in the consideration of THE COVENANT MADE WITH ABRAHAM, and its bearing upon the future development of the divine purpose. This covenant guaranteed:

FIRST. The ultimate blessing of all nations through him and his seed.

Now the Lord had said unto Abram, Get thee out of thy country, and from thy kindred, and from thy father's house, unto a land that I will show thee. And I will make of thee a great nation, and make thy name great; and thou shalt be a blessing. And I will bless them that bless thee, and curse him that curseth thee; AND IN THEE SHALL ALL FAMILIES *of the earth be blessed* (Gen. 12:1-3).

And the Scripture, foreseeing that God would justify the heathen through faith, preached before THE GOSPEL unto Abraham saying, *In thee shall all nations be blessed* (Gal. 3:8).

SECOND. The everlasting, personal possession of the territory lying between the Euphrates and the Nile, known in the terms of modern geography as Syria and Israel, and Biblically as Canaan.

And the Lord said unto Abraham, after that Lot was separated from him, Lift up now thine eyes and look from the place where thou art, northward, and southward, and eastward, and westward: for *all the land which thou seest, to thee will I give it, and to thy seed for ever.* Arise, walk through the land in the length of it and in the breadth of it; FOR I WILL GIVE IT UNTO THEE (Gen. 13: 14-17; see also 12:7; 15: 8-18; 17:8).

XII.   The promises made were renewed to Isaac and Jacob.

And the Lord appeared unto him (Isaac) and said, Sojourn in this land, and I will be with thee, and will bless thee; *for unto thee and unto thy seed I will* GIVE ALL THESE COUNTRIES, and I will perform the oath which I sware unto Abraham thy father (Gen. 26:2, 3, 4).

And God Almighty bless thee (Jacob), and give thee the blessing of Abraham, to thee and to *thy seed* with thee; *that thou mayest inherit the land wherein thou art a stranger,* which God gave unto Abraham (Gen. 28: 3, 4).

I am the Lord God of Abraham, thy father, and the God of Isaac; THE LAND WHEREON THOU LIEST, TO THEE WILL I GIVE IT, AND TO THY SEED, and in thee and in thy seed shall all the families of the earth be blessed. (Gen. 28: 13, 14).

XIII.   These promises were not fulfilled in the experience of Abraham, Isaac, and Jacob, nor have they been fulfilled at any time since.

And he (God) gave him (Abraham) *none inheritance in it, no, not so much as to set his foot on,* YET HE PROMISED THAT HE WOULD GIVE IT TO HIM FOR A POSSESSION (Acts 7:5).

By faith Abraham, when he was called to go out into a place which he should after receive for an inheritance, obeyed; and he went out, not knowing whither he went. By

A DECLARATION OF THE TRUTH REVEALED IN THE BIBLE, THE SUBLIME AND SIMPLE THEOLOGY OF THE PRIMITIVE CHRISTIANS (UNAMENDED CHRISTADELPHIANS) (continued)

faith HE SOJOURNED IN THE LAND OF PROMISE *as in a strange country,* dwelling in tabernacles with Isaac and Jacob, *the heirs with him of the same promise* (Heb. 11:8-9).

These all died in faith, *not having received the promises,* but having SEEN THEM AFAR OFF, and were persuaded of them and embraced them, and confessed that they were strangers and pilgrims on the earth (Heb. 11: 13-35, 39, 40).

Now to Abraham and his seed were the promises made. He saith not, And to seeds as of many; but as of one, And to thy seed, which is Christ . . . And if ye be Christ's then are ye Abraham's seed, and heirs according to the promise (Gal. 3:16, 29).

Now, I Paul, say that Jesus Christ was a minister of the circumcision for the truth of God, to *confirm* the promises made unto the fathers (Rom. 15:8).

Blessed be the Lord God of Israel: for he hath visited and redeemed his people, and hath raised up a horn of salvation for us (that is Jesus—see context) in the house of his servant David; as he spake by the mouth of his holy prophets, which have been since the world began; that we should be saved from our enemies, and from the hand of all that hate us: *to perform the mercy promised to* OUR FATHERS, *and to remember his holy covenant,* THE OATH WHICH HE SWARE TO OUR FATHER ABRAHAM (Luke 1: 68-73).

XIV. These promises will be fulfilled in the establishment of THE KINGDOM OF DAVID UNDER CHRIST (that is, in the setting up of the kingdom of God on Earth) as the centre of a universal empire.

FIRST, as to THE BLESSING OF ALL NATIONS:

THE EARTH SHALL BE FULL OF THE KNOWLEDGE OF THE LORD as the waters cover the sea (Isa. 11:9).

And he shall judge among the nations, and shall rebuke many people: and they shall beat their swords into ploughshares, and their spears into pruning hooks: *nation shall not lift up sword against nation, neither shall they learn war any more* (Isa. 2:4).

He shall judge the poor of the people, he shall save the children of the needy, and shall break in pieces the oppressor . . . His name shall endure for ever: his name shall be continued as long as the sun: *and men shall be blessed in him: all nations shall call him blessed* (Psa. 72:4, 17).

Behold, a king shall reign in righteousness, and princes shall rule in judgment; and a man shall be *as an hiding place from the wind, and a covert from the tempest; as rivers of water in a dry place, as the shadow of a great rock in a weary land. And the eyes of them that see shall not be dim, and the ears of them that hear shall hearken. The heart also of the rash shall understand knowledge, and the tongue of the stammerers shall be ready to speak plainly* (Isa. 32:1-4; Jer. 3:17).

The battle bow shall be cut off, *and he shall speak peace unto the heathen (nations),* and his dominion shall be from sea even to sea, and from the river even to the ends of the earth (Zech. 9:10).

The Lord is exalted: . . . and wisdom and knowledge *shall be the stability of thy times, and strength of salvation* (Isa. 33: 5, 6).

O, let the nations be glad and sing for joy, for thou shalt judge the people righteously, and govern the nations upon earth (Psa. 67:4).

SECOND, as to the INHERITANCE OF THE LAND OF PROMISE:

Then will I remember my covenant with Jacob, and also my covenant with Isaac, and also my covenant with Abraham will I remember; AND I WILL REMEMBER THE LAND (Lev. 26:42).

Then will the Lord be *jealous for his* land, and pity his people . . . *Fear not, O land;* be glad and rejoice: for the Lord will do great things (Joel 2: 18, 21).

And *the desolate land shall be tilled,* whereas it lay desolate in the sight of all that passed by; and they shall say, *This land that was desolate is become* LIKE THE GARDEN OF EDEN, and the waste and desolate and ruined cities are become fenced, and are inhabited. Then the heathen that are left round about you shall know that I the Lord build the ruined places, and plant that that was desolate: *I the Lord have spoken it and I will do it* (Ezek. 36: 34-36).

For the Lord shall comfort Zion: he will comfort all her waste places; and he will *make her wilderness* LIKE EDEN, and *her desert* LIKE THE GARDEN OF THE LORD; joy and gladness shall be found therein, thanksgiving and the voice of melody (Isa. 51:3).

Thou shalt no more be termed forsaken; neither shall THY LAND *any more be termed desolate;* but thou shalt be called Hephzibah (i.e. *my delight is in her*) and thy land Beulah (i.e. *married*): for the Lord delighteth in thee, and thy land shall be married (Isa. 62:4).

Whereas thou hast been forsaken and hated, so that no man went through thee, I will make thee *an eternal excellency, a joy of many generations* (Isa. 60:15).

And I say unto you, that many shall come from the east and west, *and shall sit down* WITH ABRAHAM, AND ISAAC, AND JACOB, *in the kingdom of heaven* (Matt. 8:11; see also Luke 13:28).

THOU WILT PERFORM THE TRUTH TO JACOB, AND THE MERCY TO ABRAHAM, WHICH THOU HAST SWORN UNTO OUR FATHERS FROM THE DAYS OF OLD (Micah 7:20).

XV. Jesus Christ will return from Heaven, AND VISIBLY APPEAR AND TAKE UP HIS RESIDENCE ON EARTH A SECOND TIME, for the purpose of bringing about the accomplishment of all these things. The second coming of Christ is therefore the true hope of the believer.

This same Jesus, which is taken up from you into heaven, *shall so come in like manner as ye have seen him go into heaven* (Acts 1:9-11).

Jesus Christ, who shall judge the quick and the dead, *at his appearing and his kingdom* (2 Tim. 4:1).

For the Son of man SHALL COME in the glory of his Father with his angels, and then he shall reward every man according to his works (Matt. 16:27).

HE SHALL SEND JESUS CHRIST, which before was preached unto you: whom the heaven must receive until the times of restitution of all things, *which God hath spoken by the mouth of all his holy prophets* since the world began (Acts 3: 20, 21).

Unto them that look for him *shall he* APPEAR THE SECOND TIME without sin unto salvation (Heb. 9:28).

The Lord himself shall descend from heaven with a shout, with the voice of the archangel, and the trump of God; and the dead in Christ shall rise first (1 Thess. 4:16).

Wherefore gird up the loins of your mind, be sober, and hope to the end for the grace that is to be brought unto you *at the revelation of Jesus Christ* (1 Pet. 1:13).

Our conversation is in heaven; *from whence* also we look for the Saviour, the Lord Jesus Christ (Phil. 3:20).

So that ye come behind in no gift; *waiting for* THE COMING OF OUR LORD JESUS CHRIST (1. Cor. 1:7).

That when he shall appear we may have confidence, and not be ashamed before him AT HIS COMING (1 John 2:28).

XVI. The Kingdom of God is the inheritance to which men are called by the gospel, and the thing presented as *the object of hope:* a proposition which destroys the popular Gospel of "Kingdoms beyond the skies."

God hath called you UNTO HIS KINGDOM and glory (1 Thess. 2:12).

Fear not, little flock, for it is your father's good pleasure to give you THE KINGDOM (Luke 12:32).

Hearken, my beloved brethren, hath not God chosen the poor of this world, rich in faith, and heirs of THE KINGDOM WHICH HE HATH PROMISED TO THEM THAT LOVE HIM? (Jas. 2:5).

Then shall the king say unto them on his right hand, Come, ye blessed of my Father, INHERIT THE KINGDOM prepared for you from the foundation of the world (Matt. 25:34).

For so an entrance shall be ministered unto you abundantly into THE EVERLASTING KINGDOM OF OUR LORD AND SAVIOUR JESUS CHRIST (2 Pet. 1:11).

And they shall come from the east, and from the west, and from the north, and from the south, and shall sit down IN THE KINGDOM OF GOD (Luke 13:29).

Jesus answered, Verily, verily, I say unto thee, except a man be born of water and of the Spirit, he cannot enter into THE KINGDOM OF GOD (John 3:5).

Now this I say, brethren, that flesh and blood cannot inherit THE KINGDOM OF GOD; neither doth corruption inherit incorruption (1 Cor. 15:50).

Know ye not that the unrighteous shall not inherit THE KINGDOM OF GOD? (1 Cor. 6:9).

XVII. The Kingdom of God will last a Thousand Years, during which Christ and his brethren will rule the mortal nations of the earth; sin and death continuing among mankind, but in a milder degree than now. At the end of that period, an entire change will take place. Christ will surrender his position of supremacy, and become subject to the Father, Who will then manifest Himself as the FATHER, STRENGTH, GOVERNOR AND FRIEND OF ALL. As a preparation for this sublime manifestation, sin and death will be abolished, but not before and extensive revolt of nations at the close of the Millennium. This revolt will succeed to the last point, and will be suppressed by a summary outburst of judgment; after which will occur a resurrection and judgment of those who shall have died during the thousand years and a judging of those who are alive at the end of that period; resulting in the immortalization of the approved and the consignment of the rejected to destruction. None will remain but a generation of righteous, redeemed, immortal persons, who shall *inhabit the earth for ever.* Christ's work will be finished, and the Father will reveal Himself without mediation.

And I saw an angel come down from heaven having the key of the bottomless pit, and a great chain in his hand. And he laid hold on the dragon, that old serpent, the Devil and Satan and bound him *a thousand years,* and cast him into the bottomless pit, and shut him up, and set a seal upon him that he should deceive the nations no more till the *thousand years* should be fulfilled, and after that to be loosed a little season. And I saw thrones, and they sat upon them, and judgment was given unto them: and I saw the souls of them that were beheaded for the witness of Jesus and for the word of God, and which had not worshipped the beast, neither his image, neither had received his mark upon their foreheads, or in their hands; and *they lived and reigned with Christ* A THOUSAND YEARS. Blessed and holy is he that hath part in the first resurrection; on such the second death hath no power, but they shall be priests of God and of Christ, *and shall reign with him a* THOUSAND YEARS. But the rest of the dead lived not again until the thousand years were finished. This is the first resurrection. *And when the thousand years are expired,* Satan shall be loosed out of his prison and shall go out to deceive the nations which are in the four quarters of the earth, Gog and Magog, to gather them together to battle: the number of whom is as the sand of the sea. And they went up on the breadth of the earth and encompassed the camp of the saints about, and the beloved city; and fire came down from God out of heaven and devoured them. And I saw the dead, small and great, stand before God; and the books were opened: and another book was opened which is the book of life; and the dead were judged out of those things which were written in the books, according to their works. And the sea gave up the dead which were in

A DECLARATION OF THE TRUTH REVEALED IN THE BIBLE, THE SUBLIME AND SIMPLE THEOLOGY OF THE PRIMITIVE CHRISTIANS (UNAMENDED CHRISTADELPHIANS) (continued)

it; and death and hell (the grave) delivered up the dead which were in them: *and they were judged every man according to their works,* and death and hell (the grave) were cast into the lake of fire. *This is the second death.* And *whosoever was not written in the book of life was cast into* THE LAKE OF FIRE (Rev. 20:1-9, 12-15).

And there was given him dominion, and glory, and A KINGDOM, *that all people, nations, and languages should serve him:* his dominion is an everlasting dominion which shall not pass away, and HIS KINGDOM that which shall not be destroyed (Dan. 7:14).

There shall be no more thence an infant of days, nor an old man that hath not filled his days; for *the child shall* DIE *an hundred years old:* but the sinner being an hundred years old shall be accursed (Isa. 65:20).

Then cometh the end *when he shall have delivered up the* KINGDOM TO GOD, even the Father; when he shall have put down all rule, and all authority and power. For he must reign, till he hath put all enemies under his feet. *The last enemy that shall be destroyed* IS DEATH. And when all things shall be subdued unto him, *then shall the Son also himself be subject unto him that put all things under him,* THAT GOD MAY BE ALL IN ALL (1 Cor. 15: 24-28).

THE THINGS CONCERNING THE NAME OF JESUS CHRIST

XVIII. That there is but ONE GOD by Whom and out of Whom all things have been created, and in Whose immensity-filling Spirit all things subsist; that He Who is thus the FATHER OF ALL dwells in UNAPPROACHABLE LIGHT styled in the Scriptures, "heaven, *his dwelling place*". He and the Spirit are one, but only in the sense in which the sun in the heavens and the light of day are one. Jesus is His manifestation by the Spirit. This proposition strikes at the root of the popular doctrine of the Trinity, which confuses the revealed relations of the Father, the Son and the Holy Spirit.

Hear, O Israel, the Lord our God is ONE Lord (Deut. 6:4).

I am the Lord, and *there is none else,* THERE IS NO GOD BESIDE ME (Isa. 45:5).

And Jesus answered him, The first of all the commandments is, Hear, O Israel, the Lord our God is ONE LORD (Mark 12:29).

And this is life eternal, that they might know thee, THE ONLY TRUE GOD, and Jesus Christ, whom thou hast sent (John 17:3).

But to us there is but ONE GOD, the Father, of whom are all things, and we in him; and one Lord Jesus Christ, by whom are all things, and we by him (1 Cor. 8: 6; Eph. 4:6).

For there is ONE GOD, and one mediator between God and men, the man Christ Jesus (1 Tim. 2:5).

The blessed and ONLY POTENTATE, the King of Kings, and Lord of Lords, who only hath immortality, *dwelling in the light which no man can approach unto* (1 Tim. 6:16).

Hear thou in HEAVEN THY DWELLING PLACE (1 Kings 8:30, 34, 39).

Our Father who art in HEAVEN (Matt. 6:9).

Unto thee lift I up mine eyes, O THOU THAT DWELLEST IN THE HEAVENS (Psa. 123:1).

XIX. That the Spirit is not a personal God distinct from the Father, but the radiant invisible power or energy of the Father; the distinction between the Father and the Spirit being not that they are two persons, but that the Spirit is the Father's power, in space-filling diffusion, forming with the Father, a unity in the stupendous scheme of creation, which is in revolution around the Supreme Source of all Power.

And the spirit of God moved upon the face of the waters (Gen. 1:2).

Thou knowest my downsitting and mine uprising; thou understandest my thought afar off. Thou compassest my path and my lying down, and art acquainted with all my ways. There is not a word in my tongue, but lo, O Lord, thou knowest it altogether. Thou has beset me behind and before, and laid thine hand upon me. Such knowledge is too wonderful for me; it is high, I cannot attain unto it. WHITHER SHALL I GO FROM THY SPIRIT, OR WHITHER SHALL I FLEE FROM THY PRESENCE? If I ascend up into heaven thou art there: if I make my bed in hell (*sheol,* the grave) behold thou art there . . . The darkness hideth not from thee, but the night shineth as the day. The darkness and the light are both alike to thee (Psa. 139:2-12).

The SPIRIT OF GOD *hath made me,* and the breath of the Almighty hath given me life (Job 33:4).

BY HIS SPIRIT *he hath garnished the heavens* (Job 26:13).

Thou sendeth forth THY SPIRIT, *they are created:* and thou renewest the face of the earth (Psa. 104:30).

And the Spirit of the Lord came mightily upon him, and he rent him (the lion) as he would have rent a kid (Judges 14:6).

And the Lord said unto Moses, Take thee Joshua the son of Nun, *a man in whom is* THE SPIRIT, and lay thine hand upon him (Num. 27:18).

Yet many years didst thou forbear them, and testifiedst against them BY THY SPIRIT IN THE PROPHETS (Neh. 9:30).

For the prohecy came not in old time by the will of man; *but holy men of God spake* AS THEY WERE MOVED BY THE HOLY GHOST (2 Pet. 1:21).

XIXA. The Holy Spirit is the Spirit of God in official manifestation. This is a mode of description almost peculiar to the New Testament. The Holy Spirit is the same Spirit mentioned in the testimonies quoted from the Old Testament, but styled Holy Spirit by way of distinction from Spirit in its free, spontaneous, universal form in nature. It is the same Spirit, gathered up, as it were, under the focalizing power of the divine will, for the bestowal of divine gifts and the accomplishment of divine results.

And the angel answered and said unto her, The Holy Ghost shall come upon thee, and the power of the Highest shall over-shadow thee; therefore also that holy thing that shall be born of thee shall be called the Son of God (Luke 1:35).

God anointed Jesus of Nazareth *with the Holy Ghost and with power;* who went about doing good, and healing all that were oppressed of the devil, for God was with him (Acts 10:38).

The Comforter, which is *the Holy Ghost* whom the Father will send in my name, he shall teach you all the things and bring all things to your remembrance whatsoever I have said unto you (John 14:26).

He shall baptize you with the Holy Ghost and with fire (Mat. 3:11).

John truly baptized with water, but ye shall be baptized with the Holy Spirit not many days hence . . . Ye shall receive *power after that the Holy Spirit is come upon you* (Acts 1:5-8).

And suddenly there came a sound from heaven *as of a rushing might wind,* and it *filled all the house* where they were sitting, and they were all filled with the Holy Spirit (Acts 2:2-4).

And as I began to speak, the Holy Spirit fell on them as on us at the beginning. Then remembered I the word of the Lord how that he said, John indeed baptized with water, but ye shall be baptized with the Holy Spirit (Acts 11:15-16).

Then laid they their hands on them, and they received the Holy Ghost; and when Simon saw that through the laying on of the apostles' hands the Holy Spirit was given, he offered them money, saying, *Give me also this power* (Acts 8:17-19).

The foregoing testimonies make plain the New Testament meaning of being baptized with the Holy Spirit, which is a very different meaning from that attached to it by professors of popular theology. It means an immersion or enswathement in spirit power, conferring miraculous gifts. No baptism of the Holy Spirit now takes place. All that can now be done is to preach the Word, and this having been given through the agency of the Spirit, working in ancient prophets and apostles, is the Spirit's instrument—the Spirit's sword, by which the Spirit makes war on the natural mind, and hews it into the similitude of the mind of the Spirit.

XX. Jesus Christ, the Son of God, is not the "second person" of an eternal Trinity, but the manifestation of the ONE ETERNAL CREATOR, who is "above all and through all" (Eph. 4:6), and "out of whom are all things" (Rom. 11:36). This Creator, is Spirit, dwelling personally in heaven yet, in His Spirit effluence filling immensity. By this Spirit-effluence, He begot Jesus, who was therefore HIS SON: by the same power He anointed him and dwelt in him, and spoke to Israel through him (Heb. 1:1). Jesus Christ, therefore, in the days of his weakness, must be considered from two points of view, one DEITY, the other MAN. The man was the son, whose existence dates from the birth of Jesus; the Deity dwelling in him was the Father, who, without beginning of days, is alone eternally pre-existent. God's relation to the Son was afterwards exemplified in the event related in Luke 1:35, by which was established what Paul styles the "mystery of godliness": "God manifest in the flesh, justified in the spirit, seen of angels, preached unto the Gentiles, believed on in the world, received up into glory" (1 Tim. 3:16).

And the angel said unto her (Mary), The Holy Spirit shall come upon thee, and the power of the Highest shall over-shadow thee; THEREFORE *also that holy thing that shall be born of thee shall be called* THE SON OF GOD (Luke 1:35).

The angel of the Lord appeared unto Joseph in a dream, saying, Joseph, thou son of David, fear not to take unto thee Mary, they wife, *for that which is conceived in her is of the Holy Spirit* (Matt. 1:20).

Unto us a child is born, unto us a son is given, and the government shall be upon his shoulder; and his name shall be called Wonderful, Counsellor, the Mighty God, the Everlasting Father, the Prince of Peace (Isa. 9:6).

And Jesus when he was baptized, went up straightway out of the water; and lo the heavens were opened unto him; and he saw the Spirit of God descending like a dove, and lighting upon him, and lo, a voice from heaven, saying, This is my beloved Son, in whom I am well pleased (Matt. 3:16-17).

The Spirit of the Lord is upon me, because he hath anointed me to preach the gospel to the poor; he hath sent me to heal the broken-hearted, to preach deliverance to the captives (Luke 4:18).

For he whom God hath sent speaketh the words of God: for God giveth not the Spirit by measure unto him. The Father loveth the Son, and *hath given all things into his hands* (John 3:34-35).

I can of mine own self do nothing: I seek not mine own will, but the will of the Father which hath sent me (John 5:30).

Jesus answered them, and said, *My doctrine is not mine,* but his that sent me (John 7:16).

I am in the Father, and the Father in me. The words that I speak unto you, I speak not of myself: but the Father that dwelleth in me, he doeth the works (John 14:10).

I go unto the Father; for my Father is greater than I (John 14:28).

Jesus of Nazareth, a MAN approved of God among you by miracles, and wonders, and signs, *which God did by him* in the midst of you, as ye yourselves also know (Acts 2:22).

God anointed Jesus of Nazareth with the Holy Spirit and with power; who went about doing good, and healing all that were oppressed of the devil, for God was with him (Acts 10:38).

XXI. That Jesus was of our nature, notwithstanding the mode of his conception and his anointing with the Holy Spirit. He was raised up as a SECOND ADAM (constituted of flesh and blood as we are, and

A DECLARATION OF THE TRUTH REVEALED IN THE BIBLE, THE SUBLIME AND SIMPLE THEOLOGY OF THE PRIMITIVE CHRISTIANS (UNAMENDED CHRISTADELPHIANS) (continued)

tempted in all points like unto us, yet without sin), to remove (by his obedience, death, and resurrection) the evil consequences resulting from the disobedience of the first Adam.

THE MAN CHRIST JESUS (1 Tim. 2:5).

God sending his own Son in THE LIKENESS OF SINFUL FLESH, *and for sin, condemned* sin in the flesh (Rom. 8:3).

Forasmuch then as the children are partakers of *flesh and blood,* he also himself likewise TOOK PART OF THE SAME (Heb. 2:14).

God sent forth his Son MADE OF A WOMAN (Gal. 4:4).

He was MADE SIN for us, who knew no sin (2 Cor. 5:21).

By man came death, BY MAN CAME *also the resurrection of the dead* . . . The first man, Adam, was made a living soul; the LAST ADAM was made a quickening spirit (1 Cor. 15:21, 45).

The gift by grace (or favour), which is by ONE MAN, *Jesus Christ,* hath abounded unto many . . . For as by one man's disobedience many were made sinners, so by the obedience of one shall many be made righteous (Rom. 5:15, 19).

He was heard in that he feared: though he were a Son, *yet learned he obedience by the things which he suffered* (Heb. 5:7, 8).

In all things it behoved him to be made LIKE UNTO HIS BRETHREN, that he might be a merciful and faithful high priest in things pertaining to God . . . *He was in all points tempted like as we are, yet without sin (Heb. 2:17; 4:15).*

XXII. The Death of Christ was not to appease the wrath of an offended God but to express the love of the Father in a necessary sacrifice for sin that the law of sin and death which came into force by the first Adam might be nullified in the second in a full discharge of its claims through a temporary surrender to its power; after which immortality by resurrection might be acquired, in harmony with the law of obedience. Thus sin is taken away, and righteousness established.

God *so loved the world* that he gave his only begotten Son, that whosoever believeth on him might not perish, but have everlasting life (John 3:16).

Behold the Lamb of God that *taketh away the sin of the world* (John 1:29).

To him give all the prophets witness, that through his name whosoever believeth in him *shall receive remission of sins* (Acts 10:43).

Neither is there salvation in ANY OTHER: FOR THERE IS NONE OTHER NAME UNDER HEAVEN *given among men,* whereby we must be saved (Acts 4:12).

Whom God hath set forth to be a propitiation through faith in his blood, to declare his righteousness for the remission of sins that are past, through the forbearance of God (Rom. 3:25).

He putteth away sin *by the sacrifice of himself* (Heb. 9:26).

Who *gave himself for our sins,* that he might deliver us from this present evil world, according to the will of God and our Father (Gal. 1:4).

Who *gave himself for us* that he might redeem us from all inquity, and purify unto himself a peculiar people, zealous of good works (Titus 2:14).

For he hath made him to be sin for us, who knew no sin; *that we might be made the righteousness of God in him* (2 Cor. 5:21).

XXIIA. God raised Jesus from the dead and exalted him to a glorified, incorruptible, immortal (because spiritual) state of existence, in which he at the present time acts as priestly mediator between the Father and those who come unto God by him.

Whom God hath raised up, having loosed the pains of death: because it was not possible that he should be holden of it (Acts 2:24).

The God of our fathers RAISED UP JESUS, whom ye slew and hanged on a tree (Acts 5:30).

Him God raised up the third day, and showed him openly; not to all the people, but unto witnesses chosen before of God, even to us, who did eat and drink with him after he rose from the dead (Acts 10:40).

God hath appointed a day in which he will judge the world in righteousness by that man whom he hath ordained; whereof he hath given assurance unto all men IN THAT HE HATH RAISED HIM FROM THE DEAD (Acts 17:31).

Jesus Christ our Lord, who was made of the seed of David according to the flesh; *and declared to be the son of God,* with power, according to the spirit of holiness, BY THE RESURRECTION FROM THE DEAD (Rom. 1:3-4).

Though he was *crucified through weakness,* YET HE LIVETH BY THE POWER OF GOD (2 Cor. 13:4).

Christ being raised from the dead *dieth no more;* DEATH HATH NO MORE DOMINION OVER HIM (Rom. 6:9).

God hath glorified his son Jesus (Acts 3:13).

GOD HATH RAISED HIM FROM THE DEAD and set him at his own right hand in the heavenly places, far above all principality, and power, and might, and dominion, and every name that is named not only in this world, but also in that which is to come (Eph. 1:20-21).

The apostle and *High Priest of our* profession, Christ Jesus (Heb. 3:1).

We have a *great High Priest* that is passed into the heavens, Jesus the Son of God. We have not an High Priest who cannot be touched with the feeling of our infirmities, but was in all points tempted like as we are, yet without sin (Heb. 4: 14-15).

We have such *an High Priest,* who is set on the right hand of the throne of the Majesty in the heavens (Heb. 8:1).

XXIII. THE DEVIL—Who is he? It is of great importance to understand this question, because the Son of God was manifested *expressly for the purpose of destroying the Devil and his works* (1 John 3:8; Heb. 2:14). The mission of Christ is, therefore, imperfectly understood when the nature of the Bible Devil is not comprehended. It will be found upon examination that the Devil is not (as is commonly supposed) a personal supernatural agent of evil, and, that in fact, *there is no such BEING in existence.* The Devil is a *Scriptural personification of sin in the flesh,* in its several phases of manifestation—subjective, individual, aggregate, social, and political, in history, current experience, and prophecy; after the style of metaphor which speaks of wisdom as a woman, riches as MAMMOM and *the god of this world,* sin as a master, etc.

Forasmuch then as the children are partakers of flesh and blood, he (Christ) also himself likewise took part of the same: *that THROUGH DEATH he might destroy him that had the power of death,* THAT IS, THE DEVIL *(diabolos)* (Heb. 2:14).

The wages of SIN *is death* (Rom. 6:23).

He put away SIN *by the sacrifice of himself* (Heb. 9:26).

Resist THE DEVIL and he will flee from you (Jas. 4:7).

Ye have not yet resisted unto blood, striving against SIN (Heb. 12:4). The DEVIL *having now put it into the heart of Judas Iscariot* (John 13:2).

[The betrayal of Christ was the result of Judas's thievish propensities; therefore, says Jesus, "It were good for that *man* that he had not been born."] Have I not chosen you twelve, and *one of you (Judas)* IS A DEVIL? (John 6:70).

Why hath *Satan filled thine heart* to lie to the Holy Spirit? . . . How is it that YE HAVE AGREED TOGETHER to tempt the Spirit of the Lord? (Acts 5:3, 9).

Every man is tempted *when he is drawn away* OF HIS OWN LUST, and enticed. Then when lust hath conceived, it bringeth forth sin; and sin, when it is finished, bringeth forth death (Jas. 1:14-15).

Wherein in time past ye walked according to the course of this world, according to *the price of the power of the air,* THE SPIRIT THAT NOW WORKETH IN THE CHILDREN OF DISOBEDIENCE (Eph. 2:2).

Give none occasion to the adversary to speak reproachfully, *for some are already turned aside* AFTER SATAN (1 Tim. 5:14-15).

Whom *I have delivered unto* SATAN, that they may learn not to blaspheme (1 Tim. 1:20).

But he turned, and said unto PETER, *Get thee behind me,* SATAN: thou art an offence unto me; for thou savourest not the things that be of God, but those that be of men (Matt. 16:23; Mark 8:33; Luke 4:8).

SATAN hindered us (1 Thess. 2:18).

And to the angel of the church in *Pergamos* write: I know thy works, and where thou dwellest, even WHERE SATAN'S SEAT IS: and thou holdest fast my name, and hast not denied my faith, even in those days wherein

Antipas was my faithful martyr, who was slain among you, WHERE SATAN DWELLETH (Rev. 2:12-13).

Be sober, be vigilant, because your adversary, *the Devil,* as a roaring lion, walketh about, seeking whom he may devour (1 Pet. 5:8).

THE DEVIL *shall cast some of you into prison* (Rev. 2:10).

And the God of peace *shall bruise* SATAN *under your feet shortly* (Rom. 16:20).

And I will put enmity between thee (the serpent) and the woman, and between thy seed and her seed; IT SHALL BRUISE THY HEAD, *and thou shalt bruise his heel* (Gen. 3:15).

But God shall wound *the head of* HIS ENEMIES (Psa. 68:21).

Thou (Israel) art my battle axe and weapons of war; for with thee will I *break in pieces* THE NATIONS, *and with thee will I destroy* KINGDOMS (Jer. 51:20).

And there appeared another wonder in heaven; and behold a GREAT RED DRAGON, having *seven heads and ten horns,* and seven crowns upon his heads . . . And the dragon was wroth with the woman, and *went to make war with the remnant of her seed,* which keep the commandments of God, and have the testimony of Jesus Christ (Rev. 12:3-17).

And he laid hold on the dragon, that old serpent, WHICH IS THE DEVIL AND SATAN, and bound him a thousand years (Rev. 20:2).

(The symbolism of the verses immediately foregoing is explained in the following.)

He shall judge among the heathen, he shall fill the places with the dead bodies; *he shall wound the heads over many countries (Psa. 110:6).*

And in the days of these kings shall the God of heaven set up a kingdom . . . *it shall break in pieces and consume all these kingdoms,* and it shall stand for ever (Dan. 2:44).

XXIIIA. Demons, devils, or so-called evil Spirits were the fanciful creation of the pagan mind. They were supposed to be a kind of demi-god inhabiting the air, and producing disease in human being by taking possession of them. The following passages show that in the Bible, the word is not used to express this idea.

They sacrifice unto *devils,* not *to* God: TO GODS *whom they knew not,* to NEW GODS that came newly up, whom your fathers feared not (Deut. 32:17; Psa. 106:37).

And he ordained him priests for the high places, and *for the devils,* and for the calves which he had made (2 Chron. 11:15: Levs. 17:7).

The things which the Gentiles sacrifice they sacrifice to *devils* (that is, to the idols in the temples) and not to God (1 Cor. 10:20).

Lord, have mercy on my son, for he is LUNATIC and sore vexed, for oftimes he falleth into the fire, and oft into the water, and they brought him to thy disciples and they could not *cure* him . . . And Jesus rebuked *the devil,* and he departed out of him, and the child was whole from that very hour (Matt. 17: 15-18).

A DECLARATION OF THE TRUTH REVEALED IN THE
BIBLE, THE SUBLIME AND SIMPLE THEOLOGY OF
THE PRIMITIVE CHRISTIANS (UNAMENDED
CHRISTADELPHIANS) (continued)

(From this, the identity of lunacy with supposed diabolical possession is apparent. The expulsion of the evil which deranged the child's faculties is the casting out of the demon).

Then was brought unto him one possessed with a devil, blind and dumb: and he healed him, insomuch that the *blind and dumb both spake and saw* (Matt. 12: 22).

And one of the multitude answered and said, Master, I have brought unto thee my son, which hath a dumb spirit (Mark 9:17).

XXIV. HUMAN NATURE—What is it? Philosophy and orthodox religion say it is a thing made up of two parts—*body* and *soul* (and some add, spirit); that the soul is the real, conscious, thinking part of man, in its nature indestructible and immortal; that when the body is destroyed in death, the soul is liberated and departs to another sphere of existence, there to undergo endless happiness or misery, according to the life developed in the body. This doctrine is known in theology as THE IMMORTALITY OF THE SOUL. This is a PAGAN FICTION *subversive of every principle of eternal truth,* as will be discovered by a consideration of the evidence, which proves:

A. That Man is a creature of dust formation, whose individuality and faculties are the attributes of his bodily *organization.*

And the Lord God formed man of the dust of the ground, and breathed into his nostrils the breath of life, and man became a living soul (Heb. *nephesh chaiyah,* living creature)—(Gen. 2:7).

In the sweat of thy face shalt thou eat bread, till thou return unto the ground; for out of it wast thou taken: for DUST THOU ART, AND UNTO DUST SHALT THOU RETURN (Gen. 3:19).

The Lord God sent him forth from the *garden of Eden to till* THE GROUND *from whence he was taken* (Gen. 3:23).

He knoweth our frame, he remembereth that WE ARE DUST (Psa. 103:14).

And Abraham answered and said, Behold now, I have taken upon me to speak unto the Lord, WHICH AM BUT DUST AND ASHES (Gen. 18:27).

Remember, I beseech thee, that *thou hast made me* AS THE CLAY; and wilt thou bring me into *dust* AGAIN? (Job. 10: 9).

For *all flesh is as grass, and all the glory of man as the flower of grass.* The grass withereth, and the flower thereof falleth away (1 Pet. 1:24; Jas. 1:10-11).

For that which befalleth the sons of men befalleth beasts; even one thing befalleth them; *as the one dieth,* SO DIETH THE OTHER; yea, they have all one breath; *so that a man hath no pre-eminence above*

a beast; for all is vanity; all go unto one place; ALL ARE OF THE DUST; *and all turn to dust again* (Eccles. 3:19-20).

Then shall *the dust return to the earth* AS IT WAS: *and the spirit (ruach,* spirit or breath, which in Eccles. 3:19, above quoted, Solomon says the beasts have as well as man) shall return unto God who gave it (Eccles. 12:7).

Thou hidest thy face, they are troubled: *thou takest away their breath,* THEY DIE, *and return to their dust* (Psa. 104:29).

Shall the clay say to him who fashioned it, What makest thou? (Isa 45:9).

We are the clay and Thou our potter (Isa. 64:8).

He that is of the earth is EARTHLY (John 3:31).

The first man is of the earth, EARTHY . . . as is the earthy, such are they also WHO ARE EARTHY . . . we have borne the image of the EARTHY (1 Cor. 15:47-49).

B. That Man is mortal (that is subject to death or *dissolution of being* in consequence of the disobedience of Adam, which brought death as the penalty of sin.

For in the day that thou (Adam) eatest thereof, thou shalt surely die (see margin, Heb. *dying thou shalt die*)—Gen. 2:17). Because thou has eaten of the tree . . . *dust thou art, and* UNTO DUST SHALT THOU RETURN (Gen. 3:19).

And now, *lest he put forth his hand and take also of the tree of life,* AND EAT AND LIVE FOR EVER (Gen. 3:22-23).

By one man sin entered into the world and DEATH BY SIN; *and so death passed upon all men, for that all have sinned* (Rom. 5:12).

In Adam all DIE (1 Cor. 15:22).

What man is he that liveth and shall not see death? *Shall he deliver* HIS SOUL *from the hand of* THE GRAVE (Psa. 89: 48; 30:3; 86:13; Job. 33:22).

All (cattle, beast and creeping thing, and EVERY MAN) *in whose nostrils was the breath of life,* of all that was in the dry land, DIED (at the flood) (Gen. 7:22).

Shall MORTAL MAN be more just than God? Shall a man be more pure than his maker? (Job 4:17).

Cease ye from man whose BREATH (*n'shamah*) IS IN HIS NOSTRILS: *for wherein is he to be accounted of?* (Isa. 2:22).

C. That in the Death State, a man, instead of having "gone to another world" is simply *a body deprived of life,* and as utterly unconscious as if he had never existed. Corruption will destroy his dead body, and he will pass away like a dream. Hence the necessity for "resurrection".

IN DEATH *there is no remembrance of thee;* in the grave, who shall give thee thanks? (Psa. 6:5).

For the living know that they shall die: but THE DEAD KNOW NOT ANYTHING, neither have they any more a reward; for the memory of them is forgotten. Also their *love,* and their *hatred,* and their *envy* is now perished; neither have they any more a portion for ever in anything that is done under the sun (Eccles. 9:5-6).

Whatsoever thy hand findeth to do, do it with thy might; *for there is no work, nor device, nor knowledge, nor wisdom,* IN THE GRAVE, *whither thou goest* (Eccles. 9:10).

Put not your trust in princes, nor in the son of man, in whom there is no help. *His* breath goeth forth, HE *returneth to his earth;* IN THAT VERY DAY HIS THOUGHTS PERISH (Psa. 146:3-4).

THE GRAVE CANNOT PRAISE THEE, *death cannot celebrate thee; they that go down into the pit* CANNOT HOPE FOR THY TRUTH. The living, the living, he shall praise thee, as I do this day (Isa. 38:18-19).

Hear my prayer, O Lord, and give ear unto my cry . . . O spare me (David) that I may receive strength *before I go hence and* BE NO MORE (Psa. 39:12-13).

For David after he had served his own generation by the will of God, *fell on sleep, and was laid unto his fathers, and saw,* CORRUPTION; but he whom God raised again saw no corruption (Acts 13:36; also 2:29-34).

D. "Soul" in the Bible means creatures in its primary use, but is also employed to express the variety of aspects in which a living creature can be contemplated, such as person, body, life, individuality, mind, disposition, breath, etc. *It never expresses the idea of immortality.*

And God said, Let the earth bring forth the living creature (the same original word translated "soul" as applied to Adam) after his kind, cattle, and creeping thing, and beast of the earth after his kind (Gen. 1:24).

And God said, Let the waters bring forth abundantly the moving creature that hath life (in the margin "*soul*"—Heb. *nephesh,*) and fowl that may fly above the earth in the open firmament of heaven (Gen. 1:20).

In whose hands is the SOUL OF *every living thing,* and the breadth of all mankind (Job 12:10).

And he stretched himself upon the child three times, and cried unto the Lord and said, O Lord my God, I pray thee let this child's soul (*nephesh*) come into him again. And the Lord heard the voice of Elijah; and the SOUL (*nephesh*) of the child came into him again, and he revived (1 Kings 17:21-22).

And it came to pass that her soul (*nephesh,* life), was in departing (for she died)—(Gen. 35:18).

It shall be even as when an hungry man dreameth, and behold, he eateth; but he awaketh, and his SOUL is empty: behold, he is faint, and his soul hath appetite (Isa. 29:8; Exod. 12:16; see margin).

Men do not despise a thief, if he steal to satisfy his SOUL when he is hungry (Prov. 6:30; cp. Lev. 17:10-12).

And levy a tribute unto the Lord of the men of war which went out to battle: ONE SOUL of five hundred, both of the *persons,* and of the beeves, and of the *asses,* and of the *sheep* (Num 31:28).

But if the priest buy any SOUL with his money, he shall eat of it, and he that is born in his house: they shall eat of his meat (Lev. 22:11).

And they smote all the SOULS that were therein with the edge of the sword, utterly destroying them: there was not any left to breathe: and he burnt Hazor with fire (Jos. 11:11; 10:32; Jer. 4:10; Job. 36:14; see margin).

Also in thy skirt is found *the blood of the souls* of the poor inocents (Jer. 2:34; Ezek. 13:18-19; 22:25-27).

So that my SOUL chooseth strangling, and death rather than my life (Job. 7-15; Psa. 105:18, see margin).

And Samson said, Let me (in the margin, Heb. *my soul*) die with the Philistines (Judges 16:30).

And it shall come to pass, that every soul which will not hear that prophet shall be destroyed from among the people (Acts 3:23).

Thou hast in love to *my soul* (that is, to me) delivered it from the pit of corruption (Isa. 38:17).

Behold, all souls are mine: as the soul of the father, so also the soul of the son is mine: the soul that sinneth, it shall die (Ezek. 18:4, 20).

For whosoever will save *his life (psuche)* shall lose it: and whosoever will lose *his life* for my sake shall find it. For what is a man profited if he shall gain the whole world and lose his own soul? (*psuche,* same word translated "life" in the previous verse; comp. also Revised Version which gives "life" in both verses): or what shall a man give in exchange for his soul *(psuche)?* (Matt. 16:25-26).

And I will say to my soul *(psuche),* Soul *(psuche),* thou hast much goods laid up for many years: take thine ease, eat, drink, and be merry. But God said unto him, Thou fool, this night thy soul *(psuche)* shall be required of thee (Luke 12:19-20).

And fear not them which kill the body but are not able to kill the soul *(psuche);* but rather fear him which is able to destroy both soul *(psuche)* and body in hell *(gehenna)*—(Matt. 10:28).

E. "Spirit" in the Scriptures, as applied to man, is no more expressive of the philosophical conception of an immortal soul than "soul", but signifies breath, life, vital energy, mind, disposition, etc., as attributes of human nature while alive.

And behold, I even I do bring a flood of waters upon the earth to destroy *all flesh wherein is the breath*

A DECLARATION OF THE TRUTH REVEALED IN THE
BIBLE, THE SUBLIME AND SIMPLE THEOLOGY OF
THE PRIMITIVE CHRISTIANS (UNAMENDED
CHRISTADELPHIANS) (continued)

(ruach) of life, from under heaven; and everything
that is in the earth shall die (Gen. 6:17).

For as the body without the spirit *(pneuma,* in the
margin, *breath),* is dead, so faith without works is
dead (Jas. 2:26).

And they stoned Stephen, calling upon God, and
saying, Lord Jesus, receive my spirit *(pneuma)* (Acts
7:59).

And Hannah answered and said, No, my lord, I am a
woman of a sorrowful *spirit (ruach)* (1 Sam. 1:15).

Who knoweth the spirit *(ruach)* of man that goeth
upward, and the spirit *(ruach)* of the beast that goeth
downward to the earth? (Eccles. 3:21).

And it came to pass, when all the kings of the
Amorites, which were on the side of Jordan westward, and all the kings of the Canaanites, which
were by the sea, heard that the Lord had dried up the
waters of Jordan from before the children of Israel,
until we were passed over, that their heart melted,
neither was there SPIRIT *(ruach) in them any more,*
because of the children of Israel (Josh. 5:1).

And they heard the voice of the Lord God walking
in the garden in the cool *(ruach,* in the margin
"wind") of the day: and Adam and his wife hid
themselves from the presence of the Lord God,
amongst the trees of the garden (Gen. 3:8).

And God made a wind *(ruach)* to pass over the
earth, and the waters assuaged (Gen. 8:1).

There is no man that hath power over the spirit
(ruach) to retain the spirit *(ruach):* neither hath he
power in the day of death: and there is no discharge
in that war: neither shall wickedness deliver those
that are given to it (Eccles. 8:8).

To the general assembly and church of the firstborn,
which are written in heaven, and to God the Judge of
all, and to the spirits of just men made perfect (Heb.
12:23).

Are they not all ministering spirits, sent forth to
minister for them who shall be heirs of salvation?
(Heb. 1:14).

Beloved, believe not every spirit *(pneuma),* but try
the spirits whether they are of God; because many
false prophets are gone out into the world. Hereby
know ye the Spirit of God; every *spirit* that confes-
seth that Jesus Christ is come in the flesh is of God
(1 John 4:1-2).

But when they saw him walking upon the sea, they
supposed it had been a spirit (in the original,
phantasma), and cried out (Mark 6:49).

XXV. The doctrine of the immortality of the soul not
being in the Bible, the question is, where has it come
from? It has been borrowed by Christendom from
pagan teaching. We direct attention to the following
quotations:

Herodotus, the oldest historian, writes as follows: "The
Egyptians say that Ceres (the goddess of corn), and
Bacchus (the god of wine), hold the chief sway in the
infernal regions; and the *Egyptians* also *were the first who
asserted the doctrine that the soul of man is immortal"*
(Herod. Book ii.; Sec. 123).

Mosheim says, "Its first promoters argued from that
known doctrine of the Platonic School, which was *also
adopted by Origen and his disciples,* that the divine nature
was diffused through all human souls; or in other words,
that the faculty of reason, from which proceed the health
and vigour of the mind, was an emanation from God into
the human soul, and comprehended it in the principles and
elements of all truth, human and *divine"* (*Ecclesiastical
History,* vol. i., p. 86).

Justin Martyr (A.D. 150) said, "For if you have conversed
with some that are indeed called Christians, and do not
maintain these opinions, but even dare to blaspheme the
God of Abraham, and the God of Isaac, and the God of
Jacob, and say that there is no resurrection of the dead,
that the souls, as soon as they leave the body, are received
up into heaven, *take care that you do not look upon these.*
But I and all those Christians, that are really orthodox in
every respect, do know that there will be a resurrection of
the body and a thousand years in Jerusalem, when it is
built again, and adorned, and enlarged, as Ezekiel, and
Esaias, and the rest of the prophets declare" (*Dialogue with
Trypho the Jew,* section 80).

An extract from a canon which was passed under Leo X.,
by the Lateran Council, shows that the doctrine of an
"immortal soul" that lives when the man is dead was
supported in those days, as it generally has been since, *by
the authority of creeds,* rather than the word of God:
"Some have dared to assert, concerning the nature of the
reasonable soul, that it is mortal; we, with the approbation
of the sacred councils, do condemn and rebrobate all such,
seeing according to the canon of Pope Clement the Fifth,
the soul is immortal; and we strictly inhibit all from
dogmatizing otherwise; and we decree that all who adhere
to the like erroneous assertions shall be shunned and
punished as heretics" (*Caranza,* p. 412, 1681).

Martin Luther ironically responded to the decree of the
Lateran Council held during the Pontificate of Pope Leo:
"I permit the Pope to make articles of faith for himself and
his faithful—such as the soul is the substantial form of the
human body,—the soul is immortal,—*with all those
monstrous opinions to be found in the Roman dunghill of
decretals;* that such as his faith is, such may be his gospel,
such his disciples, and such his Church, that the mouth
may have meat suitable for it, and the dish a cover worthy
of it" *(Luther's Works,* vol ii., folio 107, Wittenburg,
1562).

"And ye in putting them in heaven, hell and purgatory,
destroy the arguments wherewyth Christ and Paul prove
the resurrection. What God doth with them, that shall we
know when we come to them. The true faith putteth the
resurrection, which we be warned to looke for every houre.
The heathen philosophers denying that, did put that the
soules did ever lyve. And the pope joyneth the spirituall
doctrine of Christ and the fleshly doctrine of philosophers

together, things so contrary that they can not agree, no more than the Spirite and the flesh do in a Christian man. And because the fleshly mynded pope consenteth unto the healthen doctrine, therefore he corrupteth the Scripture to stablish it." William Tyndall, the translator of the Scriptures into English, who suffered martyrdom in 1536.

Gibbon declares that "The doctrine of the immortality of the soul is omitted in the law of Moses". (*Gibbon,* chap. xv).

Richard Watson remarks, "That the soul is naturally immortal, *is contradicted by Scripture,* which makes our immortality a gift dependent, on the will of the Giver" (*Institutes,* vol. ii., p. 250).

The authentic Christian doctrine has three special characteristics:

(a) It is a doctrine, not of Immortality, but of Resurrection.

(b) It regards this Resurrection as an act and gift of God, not an inherent right of the human soul as such.

(c) It is not so much a doctrine of rewards and punishments, as the proclamation of the inherent joy of love and the inherent misery of selfishness.

Nature, Man and God, by Wm. Temple.

Another consideration of the highest importance is that the natural immortality of the soul is a doctrine wholly unknown to the Holy Scriptures, and standing on no higher plane than that of an ingeniously sustained, but gravely and formidably contested, philosophical opinion. And surely there is nothing, as to which we ought to be more on our grand, than the entrance into the precinct of Christian doctrine, either without authority or by an abuse of authority, of philosophical speculations disguised as truths of Divine Revelation. They bring with them a grave restraint on mental liberty; but what is worse is, that their basis is a pretension essentially false, and productive by rational retribution of other falsehoods. Under these two heads, we may perhaps find that we have ample warrant for declining to accept the tenet of natural immortality as a truth of Divine Revelation. *Studies Subsidiary to the Works of Bishop Butler,* by W. E. Gladstone.

Careful attention to the origin of the doctrine of the necessary immortality or indestructibility of each human soul, as stated for instance by Augustine and Aquinas, will probably convince us that it was no part of the original Christian message, or of early catholic doctrine. It was rather a speculation of Platonism taking possession of the Church. *The Epistle to the Romans,* by Charles Gore.

XXVI. The true doctrine of immortality. There is a doctrine of immortality in the Bible: but it differs from the popular doctrine in every particular.

FIRST. Instead of immortality being inherent and natural, the Bible teaches it is a quality brought within reach by Christ in the Gospel, and will only be attained on condition of believing the Gospel and obeying the divine commandments.

Jesus Christ hath abolished death, *and brought life and immortality to light* THROUGH THE GOSPEL (2 Tim. 1:10).

I am the Resurrection and the Life; *he that believeth on me,* though he were *dead* YET SHALL HE LIVE (that is, by resurrection: see foregoing context) (John 6:40: John 11:25).

For the wages of sin is *death;* but the gift of God is ETERNAL LIFE *through Jesus Christ our Lord* (Rom. 6:23).

And *this is the promise that he hath promised us,* EVEN ETERNAL LIFE (1 John 2:25).

Paul, an Apostle of Jesus Christ, by the will of God, according to THE PROMISE OF LIFE, *which is in Christ Jesus* (2 Tim. 1:1).

IN HOPE OF ETERNAL LIFE, which God, that cannot lie, *promised* before the world began (Titus 1:2).

That being justified by his grace, we should be made heirs *accordings to* THE HOPE OF ETERNAL LIFE (Titus 3:7).

For we are saved *by hope;* but HOPE THAT IS SEEN IS NOT HOPE: for what a man seeth why doth he yet hope for? But if we hope for that we see not then do we with patience WAIT FOR IT (Rom. 8:24-25).

He that soweth to the Spirit shall of the Spirit reap LIFE EVERLASTING (Gal. 6:8).

God so loved the world that he gave his only begotten son, that *whosoever believeth on him* should not perish, but have EVERLASTING LIFE (John 3:16).

And this is the record, that God hath given to us ETERNAL LIFE, and this life is in his Son. He that hath the Son hath life; and he that hath not the Son of God hath not life (1 John 5:11-12).

Blessed are they that do his commandments, that they may have right to *the tree of life* (Rev. 22:14).

He that believeth on the Son HATH EVERLASTING LIFE: and he that believeth not the Son shall not see life; but the wrath of God abideth on him (John 3:36).

He that hateth his life in this world SHALL KEEP IT UNTIL LIFE ETERNAL (John 12:25).

He shall receive . . . in the world to come, ETERNAL LIFE (Mark 10:30).

To them, who by patient continuance in well doing *seek for glory* and honour and immortality (God will render: see verse 6), eternal life (Rom. 2:7).

They which shall be accounted worthy to obtain that world, and the resurrection from the dead, neither marry, nor are given in marriage; NEITHER CAN THEY DIE ANY MORE: for they are equal unto the angels; and are the children of God, *being the children of the resurrection* (Luke 20:35-36).

And I will give unto them *(my sheep) eternal life;* and THEY SHALL NEVER PERISH, neither shall any man pluck them out of my hand (John 10:28).

A DECLARATION OF THE TRUTH REVEALED IN THE BIBLE, THE SUBLIME AND SIMPLE THEOLOGY OF THE PRIMITIVE CHRISTIANS (UNAMENDED CHRISTADELPHIANS) (continued)

As thou hast given him power over all flesh, *that he should give* ETERNAL LIFE *to as many as thou hast given him* (John 17:2).

Blessed is *the man that endureth temptation;* for *when he is tried,* he shall receive THE CROWN OF LIFE, which the Lord hath promised to them that love him (Jas. 1:12).

And the world passeth away and the lust thereof: BUT HE THAT DOETH THE WILL OF GOD ABIDETH FOR EVER (1 John 2:17).

For in this we groan, earnestly desiring to be clothed upon with our house which is from heaven. For we that are in this tabernacle do groan, being burdened: not for that we would be unclothed, but clothed upon, *that mortality might be* SWALLOWED UP OF LIFE (2 Cor. 5:1-4).

So when THIS CORRUPTIBLE *shall have put on incorruption,* and THIS MORTAL *shall have put on immortality,* then shall be brought to pass the saying that is written, Death is swallowed up in victory. O death, where is thy sting? O grave, where is thy victory? (1 Cor. 15:54-55).

And God shall wipe away all tears from their eyes; and there shall be NO MORE DEATH, neither sorrow, nor crying, neither shall there be any more pain; for the former things are passed away (Rev. 21:4).

He that overcometh shall not be hurt of the second death. *To him that overcometh* will I give to eat of THE TREE OF LIFE, which is in the midst of the paradise of God (Rev. 2:11, 7).

> SECOND. The immortality of the Bible, unlike the inherent immortality of popular belief, is to be manifested *in connection with, and as the result of, the resurrection or change of* THE BODY. (The reason is evident: *immortality is life manifested through* AN UNDECAYING BODY). This proposition is established in many of the testimonies cited under the last heading; it obtains further support from the following:

And many of them that sleep in the dust of the earth *shall awake,* SOME TO EVERLASTING LIFE, *and some to shame and everlasting contempt* (Dan. 12:2).

And shall come forth; they that have done good, unto the RESURRECTION OF *(resulting in)* LIFE; and they that have done evil unto the resurrection of *(resulting in)* damnation (John 5:29).

And thou shalt be blessed; for they cannot recompense thee: for *thou shalt be recompensed* AT THE RESURRECTION OF THE JUST (Luke 14:14).

And this is the Father's will which hath sent me, that of all which he hath given me I should lose nothing, BUT SHOULD RAISE IT UP AGAIN AT THE LAST DAY (John 6:39, 40, 44).

Matha said unto him, I know that he shall rise again IN THE RESURRECTION at the last day (John 11:24).

For the Lord himself shall descend from heaven with a shout, with the voice of the archangel, and with the trump of God: AND THE DEAD IN CHRIST SHALL RISE FIRST (1 Thess. 4:16).

Awake and sing, *ye that dwell in dust;* for thy dew is as the dew of herbs, and the earth shall cast out the dead (Isa. 26:19).

There shall be *a resurrection of the dead,* both of the just and unjust (Acts 24:15).

So also is the resurrection of the dead. It is sown in corruption, it is raised in incorruption (1 Cor. 15:42-44).

Behold I shew you a mystery: We shall not all sleep, but WE (the awakened dead and those who do not sleep) SHALL ALL BE CHANGED (after judgment) . . . For the trumpet shall sound, and THE DEAD SHALL BE RAISED INCORRUPTIBLE, and we shall be changed: *for this corruptible must put on incorruption, and this mortal must put on immortality* (1 Cor. 15:51-53).

If there be no resurrection of the dead, then is Christ not risen: and if Christ be not risen, then is our preaching vain, and your faith is also vain (1 Cor. 15:13-14).

For I know that my redeemer liveth, and that he shall stand *at the latter day upon the earth;* and though after my skin worms destroy this body, yet IN MY FLESH shall I see God, whom *mine eyes shall behold,* and not another (Job. 19: 25-27).

What advantageth it me (Paul) *if the dead rise not?* (1 Cor. 15:32).

I (Paul) have suffered the loss of all things . . . if by any means *I might attain* unto THE RESURRECTION OF THE DEAD (Phil. 3:8, 11).

Now that the dead are raised, even Moses shewed at the bush, when he calleth the Lord the God of Abraham, and the God of Isaac, and the God of Jacob. For he is not a God of the dead, but of the living, for all live unto him (Luke 20:37-38).

> THIRD. The immortality of the Bible, in addition to depending upon "the resurrection of the body", is a thing to be manifested and enjoyed ON THE EARTH, instead of something to which a man ascends in starry regions after death.

Behold, the righteous shall be recompensed IN THE EARTH: much more the wicked and the sinner (Prov. 11:31).

Blessed are the meek: FOR THEY SHALL INHERIT THE EARTH (Matt. 5:5).

The earth which he hath established for ever (Psa. 78:69; Eccles. 1:4).

For the evil-doers *shall be cut off;* but those that wait upon the Lord, THEY SHALL INHERIT THE EARTH (Psa. 37:9).

But the meek shall INHERIT THE EARTH, and shall delight themselves in the abundance of peace (Psa. 37:11).

For such as he blessed of him SHALL INHERIT THE EARTH: and they that be cursed of him shall be cut off (Psa. 37:22).

The righteous SHALL INHERIT THE LAND and dwell therein, *for ever* (Psa. 37:29).

Wait on the Lord, and keep his way, and he shall exalt thee to INHERIT THE LAND: when the wicked are cut off, thou shalt see it (Psa. 37:34).

The righteous *shall never be removed;* but the wicked *shall not inhabit* THE EARTH (Prov. 10:30).

For the promise, that he should be the HEIR OF THE WORLD, was not to Abraham, or to his seed, through the law, *but through the righteousness of faith* (Rom. 4:13).

By faith Abraham, when he was called to go out into A PLACE (the land of Canaan-Acts 7:4) *which he should afterwards receive for an inheritance,* obeyed (Heb. 11:8).

And they sung a new song, saying, Thou art worthy to take the book, and to open the seals thereof; for thou wast slain, and hast redeemed us to God by thy blood out of every kindred, and tongue, and people, and nation; and hast made us unto our God kings and priests: and we SHALL REIGN ON THE EARTH (Rev. 5:9).

And the kingdom, and dominion, and the greatness of the kingdom UNDER THE WHOLE HEAVEN *shall be given to the people of the saints* of the Most High, whose kingdom is an everlasting kingdom, and all dominions shall serve and obey him (Dan. 7:27).

XXVII. The Earth the destined Inheritance of the Righteousness—It follows that THE EARTH and not "heaven above the skies", is the inheritance of the saints, and the scene of God's work with the human race.

For thus saith the Lord that created the heavens; God himself that formed the earth and made it; *he hath established it, he created it not in vain,* HE FORMED IT TO BE INHABITED (Isa. 45:18).

The heavens, even the heavens, are the Lord's; but THE EARTH HE HATH GIVEN *to the children of men* (Psa. 115:16).

And NO MAN HATH ASCENDED UP TO HEAVEN (John 3:13).

Men and brethren, let me freely speak unto you of the patriach David, that *he is both dead and buried, and his sepulchre is with us unto this day* . . . For DAVID IS NOT ASCENDED INTO THE HEAVENS: but he saith himself, The Lord said unto my Lord, Sit thou on my right hand (Acts 2:29, 34).

Little children, yet a little while I am with you. Ye shall seek me; and as I said unto the Jews, *Whither I go* YE CANNOT COME; so now I say to you (John 13:33).

In my Father's House are many mansions: if it were not so I would have told you. I go to prepare a place for you. And if I go and prepare a place for you, *I will come again and receive you unto myself;* that where I am, there ye may be also (John 14:2-3).

XXVIII. HELL.—It follows also, of necessity, that the popular theory of hell and "eternal torments" is a fiction. The word "hell" occurs in the English Bible, but a comparison of the texts quoted below will show that its significance is totally different from that which ignorance and supersitition have come to

attach to it; that, in fact, it, almost without exception, means the grave.

O, that thou wouldst hide me in the *grave (sheol),* that thou wouldst keep me secret, until thy wrath be passed, that thou wouldst appoint me a set time, and remember me (Job 14:13).

And they shall not lie with the mighty that are fallen of the uncircumcised, which are *gone down to hell (sheol, grave),* WITH THEIR WEAPONS OF WAR: and *they have laid their swords under their heads,* but their iniquities shall be upon their bones, though they were the terror of the mighty in the land of the living (Ezek. 32:27, compare with Ezek. 31:14-17).

The wicked shall be turned into hell *(sheol, grave),* and all nations that forget God (Psa. 9:17).

Let the wicked be ashamed, and let them be silent in the grave *(sheol)* (Psa. 31:17).

For thou wilt not leave my soul in hell *(sheol, grave;* see Peter's application of this to the resurrection of Christ—Acts 2:27, 30-32); neither wilt thou suffer thine Holy One to see corruption (Psa. 16:10).

The sorrows of death compassed me, and the pains of hell *(sheol, grave)* got hold upon me: I found trouble and sorrow (Psa. 116:3).

Then Jonah prayed unto the Lord his God out of the fish's belly, and said, I cried by reason of my affliction unto the Lord, and he heard me; out of the belly of hell (margin, *the grave),* cried I, and thou heardest my voice (Jonha 2:1-3).

For great is thy mercy towards me: and thou has delivered my soul from the lowest hell [*sheol* (see margin) *grave*] (Psa. 86:13).

But those that seek my soul, to destroy it, shall go into the lower parts of the earth *(grave)* (Psa. 63:9).

And thou, Capernaum, which art exalted unto heaven, shall be brought down to hell *(hades, grave):* for if the mighty works which have been done in thee had been done in Sodom, it would have remained until this day (Matt. 11:23).

And I say also unto thee, that thou art Peter, and upon this rock I will build my church; and the gates of hell *(hades, grave)* shall not prevail against it (Matt. 16:18).

He (David) seeing this before, spake of the resurrection of Christ, that his soul was not left in hell *(hades, grave),* neither his flesh did see corruption (Acts 2:31).

I am he that liveth and was dead; and behold I am alive for evermore. Amen; and have the keys of hell *(hades, grave),* and of death (Rev. 1:18).

O death, where is thy sting? O grave *(hades),* where is thy victory? (1 Cor. 15:55; see Hosea 13:14).

And death and hell *(hades, grave)* delivered up the *dead* which were in them; and they were judged according to their works. And death and hell *(hades, grave)* were cast into the lake of fire (Rev. 20:13-14).

XXVIII. Gehenna—There is another class of texts in which the word "hell" occurs, which have to be differently understood from those quoted in the foregoing section: in this the original is *Gehenna.* A

A DECLARATION OF THE TRUTH REVEALED IN THE BIBLE, THE SUBLIME AND SIMPLE THEOLOGY OF THE PRIMITIVE CHRISTIANS (UNAMENDED CHRISTADELPHIANS) (continued)

reference to the passages and notes below will, however, show that they give as little countenance to the hell of popular theology as those in which the word "hell" simply means grave. They refer to a locality in the land of Israel, which was, in past times, the scene of judicial inflictions, and which is again to become so on a larger scale.

And if thy hand offend thee, cut it off; it is better for thee to enter into life maimed than having two hands to go into hell (*Gehenna, valley of Hinnom*), into the fire that never shall be quenched: where their worm dieth not, and the fire is not quenched (Mark 9:43).

And fear not them which kill the body but are not able to kill the soul (*psuche,* life), but rather fear him which is able to destroy both soul (*psuche,* life) and body in hell (*Gehenna*) (Matt. 10:28).

For it is the day of the Lord's vengeance, and the year of recompences for the controversy of Zion. And the streams thereof shall be turned into pitch, and the dust thereof into brimstone, and the land thereof shall become burning pitch. It shall not be quenched night nor day; the smoke thereof shall go up for ever; from generation to generation it shall lie waste; none *shall pass* through it for ever and ever (Isa. 34:8-10; see Jer. 7:17-20; 17:27; 2 Chron. 34:25).

Whose fan is in his hand, and he will thoroughly purge his floor, and gather his wheat into the garner:; but *he will burn up the chaff with unquenchable fire* (Matt. 3:12).

The sinners in Zion are afraid; fearfulness hath surprised the hypocrites. Who among us shall dwell with the devouring fire? Who among us shall dwell with everlasting burnings? (Isa. 33:14).

For our God is a consuming fire. (Heb. 12:29).

Behold the day cometh that shall *burn as an oven,* and all the proud, yea, and all that do wickedly shall be stubble, and the day that cometh shall *burn them up,* THAT IT SHALL LEAVE THEM NEITHER ROOT NOR BRANCH. But unto you that fear my name shall the sun of righteousness arise with healing in his wings. And ye shall go forth and grow up as calves of the stall, and *ye shall tread down the wicked,* FOR THEY SHALL BE ASHES UNDER THE SOLES OF YOUR FEET in the day that I shall do this, saith the Lord of Hosts (Mal. 4:1-3).

XXIX. The Destiny of the Wicked. If the hell of popular belief is a mere figment of the imagination it will be asked, What then is the destiny of the wicked according to the Scripture? The answer justified by the foregoing and subjoined testimonies is that they will be put out of existence by divine judgment, with attendant circumstances of shame and suffering.

But *the wicked shall perish,* and the enemies of the Lord shall be as the fat of lambs; they shall consume; INTO SMOKE SHALL THEY CONSUME AWAY (Psa. 37:20).

For the day of the Lord is near upon all the heathen. For as ye have drunk upon my holy mountain, so shall the heathen drink continually, yea, they shall drink, and they shall swallow down, and they shall be AS THOUGH THEY HAD NOT BEEN (Obad. 15-16).

For yet a little while, and the wicked *shall not be:* yea, thou shalt diligently consider his place, and *it shall not be* (Psa. 37:10).

Wait on the Lord, and keep his way, and he shall exalt thee to inherit the land: when the wicked are cut off, thou shalt see it. But *the transgressors shall be destroyed together:* the end of the wicked shall be cut off (Psa. 37:34, 38).

Who shall be punished with EVERLASTING DESTRUCTION from the presence of the Lord, and from the glory of His power, when he shall come to be glorified in his saints, and to be admired in all them that believe (2 Thess. 1:9-10).

The Lord preserveth all them that love him; but ALL THE WICKED WILL HE DESTROY (Psa. 145:20).

Let the sinners be CONSUMED OUT OF THE EARTH, and let the wicked be no more (Psa. 104:35).

For we are unto God a sweet savour of Christ, in them that are saved, and in them that perish; to the one we are the savour of DEATH UNTO DEATH; and to the other the savour of life unto life (2 Cor. 2:15-16).

Whoso despiseth the word SHALL BE DESTROYED: but he that feareth the commandment shall be rewarded (Prov. 13:13).

And these shall go away into *everlasting punishment:* but the righteous into life eternal (Matt. 25:46).

XXX. The irresponsible of Mankind—There is a class, forming by far the largest part of mankind, who have never heard the Gospel, and are in the darkness of complete barbarism. What is to be done with them? Popular theology says (sometimes), They will go to hell; and at other times, They will be admitted to heaven. The first assumption *outrages justice;* the second *violates every divine principle.* We submit, on the strength of the following passages, that they are exempted from responsibility, and will pass away in death, as though they had never existed. THEY WILL NEVER SEE THE LIGHT OF RESURRECTION.

O Lord, our God, other lords besides thee have had dominion over us . . . They are dead, *they shall not live:* they are deceased, THEY SHALL NOT RISE; therefore thou hast visited and DESTROYED them, *and made all their memory to perish* (Isa. 26:13-14).

In their heat I will make their feasts, and I will make them drunken, that they may rejoice, and *sleep a perpetual sleep, and not awake, saith the Lord* (Jer. 51:39).

The man that wandereth out *of the way of understanding* SHALL REMAIN IN THE CONGREGATION OF THE DEAD (Prov. 21:16; Jer. 51:57).

By one man *sin* entered into the world, and *death* by sin, and so *death passed* upon ALL MEN, for that all have sinned (Rom. 5:12).

That ye henceforth walk not as other Gentiles walk, having the *understanding darkened,* being ALIENATED FROM THE LIFE OF GOD *through the ignorance that is in them* because of the blindness of their heart (Eph. 4:17-18).

If our Gospel be hid, IT IS HID *to them that are lost* (2 Cor. 4:3).

Man that is in honour and UNDERSTANDETH NOT, *is like the beasts* THAT PERISH (Psa. 49:20).

There shall be a resurrection of the dead, both of the just and unjust (at Christ's coming) (Acts 24:15).

The Lord Jesus Christ, who shall judge the quick and the dead AT HIS APPEARING and *his kingdom* (2 Tim. 4:1).

For we must *all appear before the judgment seat of Christ,* that every one may receive the things done in his body according to that he hath done, whether it be good or bad (2 Cor. 5:10).

We shall all *stand before the judgment seat* of Christ . . .
So then every one of US SHALL GIVE *account of himself* to God (Rom. 14:10-12).

XXXI. The Judgment-Seat of Christ—That at the return of Jesus Christ from heaven, to establish his kingdom on earth, he will, first of all, summon before him for judgment the whole of those who are responsible to his judgment. Those that are dead he will cause to come forth from the dust, and assemble them with the living to his presence. Faithful and unfaithful will be mustered together before his judgment-seat, for the purpose of having it declared, after account rendered, who is worthy of being *invested with immortality* and promoted to the kingdom, and who is deserving of rejection, and *re-consignment to corruption after punishment.* (This precludes the idea created by a superficial reading of the apostolic testimony, that there are no judgments for the saints, and that the resurrection at the coming of Christ will be confined to the accepted, who according to this theory, awake to instantaneous incorruption and immortality).

Every idle word that men shall speak, they SHALL GIVE ACCOUNT thereof in the day of judgment. For by thy words thou shalt be justified, and by thy words thou shalt be condemned (Matt. 12:36-37).

All that are in the graves shall hear his voice, and *shall come forth:* they that have done good unto the resurrection of (*to receive*) life, and they that have done evil unto the resurrection of (*to receive*) damnation (John 5:28-29).

For he that soweth to his flesh shall of the flesh REAP (after judgment) *corruption,* but he that soweth to the Spirit shall of the Spirit REAP (after judgment) life *everlasting* (Gal. 6:8).

Little children, abide in him; that when he shall appear, we may have confidence, and *not be ashamed* before him AT HIS COMING (1 John 2:28).

If that evil servant shall say in his heart, My lord delayeth his coming . . . the lord of that servant SHALL COME in a day when he looketh not for him . . . and shall cut him asunder (Matt. 24:48-51). Of him also shall the Son of Man be ashamed WHEN HE COMETH in the glory of his Father with the holy angels (Mark 8:38).

For the Son of Man *shall come* in the glory of his Father, with his angels, and THEN he shall reward EVERY (good and evil servants) man according to his works (Matt. 16:27).

He shall set the sheep on his right hand, but the goats on the left. Then shall the king say unto them on his right hand, Come ye blessed my Father inherit the kingdom prepared for you from the foundation of the world . . .
Then shall he say also unto them on the left hand, Depart from me, ye cursed, into everlasting (aionian) fire . . .
And these shall go away into everlasting punishment, but the righteous into (shall have) life eternal (Matt. 25:31-46; Dan 12:2).

And it came to pass that when HE was returned, having received THE KINGDOM then he commanded these servants to be called to him, to whom he had given the money, that *he might know how much every man had gained* by trading (Luke 19:15).

There shall be weeping and gnashing of teeth, when ye shall see Abraham, Isaac, and Jacob, and all the prophets in the kingdom of God, and you yourselves *thrust out* (Luke 13:25-30).

It is appointed unto men once to die, but after this (that is, when the deathstate ends in resurrection) the judgment (Heb. 9:27; Rev. 22:11-12). Who SHALL *give account* to him that is ready to judge both the quick and the dead (1 Pet. 4:5; 1:17; 1 Cor. 3:13; Rev. 11:18; John 12:48).

Therefore, judge nothing before the time, *until the Lord come,* who will both bring to light the hidden things of darkness, and will make manifest the counsels of the hearts (1 Cor. 4:5).

XXXII. BAPTISM is an act of obedience required of all who believe the Gospel. It is a bodily immersion in, and not a face-sprinkling or headpouring with water. Its administration to infants, in any form, is unauthorized and useless: it is only enjoined on those who have intelligence enough to believe the glad tidings of the kingdom of God and the things concerning the name of Jesus Christ. To such it is the means of that present union with Christ which is preparatory to perfect assimilation at the resurrection. It is, therefore, necessary to salvation.

Go ye into all the world and preach the gospel to every creature. He that believeth and is baptized shall be saved: but he that believeth not shall be damned (Mark 16:15-16).

Jesus answered, Verily, verily, I say unto you, Except a man be *born of water* and of the Spirit, he cannot enter into the kingdom of God (John 3:5).

Then Peter said unto them, Repent and *be baptized* every one of you, in the name of Jesus Christ . . . Then they that gladly receive his word *were baptized* (Acts 2:38-41).

And when they (the people of Samaria believed Philip preaching the things concerning the kingdom of God and the name of Jesus Christ, *they were baptized,* both MEN AND WOMEN (Acts 8:12).

And he commanded the chariot to stand still; and they
went down *into the water,* both Philip and the eunuch: and
HE BAPTIZED HIM (Acts 8:38).

Paul (after his conversion) arose and WAS BAPTIZED
(Acts 9:18).

Lydia was BAPTIZED, and her household (Acts 16:15).

The keeper of the prison (at Philippi) . . . *was BAP-
TIZED, he and all his straightway . . . believing in God
with all his house* (Acts 16:27, 33, 34).

When they (twelve men at Ephesus) *heard this,* they were
baptized in the name of the Lord Jesus (Acts 19:5).

The like figure whereunto even BAPTISM DOTH ALSO
NOW SAVE us (not the putting away of the filth of the
flesh, but the answer of a good conscience toward God) by
the resurrection of Jesus Christ (1 Pet. 3:21).

Know ye not that so many of us as were baptized into
Jesus Christ were BAPTIZED INTO HIS DEATH?
Therefore, WE ARE BURIED WITH HIM BY BAP-
TISM into death: that like as Christ was raised up from
the dead by the glory of the Father even so we also should
walk in newness of life. For if we have been planted
together in the likenss of his death, we shall be also in the
likeness of his resurrection (Rom. 6:3-5).

For as many of you as have been BAPTIZED INTO
Christ have put on Christ . . . and if ye be Christ's then
are ye Abrahams's seed, and heirs according to the
promise (Gal. 3:27-29).

XXXIII. How can so many be wrong? It is usual to rely
on numbers in deciding questions of religious belief.
This disposition takes the form of the question: "Can
so many hundreds of thousands of people, including
thousands of clergymen and ministers, be in the
wrong?" As a general answer to this, attention is
invited to the following testimonies, which declare
the fewness of those who receive the truth.

Enter ye in at the strait gate; for wide is the gate and broad
is the way that leadeth to destruction, and *many there be
that go in thereat* (Matt. 7:13).

Strait is the gate and narrow is the way which leadeth unto
life, and FEW THERE BE THAT FIND IT (Matt. 7:14).

Many are called, but FEW ARE CHOSEN (Matt. 22:14).

Hearken, my beloved brethren, Hath not God chosen *the
poor of this world, rich in faith,* and heirs of the kingdom
which he hath promised to them that love him? (Jas. 2:5).

For ye see your calling, brethren, how that *not many wise
men after the flesh,* not many mighty, nor many noble, are
called (1 Cor. 1:26-27).

For the WISDOM OF THIS WORLD is foolishness with
God (1 Cor. 3:19).

God hath chosen *the foolish things* of the world to
confound the wise; and God hath chosen *the weak things*
of the world to confound the things which are mighty; and
base things of the world, and *things which are despised,* hath

God chosen, yea, and things which are not, to bring to
nought things that are (1 Cor. 1:27-28).

I pray for them: *I pray not for the world,* but FOR THEM
WHICH THOU HAST GIVEN ME; for they are thine.
Neither pray I for these alone, but for them also which
shall believe on me through their word (John 17:9, 20).

As concerning THIS SECT, we know that *everywhere it is
spoken against* (Acts 28:22).

Blessed are ye when men shall hate you, and when they
shall separate you from their company, and shall reproach
you, and cast out your name as evil, for the Son of Man's
sake (Luke 6:22).

If *ye be reproached for the name of Christ* happy are
ye; . . . Yet, if any man suffer as a Christian, let him not
be ashamed (1 Pet. 4:14-16).

I have given them thy word, and the world hath hated
them because they are not of the world, as I am not of the
world (John 17:14).

XXXIV. Popular Error and Divine Truth in Contrast—
The true test to apply in the determination of
religious truth is the one given by Isaiah (8:20): "TO
THE LAW AND TO THE TESTIMONY; if they
speak not according to this word, *it is because there is*
NO LIGHT *in them."* This principle is extensively
applied in the classification of Scripture testimony
contained in this pamphlet as a whole. To bring the
matter to a focus, the following tabularized contrast
of popular tradition with the word of God is here
presented:

POPULAR TRADI- TION	THE WORD OF GOD
"I can imagine that when a man dies *suddenly,* one of the first emotions he experiences in the next world will be surprise . . . He looks about him, 'Oh, that glory, how resplendent yon throne!' He listens to harps of glory, and he can scarce believe it is true. I, the chief of sinners, and yet *in heaven;* and then, when he is conscious that he is *really in heaven,* 'Oh! what everlasting joy'." *C. H. Spurgeon,* Sermon No. 349, p. 311.	And *no man hath ascended up to heaven* (John 3:13). For David *is not ascended* into the heavens (Acts 2:34). As for me, I will behold thy face in righteousness: I shall be satisfied, *when I awake, with thy likeness (Psa. 17:15).*
"I'll praise my Maker with my breath, And when my voice *is fast in death,* Praise shall my nobler powers employ." *Dr. Watts*	For the living know that they shall die: but the dead *know not anything,* neither have they any more a reward; for the memory of them is forgotten. Also their love and their hatred, and their envy, *is now perished;* neither have they any more a portion for

ever in anything that is done under the sun (Eccl. 9:5-6).

His breath goeth forth, he returneth to his earth, *in that very day* HIS THOUGHTS PERISH (Psa. 146:4).

The *dead praise not* the Lord, neither any that go down into silence (Psa. 115:17).

For *in death there* is no remembrance of thee: *in the grave,* who shall give thee thanks? (Psa. 6:5).

"The souls of believers a death do *immediately* pass into glory." *Meth. and Presby. Cathechism.*

God will redeem my soul *from the power of* THE GRAVE (Psa. 49:15).

And this is the Father's will which hath sent me, that of all which he hath given me I should lose nothing , but should *raise it up* again at THE LAST DAY (John 6:39; 11:24; I Thess. 4:13-16).

"With Thee we'll *reign,*
With Thee we'll rise,
And kingdoms gain,
Beyond the skies."

But go thou (Daniel) thy way till the end be, for *thou shalt rest,* and stand in thy lot *at the end of the days* (Dan. 12:13; Job 19:25).

"Beyond the bounds of
  time and space,
The saints' secure abode."
Dr. Watts

Blessed are the meek, for they shall inherit the earth (Matt. 5:5).

Thou hast made us unto our God kings and priests, and we shall *reign on the earth* (Rev. 5:10).

"A never dying soul to
  save,
And fit it for the sky."
Chas. Wesley

And the kingdom and dominion and the greatness of the kingdom UNDER THE WHOLE HEAVEN shall be given to the people of the saints of the Most High (Dan. 7:27).

"Up to the courts here
  angels dwell
It *mounts* triumphant
  there;

The soul that sinneth, it shall die (Ezek. 18:4, 20).

He casteth the wicked

Or devils plunge it *down to hell,*
In infinite despair."
Dr. Watts

"When the poor soul shall find itself in the hands of angry fiends, it shall seem in that first moment as though it had been athirst for a thousand years. What will be his surprise. 'And am I,' he will say, 'really here? I was in the streets of *London* but *a moment ago;* I was singing a song but an *instant ago;* and here am I *in hell.' "—Chas. H. Spurgeon,* Sermon No. 369, p. 312.

down to the ground (Psa. 147:6).

The wicked is *reserved to the day of* destruction; they shall be *brought forth* to the *day of wrath* (Job. 21:30).

As smoke is driven away, so drive them away; as wax melteth before the fire, so let the *wicked perish* AT THE PRESENCE OF GOD (Psa. 68:2). But the wicked *shall perish,* and the enemies of the Lord shall be as the *fat of lambs;* they shall consume; *into smoke they shall consume away* (Psa. 37:20).

IN VAIN DO THEY WORSHIP ME, TEACHING FOR DOCTRINES THE COMMANDMENTS OF MEN (Matt. 15:9).

IF ANY MAN SPEAK, LET HIM SPEAK AS THE ORACLES OF GOD (1. Pet. 4:11).

XXXV. Departure from the truth foretold—The thoughtful mind, on which the testimony cited in the foregoing thirty-four sections may have made an impression, will enquire, How comes the religious world, with the Bible circulated so freely, and honored so universally, to be so much astray? Without attempting in this limited work to indicate the process by which the result has been arrived at, we call attention to the fact apparent on the face of the subjoined Scriptural quotations, that the truth of apostolic prophecy requires that *the world at the present time should be in a state of complete and universal apostasy.*

There shall come in the last days scoffers, walking after their own lust, and saying, WHERE IS THE PROMISE OF HIS COMING? For since the fathers fell asleep, all things continue as they were from the beginning of the creation (2 Pet. 3:3-4).

A DECLARATION OF THE TRUTH REVEALED IN THE BIBLE, THE SUBLIME AND SIMPLE THEOLOGY OF THE PRIMITIVE CHRISTIANS (UNAMENDED CHRISTADELPHIANS) (continued)

The time will come when *they will not endure sound doctrine;* but after their own lusts shall they HEAP TO THEMSELVES TEACHERS, having itching ears. And *they shall turn away their ears* FROM THE TRUTH, AND SHALL BE TURNED UNTO FABLES (2 Tim. 4:3-4).

When the Son of Man cometh, shall he find faith on the earth? (Luke 18:8).

Now the Spirit speaketh expressly that in the *latter days some shall depart from the faith (tes pistios),* giving heed to seducing spirits and doctrines of devils; speaking lies in hypocrisy; having their conscience seared with a hot iron; FORBIDDEN TO MARRY, and commanding to abstain from meats, which God hath created to be received with thanksgiving of them which BELIEVE and KNOW THE TRUTH (1 Tim. 4:1-3).

For I know this, that after my departing, shall grievous wolves enter in among you, not sparing the flock. Also of your own selves shall men arise, *speaking perverse things,* to draw away disciples after them (Acts 20:29-30).

And for this cause God shall send them *strong delusions,* that they should believe A LIE (2 Thess. 2:11).

For the mystery of iniquity *doth already work* (in Paul's day); only he who now letteth (that is, hindereth), will let (or hinder), until he *(paganism)* be taken out of the way. And then shall that wicked *(the Papacy)* be revealed, whom the Lord shall consume with the spirit of his mouth, and shall destroy with the brightness of His coming (2 Thess. 2:7-8).

And upon her forehead (the forehead of the woman representing Papal Rome—see Rev. 17:18) was a name written, Mystery, Babylon the Great *(Papacy),* The Mother of Harlots *(that is, of State Religions),* and Abominations *(the innumerable sects) of the Earth* (Rev. 17:5).

For behold, the darkness shall cover the earth, and gross darkness the people (Isa. 60:2).

As the days of Noah were, so also shall the coming of the Son of Man be. For as in the days that were before the flood they were eating and drinking, marrying, and giving in marriage, until the day Noah entered into the ark, and knew not until the flood came and took them all away; so shall also the coming of the Son of Man be (Matt. 24:37-39).

XXXVI. Coming Deliverance—It is a common belief that the world's deliverance from the state of things portrayed in the foregoing testimonies is to be effected by the preaching of the gospel. The erroneousness of this view will be apparent from the following testimonies, which teach that it is to result from divine intervention:

Gentiles shall come UNTO THEE from the ends of the earth, and shall say, Surely *our fathers have inherited* lies, vanity and things wherein there is no profit. Therefore, behold, I will *this once* cause them to know, I will cause

them to know mine hand and my might; and they shall know that my name is the Lord (Jer. 16:19-21).

For *when thy judgments are in the earth* THE INHABITANTS OF THE WORLD SHALL LEARN RIGHTOUSNESS (Isa. 26:9).

And in this mountain shall the Lord of Hosts make unto all people a feast of fat things . . . And he will destroy in this mountain the face of the covering cast over all people, and the veil that is spread over all nations (Isa. 25:6-7).

Thus saith the Lord of Hosts: In those days it shall come to pass that ten men shall take hold out of *all languages of the nations,* even shall take hold of the skirt of him that is a Jew, saying, We will go with you: for we have heard that God is with you. Yea, many people and strong nations *shall come to seek* the Lord of Hosts in Jerusalem, and to pray before the Lord (Zech 8:23, 22; Mic. 5:2; Isa. 2:3).

And it shall come to pass, that *every one that is left of all the nations* which came against Jerusalem shall even go up from year to year to worship the King, the Lord of Hosts, and to keep the feast of tabernacles (Zech. 14:16).

For the earth *shall be filled* with the knowledge of the glory of the Lord, as the waters cover the sea (Hab. 2:14).

In conclusion, the time is near for the occurrence of the great events outlined in the Scriptures of Truth, and set forth in this pamphlet. The reader is referred to works advertised herewith, for the evidence that *we are now nearing the time of the advent.* May the reader be induced to accept THE TRUTH herein defined, and be found worthy of the inheritance then to be manifested.

AMEN.

"PROVE ALL THINGS: HOLD FAST THAT WHICH IS GOOD" (1. Thess. 5:21).

Notes: *Unamended Christadelphians follow Christadelphian belief on most points. They do not, however, accept the perspective on resurrectional responsibility. They teach instead that all humans will be resurrected to be judged by Christ at the end of time. See items 29-31 of the declaration. This statement is circulated in North America by the Brethren of Messiah, an Unamended organization in Canada.*

*   *   *

DOCTRINES CHRISTADELPHIANS BELIEVE AND TEACH (UNAMENDED CHRISTADELPHIANS)

That the Bible is the only source now extant of Knowledge concerning God and His purposes, and it was given wholly by the unerring inspiration of God in the writers, and that such errors as have since crept in are due to transcription or translation.

That there is but ONE God, the Father, dwelling in heaven, who, out of His own underived energy created heaven and earth, and all that in them is.

That Jesus Christ is the Son of God (not "God the Son", a phrase not found in Scriptures), begotten of the Virgin Mary by the power of the Holy Spirit.

That God is omnipresent by means of His spirit flowing out from His personal presence. This spirit power is universal in upholding all things in the natural world. For the performance of work that is supernatural and sacred the same spirit by special concentration of the Divine Will becomes Holy Spirit for the holy or sacred work determined to be done.

That man is mortal; a creature of the dust. Immortality is not a present possession, but will be bestowed upon the worthy at the resurrection.

That man in death is unconscious, and depends upon a resurrection for a future life.

That death came into the world through the disobedience of one man. "Wherefore, as by one man sin entered into the world, and death by sin; and so death passed upon all men, in whom all have sinned." (Rom. 5-12).

That as death came into the world through sin, it can only be abolished through the righteousness of One who was raised up of the condemned race of Adam, in the line of Abraham and David, who though wearing the condemned nature was to obtain a title to resurrection by perfect obedience, and by dying abrogate the law of condemnation for HIMSELF, and all who should believe and obey Him.

That at the appearing of Christ prior to the establishment of the Kingdom, the responsible (faithful and unfaithful), dead and living of both classes, will be summoned before His judgment seat "to be judged according to their works"; "and receive in body according to what they have done, whether it be good or bad."

That the gospel concerns the "Kingdom of God" (for the establishment of which Christ taught his disciples to pray, and of which the prophet Daniel says, "the God of Heaven shall set up"), and the "Things Concerning the Name of Jesus Christ," a knowledge and adherence to which are necessary for salvation.

That the kingdom when established will be the kingdom of Israel restored, in the territory it formerly occupied, viz., the land bequeathed to Abraham and his seed (the Christ), by covenant.

That baptism into the name of the Lord Jesus Christ, after knowledge of God's plan, and a faithful walk therein, is essential to salvation.

Notes: *This statement is a much briefer form of the essentials of the belief of Unamended Christadelphians. It is published periodically in* The Christadelphian Advocate, *a leading Unamended journal published in Richmond, Virginia.*

Chapter 4

Independent Fundamentalist Family

Fundamentalism/Evangelicalism

STATEMENT OF FAITH (NATIONAL ASSOCIATION OF EVANGELICALS)

1. We believe the Bible to be the inspired, the only infallible, authoritative Word of God.

2. We believe that there is one God, eternally existent in three persons: Father, Son and Holy Spirit.

3. We believe in the deity of our Lord Jesus Christ, in His virgin birth, in His sinless life, in His miracles, in His vicarious and atoning death through his shed blood, in His bodily resurrection, in His ascension to glory.

4. We believe that for the salvation of lost and sinful man, regeneration by the Holy Spirit is absolutely essential.

5. We believe in the present ministry of the Holy Spirit by whose indwelling the Christian is enabled to live a godly life.

6. We believe in the resurrection of both the saved and the lost; they that are saved unto the resurrection of life and they that are lost unto the resurrection of damnation.

7. We believe in the spiritual unity of believers in our Lord Jesus Christ.

Notes: *Growing out of Plymouth Brethren perspectives, Fundamentalism has adopted as its focus the authority of scripture and the dispensational approach to its interpretation. That dispensation is highlighted by a particular view of eschatology termed "premillennialism." According to premillennialists, Jesus' second coming is imminent and will be followed by the millennium, a thousand years of peace on earth under Christ's personal reign. This will be followed by the final judgment of humankind. The millennium is mentioned prominently in the Book of Revelation, the last book of the Bible.*

Premillennialism is contrasted with other popular eschatologies. According to amillennialism, there will be no millennium. Postmillennialism teaches that the human race will grow into the millennium, and Christ will return only after such a period. Both amillennialism and postmillennialism tend to place less emphasis upon eschatology in their overall presentation of the Christian faith.

During the twentieth century, fundamentalists have spent much of their time defining the nature of scriptural authority. A major difference has centered around two technical terms, "inerrancy" and "infallibility." All fundamentalists affirm the infallibility of scripture (i.e., the Bible is sufficient, complete and trustworthy in matters of humanity's relationship to God). The Bible contains all that God intended to communicate to his human children. The affirmation of the Bible as the Word of God is usually equated with an affirmation of infallibility.

Inerrancy, on the other hand, deals with Biblical statements concerning scientific, historical, poetic, or prophetic matters. To believe in inerrancy is to affirm the Bible is without error on such matters, even in the face of scientific evidence or historical data to the contrary. Statements of faith from fundamentalist churches will often affirm both infallibility and inerrancy. The absence of such statements may merely indicate that the statements predate the development of the terminology and no effort has been made to update them, or may indicate a willingness to tolerate a range of opinion on the subject, especially of inerrancy. Those who believe in inerrancy are generally considered fundamentalists, and those who do not (or tolerate those who do not) are considered conservative evangelicals. The National Association of Evangelicals is the most prominent of several conservative evangelical ecumenical organizations.

Fundamentalists are also concerned with the nature of the Bible's inspiration. They commonly affirm plenary (or verbal) inspiration; that is, the very words, not just thoughts and concepts, were inspired and hence bear the authority of God's revelation. In this regard, fundamentalists have taken into account the problems of textual scholarship. Only the original manuscripts of the Biblical books are held to be ultimately infallible and inerrant. However, none of these original manuscripts are known to be in existence today. The earliest manuscripts available are much later copies of the originals. It is the fundamentalists' belief that these later copies have faithfully retained all matters of importance.

STATEMENT OF FAITH (NATIONAL ASSOCIATION OF EVANGELICALS) (continued)

Quite apart from its statements on scripture, Fundamentalism manifests a continuation of the Reformed theological tradition in the constant affirmation of the total depravity of man and the eternal security of the believer. Because of these affirmations, many from a Methodist tradition (including Holiness and Pentecostal churches), while affirming the infallibility, inerrancy, and/or plenary inspiration of the Bible, have refused to be identified with the fundamentalist movement as a whole and will not attend fundamentalist conferences.

Statements issued by fundamentalist bodies are generally quite brief. Inheriting the Plymouth Brethren reluctance to write "creeds," the fundamentalists have done so only to refute "modernist" theologies, which they believe deny essentials (fundamentals) of the faith. Thus their statements will, on occasion, deal only with crucial matters considered to be under attack.

*　　*　　*

DOCTRINAL STATEMENT (AMERICAN COUNCIL OF CHRISTIAN CHURCHES)

Among other equally biblical truths, we believe and maintain the following:

a. The plenary divine inspiration of the Scriptures in the original languages, their consequent inerrancy and infallibility, and, as the Word of God, the supreme and final authority in faith and life;

b. The Triune God: Father, Son, and Holy Spirit;

c. The essential, absolute, eternal deity, and the real and proper, but sinless, humanity of our Lord Jesus Christ;

d. His birth of the Virgin Mary;

e. His substitutionary, expiatory death, in that He gave His life "a ransom for many";

f. His resurrection from among the dead in the same body in which He was crucified, and the second coming of this same Jesus in power and great glory;

g. The total depravity of man through the fall;

h. Salvation, the effect of regeneration by the Spirit and the Word, not by works but by grace through faith;

i. The everlasting bliss of the saved, and the everlasting suffering of the lost;

j. The real spiritual unity in Christ of all redeemed by His precious blood;

k. The necessity of maintaining, according to the Word of God, the purity of the Church in doctrine and life.

Notes: *Conservative even by Fundamentalist standards, the American Council of Christian Churches affirms plenary inspiration, infallibility, and inerrancy.*

THE CONFERENCE TESTIMONY (PROPHETIC BIBLE CONFERENCE OF 1914)

The brethren gathered for the International Conference on the Prophetic Scriptures heartily endorse the declarations made by the previous prophetic conferences; but also feel it their solemn duty, in view of existing conditions in the professing church, to restate and reaffirm their unswerving belief in the following fundamental truths of our holy faith:

1. We believe that the Bible is the Word and Revelation of God and therefore our only authority.

2. We believe in the Deity of our Lord Jesus Christ, that He is very God by whom and for whom "all things were created."

3. We believe in His virgin birth, that He was conceived by the Holy Spirit and is therefore God manifested in the flesh.

4. We believe in salvation by divine sacrifice, that the Son of God gave "His life a ransom for many" and bore "our sins in His own body on the tree."

5. We believe in His physical resurrection from the dead and in His bodily presence at the right hand of God as our Priest and Advocate.

6. We believe in the universality and heinousness of sin, and in salvation by Grace, "not of works lest any man should boast"; that Sonship with God is attained only by regeneration through the Holy Spirit and faith in Jesus Christ.

7. We believe in the Personality and Deity of the Holy Spirit, who came down upon earth on the day of Pentecost to indwell believers and to be the administrator in the church of the Lord Jesus Christ; Who is also here to "reprove the world of sin, and of righteousness, and of judgment."

8. We believe in the great commission which our Lord has given to His church to evangelize the world, and that this evangelization is the great mission of the church.

9. We believe in the second, visible and imminent coming of our Lord and Saviour Jesus Christ to establish His world-wide Kingdom on the earth.

10. We believe in a Heaven of eternal bliss for the righteous and in the conscious and eternal punishment of the wicked.

Furthermore, we exhort the people of God in all denominations to stand by these great truths, so much rejected in our days, and to contend earnestly for the faith which our God has, in His Holy Word, delivered unto the saints.

Notes: *Fundamentalist forces were rallied through a series of conferences held in the late nineteenth and early twentieth centuries which focused upon biblical and prophetic themes. Many of these conferences passed statements [see George W. Dollar's A History of Fundamentalism in America (Greenville, SC: Bob Jones University Press, 1973), pp. 27-66, for some sample texts]. The statement reproduced here follows the trend of previous statements, but was distinguished in 1915 by its insertion in the catalog of*

Moody Biblical Institute at the direction of the trustees. A more formal statement was adopted by Moody in 1928.

* * *

DOCTRINAL STATEMENT [DALLAS (TEXAS) THEOLOGICAL SEMINARY]

Article I. THE SCRIPTURES

We believe that "all Scripture is given by inspiration of God," by which we understand the whole Bible is inspired in the sense that holy men of God "were moved by the Holy spirit" to write the very words of Scripture. We believe that this divine inspiration extends equally and fully to all parts of the writings—historical, poetical, doctrinal, and prophetical—as appeared in the original manuscripts. We believe that the whole Bible in the originals is therefore without error. We believe that all the Scriptures center about the Lord Jesus Christ in His person and work in His first and second coming, and hence that no portion, even of the Old Testament, is properly read, or understood until it leads to Him. We also believe that all the Scriptures were designed for our practical instruction. (Mark 12: 26, 36; 13:11; Luke 24:27, 44; John 5:39; Acts 1:16; 17:2-3; 18:28; 26:22-23; 28:23; Rom. 15:4; 1 Cor. 2:13; 10:11; 2 Tim. 3:16; 2 Peter 1:21.)

Article II. THE GODHEAD

We believe that the Godhead eternally exists in three persons—the Father, the Son, and the Holy Spirit—and that these three are one God having precisely the same nature, attributes, and perfections, and worthy of precisely the same homage, confidence, and obedience. (Matt. 28:18-19; Mark 12:29; John 1:14; Acts 5:3-4; 2 Cor. 13:14; Heb. 1:1-3; Rev. 1:4-6.)

Article III. ANGELS, FALLEN AND UNFALLEN

We believe that God created an innumerable company of sinless, spiritual beings, known as angels; that one, "Lucifer, son of the morning"—the highest in rank—sinned through pride, thereby becoming Satan; that a great company of the angels followed him in his moral fall, some of whom became demons and are active as his agents and associates in the prosecution of his unholy purposes, while others who fell are "reserved in everlasting chains under darkness unto the judgment of the great day." (Isa. 14:12-17; Ezek. 28:11-19; 1 Tim. 3:6; 2 Peter 2:4; Jude 1:6.)

We believe that Satan is the originator of sin, and that, under the permission of God, he, through subtlety, led our first parents into transgression, thereby accomplishing their moral fall and subjecting them and their posterity to his own power; that he is the enemy of God and the people of God, opposing and exalting himself above all that is called god or that is worshiped; and that he who in the beginning said, "I will be like the most High," in his warfare appears as an angel of light, even counterfeiting the works of God by fostering religious movements and systems of doctrine, which systems in every case are characterized by a denial of the efficacy of the blood of Christ and of salvation by grace alone. (Gen. 3:1-19; Rom. 5:12-14; 2 Cor. 4:3-4; 11:13-15; Eph. 6:10-12; 2 Thess. 2:4; 1 Tim. 4:1-3.)

We believe that Satan was judged at the cross though not then executed, and that he, a usurper, now rules as the "god of this world;" that, at the second coming of Christ, Satan will be bound and cast into the abyss for a thousand years, and after the thousand years he will be loosed for a little season and then "cast into the lake of fire and brimstone," where he "shall be tormented day and night for ever and ever." (Col. 2:15; Rev. 20:1-3, 10.)

We believe that a great company of angels kept their holy estate and are before the throne of God, from whence they are sent forth as ministering spirits to minister for them who shall be heirs of salvation. (Luke 15:10; Eph. 1:21; Heb. 1:14; Rev. 7:12.)

We believe that man was made lower than the angels; and that, in His incarnation, Christ took for a little time this lower place that he might lift the believer to His own sphere above the angels. (Heb. 2:6-10.)

Article IV. MAN CREATED AND FALLEN

We believe that man was originally created in the image and after the likeness of God, and that he fell through sin, and, as a consequence of his sin, lost his spiritual life, becoming dead in trespasses and sins, and that he became subject to the power of the devil. We also believe that this spiritual death, or total depravity of human nature, has been transmitted to the entire human race of man, the Man Christ Jesus alone being excepted; and hence that every child of Adam is born into the world with a nature which not only possesses no spark of divine life, but is essentially and unchangeably bad apart from divine grace. (Gen. 1:26; 2:17; 6:5; Ps. 14:1-3; 51:5; Jer. 17:9; John 3:6; 5:40; 6:53; Rom. 3:10-19; 8:6-7; Eph. 2:1-3; 1 Tim. 5:6; 1 John 3:8.)

Article V. THE DISPENSATIONS

We believe that the dispensations are stewardships by which God administers His purpose on the earth through man under varying responsibilities. We believe that the changes in the dispensational dealings of God with man depend on changed conditions or situations in which man is successively found with relation to God, and that these changes are the result of the failures of man and the judgments of God. We believe that different administrative responsibilities of this character are manifest in the biblical record, that they span the entire history of mankind, and that each ends in the failure of man under the respective test and in an ensuing judgment from God. We believe that three of these dispensations or rules of life are the subject of the Mosaic Law, the present dispensation of grace, and the future dispensation of the millennial kingdom. We believe that these are distinct and are not to be intermingled or confused, as they are chronologically successive.

We believe that the dispensations are not ways of salvation nor different methods of administering the so-called Covenant of Grace. They are not in themselves dependent on covenant relationships but are ways of life and responsibility to God which test the submission of man to His revealed will during a particular time. We believe, that, if man does trust in his own efforts to gain the favor of God or salvation under any dispensational test, because of inherent sin his failure to satisfy fully the just requirements of God is inevitable and his condemnation sure.

We believe that according to the "eternal purpose" of God (Eph. 3:11) salvation in the divine reckoning is always "by grace, through faith," and rests upon the basis of the shed blood of Christ. We believe that God has always been gracious, regardless of the ruling dispensation, but that man has not at all times been under an administration or stewardship of grace as is true in the present dispensation. (1 Cor. 9:17; Eph. 3:2; 3:9, A.S.V.; Col. 1:25; 1 Tim. 1:4, A.S.V.)

We believe that it has always been true that "without faith it is impossible to please" God (Heb. 11:6), and that the principle of faith was prevalent in the lives of all the Old Testament saints. However, we believe that it was historically impossible that they should have had as the conscious object of their faith the incarnate, crucified Son, the Lamb of God (John 1:29), and that it is evident that they did not comprehend as we do that the sacrifices depicted the person and work of Christ. We believe also that they did not understand the redemptive significance of the prophecies or types concerning the sufferings of Christ (1 Peter 1:10-12): therefore, we believe that their faith toward God was manifested in other ways as is shown by the long record in Hebrews 11:1-40. We believe further that their faith thus manifested was counted unto them for righteousness (cf. Rom. 4:3 with Gen. 15:6; Rom. 4:5-8; Heb. 11:7).

Article VI. THE FIRST ADVENT

We believe that, as provided and proposed by God and as preannounced in the prophecies of the Scriptures, the eternal Son of God came into this world that He might manifest God to men, fulfill prophecy, and become the Redeemer of a lost world. To this end He was born of the virgin, and received a human body and a sinless human nature. (Luke 1:30-35; John 1:18; 3:16; Heb. 4:15.)

We believe that, on the human side, He became and remained a perfect man, but sinless throughout His life; yet He retained His absolute deity, being at the same time very God and very man, and that His earth-life sometimes functioned within the sphere of that which was human and sometimes within the sphere of that which was divine. (Luke 2:40; John 1:1-2; Phil. 2:5-8.)

We believe that, in fulfillment of prophecy He came first to Israel as her Messiah-King, and that, being rejected of that nation, He, according to the eternal counsels of God, gave His life as a ransom for all. (John 1:11; Acts 2:22-24; 1 Tim. 2:6.)

We believe that, in infinite love for the lost, He voluntarily accepted His Father's will and became the divinely provided sacrificial Lamb and took away the sin of the world; bearing the holy judgments against sin which the righteousness of God must impose. His death was, therefore, substitutionary in the most absolute sense—the just for the unjust—and by His death He became the Savior of the lost. (John 1:29; Rom. 3:25-26; 2 Cor. 5:14; Heb. 10:5-14; 1 Peter 3:18.)

We believe that, according to the Scriptures, He arose from the dead in the same body, though glorified, in which He had lived and died, and that His resurrection body is the pattern of that body which ultimately will be given to all believers. (John 20:20; Phil. 3:20.)

We believe that, on departing from the earth, He was accepted of His Father and that His acceptance is a final assurance to us that His redeeming work was perfectly accomplished. (Heb. 1:3.)

We believe that He became Head over all things to the church which is His body, and in this ministry He ceases not to intercede and advocate for the saved. (Eph. 1:22-23; Heb. 7:25; 1 John 2:1.)

Article VII. SALVATION ONLY THROUGH CHRIST

We believe that, owing to universal death through sin, no one can enter the kingdom of God unless born again; and that no degree of reformation however great, no attainments in morality however high, no culture however attractive, no baptism or other ordinance however administered, can help the sinner to take even one step toward heaven: but a new nature imparted from above, a new life implanted by the Holy Spirit through the Word, is absolutely essential to salvation, and only those thus saved are sons of God. We believe, also, that our redemption has been accomplished solely by the blood of our Lord Jesus Christ, who was made to be sin and was made a curse for us, dying in our room and stead; and that no repentance, no feeling, no faith, no good resolutions, no sincere efforts, no submission to the rules and regulations of any church, nor all the churches that have existed since the days of the Apostles can add in the very least degree to the value of the blood, or to the merit of the finished work wrought for us by Him who united in His person true and proper deity with perfect and sinless humanity. (Lev. 17:11; Isa. 64:6; Matt. 26:28; John 3:7-18; Rom. 5:6-9; 2 Cor. 5:21; Gal. 3:13; 6:15; Eph. 1:7; Phil. 3:4-9; Titus 3:5; James 1:18; 1 Peter 1:18-19, 23.)

We believe that the new birth of the believer comes only through faith in Christ and that repentance is a vital part of believing, and is in no way, in itself, a separate and independent condition of salvation; nor are any other acts, such as confession, baptism, prayer, or faithful service, to be added to believing as a condition of salvation. (John 1:12; 3:16, 18, 36; 5:24; 6:29; Acts 13:39; 16:31; Rom. 1:16-17; 3:22, 26; 4:5; 10:4; Gal. 3:22.)

Article VIII. THE EXTENT OF SALVATION

We believe that when an unregenerate person exercises that faith in Christ which is illustrated and described as such in the New Testament, he passes immediately out of spiritual death into spiritual life, and from the old creation into the new; being justified from all things, accepted before the Father according as Christ His Son is accepted, loved as Christ is loved, having his place and portion as linked to Him and one with Him forever. Though the saved one may have occasion to grow in the realization of his blessings and to know a fuller measure of divine power through the yielding of his life more fully to God, he is, as soon as he is saved, in possession of every spiritual blessing and absolutely complete in Christ, and is, therefore, in no way required by God to seek a so-called "second blessing," or a "second work of grace." (John 5:24; 17:23; Acts 13:39; Rom. 5:1; 1 Cor. 3:21-23; Eph. 1:3; Col. 2:10; 1 John 4:17; 5:11-12.)

Article IX. SANTIFICATION

We believe that sanctification, which is a setting apart unto God, is three-fold: It is already complete for every saved person because his position toward God is the same as Christ's position. Since the believer is in Christ, he is set apart unto God in the measure in which Christ is set apart unto God. We believe, however, that he retains his sin nature, which cannot be eradicated in this life. Therefore, while the standing of the Christian in Christ is perfect, his present state is no more perfect than his experience in daily life. There is, therefore a progressive sanctification wherein the Christian is to "grow in grace" and to "be changed" by the unhindered power of the Spirit. We believe, also, that the child of God will yet be fully sanctified in his state as he is now sanctified in his standing in Christ when he shall see his Lord and shall be "like Him." (John 17:17; 2 Cor. 3:18, 7:1; Eph. 4:24; 5:25-27; 1 Thess. 5:23; Heb. 10:10, 14; 12:10.)

Article X. ETERNAL SECURITY

We believe that, because of the eternal purpose of God toward the objects of His love, because of His freedom to exercise grace toward the meritless on the ground of the propitiatory blood of Christ, because of the very nature of the divine gift of eternal life, because of the present and unending intercession and advocacy of Christ in heaven, because of the immutability of the unchangeable covenants of God, because of the regenerating, abiding presence of the Holy Spirit in the hearts of all who are saved, we and all true believers everywhere, once saved shall be kept saved forever. We believe, however, that God is a holy and righteous Father and that, since He cannot overlook the sin of His children, He will when they persistently sin chasten them and correct them in infinite love; but having undertaken to save them and keep them forever, apart from all human merit, He, who cannot fail, will in the end present every one of them faultless before the presence of His glory and conformed to the image of His Son. (John 5:24; 10:28; 13:1; 14:16-17; 17:11; Rom. 8:29; 1 Cor. 6:19; Heb. 7:25; 1 John 2:1-2; 5:13; Jude 1:24.)

Article XI. ASSURANCE

We believe it is the privilege, not only of some, but of all who are born again by the Spirit through faith in Christ as revealed in the Scriptures, to be assured of their salvation from the very day they take Him to be their Savior and that this assurance is not founded upon any fancied discovery of their own worthiness or fitness, but wholly upon the testimony of God in His written Word, exciting within His children filial love, gratitude, and obedience. (Luke 10:20; 22:32; 2 Cor. 5:1; 6-8; 2 Tim. 1:12; Heb. 10:22; 1 John 5:13.)

Article XII. THE HOLY SPIRIT

We believe that the Holy Spirit, the Third Person of the blessed Trinity, though omnipresent from all eternity, took up His abode in the world in a special sense on the day of Pentecost according to the divine promise, dwells in every believer, and by His baptism unites all to Christ in one body, and that He, as the Indwelling One, is the source of all power and all acceptable worship and service. We believe that He never takes His departure from the church, nor from the feeblest of the saints, but is ever present to testify of Christ; seeking to occupy believers with Him and not with themselves nor with their experiences. We believe that His abode in the world in this special sense will cease when Christ comes to receive His own at the completion of the church. (John 14:16-17; 16:7-15; 1 Cor. 6:19; Eph. 2:22; 2 Thess. 2:7.)

We believe that, in this age, certain well-defined ministries are committed to the Holy Spirit, and that it is the duty of every Christian to understand them and to be adjusted to them in his own life and experience. These ministries are: The restraining of evil in the world to the measure of the divine will; the convicting of the world respecting sin, righteousness, and judgment; the regenerating of all believers; the indwelling and anointing of all who are saved, thereby sealing them unto the day of redemption; the baptizing into the one body of Christ of all who are saved; and the continued filling for power, teaching, and service of those among the saved who are yielded to Him and who are subject to His will. (John 3:6; 16:7-11; Rom. 8:9; 1 Cor. 12:13; Eph. 4:30; 5:18; 2 Thess. 2:7; 1 John 2:20-27.)

We believe that some gifts of the Holy Spirit such as speaking in tongues and miraculous healings were temporary. We believe that speaking in tongues was never the common or necessary sign of the baptism nor of the filling of the Spirit, and that the deliverance of the body from sickness or death awaits the consummation of our salvation in the resurrection. (Acts 4:8, 31: Rom. 8:23; 1 Cor. 13:8.)

Article XIII. THE CHURCH A UNITY OF BELIEVERS

We believe that all who are united to the risen and ascended Son of God are members of the church which is the body and bride of Christ, which began at Pentecost and is completely distinct from Israel. Its members are constituted as such regardless of membership or nonmembership in the organized churches of earth. We believe that by the same Spirit all believers in this age are baptized into, and thus become, one body that is Christ's, whether Jews or Gentiles, and having become members one of another, are under solemn duty to keep the unity of the Spirit in the bond of peace, rising above all sectarian differences, and loving one another with a pure heart fervently. (Matt. 16:16-18; Acts 2:42-47; Rom. 12:5; 1 Cor. 12:12-27; Eph. 1:20-23; 4:3-10; Col. 3:14-15.)

Article XIV. THE SACRAMENTS OR ORDINANCES

We believe that water baptism and the Lord's Supper are the only sacraments and ordinances of the church and that they are a scriptural means of testimony for the church in this age. (Matt. 28:19; Luke 22:19-20; Acts 10:47-48; 16:32-33; 18:7-8; 1 Cor. 11:26.)

Article XV. THE CHRISTIAN'S WALK

We believe that we are called with a holy calling, to walk not after the flesh, but after the Spirit, and so to live in the power of the indwelling Spirit that we will not fulfill the lust of the flesh. But the flesh with its fallen, Adamic nature, which in this life is never eradicated, being with us to the end of our earthly pilgrimage, needs to be kept by the Spirit constantly in subjection to Christ, or it will surely manifest its presence in our lives to the dishonor of our Lord. (Rom. 6:11; 8:2, 4, 12-13; Gal. 5:16; Eph. 4:22-24; Col. 2:1-10; 1 Peter 1:14-16; 1 John 1:4-7; 3:5-9.)

Article XVI. THE CHRISTIAN'S SERVICE

We believe that divine, enabling gifts for service are bestowed by the Spirit upon all who are saved. While there is a diversity of gifts, each believer is energized by the same Spirit, and each is called to his own divinely appointed service as the Spirit may will. In the apostolic church there were certain gifted men-apostles, prophets, evangelists, pastors, and teachers—who were appointed by God for the perfecting of the saints unto their work of the ministry. We believe also that today some men are especially called of God to be evangelists, pastors and teachers, and that it is to the fulfilling of His will and to His eternal glory that these shall be sustained and encouraged in their service for God. (Rom. 12:6; 1 Cor. 12:4-11; Eph. 4:11.)

We believe that, wholly apart from salvation benefits which are bestowed equally upon all who believe, rewards are promised according to the faithfulness of each believer in his service for his Lord, and that these rewards will be bestowed at the judgment seat of Christ after He comes to receive His own to Himself. (1 Cor. 3:9-15; 9:18-27; 2 Cor. 5:10.)

Article XVII. THE GREAT COMMISSION

We believe that it is the explicit message of our Lord Jesus Christ to those whom He has saved that they are sent forth by him into the world even as He was sent forth of His Father into the world. We believe that, after they are saved, they are divinely reckoned to be related to this world as strangers and pilgrims, ambassadors and witnesses, and that their primary purpose in life should be to make Christ known to the whole world. (Matt. 28:18-19; Mark 16:15; John 17:18; Acts 1:8; 2 Cor. 5:18-20; 1 Peter 1:17; 2:11.)

Article XVIII. THE BLESSED HOPE

We believe that, according to the Word of God, the next great event in the fulfillment of prophecy will be the coming of the Lord in the air to receive to Himself into heaven both His own who are alive and remain unto His coming, and also all who have fallen asleep in Jesus, and that this event is the blessed hope set before us in the Scripture, and for this we should be constantly looking. (John 14:1-3; 1 Cor. 15:51-52; Phil. 3:20; 1 Thess. 4:13-18; Titus 2:11-14.)

Article XIX. THE TRIBULATION

We believe that the translation of the church will be followed by the fulfillment of Israel's seventieth week (Dan. 9:27; Rev. 6:1; 19:21) during which the church, the body of Christ, will be in heaven. The whole period of Israel's seventieth week will be a time of judgment on the whole earth, at the end of which the times of the Gentiles will be brought to a close. The latter half of this period will be the time of Jacob's trouble (Jer. 30:7), which our Lord called the great tribulation (Matt. 24:15-21). We believe that universal righteousness will not be realized previous to the second coming of Christ, but that the world is day by day ripening for judgment and that the age will end with a fearful apostasy.

Article XX. THE SECOND COMING OF CHRIST

We believe that the period of great tribulation in the earth will be climaxed by the return of the Lord Jesus Christ to the earth as He went, in person on the clouds of heaven, and with power and great glory to introduce the millennial age, to bind Satan and place him in the abyss, to lift the curse which now rests upon the whole creation, to restore Israel to her own land and to give her the realization of God's covenant promises, and to bring the whole world to the knowledge of God. (Deut. 30:1-10; Isa. 11:9; Ezek. 37:21-28; Matt. 24:15-25; 46; Acts 15:16-17; Rom. 8:19-23; 11:25-27; 1 Tim. 4:1-3; 2 Tim. 3:105; Rev. 20:1-3.)

Article XXI. THE ETERNAL STATE

We believe that at death the spirits and souls of those who have trusted in the Lord Jesus Christ for salvation pass immediately into His presence and there remain in conscious bliss until the resurrection of the glorified body when Christ comes for His own, whereupon souls and body reunited shall be associated with Him forever in glory; but the spirits and souls of the unbelieving remain after death conscious of condemnation and in misery until the final judgment of the great white throne at the close of the millennium, when soul and body reunited shall be cast into the lake of fire, not to be annihilated, but to be punished with everlasting destruction from the presence of the Lord, and from the glory of His power. (Luke 16:19-26; 23:42; 2 Cor. 5:8; Phil. 1:23; 2 Thess. 1:7-9; Jude 1 6-7; Rev. 20:11-15.)

Notes: *The Dallas Theological Seminary is among the most prominent schools serving the Independent Fundamentalist community. Several church bodies, such as the Independent Bible Church Movement, have grown directly out of the Seminary through the bonding together of alumni. The Seminary's lengthy statement gives substance to the many brief documents published by fundamentalist churches on their doctrine. The article on sanctification places the statement squarely in the Reformed theological position (of the Westminster Confession) as opposed to the Wesleyan-Methodist tradition. The eschatological statements (articles 18-21) provide a concise presentation of premillennial doctrine. The statement also includes the idea of Christ's appearance prior to the seventh dispensational period known as the tribulation and His true second coming to establish the millennium following that tribulation period. This position is frequently termed "pretribulation" (or simply "pretrib") premillennialism.*

ARTICLES OF FAITH (AMERICAN EVANGELICAL CHRISTIAN CHURCHES)

The A.E.C.C. was founded as an inter-doctrinal ecclesiastical body. Inter-doctrinal because we feel that its Seven Articles of Faith to which each member must subscribe are the first and foremost doctrines of the Bible and are found in both Calvinistic and Arminian teachings.

The Seven Articles of Faith are set forth as follows:

1. The Bible as the written word of God.
2. The Virgin Birth.
3. The Deity of Jesus the Christ.
4. Salvation through the Atonement.
5. The guidance of our life through prayer.
6. The return of the Saviour.
7. The establishment of the kingdom of God on earth.

We call the above seven points "The Essentials" and beyond these the A.E.C.C. does not stress any denominational doctrines. Anyone who can subscribe thereto may become a member of the organization and is welcome to fellowship with us. If the individual holds to certain views, not in conflict to these, in dress, observance of holy days, the eating of or abstinence of certain foods, etc., we feel that he or she should be allowed the liberty to do so.

Notes: *This short statement provides significant room for different opinions on a variety of controversial issues among evangelicals.*

*   *   *

WHAT WE BELIEVE (AMERICAN MISSION FOR OPENING CHURCHES)

1. We believe that all Scripture is the infallible, divinely inspired Word of God; inerrant in the original autographs; and is the guide for Christian faith and practice. II Tim. 3:16,17

2. We believe in one God eternally existing in three Persons: Father, Son, and Holy Spirit. Matt. 28:18,19; Mark 12:29

3. We believe that Jesus Christ was begotten by the Holy Spirit, born of the Virgin Mary, and is true God and true man. Matt. 1:16,18,21,25

4. We believe that the Holy Spirit, the Third Person of the Godhead, dwells in every believer, sealing them unto the day of redemption, and by His baptism unites all to Christ in one body. John 16:8-11; 1 Cor. 12:12-14, Eph. 1:13,14

5. We believe that man, who was created in the image of God, sinned and thereby incurred physical death as well as that spiritual death which is separation from God and that all human beings are born with a sinful nature. Gen. 1:26,27; 3:1-13; Psalm 51:5

6. We believe that Jesus Christ died for our sins according to the Scriptures as a representative and substitutionary sacrifice; and all who believe in Him are justified by faith and regenerated by the Holy Spirit, becoming children of God. 1 Tim. 1:15; Acts 4:12; John 1:12,13

7. We believe in the literal, physical resurrection of our Lord, His ascension into Heaven, and His present life there for us as High Priest and Advocate. John 20:11-18, 19-24; Acts 1:10; Heb. 8:1

8. We believe in the personal, imminent, pretribulational and premillennial coming of the Lord Jesus Christ for His redeemed ones. I Thess. 4:13-17

9. We believe in the bodily resurrection of the just and unjust, the everlasting blessedness of the saved and everlasting punishment of the lost. Acts 24:15; Rev. 20:5,6

Notes: *The statement of the American Mission is similar to those of both the Independent Fundamental Churches of America and the Bethany Bible Church.*

*   *   *

DOCTRINE AND TENETS (BERACHAH CHURCH)

The following basic doctrines contained in the Holy Scriptures are adopted:

1. THE HOLY SCRIPTURES

We believe the Holy Scriptures to be the inspired Word of God, authoritative, inerrant, and God-breathed (II Timothy 3:16-17; II Peter 1:20-21; Matthew 5:18; John 16:12-13).

2. THE GODHEAD

We believe in one Triune God, existing in three persons, Father, Son and Holy Spirit, eternal in being, identical in nature, equal in power and glory and having the same attributes and perfections, (Deuteronomy 6:4; II Corinthians 13:14).

3. THE TOTAL DEPRAVITY OF MAN

We believe that man was created in the image and likeness of God but that in Adam's sin the race fell, inherited a sinful nature, became alienated from God, and is totally unable to retrieve his lost condition (Genesis 1:26-27; Romans 3:22-23; 5:12; Ephesians 2:12).

4. THE PERSON AND WORK OF CHRIST

We believe that the Lord Jesus Christ, the eternal Son of God, became man, without ceasing to be God, having been conceived of the Holy Spirit and born of the virgin Mary, in order that He might reveal God and redeem sinful man; that He accomplished our redemption through His spiritual death on the cross as a substitutionary sacrifice; that our redemption is made sure to us by his literal physical resurrection from the dead (John 1:1-2, 14; Luke 1:35; Romans 3:24-25; 4:25; I Peter: 3-5); that the Lord Jesus Christ is now in Heaven, exalted at the right hand of God, where as the High Priest for His people, He fulfills the ministry of Representative, Intercessor and Advocate (Hebrews 9:24; 7:25; Romans 8:34; I John 2:1-2).

5. THE PERSONALITY AND WORK OF THE HOLY SPIRIT

We believe that the Holy Spirit is a person who convicts the world of sin, indwells all believers in the present age, baptizes them into the body of Christ, seals them unto the day of redemption, and that it is the duty of every believer to be filled with the Holy Spirit (Romans 8:9; I Corinthians 12:12-14; Ephesians 1:13-14; 5:18).

6. SALVATION

We believe that salvation in every dispensation is the gift of God brought to man by grace and received by personal faith in the Lord Jesus Christ, whose efficatious death on the cross provided man's reconciliation to God. (Ephesians 2:8-20; John 1:12; Ephesians 1:7).

7. THE ETERNAL SECURITY OF BELIEVERS

We believe that all believers are kept secure forever (Romans 8:1, 38-39; John 10:27-30; I Corinthians 1:4-8).

8. THE CHURCH

We believe that the Church, which is now the body and shall be the bride of Christ, is a spiritual organism made up of all born-again persons of this age irrespective of their affiliation with Christian organizations (Ephesians 1:22-23; 5:25-27; I Corinthians 12:12-14).

9. THE PERSONALITY OF SATAN

We believe in the personality of Satan, who is the open and declared enemy of God and man (Job 1:6-7; Matthew 4:2-11; Isaiah 14:12-17).

10. THE BLESSED HOPE

We believe that the next great event in the fulfillment of prophecy will be the coming of the Lord Jesus in the air to receive to Himself the dead in Christ and believers who are alive at His coming, otherwise known as the Rapture and Translation of the Church (I Corinthians 15:51-57; I Thessalonians 4:13-18; Titus 2:11-14).

11. THE TRIBULATION

We believe that the Rapture of the Church will be followed by the fulfillment of Israel's seventieth week, the latter half of which is the time of Jacob's trouble, the great tribulation (Daniel 9:27; Jeremiah 30:7; Matthew 24:15-21; Revelation 6:1-19; 21).

12. THE SECOND COMING OF CHRIST

We believe that the great tribulation will be climaxed by the (premillennial) return of the Lord Jesus Christ to earth to set up his kingdom (Zechariah 14:4-11; Matthew 24:15-25; 46; II Thessalonians 1:7-10; Revelation 20:6).

13. THE ETERNAL STATE

We believe that the soul and human spirit of those who have believed in the Lord Jesus Christ for salvation do at death immediately pass into His presence, and there remain in the conscious bliss until the resurrection of the body at His coming, when soul, human spirit and body reunited shall be associated with Him forever in the glory; but the souls of unbelievers remain after death in conscious misery until the final judgement of the Great White Throne at the close of the millennium, when soul and body reunited shall be cast into the lake of fire, not to be annihilated, but to be punished with everlasting destruction from the presence of the Lord and from the glory of His power (Luke 16:19-26; 23:43; II Corinthians 5:8; Philippians 1:23; II Thessalonians 1:7-9; Jude, verses 6-7; Revelation 20:11-15).

14. THE RESPONSIBILITY OF BELIEVERS

To "Grow in grace and knowledge of the Lord Jesus Christ," to the end that His life is consistent with the Lord's plan thus bringing both blessing to the believer and honor to the Lord.

15. CHURCH ORDINANCES

We believe that the Lord Jesus Christ instituted the Lord's Supper to be observed until His return (Matthew 28:19-20: I Corinthians 11:23-26).

16. SOVEREIGNTY

We believe that God, existing as Father, Son and Holy Spirit, is sovereign, and exercises supreme and absolute rule over all creation as a part of and consistent with the essence and attributes of deity. (I Chronicles 29:11, 12; Daniel 4:35; Psalms 24:1; Ephesians 1:11; I Timothy 6:15).

17. SPIRITUALITY

We believe that spirituality is an absolute condition in the life of a believer in this dispensation wherein he is filled or controlled by the Holy Spirit, walking in love and fellowship with the Lord Jesus Christ.

We believe that spirituality is distinct from maturity, that a believer becomes carnal through any act of mental, verbal or overt sin and that spirituality or fellowship with Christ is restored solely by personal confession of that sin to God the Father. (John 15:7, 8; II Corinthians 5:6; Galatians 5:16; Ephesians 5:18; Romans 6:11-13; I John 1:9, I John 1:5; 2:2; I Corinthians 11:30, 31).

18. SPIRITUAL GIFTS

We believe that God the Holy Spirit in grace and apart from human merit sovereignly bestows spiritual gifts to believers in this dispensation. Some of the permanent spiritual gifts which exist today are pastor-teacher, evangelist, administrator. We further believe that the temporary spiritual gifts ceased with the completion of the Canon of Scripture and these were: Apostleship, Prophecy, Speaking in Tongues, Interpreting Tongues, Healing and Working of Miracles. (I Corinthians 12, 13; Ephesians 4:7-12; Romans 12:4-8). Any member practicing these temporary gifts shall be subject to immediate dismissal.

B. TENETS

1. This Church shall not at any time become a member, sanction, or support any denomination, association of Churches or religious organization of any kind.

2. This Church shall not solicit anyone to become a member. Those who desire to affiliate with this Church may do so by complying with the provision of Article V.

3. This Church shall not knowingly accept gifts from unbelievers nor make individual solicitation of funds or pledges among believers.

Notes: *The Berachah Church was formed by a graduate of Dallas Theological Seminary, and the church's statement in large part is derived from the one published by the school.*

*   *   *

STATEMENT OF FAITH (BETHANY BIBLE CHURCH)

1. We believe in the Scriptures of the Old and New Testaments as being verbally inspired and completely inerrant in the original writings and of supreme and final authority in faith and life.

2. We believe in one God, eternally existing in three persons: Father, Son and Holy Spirit.

3. We believe that Jesus Christ was begotten of the Holy Spirit and born of the Virgin Mary and is true God and true man.

4. We believe that man was created in the image of God; that he sinned and thereby incurred not only physical death but also that spiritual death which is separation from God; and that all human beings are born with a sinful nature and in the case of those who reach moral responsibility, become sinners in thought, word and deed.

5. We believe that the Lord Jesus Christ died for our sins according to the scriptures as a representative and substitutionary sacrifice, and that all who believe in Him are justified on the ground of His shed blood.

6. We believe in the resurrection of the crucified body of our Lord, in His ascension into Heaven, and His present life for us as High Priest and Advocate.

7. We believe in "that blessed hope," the personal, premillennial and imminent return of our Lord and Saviour, Jesus Christ.

8. We believe that all who receive by faith the Lord Jesus Christ are born of the Holy Spirit and thereby become children of God, a relationship in which they are eternally secure.

9. We believe in the bodily resurrection of the just and of the unjust; the everlasting blessedness of the saved and the everlasting conscious punishment of the lost.

Notes: *The Bethany Bible Church congregation and its associated churches have a close relationship with Dallas Theological Seminary, where most of the ministers graduated.*

*   *   *

STATEMENT OF FAITH (CHURCH OF CHRISTIAN LIBERTY)

We believe in and earnestly contend for the verbal, plenary inspiration and consequent inerrancy of the Scriptures; the Trinity of the Godhead; the Deity and Virgin Birth of Christ; the Person and work of the Holy Spirit; the Genesis account of creation; the fall and resulting total depravity of man by nature; the sovereign unconditional election of God; the particular redemption wrought by the death of Jesus Christ; the irresistible grace of God; the

perseverance and preservation of the saints; salvation by grace through faith apart from works; the maintenance of good works by believers as evidence of their faith; the independence of the local church; the Bible as its only rule of faith and practice; a regenerated church membership; the baptism of believers; the Lord's Table as a memorial of His once-for-all death; the priesthood of believers; the bodily resurrection, ascension, and personal, visible, return of Christ; the personality of the Devil; the resurrection of the just and the unjust; and the everlasting happiness of the just in Heaven and the everlasting conscious suffering of the unjust in the lake of fire.

Notes: *The founder of the Church of Christian Liberty graduated from Trinity Theological Seminary, the school sponsored by the Evangelical Free Church.*

*   *   *

STATEMENT OF FUNDAMENTAL TRUTHS (INDEPENDENT CHRISTIAN CHURCHES INTERNATIONAL)

We believe in the complete and entire Divine inspiration of the Bible (both the Old and New Testaments); the creation of many by the direct act of Jehovah God; the incarnation and virgin birth of our blessed Lord and Saviour, Jesus Christ: the Son of God; His vicarious atonement for the sins of mankind by the shedding of His blood on the cross; His literal physical death and His bodily resurrection from the tomb; His power to save men from sin; the adoption into the family of God through the regeneration by the Holy Spirit; and the gift of eternal life by the grace of God.

We accept the Bible as our all-sufficient rule of faith and practice. Therefore, this STATEMENT OF FUNDAMENTAL BELIEFS is intended only as a basis of fellowship among us in order that we might all "speak the same thing" (I Corinthians 1:10 and Acts 2:42). The human phraseology which is employed in this statement is not inspired, but the truths set forth in it are held to be essential to a fundamental ministry. No claim is made that it contains all truths in the Bible, but that it covers our present needs regarding these fundamental matters.

1. THE SCRIPTURES INSPIRED

The Bible is the inspired Word of God, a revelation from God to man. It is the infallible rule of faith and conduct, and is superior to conscience and reason, while not being contrary to reason. (II Timothy 3:15-16; II Peter 1:21; I Peter 1:23-25 and Hebrews 4:12).

2. THE ONE TRUE GOD

The one true God has revealed Himself as the eternally self-existent, self-revealed "I AM"; and has further revealed Himself as embodying the principles of relationship and association, ie., as the Father, Son and Holy Spirit. (Deuteronomy 6:4; Mark 12:29; Isaiah 43:10; Matthew 28:19 and Luke 3:22).

3. MAN, HIS FALL AND REDEMPTION

Man was created good and perfect; for God said: "Let us make man in our image, after our likeness." But man, by voluntary transgression, fell, and his only hope of redemp-

tion is in Jesus Christ. (Genesis 1:26-31; 3:1-17 and
Romans 5:12-21).

4. THE SALVATION OF MAN

(a) CONDITIONS OF SALVATION: The grace of
God, which brings salvation, has appeared to all
men, through the preaching of repentance toward
God and faith toward the Lord Jesus Christ. Man is
therefore saved by the washing of regeneration and
the renewing of the Holy Spirit, and being justified
by the grace through faith of both God and man, he
becomes an heir of God according to the hope of
eternal life. (Titus 2:11; 3:5-7; Romans 10:8-15 and
Luke 24:47).

(b) THE EVIDENCE OF SALVATION: The inward
evidence to the believer of his salvation is the direct
witness of the Spirit (Romans 8:16). The outward
evidence to all men is a life of righteousness and true
holiness.

5. BAPTISM IN WATER

The ordinance of Baptism by a burial with Christ should
be observed as commanded in the Holy Writ by all who
have truly repented and in their hearts have really believed
in Christ as Saviour and Lord. In so doing, they have the
body washed in pure water as an outward sign or symbol
of cleansing, while their hearts have already been sprinkled
with the blood of Christ as an inner cleansing. Thus, they
proclaim to the world that they have died with Christ to
sin, and that they have also been raised with Him to live
and walk in newness of life. (Matthew 28:19; Acts 10:47-
48; Romans 6:4 and Hebrews 10:22).

6. THE LORD'S SUPPER

The Lord's Supper, consisting of the elements, is the
symbol expressing our sharing the divine nature of our
Lord Jesus Christ (II Peter 1:4); a memorial of His
suffering and death (I Corinthians 11:26) and a prophecy
of His second advent (I Corinthians 11:26); and is
commended to all believers as such a sign until He returns.

7. ENTIRE SANCTIFICATION

The Scriptures teach a life of holiness without which no
man can see the Lord. By the power of the Holy Spirit we
are able to obey the command, "be ye holy, for I am holy."
Entire sanctification is the will of God for all believers, and
should earnestly be pursued by walking in obedience to
God's word. (Hebrews 12:14; I Peter 1:15-16; I Thessalonians 5:23-24 and I John 2:6).

8. THE CHURCH

The Church is the body of Christ, the habitation of God
through the Spirit, with Divine appointments for the
fulfillment of her great commission. Each believer is an
integral part of that General Assembly and the Church of
the First-born, which are written in Heaven. (Ephesians
1:22-23; 2:19-22 and Hebrews 1:23).

9. THE MINISTRY AND EVANGELISM

A divinely called and Scripturally appointed and ordained
ministry has been provided for by our Lord for a two-fold

purpose: (1) The evangelization of the world, and (2) the
edifying of the Body of Christ. (Mark 16:15-20 and
Ephesians 4:11-13).

10. DIVINE HEALING

Deliverance from sickness is provided for in the atonement, just as is salvation from sin. (Isaiah 53:4-5; Matthew
8:16-17 and James 5:14-16).

11. THE BLESSED HOPE

The resurrection of those who have fallen asleep in Christ
and their translation together with those who are alive and
remaining unto the day of the coming of the Lord is the
imminent and blessed hope of the Church. (I Thessalonians 4:16-17; Romans 8:2; Titus 2:13 and I Corinthians
15:51-52).

12. THE MILLENNIAL REIGN OF JESUS

The revelation of the Lord Jesus from Heaven, the
salvation of mankind then completed, and the millennial
reign of Christ is the Scriptural promise of the world's
hope. (II Thessalonians 1:7; Revelation 19:11-14 and 20:1-
7).

13. THE LAKE OF FIRE

The devil and his angels, the beast and the false prophet,
and whosoever is not found written in the Book of Life,
shall be sentenced to everlasting punishment in the lake
which burns with fire and brimstone, which is the second
death. (Revelation 19:20 and 20:10-15).

14. THE NEW HEAVENS AND NEW EARTH

We, according to His promise, look for new heavens and a
new earth, wherein dwelleth righteousness. (II Peter 3:13
and Revelation 21 and 22).

Notes: *The beliefs of the loosely affiliated churches belonging to the Independent Christian Churches International
are held as fallible summaries which set forth their attempts
briefly to specify essential Biblical Truth. The statement
reproduced here, less detailed than those of many fundamentalist churches, differs in that it does not affirm either
the inerrancy of the Bible or dispensationalism. The Trinity,
baptism by immersion, and a premillennial eschatology are
affirmed.*

*   *   *

FAITH AND DOCTRINE (INDEPENDENT FUNDAMENTAL CHURCHES OF AMERICA)

Each person, church, or organization, in order to become
or remain a member of the IFCA, shall be required to
subscribe to the following articles of faith:

1. THE HOLY SCRIPTURES

We believe the Holy Scriptures of the Old and New
Testaments to be the verbally inspired Word of God, the
final authority for faith and life, inerrant in the original
writings, infallible and God-breathed (II Tim. 3:16, 17; II
Peter 1:20, 21; Matt. 5:18; John 16:12, 13).

2. THE GODHEAD

We believe in one triune God, eternally existing in three
persons—Father, Son, and Holy Spirit—coeternal in
being, co-identical in nature, co-equal in power and glory,

and having the same attributes and perfections (Deut. 6:4; II Cor. 13:14).

3. THE PERSON AND WORK OF CHRIST

a. We believe that the Lord Jesus Christ, the eternal Son of God, became man, without ceasing to be God, having been conceived by the Holy Spirit and born of the Virgin Mary, in order that He might reveal God and redeem sinful men (John 1:1, 2, 14; Luke 1:35).

b. We believe that the Lord Jesus Christ accomplished our redemption through His death on the cross as a representative, vicarious, substitutionary sacrifice; and, that our justification is made sure by His literal, physical resurrection from the dead (Rom. 3:24, 25; I Peter 2:24; Eph. 1:7; I Peter 1:3-5).

c. We believe that the Lord Jesus Christ ascended to heaven, and is now exalted at the right hand of God, where, as our High Priest, He fulfills the ministry of Representative, Intercessor, and Advocate (Acts 1:9, 10; Heb. 9:24; 7:25; Rom. 8:34; I John 2:1, 2).

4. THE PERSON AND WORK OF THE HOLY SPIRIT

a. We believe that the Holy Spirit is a person who convicts the world of sin, of righteousness, and of judgment; and, that He is the supernatural agent in regeneration, baptizing all believers into the body of Christ, indwelling and sealing them unto the day of redemption (John 16:8-11; II Cor. 3:6; I Cor. 12:12-14; Rom. 8:9; Eph. 1:13, 14).

b. We believe that He is the divine Teacher who guides believers into all truth; and, that it is the privilege and duty of all the saved to be filled with the Spirit (John 16:13; I John 2:20, 27; Eph. 5:18).

5. THE TOTAL DEPRAVITY OF MAN

We believe that man was created in the image and likeness of God, but that in Adam's sin the race fell, inherited a sinful nature, and became alienated from God; and, that man is totally depraved, and, of himself, utterly unable to remedy his lost condition (Gen. 1:26, 27; Rom. 3:22, 23; 5:12; Eph. 2:1-3, 12).

6. SALVATION

We believe that salvation is the gift of God brought to man by grace and received by personal faith in the Lord Jesus Christ, whose precious blood was shed on Calvary for the forgiveness of our sins (Eph. 2:8-10; John 1:12; Eph. 1:7; I Peter 1:18, 19).

7. THE ETERNAL SECURITY AND ASSURANCE OF BELIEVERS

a. We believe that all the redeemed, once saved, are kept by God's power and are thus secure in Christ forever (John 6:37-40; 10:27-30; Rom. 8:1, 38, 39; I Cor. 1:4-8; I Peter 1:5).

b. We believe that it is the privilege of believers to rejoice in the assurance of their salvation through the testimony of God's Word; which, however, clearly forbids the use of Christian liberty as an occasion to the flesh (Rom. 13:13, 14; Gal. 5:13; Titus 2:11-15).

8. THE TWO NATURES OF THE BELIEVER

We believe that every saved person possesses two natures, with provision made for victory of the new nature over the old nature through the power of the indwelling Holy Spirit; and, that all claims to the eradication of the old nature in this life are unscriptural (Rom. 6:13; 8:12, 13; Gal. 5:16-25; Eph. 4:22-24; Col. 3:10; I Peter 1:14-16; I John 3:5-9).

9. SEPARATION

We believe that all the saved should live in such a manner as not to bring reproach upon their Saviour and Lord; and, that separation from all religious apostasy and all worldly and sinful pleasures, practices and associations is commanded of God (II Tim. 3:1-5; Rom. 12:1, 2; 14:13; I John 2:15-17; II John vss. 9-11; II Cor. 6:14-7:1).

10. MISSIONS

We believe that it is the obligation of the saved to witness by life and by word to the truths of Holy Scripture and to seek to proclaim the Gospel to all mankind (Mark 16:15; Acts 1:8; II Cor. 5:19, 20).

11. THE MINISTRY AND SPIRITUAL GIFTS

a. We believe that God is sovereign in the bestowment of all His gifts; and, that the gifts of evangelists, pastors, and teachers are sufficient for the perfecting of the saints today; and, that speaking in tongues and the working of sign miracles gradually ceased as the New Testament Scriptures were completed and their authority became established (I Cor. 12:4-11; II Cor. 12:12; Eph. 4:7-12).

b. We believe that God does hear and answer the prayer of faith, in accord with His own will, for the sick and afflicted (John 15:7; I John 5:14, 15).

12. THE CHURCH

a. We believe that the Church, which is the body and the espoused bride of Christ, is a spiritual organism made up of all born-again persons of this present age (Eph. 1:22, 23; 5:25-27; I Cor. 12:12-14; II Cor. 11:2).

b. We believe that the establishment and continuance of local churches is clearly taught and defined in the New Testament Scriptures (Acts 14:27; 20:17, 28-32; I Tim. 3:1-13; Titus 1:5-11).

13. DISPENSATIONALISM

We believe in the dispensational view of Bible interpretation but reject the extreme teaching known as "hyper dispensationalism" such as that teaching which opposes either the Lord's table or water baptism as a Scriptural means of testimony for the church in this age (Matt. 28:19, 20; Acts 2:41, 42; 18:8; I Cor. 11:23-26).

14. THE PERSONALITY OF SATAN

We believe that Satan is a person, the author of sin and the cause of the fall; that he is the open and declared enemy of God and man; and, that he shall be eternally punished in the lake of fire (Job 1:6, 7; Isa. 14:12-17; Matt. 4:2-11; 25:41; Rev. 20:10).

FAITH AND DOCTRINE (INDEPENDENT FUNDAMENTAL
CHURCHES OF AMERICA) (continued)

15. THE SECOND ADVENT OF CHRIST

We believe in that "blessed hope," the personal, imminent, pre-tribulation and premillennial coming of the Lord Jesus Christ for His redeemed ones; and in His subsequent return to earth, with His saints, to establish His millennial kingdom (I Thess. 4:13-18; Zech. 14:4-11; Rev. 19:11-16; 20:1-6; I Thess. 1:10; 5:9; Rev. 3:10).

16. THE ETERNAL STATE

a. We believe in the bodily resurrection of all men, the saved to eternal life, and the unsaved to judgment and everlasting punishment (Matt. 25:46; John 5:28, 29; 11:25, 26; Rev. 20:5, 6, 12, 13).

b. We believe that the souls of the redeemed are, at death, absent from the body and present with the Lord, where in conscious bliss they await the first resurrection, when spirit, soul and body are reunited to be glorified forever with the Lord (Luke 23:43; Rev. 20:4-6; II Cor. 5:8; Phil. 1:23; 3:21; I Thess. 4:16, 17).

c. We believe that the souls of unbelievers remain after death, in conscious misery until the second resurrection, when with soul and body reunited they shall appear at the great white throne judgment, and shall be cast into the lake of fire, not to be annihilated, but to suffer everlasting conscious punishment (Luke 16:19-26; Matt. 25:4-46; II Thess. 1:7-9; Jude vss. 6,7; Mark 9:43-48; Rev. 20:11-15).

SECTION 2. FELLOWSHIP COVENANT

In subscribing to these articles of faith, we by no means set aside, or undervalue, any of the Scriptures of the Old and New Testaments; but we deem the knowledge, belief and acceptance of the truth as set forth in our doctrinal statement, to be essential to sound faith and fruitful practice, and therefore requisite for Christian fellowship in the IFCA.

Notes: *The Independent Fundamental Churches of America (IFCA) is among the most influential of fundamentalist bodies. It draws many of its pastors from Dallas Theological Seminary and Moody Biblical Institute graduates.*

*   *   *

STATEMENT OF FAITH (INTERNATIONAL MINISTERIAL FELLOWSHIP)

The International Ministerial Fellowship accepts the Holy Scriptures as the revealed will of God, the all-sufficient rule for faith and practice; and for the purpose of maintaining general unity adopts the following Statement of Fundamental Truths:

1. We believe the Bible to be the inspired, the only infallible, authoritative Word of God.

2. We believe that there is one God eternally existent in three persons: Father, Son and Holy Spirit.

3. We believe in the deity of our Lord Jesus Christ, in His virgin birth, in His sinless life, in His miracles, in His vicarious and atoning death through His shed blood, in His bodily resurrection, in His ascension to the right hand of the Father, and in his personal return in power and glory.

4. We believe that for the salvation of lost and sinful man, regeneration by the Holy Spirit is absolutely essential.

5. We believe in the present ministry of the Holy Spirit by whose indwelling the Christian is enabled to live a godly life.

6. We believe that the baptism of the Holy Spirit, according to Acts 2:4, is given to believers who ask for it.

7. We believe in the sanctifying power of the Holy Spirit by Whose indwelling the Christian is enabled to live a holy life.

8. We believe in the resurrection of both the saved and the lost: they that are saved unto the resurrection of life and they that are lost unto the resurrection of damnation.

9. We believe in the spiritual unity of believers in our Lord Jesus Christ.

Notes: *This brief statement was adopted in 1984.*

*   *   *

DOCTRINAL STATEMENT (MOODY BIBLICAL INSTITUTE)

In view of the present unrest concerning doctrinal questions within the sphere of evangelical Christianity, and to answer inquiries regarding the position of the Moody Bible Institute thereupon, be it *Resolved*, That this Board of Trustees places on record the following statement of faith as that to which its members severally subscribe, and to which it requires the subscription of the members of the faculty of the Educational Branch and all the official heads of the Institute, to wit:

ARTICLE I. God is a Person who has revealed Himself as a Trinity in unity, Father, Son and Holy Spirit—three Persons and yet but one God (Deut. 6:4; Matt. 28:19; I Cor. 8:6).

ARTICLE II. The Bible, including both the Old and the New Testaments, is a divine revelation, the original autographs of which were verbally inspired by the Holy Spirit (II Tim. 3:16; II Pet. 1:21).

ARTICLE III. Jesus Christ is the image of the invisible God, which is to say, He is Himself very God; He took upon Him our nature, being conceived by the Holy Ghost and born of the Virgin Mary; He died upon the cross as a substitutionary sacrifice for the sin of the world; He arose from the dead in the body in which He was crucified; He ascended into heaven in that body glorified, where He is now, our interceding High Priest; He will come again personally and visibly to set up His kingdom and to judge the quick and the dead (Col. 1:15; Phil. 2:5-8; Matt. 1:18-25; I Pet. 2:24, 25; Luke 24; Heb. 4:14-16; Acts 1:9-11; I Thess. 4:16-18; Matt. 25:31-46; Rev. 11:15-17; 20:4-6, 11-15).

ARTICLE IV. Man was created in the image of God but fell into sin, and, in that sense, is lost; this is true of all men, and except a man be born again he cannot see the kingdom of God; salvation is by grace through faith in Christ who His own self bare our sins in His own body on the tree; the retribution of the wicked and unbelieving and the reward of the righteous are everlasting, and as the reward is conscious, so is the retribution (Gen. 1:26, 27; Rom. 3:10, 23; John 3:3; Acts 13:38, 39; 4:12; John 3:16; Matt. 25:46; II Cor. 5:1; II Thess. 1:7-10.)

ARTICLE V. The Church is an elect company of believers baptized by the Holy Spirit into one body; its mission is to witness concerning its Head, Jesus Christ, preaching the gospel among all nations; it will be caught up to meet the Lord in the air ere He appears to set up His kingdom (Acts 2:41; 15:13-17; Eph. 1:3-6; I Cor. 12:12, 13; Matt. 28:19, 20; Acts 1:6-8; I Thess. 4:16-18).

Notes: *This statement was adopted in 1928 by the trustees of Moody Biblical Institute. It superseded an earlier statement placed in the institute's catalog in 1915.*

*   *   *

DOCTRINAL STATEMENT (MOODY MEMORIAL CHURCH)

1. We believe the Holy Scriptures to be the inspired Word of God absolutely authoritative and infallible.

2. We believe in one God existing in three persons, Father, Son, and Holy Spirit, co-equal and eternal.

3. We believe that man was created in innocence but fell in Adam and is now totally unable to retrieve his lost condition.

4. We believe that salvation has been provided through our Lord Jesus Christ who was born of the virgin Mary, suffered and died for our sins upon the Cross, rose from the dead, ascended to God's right hand, and is coming again in power and great glory.

5. We believe that the Church is the Body of Christ formed by the baptism of the Holy Spirit, and that all believers are members thereof and are a holy and royal priesthood.

6. We believe in the eternal security and everlasting blessedness of the saved and the eternal judgment of all who reject our Lord Jesus Christ.

7. We believe that Christ instituted the ordinances of baptism and the Lord's Supper to be observed until He come.

8. We believe that it is the responsibility of all who are saved to seek to win others to Christ.

Notes: *Though closely related to Moody Biblical Institute, Moody Church is completely autonomous and has adopted its own statement of doctrine.*

FAITH AND DOCTRINE (OHIO BIBLE CHURCH)

13. BAPTISM

A. We believe immersion to be the New Testament mode of baptism to be administered upon personal acceptance and public confession of Christ as Saviour. We believe Christ Himself established and commanded the ordinance to symbolize the believer's death to the old life of sin and his spiritual resurrection to the new life in Christ (Acts 2:41; 8:12; 9:18; 10:47, 48; Romans 6:3-6).

B. Since baptism is not essential to salvation we recognize the sovereign right of any local church to accept for membership those who have not yet been baptized or who have been baptized by other modes if it so desires.

Notes: *The statement of the Ohio Bible Church is identical to that of the Independent Fundamental Churches of America except in its addition of an article on baptism, reproduced here.*

*   *   *

Grace Gospel Movement

DOCTRINAL STATEMENT (BEREAN BIBLE SOCIETY)

We hold the following doctrinal beliefs:

The verbal inspiration and plenary authority of the BIBLE in its original writings.

The eternal trinity of the GODHEAD.

The eternal deity, the virgin birth, the spotless humanity and the vicarious death of THE LORD JESUS CHRIST.

The personality and deity of the HOLY SPIRIT.

The total depravity of MAN by nature.

SALVATION by grace, through faith in the crucified, risen and glorified Christ.

The essential unity of all believers of the present dispensation as members of the ONE TRUE CHURCH, the Body of Christ.

The GIFTS enumerated in EPHESIANS 4:7-16, and that these alone are necessary for the building up of the Body of Christ.

The privilege and duty of all the saved to WALK as children of light.

The communion of the LORD'S SUPPER as revealed through Paul for the members of the Body of Christ "till He come."

One divine BAPTISM, the operation of the Holy Spirit, by which all true believers are made members of the Body of Christ, being identified with Him in His death, burial and resurrection. In the light of I COR. 1:17, EPH. 4:5 and COL. 2:12 we affirm that water baptism has no place in God's spiritual program for the Body of Christ in the present dispensation of grace.

The RESURRECTION of the body.

The pre-tribulation RAPTURE of the Church.

The personal, pre-millennial RETURN OF CHRIST to reign on earth.

The ETERNAL PUNISHMENT of the unsaved dead.

The GOSPEL which Paul called "my gospel," and "the gospel of the grace of God," as God's specific message for the world today.

Notes: *The Grace Gospel Movement, often called ultra-dispensationalism, resembles fundamentalism, out of which it came. The movement developed some unique views, however. Among the most important views is that only a few of Paul's epistles, especially the Epistle to the Ephesians, were meant for this present church age or dispensation. Among other peculiarities, their unique position has led them to abandon water baptism, though the Lord's Supper is retained as an ordinance.*

One of the two most prominent Grace Gospel organizations, the Berean Bible Society does not differ from the older Grace Gospel Fellowship on essential doctrinal points. Notice the citation of Ephesians concerning spiritual gifts (an anti-pentecostal statement) and the item on baptism (apart from which any fundamentalist could accept this statement).

* * *

DOCTRINAL STATEMENT (GRACE GOSPEL FELLOWSHIP)

"I therefore, the prisoner of the Lord, beseech you that ye walk worthy of the vocation wherewith ye are called, with all lowliness and meekness, with long-suffering, forbearing one another in love; endeavoring to keep the unity of the Spirit in the bond of peace. There is one body, and one Spirit, even as ye are called in one hope of your calling; one Lord, one faith, one baptism, one God and Father of all, who is above all, and through all, and in you all. But unto every one of us is given grace according to the measure of the gift of Christ" (Eph. 4:1-7).

We affirm that the seven-fold unity expressed in this passage is the Holy Spirit's doctrinal statement for the Church, which is the Body of Christ. We believe that all the expressions of doctrinal position and requirements for this Dispensation of the Grace of God must be in full accord with the Holy Spirit's outline. We recognize other doctrinal unities for other dispensations, but we affirm that Ephesians 4:4-6 stands alone as the doctrinal unity for this dispensation.

Desiring to be in full accord with the Mind of the Spirit, we hold and require the following doctrinal beliefs:

THE BIBLE

The entire Bible in its original writings is verbally inspired of God and is of plenary authority (2 Tim. 3:16, 17; 2 Pet. 1:21).

THE GODHEAD

There is one God, eternally existing in three Persons: Father, Son, and Holy Spirit (Deut. 6:4; I Tim. 2:5; Eph. 4:4-6; Matt. 28:19; 2 Cor. 13:14).

THE PERSON OF CHRIST

Jesus Christ was begotten by the Holy Spirit and born of the Virgin Mary and is true God and true man (Lk. 1:35; Phil. 2:6-9; Rom. 1:3, 4).

TOTAL DEPRAVITY

All men by nature are dead in trespasses and sins and are, therefore, totally unable to do anything pleasing to God (Eph. 2:1-3; Rom. 3:9-12).

REDEMPTION

God justifies ungodly sinners by His grace upon the ground of the blood of Christ through the means of faith. This complete salvation is bestowed as the free gift of God apart from man's works (Rom. 3:24-28; 5:1, 9; Eph. 2:8, 9).

ETERNAL SECURITY

All of the saved are eternally secure in Christ (Col. 3:1-4; Phil. 1:6; Rom. 8:1; 8:29-34; Rom. 8:38, 39; John 10:27-29; Eph 1:13-14).

PERSONALITY AND WORK OF THE HOLY SPIRIT

The Holy Spirit is a Person, Who convicts the world of sin and Who regenerates, baptizes, indwells, enlightens, and empowers (John 16:8; Tit. 3:5; 1 Cor. 12:13; Eph. 1:13, 17, 18; 3:16).

THE CHURCH

In the present dispensation there is only one true Church, which is called the Body of Christ (I Cor. 12:13; Eph. 1:22, 23; 3:6). The historical manifestation of the Body of Christ began with the Apostle Paul before he wrote his first epistle (I Thess. 2:14-16 cf. Acts 13:45, 46; Phil. 1:5, 6 cf. Acts 16; I Cor. 12:13, 27 cf. Acts 18).

GIFTS

The only gifts necessary for the ministry of the Body of Christ are those enumerated in Ephesians 4:7-16. Of these, only the gifts of Evangelists, Pastors, and Teachers are in operation today. All of the sign gifts of the Acts period, such as tongues, prophecy, and healing (I Cor. 12:1-31), being temporary in character, have ceased (I Cor. 13:8-11).

WALK

By reason of Christ's victory over sin and of His indwelling Spirit, all of the saved may and should experience deliverance from the power of sin by obedience to Romans 6:11; but we deny that man's nature of sin is ever eradicated during this life (Rom. 6:6-14; Gal. 5:16-25; Rom. 8:37; II Cor. 2:14; 10:2-5).

LORD'S SUPPER

The communion of the Lord's Supper as revealed through the Apostle Paul in I Corinthians 11:23-26 is for members of the Body of Christ to observe "until He comes."

There is no place in Scripture where the Lord's supper and water baptism are linked together either as ordinances or as sacraments for the Church.

BAPTISM

All saved persons have been made members of the Body of Christ by one divine baptism (I Cor. 12:13). By that one baptism every member of the Body of Christ is identified with Christ in His death, burial, and resurrection. In the light of the statement concerning the one baptism in Ephesians 4:5, the statements concerning baptism in Colossians 2:12 and Romans 6:3, 4, and Paul's statement in I Corinthians 1:17 that "Christ sent me not to baptize, but to preach the gospel," we conclude that water baptism has no place in God's spiritual program for the Body of Christ in this Day of Grace.

RESURRECTION

Jesus Christ was resurrected bodily from the dead (Luke 24:39-43). Therefore (I Cor. 15:21), all men will have a bodily resurrection (Acts 24:15): the saved to everlasting glory and the unsaved to everlasting punishment (John 5:29; Rev. 20:11-15).

SECOND COMING OF CHRIST

The rapture of the Church and the second coming of Christ will be pre-millennial. He will come first to receive the Church unto Himself (I Thess. 4:13-18; Phil. 3:20, 21) and then come to receive His Millennial Kingdom, over which He will reign (Zech. 14:4, 9; Acts 1:10, 11; Rev. 19:11-16; 20:4-6). Because of the nature of the Body of Christ, the resurrection and rapture of the Church, which is His Body, will take place before the Great Tribulation (Jer. 30:7; Matt. 24:15-31) at His appearing in the air (I Thess. 4:13-18; Phil. 3:20, 21; Titus 2:13, 14; I Cor. 15:51-53). The resurrection of the other saved dead will occur after the Tribulation (Rev. 20:4-6).

STATE OF THE DEAD

Nowhere does Scripture extend the hope of salvation to the unsaved dead but instead reveals that they will ever continue to exist in a state of conscious suffering (Luke 16:23-28; Rev. 14:11; 20:14, 15; Col. 3:6; Rom. 1:21-32; John 3:36; Phil. 3:19; II Thess. 1:9). The teachings of Universalism, of probation after death, of annihilation of the unsaved dead, and of the unconscious state of the dead, saved or unsaved (Luke 16:23-28; Phil. 1:23; II Cor. 5:6-8), are opposed by us as being thoroughly unscriptural and dangerous doctrines.

MISSION

The mission and commission of the Church, which is His Body, is to proclaim the message of reconciliation (II Cor. 5:14-21) and endeavor to make all men see what is the Dispensation of the Mystery (Eph. 3:8, 9). In this, we should follow the Apostle Paul (I Cor. 4:16; 11:1; Phil. 3:17; I Tim. 1:11-16). That distinctive message which the Apostle of the Gentiles (Rom. 11:13, 15:16) calls "my gospel" (Rom. 2:16; 16:25) is also called the "gospel of the grace of God" (Acts 20:24). We, like Paul, must preach the entire Word of God in the light of *this* Gospel (II Tim. 4:2; Gal. 1:8, 9) and strive to reach those in the regions beyond where Christ is not yet named (Rom. 15:20; II Cor. 10:16).

Notes: *This statement most clearly spells out the essential position concerning the Epistle to the Ephesians among Grace Gospel churches. Also note the statement of "Gifts" and "Baptism."*

*　　*　　*

WE BELIEVE IN . . . (LAST DAY MESSENGER ASSEMBLIES)

We believe in:

1. The verbal inspiration of the Word of God (2 Tim. 3:16).

2. The deity of Jesus Christ, and the trinity of the Godhead (Titus 2:13, 2 Cor. 13:14).

3. The total depravity of man, and everlasting punishment of the rejecters of Christ (Romans 3, John 3:36, Rev. 20:15).

4. Redemption by the blood of Christ, by grace, not of works (Titus 3:5, Eph. 2:8-9).

5. Everlasting life and security of the believer (John 10:28).

6. The personality and punishment of Satan (Job 1, Rev. 20).

7. The imminent rapture of the church, followed by the Great Tribulation and the millennial reign of Christ on earth (1 Thess. 4:16-17, Matt. 24, Rev. 20).

Notes: *This statement has been regularly printed in the* Last Day Messenger, *the periodical which unofficially ties together the assemblies.*

*　　*　　*

STATEMENT OF BELIEFS (THE WAY INTERNATIONAL)

1. We believe the scriptures of the Old and New Testaments were *Theopneustos*, "God-breathed," and perfect as originally given; that the Scriptures, or the Word of God, are of supreme, absolute and final authority for believing and godliness.

2. We believe in one God, the creator of the heavens and earth; in Jesus Christ, God's only begotten Son our lord and savior, whom God raised from the dead; and we believe in the workings of the Holy Spirit.

3. We believe that the virgin Mary conceived Jesus Christ by the Holy Spirit; that God was in Christ, and that Jesus Christ is the "mediator between God and men," and is "the man Christ Jesus."

4. We believe that Adam was created in the image of God, spiritually; that he sinned and thereby brought upon himself immediate spiritual death, which is separation from God, and physical death later, which is the consequence of sin; and that all human beings are born with a sinful nature.

5. We believe that Jesus Christ died for our sins according to the Scriptures, as a representative and substitute for us, and that all who believe that God raised him from the dead are justified and made righteous, born again by the Spirit of God, receiving

eternal life on the grounds of His eternal redemption, and thereby are the sons of God.

6. We believe in the resurrection of the crucified body of our Lord Jesus Christ, his ascension into heaven and his seating at the right hand of God.

7. We believe in the blessed hope of Christ's return, the personal return of our living lord and savior Jesus Christ and our gathering together unto him.

8. We believe in the bodily resurrection of the just and the unjust.

9. We believe in the receiving of the fullness of the holy spirit, the power from on high, plus the corresponding nine manifestations of the holy spirit, for all born-again believers.

10. We believe it is available to receive all that God promises us in His Word according to our believing faith. We believe we are free in Christ Jesus to receive all that he accomplished for us by his substitution.

11. We believe the early Church flourished rapidly because they operated within a Root, Trunk, Limb, Branch and Twig setup, decently and in order.

Notes: *The Way International departs from other Grace Gospel groups on several major points, especially in its denial of the Trinity and its acceptance of the charismatic gifts of I Corinthians 12. Compare item 9 with the item on gifts in the Grace Gospel Fellowship's statement.*

*   *   *

Miscellaneous Bible Students

THE BELIEFS AND PRACTICES (THE LOCAL CHURCH)

OUR BELIEF

1. We believe that the Holy Bible is the complete divine revelation verbally inspired by the Holy Spirit.

2. We believe that God is the only one Triune God— the Father, the Son, and the Spirit—co-existing equally from eternity to eternity.

3. We believe that the Son of God, even God Himself, became incarnated to be a man by the name of Jesus, born of the virgin Mary, that He might be our Redeemer and Savior.

4. We believe that Jesus, a genuine man, lived on this earth for thirty-three and a half years to make God the Father known to men.

5. We believe that Jesus, the Christ anointed by God with His Holy Spirit, died on the cross for our sins and shed His blood for the accomplishment of our redemption.

6. We believe that Jesus Christ, after being buried for three days, resurrected from the dead physically and

spiritually and that, in resurrection, He has become the life-giving Spirit to impart Himself into us as our life and our everything.

7. We believe that after His resurrection Christ ascended to the heavens and that God has made Him the Lord of all.

8. We believe that after His ascension Christ poured down the Spirit of God to baptize His chosen members into one Body and that the Spirit of God, who is also the Spirit of Christ, is moving on this earth today to convict sinners, to regenerate God's chosen people, to dwell in the members of Christ for their growth in life, and to build up the Body of Christ for His full expression.

9. We believe that at the end of this age Christ will come back to take up His members, to judge the world, to take possession of the earth, and to establish His eternal kingdom.

10. We believe that the overcoming saints will reign with Christ in the millennium and that all the believers in Christ will participate in the divine blessings in the New Jerusalem in the new heaven and new earth for eternity.

OUR STANDING

1. We stand on the Holy Scriptures, not according to any traditional interpretation, but according to the pure Word of God.

2. We stand on Christ, the living rock, the foundation stone, the Head of the Body, and the life and reality of the church.

3. We stand on the genuine unity of the Body of Christ. We are not sectarian, nor denominational, nor nondenominational, nor interdenominational.

4. We stand on the ground of the oneness of all believers in each locality; we recognize all the blood-redeemed and Spirit-regenerated believers in Christ as members of the one church in each city.

OUR MISSION

1. To preach the gospel of grace and of the kingdom to sinners that they may be saved.

2. To minister the life supply to believers that they may grow in Christ.

3. To establish the church in each city that the believers may become a local corporate expression of Christ in practicality.

4. To release the living and rich word of God from the Holy Scriptures that the believers may be nourished to grow and mature.

5. To build up the Body of Christ so that the Bride may be prepared for the coming back of Christ as the Bridegroom.

OUR HOPE

1. We hope that as many as are ordained by God to eternal life will believe in the Lord Jesus.

2. We hope that all regenerated Christians will seek the growth in life, not the mere increase of knowledge.

3. We hope that all seeking Christians will see the vision of the church and come into the practical church life in their locality.

4. We hope that the Lord will have a remnant of overcomers that His Bride may be prepared.

5. We hope that the coming back of the Lord will be hastened by our growth and that we may participate in the blessed rapture and in His coming kingdom.

CONCERNING THE RECOVERY

We in the local churches are for God's recovery. A basic definition of what we mean by recovery is necessary for an accurate understanding of our testimony.

1. The word "recover" means to obtain again something that has been lost, or to return something to a normal condition. "Recovery" means the restoration or return to a normal condition after a damage or a loss has been incurred. To say that God is recovering certain matters means that in the course of church history they have been lost, misused, or corrupted and that God is restoring them to their original state or condition.

2. Because the church has become degraded through the many centuries of its history, it needs to be restored according to God's original intention. Concerning the church, our vision is governed not by the present situation nor by traditional practice, but by God's original intention and by His unchanging standard as revealed in His Word. We regard the New Testament revelation of the church not merely as a historical antecedent, but as the norm for church practice in the present day.

3. God's recovery did not begin in the twentieth century. Although it is difficult to fix an exact date for its beginning, it is convenient to set it at the time of the Reformation. The recovery has gone through several stages since the Reformation, passing through the partial recovery of the church life in Bohemia under the leadership of Zinzendorf, moving on to the unveiling of the many precious Bible truths through the Plymouth Brethren, and then going on to the genuine experience of the inner life. Now it has reached its present stage with the establishment of genuine local churches as the expression of the Body of Christ.

4. In His recovery today the Lord is doing two things. He is recovering the experience of the riches of Christ—that is, the enjoyment of Christ as our life and our everything—and He is recovering the practice of the church life. These two matters go hand in hand, for the practical church life is the issue of the enjoyment of the riches of Christ. We in the Lord's recovery today testify that Christ is unsearchably rich, that He is the all-inclusive One for our enjoyment. Furthermore, we testify that the Lord has burdened us for the practice of the church life according to the revelation of the pure Word of God.

CONCERNING SALVATION

1. In Christ God has provided for man a full and complete salvation. This full salvation includes our whole being: spirit, soul, and body. In God's salvation, man's spirit is regenerated, his soul is being transformed, and his body will be transfigured.

2. In order to be saved, one must have a living faith in the Person and work of Jesus Christ, the Son of God. Every genuinely saved one has what the Bible calls the "common faith" (Titus 1:4), which includes what we must believe in order to be saved: we must believe that the Bible is the complete divine revelation wholly inspired by God; that there is a unique Triune God, the Father, the Son, and the Spirit; that Jesus Christ is the Son of God incarnated to be a man; that Christ died on the cross for our sins, shedding His blood for our redemption; that on the third day He was bodily raised from the dead; that He had been exalted to the right hand of God and made the Lord of all; and that He is coming again for His own and to set up His kingdom on earth.

3. Eternal salvation is by grace through faith, not by our works.

4. In order to be saved, one must have a living contact with Jesus Christ. Therefore, in bringing unbelievers to salvation, we emphasize prayer and calling on the name of the Lord. According to Romans 10:9 and 10, if a man is to be saved, he must believe in his heart and confess with his mouth.

5. Once a person has been saved, he may have both the assurance of salvation and the security of salvation. Once we are saved, we are saved forever.

CONCERNING THE CHRISTIAN LIFE

1. REGENERATION. The Christian life begins with regeneration. To be regenerated is to be born of the Spirit in our spirit (John 3:6) through the redemption of Christ and thereby to have the life and nature of God imparted into our spirit. This makes our spirit alive with the very life of God.

2. SEPARATION. The true Christian life requires a proper separation from this corrupt and evil world. This separation is not according to legalistic, man-made rules; it is according to the life and nature of the holy One who dwells within us. We are separated unto God by the redeeming blood of Christ, by the Holy Spirit, and in the name of the Lord Jesus. In order to live a proper Christian life, we must maintain such a separated position. Although we are not of the world, we nevertheless live a godly life in the world.

3. CONSECRATION. The Christian life is a life of consecration. To be consecrated to the Lord means that we are utterly given to the Lord, not to do something for Him nor to become something, but to make ourselves available to Him as a living sacrifice so that He may work on us and in us according to His good pleasure. We consecrate to the Lord because we love Him and delight to belong to Him. We also recognize that we already belong to Him because He has purchased us with His precious blood. We in the local churches are living not for

ourselves, but for God and for the fulfillment of His eternal purpose.

4. LOVING THE LORD. In our Christian life we emphasize loving the Lord. Above all else, God desires that we love Him. We testify that our Lord Jesus Christ is the altogether lovely One, that He has won our hearts, and that we love Him, not with a love of our own, but with the very love with which He first loved us.

5. THE WORD OF GOD. The Bible occupies a very important place in our Christian life. All those in the local churches are encouraged to read the Word in a regular way, even to read it through once a year. We read the Word, we study the Word, and we take the Word by prayer as spiritual food. All teachings, inspirations, and guidance which claim the Holy Spirit as their source must be checked by God's revelation in His Word. Although the Bible reveals the mind of God concerning so many matters, to us the Bible is not primarily a book of doctrine; instead, it is mainly a book of life. We come to the Word not merely for knowledge, but, through a prayerful reading of the Scripture, to contact the Lord Jesus, who is Himself the living Word.

6. PRAYER. The Christian life is also a life of prayer. In prayer we enjoy sweet, intimate personal communion with the Lord. By prayer we declare our dependence on God, our submission to Him, and our desire to cooperate with Him in the fulfillment of His purpose. All those in the local churches are encouraged to have a time of personal prayer every day.

7. THE EXPERIENCE OF CHRIST. We have seen from God's revelation in the Bible that the Christian life is actually Christ Himself living in us. For this reason, we lay great emphasis on the experience of Christ. According to the New Testament Epistles, Christ is revealed in us, is living in us, is being formed in us, is making His home in us, is being magnified in us, and is becoming all in all to us. Instead of imitating Christ according to an outward pattern, we seek to live out Christ and to live by Christ by allowing the indwelling Christ to occupy our whole inward being and to express Himself through us in our daily living.

8. A CRUCIFIED LIFE. As genuine Christians, we are to live a crucified life. We are not ashamed of the cross of Christ, and we do not shrink back from following the Lord along the narrow pathway of the cross. If we would truly experience Christ and live by Him, we need to experience daily the subjective work of the cross in our lives. We have seen something of the ugliness of man's fallen flesh in the eyes of God, and we agree with God's judgment upon it. Moreover, we have seen that both the self and the natural man are opposed to God. Therefore, we welcome the inward working of the death of Christ so that we may experience Christ and live by Him in the riches of His resurrection life.

9. NOURISHMENT. If we would live a normal Christian life, we need to be nourished daily with spiritual food and spiritual drink. For this reason, we emphasize the partaking of Christ as our spiritual food and drink. In the Spirit and through the Word, we enjoy Him as our life supply. As He Himself said, "He that eateth me, even he shall live by me" (John 6:57). The Lord is the living bread, the bread of life, and the bread of God who came down from heaven to give life to the world (John 6:33, 35, 51), and we are nourished by Him day by day.

10. THE GROWTH IN LIFE. In the local churches we emphasize the fact that in the Christian life we should grow normally in life. We are not content to remain spiritual infants. The divine life, like the human life, must have a normal development leading to maturity. Therefore, as seekers of the Lord, we pursue the growth in life. We desire to be a full-grown man to express the Lord, to represent Him with His authority, and to engage in spiritual warfare to defeat His enemy.

11. HUMAN LIVING. As Christians, we also live a normal human life, free from extremes and balanced in every way. We desire that our entire being, spirit, soul, and body, be maintained for the glory of God. We seek to express the humanity of Jesus in all our relationships and bear a worthy testimony of Him in all walks of human life: at home, at school, in our neighborhoods, and at our places of employment. To us, the Christian life cannot be divorced from our daily human life. We find that the more we grow in Christ, the more truly human we become, and the more we enjoy in a practical way the uplifted, transformed humanity of Jesus.

12. THE SPIRIT. The Christian life is a life of walking according to the Spirit. To walk in the Spirit is to have our living and our being according to the Spirit. Therefore, we need to set our mind on the Spirit and put to death the practices of the body (Rom. 8:6, 13). When we walk according to the Spirit, all the righteous requirements of God are fulfilled in us spontaneously. Only by living in the Spirit and walking according to the Spirit will the divine things revealed in the Scriptures become real to us. Hence, to be a normal Christian we must know the Spirit, live in the Spirit, and walk according to the Spirit.

13. TRANSFORMATION. Many Christians know of the regeneration of the spirit and the transfiguration of the body, but they neglect the crucial matter of the transformation of the soul. Nevertheless the Bible says, "Be ye transformed by the renewing of your mind" (Rom. 12:2). Therefore, we recognize the need to be dispositionally transformed in our souls by the inward working of the Spirit of life. As we are transformed, an inward change takes place in our very being. As our soul is permeated with the element of God, it is purified and sanctified. It can thereby fulfill its God-created function to express the Lord who dwells in our regenerated spirit. This transformation of the soul is intimately related to our

readiness to meet the Lord at His coming. Those who would dwell in His holy and glorious presence must not merely be positionally sanctified, but be dispositionally transformed. This transformation requires the operation of the cross negatively and the working of the Spirit of life positively.

14. TRANSFIGURATION. Finally, at the culmination of the Christian experience in life, our body will be transfigured and made like the Lord's glorious body (Phil. 3:21). In the Bible this is called the redemption of the body, the fullness of sonship. Therefore, the Christian life begins with regeneration, passes through transformation, and consummates with the transfiguration of the body.

CONCERNING THE CHURCH LIFE

1. A CORPORATE LIFE. By its very nature the Christian life, which is the living out of Christ as life from within us, is a corporate life. Many expressions in the New Testament confirm this: we are sheep in God's flock, we are living stones in God's building, we are branches in the vine, we are members of the Body of Christ. Although we remain individuals, as Christians we should no longer live individualistically, that is, caring only for our own interests, activities, and goals. On the contrary, God desires that we live a corporate life, conscious of the Body of Christ, mindful of the things of others, and concerned for the building up of the church. Therefore, we are experiencing a recovery not only of the normal Christian life, but also of the normal church life.

2. THE HEADSHIP OF CHRIST. In the church life we all need to honor the headship of Christ. We are the Body, and He is the unique Head of the Body. No one and nothing can presume to usurp Christ's headship. We cannot tolerate any system, organization, or leadership that insults the headship of Christ. Among us there is no permanent, official, organized leadership. Furthermore, there is no hierarchy. Rather, all the members of the Body are encouraged to have direct fellowship with the Head and receive from Him all directions concerning their life and movements. We recognize no subheads, no intermediaries between Christ and the members of His Body.

3. FELLOWSHIP. Even as we honor the headship of Christ, we also enjoy the fellowship of the Body of Christ. We recognize that, in Christ, we should no longer live in an individualistic way. On the contrary, we greatly value the fellowship among the members of the Body. How we enjoy the flow of life that circulates through the Body of Christ! We testify that this flow, this fellowship, is a blessed reality.

4. ONENESS. Another vital concern in the church life is the keeping of the oneness. Before He was crucified, the Lord prayed that those who believe in Him would be one even as He and the Father are one. Therefore, we must diligently maintain the unique oneness of the Body of Christ, which is expressed in local churches established on the ground of oneness with all believers in a locality. We must care for the oneness; therefore, we must repudiate all division and abhor it. What a shame and a reproach to the testimony of the Lord is the divisive state of today's Christians! In the church life, we stand for the unique oneness of Christ's Body. In order to maintain this oneness, we meet as believers on the ground of oneness, we receive all believers according to the common faith, and we seek to grow in Christ so that we may be with Him in the Father and in the Father's glory, where we are perfected into one. We believe that the Lord's prayer in John 17 will be answered on earth and that as we are perfected into one, the world will believe and know that the Father has sent the Son.

5. MUTUAL CARE FOR ONE ANOTHER. In the practice of the church life, we care for the saints, the believers in Christ, in a practical way. We delight to bear one another's burdens, to extend hospitality to visitors, to open our homes for fellowship, and to meet the practical needs of the brothers and sisters through loving service in the name of Christ. We encourage one another, refresh one another, minister Christ as life to one another, and build up one another. Our church life is not limited to meetings in our place of meeting; it goes on all the time.

6. THE CONSCIENCE. In the church life we also honor the conscience of others. This means that all the believers in Christ have the liberty to follow the Lord according to their conscience and in the light they have received from God through His Word. There is no external control molding and manipulating our daily lives, and there is no authoritarian disregard of our conscience. There is no coercion nor compulsion. Rather, all are encouraged to deal thoroughly with their conscience in the sight of God and to maintain a conscience void of offense toward God and toward man. Thus, we care for our conscience and for the conscience of others.

7. MEETINGS. Because the church life is a meeting life, we usually have meetings several times a week. To us, meetings are not a drudgery; they are an enjoyment. In the church meetings we are supplied, instructed, strengthened, encouraged, enlightened, inspired, equipped, built up, and commissioned by the Lord. In the proper church life there is a balance between the personal Christian life and the corporate meeting life. The personal time with the Lord cannot replace the meetings, and the meetings cannot replace the personal time. We delight to meet with Him individually, and we enjoy even more the meeting with Him corporately. We testify that in the church meetings the resurrected Christ truly is with us as we are gathered into His name.

8. THE FUNCTION OF ALL THE MEMBERS. In the church life every member of the Body can function. Although we do not all have the same function, we all have a function, and the function of every member is appreciated. We absolutely repudiate the clergy-laity system as a strategy of Satan to

THE BELIEFS AND PRACTICES (THE LOCAL
CHURCH) (continued)

frustrate the function of the members of the Body of
Christ. In the local churches we have no clergy and
we have no laity; rather, we are members of the
Body, all of whom have the right to function
according to their measure. Furthermore, we have
no pastor and no janitor. All the saints may share in
the meetings, and all may also partake of the
cleaning service.

Notes: *Of several groups growing out of the Plymouth
Brethren tradition, The Local Church alone has produced a
lengthy doctrinal statement, in part to refute charges that
the church was doctrinally unsound. The statement affirms
most of the traditional Christian beliefs in the authority of
scripture, the Trinity, the incarnation, the virgin birth, the
substitutionary atonement, and so on. It also systematically
details some of the church's peculiar beliefs such as its
ecclesiology, i.e., its doctrine of the church (from which its
name derives) and its idea of God's present work of recovery.*

Chapter 5
Adventist Family

Sunday Adventist

DECLARATION OF PRINCIPLES (ADVENT CHRISTIAN CHURCH)

I. We believe that the Bible is the inspired Word of God, being in its entirety a revelation given to man under Divine inspiration and providence; that its historic statements are correct, and that it is the only Divine and infallible standard of faith and practice. (*Romans 15:4; II Timothy 3:15, 16; John 17:17*)

II. We believe, as revealed in the Bible:

(a) In one God, our Father, eternal, and infinite in His wisdom, love and power, the Creator of all things, "in whom we live, and move, and have our being." (*Genesis 1:1; Isaiah 40:28; Matthew 6:6*)

(b) And in Jesus Christ, our Lord, the only begotten Son of God, conceived of the Holy Spirit, born of the Virgin Mary; who came into our world to seek and to save that which was lost; who died for our sins, who was raised bodily from the dead for our justification; who ascended into heaven as our High Priest and Mediator, and who will come again in the end of this age, to judge the living and the dead, and to reign forever and ever. (*I Timothy 3:16*)

(c) And in the Holy Spirit, the Comforter, sent from God to convince the world of sin, of righteousness and of judgment, whereby we are sanctified and sealed unto the day of redemption. (*John 14:16, 26; 16:7-11; Ephesians 1:13*)

III. We believe that man was created for immortality, but that through sin he forfeited his Divine birthright; that because of sin, death entered into the world, and passed upon all men; and that only through faith in Jesus Christ, the divinely ordained Life-giver, can men become "partakers of the divine nature," and live forever. (*II Timothy 1:10; Romans 2:7; I Corinthians 15:22, 51-54*)

IV. We believe that death is a condition of unconsciousness to all persons, righteous and wicked; a condition which will remain unchanged until the resurrection at Christ's second coming, at which time the righteous will receive everlasting life while the wicked will be "punished with everlasting destruction"; suffering complete *extinction of being*. (*Ecclesiastes 9:5; Job 14:14; John 5:28, 29; Matthew 10:28*)

V. We believe that salvation is free to all those who, in this life and in this age, accept it on the conditions imposed, which conditions are simple and inflexible; namely, turning from sin, repentance toward God, faith in the Lord Jesus Christ, and a life of consecration to the service of God; thus excluding all hope of a future probation, or of universal salvation. (*John 3:16; II Corinthians 6:2; Luke 13:25-28*)

VI. We believe that Jesus Christ, according to His promise, will come again to this earth, even "in like manner" as He went into heaven—personally, visibly and gloriously—to reign here forever; and that this coming is the hope of the Church, inasmuch as upon that coming depend the resurrection and the reward of the righteous, the abolition of sin and its consequences, and the renewal of the earth—now marred by sin—to become the eternal home of the redeemed, after which event the earth will be forever free from sin and death. (*Acts 1:11; I Thessalonians 4:16, 17; Revelation 22:12, 20*)

VII. We believe that Bible prophecy has indicated the approximate time of Christ's return; and comparing its testimony with the signs of our times, we are confident that He is near, "even at the doors," and we believe that the great duty of the hour is the proclamation of this soon-coming redemption, the defense of Bible authority, inspiration and truth, and the salvation of lost men. (*II Peter 1:19-21; Matthew 24:42-45; Revelation 22:17*)

VIII. We believe the Church of Christ is an institution of Divine origin, which includes all true Christians of whatever name; but that local church organizations should be independent of outside control, congregational in government, and subject to no dictation of priest, bishop or pope—although true fellowship and unity of action should exist between all such organizations. (*Matthew 16:18; Ephesians 5:25; Ephesians 4:15*)

IX. We believe that the only ordinances of the Church of Christ are Baptism and the Lord's Supper; immersion being the only true baptism. (*Matthew 28:19; Romans 6:3-5; I Corinthians 11:23-26*)

X. We believe that the first day of the week, as the day set apart by the early Church in commemoration of Christ's resurrection, should be observed as the Christian Sabbath, and used as a day of rest and religious worship. (*Psalms 118:22-24; Luke 24:1-12; I Corinthians 16:2*)

XI. We believe that war is contrary to the spirit and teachings of our Lord and Master, Jesus Christ; that it is contrary to the spirit of true brotherhood, and inimical to the welfare of humanity. We believe that Christ's followers are under obligation to use their influence against war; that they are justified in refusing to bear arms for conscience' sake in loyalty to their divine Master.

Notes: *Historically, Adventists have a relationship to the Baptists and their beliefs have followed a Baptist pattern. Baptism by immersion is practiced and affirmed in most statements. However, most statements lack clear affirmation of the doctrine of the Trinity.*

The declaration of the Advent Christian Church highlights distinguishing doctrines of the church: conditional immortality (item 3) and soul sleep (item 4). The doctrine of God (item 2) is so stated that both Trinitarian and non-Trinitarian views could be included. While affirming God the Father, Son, and Holy Spirit, neither the Trinity nor the personhood of the Holy Spirit are specifically mentioned. The church also continues the pacifism of the first generation of Adventists.

* * *

A SIMPLE STATEMENT OF FAITH [CHURCH OF GOD GENERAL CONFERENCE (ABRAHAMIC FAITH)]

This simplified Statement of Faith is included in the Constitution and By-Laws of the Church of God General Conference. While it is not a creed, it is a summary of the truths commonly believed and taught in the Church of God.

A. GOD. We believe that only one person is God, and that He is a literal (corporeal) being—almighty, eternal, immortal, and the Creator of all things. (Deut. 6:4; Isa. 45:18; 1 Tim. 2:5.)

B. JESUS CHRIST. We believe that Jesus Christ, born of the virgin Mary, is the sinless and only begotten Son of God. He did not personally pre-exist. (Luke 1:32, 33; 3:22; 1 Pet. 1:18, 19.)

C. THE HOLY SPIRIT. We believe that the Holy Spirit is not a person, but is God's divine power and influence manifest in God's mighty works and in the lives of His people. (Gen. 1:2; Rom. 8:1.)

D. THE BIBLE. We believe that the Bible is the Word of God, given by divine inspiration, and that it is the only authoritative source of doctrine and practice for Christians. (2 Tim. 2:15; Heb. 4:12; 2 Pet. 1:3.)

E. MAN. We believe that man was created innocent, but through disobedience to God fell under condemnation of death—the cessation of all life and consciousness. All men, being both sinful and mortal, are in need of salvation. (Gen. 2:7, 17; 3:4, 19; 5:5; Eccl. 9:4, 10; Rom. 3:9-11; 6:23.)

F. SALVATION. We believe that salvation is by the grace of God, through the atoning blood of Christ, and that it consists of God's forgiveness of sin, the imparting of His Spirit to the believer, and finally the gift of immortality at the resurrection when Christ returns. The steps in the gospel plan of salvation are:

1) Belief of the gospel of the Kingdom and the things concerning Jesus Christ (Acts 8:12; Rom. 1:16);

2) Sincere repentance for sin, which may be evidenced by confession and restitution (Acts 2:38);

3) Baptism—which is immersion—in the name of Jesus Christ for the remission of sins (Mark 16:15, 16; Rom. 6:1-6; Acts 22:16);

4) Growth in grace and in the knowledge of our Lord Jesus Christ (1 Pet. 2:1-3).

G. THE CHURCH OF GOD. We believe that the Church of God is the Scriptural name for that body of people who have been called out from among all nations through obedience to the gospel plan of salvation. Christ is the Head of the Church; and the nature, work, and government of the Church are set forth in the New Testament. (2 Cor. 1:1; Eph. 5:23-25.)

H. THE CHRISTIAN LIFE. We believe that the Christian life is primarily a life of consecrated discipleship to Jesus Christ as Lord, Saviour, and Teacher. It will be based on the standards which He taught and exemplified. Thus, it will be characterized by prayerful dependence on God, study of His Word, and faithful stewardship of time and possessions—with tithing as a practical expression of such stewardship. The Church of God will recognize those members who, because of their religious convictions, claim exemption from military service. (1 Tim. 4:11-16; Titus 2:11-14; Mal. 3:10.)

I. ISRAEL. We believe that "Israel" is the name of the literal descendants of Abraham through Jacob. As God's chosen nation, Israel was given the land of Palestine, but because of disobedience they were scattered throughout the world. In accordance with God's covenant with them, they will be restored to Palestine as the head of the nations in the Kingdom of God. (Ezek. 36:21-32.)

J. THE KINGDOM OF GOD. We believe that the Kingdom of God will be established on earth when Christ returns personally and visibly to reign as King in Jerusalem over the whole earth, with the Church as joint-heirs with Him. His Millennial reign will be followed by the final judgment and destruction of the wicked, after which will be established "New Heavens and a New Earth" wherein there will be no more death and God will be all in all. (Acts 1:11; 1 Thess. 4:16, 17; Rev. 5:9, 10; 20:4, 5; 21:1-4, 7, 8; 2 Pet. 2:12-14.)

Notes: *The Church of God General Conference specifically denies the Trinity (in its affirmation of one God), the preexistence of Jesus Christ, and the personhood of the Holy Spirit.*

*   *   *

DECLARATION OF FAITH (PRIMITIVE ADVENT CHRISTIAN CHURCH)

SECTION ONE

We believe in God, the Father Almighty, creator of heaven and earth, and in His Son, the Lord Jesus Christ, our Saviour from sin and death, and in the Holy Spirit our ever present sanctifier, comforter and guide.

SECTION TWO

We believe the Bible is the inspired Word of God, containing a revelation given to man by Divine inspiration, that its historic statements are true, that it is the only Divine standard of faith and practice.

SECTION THREE

We believe the teachings of our Lord Jesus Christ and his holy apostles are a full and sufficient statement of the duties and the faith of the church, and we reject all modern visions and revelations, so-called.

SECTION FOUR

We believe in conditional immortality. That man was created for immortality, but through sin he forfeited his divine birthright; that because of sin death entered into the world and was passed upon all men, and that only through faith in the Lord Jesus Christ can man become "partakers of the divine nature" and live forever. See Matt. 25:46, John 3:16, Rom. 6:23, 11:5-9, 1st Tim. 6:14.

SECTION FIVE

We believe that Jesus Christ died for our sins, that he was buried, that he arose from the dead the third day immortal; that he ascended bodily from earth to heaven, where he sitteth at the right hand of God the Father, there to make intercession for us; and from thence he shall come again personally to judge the living and the dead, and to establish his everlasting kingdom under the whole heavens, that his glorious coming is near and is daily to be watched for.

SECTION SIX

We believe that death is a condition of unconsciousness to all persons, righteous or wicked: a condition which will remain unchanged until the resurrection at the coming of Christ, at which time the righteous will receive everlasting life and the wicked will be punished with everlasting destruction, suffering extinction of being.

SECTION SEVEN

We believe in a change of heart at conversion. That salvation is free to all who in this life accept it on the conditions imposed, namely, repentance toward God, and faith in Jesus Christ with a life of consecration to the service of God; thus excluding all hope of a universal salvation or future probation. Acts 2:38, 3:19, 16:31, Hebrews 12:14.

SECTION EIGHT

We believe in the second coming of Jesus Christ, personally, visibly, and gloriously, to reign forever. At which time the dead will be raised, the world judged in righteousness, sin and its consequences abolished, and the everlasting kingdom, the eternal home of the redeemed set up on the new earth forever free from sin and death. That the earth made new will be inhabited by the righteous forever, and their reward will be eternal life with glory, honor, peace and fullness of joy forever.

SECTION NINE

We believe that the second coming of Christ will be the day of final judgment to all men, both saint and sinner. That all men will receive their final reward at that day, according as their works have been.

SECTION TEN

We believe the Bible sets forth three ordinances to be observed by the Christian Church, namely:

1. Baptism by immersion.

2. The Lord's Supper, by partaking of unleavened bread and wine.

3. Feet washing, to be observed by the saints washing one anothers feet.

We further believe that there is no substitute set forth in the scriptures to take the place of either of the above named ordinances.

SECTION ELEVEN

We believe that backsliders lose their covenant favor with God and that before they can be renewed in his favor they must again do the first works, including repentance toward God, faith in the Lord Jesus Christ and baptism.

SECTION TWELVE

We do not believe in opposing other denominations, but we believe in fighting the good fight of faith in Christian fellowship, love, peace and unity in the spirit of God.

Notes: *This statement is derived from that of the Advent Christian Church. The section on pacifism has been dropped, and a statement on foot washing as an ordinance has been added.*

Seventh-Day Adventist

FUNDAMENTAL BELIEFS (SEVENTH-DAY ADVENTIST CHURCH)

Seventh-day Adventists accept the Bible as their only creed and hold certain fundamental beliefs to be the teaching of the Holy Scriptures. These beliefs, as set forth here, constitute the church's understanding and expression of the teaching of Scripture. Revision of these statements may be expected at a General Conference session when the church is led by the Holy Spirit to a fuller understanding of Bible truth or finds better language in which to express the teachings of God's Holy Word.

1. THE HOLY SCRIPTURES

The Holy Scriptures, Old and New Testaments, are the written Word of God, given by divine inspiration through holy men of God who spoke and wrote as they were moved by the Holy Spirit. In this Word, God has committed to man the knowledge necessary for salvation. The Holy Scriptures are the infallible revelation of His will. They are the standard of character, the test of experience, the authoritative revealer of doctrines, and the trustworthy record of God's acts in history. (2 Peter 1:20, 21; 2 Tim. 3:16, 17; Ps. 119:105; Prov. 30:5, 6; Isa. 8:20; John 17:17; 1 Thess. 2:13; Heb. 4:12.)

2. THE TRINITY

There is one God: Father, Son, and Holy Spirit, a unity of three co-eternal Persons. God is immortal, all-powerful, all-knowing, above all, and ever present. He is infinite and beyond human comprehension, yet known through His self-revelation. He is forever worthy of worship, adoration, and service by the whole creation. (Deut. 6:4; Matt. 28:19; 2 Cor. 13:14; Eph. 4:4-6; 1 Peter 1:2; 1 Tim. 1:17; Rev. 14:7.)

3. THE FATHER

God the eternal Father is the Creator, Source, Sustainer, and Sovereign of all creation. He is just and holy, merciful and gracious, slow to anger, and abounding in steadfast love and faithfulness. The qualities and powers exhibited in the Son and the Holy Spirit are also revelations of the Father. (Gen. 1:1; Rev. 4:11; 1 Cor. 15:28; John 3:16; 1 John 4:8; 1 Tim. 1:17; Ex. 34:6, 7; John 14:9.)

4. THE SON

God the eternal Son became incarnate in Jesus Christ. Through Him all things were created, the character of God is revealed, the salvation of humanity is accomplished, and the world is judged. Forever truly God, He became also truly man, Jesus the Christ. He was conceived of the Holy Spirit and born of the virgin Mary. He lived and experienced temptation as a human being, but perfectly exemplified the righteousness and love of God. By His miracles He manifested God's power and was attested as God's promised Messiah. He suffered and died voluntarily on the cross for our sins and in our place, was raised from the dead, and ascended to minister in the heavenly sanctuary in our behalf. He will come again in glory for the final deliverance of His people and the restoration of all things. (John 1:1-3, 14; Col. 1:15-19; John 10:30; 14:9; Rom. 6:23; 2 Cor. 5:17-19; John 5:22; Luke 1:35; Phil. 2:5-11; Heb. 2:9-18; 1 Cor. 15:3, 4; Heb. 8:1, 2; John 14:1-3.)

5. THE HOLY SPIRIT

God the eternal Spirit was active with the Father and the Son in Creation, incarnation, and redemption. He inspired the writers of Scripture. He filled Christ's life with power. He draws and convicts human beings; and those who respond He renews and transforms into the image of God. Sent by the Father and the Son to be always with His children, He extends spiritual gifts to the church, empowers it to bear witness to Christ, and in harmony with the Scriptures leads it into all truth. (Gen. 1:1, 2; Luke 1:35; 4:18; Acts 10:38; 2 Peter 1:21; 2 Cor. 3:18; Eph. 4:11, 12; Acts 1:8; John 14:16-18, 26; 15:26, 27; 16:7-13.)

6. CREATION

God is Creator of all things, and has revealed in Scripture the authentic account of His creative activity. In six days the Lord made "the heaven and the earth" and all living things upon the earth, and rested on the seventh day of that first week. Thus He established the Sabbath as a perpetual memorial of His completed creative work. The first man and woman were made in the image of God as the crowning work of Creation, given dominion over the world, and charged with responsibility to care for it. When the world was finished it was "very good," declaring the glory of God. (Gen. 1; 2; Ex. 20:8-11; Ps. 19:1-6; 33:6, 9; 104; Heb. 11:3.)

7. THE NATURE OF MAN

Man and woman were made in the image of God with individuality, the power and freedom to think and to do. Though created free beings, each is an indivisible unity of body, mind, and soul, dependent upon God for life and breath and all else. When our first parents disobeyed God, they denied their dependence upon Him and fell from their high position under God. The image of God in them was marred and they became subject to death. Their descendants share this fallen nature and its consequences. They are born with weaknesses and tendencies to evil. But God in Christ reconciled the world to Himself and by His Spirit restores in penitent mortals the image of their Maker. Created for the glory of God, they are called to love Him and one another, and to care for their environment. (Gen. 1:26-28; 2:7; Ps. 8:4-8; Acts 17:24-28; Gen. 3; Ps. 51:5; Rom. 5:12-17; 2 Cor. 5:19, 20; Ps. 51:10; 1 John 4:7, 8, 11, 20; Gen. 2:15.)

8. THE GREAT CONTROVERSY

All humanity is now involved in a great controversy between Christ and Satan regarding the character of God, His law, and His sovereignty over the universe. This conflict originated in heaven when a created being, endowed with freedom of choice, in self-exaltation became Satan, God's adversary, and led into rebellion a portion of the angels. He introduced the spirit of rebellion into this world when he led Adam and Eve into sin. This human sin resulted in the distortion of the image of God in humanity, the disordering of the created world, and its eventual devastation at the time of the worldwide flood. Observed by the whole creation, this world became the arena of the universal conflict, out of which the God of love will ultimately be vindicated. To assist His people in this controversy, Christ sends the Holy Spirit and the loyal angels to guide, protect, and sustain them in the way of salvation. (Rev. 12:4-9; Isa. 14:12-14; Eze. 28:12-18; Gen. 3; Rom. 1:19-32; 5:12-21; 8:19-22; Gen. 6-8; 2 Peter 3:6; 1 Cor. 4:9; Heb. 1:14.)

9. THE LIFE, DEATH, AND RESURRECTION OF CHRIST

In Christ's life of perfect obedience to God's will, His suffering, death, and resurrection, God provided the only means of atonement for human sin, so that those who by faith accept this atonement may have eternal life, and the whole creation may better understand the infinite and holy love of the Creator. This perfect atonement vindicates the righteousness of God's law and the graciousness of His character; for it both condemns our sin and provides for our forgiveness. The death of Christ is substitutionary and expiatory, reconciling and transforming. The resurrection of Christ proclaims God's triumph over the forces of evil, and for those who accept the atonement assures their final victory over sin and death. It declares the Lordship of Jesus Christ, before whom every knee in heaven and on earth will bow. (John 3:16; Isa. 53; 1 Peter 2:21, 22; 1 Cor. 15:3, 4, 20-22; 2 Cor. 5:14, 15, 19-21; Rom. 1:4; 3:25; 4:25; 8:3, 4; 1 John 2:2; 4:10; Col. 2:15; Phil. 2:6-11.)

10. THE EXPERIENCE OF SALVATION

In infinite love and mercy God made Christ, who knew no sin, to be sin for us, so that in Him we might be made the righteousness of God. Led by the Holy Spirit we sense our need, acknowledge our sinfulness, repent of our transgressions, and exercise faith in Jesus as Lord and Christ, as Substitute and Example. This faith which receives salvation comes through the divine power of the Word and is the gift of God's grace. Through Christ we are justified, adopted as God's sons and daughters, and delivered from the lordship of sin. Through the Spirit we are born again and sanctified; the Spirit renews our minds, writes God's law of love in our hearts, and we are given the power to live a holy life. Abiding in Him we become partakers of the divine nature and have the assurance of salvation now and in the judgment. (2 Cor. 5:17-21; John 3:16; Gal. 1:4; 4:4-7; Titus 3:3-7; John 16:8; Gal. 3:13, 14; 1 Peter 2:21, 22; Rom. 10:17; Luke 17:5; Mark 9:23, 24; Eph. 2:5-10; Rom. 3:21-26; Col. 1:13, 14; Rom. 8:14-17; Gal. 3:26; John 3:3-8; 1 Peter 1:23; Rom. 12:2; Heb. 8:7-12; Eze. 36:25-27; 2 Peter 1:3, 4; Rom. 8:1-4; 5:6-10.)

11. THE CHURCH

The church is the community of believers who confess Jesus Christ as Lord and Saviour. In continuity with the people of God in Old Testament times, we are called out from the world; and we join together for worship, for fellowship, for instruction in the Word, for the celebration of the Lord's Supper, for service to all mankind, and for the worldwide proclamation of the gospel. The church derives its authority from Christ, who is the incarnate Word, and from the Scriptures, which are the written Word. The church is God's family; adopted by Him as children, its members live on the basis of the new

covenant. The church is the body of Christ, a community of faith of which Christ Himself is the Head. The church is the bride for whom Christ died that He might sanctify and cleanse her. At His return in triumph, He will present her to Himself a glorious church, the faithful of all the ages, the purchase of His blood, not having spot or wrinkle, but holy and without blemish. (Gen. 12:3; Acts 7:38; Eph. 4:11-15; 3:8-11; Matt. 28:19, 20; 16:13-20; 18:18; Eph. 2:19-22; 1:22, 23; 5:23-27; Col. 1:17, 18.)

12. THE REMNANT AND ITS MISSION

The universal church is composed of all who truly believe in Christ, but in the last days, a time of widespread apostasy, a remnant has been called out to keep the commandments of God and the faith of Jesus. This remnant announces the arrival of the judgment hour, proclaims salvation through Christ, and heralds the approach of His second advent. This proclamation is symbolized by the three angels of Revelation 14; it coincides with the work of judgment in heaven and results in a work of repentance and reform on earth. Every believer is called to have a personal part in this worldwide witness. (Rev. 12:17; 14:6-12; 18:1-4; 2 Cor. 5:10; Jude 3, 14; 1 Peter 1:16-19; 2 Peter 3:10-14; Rev. 21:1-14.)

13. UNITY IN THE BODY OF CHRIST

The church is one body with many members, called from every nation, kindred, tongue, and people. In Christ we are a new creation: distinctions of race, culture, learning, and nationality, and differences between high and low, rich and poor, male and female, must not be divisive among us. We are all equal in Christ, who by one Spirit has bonded us into one fellowship with Him and with one another; we are to serve and be served without partiality or reservation. Through the revelation of Jesus Christ in the Scriptures we share the same faith and hope, and reach out in one witness to all. This unity has its source in the oneness of the triune God, who has adopted us as His children. (Rom. 12:4, 5; 1 Cor. 12:12-14; Matt. 28:19, 20; Ps. 133:1; 2 Cor. 5:16, 17; Acts 17:26, 27; Gal. 3:27, 29; Col. 3:10-15; Eph. 4:14-16; 4:1-6; John 17:20-23.)

14. BAPTISM

By baptism we confess our faith in the death and resurrection of Jesus Christ, and testify of our death to sin and of our purpose to walk in newness of life. Thus we acknowledge Christ as Lord and Saviour, become His people, and are received as members by His church. Baptism is a symbol of our union with Christ, the forgiveness of our sins, and our reception of the Holy Spirit. It is by immersion in water and is contingent on an affirmation of faith in Jesus and evidence of repentance of sin. It follows instruction in the Holy Scriptures and acceptance of their teachings. (Rom. 6:1-6; Col. 2:12, 13; Acts 16:30-33; 22:16; 2:38; Matt. 28:19, 20.)

15. THE LORD'S SUPPER

The Lord's Supper is a participation in the emblems of the body and blood of Jesus as an expression of faith in Him, our Lord and Saviour. In this experience of communion Christ is present to meet and strengthen His people. As we partake, we joyfully proclaim the Lord's death until He comes again. Preparation for the Supper includes self-

FUNDAMENTAL BELIEFS (SEVENTH-DAY ADVENTIST
CHURCH) (continued)

examination, repentance, and confession. The Master
ordained the service of foot washing to signify renewed
cleansing, to express a willingness to serve one another in
Christlike humility, and to unite our hearts in love. The
communion service is open to all believing Christians. (1
Cor. 10:16, 17; 11:23-30; Matt. 26:17-30; Rev. 3:20; John
6:48-63; 13:1-17.)

16. SPIRITUAL GIFTS AND MINISTRIES

God bestows upon all members of His church in every age
spiritual gifts which each member is to employ in loving
ministry for the common good of the church and of
humanity. Given by the agency of the Holy Spirit, who
apportions to each member as He wills, the gifts provide
all abilities and ministries needed by the church to fulfill
its divinely ordained functions. According to the Scriptures, these gifts include such ministries as faith, healing,
prophecy, proclamation, teaching, administration, reconciliation, compassion, and self-sacrificing service and
charity for the help and encouragement of people. Some
members are called of God and endowed by the Spirit for
functions recognized by the church in pastoral, evangelistic, apostolic, and teaching ministries particularly needed
to equip the members for service, to build up the church to
spiritual maturity, and to foster unity of the faith and
knowledge of God. When members employ these spiritual
gifts as faithful stewards of God's varied grace, the church
is protected from the destructive influence of false doctrine, grows with a growth that is from God, and is built
up in faith and love. (Rom. 12:4-8; 1 Cor. 12:9-11, 27, 28;
Eph. 4:8, 11-16; Acts 6:1-7; 1 Tim. 2:1-3; 1 Peter 4:10, 11.)

17. THE GIFT OF PROPHECY

One of the gifts of the Holy Spirit is prophecy. This gift is
an identifying mark of the remnant church and was
manifested in the ministry of Ellen G. White. As the
Lord's messenger, her writings are a continuing and
authoritative source of truth which provide for the church
comfort, guidance, instruction, and correction. They also
make clear that the Bible is the standard by which all
teaching and experience must be tested. (Joel 2:28, 29;
Acts 2:14-21; Heb. 1:1-3; Rev. 12:17; 19:10.)

18. THE LAW OF GOD

The great principles of God's law are embodied in the Ten
Commandments and exemplified in the life of Christ. They
express God's love, will, and purposes concerning human
conduct and relationships and are binding upon all people
in every age. These precepts are the basis of God's
covenant with His people and the standard in God's
judgment. Through the agency of the Holy Spirit they
point out sin and awaken a sense of need for a Saviour.
Salvation is all of grace and not of works, but its fruitage is
obedience to the Commandments. This obedience develops
Christian character and results in a sense of well-being. It
is an evidence of our love for the Lord and our concern for
our fellow men. The obedience of faith demonstrates the
power of Christ to transform lives, and therefore strengthens Christian witness. (Ex. 20:1-17; Ps. 40:7, 8; Matt.

22:36-40; Deut. 28:1-14; Matt. 5:17-20; Heb. 8:8-10; John
16:7-10; Eph. 2:8-10; 1 John 5:3; Rom. 8:3, 4; Ps. 19:7-14.)

19. THE SABBATH

The beneficent Creator, after the six days of Creation,
rested on the seventh day and instituted the Sabbath for all
people as a memorial of Creation. The fourth commandment of God's unchangeable law requires the observance
of this seventh-day Sabbath as the day of rest, worship,
and ministry in harmony with the teaching and practice of
Jesus, the Lord of the Sabbath. The Sabbath is a day of
delightful communion with God and one another. It is a
symbol of our redemption in Christ, a sign of our
sanctification, a token of our allegiance, and a foretaste of
our eternal future in God's kingdom. The Sabbath is God's
perpetual sign of His eternal covenant between Him and
His people. Joyful observance of his holy time from
evening to evening, sunset to sunset, is a celebration of
God's creative and redemptive acts. (Gen. 2:1-3; Ex. 20:8-
11; Luke 4:16; Isa. 56:5, 6; 58:13, 14; Matt. 12:1-12; Ex.
31:13-17; Eze. 20:12, 20; Deut. 5:12-15; Heb. 4:1-11; Lev.
23:32; Mark 1:32.)

20. STEWARDSHIP

We are God's stewards, entrusted by Him with time and
opportunities, abilities and possessions, and the blessings
of the earth and its resources. We are responsible to Him
for their proper use. We acknowledge God's ownership by
faithful service to Him and our fellow men, and by
returning tithes and giving offerings for the proclamation
of His gospel and the support and growth of His church.
Stewardship is a privilege given to us by God for nurture
in love and the victory over selfishness and covetousness.
The steward rejoices in the blessings that come to others as
a result of his faithfulness. (Gen. 1:26-28; 2:15; 1 Chron.
29:14; Haggai 1:3-11; Mal. 3:8-12; 1 Cor. 9:9-14; Matt.
23:23; Rom. 15:26, 27.)

21. CHRISTIAN BEHAVIOR

We are called to be a godly people who think, feel, and act
in harmony with the principles of heaven. For the Spirit to
recreate in us the character of our Lord we involve
ourselves only in those things which will produce Christ-
like purity, health, and joy in our lives. This means that
our amusement and entertainment should meet the highest
standards of Christian taste and beauty. While recognizing
cultural differences, our dress is to be simple, modest, and
neat, befitting those whose true beauty does not consist of
outward adornment but in the imperishable ornament of a
gentle and quiet spirit. It also means that because our
bodies are the temples of the Holy Spirit, we are to care for
them intelligently. Along with adequate exercise and rest,
we are to adopt the most healthful diet possible and
abstain from the unclean foods identified in the Scriptures.
Since alcoholic beverages, tobacco, and the irresponsible
use of drugs and narcotics are harmful to our bodies, we
are to abstain from them as well. Instead, we are to engage
in whatever brings our thoughts and bodies into the
discipline of Christ, who desires our wholesomeness, joy,
and goodness. (Rom. 12:1, 2; 1 John 2:6; Eph. 5:1-21; Phil.
4:8; 2 Cor. 10:5; 6:14-7:1; 1 Peter 3:1-4; 1 Cor. 6:19, 20;
10:31; Lev. 11:1-47; 3 John 2.)

22. MARRIAGE AND THE FAMILY

Marriage was divinely established in Eden and affirmed by Jesus to be a lifelong union between a man and a woman in loving companionship. For the Christian a marriage commitment is to God as well as to the spouse, and should be entered into only between partners who share a common faith. Mutual love, honor, respect, and responsibility are the fabric of this relationship, which is to reflect the love, sanctity, closeness, and permanence of the relationship between Christ and His church. Regarding divorce, Jesus taught that the person who divorces a spouse, except for fornication, and marries another, commits adultery. Although some family relationships may fall short of the ideal, marriage partners who fully commit themselves to each other in Christ may achieve loving unity through the guidance of the Spirit and the nurture of the church. God blesses the family and intends that its members shall assist each other toward complete maturity. Parents are to bring up their children to love and obey the Lord. By their example and their words they are to teach them that Christ is a loving disciplinarian, ever tender and caring, who wants them to become members of His body, the family of God. Increasing family closeness is one of the earmarks of the final gospel message. (Gen. 2:18-25; Matt. 19:3-9; John 2:1-11; 2 Cor. 6:14; Eph. 5:21-33; Matt. 5:31, 32; Mark 10:11, 12; Luke 16:18; 1 Cor. 7:10, 11; Ex. 20:12; Eph. 6:1-4; Deut. 6:5-9; Prov. 22:6; Mal. 4:5, 6.)

23. CHRIST'S MINISTRY IN THE HEAVENLY SANCTUARY

There is a sanctuary in heaven, the true tabernacle which the Lord set up and not man. In it Christ ministers on our behalf, making available to believers the benefits of His atoning sacrifice offered once for all on the cross. He was inaugurated as our great High Priest and began His intercessory ministry at the time of His ascension. In 1844, at the end of the prophetic period of 2300 days, He entered the second and last phase of His atoning ministry. It is a work of investigative judgment which is part of the ultimate disposition of all sin, typified by the cleansing of the ancient Hebrew sanctuary on the Day of Atonement. In that typical service the sanctuary was cleansed with the blood of animal sacrifices, but the heavenly things are purified with the perfect sacrifice of the blood of Jesus. The investigative judgment reveals to heavenly intelligences who among the dead are asleep in Christ and therefore, in Him, are deemed worthy to have part in the first resurrection. It also makes manifest who among the living are abiding in Christ, keeping the commandments of God and the faith of Jesus, and in Him, therefore, are ready for translation into His everlasting kingdom. This judgment vindicates the justice of God in saving those who believe in Jesus. It declares that those who have remained loyal to God shall receive the kingdom. The completion of this ministry of Christ will mark the close of human probation before the Second Advent. (Heb. 8:1-5; 4:14-16; 9:11-28; 10:19-22; 1:3; 2:16, 17; Dan. 7:9-27; 8:13, 14; 9:24-27; Num. 14:34; Eze. 4:6; Lev. 16; Rev. 14:6, 7; 20:12; 14:12; 22:12.)

24. THE SECOND COMING OF CHRIST

The second coming of Christ is the blessed hope of the church, the grand climax of the gospel. The Saviour's coming will be literal, personal, visible, and worldwide. When He returns, the righteous dead will be resurrected, and together with the righteous living will be glorified and taken to heaven, but the unrighteous will die. The almost complete fulfillment of most lines of prophecy, together with the present condition of the world, indicates that Christ's coming is imminent. The time of that event has not been revealed, and we are therefore exhorted to be ready at all times. (Titus 2:13; Heb. 9:28; John 14:1-3; Acts 1:9-11; Matt. 24:14; Rev. 1:7; Matt. 26:43, 44; 1 Thess. 4:13-18; 1 Cor. 15:51-54; 2 Thess. 1:7-10; 2:8; Rev. 14:14-20; 19:11-21; Matt. 24; Mark 13; Luke 21; 2 Tim. 3:1-5; 1 Thess. 5:1-6.)

25. DEATH AND RESURRECTION

The wages of sin is death. But God, who alone is immortal, will grant eternal life to His redeemed. Until that day death is an unconscious state for all people. When Christ, who is our life, appears, the resurrected righteous and the living righteous will be glorified and caught up to meet their Lord. The second resurrection, the resurrection of the unrighteous, will take place a thousand years later. (Rom. 6:23; 1 Tim. 6:15, 16; Eccl. 9:5, 6; Ps. 146:3, 4; John 11:11-14; Col. 3:4; 1 Cor. 15:51-54; 1 Thess. 4:13-17; John 5:28, 29; Rev. 20:1-10.)

26. THE MILLENNIUM AND THE END OF SIN

The millennium is the thousand-year reign of Christ with His saints in heaven between the first and second resurrections. During this time the wicked dead will be judged; the earth will be utterly desolate, without living human inhabitants, but occupied by Satan and his angels. At its close Christ with His saints and the Holy City will descend from heaven to earth. The unrighteous dead will then be resurrected, and with Satan and his angels will surround the city; but fire from God will consume them and cleanse the earth. The universe will thus be freed of sin and sinners forever. (Rev. 20; 1 Cor. 6:2, 3; Jer. 4:23-26; Rev. 21:1-5; Mal. 4:1; Eze. 28:18, 19.)

27. THE NEW EARTH

On the new earth, in which righteousness dwells, God will provide an eternal home for the redeemed and a perfect environment for everlasting life, love, joy, and learning in His presence. For here God Himself will dwell with His people, and suffering and death will have passed away. The great controversy will be ended, and sin will be no more. All things, animate and inanimate, will declare that God is love; and He shall reign forever. Amen. (2 Peter 3:13; Isa. 35; 65:17-25; Matt. 5:5; Rev. 21:1-7; 22:1-5; 11:15.)

Notes: *The Seventh-Day Adventist Church is Trinitarian in belief. Besides its sabbatarianism, it is distinguished most by its particular beliefs concerning spiritual gifts and the prophetic ministry of founder Ellen G. White (items 16 and 17). A number of the items in this statement concern eschatology.*

BELIEFS (SEVENTH-DAY ADVENTIST REFORM MOVEMENT)

"In the mouth of two or three witnesses shall every word be established." *2 Corinthians 13:1.*

1. There is an intelligent Supreme Being called God, whose activities are visible throughout nature. He created the universe, this earth, and every living organism. *Acts 17:23-28; Genesis 1:1; Colossians 1:16.*

2. Jesus Christ is His Son who existed in heaven before being born on earth. Together with His Father He created this world. *John 20:31; 17:5; 1:1-3, 14.*

3. The Holy Spirit is the third person in the divine family. *1 John 5:5, 6; John 16:7, 8, 13.*

4. God's will for man was recorded by select men who were inspired by the Holy Spirit. Those writings were gathered into one volume called "The Bible." *2 Peter 1:21; 2 Timothy 3:16, 17.*

5. God created human beings to be happy, content, and immortal. *Proverbs 8:30, 31; Genesis 1:29; 2:9.*

6. The whole universe, including our world and its creatures, is controlled by divine laws. *Job 38, 39.*

7. There is clear evidence of other, invisible beings, called angels, who were created before man. *1 Corinthians 15:39, 40; Job 38:4, 7; Genesis 3:24.*

8. One of the angels, called Lucifer, or Satan, perverted his liberty and began to counterwork and disrupt the existing harmony. For this reason he was cast out of heaven. *Isaiah 14:12-17; Ezekiel 28:12-19; Luke 10:18; Revelation 12:9.*

9. He confused and deceived the first human pair into trying a new experience by stepping outside God's order into forbidden territory. *Genesis 3.*

10. Trespassing against God's law is called "sin." Man's nature became sinful and degenerated through continued sinful practices. *1 John 3:4; Ephesians 2:3; Psalm 51:5.*

11. God's character is love, as seen in the beauty of nature. *1 John 4:8, 16; Philippians 4:7-9.*

12. He is the source of all higher intelligence. With His Son He devised a plan to counteract the degeneration of transgression by creating a unique plan for restoration, called "The Plan of Redemption." *Colossians 2:2, 3; Matthew 20:28; 1 Timothy 2:5, 6.*

13. The sure result of transgression and sin is eternal death unless the redemption of Christ is accepted. *Romans 6:23; 5:12; Colossians 1:13, 14; John 3:16.*

14. So that justice may be carried out, God requires the life of very sinner, which means the shedding of his blood. *Ezekiel 18:19, 20; Hebrews 9:22; Exodus 12:13.*

15. The Plan of Redemption provided for Christ to become the sinner's substitute, paying for our guilt with His own blood. *Hebrews 2:9; Romans 5:6, 8; Hebrews 9:11, 12.*

16. The sinner must accept this substitute ransom payment by faith in order to receive forgiveness. *Romans 3:22-25, 28, 31; Isaiah 1:18.*

17. The sinner must accept Christ as his personal Saviour and Redeemer. *John 20:31; 3:15, 16, 36.*

18. The Holy Spirit convinces the sinner that all things earthly are transitory and not worth living for. His outlook on life will be drawn to eternal subjects, and his affections and longings will completely change. This is the experience of the "new birth," or "conversion." *James 4:14; Ecclesiastes 2:11; Psalm 144:3, 4; John 3:3-8.*

19. This change of heart is attested to publicly by being baptized by immersion, representing the death of the old man and the birth of the new. *Romans 6:3-11; 1 Peter 3:21.*

20. In the Old Testament, animals that were slain for the guilty sinner symbolized Christ, the true Sin Bearer and sacrificial Lamb. *Exodus 12:5, 6, 13; Hebrews 8:5; John 1:29.*

21. When Christ died, the symbolic laws connected with the temple service ended. *Matthew 27:51; Colossians 2:14-17.*

22. Christ's blood does not cover premeditated, willful sins but only weakness and ignorance. *Hebrews 10:26, 27; 4:15; Acts 17:30.*

23. Salvation cannot be earned by good works, for man is saved by unmerited grace alone. *Romans 3:24; Ephesians 2:8; Romans 9:16.*

24. God's law consisting of ten commandments checks human behavior, shows sins when committed, and therefore must be obeyed. *Matthew 19:17-19; Romans 7:7, 8; Matthew 5:19.*

25. Obedience to God's law, motivated by love, shows that the person's faith is genuine. *1 John 5:2, 3; James 2:14, 18, 24, 26.*

26. God rested on the seventh day of the creation week and commanded mankind to rest also. This obedience shows that we recognize and worship Him as our Creator. The Lord's day is not the pagan day of sun worship, Sunday, but the seventh day of the week, Saturday. *Genesis 2:1-3; Exodus 20:8-11; Romans 1:25; Mark 2:28.*

27. This lifespan is an education for the afterlife. The change in a Christian's life is effected by the working of the Holy Spirit. A new, divine nature eventually replaces the old, sinful nature. This is called sanctification. At death, all opportunities for perfecting character cease. *Colossians 3:1-3; 2 Peter 1:4-8; 1 Thessalonians 4:3; Hebrews 9:27.*

28. Death is an unconscious sleep of body and soul, but it will not last forever. Through a miraculous resurrection, human beings will one day become alive again. *Ecclesiastes 9:5, 6; John 5:25-29.*

29. Those who accepted Christ as their Saviour before they died will be raised at His second coming to receive a new body that will never die. *1 Thessalonians 4:16; 1 Corinthians 15:53, 54.*

30. Christ's second coming is imminent and will be an actual happening visible to all people on earth. *Matthew 24:42; Acts 1:10, 11; Revelation 1:7.*

31. In Noah and Lot's times all unbelievers were destroyed by physical elements (water and fire). Likewise, in the last days literal fire will destroy the wicked, making this earth a desolate wilderness. *2 Peter 3:5-7; 2:4-6; Malachi 4:1; Joel 2:3.*

32. The destruction of the unbelievers will bind Satan for a thousand years, because he will have no one to deceive, for all people are then dead. *Revelation 20:1, 2; 2 Peter 2:4.*

33. During the 1,000 years (millennium), judgment is held in heaven to determine the degree of the unbelievers' guilt. *Revelation 20:4, 12; 1 Corinthians 6:2, 3.*

34. At the millennium's end, the unbelievers will be resurrected to hear their sentence of doom and receive their punishment. *John 5:29; Revelation 20:5, 9, 14, 15.*

35. The earth will be renovated and made new like Eden, and God's kingdom will be established forever. *Revelation 21:1, 5, 3; Daniel 2:44.*

36. A large part of the Bible is prophetic, and the historic fulfillment of these predictions proves that the Bible is inspired. *2 Peter 1:19; Luke 24:44-46; Acts 8:30-35.*

37. The books Daniel and The Revelation of the Bible predict the rise and fall of the empires of antiquity and their characteristics, as well as the religious developments up to our own time. These prophecies help the Christian understand present-day events. *Daniel 7:3-8, 17; Revelation 13; Matthew 24:15; Revelation 1:3.*

38. Since Daniel 7 and 8 use symbols throughout, the 2,300-day period of Daniel 8:14 is also symbolic and represents 2,300 literal years. Since the period's beginning is historically set at 457 B.C., it extends to 1844, at which time an investigative judgment of all Christians began in the heavenly sanctuary. *Numbers 14:34; Ezekiel 4:6; Ezra 7:12-26; Daniel 7:9, 10.*

39. The gift of the Spirit of prophecy is given to the remnant church of the last days to warn and guide them. *Revelation 12:17; 19:10; 2 Chronicles 20:20.*

40. Earthly governments are ordained by God and should be obeyed within their rightful sphere. *Romans 13:1-7; Titus 3:1.*

41. All governments are under God and therefore under obligation to obey Him. *Daniel 2:21; 4:17; Psalm 2:10, 11.*

42. If governments command the Christian to destroy the life of any fellow human being in peace or war, he is obliged to obey God's superior law first. The Christian cannot support warfare. *Luke 3:14; Matthew 26:52; Acts 4:19; 5:29.*

43. Marriage is a lifelong partnership. Divorce and remarriage are contrary to God's will. *Romans 7:2, 3; Matthew 19:6-9.*

44. Since Christ sacrificed everything for us and everything belongs to Him, it is a blessing to return to Him that portion of our income which He claims as His. *Matthew 23:23; Hebrews 7:8; Malachi 3:8-11.*

45. The physical body belongs to God, and we must keep it in good, healthy condition with proper food, rest, cleanliness, exercise, etc. *1 Corinthians 3:16, 17; 6:19, 20.*

46. Narcotics, stimulants, drugs, etc. are unnatural and destroy the body and mind. *Proverbs 20:1; 23:29-32; Luke 1:15.*

47. In His original plan, God never intended the living creatures to be man's food. *Genesis 1:29; Exodus 16:3, 4; Numbers 11:18-20, 33.*

48. Extreme fashions, dictated by modern society, are unhealthful, immoral, and contrary to Christian ethics. *1 Timothy 2:9, 10; 1 Peter 3:1-5.*

49. God recognizes only one true church, whether small or large—the one which keeps His commandments, has the Spirit of prophecy, and is separate from the world. It is His agency on earth, and He works through it to accomplish His purpose. *Ephesians 4:5; Solomon's Song 6:8-10; Matthew 28:19, 20; Revelation 12:17.*

50. God's church carries the responsibility of proclaiming the last warning preparatory to Christ's second coming. *Revelation 14:6-12; Matthew 24:14; Revelation 18:1-4.*

Notes: *The Seventh-Day Adventist Reform Movement departs from traditional Christian belief primarily in its position on Christ's atonement. Christ's atonement does not apply to willful sin, only ignorance and weakness (item 22). Pacifism is affirmed (item 42).*

*   *   *

Church of God Adventist

FUNDAMENTAL BELIEFS (ASSOCIATED CHURCHES OF GOD)

1. GOD

We believe that one God, the heavenly Father, is the supreme Deity of the universe (Eph. 4:6; I Cor. 8:4-6; 15:24-28). He is composed of spirit and is eternal (John 4:24; I Tim. 1:17). He is a personal Being of supreme love, wisdom, knowledge, judgment, mercy and power; He possesses every attribute of perfect character (Matt. 5:48; I John 4:8; Prov. 2:6-8; Isa. 40:12-31). He is Creator of the heavens and the earth and all that is in them and the source of life (Gen. 1; Acts 17:24-29; John 5:26).

2. JESUS CHRIST

We believe that Jesus of Nazareth is the Son of God, conceived of the Holy Spirit and born in the human flesh of the virgin Mary (Matt. 1:18-25; Luke 1:34-35). Before His human birth, Christ existed eternally with God and as God (John 1:1-2, 14; Rev. 1:8). God created everything in the universe by and through Jesus Christ (Col. 1:16; John

FUNDAMENTAL BELIEFS (ASSOCIATED CHURCHES OF GOD) (continued)

1:3). Jesus is the Christ, or Messiah, sent from God to be our Saviour and Redeemer (John 1:29; 3:15-17; Acts 4:12).

3. HOLY SPIRIT

We believe that the Holy Spirit is the spirit of God the Father and of Jesus Christ. The Holy Spirit is not a person but rather it is the power of God by which all things were made (Gen. 1:2; Psalm 104:30). Through the Holy Spirit God is omnipresent (Psalm 139:7-11). Through the Holy Spirit God the Father imparts His life, power, mind, and attributes, and Jesus Christ abides and lives in true Christians (Luke 24:49; Acts 1:8; 2:38; 5:32; John 1:12; 14:16-17, 23; 15:4-5; I John 3:24; 4:13; 5:12; Rom. 5:5; 8:9; II Tim. 1:7; Gal. 5:22-23).

4. THE BIBLE

We believe that the Scriptures of the Old and New Testaments are God's revelation to man. The original writings were divinely inspired (II Tim. 3:16; II Pet. 1:21). The Bible is the source of divine truth and wisdom (John 17:17; Prov. 2:6) and all doctrines and philosophies contrary to the Bible are false (Rom. 3:4). The Bible reveals God's will and plan of salvation and contains God's instruction for man (II Tim. 3:15-17; Prov. 1:2-7; Matt. 4:4).

5. SATAN

We believe that Satan, the Devil, is a literal spirit being. He is the adversary of God and His people and is the deceiver of mankind (Rev. 12:9; II Cor. 4:4; I Pet. 5:8; Matt. 4:1,3; John 8:44; Eph. 6:11-12). Demons are those angels who sinned against God (Rev. 12:9,4; II Pet. 2:4).

6. MAN

We believe that man is a physical, mortal being created in the image of God from the elements and given the breath of life by God (Gen. 1:26-27; 2:7). Man is subject to corruption and death and does not have eternal life inherent in himself prior to receiving the gift of God's Holy Spirit (Gen. 2:17; 3:3-4, 19, 22; Eccl. 3:19-20; Ezek. 18:4, 20; I Cor. 15:45, 47, 50-54; Rom. 5:12; 6:23; I John 3:14-15; 5:11-12). Though there is a spirit in man (Job 32:8; I Cor. 2:11), we believe that spirit is not the conscious being apart from the body; death is the cessation of both life and consciousness (Rom. 6:23; Psa. 6:5; 115:17; 146:4; Eccl. 9:4-6, 10; Acts 2:29, 34; John 3:13; I Cor. 15:20-23, 52-54).

7. GOD'S PURPOSE FOR MAN

We believe that God's purpose for each human being is that he ultimately become a member of His divine Family, composed of spirit and possessing eternal life and the attributes of Godly character (John 1:12-13; Rom. 8:14-19, 28-29; I Cor. 15:39-54; Heb. 2:5-10). It is God's desire that all men be saved and come to the knowledge of the truth; He has a step-by-step plan by which He is fulfilling His purpose and bringing all men to the full knowledge and stature of Jesus Christ (Acts 4:12; John 6:44; 17:2-8, 17-21; 15:16; Matt. 28:18-20; Acts 1:7-8; 2:22-39; 3:17-26; Eph. 4:11-15; Rom. 1:16; 11:22-26; II Pet. 3:9; I Tim. 2:4-6).

8. SIN

We believe that all men have sinned and come short of the glory of God (Rom. 3:10, 23; 5:12). Sin is the transgression of God's law (I John 3:4). By the law is the knowledge of sin (Rom. 3:20; 7:7); to him who knows to do good and does it not, to him it is sin (James 4:17); whatever is not of faith is sin (Rom. 14:23). The penalty for sin is death (Rom. 6:23).

9. SACRIFICE OF CHRIST

We believe that God sent Jesus Christ to this earth to die for the sins of the world. Though tempted in all points as we are, Christ lived without sin and gave His life as the full atonement for the sins of all mankind (John 3:16-17; I John 2:1-2; Rom. 5:6-11; 6:23; Heb. 4:15). He was crucified, died, was buried, and was resurrected after three days and three nights in the grave (I Cor. 15:3-4; Matt. 12:40). He ascended to heaven where He now sits at the right hand of the Father as our High Priest and Advocate (Heb. 1:2-3; 4:14-16; 7:25-27; 12:2).

10. FORGIVENESS OF SINS

We believe that all who repent of their sins, believe the gospel of Jesus Christ, accept Him as their personal Saviour and, following the example of Christ, are baptized by immersion, are forgiven their sins by God's grace, through faith in Christ's blood (Mark 1:15; 16:15-16; Matt. 3:2,6,8,13-17; Acts 2:38-39; 4:12; Rom. 1:16; 3:23-25; 5:1-2; 6:3-6; Eph. 1:7).

11. GIFT OF THE HOLY SPIRIT

We believe that all who repent and are forgiven of past sins through Christ can receive the gift of God's Holy Spirit through the laying on of hands (Acts 2:38; 8:15-17; 19:1-6; Heb. 6:1-2). God's Holy Spirit literally comes and abides in them, bearing the fruits of God's Spirit in the individual's life (John 14:16-17, 23; 15:1-8; Gal. 5:16-25; Rom. 6:4-6, 12-22). Those who have God's Holy Spirit in this life, and are led by it, shall be changed from mortal to immortal at the return of Jesus Christ (Rom. 5:8-10; 8:1-18; I Cor. 15:50-58).

12. THE TEN COMMANDMENTS

We believe that God's way of life is expressed in His Ten Commandments (Ex. 20, Deut. 5) as magnified by Christ in explaining their full spiritual intent (Matt. 5, 6, 7) and summarized by Him in the two great spiritual principles of love toward God and love toward neighbor (Matt. 22:36-40). We believe God's Commandments are spiritual precepts (Rom. 7:12-14) that were in effect prior to the Old Covenant (Rom. 4:15; I John 3:4; Gen. 4:7; Rom. 5:12-14; Gen. 26:5) and were taught by Christ and the Apostles as a fundamental part of the New Covenant (Matt. 5:17-48; 7:12-29; 19:16-19; Rom. 6:4-6, 12-22; I Cor. 7:19; Heb. 8:6-10; 10:16; James 2:8-12; I John 2:3-5; 3:24; 5:2-3; Rev. 21:8; 22:14).

13. OBEDIENCE

We believe that Jesus Christ lived without sin as an example for us (John 15:9-12; I Pet. 2:21-25; I John 2:6; Eph. 5:1-2; I Cor. 11:1). Though justification and salvation are a gift of God through faith in Christ's blood (Rom. 3:23-25; 5:1-2; 6:23) and are not earned by obedience

(Rom. 3:20, 23; Gal. 2:16; Eph. 2:8-10), those who abide in Christ should live as He lived (I John 2:3-6). Christ and the love of God dwelling in them will be keeping God's Commandments (John 14:15-24; I John 3:24; 5:2-3; Rom. 5:8-10; Gal. 5:16-25). ". . . to whom ye yield yourselves servants to obey, his servants ye are to whom ye obey; whether of sin unto death, or of obedience unto righteousness" (Rom. 6:16-23; 2:5-11; I Cor. 6:9-10; Gal. 5:19-23; II Pet. 1:5-11).

14. SPIRITUAL CHRISTIANITY

We believe that the emphasis in true Christianity is on the spiritual more than on the physical (II Cor. 3:6, 16-18; Matt. 5:20; Gal. 5:13-25; Rom. 8:1-9). God is spirit and they who worship Him must worship in spirit and in truth (John 4:23-24). God is primarily concerned with the heart, mind, attitude, spirit and character of man (Acts 10:34-35; 15:8; Phil. 2:2-8; Rom. 2:23-29). The kingdom of God is not meat and drink, but righteousness, peace, and joy in the Holy Spirit (Rom. 14:17). Christianity is not established on human teachings regarding ". . . touch not; taste not; handle not; which all are to perish with the using . . . " (Col. 2:20-22).

Christ explained true Christianity by amplifying God's Commandments to reveal their positive spiritual intent (Matt. 5,6,7). The New Covenant involves internalizing those spiritual laws and having them written in our hearts and minds (Heb. 10:16; II Cor. 3:3). Spiritual Christianity leads to a positive orientation with an outward expression of the fruits of God's Spirit—love, joy, peace, judgment, mercy, and faith (Matt. 23:23; Gal. 5:22-23).

15. CHRISTIAN INDIVIDUALITY & RESPONSIBILITY

We believe that each person is a unique individual and personality. He has the responsibility in this life not only of growing in Christian character and Godliness but also of fully developing his mind, personality, talents and abilities (Rom. 12:3-8; I Cor. 12:4-11; 3:10-14; 6:19-20; Eph. 4:7, 15-16; Luke 19:11-26; Matt. 25:15). Each human being has the God-given right to maintain his individuality, self-respect, and human dignity, and is personally responsible before God for his own mind, conscience, and convictions.

16. THE CHURCH

We believe that God's Church, the body of Christ, is a spiritual organism composed of all people who have God's Holy Spirit (I Cor. 12:12-14; Rom. 8:9; I John 4:13). It has only one Head, which is Christ (Eph. 1:22-23; Col. 1:18). The spiritual body of Christ is not limited to any one organization on earth; membership in that body is not determined by adherence to the teachings of any one man or group of men; members of Christ's body are those who live in Christ and in whom Christ dwells (John 14:23; 15:4-5; I Cor. 1:12-13; 3:1-11; Eph. 4:4-6; Matt. 7:16-23; I John 2:3-5; 3:23-24).

17. CHURCH ORGANIZATION AND GOVERNMENT

We believe that Christians should be organized in order to effectively serve God, each other, and mankind (I Cor. 12:7, 15-27; 14:33; 1:10; Eph. 4:3-7, 11-13). Such an organization should have proper order and government to facilitate coordination of effort and the effectual working of God's Spirit through all the members (I Cor. 12:4-11; 14:40; Eph. 4:11-16; Rom. 12:3-8). But that government should not restrict or impede the individual's spiritual growth, subvert his personal conscience or convictions, or interfere with the working of God's Spirit in his mind and life. The government of God in a Christian's life is not the human authority within an organization; rather, it is the direct authority of Jesus Christ and the Word of God that is accepted personally and voluntarily by each member of the body of Christ (Eph. 1:22; I Tim. 2:5; Matt. 23:10; Rom. 14:4; Acts 5:27-29).

18. COMMISSION TO THE CHURCH

We believe that Christ's commission to His Church is set forth in Mark 16:15-16, Luke 24:47, and Matthew 28:19-20: "Go ye therefore, and teach [make disciples of] all nations, baptizing them in the name of the Father, and of the Son, and of the Holy Spirit: Teaching them to observe all things whatsoever I have commanded you. . . . " This work of the Church involves preaching the good news of Jesus Christ and the Kingdom of God to the world; it involves being a light and example of God's way (Matt. 5:16; John 15:8, 16; Phil 2:15-16); it involves baptizing and teaching those who repent; and it involves edifying the body of Christ, feeding the flock of God, and perfecting the saints (Matt. 5:48; Eph. 4:12-13; John 21:15-17; I Pet. 5:2). God has placed every member in the body of Christ in order to fulfill the various facets of this commission (I Cor. 12:7-11, 18-20, 27-30: Eph. 4:4,7,11-16).

19. FINANCING THE COMMISSION TO THE CHURCH

We believe that Christ's commission to the Church should be financed through the freewill offerings of the Church (Matt. 6:19-33; I Cor. 9:1-14; II Cor. 11:8-9; 12:13; Phil. 4:14-19; Gal. 6:6-8; I Tim. 5:17-18), not by having to charge the public for the gospel (Matt. 10:7-8; III John 5-8), nor by prescribing a specific amount or percentage that the Church members must give as was done under the Old Testament tithing laws. It is the responsibility of every Christian to give generously to support the various facets of the work of the Church and of the ministry of Jesus Christ; ". . . He which soweth sparingly shall reap also sparingly; and he which soweth bountifully shall reap also bountifully" (II Cor. 9:6-11; Prov. 3:9-10; I Tim. 6:17-19; Mark 12:41-44; Luke 6:38).

20. NEW TESTAMENT PASSOVER

We believe that we should annually, each Passover, observe the anniversary of Christ's death by partaking of the bread and the wine that symbolize His broken body and shed blood (Matt. 26:26-29; I Cor. 11:23-30).

21. NEW TESTAMENT SABBATH

We believe that the seventh day of the week, from Friday sunset to Saturday sunset, is God's Sabbath (Gen. 2:2-3; 1:5; Lev. 23:32). We are to rest from our labors on this day following the example of God (Gen. 2:1-3; Ex. 20:11). We are to observe the Sabbath according to the teachings and example of Jesus Christ in the New Testament (Mark 2:23-28; 3:1-4; Matt. 12:7-12; Luke 4:16; Mark 6:2) and following the practice of the Apostles and the New Testament Church (Acts 13:42-44; 17:2; 18:4).

22. RETURN OF CHRIST

We believe that Jesus Christ will return to this earth, personally and visibly, in power and glory, before His one thousand year reign on earth (Acts 1:11; 3:19-21; I Thess. 4:16; Rev. 1:7; 11:15; 19:11-16; 20:4,6; Matt. 24:23-30; 25:31; Dan. 2:44; Zech. 14:3-4, 9). He will reign with love and justice over all nations as King of kings and Lord of lords (Isa. 11:1-10; Rev. 19:16).

23. RESURRECTION OF SAINTS

We believe that the dead in Christ will be resurrected to eternal life at Christ's return, and that those Christians who are alive at that time will be changed from mortal to immortal (I Thess. 4:13-17; I Cor. 15:50-54; Phil. 3:20-21). They will be composed of spirit and have eternal life as immortal members of God's divine Family (Rev. 2:11; 20:6; 21:7; I John 3:2; Rom. 8:11, 16-17). They will rule with Christ over the nations for the one-thousand-year reign of God's Kingdom on earth (Rev. 20:4-6; 1:5-6; 2:25-27; 5:10; Dan. 7:18,22,27; Luke 1:31-33; 22:29-30; Matt. 19:28; Ezek. 37:23-25).

24. GENERAL RESURRECTION

We believe that God will resurrect to physical life again all who have not had a full, complete opportunity to know God and Christ, to understand God's purpose and truth, and to develop Godly character through the experiences of life (Acts 4:12; John 17:2-3; I John 5:11-12, 19-20; Heb. 8:8-12; Rev. 20:5; Matt. 12:41-42; Ezek. 37; Rom. 11:25-32; John 5:21-30).

It is God's desire that all men be saved and come to the knowledge of the truth (I Tim. 2:4-6; II Pet. 3:9). God will judge people according to their works after they receive knowledge and understanding and have had opportunity to use God's Holy Spirit to live God's way of life; God will not eternally condemn people because of sins committed in ignorance of the true God and His way (Acts 17:23-31; James 4:17; Rom. 7:7; John 6:37-40, 44-45; Acts 10:34-35; Rev. 20:5, 11-12; Ezek. 37:13-14; I Tim. 2:6; Heb. 9:25-28; John 3:16-17).

Notes: *The Church of God Adventist churches are sabbatarian, but did not follow the revelations given to Ellen G. White, founder of the Seventh-Day Adventist Church. Many not only worship on Saturday, but keep the Old Testament (Jewish) holy days.*

The Associated Churches of God follows the non-Trinitarian perspective of its parent organization, the Worldwide Church of God. Statements on church government (item 17) and church finances (item 19) reflect issues that led to the founding of the church.

FUNDAMENTAL BELIEFS (CHURCH OF GOD EVANGELISTIC ASSOCIATION)

FOREWORD

The fundamental beliefs of the Church of God Evangelistic Association are based on the careful study of the Holy Scriptures. We adhere to these precepts and are dedicated to teach and live by them. THEY DO NOT, HOWEVER, FORM A CLOSED CREED. Individually and collectively we recognize the need for continual study, growth, and change. We seek to grow in knowledge and understanding "Till we all come in the unity of the faith, and of the knowledge of the Son of God, unto a perfect man, unto the measure of the stature of the fullness of Christ" (Eph. 4:13).

We do not believe that compliance with all of our fundamental beliefs is required of each individual for salvation. On the other hand, the Bible does set specific standards and outlines definite requirements for salvation. Our beliefs concerning those basic requisites are essentially explained in sections 10 through 13, with some elaboration in other sections.

The Church of God Evangelistic Association is committed to teach the Word of God, not to legislate its present understanding on others. We believe Christians should not judge one another in matters of individual conscience and understanding (Matt. 7:1-2; Rom. 14:4, 12-13, 17-23; 15:1-2; James 4:11-12).

For further explanation on any of these subjects or for information on scriptural teachings not covered in this statement of belief, write to the Church of God Evangelistic Association, 11824 Beaverton, Bridgeton, Missouri 63044. Phone (314) 739-4490.

1. GOD

We believe that one God, the heavenly Father, is the supreme Diety of the universe (Eph. 4:6; I Cor. 8:4-6; 15:24-28). He is composed of spirit and is eternal (John 4:24; I Tim. 1:17). He is a personal Being of supreme love, wisdom, knowledge, judgement, mercy and power. He possesses every attribute of perfect character (Matt. 5:48; I John 4:8; Prov. 2:6-8; Isa. 40:12-31). He is Creator of the heavens and the earth and all that is in them and the source of life (Gen. 1; Acts 17:24-29; John 5:26).

2. JESUS CHRIST

We believe that Jesus of Nazareth is the Son of God, conceived of the Holy Spirit and born in the human flesh of the virgin Mary (Matt. 1:18-25; Luke 1:34-35). Before His human birth, Christ existed eternally with God and as God (John 1:1-2, 14; Rev. 1:8). God created everything in the universe by and through Jesus Christ (Col. 1:16; John 1:3). Jesus is the Christ, or Messiah, sent from God to be our Saviour and Redeemer (John 1:29; 3:15-17; Acts 4:12).

3. HOLY SPIRIT

We believe that the Holy Spirit is the spirit of God the Father and of Jesus Christ. The Holy Spirit is not a person but rather it is the power of God by which all things were made (Gen. 1:2; Psalm 104:30). Through the Holy Spirit God is omnipresent (Psalm 139:7-11). Through the Holy Spirit God the Father imparts His life, power, mind, and attributes, and Jesus Christ abides and lives in true Christians (Luke 24:49; Acts 1:8; 2:38; 5:32; John 1:12; 14:16-17, 23; 15:4-5; I John 3:24; 4:13; 5:12; Rom. 5:5; 8:9; II Tim. 1:7; Gal. 5:22-23).

4. THE BIBLE

We believe that the Scriptures of the Old and New Testaments are God's revelation to man. The original writings were divinely inspired (II Tim. 3:16; II Pet. 1:21). The Bible is the source of divine truth and wisdom (John 17:17; Prov. 2:6) and all doctrines and philosophies contrary to the Bible are false (Rom. 3:4). The Bible reveals God's will and plan of salvation and contains God's instruction for man (II Tim. 3:15-17; Prov. 1:2-7; Matt. 4:4).

5. SATAN

We believe that Satan, the Devil, is a literal spirit being. He is the adversary of God and His people and is the deceiver of mankind (Rev. 12:9; II Cor. 4:4; I Pet. 5:8; Matt. 4:1, 3; John 8:44; Eph. 6:11-12). Demons are those angels who sinned against God (Rev. 12:9, 4; II Pet. 2:4).

6. MAN

We believe that man is a physical, mortal being created in the image of God from the elements and given the breath of life by God (Gen. 1:26-27; 2:7). Man is subject to corruption and death and does not have eternal life inherent in himself prior to receiving the gift of God's Holy Spirit (Gen. 2:17; 3:3-4, 19, 22; Eccl. 3:19-20; Ezek. 18:4, 20; I Cor. 15:45, 47, 50-54; Rom. 5:12; 6:23; I John 3:14-15; 5:11-12). Though there is a spirit in man (Job 32:8; I Cor. 2:11), we believe that spirit is not the conscious being apart from the body; death is the cessation of both life and consciousness (Rom. 6:23; Psa. 6:5; 115:17; 146:4; Eccl. 9:4-6, 10; Acts 2:29, 34; John 3:13; I Cor. 15:20-23, 52-54).

7. GOD'S PURPOSE FOR MAN

We believe that God's purpose for each human being is that he ultimately become a member of His divine Family, composed of spirit and possessing eternal life and the attributes of Godly character (John 1:12-13; Rom. 8:14-19, 28-29; I Cor. 15:39-54; Heb. 2:5-10). It is God's desire that all men be saved and come to the knowledge of the truth; He has a step-by-step plan by which He is fulfilling His purpose and bringing all men to the full knowledge and stature of Jesus Christ (Acts 4:12; John 6:44; 17:2-8, 17-21; 15:16; Matt. 28:18-20; Acts 1:7-8; 2:22-39; 3:17-26; Eph. 4:11-15; Rom. 1:16; 11:22-26; II Pet. 3:9; I Tim. 2:4-6).

8. SIN

We believe that all men have sinned and come short of the glory of God (Rom. 3:10, 23; 5:12). Sin is the transgression of God's law (I John 3:4). By the law is the knowledge of sin (Rom. 3:20; 7:7); to him who knows to do good and does it not, to him it is sin (James 4:17); whatever is not of faith is sin (Rom. 14:23). The penalty for sin is death (Rom. 6:23).

9. SACRIFICE OF CHRIST

We believe that God sent Jesus Christ to this earth to die for the sins of the world. Though tempted in all points as we are, Christ lived without sin and gave His life as the full atonement for the sins of all mankind (John 3:16-17; I John 2:1-2; Rom. 5:6-11; 6:23; Heb. 4:15). He was crucified, died, was buried, and was resurrected after three days and three nights in the grave (I Cor. 15:3-4; Matt. 12:40). He ascended to heaven where He now sits at the right hand of the Father as our High Priest and Advocate (Heb. 1:2-3; 4:14-16; 7:25-27; 12:2).

10. FORGIVENESS OF SINS

We believe that all who repent of their sins, believe the gospel of Jesus Christ, accept Him as their personal Saviour and, following the example of Christ, are baptized by immersion, are forgiven their sins by God's grace, through faith in Christ's blood (Mark 1:15; 16:15-16; Matt. 3:2, 6, 8, 13-17; Acts 2:38-39; 4:12; Rom. 1:16; 3:23-25; 5:1-2; 6:3-6; Eph. 1:7).

11. GIFT OF THE HOLY SPIRIT

We believe that all who repent and are forgiven of past sins through Christ can receive the gift of God's Holy Spirit through the laying on of hands (Acts 2:38; 8:15-17; 19:1-6; Heb. 6:1-2). God's Holy Spirit literally comes and abides in them, bearing the fruits of God's Spirit in the individual's life (John 14:16-17, 23; 15:1-8; Gal. 5:16-25; Rom. 6:4-6, 12-22). Those who have God's Holy Spirit in this life, and are led by it, shall be changed from mortal to immortal at the return of Jesus Christ (Rom. 5:8-10; 8:1-18; I Cor. 15:50-58).

12. THE TEN COMMANDMENTS

We believe that God's way of life is expressed in His Ten Commandments (Ex. 20, Deut. 5) as magnified by Christ in explaining their full spiritual intent (Matt. 5, 6, 7) and summarized by Him in the two great spiritual principles of love toward God and love toward neighbor (Matt. 22:36-40). We believe God's Commandments are spiritual precepts (Rom. 7:12-14) that were in effect prior to the Old Covenant (Rom. 4:15; I John 3:4; Gen. 4:7; Rom. 5:12-14; Gen. 26:5) and were taught by Christ and the Apostles as a fundamental part of the New Covenant (Matt. 5:17-48; 7:12-29; 19:16-19; Rom. 6:4-6, 12-22; I Cor. 7:19; Heb. 8:6-10; 10:16; James 2:8-12; I John 2:3-5; 3:24; 5:2-3; Rev. 21:8; 22:14).

13. OBEDIENCE

We believe that Jesus Christ lived without sin as an example for us (John 15:9-12; I Pet. 2:21-25; I John 2:6; Eph. 5:1-2; I Cor. 11:1). Though justification and salvation are a gift of God through faith in Christ's blood (Rom. 3:23-25; 5:1-2; 6:23) and are not earned by obedience (Rom. 3:20, 23; Gal. 2:16; Eph. 2:8-10), those who abide in Christ should live as He lived (I John 2:3-6). Christ and the love of God dwelling in them will be keeping God's Commandments (John 14:15-24; I John 3:24; 5:2-3; Rom. 5:8-10; Gal. 5:16-25). ". . . to whom ye yield yourselves servants to obey, his servants ye are to whom ye obey; whether of sin unto death, or of obedience unto righteousness" (Rom. 6:16-23; 2:5-11; I Cor. 6:9-10; Gal. 5:19-23; II Pet. 1:5-11).

14. SPIRITUAL CHRISTIANITY

We believe that the emphasis in true Christianity is on the spiritual more than on the physical (II Cor. 3:6, 16-18; Matt. 5:20; Gal. 5:13-25; Rom. 8:1-9). God is spirit and they who worship Him must worship in spirit and in truth (John 4:23-24). God is primarily concerned with the heart, mind, attitude, spirit and character of man (Acts 10:34-35; 15:8; Phil. 2:2-8; Rom. 2:23-29). The kingdom of God is not meat and drink, but righteousness, peace, and joy in the Holy Spirit (Rom. 14:17). Christianity is not established on human teachings regarding ". . . touch not; taste not; handle not; which all are to perish with the using . . . " (Col. 2:20-22).

Christ explained true Christianity by amplifying God's Commandments to reveal their positive spiritual intent (Matt. 5, 6, 7). The New Covenant involves internalizing those spiritual laws and having them written in our hearts and minds (Heb. 10:16; II Cor. 3:3). Spiritual Christianity leads to a positive orientation with an outward expression of the fruits of God's Spirit—love joy, peace, judgment, mercy, and faith (Matt. 23:23; Gal. 5:22-23).

15. CHRISTIAN INDIVIDUALITY & RESPONSIBILITY

We believe that each person is a unique individual and personality. He has the responsibility in this life not only of growing in Christian character and Godliness but also of fully developing his mind, personality, talents and abilities (Rom. 12:3-8; I Cor. 12:4-11; 3:10-14; 6:19-20; Eph. 4:7, 15-16; Luke 19:11-26; Matt. 25:15). Each human being has the God-given right to maintain his individuality, self-respect, and human dignity, and is personally responsible before God for his own mind, conscience, and convictions.

16. THE CHURCH

We believe that God's Church, the body of Christ, is a spiritual organism composed of all people who have God's Holy Spirit (I Cor. 12:12-14; Rom. 8:9; I John 4:13). It has only one Head, which is Christ (Eph. 1:22-23; Col. 1:18). The spiritual body of Christ is not limited to any one organization on earth; membership in that body is not determined by adherence to the teachings of any one man or group of men; members of Christ's body are those who live in Christ and in whom Christ dwells (John 14:23; 15:4-5; I Cor. 1:12-13; 3:1-11; Eph. 4:4-6; Matt. 7:16-23; I John 2:3-5; 3:23-24).

17. CHURCH ORGANIZATION AND GOVERNMENT

We believe that Christians should be organized in order to effectively serve God, each other, and mankind (I Cor. 12:7, 15-27; 14:33; 1:10; Eph. 4:3-7, 11-13). Such an organization should have proper order and government to facilitate coordination of effort and the effectual working of God's Spirit through all the members (I Cor. 12:4-11; 14:40; Eph. 4:11-16; Rom. 12:3-8). But that government should not restrict or impede the individual's spiritual growth, subvert his personal conscience or convictions, or interfere with the working of God's Spirit in his mind and life. The government of God in a Christian's life is not the human authority within an organization; rather, it is the direct authority of Jesus Christ and the Word of God that is accepted personally and voluntarily by each member of

the body of Christ (Eph. 1:22; I Tim. 2:5; Matt. 23:10; Rom. 14:4; Acts 5:27-29).

18. COMMISSION TO THE CHURCH

We believe that Christ's commission to His Church is set forth in Mark 16:15-16, Luke 24:47, and Matthew 28:19-20: "Go ye therefore, and teach (make disciples of) all nations, baptizing them in the name of the Father, and of the Son, and of the Holy Spirit: Teaching them to observe all things whatsoever I have commanded you . . . " This work of the Church involves preaching the good news of Jesus Christ and the Kingdom of God to the world; it involves being a light and example of God's way (Matt. 5:16; John 15:8, 16; Phil. 2:15-16); it involves baptizing and teaching those who repent; and it involves edifying the body of Christ, feeding the flock of God, and perfecting the saints (Matt. 5:48; Eph. 4:12-13; John 21:15-17; I Pet. 5:2). God has placed every member in the body of Christ in order to fulfill the various facets of this commission (I Cor. 12:7-11, 18-20, 27-30; Eph. 4:4, 7, 11-16).

19. FINANCING THE COMMISSION TO THE CHURCH

We believe that Christ's commission to the Church should be financed through the freewill offerings of the Church (Matt. 6:19-33; I Cor. 9:1-14; II Cor. 11:8-9; 12:13; Phil. 4:14-19; Gal. 6:6-8; I Tim. 5:17-18), not by having to charge the public for the gospel (Matt. 10:7-8; III John 5:8). It is the responsibility of every Christian to give generously to support the various facets of the work of the Church and of the ministry of Jesus Christ; ". . . He which soweth sparingly shall reap also sparingly; and he which soweth bountifully shall reap also bountifully" (II Cor. 9:6-11; Prov. 3:9-10; I Tim. 6:17-19; Mark 12:41-44; Luke 6:38).

20. NEW TESTAMENT PASSOVER

We believe that we should annually, each Passover, observe the anniversary of Christ's death by partaking of the bread and the wine that symbolize His broken body and shed blood (Matt. 26:26-29; I Cor. 11:23-30).

21. NEW TESTAMENT SABBATH

We believe that the seventh day of the week, from Friday sunset to Saturday sunset, is God's Sabbath (Gen. 2:2-3; 1:5; Lev. 23:32). We are to rest from our labors on this day following the example of God (Gen. 2:1-3; Ex. 20:11). We are to observe the Sabbath according to the teachings and example of Jesus Christ in the New Testament (Mark 2:23-28; 3:1-4; Matt. 12:7-12; Luke 4:16; Mark 6:2) and following the practice of the Apostles and the New Testament Church (Acts 13:42-44; 17:2; 18:4).

22. RETURN OF CHRIST

We believe that Jesus Christ will return to this earth, personally and visibly, in power and glory, before His one thousand year reign on earth (Acts 1:11; 3:19-21; I Thess. 4:16; Rev. 1:7; 11:15; 19:11-16; 20:4, 6; Matt. 24:23-30; 25:31; Dan. 2:44; Zech. 14:3-4, 9). He will reign with love and justice over all nations as King of kings and Lord of lords (Isa. 11:1-10; Rev. 19:16).

23. RESURRECTION OF SAINTS

We believe that the dead in Christ will be resurrected to eternal life at Christ's return, and that those Christians who are alive at that time will be changed from mortal to immortal (I Thess. 4:13-17; I Cor. 15:50-54; Phil. 3:20-21). They will be composed of spirit and have eternal life as immortal members of God's divine Family (Rev. 2:11; 20:6; 21:7; I John 3:2; Rom. 8:11, 16-17). They will rule with Christ over the nations for the one-thousand-year reign of God's Kingdom on earth (Rev. 20:4-6; 1:5-6; 2:25-27; 5:10; Dan. 7:18, 22, 27; Luke 1:31-33; 22:29-30; Matt. 19:28; Ezek. 37:23-25).

24. GENERAL RESURRECTION

We believe that God will resurrect to physical life again all who have not had a full, complete opportunity to know God and Christ, to understand God's purpose and truth, and to develop Godly character through the experiences of life (Acts. 4:12; John 17:2-3; I John 5:11-12, 19-20; Heb. 8:8-12; Rev. 20:5; Matt. 12:41-42; Ezek. 37; Rom. 11:25-32; John 5:21-30).

It is God's desire that all men be saved and come to the knowledge of the truth (I Tim. 2:4-6; II Pet. 3:9). God will judge people according to their works after they receive knowledge and understanding and have had opportunity to use God's Holy Spirit to live God's way of life; God will not eternally condemn people because of sins committed in ignorance of the true God and His way (Acts 17:23-31; James 4:17; Rom. 7:7; John 6:37-40, 44-45; Acts 10:34-35; Rev. 20:5, 11-12; Ezek. 37:13-14; I Tim. 2:6; Heb. 9:25-28; John 3:16-17).

25. HOLY DAYS

We believe the Holy Days are for Christians today to understand the unfolding plan of God for all mankind. We believe they ARE shadows of good things to come as well (Col. 2:16-17). The Feasts are Festivals of the Lord (Jesus Christ) (Lev. 23:1-2). They are statutes forever (Lev. 23:14,21,31,41). Feasts of Christ are times of great rejoicing (Lev. 23:40; Deut. 16:11,14,15; Neh. 8:10-12, 17). Jesus, our example of pleasing the heavenly Father, kept them (Jn. 5:30; 8:29; Lk. 2:41-42; Jn. 2:13; 7:2,8,10,14, 37). The original Apostles kept them (Acts 2; 18:21; 20:16; 1 Cor. 5:7-8). If anyone will observe the Holy Days of God, that person will KNOW the doctrine is of God (Jn. 7:17).

Notes: *A Bible-oriented church, the association explains the nature of its statement in its prefatory remarks. Compare this statement to that of the Associated Church of God which, like the association, was also formed by former members of the Worldwide Church of God.*

* * *

DOCTRINES (CHURCH OF GOD INTERNATIONAL)

The Church of God, International, claims for its basic and entire doctrines, the most ancient and purest examples of Holy Writ: the Bible in its entirety as originally inspired. We believe in Jesus Christ, born of woman, become man in the flesh, crucified and buried, resurrected the third day according to the scriptures, ascended to heaven to become High Priest and Author of our Salvation, and who awaits His Father's time to return to this earth as conquering King, and Divine Ruler of the world for one thousand years. We believe in the Ten Commandments of God as magnified by the teachings and life's examples of Jesus Christ of Nazareth, and believe that Jesus Christ has given, as He promised, that "other comforter," through whose indwelling presence the Church is being led, through the ages, into "all truth."

Notes: *Only a brief statement was adopted for the constitution of the Church of God International, and it does not deal with most of the particular beliefs to which church members adhere.*

* * *

WHAT THE "CHURCH OF GOD" BELIEVES, AND WHY [CHURCH OF GOD (SEVENTH-DAY, SALEM, WEST VIRGINIA)]

1. We believe the Bible is the book through which God has revealed His will to man, and that all contrary teachings are false and spurious.

    REASON: "All scripture is given by inspiration of God."—2 Tim. 3:16.

2. We believe in examining everything in the light of the Bible, weighing everything in the balance of the Bible and if it will not stand the test, reject it, but if it will stand the test, accept it.

    We believe in granting liberty of thought, and speech, and we stand for an open forum where advanced light can be given, thus stimulating a growth in knowledge.

    REASON: 1 Thess. 5:21, "Prove all things; hold fast that which is good." "Grow in grace . . . and knowledge."—2 Peter 3:18.

3. We believe in God the Father, the Creator of heaven and earth.

    REASON: "In the beginning God created the heaven and the earth."—Gen. 1:1.

4. We believe that Christ is the Son of God, that after His death, burial, and resurrection, He ascended to heaven and is now at the right hand of the throne of God.

    REASON: ". . . This is my beloved Son, in whom I am well pleased."—Matt. 3:17. "He was received up into heaven, and sat on the right hand of God."—Mark 16:19.

5. We believe that Christ was in the grave just three days and three nights, that He was resurrected in the end of the Sabbath, and placed in the tomb just three days and three nights previous.

    REASON: He said He would be in the heart of the earth three days and three nights. Matt. 12:40. It was in the end of the Sabbath when the earthquake occurred, when the angel descended, when the stone was rolled away and when the resurrection occurred. Matt. 28:1-6.

WHAT THE "CHURCH OF GOD" BELIEVES, AND WHY [CHURCH OF GOD (SEVENTH-DAY, SALEM, WEST VIRGINIA)] (continued)

6. We believe that the Commandments of God and the Faith of Jesus are the standards of righteousness by which the future destiny of man will be determined in the day of judgment.

REASON: In Rev. 14:9-11, an account of the destruction of the wicked is given, and in verse 12 we are told that the saints or the ones saved are those who keep the commandments of God and the Faith of Jesus. See also Rev. 12:17; Rev. 22:14; 1 John 5:3; and James 2:10-12.

7. We believe in the literal, personal, visible return of Christ to the earth at the end of this age.

REASON: The inspired apostles Peter and Paul say He will come personally and literally. Acts 3:20, 21; 1 Thess. 4:16, 17; 2 Thess. 1:7, 8. John and James also testify the same. The angel from heaven said in Acts 1:11, "This same Jesus which is taken up from you into heaven, shall so come in like manner as ye have seen him go into heaven." Jesus Himself said He would come again and the event would be as the lightning flashing from the sky. Matt. 24:27.

8. We believe God's people will be posted regarding this event and will therefore be looking for His return.

REASON: "But ye, brethren, are not in darkness, that that day should overtake you as a thief. Ye are all the children of light. . . . "—1 Thess. 5:4, 5. ". . . If therefore thou shall not watch, I will come on thee as a thief."—Rev. 3:3.

Speaking of His coming and giving a series of events which will transpire before He returns, Christ says, "So likewise ye, when ye shall see all these things, know that it is near, even at the doors."—Matt. 24:33.

9. We believe that when people die they become unconscious and remain in the grave in this condition until the judgment. We believe that their thoughts perish, and all hatred, love, and envy ceases.

REASON: "For the living know that they shall die: but the dead know not anything . . . "—Eccl. 9:5. "Also their love, and their hatred, and their envy, is now perished . . . "—Verse 6. Psa. 146:6, "His breath goeth forth, he returneth to his earth; in that very day his thoughts perish."

10. We believe the righteous dead will be resurrected at the coming of Christ.

REASON: 1 Thess. 4:16, ". . . The Lord himself shall descend from heaven with a shout, with the voice of the archangel, and with the trump of God: and the dead in Christ shall rise first."

1 Cor. 15:52, "In a moment, in the twinkling of an eye at the last trump; for the trumpet shall sound and the dead shall be raised incorruptible, and we shall be changed."

1 Cor. 15:22, 23, "For as in Adam all die, even so in Christ shall all be made alive. But every man in his own order: Christ the firstfruits; afterward they that are Christ's at his coming."

11. We believe that the signs of the times indicate the nearness of Christ's return.

REASON: "This know also, that in the last days perilous times shall come."—2 Tim. 3:1. This is a time of worldliness and pleasure, covetousness and ungodliness. It is a time when knowledge is increased as never before. Dan. 12:4 says, ". . . Seal the book, even to the time of the end: many shall run to and fro, and knowledge shall be increased." The prophecies of God have nearly all been fulfilled: Dan. 2; Matt. 24; Luke 21; Dan. 7, and many others.

12. We believe that the living and the dead will be judged and receive their reward at the coming of Christ at the end of this age.

REASON: "I charge thee therefore before God, and the Lord Jesus Christ, who shall judge the quick and the dead at his appearing and his kingdom."—2 Tim. 4:1. As this was spoken in 66 A.D., it was a future event at that time and as no occurrence of this nature has ever transpired since, it is yet future.

It would be absurd to think of the dead receiving their reward before they were judged. This would be an impossibility. They are judged when Christ comes, therefore, they could not receive their reward before that time. This is the exact teaching of Christ. In Rev. 22:12, He says, ". . . Behold, I come quickly; and my reward is with me, to give every man according as his work shall be." This does away with the belief that people are now in heaven receiving their reward, which would place the judgment in the past. To believe that the judgment was in the past would necessitate our denying the plain statements of our Savior.

13. We believe in the inspired church name, "Church of God."

REASON: It is the only church name found in the Bible. There are over six hundred different church denominations, but not one of them is mentioned in the Bible as pertaining to the name of a church. In one place the statement, "The churches of Christ," is made, but in every other place (twelve in all) the name "Church of God" is given. It was the Church of God that Christ purchased with His own blood (Acts 20:28); it was the Church of God which Paul persecuted before his conversion (1 Cor. 15:9; Gal. 1:13); it was the Church of God of which he afterwards became a member (1 Cor. 12:12, 13).

14. We believe that among the different instruments of law given by God the Father, the Ten Commandments were far superior to any other, that they constitute the fundamental organic code of all law and the constitution of the supreme court of heaven.

REASON: They were thundered from Sinai's quaking summit, with a voice that shook the earth. See Ex. 19:16-18. They were written with the finger of

God on tables of stone. See Ex. 31:18; 32:15, 16. No other code of law in the Bible was written with the finger of God on tables of stone, but the other documents were written by Moses in a book. However, this was not true of the Ten Commandments. God did this work Himself, writing with His own finger on tables of stone. By this very act we see that He magnified them above all else, that they were exalted by the Almighty and considered superior to all other documents or codes.

15. We believe that the wages of sin is death, and that all sinners will be destroyed out of the earth.

    REASON: "The wages of sin is death."—Rom. 6:23. "Behold, the day of the Lord cometh, cruel both with wrath and fierce anger, to lay the land desolate: and he shall destroy the sinners thereof out of it."— Isa. 13:9.

16. We believe that sin is the transgression of the law.

    REASON: "Whosoever committeth sin transgresseth also the law: for sin is the transgression of the law."—1 John 3:4.

17. We believe that one becomes a sinner in the sight of God just as soon as he breaks any one of the commandments of this eternal code of law. To break any one of them makes him a transgressor of the law, and therefore a sinner.

    REASON: "For whosoever shall keep the whole law, and yet offend in one point, he is guilty of all. For he that said, Do not commit adultery, said also, Do not kill. Now if thou commit no adultery, yet if thou kill, thou art become a transgressor of the law."—James 2:10, 11.

    NOTE: This eternal document of ten commandments contains the two above named precepts. Therefore, beyond any question of doubt, this was the law to which the apostle referred. This was twenty-seven years after Christ's ascension.

    James informed the people of that day that if they kept all the commandments and yet violated just one, they were guilty of all. That is, as "sin is the transgression of the law," to transgress in only one point would make the guilty party a sinner, showing that this code of law which God wrote on tables of stone is still in force.

18. We believe that as the fourth precept, or article of the constitution of high heaven forbids labor on the seventh day of the week, and commands that this day be kept holy, it would be a violation of the law to desecrate it, the same as to break any one of the other ten, and thereby make the guilty party a sinner in the eyes of God.

    REASON: "For whosoever shall keep the whole law, and yet offend in one point, he is guilty of all."— James 2:10. "For this is the love of God, that we keep his commandments: and his commandments are not grievous."—1 John 5:3.

Those who are saved in the end of the world are the ones who have kept the commandments of God, and the faith of Jesus. See Rev. 14:12.

19. We believe that the life which Christ lived while on earth is the life that will save, and that all Christians should accept Him as their example, and follow in His footsteps. If they will do this they will not be in darkness, but will have the light of life.

    REASON: "In him was life; and the life was the light of men."—John 1:4. ". . . He that followeth me shall not walk in darkness, but shall have the light of life."—John 8:12.

20. We believe that all professed Christians who keep Sunday for the Sabbath are not living in accordance with their name, as they do not follow Christ in this practice.

    REASON: We have no record that Christ, in all His life, mentioned the first day of the week, neither did He keep it as a sacred or holy day, but to the contrary He kept the seventh day Sabbath all His life. "And he came to Nazareth, where he had been brought up: and as his custom was, he went into the synagogue on the Sabbath day, and stood up for to read."—Luke 4:16. The following verses tell of the sermon He preached. Christ's mother and the holy women kept the Sabbath day according to the commandment. Luke 23:56.

21. We believe that the commandments which were nailed to the cross included only the code of commandments contained in the sacrifical ordinance, that is, the atonement for sin by animal sacrifices, the yearly sabbath days, governed by the day of the month or moon, the feasts and holy days included in the same code of law. We believe that Christ's death on the cross did not in any way effect the Ten Commandment Law of God which is, and will forever be, the constitution for the supreme court of heaven and earth.

    Reason: "Having abolished in his flesh the enmity, even the law of commandments contained in ordinances."—Eph. 2:15. (Not the Ten Commandments.) In speaking of the sacrificial commandments Paul says, "Which stood only in meats and drinks, and divers washings, and carnal ordinances, imposed on them until the time of reformation. But Christ being come an high priest of good things . . . by his own blood he entered in once into the holy place, having obtained eternal redemption for us."—Heb. 9:10-15.

    The ten commandments did not cease at the cross, for 57 years afterward, John tells us that "this is the love of God, that we keep his commandments: and his commandments are not grievous."—1 John 5:3. Sixty-three years after the cross, he told the people that the ones who are saved in the end of the world are those who keep the commandments of God and the faith of Jesus. See Rev. 14:12. The seventh day Sabbath was also sacred and holy 31 years after the cross, as Paul mentions the seventh day, and tells the

WHAT THE "CHURCH OF GOD" BELIEVES, AND WHY
[CHURCH OF GOD (SEVENTH-DAY, SALEM, WEST
VIRGINIA)] (continued)

people to enter into that rest as God did, and that
there remained a rest (i.e., "the keeping of a
Sabbath") to the people of God. See Heb. 4:4-11.

22. We believe that the foreknowledge of God is portrayed in the scriptures of truth by divine prophecy,
and that God purposed the authenticity of His word
to be proven by the response of history to the call of
prophecy.

Reason: Isa. 41:22,23, "Let them bring them forth,
and shew us what shall happen: let them shew the
former things, what they be, that we may consider
them, and know the latter end of them; or declare us
things for to come. Shew the things that are to come
hereafter, that we may know that ye are
gods. . . . "

Deut. 18:22, "When a prophet speaketh in the name
of the Lord, if the thing follow not, nor come to pass,
that is the thing which the Lord hath not spoken. . . . "

23. We believe that there is but one faith of which God is
the Author, and that there is only one form of
baptism acceptable to Him.

REASON: "One Lord, one faith, one baptism."—
Eph. 4:5.

24. We believe this one faith is the one revealed to us in
His Word through the life and teachings of Christ
and the gospel of the apostles, and that any other
gospel foreign to such teachings, regardless of the
claim of divinity, is not genuine but counterfeit.

REASON: John 1:4 says, "In him was life; and the
life was the light of men." Paul says, "But though
we, or an angel from heaven, preach any other gospel
unto you than that which we have preached unto
you, let him be accursed."—Gal. 1:8.

25. We believe the one form of baptism acceptable to
God is immersion, being buried in the watery grave,
which is typical of the burial and resurrection of
Christ.

REASON: "Know ye not, that so many of us as were
baptized into Jesus Christ were baptized into his
death? Therefore we are buried with him by baptism
into death: that like as Christ was raised up from the
dead by the glory of the Father, even so we also
should walk in newness of life. For if we have been
planted together in the likeness of his death, we shall
be also in the likeness of his resurrection."—Rom.
6:3-5.

Matt. 3:16, "And Jesus, when he was baptized, went
up straightway out of the water." We read in John
8:12, ". . . I am the light of the world: he that
followeth me shall not walk in darkness, but shall
have the light of life."

We read in Col. 2:12, "Buried with him in baptism,
wherein also ye are risen with him through the faith

of the operation of God, who hath raised him from
the dead."

NOTE: This is the gospel of the apostles, and Paul
says as follows, "But though . . . an angel from
heaven, preach any other gospel . . . let him be
accursed." Is there a different gospel being preached
today, and can we discern the genuine from the
counterfeit?

26. We believe that faith is the essential quality through
which soul salvation is gained, and not through dead
works.

REASON: Gal. 2:16, "Knowing that a man is not
justified by the works of the law (sacrificial code),
but by the faith of Jesus Christ. . . . that we might
be justified by the faith of Christ."

Gal. 3:26,27, "For ye are all the children of God by
faith in Christ Jesus. For as many of you as have
been baptized into Christ have put on Christ."

NOTE: After Christ, the great sacrificial Lamb, had
been slain, redemption and remission of sins could
only be received through faith in Him, and not by
the works of the law which commanded the killing of
lambs for a sin offering. This law ceased at the cross
but those who rejected Christ continued the works of
the law and the killing of animal sacrifices.

Speaking of the Ten Commandment Law, written on
stone by the finger of God, Paul says, "For not the
hearers of the law are just before God, but the doers
of the law shall be justified."—Rom. 2:13.

27. We believe that the individual having faith, will be
prompted to higher ideals, and will conform his life
to the requirements of God, and his faith will be
manifested by works.

REASON: ". . . Shew me thy faith without thy
works, and I will shew thee my faith by my
works."—James 2:18. "Even so faith, if it hath not
works, is dead, being alone."—James 2:17.

"Not every one that saith unto me, Lord, Lord, shall
enter into the kingdom of heaven: but he that doeth
the will of my Father which is in heaven." Matt.
7:21.

28. We believe that in the day of judgment many will be
disappointed and rejected who have believed in
Christ and performed works in His name. Therefore,
we admonish every one to carefully consider the
following:

REASON: "There is a way which seemeth right unto
a man, but the end thereof are the ways of death."—
Prov. 14:12. "Many will say to me in that day. Lord,
Lord, have we not prophesied in thy name? and in
thy name have cast out devils? and in thy name done
many wonderful works? And then will I profess unto
them, I never knew you: depart from me, ye that
work iniquity."—Matt. 7:21, 22. ". . . . The devils
also believe, and tremble."—Jas. 2:19. "Wherefore
let him that thinketh he standeth take heed lest he
fall."—1 Cor. 10:12.

29. We believe that the benefits of God's plan of salvation will be realized only by those who, through faith, accept it as divine, make use of it in accordance with God's purpose, and conform their lives to His requirements, to do His will continually.

REASON: "Here is the patience of the saints: here are they that keep the commandments of God, and the faith of Jesus."—Rev. 14:12. "Blessed are they that do his commandments, that they may have right to the tree of life, and may enter in through the gates into the city."—Rev. 22:14. "Not every one that saith unto me, Lord, Lord, shall enter into the kingdom of heaven; but he that doeth the will of my Father which is in heaven."—Matt. 7:21.

30. We believe that man is mortal and therefore, is subject to death.

REASON: "Shall mortal man be more just than God? . . . "—Job 4:17.

31. We believe that man will put on immortality at the resurrection rather than at death.

REASON: 1 Cor. 15:51-53, "Behold, I shew you a mystery; we shall not all sleep, but we shall all be changed, In a moment, in the twinkling of an eye, at the last trump: for the trumpet shall sound, and the dead shall be raised incorruptible, and we shall be changed. For this corruptible must put on incorruption, and this mortal must put on immortality."

32. We believe that God only hath immortality.

REASON: 1 Tim. 6:16, "Who only hath immortality, dwelling in the light which no man can approach unto; whom no man hath seen, nor can see: to whom be honour and power everlasting. Amen."

33. We believe that the dead are unconscious between death and the resurrection.

REASON: Eccl. 9:5, "For the living know that they shall die: but the dead know not any thing. . . . "

Psalms 146:4, "His breath goeth forth, he returneth to his earth; in that very day his thoughts perish."

34. We believe that the soul of man, which is in many places translated "person" means the essentials of life; the real person dies.

REASON: "The soul that sinneth, it shall die."—Ezek. 18:4,20.

35. We believe that the wicked will be totally destroyed, that they will be consumed as stubble fully dry.

REASON: Nahum 1:10, ". . . they shall be devoured as stubble fully dry."

Mal. 4:1, "For, behold, the day cometh, that shall burn as an oven; and all the proud, yea, and all that do wickedly, shall be stubble: and the day that cometh shall burn them up, saith the Lord of hosts, that it shall leave them neither root nor branch." 2 Thess. 1:9, "Who shall be punished with everlasting destruction from the presence of the Lord, and from the glory of his power."

36. We believe that the righteous will be rewarded and recompensed in the earth and that they will never be permanently removed.

REASON: Prov. 10:30, "The righteous shall never be removed: but the wicked shall not inhabit the earth."

Prov. 11:31, "Behold, the righteous shall be recompensed in the earth: much more the wicked and the sinner."

Matt. 5:5, "Blessed are the meek, for they shall inherit the earth . . . "

37. We believe that the kingdom of God will be established on the earth, and is a future event.

REASON: "And the kingdom and dominion, and the greatness of the kingdom under the whole heaven, shall be given to the people of the saints of the most High, whose kingdom is an everlasting kingdom, and all dominions shall serve and obey him."—Dan. 7:27.

Paul says in 2 Tim. 4:1, "I charge thee therefore before God, and the Lord Jesus Christ, who shall judge the quick and the dead at his appearing and his kingdom." In verse eight he says, "Henceforth there is laid up for me a crown of righteousness, which the Lord, the righteous judge, shall give me at that day. . . . "

Acts 14:22, "Confirming the souls of the disciples, and exhorting them to continue in the faith, and that we must through much tribulation enter into the kingdom of God."

NOTE: The kingdom at this time was recognized by the apostles as future. We have no history to prove that it has ever been established and surrounding conditions indicate plainly that it is not present with us today, so we may conclude that it is yet future. "When the Son of man shall come in his glory, and all the holy angels with him, then shall he sit upon the throne of his glory."—Matt. 25:31.

38. We believe there have been four universal kingdoms to rule the world, Babylon, Medo-Persia, Greece, and Rome, and that the dream of Nebuchadnezzar, as interpreted by Daniel, was consequently true. The fifth universal kingdom yet to be established, represented by the stone cut out of the mountain without hands, will be the kingdom of God.

REASON: Daniel, speaking to Nebuchadnezzar, said, "Thou art this head of gold. And after thee shall arise another kingdom inferior to thee, and another third kingdom of brass, which shall bear rule over all the earth. And the fourth kingdom shall be strong as iron."—Dan. 2:38-40. After stating that the kingdoms of earth would be divided in their last stages of existence, he said, "And in the days of these kings shall the God of heaven set up a kingdom, which shall never be destroyed: and the kingdom shall not be left to other people, but it shall break in pieces and consume all these kingdoms, and it shall stand for ever."—verse 44.

39. We believe that Christ's return to the earth will be at a time of war, bloodshed and strife—a time when nations, in their divided state, are angry, and there is a time of trouble such as was never before witnessed.

REASON: Rev. 16:14,15, "For they are the spirits of devils, working miracles, which go forth unto the kings of the earth and of the whole world, to gather them to the battle of that great day of God Almighty. Behold, I come as a thief. Blessed is he that watcheth, and keepeth his garments, lest he walk naked, and they see his shame."

Dan. 12:1,2, "And at that time shall Michael stand up, the great prince which standeth for the children of thy people: and there shall be a time of trouble, such as never was since there was a nation even to that same time: and at that time thy people shall be delivered, every one that shall be found written in the book. And many of them that sleep in the dust of the earth shall awake, some to everlasting life, and some to shame and everlasting contempt."

Rev. 11:18, "And the nations were angry, and thy wrath is come, and the time of the dead, that they should be judged, and that thou shouldest give reward unto thy servants the prophets, and to the saints, and them that fear thy name, small and great; and shouldest destroy them which destroy the earth."

40. We believe that the ordinance of the Lord's Supper, as Christ instituted it, should be observed yearly. We believe that the wine and bread are typical of His shed blood, and broken body.

REASON: "And he took the cup, and gave thanks, and said, Take this, and divide it among yourselves: For I say unto you, I will not drink of the fruit of the vine, until the kingdom of God shall come. And he took bread, and gave thanks, and brake it, and gave unto them, saying, This is my body which is given for you: this do in remembrance of me. Likewise also the cup after supper, saying, This cup is the new testament in my blood, which is shed for you."—Luke 22:17-20.

This was the passover supper, and was to be a perpetual ordinance. We read the words of the Savior in verse 16, "For I say unto you, I will not any more eat thereof, until it be fulfilled in the kingdom of God." He repeats the same in verse 18, making it all the more emphatic that this ordinance would reach even into the kingdom of God.

As God is a God of order, He has set a time for this ordinance which we find to be once a year. "Thou shalt therefore keep this ordinance in his season from year to year."—Exod. 13:10. ". . . Behold, there is a feast of the Lord in Shiloh yearly. . . . "—Judges 21:19.

This feast of the Lord, commonly called the passover, was instituted by God on the 14th day of the first month and was kept by His chosen people for many centuries on that day. The sacrificial lamb, which for hundreds of years was slain on this day, pointed forward to Christ. The bread and wine which Christ instituted on the same day points backward to Him.

The foregoing forty principles, which the Church of God accepts, are Bible facts and we believe these truths should be sounded to the world. Let us with one voice send out the message for our day. The warning cry and message of salvation must go to earth's remotest bounds.

Notes: *This statement is derived from, and closely resembles, older Church of God statements. A number of notes supporting the individual affirmations have been added.*

*   *   *

WHAT THE CHURCH OF GOD BELIEVES AND WHY (GENERAL CONFERENCE OF THE CHURCH OF GOD)

THE BIBLE

1. The Holy Bible, including the divisions commonly known as the Old Testament and the New Testament, is the divinely inspired Word of God. No other writing is so inspired. The Bible is infallible in teaching, and contains the complete will and revelation of God to man. 2 Peter 1:19-21; Isa. 45:23; Heb. 4:12; Matt. 24:35; 2 Tim. 3:16, 17.

GOD, THE CREATOR

2. The Supreme Deity of the universe is God. He is the Almighty Creator and Sustainer of the heaven, the earth, and all things therein. Acts 17:24-28; Acts 14:15; Gen. 1:1; Rev. 14:7; Psa. 124:8; Neh. 9:6; Isa. 40:28; Isa. 44:24; Psa. 55:22.

JESUS, THE SON OF GOD

3. Jesus of Nazareth is the only begotten Son of God, conceived of the Holy Spirit and born of the Virgin Mary. He is the Christ, or Messiah, sent from God to be our Saviour and Redeemer. John 3:16; 1 John 4:9; Matt. 16:16; Isa. 7:14; John 1:18; John 6:65; John 4:25, 26; Matt. 1:18-25; Matt. 14:33; Luke 1:26-36; Luke 2:6-32; Luke 4:14-21; Acts 4:12; Titus 2:14.

THE HOLY SPIRIT

4. The Holy Spirit (also called the Holy Ghost) is the Comforter promised by our Lord, who will abide in the hearts of those who diligently seek Him; and who will guide us into all godly truths, and give us power to witness for Him; evidence of whose presence is manifest both in word and in "fruit of the Spirit," and in keeping the commandments of God. John 14:15-19, 26; John 16:13; Luke 11:9-13; Acts 1:8; Romans 5:5; Gal. 5:22-26; 1 Cor. 12:7-11.

SATAN

5. Satan is "that old serpent, which is called the Devil"; he is the adversary of God and His people. Rev. 20:2; 1 Peter 5:8; 2 Cor. 11:14; Matt. 13:39; Eph. 6:10-12;

Luke 10:18; John 8:44; Rev. 12:9; 2 Cor. 11:15; Rev. 20:10.

THE FALL OF MAN

6. Man was created a perfect being, but through disobedience fell, bringing imperfection, death, and God's curse upon all mankind. Gen. 1:26-31; Gen. 3:8-20; 1 Cor. 15:21, 22; Romans 5:12.

THE PLAN OF SALVATION

7. The Plan of Salvation was made by God the Father as the way of escape for man from the results of the fall. In this plan God gave His Son, Jesus, who paid the penalty for mankind, and made possible our salvation and redemption to eternal life. 2 Peter 3:9; 2 Thess. 2:13; John 3:16; John 10:1, 7; Acts 4:12; Romans 5:11; 1 Peter 1:18, 19; 1 Peter 2:24; 1 John 2:2-4; Heb. 9:13, 14, 28.

THE BLOOD OF CHRIST

8. The blood of Christ was shed for the remission of sins, and the atonement was made on the Cross. Matt. 26:28; Matt. 20:28; Romans 5:6-13; Romans 3:25; Luke 24:47; Acts 10:43; Phil. 2:8-12; Col. 1:19-23; Titus 2:13, 14; 1 Cor. 15:1-5.

ACCEPTING CHRIST

9. To secure the benefits of the Plan of Salvation, each individual must believe on the Lord Jesus Christ and accept Him as his personal Saviour, obey the terms of the gospel, and pattern his life after the example of Christ. Acts 4:12; Luke 24:47; Rom. 10:6-10; 1 John 5:10-14; Romans 6:16-18; 1 Peter 2:21; John 13:15.

THE TERMS OF THE GOSPEL

10. The terms of the gospel include faith in God, and in His Son, Jesus Christ, repentance and confession of sin, including restitution where possible, baptism by immersion in water, signifying the burial of the old life of sin and the arising to a new life of obedience to God. Heb. 11:6; Rom. 10:9, 10, 17; Rom. 6:1; 1 John 5:10-14; 1 John 5:1-9; Gal. 3:26, 27; Luke 13:3; Luke 24:47; Luke 19:8; Acts 2:38; Acts 3:19; Eph. 4:21-25; Col. 2:12.

THE TEN COMMANDMENTS

11. The Ten Commandments are the eternal, constitutional Law of God, and are to be observed by the people of God in this age. Ex. 20:2-17; James 2:9, 10; 1 Cor. 7:19; Matt. 5:18; Matt. 19:16-23; 1 John 2:4; 1 John 3:4; John 12:50; 2 Kings 17:37.

THE SABBATH

12. The fourth commandment enjoins the observance of the Sabbath, the seventh day of the week, commonly called Saturday. It is to be kept as sacred and holy time, from sunset Friday until sunset Saturday. It is given to all the people of God as a memorial of His creation. Gen. 2:2, 3; Ex. 20:8-11; Isa. 58:13; Heb. 4:4-11; Luke 4:16; Luke 23:56; Matt. 28:1; Acts 13:14, 42, 44; Acts 16:13; Mark 2:27, 28; Lev. 23:32; Mark 1:32.

THE LORD'S SUPPER

13. The Lord's Supper is an ordinance given to the Church as a memorial of the death of Christ, and it should be observed annually (on the beginning of the fourteenth of the Hebrew month Nisan). Unleavened bread and unfermented grape juice should be used in this service as emblems of the broken body and the shed blood of Christ. Lev. 23:5, 27, 32; Matt. 26:26-29; Luke 22:7-21, 29, 30; 1 Cor. 11:1, 2, 18-31; 1 Cor. 5:7; John 19:14, 15, 31.

FEET WASHING

14. The ordinance of feet washing was given by Jesus as an example for us, to teach humility, and is to be practiced in connection with the observance of the Lord's Supper. John 13; Luke 14:11; James 4:10; 1 Peter 2:21; 1 Tim. 5:9, 10.

CHURCH ORGANIZATION

15. Salvation is through faith in Christ, but for the purpose of co-operation in the proclamation of the gospel, and the upholding of true Bible standards and doctrines, and for the fellowship of the believers, the Church should be organized in accordance with the Bible plan. Acts 6:1-8; Acts 1:23-26; 1 Cor. 12:27-30; Eph. 2:19, 20; Eph. 4:10-17; 1 Tim. 5:17; 1 Tim. 3:1-5; Heb. 13:17; Titus 1:5-7.

CHURCH NAME

16. The organization of the people of God should be known by the Bible name—The Church of God. Acts 20:28; Eph. 3:14, 15; John 17:11, 12; Dan. 9:19; Jer. 15:16; 1 Cor. 15:9; 1 Cor. 1:2; 1 Cor. 11:22; 1 Tim. 3:15; Deut. 28:10.

TITHES AND OFFERINGS

17. The Bible plan of financial support for the gospel work is the paying of the tithes and offerings, by the members of the church. The tithe is one-tenth part of the increase, and should be paid as a part of the Christian obligation. Offerings are also a part of the Christian obligation to the Lord, and should be given liberally as one is prospered of Him. Matt. 23:23; 1 Cor. 9:13, 14; Lev. 27:30; Mal. 3:8-10.

LAW OF CLEAN AND UNCLEAN

18. The people of God and the followers of Christ in this age are to use for food those things which were given by God for that purpose, as distinguished from those things designated as unclean for human use. Gen. 7:1, 2, 20; Lev. 11:4-20; 1 Tim. 4:5; Isa. 66:15-17.

UNCLEAN HABITS

19. The body is the temple of the Holy Ghost, and God's people should be clean, refraining from any practice which would defile their bodies. Therefore, the smoking, chewing or snuffing of tobacco; the drinking of intoxicating liquors, and the habitual use of narcotic drugs, are not to be practiced by the members of the Church of God. 1 Cor. 3:16, 17; 2 Cor. 6:16-18; 2 Cor. 7:1; 1 John 2:15-17; James 1:14, 15; Gal. 5:19-21; Prov. 23:21-23, 29-32; Eph. 5:18; 1 Tim. 3:3.

20. Since Christians are to love their enemies and work for the salvation of mankind, we stand opposed to carnal warfare. Ex. 20:13; Matt. 5:44; Romans 12:17-21; 2 Cor. 10:4; Eph. 6:12.

PRAYER

21. God's people are to pray to Him, through and in the name of Jesus, their Mediator and High Priest at the right hand of God in heaven. We believe in the efficacy of prayer in the name of Jesus for all our needs, and that answer will be given in accordance with God's will for us. 1 Tim. 2:8; Phil. 4:6; John 14:13, 14; Heb. 7:25; Heb. 12:2; Heb. 4:14-16; Romans 8:34; 1 Tim. 2:5; 1 John 5:14; Luke 18:1; Matt. 7:7, 8; Matt. 6:5-9; James 1:6.

PRAYER FOR THE SICK

22. The Bible teaches both individual and collective prayer for the healing of the sick, and also the calling for the elders of the Church to anoint and pray for the sick, and that God hears and answers the prayer of faith. James 5:13-16; James 1:6; John 5:14, 15; Psalm 103:1-3.

23. We believe that Jesus Christ, the Son of God, was in the plan of salvation before the foundation of the world. He was the Word spoken of in John 1:1, 2, and His birth of the virgin Mary was in fulfillment of, "And the Word was made flesh, and dwelt among us. . . . " John 1:1, 2, 14; John 8:57, 58; Gen. 11:7; John 17:5; Col. 1:16-18.

CRUCIFIXION OF JESUS

24. The Bible teaches that Jesus was crucified on the day of the week commonly known as Wednesday, and He was in the tomb three days and three nights, arising therefrom in the end of the Sabbath, thus fulfilling the prophecy of His sign as recorded in Matt. 12:39, 40; Matt. 28:1-8; Dan. 9:27; 1 Cor. 15:3, 4; Mark 16:1-6; Mark 15:42; John 20:1-10; John 19:14; Luke 24:1-8; Luke 23:54-56.

MILLENNIAL REIGN

25. At the second advent of Christ, He will establish His kingdom on the earth, and the redeemed will reign with Him on the earth for a period of one thousand years. This is the "regeneration" (Matt. 19:28), and also the "times of restitution" (Acts 3:21). At the close of the millennium, Christ will have "put all enemies under His feet," and will deliver up the kingdom to God that God may be all in all. 1 Cor. 15:24, 25, 28; Zech. 14:4-9; Rev. 11:15; Rev. 20:4-6; Rev. 21:1-5; Rev. 19:16; Matt. 25:34; Matt. 5:5; Psalm 37:11; Rev. 5:10; Dan. 7:27; Isa. 2:2-4; Micah 4:1-5.

NEW EARTH

26. At the close of the millennium, the restitution will be complete, and the earth will have been made new; the New Earth will be the eternal home of the saved. Rev. 21:1-8; Prov. 10:30; Isa. 45:8, 9.

THE KINGDOM

27. The Kingdom is divided into three phases: (1) The Spiritual Kingdom of Grace, (2) The Millennial Reign of Christ, (3) The Eternal Kingdom of God. We are now in the Kingdom of Grace during which Christ reigns in the hearts of the believers, through the Holy Spirit. During the millennium, Christ will reign on the throne of His glory, literally, and jointly, with the redeemed for one thousand years. Following the millennium will be the third phase, The Eternal Kingdom of God, in which God will be all in all. Heb. 4:16; Matt. 25:31; Rev. 20:6; 1 Cor. 15:24-28; Romans 12:2; Col. 1:12-14; 1 Peter 2:5-9; Acts 26:18.

Please see Scriptures under Articles 25 and 26.

REGATHERING OF ISRAEL

28. The regathering of literal Israel to the land of Palestine, as portrayed in the prophecies, is in process of fulfillment, and is the sign of the soon coming of Christ. Jer. 31:9; Isa. 61:4; Luke 21:24; Ezek. 21:25-27; Ezek. 37:21-28.

SECOND COMING OF CHRIST

29. The personal and visible return of Christ to this earth will be to establish His kingdom. He will come in the clouds of heaven in the same manner as was His departure into heaven. Acts 1:10, 11; John 14:1-3; Rev. 1:7; Acts 3:20; Job 19:25-27.

PROPHECY

30. "Prophecy came not in old time by the will of man: but holy men of God spake as they were moved by the Holy Ghost," and it is given to us to study that we might watch, as we travel the highway of time, for the prophetic signboards, showing us where we are living in respect to the second coming of Christ. 2 Peter 1:19-21; Romans 15:4; Matthew 24; Psa. 119:105.

SIGNS OF THE TIMES

31. Considering the fulfillment of the signs in the political, religious, physical, and social world, we believe that we are living in the time of the end, and that the second advent of Christ is very near. Luke 21:25; Luke 17:26-31; Rev. 11:18; Matt. 24:6, 7, 36-40; 2 Tim. 4:3, 4; 2 Tim. 3:1-7, 13.

STATE OF THE DEAD

32. When man dies, he is unconscious, and in the grave awaits the resurrection, at which time the righteous will receive immortality, and the wicked, eternal death. Psa. 146:4; Eccl. 9:5, 6; 1 Cor. 15:42-56; Job 17:13; Rev. 20:11-15; Job 14:13, 14.

PUNISHMENT OF THE WICKED

33. The wicked dead will be resurrected at the end of the thousand-year reign of Christ, to receive final judgment, be cast into the Lake of Fire, which is the second death, and will be completely destroyed. Rev. 20:5, 11-15; Mal. 4:1.

WORLDLINESS

34. The Scriptures condemn worldliness, which includes the lust of the flesh, the lust of the eye, and the pride

of life. Attendance at the movie theaters, pool halls, and dances, and the excessive use of jewelry are of the world, and should be eradicated from the lives of the people of God. 1 John 2:15, 16; John 17:16; Romans 12:2; Gal. 5:17-26; 1 Peter 3:3, 4; 1 Tim. 2:9; Romans 8:12-14; Col. 3:1-10.

PAGAN DAYS

35. The days commonly known as Christmas, Lent, Easter, Good Friday, and Sunday are of pagan origin, and are not Biblical; therefore, they should not be observed by members of the Church of God. (In addition to the Scriptures, please see profane history and other reference books for origins of the above-mentioned days.)

THE PLAGUES

36. We believe that the wrath of God against sin and sinners reaches its fullness before and at the time of the second advent of Christ in the seven last plagues described in Rev. 16. These plagues represent events in the world which cause great trouble and distress. It is a part of the message of the Church to warn the world against the troubles and distress to come as the result of sin.

THIRD ANGEL'S MESSAGE

37. An evil power known as the beast exists prior to and at the time of the second advent of Christ. A message known as the Third Angel's Message should be, and is being given by the Church of God as a warning against that evil power. This is a part of the gospel by the acceptance of which people may escape the wrath of God. Rev. 13:1-10; Rev. 14:9-11; Rev. 17:7-14; Rev. 15:1.

MARRIAGE AND DIVORCE

38. We believe marriage to be a sacred ordinance of God, and that as such it belongs to the Church. Because of this fact our people should secure the services of one of our ministers to perform the marriage ceremony.

We believe that any marriage contract entered into between husband and wife at a time prior to the conversion of either party to the marriage, should be recognized as acceptable to the Church if recognized by civil law at the time either party is converted.

We believe that after one has been converted and is in fellowship in the Church, divorce is not to be tolerated, except for Bible reason. Matt. 5:32.

Notes: *This oldest branch of the Church of God perpetuates a peculiar set of beliefs held by most branches of the "Adventist" Church of God bodies. These include the annual practice of the Lord's Supper, foot washing, adherence to the Old Testament dietary laws, condemnation of popular holidays such as Christmas and Easter, and the understanding that annihilation, not eternal torment, is the result of sin.*

FUNDAMENTAL ARTICLES OF FAITH (GENERAL COUNCIL OF THE CHURCHES OF GOD)

"Forasmuch as many have taken in hand to set forth in order a declaration of those things most commonly believed among us" (Luke 1:1).

A. GENERAL STATEMENT

The Churches of God (7th Day) cherish liberty of thought as an essential condition for the guidance of the Holy Spirit. Therefore we have no binding creed to which members must subscribe. However, there are certain fundamental truths which have been binding upon Christians through all ages. Therefore, these are the historic doctrines taught by the Church of God, which we reaffirm as the fundamental principles of the faith.

These statements of faith approved by the General Council are passed on to the churches of God for such action as the Spirit of God may direct. It is believed that they will be helpful in giving Christian training to our children, in establishing our people in the faith, and making known our essential doctrines to others.

B. POLITY

The Church of God (7th Day) is, historically, congregational in polity. We desire that our churches and their members continue to enjoy this blessed freedom of local autonomy. Therefore, the statements set forth here are simply an exhibition of the things most commonly believed among us and is not adopted as having binding force in itself, nor is the inspiration of the phraseology contended for.

THE FUNDAMENTAL ARTICLES OF FAITH

1. THE BIBLE

We believe the Bible (both Old and New Testament) to be the inspired Word of God, containing the revelation of God given to man under Divine supervision and providence; that its historic statements are correct and that it is the only rule for faith and practice (Romans 15:4; 2 Timothy 3:15, 16; John 17:17).

2. THE GODHEAD

We believe, as revealed in the Bible—

a. In the one true God the Father who is the eternal and supreme Deity. He is infinite in His wisdom, love and power, the Creator and Sustainer of all things, "in whom we live, and move, and have our being" (Genesis 1:1; Isaiah 40:28; Matthew 6:6).

b. In Jesus Christ, our Lord and Savior, the only begotten Son of God; who came into the world to seek and to save that which was lost. We believe in His deity, in His virgin birth, in His sinless life, in His miracles, in His vicarious and atoning death on Calvary, in His bodily resurrection late on the Sabbath day, in His ascension to the right hand of God in heaven, in His ministry as our High Priest and Mediator, in His personal return to the earth at the end of this age to establish His kingdom and rule this earth in great power and glory, judging the living and the dead (1 Timothy 3:16).

FUNDAMENTAL ARTICLES OF FAITH (GENERAL COUNCIL
OF THE CHURCHES OF GOD) (continued)

c.   And in the Holy Spirit, the promised Comforter, which is the agency of the Father and the Son to convince the world of sin, of righteousness and of judgment to come. But this same Spirit of God we are sanctified and sealed unto the day of redemption. For those who diligently seek Him, He will lead and guide into all truth and empower the believer for witnessing and service (John 14:16, 26; 16:7-11; Ephesians 1:13).

3. CRUCIFIXION AND RESURRECTION OF CHRIST

We believe the Scriptures plainly teach that Jesus Christ was crucified in the middle of the week, on the day we call Wednesday, and He was in the tomb three days and three nights. He arose towards the end of the Sabbath day (Saturday) and thus fulfilled the sign given by Jesus in Matthew 12:39-40.

4. MAN'S CONDITION

We believe man was created for immortality, but through sin he forfeited his Divine birthright; that because of sin, death entered into the world, and passed upon all men; and that only through faith in Jesus Christ can depraved man become "partakers of the divine nature," and live forever (2 Timothy 1:10; Romans 2:7; 1 Corinthians 15:22, 51-54).

5. STATE OF THE DEAD

We believe that death is a condition of unconsciousness (sleep) to all persons, both the just and the unjust, a condition which shall remain unchanged until the great resurrection at Christ's second advent, at which time the righteous will receive eternal life, while at their appointed time the wicked will be "punished with everlasting destruction," suffering the complete extinction of being, this is the second death (Ecclesiastes 9:5; Job 14:14; John 5:28-29; Matthew 10:28).

6. MAN'S SALVATION

We believe that man in his state of depravity cannot extricate himself and, therefore, God provided salvation free to all those who, in this life and this age, accept it on the conditions imposed, which conditions are simple; namely, turning from sin, repenting before God, exercising faith in our Lord Jesus Christ and His precious blood, making restitution where possible, and obeying the command to be baptized in the name of the Lord Jesus and receive the gift of the Holy Spirit. A life of consecration to Christ and obedience to His commandments must follow in order to obtain eternal life (John 3:16; 2 Corinthians 6:2; Luke 13:25-28; Acts 2:38).

7. A HOLY LIFE AND SANCTIFICATION

We believe that God is holy and requires that His children be holy and sanctified. Sanctification means a cleansing from sin, separation from the world, and consecration to God. The sanctification of a Christian is attained through faith in the Word, faith in the blood of Jesus and the work of the Holy Spirit in the believer's life. Sanctification is effected instantaneously at the time of conversion, and

continuously, each day as the believer walks with God (1 Peter 3:15; 1 Corinthians 1:2; 1 Corinthians 6:11).

8. THE CHURCH

We believe "The Church of God" to be the common Bible name for God's Church and that the church is of divine origin, established upon the foundation of the prophets and apostles with Jesus Christ being the chief cornerstone. This spiritual body includes all true Christians who have been "called out" of the world and gathered into it. Jesus Christ is the Head of the church of God, which is His body; and all the local churches should be independent of outside control, congregational in government, under the spiritual oversight of the godly elders and under the direction of the Holy Spirit, and subject to no priest, bishop or overseer—although true Christian fellowship and unity of action should exist between all local churches of God (Matthew 16:18; Ephesians 5:25, 4:15, 2:19-22; Acts 20:28).

9. ORDINANCES OF THE CHURCH

We believe Christ has placed in His church certain ordinances that all of the children of God should participate in. We believe they are:

a.   Christian baptism of believers by immersion as the only true water baptism. After repentance of sin the believer is to be baptized into Christ for the remission of sin and as a public witness to his acceptance of Christ as Lord and Savior, a symbol of death to sin, and a pledge to walk in "newness of life" in Christ Jesus.

b.   The Lord's Supper, which commemorates the suffering and death of our Lord Jesus Christ, "Till He comes," and is a memorial that should be observed yearly at the beginning of the 14th of Nisan (Abib) with unleavened bread and "fruit of the vine," which represent the broken body and shed blood of Christ. It is also a loving symbol of Christian fellowship, and a pledge of renewed allegiance to our risen Lord and Savior.

c.   The observance of the act of humility, the washing of the saints' feet, should be held in connection with the Lord's Supper. Jesus said, "If I then, your Lord and Master have washed your feet, ye also ought to wash one another's feet" (Acts 2:38; 1 Corinthians 11:23-26; Matthew 28:19; Romans 6:3-5; John 13:4-17).

10. THE TEN COMMANDMENT LAW AND THE SABBATH DAY

We believe the Ten Commandments are the eternal law of God and this law is still binding upon all Christians. Christ did not come to destroy it but, instead, to magnify it. Therefore, the Scriptures enjoin the observance of the fourth commandment, which declares the observance of the 7th day of the week as the Christian Sabbath (which is commonly called Saturday). It should be observed from sunset on Friday until sunset on Saturday and is to be observed as a day of rest and religious worship. However, the handwriting of ordinances that was against us was blotted out and taken out of the way, by Christ nailing it to His cross (Exodus 20:2-17; Deuteronomy 9:10; Matthew 5:17; 19:16-22; 5:18; James 2:8-12; 1 Corinthians 7:19;

Romans 3:20; Genesis 2:3; Matthew 28:1; Leviticus 23:32; Mark 2:27-28; Colossians 2:14).

11. PRAYER AND DIVINE HEALING

We believe prayer is the privilege and duty of every Christian, and it is a drawing near to God in spiritual communion, in order to worship Him and praise Him for His mercies and to bring our requests to Him and to intercede on behalf of others. Prayer should be made to God in the name of Jesus Christ, in the power of the Holy Spirit, and with understanding. We believe in the "laying on of hands" of the elders and the prayer of faith for divine healing (Acts 5:15-16; 28:9; James 5:14-16; 1 Timothy 2:8; Luke 4:6; John 14:13; Romans 3:34; Philippians 4:6).

12. THE SECOND COMING AND THE KINGDOM OF GOD

We believe that Jesus Christ, according to His promise, will come again to this earth, even "in like manner" as He went into heaven—personally, visibly and gloriously—to reign here on earth with His holy saints for a thousand years; and that this coming is the blessed hope of the church, inasmuch as upon that coming depend the resurrection of the dead and the reward of the righteous, the abolition of sin and its fruits, and the renewal of the earth now marred by sin, which will become the eternal home of the redeemed, after which event the earth will forever be free from sin and the curse of death (Acts 1:11; 1 Thessalonians 4:16-17; Revelation 22:12-20; Matthew 25:31-32; 1 Corinthians 15:24-28; Acts 3:21; Revelation 19:11-16; Daniel 7:27; 2 Peter 3:13; Proverbs 10:30; Matthew 5:5).

13. SIGNS OF THE TIMES

We believe that Bible prophecy has indicated the approximate time or season of Christ's return; comparing testimony with the signs of the times (such as the regathering of Israel). We are confident that He is near, "even at the doors," and we believe that the great duty of the hour is the proclamation of this soon coming redemption, the defense of the Bible truth and authority, warning the nations to flee the wrath to come and following the last command of our Savior to His disciples to preach (teach) this message to all of the world, and to remember His promise that He would be with us even till the end of the age (2 Peter 1:19-21; Matthew 24:42-45; Revelation 22:17; 11:18; 2 Timothy 3:1-7; Romans 15:4).

—Even So, Come Lord Jesus—Amen

STANDING RESOLUTIONS

Realizing the need for higher standards in the church of today, we recommend that the following resolutions be presented to the General Council. In no way are they designed to be "high church dictation or religious legislation," but resolutions formulated as guides for our churches and a testimony to the world of our determination to hold fast to that which is good in the face of the present moral and spiritual decline in the United States and elsewhere.

BE IT RESOLVED that we accept the Bible plan for financing the general ministry of the church. We believe the paying of tithes and giving freewill offerings the duty and obligation of all Christians. By dedicated Christian stewardship the work of the church can be greatly blessed.

BE IT RESOLVED that the General Council go on record as being opposed to worldliness. The Scriptures condemn worldliness and it involves our manner of speech, actions, patronizing of certain places of amusement, immodesty of dress and the participation in certain things that a Christian should not participate in or be a part of.

BE IT RESOLVED that we maintain the following position concerning defiling habits, since our bodies are the temples of the Holy Spirit. Each child of God should refrain from all fleshly lusts, and this would include tobacco, narcotic drugs, and intoxicating liquors.

BE IT RESOLVED that we reaffirm our position on marriage. We believe it is a sacred ordinance instituted by God, and thus it belongs to the church. Divorce is a present day evil and since it breaks the law of God and weakens the homes of our nation, we therefore encourage our members to avoid this evil, except for the Bible reason.

BE IT RESOLVED that we now reaffirm our faith in the commandments of God and the faith of Jesus. Therefore, as we near the second advent of our Savior, let us boldly declare the traditional faith of our fathers with new zeal and devotion that all men might hear the Gospel and escape the wrath to come. May we use every means at our disposal to spread the Gospel of Jesus Christ.

STATEMENT ON CARNAL WARFARE

Whereas the General Council of the Churches of God (7th Day) recognizes that the young people who refuse military service for reasons of religious conscience have taken a position that is upright, honest, and above reproach; therefore,

BE IT RESOLVED, that we as Christians stand opposed to carnal warfare, and whereas there is a sincere difference of opinion as to the duty of a Christian concerning military service, some of the members of our churches being conscientiously opposed to any participation in war on the ground that war is contrary to the teaching of Christ, and others believing that they can conscientiously serve the cause of righteousness through such participation, therefore,

BE IT RESOLVED, that we recognize the need of maintaining fellowship in spite of these differences of opinion, pledging our moral support and protection to those who follow the voice of conscience.

We invite the conscientious objectors among our people to register their conviction in writing with the corresponding secretary of the General Council with respect to their status.

Notes: *The council is in general agreement with the General Conference of the Church of God but has added an item on pacifism to its statement.*

DOCTRINAL POINTS OF THE FAITH
(SEVENTH DAY CHURCH OF GOD)

Inasmuch as the Church, as an organized body of believers, accepts and upholds certain tenets of faith, and as the licensed, and ordained ministers, and officers of the Church have accepted these articles of faith without reservations, and such are the faith of the body at large, the same are published as follows, that each member may acquaint themselves better with the Faith of The Church of God. II Tim. 3:15; 1 Tim. 4:6, 16; John 7:16, 17; II Tim. 3:16, 17; Matt. 4:4.

DOCTRINE

Doctrine shall in all cases be according to the Holy Bible as it is summed up in the Saviour, and inasmuch as the Scriptures clearly teach the following points of doctrine, the same are listed as essential parts of "the Whole Armour" of our faith; Eph. 6:11.

1. THAT the Bible, the Old and New Testaments, is inspired as no other writings is, and is complete, infallible, and expresses God's complete will for man.—II Tim. 3:16; Rom. 15:4; II Peter 1:20; Rev. 22:18, 19; Deut. 4:2; Deut. 12:32.

2. THAT Jehovah alone is God, the Creator of the heaven, the earth, the sea, and all that is therein.—Gen. 1:1; Jer. 10:10, 12; Eph. 3:9; Heb. 1:10; Rev. 10:6.

3. THAT Jesus of Nazareth is the only begotten Son of God, conceived of the Holy Spirit, born of the virgin Mary, and is our Lord, Saviour, and Redeemer.—Matt. 1:18-21; 3:17; Luke 1:28-35; John 3:16.

4. THAT Jesus proved His Messiahship by remaining in the tomb exactly three days and three nights, rising in the end of the Sabbath.—Matt. 12:40; Dan. 9:26, 27; Crucified in the midst of the week, Wednesday.—Matt. 28:1-6 (Rose on Sabbath).

5. THAT the Holy Spirit is "the Comforter," which abides in the believer and He is manifested by the power, and the fruits of the Spirit, as in Acts 2nd Chapter, John 16:7-14, and Gal. 5:22-26. Manifestations regulated according to I Corinthians 14th chapter.

6. THAT Satan is a personality, and as "the devil," he is an adversary of God and the children of God.—Isaiah 14:12-20; Ezek. 28:13-19; Rev. 12:7-9; John 8:44.

7. THAT man was created perfect originally, but through disobedience fell, bringing imperfection, death, and God's wrath upon mankind.—Gen. 3:17-19; Matt. 19:8; Romans 5:12, 17; I Cor. 15:21, 22; Gen. 1:26-28.

8. THAT the Christian's life must be patterned after the example of the perfect man—Christ Jesus, who shall have pre-eminence in all things.—II Cor. 5:17; I Peter 2:21-25; I John 2:6; I John 3:5; Col. 1:18.

9. THAT an inspired Bible name for God's called out assembly is the "Church of God." These saints will faithfully uphold all the principles of the Kingdom of God.—Acts 20:28; I Cor. 15:9; Gal. 1:13; I Cor. 1:2; I Tim. 3:15; Ex. 19:5, 6.

10. THAT the apostolic organization and government of God's Kingdom is the only one taught in the Bible for the Church of God.—Isa. 9:6; I Cor. 12:28; Eph. 4:11-16.

11. THAT "Pure Religion," personally experienced by the one regenerated by its power, is the only safe one to trust in.—John 3:1-12; Romans 6:1-12; Romans 13:14; Gal. 3:26, 27; Matt. 19:28; James, 1:27.

12. THAT repentance must be preached.—Matt. 4:17; Mark 6:7, 12; Luke 13:3; Luke 24:47; Acts 2:38; Acts 17:30, 31.

13. THAT conversion is essential to salvation.—Luke 22:32; Acts 3:19; Psalms 19:7.

14. THAT the sanctification of holy living is commanded for the people of God.—John 17:17; Acts. 26:18; I Cor. 1:2; I Cor. 6:11; II Tim. 2:21; Heb. 13:12; I Peter 3:15; I Peter 1:15.

15. THAT baptism by immersion for the remission of sins is vital and typical of the burial and resurrection of Christ.—Romans 6:3-6; Matt. 3:16; Col. 2:11, 12.

16. THAT there is efficacy in the fervent prayer of the righteous.—Prov. 15:8; John 14:13; Matt. 21:22; James 5:16; I John 3:22; I John 5:14.

17. THAT the prayer of faith and anointing will save the sick.—James 5:14-16; Mark 6:13; Acts 5:15, 16; Acts 9:17; Acts 28:8.

18. THAT the laying on of hands is to be practiced.—see above references and Acts 8:14-18; Acts 19:6; II Tim. 1:6.

19. THAT the Passover is to be observed annually on the beginning of the 14th of Abib, and after the example of Jesus.—Ex. 12:6; Ex. 13:10; Lev. 23:5; Luke 22:8-17. The Lord's Supper is a perpetual ordinance until it is fulfilled in the Kingdom of God. (Verses 16, 18).

20. THAT we ought to wash one another's feet.—John 13:1-17.

21. THAT we should observe the seventh day of the week, from even to even, as "the Sabbath of the Lord".—Gen. 2:2, 3; Eccl. 3:14; Ex. 20:8-11; Ex. 31:14-17; Ezek. 20:12; Isa. 58:13; Isa. 56:2, 7; Luke 4:16; Mark 2:27, 28; Matt. 12:10, 12. Evening is at sunset, when the day ends and another begins.—Gen. 1:5, 8, 13, 14: Deut. 16:6; Mark 1:32; Lev. 23:32 (last part); II Chron. 18:34; Neh. 13:19; Heb. 4:3-12.

22. THAT we recognize the Bible calendar, and "observe" the Seven Annual Holy Days of God as "The Way" to fulfill: "Come to the Marriage Feast" of Matt. 22—Lev. 23rd chapter; Ex. 23:14-17; Matt. 23:1-3; Matt. 28:18-20.

23. THAT the paying of "the tithe" of all "increase" is a continued obligation.—Gen. 14:18-20; Heb. 6:20; Heb. 7:1, 2; Lev. 27:32; Num. 18:21; Deut. 8:18; Prov. 3:9; Psa. 24:1, Mal. 3:8, 10; Matt. 23:23; I Cor. 9:11-14; Romans 15:27; Phil. 4:17, 18.

24. THAT all carnal warfare, and the participation therein is condemned, as declared by the Master and our earliest belief.—Ex. 20:13; Matt. 5:21, 22; Romans 13:8-10; Matt. 26:52; John 18:36; Rev. 13:10.

25. THAT the law of the clean and unclean is still to be observed in this age.—Lev. 11th chapter; Eccl. 3:14; Mal. 3:6; James 1:17; Acts 15:20, 29; II Cor. 6:16-18; Rev. 16:13; Isa. 65:4; Isa. 66:11-17.

26. THAT the use of intoxicating liquors, alcoholic stimulants, narcotics, tobacco, and any habit-forming drugs, is condemned.—I Cor. 9:25; Prov. 23:29, 30; Dan. 1:8, 12; Gal. 5:19-21; I Cor. 3:16, 17; I Cor. 5:11; I Cor. 6:10.

27. THAT our perfecting thru the continuation in the observance of "the Law of God," should be taught as Jesus directed. This is "The Law of Life in Christ."—Isa. 42:21; Matt. 5:17-32; Matt. 19:17; Matt. 22:34-40; Romans 8:1, 2; I Cor. 9:21; James 2:10, 11; I John 5:3; Rev. 14:12; Rev. 22:14.

28. THAT sin is the transgression of "the Law" as Jesus demonstrated it.—Romans 6:23; I John 3:4; John 8:1-11; John 16:9.

29. THAT justification from sins is through Christ alone.—John 1:29; Romans 3:24-31; Romans 4:24, 25; Romans 5:1.

30. THAT the return of Jesus Christ will be literal, visible, personal, and is imminent.—Acts 1:11; Acts 3:20, 21; I Thess. 4:16, 17; II Thess. 1:7, 8; Matt. 24:15-31; Rev. 1:7.

31. THAT the throne of David will be established at Jerusalem by the person of Jesus Christ.—Zech. 14:4; Dan. 2:44, 45; Dan. 7:13, 14, 27; Rev. 5:9, 10; Micah 4:8; Luke 1:23, 33; Isa. 24:20-23.

32. THAT the institution of the millennial reign of the kingdom of heaven is at the return of Jesus.—See above; also Rev. 20:4.

33. THAT judgment is upon the house of God during the gospel age.—I Peter 4:17; John 3:18-21.

34. THAT the righteous are resurrected and rewarded at the coming of Jesus.—I Thess. 4:16, 17; I Cor. 15:22, 23, 52; Rev. 20:6; Matt. 25:31-46.

35. THAT the meek shall inherit the earth.—Matt. 5:5; Psalms 37:11, 34; Prov. 10:30; Rev. 5:9, 10; Rev. 21:2, 3.

36. THAT there shall be a final regathering of the dispersed nation of Israel.—Ezek. 37:21, 22; Joel 3:1; Jer. 31:8, 9; Isa. 61:4.

37. THAT the wicked dead are resurrected to final judgment, and not to probation.—Eccl. 3:17; Eccl. 12:14; Acts 17:31; II Cor. 5:10; II Peter 2:9; Rev. 20:7, 8, 12, 15.

38. THAT the wicked are destroyed.—Ezek. 18:4; Romans 6:23; Nahum 1:10; Mal. 4:1-3; Psalms 37:10, 20, 38; Rev. 20:10, 15; Rev. 21:8; Rev. 22:10.

39. THAT the Third Angel's Message is a present day message, and will continue to the advent of Jesus.—Rev. 14:9.

40. THAT the seven last plagues are literal, and fall at the termination of this Gospel age.—Rev. 14:9, 10.

41. THAT we shall practice fellowship in the brotherhood of Christ according to:—Prov. 4:18; I John 1:7; I John 5:1; Eph. 4:11-16; I Cor. 1:1-3.

Notes: *The doctrinal points were adopted as revised in 1965. No member is allowed to teach any doctrine contrary to these statements.*

*　　*　　*

DOCTRINE, AND BASIS FOR FELLOWSHIP (WORLDWIDE CHURCH OF GOD)

Section 1. Basic Doctrine: The doctrine of this Church shall be that of a plain and literal understanding of the Holy Bible, believing it means exactly what it says; —of the Bible alone, and not as interpreted by any other book or person, but it is a point of basic doctrine in this Church that we understand the Bible to reveal a divine Creator, the Almighty God, a divine Saviour, the Son of God, Jesus Christ, who came in the human flesh, proclaimed the Gospel of the coming world-ruling Kingdom of God, which it is obligatory for all Christians to believe; who died to pay the penalty of our sins in our stead; who was raised from the dead after three days and three nights in the grave by God the Father; who ascended to the right hand of the Father in heaven; who is soon coming again literally and in Person to earth to set up the Kingdom of God, and as King of kings and Lord of lords, to rule all nations by this world-ruling Kingdom for one thousand years; we believe in the Commandments of God and the faith of Jesus Christ our Lord.

Section 2. Belief on Bearing Arms: It is the conviction and firm belief of this Church and its membership that Christian disciples of Christ are forbidden by Him and the Commandments of God to kill, or in any manner directly or indirectly to take human life, by whatsoever means; and we believe that bearing arms is directly contrary to this fundamental doctrine of our belief; and we therefore conscientiously refuse to bear arms or to come under the military authority.

Section 3. Basis for Fellowship: The basis for fellowship in this Church or any of its local congregations shall be LOVE alone, plus the adherence to and belief in the general basic doctrine stated in Section 1 above, and the requirement of repentance of sin (the transgression of God's law), and the acceptance of Jesus Christ as personal Saviour, and the receiving of the Holy Spirit of God evidenced by the fruits of the Spirit (Gal. 5) in the member's life.

Notes: *This brief statement is taken from the constitution of the church. It emphasizes the church's belief in the soon-coming kingdom of God and its refusal to participate in war. A number of church bodies, such as the Church of God International and the Associated Churches of God, have*

DOCTRINE, AND BASIS FOR FELLOWSHIP (WORLDWIDE CHURCH OF GOD) (continued)

arisen from the Worldwide Church of God and continue these emphases.

* * *

Sacred Name Groups

MAJOR POINTS OF DOCTRINE (ASSEMBLIES OF THE CALLED OUT ONES OF YAH)

1. "Yah" name we know.

2. "Yah's" name we are called by.

3. "Yah's" name and word we publish.

4. "Yah's" voice through "Yeshuah" we know and hear.

5. "Yah" has called us out.

6. "Yah" through "Yeshuah" is our salvation and joy.

7. "Yah's" Son, "Yeshuah," is our Saviour.

8. "Yah's" repentance, baptisms, commandments, laws and statutes we obey and the testimony of "Yeshuah."

9. "Yah's" gifts of the Holy Spirit we recognize and cherish.

10. "Yah's" prophecies we see and believe.

11. "Yah's" signs and seals we know and keep.

12. "Yah's" great power is the living power of the Holy Spirit, making us the "Called Out Ones" of "Yah" all in one accord through the Son, "Yeshuah," with the Heavenly Father, "Yah."

13. "Yah" is not a liar, but all men are.

Notes: *The Sacred Name groups are distinguished by their use of Hebrew transliterations as the actual name of the Creator (Yah, Yahweh, Yahvah, etc.) and his Son (Yeshuah, Yahshua, etc.) in place of the more common designations, God and Jesus. On other points they are very close to other Church of God Adventists.*

The Assemblies of the Called Out Ones of Yah uses "Yah" and "Yeshuah" for the names of the Creator and His Son. Members practice the charismatic gifts of the Holy Spirit usually associated with pentecostal churches.

* * *

BELIEFS [ASSEMBLY OF YAHVAH (ALABAMA)]

The Assembly of Yahvah teaches that "according to the Holy Spirit inspired scriptures, "Yahvah is the oldest and most correct rendering of the four sacred consonants from the Hebrew scriptures into the English scriptures, and the true and correct abbreviated form Yahshua, is the Saviour's name, as transferred from the language (Hebrew) in which the Saviour himself revealed it." "The keeping of all ten commandments including the observance of the seventh day Sabbath as taught in the fourth commandment." "That Yahshua is the only begotton Son of Yahvah, formed by the Holy Spirit, born of the virgin Mary (Miriam)." "That Salvation is only through the blood of Yahshua the Messiah and repentance, conversion, sanctification, the immersion (in water) must be preached." "That the baptism of the Holy Spirit and the nine gifts of the spirit are for the followers of Yahvahshua today, and all must live a clean, humble, Holy Spirit filled life." "A decent dress code for both sexes according to the Holy inspired Word and the abstaining from the habitual use of intoxicating liquors and drugs."

Notes: *The Alabama branch of the assembly is specifically charismatic and believes in the nine gifts of the spirit. The Creator and His Son's names are Yahvah and Yahshua.*

* * *

DOCTRINE [ASSEMBLY OF YAHVAH (OREGON)]

1. That "All scripture is given by inspiration of Yahvah, and is profitable for doctrine, for reproof, for correction, for instruction in righteousness: That the man of Yahvah may be perfect, thoroughly furnished unto all good works."

2. According to the Holy Spirit inspired Scriptures, "Yahvah" is the oldest and most correct rendering of the four Sacred Consonants from the Hebrew Scriptures into the English Scriptures; therefore "Yahvah" is the correct Name of the Creator, and Yahshua is the true and correct abbreviated form to use in English for the Saviour's Name, as transferred from the language (Hebrew) in which the Saviour Himself revealed it.

3. THAT Yahvah in six days made heaven and earth, the sea, and all that in them is, and rested the seventh day.

4. THAT Yahshua is the only begotten Son of Yahvah, formed by the Holy Spirit, born of the Virgin Miriam (Mary).

5. THAT Yahshua prove His Messiahship by remaining in the tomb exactly 3 days and 3 nights, rising in the end of, or late on the Sabbath.

6. THAT the baptism of the Holy Spirit and the nine gifts of the Spirit are for the followers of Yahshua today, and each follower of Yahshua must live a clean, humble, Holy Spirit-filled life; manifestations of the Spirit regulated according to 1 Corinthians 12th and 14th chapters.

7. THAT the inspired scriptural name for Yahvah's children is "The Assembly of Yahvah."

8. THAT Adam who was created perfect originally, through disobedience to Yahvah fell, bringing death, and the wrath of Yahvah upon mankind.

9. THAT experimental salvation, or salvation personally experienced by the one regenerated by the power of the Holy Spirit, is the only safe one to trust in.

10. THAT repentance, conversion, sanctification, and immersion (in water) must be preached.

11. THAT prayer and anointing will heal the sick.

12. THAT the passover, which consists of unleavened bread and the fruit of the vine (grape juice), is to be observed annually in honor of our Saviour's death, in the beginning (dark part) of the 14th of Abib.

13. THAT, according to the example of our Saviour, we ought to wash one another's feet.

14. THAT the seventh day of the week shall be observed from evening to evening as Yahvah's Sabbath.

15. THAT the paying of tithe should be practiced by Yahvah's children.

16. THAT all carnal warfare is condemned.

17. THAT the law of clean and unclean is still to be observed and taught.

18. THAT the habitual use of intoxicating liquors, alcoholic stimulants, narcotics, tobacco and any habit-forming drug, is condemned.

19. THAT the perfection and continuity of the law of Yahvah, the Ten Commandments, should be taught.

20. THAT the return of Yahshua will be literal, perceivable to the eye, personal and is impending.

21. THAT the Kingdom of Yahvah will be established under the leadership and in the person of Yahshua the Messiah on the throne of David at Jerusalem during the restitution of all things or during the one thousand year reign of the Saviour on earth, beginning at the second coming of Yahshua.

22. THAT the righteous are resurrected and rewarded at the second coming of Yahshua.

23. THAT the saints shall inherit the earth and will reign with the Saviour on earth during the millennium and throughout eternity.

24. THAT the dead are unconscious.

25. THAT the wicked dead are resurrected to final judgment, and not to a second trial or chance.

26. THAT the wicked will be eternally destroyed.

27. THAT the seven last plagues are literal, and will fall at the conclusion of this age.

In addition to the Statements or Belief and our Stand on Israel, here is how we stand on other scriptural points:

WATER BAPTISM CEREMONY. We believe that "Yahvah-shua the Messiah" is the correct form to use in the ceremony of water baptism, and that this is a complete fulfillment of the command given by our Saviour in Matt. 28:19, "Go ye therefore, and teach all nations, baptizing them in the name (not names) of the Father, and of the Son, and of the Holy Spirit." "Yahvah" (pronounced Yah Vah, Yahvah) is the Father's NAME, "Yahvah" is His Son's NAME, and it was in the Son's NAME that the Holy Spirit came, and please remember that the Son came in His Father's NAME, "Yahvah." "Shua" is the official title or term applied to the Son which shows what His Father does through Him, that is, "save or redeem." So when the ONE full correct form of the Son's NAME, "Yahvah-Shua the Messiah" is used in baptizing, this fulfills Matt. 28:19.

PASSOVER CALCULATION. We believe the Passover should be observed exactly 14 days from the time the first New Moon nearest the true Spring Equinox first becomes visible after the conjunction of the sun and moon, which is marked new moon on our calendars.

THE NEW COVENANT AND THE HUNDRED AND FORTY-FOUR THOUSAND. We believe just what the Scriptures state concerning this number and that is, that twelve thousand were sealed from each of the 12 fleshly tribes of (a man named) Israel. We believe that this work was accomplished under the personal ministry of our Saviour and the apostles and the early assembly. In other words, we believe the hundred and forty-four thousand were the FIRST to hear and accept the kingdom message, the FIRST to be sealed in the beginning of this great harvest age, "being the first fruits unto Yahvah and the lamb." (Rev. 14:4). We are living in the END of the harvest and for that reason, no sect, organization, association or individuals can constitute the "hundred and forty-four thousand."

We believe that Yahvah-Shua (Yahshua), was and is the mediator and testator of the New Testament, and He sealed it with His own blood. And according to Heb. 8:6-13; 9:15-17; 10:15-22; 1 Cor. 11:25, we believe that Yahvah-shua made the New Testament with the "house of Israel (10 tribes) and the house of Judah (2 tribes, Benjamin and Judah)" when He was there the first time.

After the hundred and forty-four thousand were sealed, we see that the work of the "great multitude" (Rev. 7:9) began, which meant spreading the "kingdom news" to any and all nations, therefore the "great multitude" is composed of believers redeemed from all nations, regardless of race or color. This work evidently started at the house of Cornelius and will continue unto the second coming of our Saviour or thereabout. Rev. 7:9; Acts 10:28-35; 13:46; Rom. 1:16.

THE MILLENNIUM. We do not believe that the Saviour will reinstate any part of the Mosaic or sacrificial system, in the millennium, which He died to abolish, but instead He will restore the entire earth to its original Edenic state and beauty, and will give to the saints of the Most High the dominion promised to Adam, that is, the whole earth. Dan. 7:18,27; 2 Pet. 3:13; Micah 4:8; Gen. 1:26-29.

WOMEN PREACHERS. We do not find one single text of Scripture that "women" ever received the titles evangelist, apostle, bishop, pastor or overseer. We do find that "women" were among those who were called "fellow-laborers" (Phil. 4:3), together with some men "helpers" (Rom. 16:3), "prophetess" (Luke 2:36), and "teachers" according to Titus 2:3-5.

Under these tithes we believe that "women" (the sisters) can fulfill any obligation put on them through the spirit toward Yahvah and His service. They can pray, sing prophesy under divine inspiration as a prophetess, be a personal witness for the Saviour and teach according to Titus 2:3-5. But all must be in harmony with 1 Tim. 2:11, 12; 1 Cor. 14:34, 35.

PENTECOST AND FEAST OF TABERNACLES. While we do not consider Pentecost and Feast of Taberna-

DOCTRINE [ASSEMBLY OF YAHVAH (OREGON)] (continued)

cles as binding on the saints of this age as we do the Passover and Ten Commandments, yet we have no objection to holding Campmeetings at these seasons. And it is the privilege of the individual or assemblies who so desired to observe these feasts. But we do not feel it best to open the Eliyah Messenger and the tracts we put out for advocating the observance of Pentecost and Tabernacles to the extent that some have, and are advocating.

Notes: *The Oregon branch of the assembly is non-Pentecostal. Yahvah and Yahshua are the names used for the Creator and His Son.*

*   *   *

STATEMENT OF DOCTRINE (ASSEMBLIES OF YAHWEH)

THE BASIS OF OUR FAITH

1. We affirm that in order to interpret the inspired Scriptures correctly, we must use the Old Testament as a basis for our faith. We must therefore interpret the New Testament through the teachings of the Old, recognizing complete harmony in the Word, thereby achieving sound doctrine, John 10:35. In the New Testament we find that repeated reference is made to the law, the Psalms, and the prophets: in other words, the Word of Almighty Yahweh, Matt. 4:4; John 5:39; Luke 24:44-46; 2 Timothy 3:14-17; Isaiah 8:16, 20; Acts 17:11. The Old Testament Scriptures saw partial fulfillment in the accounts that are recorded in the New, while they will find complete fulfillment in the years that will follow the Second Coming of our Savior.

2. We affirm that there is one Almighty Heavenly Father who is above all, and to whom we owe our reverence and worship, Deut. 6:4, 13; Matt. 4:10; 1 Cor. 8:4-6.

3. We affirm that the Messiah has come in human form as the man recognized as the Savior in the New Testament Scriptures, that He pre-existed with the Father, John 16:28-30; Psalm 2; Micah 5:2; John 17:5; Phil. 2:5-8; that He was born of a virgin, Matt. 1:18, 23; Luke 1:26-38; that He lived a sinless life, 1 Peter 2:22; that through His death upon the tree of Calvary we may have atonement for our sins, Isaiah 53; Hebrews 9; and that He rose again the third day, Matt. 12:40; 1 Cor. 15:1-8; to give us a hope of a resurrection also, Romans 5:6-12; 1 John 5:9-13.

4. We affirm that it is necessary and most important to our salvation that we accept the revealed, personal Name of our Heavenly Father YAHWEH and the Name of His Son, our Savior YAHSHUA the MESSIAH. We affirm also that the most accurate transliteration of these Names from the Hebrew into the English is by the spellings employed above, Exodus 3:14-15; Psalm 68:4; Psalm 83:18; Isaiah 42:8; Isaiah 52:6; Acts 4:12.

5. We affirm that the Holy Spirit is the mighty power from the Heavenly Father and the Messiah dwelling within us so that we may have the ability and strength to bring our lives into a state of perfection pleasing to our Heavenly Father, John 14:15-27. We find the trinitarian doctrine to be foreign to the inspired Scriptures. The Holy Spirit is imparted to the obedient believers by the laying on of hands of the elders of the Assemblies of Yahweh after baptism, Acts 19:1-6; Acts 8:14-24; 1 Timothy 4:14; Acts 2:38; Acts 5:32.

6. We affirm that as obedient children it is necessary to keep all the commandments, statutes, and judgments (except the ritual and animal sacrifice laws) which the Heavenly Father gave to Israel to make them a separate people, Lev. 20:7-8; Deut. 6:6-9, 25; Deut. 7:6-11; Matt. 5:17-20; Romans 7:12. It is now possible through the Holy Spirit to keep these commandments by faith for our salvation, Eph. 2:8-10; James 2:17-20. We now keep a spiritual sacrifice rather than animal sacrifices, meal, and drink offerings, Hebrews 13:15-16; 1 Peter 2:5; Romans 12:1; Phil. 4:18.

7. We affirm that sin is the transgression of the law of Yahweh, Lev. 4:2, 13, 27; 1 John 3:4.

8. We affirm that in order to be free from sin, a person must accept the shed blood of Yahshua the Messiah as his atonement and live in submission to the will of our Heavenly Father by keeping His laws, Micah 6:6-8; 1 John 1:7; 1 John 2:2; Hebrews 10:26-31; Eph. 1:6-7. Yahweh has extended grace (unmerited kindness or mercy) to all who keep His law, Rom. 3:24. Grace is not license to do as you please, Jude 4.

9. We affirm that water baptism is a necessary act following repentance, Acts 2:38; Matt. 3:13-17; that this baptism is immersion in water, backward, one time, into the Name of Yahshua the Messiah; Rom. 6:3-6; John 5:43; John 14:26; that this baptism symbolically indicates an inner cleansing, Romans 6:7-23; 1 Cor. 10:1-10. We also affirm that baptism, except in rare instances, is a necessary step in receiving the Holy Spirit, 1 Pet. 3:21.

10. We affirm that obedience to the commandments of Almighty Yahweh includes observing and keeping holy His commanded observances of Leviticus 23 and Numbers 28-29.

11. We affirm that the weekly seventh-day Sabbath (commonly called Saturday) is upheld in both Old and New Testament Scriptures, Exodus 20:8-11; Mark 2:27-28; Luke 4:16; Hebrews 4:4, 9. The Sabbath is a sign between Yahweh and His people, Ex. 31:12-17.

12. We affirm that the scriptural months are determined by the visible new moons, Deut. 16:1. The first day of each month is delineated by the appearance of the crescent. We find that the Scriptures indicate further that the law will go forth from Zion in the Millennium, Isaiah 2:3; the holy days will then be set from Jerusalem, Isaiah 66:23. The scriptural day begins and ends with sunset, Lev. 23:32; Mark 1:32.

13. We affirm that the Passover Memorial Supper in this New Testament era is the annual observance of our Savior's death. The Passover Memorial is to be observed on the evening of the 14th day of the scriptural month of Abib, soon after sundown, at the commencement of the day, Exodus 12:3-14; Numbers 28:16; 1 Cor. 5:7-8; 1 Cor. 11:23.

14. The Passover observance utilizes the emblems that are to be partaken in this New Testament era. The unleavened bread (matzoth) is the symbol of the broken body of our Savior, 1 Cor. 10:16; Exodus 23:18. The symbol of our Savior's shed blood is understood to be the fruit of the vine (Heb. tirosh, 'asis—grape juice), Matt. 26:27-29; Isaiah 65:8-9; Deut. 32:14. We find the Passover day to necessitate the use of unleavened bread, but it is not a Sabbath of rest, Deut. 16:3-4. It is the preparation for the feast, the day before the annual Sabbath, Mark 15:42; Luke 23:54; John 19:31, 42; Exodus 12:18; Exodus 34:25. Foot washing precedes the taking of the emblems, John 13.

15. We affirm that the Feast of Unleavened Bread is observed from the 15th to the 21st (inclusive) of the month of Abib; during this period we eat unleavened bread with our meals, Lev. 23:6, while symbolically cleansing ourselves of everything that corrupts, meaning false doctrine (teaching) which leads to sin, 1 Cor. 5:6-8; Matt. 16:12; Mark 8:14-15; Luke 12:1. The first and last days of this observance are to be kept as holy Sabbaths and convocations for the worship and praise of our Heavenly Father, Exodus 12:15-20; Numbers 28:17-25; Acts 20:6-7.

16. We affirm that the Feast of Shavuoth (Pentecost) is to be observed seven weeks after Passover, beginning our count with the day following the weekly Sabbath falling on Passover or during the week of Unleavened Bread, Joshua 5:10-12, NEB. Shavuoth (Feast of Weeks) is always observed on the first day of the week, Lev. 23:9-21; Acts 2. We find that it was the day of the outpouring of the Holy Spirit upon the New Testament assembly and was also the time when Israel ratified the convenant law with Yahweh given to Israel at Mt. Sinai.

17. We affirm that we shall observe the Feast of Trumpets in anticipation of our Savior's return from heaven for His bride, the assembly, Lev. 23:24-25; Numbers 10:1-10; Numbers 29:1; 1 Thess. 4:16.

18. We affirm that the fast of Atonement (Yom Kippur) is to be observed as a memorial of our Savior's atonement for us on the tree of Calvary. This day is to be observed as a strict Sabbath and fast day, Lev. 23:27-32; Acts 27:9.

19. We affirm that the Feast of Tabernacles is to be observed in this New Testament era as a preview of the Kingdom of Yahweh and the Millennium, Lev. 23:34-39; John 7:1-39; Zech. 14:16-21. The Feast of Tabernacles is a feast of seven days, the first day being a holy convocation, while the eighth day, called the Last Great Day, is to be observed as a holy convocation also, John 7:37.

20. We affirm that our Savior Yahshua the Messiah will establish the Kingdom of Yahweh, the Kingdom of the Heavens, on this earth, Ps. 115:16; Prov. 11:31; Matt. 5:5; Rev. 5:10. This Millennial Kingdom will prevail for 1,000 years and will be set up by Yahshua the Messiah at His Second Coming. At that time righteousness will be established as the order of the day, and this earth will be rebuilt into an Edenic paradise which man lost originally through sin, Isaiah 11:1-10; Matt. 6:10. After the Millennium, a new heaven and earth will be brought forth, Isaiah 66:22; Rev. 21:1.

21. We affirm that the Scriptures teach eternal punishment for the wicked, that this punishment is complete destruction in the lake of fire (Gehenna), and we disavow an eternal torment in an ever-burning hell, 2 Thess. 1:7-10; Mal. 4:1-3; Psalm 37:20-22; Isaiah 33:12; Matt. 25:46; Jude 7. We affirm that the Bible teaches the existence of a literal devil (Satan), Genesis 3:1-15, Isaiah 14:12-20, Zech. 3:1-2, Matt. 4:1-11, 1 Peter 5:8, Rev. 12:9. Satan will be destroyed at the end of the Millennium, Ezek. 28:18-19, Romans 16:20, Rev. 20:7-10.

22. We affirm that adherence to the law of clean meats in Lev. 11 and Deut. 14 remains in effect and binding in our era, and that it is important to our physical health, 2 Cor. 6:16-18.

23. We affirm that the Scriptures teach anointing with oil in the Name of Yahweh and in the Name of Yahshua the Messiah for healing of illness. This anointing service should be done by at least two elders if possible, James 5:13-20; Ex. 15:26.

24. We affirm that in order to preach this true doctrine of salvation around the world, every member of the body of the Messiah is obligated by scriptural law to tithe (10 percent of his increase) to the Assemblies of Yahweh, Prov. 3:9. These tithes are to be paid to the headquarters treasury so that no duplication of the ministry shall occur, Mal. 3:8-12; Lev. 27:30-33; Matt. 23:23. The Assemblies of Yahweh teaches also the second (feast day) tithe, Deut. 14:22-26, and the third (third year poor fund) tithe, Deut. 14:27-29; Deut. 26:12-17.

Notes: *This statement of the largest of the Sacred Name bodies was issued to bring unity to the movement. It is the most complete and systematic of the statements from the various Sacred Name organizations. Yahweh is the accepted name of the Creator.*

*   *   *

STATEMENT OF THE ASSEMBLIES OF YAHWEH (MICHIGAN)

This magazine is published for the glory of our Heavenly Father and His only begotten Son, our Saviour. It upholds the original inspired Scriptures—". . . the whole counsel of Yahweh." (Acts 20:27). Its aim is to remove the names substituted by man for the Memorial Name of the Creator and his Son, the Saviour of the world. Therefore, the originally inspired name Yahweh, the title Elohim (Mighty One) and the name Yahshua, the Messiah will be found on its pages. It upholds the Ten Commandments: restoring the Sacred Name in the third and the observing of the 7th Day Sabbath (Saturday) in the fourth. It stands for baptism by immersion in the Name of Yahshua the Messiah according to Acts 2:38 and Matthew 28:19; the ordinance of feet washing and the commemoration of Messiah's death at the Passover Season; the Feasts of Unleavened, Weeks, and Tabernacles, and the annual Sabbaths in Leviticus 23. It advocates tithing and the observance of all Yahweh's health laws including clean foods. It teaches justification by faith in the blood of Yahshua and advocates healing of the whole man—physically and spiritually. It stresses the importance of the sanctified life and the power of the Holy Spirit by which Yahweh works in us—". . . to will and do of His good pleasure." Philippians 2:13. It is supported entirely by the "Called Out Ones of Yahweh," which is the meaning of "The Assembly of Yahweh." It is of His People and for His People: all those who have heard and heeded the call of Revelation 18:4.

Notes: *Possibly the oldest Sacred Name congregations are associated with* The Faith, *a periodical begun in the mid-1930s. Each issue carries a declaration of basic affirmations which distinguish the Sacred Name cause from the Church of God Adventists as a whole.*

*　　*　　*

Jehovah's Witnesses Groups

WE BELIEVE (CHRISTIAN MILLENNIAL CHURCH)

GOD

We believe in ONE GOD; and that in the beginning He created Heaven and earth. That He is immortal, Divine and self-existing; having no beginning and will have no end.

That He is the Father of our Lord Jesus Christ. God is perfect in His four attributes of power, justice, wisdom and love. And that such attributes lie plain before the eyes of men; revealed to them in nature. In its universal order and beauty. To all who obey Him; through accepting and belief in His Son Jesus Christ; by recognizing His sovereignty; will receive eternal life.

For further reading: Genesis 1:1; Psalms 90:2; 83:18; 103:19; Deut. 32:4; I Chron. 29:10-13; Isa. 40:12-15; 42:9; 44:68; 46:8-11; 48:3; Rom. 1:19; I Tim. 1:17; I Tim. 6:16; John 3:36; 5:24; Titus 1:2.

JESUS CHRIST

Jesus Christ is the very first and only creation of God; the only begotten Son of God. As such He was known as the *Logos* or the Word. A most glorious Spirit Being in Heaven, who created all things under the guidance and direction of His Heavenly Father. In God's due time, Jesus willingly gave up His Heavenly glory, to be born to a virgin Mary; and was a perfect human being.

Jesus became the Savior and Redeemer of the human race, by giving His perfect life on the cross of Calvary, a ransom for Adam's life; thus satisfying Divine Justice. He was therefore rewarded by God His Father for His "faithfulness unto death"; by being raised from the dead, and given all power in Heaven and on earth; along with glory, honor and immortality; to be seated on His Father's right hand in the highest Heaven.

For further reading: John 1:1, 2; 3:16; Matt. 26:42; Luke 1:26-38; 19:10; Acts 1:6-11; 2:24; Col. 1:16; I Tim. 2:3-6; Heb. 8:1; Rev. 3:14.

THE HOLY BIBLE

The Bible is a collection of sixty-six books; written by the prophets, apostles and other men of God, who wrote under God's inspiration and direction, given them through God's Holy Spirit. From Genesis to Revelation, the Bible is God's message to men, revealing His will for mankind, and His wonderful plan for the redemption and salvation of the world. It tells of our legacy of eternal life—a reward for obedience to His just laws.

For further reading: John 17:3, 17; Ps. 119:1-5; 2 Tim. 3:16 & 17.

GOD'S PLAN OF THE AGES

God's Plan, as revealed in the Holy Bible, encompasses a period of about 7,000 years. From the creation of Adam to the end of Christ's (thousand-year) reign. Redemption through the blood of Jesus, is woven like a golden thread throughout the Bible; from Genesis to Revelation.

Genesis reveals the fall of man into sin and death, as well as the promise of the "seed"; Jesus; to expiate and atone for that sin of disobedience in the Garden of Eden. Then throughout the Old Testament the 'thread' is picked up, and extended to the actual giving of Christ's life on the cross. It further predicts the return of Christ to this earth, when He will set up God's Kingdom with His elected Church. During this first thousand years, God's purpose will be accomplished: A resurrection of all the dead; the just AND unjust. The just to reign with Christ; the unjust to have their trial or decision period; which includes every person who ever lived. Including the restoration of the earth and its order of things. Thus, at the end of His reign, Christ will turn over this perfected, sinless world to God, so God can be all in all.

For further reading: Genesis 3:1-19; Matt. 1:21; John 3:17; John 5:28; 14:1-3; I Cor. 15:20-28; I Tim. 2:3-6; I John 4:14; Rev. 11:15-18; Rev. 20:11, 12.

SATAN

Originally, Satan was created by God as a beautiful, powerful and wise cherub whose name was Lucifer. He was placed by God in the Garden of Eden to care for our first parents, Adam and Eve. However, Lucifer's heart was full of pride, ambition and a desire to be like the Most High, and desired to be worshipped as He is worshipped. So Lucifer lied to Eve, which led to her disobeying God. Adam soon followed, thus plunging all mankind into sin and death. Satan also seduced or influenced a great multitude of angels to follow him, and do his bidding, before the great Flood. Afterwards they were placed in everlasting chains until the Judgment Day.

But Satan and other his demoniacal associates are still very active in the world today: influencing and causing fear and confusion among people of all nations. He has very cleverly learned to use all means of communications: Television, movies, radio, stage plays, books, pornographic magazines, etc.

At the very beginning of Christ's Kingdom on earth, Satan will be imprisoned in a "bottomless abyss," so as not to deceive the nations. At the end of the Millennium, Satan will be destroyed.

For further reading: Genesis 3:1-6; Isa. 14:1-15; Ezek. 28:11-19; Matt. 4:1-11; II Cor. 4:4; John 14: 30; Jude 6; Ephes. 2:2; Rev. 20:7-10.

SIN

The Bible declares that sin is disobedience to the expressed will of God. And that the penalty for sin is DEATH: not eternal torment. For God warned Adam he would die if he disobeyed Him. But Adam willfully disobeyed His Creator, and with Eve was sentenced to death.

So by heredity, all Adam's children, all mankind, have been born under his condemnation. Therefore, no matter how they live, where they live, what race or nationality they are, all mankind is appointed to die.

For further reading: Genesis 3:17-19; Psa. 51:5; Rom. 2:23; 6:23; 5:12; Heb. 9:27; James 1:15; I Tim. 2:6; Rev. 1:5.

Man can be freed from slavery to sin by accepting the Lord Jesus Christ as His Lord or Master, and Savior; which is indicated by repentance and true conversion which leads to baptism; thus indicating he is a "new creature" in Christ Jesus. As redeemed by the Lord, they will; upon His return to earth; be resurrected and rewarded with eternal life. Then, by the end of Christ's reign, sin and death will have been completely eradicated from the face of the earth.

For further reading: I Peter 2:24, Acts 2:38, I John 2:12 and I Corinthians 15:26, 27.

ADAMIC DEATH

Adamic death is the result of sin. It has engulfed all of mankind because "all have sinned." So all mankind is under this sentence of death, as pronounced on father Adam: "Thou wast made of dust, and unto dust shalt thou return." Genesis 3:19. This is called Adamic death.

Death is a cessation of life; not a continuation of life somewhere else. The Bible reveals that when a man dies he loses all consciousness, knowledge, feeling, wisdom, etc. Man is placed into the grave (*sheol* in Hebrew; *hades* in Greek) where he sleeps until Christ's return, and the resurrection of the dead. Eccles. 9:5 and 10; John 5:28 & 29; I Cor. 15:22; Rom. 3:23; I Tim. 2:14; Ezek. 18:2-23; Isaiah 35:10.

SECOND DEATH

The second death is different from the first, or Adamic death, in that it means total destruction of the sinner; with no hope of a second resurrection.

Second death is vividly illustrated by the Valley of Hinnom, south of Jerusalem; the valley at the time of Christ, which was used as a garbage dump and incinerator for the city of Jerusalem. Its Greek name was *gehenna*. The fires in the Valley of Hinnom were always kept alive to burn and completely destroy all the trash, garbage and carcasses that were thrown or dumped there. No living thing was ever thrown into the fires; only the bodies of animals and of executed criminals. And what the fire did not destroy, worms did. Thus showing the complete annihilation of whatever was put into it. At the end of the Millennium, Adamic death and hell (the grave) will be thrown into Gehenna (destroyed). This is also pictured as "the lake burning with fire and brimstone"; where also Satan and his unrepentant fallen angels (demons) and obstinate sinners will be thrown. Forever more destroyed; thus ending all death. For further reading: Psalms 145:20; Matt. 10:28; Rev. 20:7-10; 20:14; 21:8.

ISRAEL

From Moses to Jesus, the people of Israel as a nation were God's chosen people. To them the Law was given; the prophets sent; the promises made. But the nation continually failed to obey God and His Law, which culminated in their rejection and crucifixion of Jesus. As a result of this rejection, Israel was destroyed as a nation, and dispersed throughout the Roman Empire. In God's Plan, favor came instead, to the Gentile (non-Jew) converts, who accepted Christ.

Nevertheless, prophecies declare that God is going to restore a relationship with the nation of Israel; restoring them as a nation and allowing His full favor to be theirs again when they accept Christ as their Messiah. The present state of Israel and events in the Middle East verify the fulfilling of these prophecies.

For further reading: Exodus 19:5,6; Zech. 12:10; Isa. 51:1-3; Mal. 2:1-9; Matt. 23:39; Luke 23:18-25; Acts 7:51-53; Rom. 11:26; Ezek. 37:1-14.

GRACE

Grace is a gift of God to us. It is His gracious favor shown unto us. None of us are deserving of such but God in His mercy provides grace through our faith in Christ Jesus. It is through His favor or Grace that we are accepted into His family as His children.

For further reading: Psa. 84:11; Acts 15:11; Romans 5:15-17; Ephes. 2:8; II Tim. 2:1; II Peter 3:18 and Romans 6:23.

SALVATION

Salvation of the human race was accomplished by the death of Christ Jesus on the cross. Since all men are under the condemnation of sin and death (see SIN and ADAMIC DEATH), to be saved one must repent of his sins and accept Jesus as Lord and Savior of his life. The Lord promised that anyone taking this step will be forgiven their sins, and if obedient unto death, will receive eternal life at the resurrection.

For further reading: Luke 9:10; Acts 2:37, 38; Rom. 5:6; I Cor. 15:3; II Cor. 6:2; Hebrews 5:9 and John 3:36.

CONSECRATION

The next logical step for the converted or saved Christian is to consecrate or dedicate his life to Christ. His life is then devoted to the service of the Lord, and learning obedience in all things of God. The exterior manifestation of this important step is baptism by water immersion. This baptism symbolizes the Christian's death to self and the world, and a rebirth or resurrection to a new life in Christ. As a new creature, the Christian should present his body a "living sacrifice"; leading a God-directed life, and thus establishing a close and intimate relationship with God as a son or daughter.

For further reading: Ephes. 5:26; I Thess. 4:3; 5:23; Heb. 2:11; 10:10; 13:12; I Pet. 3:11 and Romans 12:1 and 2.

BAPTISM

Baptism by immersion was ordered by Christ, so is considered mandatory. The immersion into water signifies the believer's death to self-will; the coming up out of the water, his intention to live "in Christ," or for Him. This then considers him to be a "new creature" in Christ; a member of God's New Creation. To which He has promised glory, honor and immortality; the Divine Nature, provided he or she remains faithful unto death.

For further reading: Rom. 6:1-11; 12:1,2; I Cor. 12:13; Gal. 3:27, Col. 3:1-4; Rev. 2:10.

GOD'S HOLY SPIRIT

God's Holy Spirit was shed on the gathered disciples at Pentecost. Ever since, it has been shed upon His disciples in varied measure, right to this day. And will be poured out upon all flesh; for His Spirit will work on the hearts of man in the next age also.

The Holy Spirit is a wondrous gift of God. It is like energy generating from Him. It is His power, His influence, which gives Christians guidance, enlightenment, comfort, wisdom, strength and joy. Without it, life for the Christian would be impossible, and he or she would miss many of the promised blessings of God.

For further reading: Luke 11:13; John 14:26; Acts 2:1-12; Joel 2:28,29; Rom. 5:5; 15:13; I Cor. 6:19; Ephes. 1:13; I Thess. 4:8; and I Pet. 1:12.

THE END OF THE WORLD

The Bible tells us that "this present evil world," dominated by Satan, is going to pass away during "the Great Day of the Wrath of the Lord God Almighty." On that day will be seen the "death" of this present evil world, as prophetically described in Daniel 2:35, and Malachi 4:1. Then follows the "birth" of God's new world of tomorrow, wherein "dwelleth righteousness." Everything on earth that is based on greed, selfishness, dishonesty, lust, violence, evil principles and wickedness will be destroyed forever. This destruction and purification will influence many to turn to God, and be in a condition to welcome the Kingdom then established on the earth.

For further reading: Matt. 4:8,9; II Cor. 4:4; John 13:31; 14:30; 16:11; Rev. 21:5; II Pet. 3:8-13; Mal. 4:1; James 5:1-6; Ezek. 7:19; Isa. 2:7-19; Rev. 6:15-17; Jer. 25:30-33; Isa. 34:1-4; Zech. 14:1-5; Rev. 19:11-21.

THE KINGDOM

God's Kingdom is seen in the New Testament as being made up of two phases—the spiritual Kingdom of God in Heaven, which has ever existed and will ever exist; and the earthly Kingdom of God, which will come into existence following the return of our Lord and Savior, Jesus Christ.

Now, during this Gospel Age, Christians who have dedicated their lives to God, and been baptized in obedience to the doing of His will, are said to be delivered from the power of darkness, (Satan's), and delivered unto the Kingdom of Christ. (Coloss. 1:13). They are said to be living (in Spirit) in the "heavenlies" with Christ Jesus. What is true now in spirit, will, at the return of Jesus, be an accomplished fact. For with Jesus, God's Kingdom reign will commence, and continue until God's plan of salvation and restoration is fulfilled through and by them.

For further reading: Col. 1:13 & 14; Ps. 2:7-9; Ps. 145:13; Isa. 9:7; Dan. 2:35,44; Dan. 7:13,14; Matt. 6:10, 33; 25:34; Luke 1:33; Luke 12:32; Eph. 5:4; I Thes. 2:12; Heb. 12:28; Rev. 11:15.

THE MILLENNIUM AND RESTORATION

The term "millennium" means one thousand years. It is applied to Christ's Kingdom on earth; which is to be established following His return from Heaven. During this period, Satan will be bound in a bottomless pit, so as not to deceive the people who will be resurrected on earth at that time. Christ and His Church will be the absolute, worldwide rulers of this Kingdom. The resurrection and judgment period of the "unjust" will then commence. Each person will have an individual trial or decision period, in which to decide as to whether or not they will accept God's righteous ways and live on forever, or reject His ways and thus die the Second Death. But each will have a full opportunity for instruction and rehabilitation, by coming to a full knowledge of Truth. For further reading: Acts 3:19-24; Rev. 20:3,4; John 5:28,29; Isa. 2:4; John 12:48. A final judgment will take place at the end of the Millennium, when Satan is loosed for a short period of time, for the testing of mankind; and will make one final attempt to deceive the people. Those who side with him will be destroyed along with Satan and his evil forces. This destruction is called the Second Death, from which there is no return.

The then proved faithful ones will continue to live on forever, completely restored to perfection, in a completely restored earth, as God always intended it to be, but thwarted in the Garden of Eden through Adam's disobedience.

Wars, violence, sorrow, sickness, suffering and death will no longer exist. They will be nothing more than memories of a painful past, and a remembrance of God's loving mercy provided through their Savior's sacrifice.

For further reading: Isa. 9:6,7; 11:1-10; 25:6-9; 26:9; 33:24; 35:1-10; 65:17-25; Acts 24:15; John 5:28, 29; Rev. 29:1-3; 11-14; I Cor. 15:24-28.

A NEW HEAVEN AND A NEW EARTH

In several places the Bible speaks of a "new heaven and a new earth," as opposed to the present heaven and present earth. We understand the old "heaven" is not God's Heaven, for it is eternal and will never pass away. But rather is Satan's lower abode of existence from which he presently rules; influencing mankind to do evil. Paul reveals to us this "heaven" is made up of "principalities, powers, rulers of darkness, and of spiritual wickedness in high places." (Ephes. 6:12). See also Ephes. 2:2; Col. 2:15. Satan is called the "god (mighty one) of this world" in II Cor. 4:4, and was called by Jesus "the prince of this world." (John 14:30). And Satan boasted to Jesus that he would give all the kingdoms of this world to Him, if He would bow down and worship him. Of course Jesus did not contest this boast. (Matt. 4:8-10). With the Lord's return this present dispensation or civilization will pass away. Just as the first dispensation was destroyed at the time of Noah by the Great Flood, so will this dispensation pass away; though not by a flood. The New English Bible explains it as "The heavens will disappear with a great rushing sound; the elements will disintegrate in flames, and the earth with all that is in it, will be laid bare." II Peter 3:10. But the earth will not be destroyed. God's plan is to make it glorious. (Num. 14:21). His footstool (Isa. 66:1). Eccles. 1:4 reminds us it will last forever.

Thus purified and renewed, this will be a beautiful "new earth, where righteousness shall abide." (Isa. 65:7; II Peter 3:12; Rev. 21:1-4).

THE RESURRECTION AND THE SOUL

The whole world has been led to believe that man has within himself something called an "immortal soul," which at death of the body goes off somewhere into space, be it heaven, hell, purgatory, nirvana, Valhalla, happy hunting ground, etc. This belief is NOT taught in the Bible, for nowhere in the Bible do we find the term "immortal soul," or that the soul is immortal. Rather we find that man IS a soul; not has one, for Genesis 2:7 states: "God breathed into man the breath of life and he BECAME a living soul." And Ezekiel 18:4, 20 tells us: "the soul that sinneth, it shall die." In sentencing Adam God made no mention of Adam's soul going anywhere after Adam's death. Rather, He plainly said: "for thou art dust, and unto dust shalt thou return." Period. (Gen. 3:19).

This means then, that man IS a soul: A conscious being, capable of thinking and feeling, and when dead he is incapable of thinking and feeling. (Eccles. 9:5 & 10). Therefore we conclude that according to the Scriptures, the grave awaits us all, good and bad, and there is no eternal torment awaiting the wicked dead, but instead the resurrection from the grave. (John 5:28 & 29).

If man had an immortal soul, there would be no need of a resurrection, for immortality means being imperishable; therefore in no need for a resurrection. God has designed the resurrection because man, the living soul, ceases to exist at the time of death. Paul clearly states that "if there is no resurrection, they also which have fallen asleep (died) are perished." Thus we see the dead are truly dead in the grave; not in Heaven or a place of torment, and without the resurrection would remain dead—perished forever. (I Corinthians 15:18).

So we must make a choice. We can either believe in the immortality of the soul (a doctrine taught by men) or in the resurrection of the dead; as taught by God and the Lord Jesus Christ, in the Bible. We cannot believe in both. We choose to believe God and His Word. How about you?

For further reading: Psa. 115:17; Isa. 26:19; John 5:26-28; I. Cor. 15:21, 22, 35-57; John 11:25; Rev. 12, 13.

SHEOL, HADES, HELL AND THE GRAVE

As noted in our discussion of Adamic death, hell is a translation of the Hebrew word *sheol*; and of the Greek word *hades*. The original meaning of these words was hole, pit, grave, tomb, a place of silence where the living placed their dead. However, centuries after the Apostles fell asleep a new meaning of heathen origin was introduced, and believed and adopted by the clergy.

The place called "hell" was described as a place of boiling and burning with fire and brimstone, where the immortal souls of sinners would be sent upon the death of their bodies. There, the devil with pitchfork, was said to inflict pain and everlasting torture upon them. But never consumed. (A question: since a soul is not made of matter, in this human theory, how then can it be roasted and burned?)

This Satanic doctrine, borrowed from heathen religions, has caused fear in the hearts of the people, thus keeping them in absolute subjection to the clergy. No such place of punishment is mentioned in the Bible, for sinners. Though in Revelation they have taken the symbolic language used in chapters 20:14 & 15, and 21:8, to indicate such a place of torment does exist. However note carefully in 20:14 that *death* and *hell* were cast into the lake of fire. How then can hell, if it be the lake of fire, be cast into hell? Notice the rest of this verse as well as 21:8 gives the proper explanation as to what the lake of fire really is: "This is the second death."

What then is the lake of fire, since it is not a literal lake? Revel. 21:8 further confirms the lake of fire to be the second death, or total destruction. Thus we can truly believe what is stated in Romans 6:23: "For the wages of sin is DEATH," but the gift of God is Eternal LIFE through Jesus Christ our Lord." Thank God for He is love and would never torture man, no matter how evil they may be, just as you or I would never think of torturing an animal or child. And thank Him for promising that in due time the grave itself will be defeated and abolished, for "the last enemy to be destroyed is death." (I Corin. 15:26). Praise God for this.

THE TRINITY

One doctrine which is believed by almost all of mainstream Christianity, is the doctrine of "The Trinity." This doctrine has led a great many people to believe that God did not send His Son Jesus into the world to become the Savior of mankind, but rather that God Himself (though the scriptures state Him to be immortal, therefore death-proof) incarnated Himself into Mary's womb, and was born half man and half God. A demi-god. Interestingly enough, the word "Trinity" is never used in the Bible.

WE BELIEVE (CHRISTIAN MILLENNIAL CHURCH) (continued)

Furthermore, history tells us that it was at the Council of Nice, in 325 A.D. that the majority of the 318 bishops officially adopted the doctrine of the Trinity as most now know it—a doctrine of which the Apostles knew nothing.

The Bible records God as the Father, the Giver of life. That He created Jesus as His only begotten Son, sending Jesus to earth through a woman, Mary. (Luke 1:26-28; John 1:14; 3:16); to be the Savior of the world. Which was accomplished by His death on the cross, thus ransoming Adam, and providing redemption for the whole human race. Both the living and the dead. (Matthew 20:28; I. Tim. 2:6).

It was God who awoke Jesus from His three-day sleep in death. Forty days later God received Him back into Heaven, and rewarded Him by making Him head of *all* things, including the Church. He is now seated on the right hand of God, a Divine immortal being, so "Christ dieth no more." (Ephes. 1:2-22; Rom. 6:9; Rev. 1:18). We see then, that it is evident that there are here but two separate entities—God the Father, and Jesus, His Son.

As for the Holy Spirit being a third entity or third person of a Triune God, the Bible tells us rather, that the Holy Spirit is used in reference to God Himself, when speaking of His power, wisdom and understanding which accomplishes His mighty words, in both the material and spiritual worlds.

We who are His sons and daughters in Christ, are the blessed recipients of this power or Spirit. This same Holy Spirit which was given to Jesus when He was baptized by John in the Jordan. (Matthew 3:13-17; Acts 2:38, John 14:26).

Many use I John 5:6 to prove the Father, Son and Holy Spirit are one. However, in reading other translations than the King James, we find it properly reads: "For there are three witnesses: the Spirit, the water, and the blood, and these three are in agreement." We therefore affirm there is ONE GOD, and we say with the Apostle Peter: "To Him be glory and dominion for ever and ever . . . Amen."

—written by Gaetano Boccaccio

—edited by Dawn Kersula

Notes: *Though many groups derive from what is today known as Jehovah's Witnesses, most became independent organizations prior to the Witnesses' acceptance of "Jehovah" as God's name; hence they do not call God "Jehovah." These groups are non-Trinitarian, believing that Jesus is not God but the first creation of God. Most of the groups have not published doctrinal statements.*

The Christian Millennial Church broke with the Jehovah's Witnesses (then known as the Millennial Dawn Bible Students) over the doctrine of the ransom atonement (item 2).

BELIEFS (DAWN BIBLE STUDENTS ASSOCIATION)

THE BELIEFS. The Bible is accepted as the inspired Word of God, and the only infallible authority to guide a Christian in his life and belief.

CREATION AND FALL. Man was created in the image of God, and given the opportunity to live in an earthly paradise forever, on conditions of obedience. He disobeyed, and was driven out of his garden home to die.—Gen. 1:26-31; 3:16-19

SIN'S PENALTY. "In the day that thou eatest thereof thou shalt surely die." (Gen. 2:17) "The wages of sin is death." (Rom. 6:23) "The soul that sinneth it shall die." (Ezek. 18:4, 20) "Fear not them which kill the body, but are not able to kill the soul: but rather fear him which is able to destroy [not torment] both soul and body in hell."—Matt. 10:28

REDEMPTION. Jesus took the sinner's place in death. Thus he became the satisfaction, the "propitiation for our sins: and not for ours only, but also for the sins of the whole world." (I John 2:2) To accomplish this redemption Jesus "poured out his soul unto death." (Isa. 53:12) Jesus gave himself a "ransom for all." (I Tim. 2:3-6) Having died for the world, Jesus was raised from the dead by the power and glory of his Heavenly Father. (Acts 2:24; Eph. 1:19, 20) His soul was not left in death, the Bible hell. (Ps. 16:10) Now he "ever liveth to make intercession" for us.—Heb. 7:25

SALVATION. "The gift of God is eternal life through Jesus Christ our Lord." (Rom. 6:23) Salvation from death, through Christ, is made possible through a resurrection of the dead, Jesus himself being the "firstfruits" of the resurrection. If Christ had not been raised from the dead, then there would have been no hope of a resurrection for others, and "they also which are fallen asleep in Christ are perished."—I Cor. 15:17-19

The church of Christ comes forth in the "first resurrection," to "live and reign with Christ a thousand years." (Rev. 20:4, 6) Then there will be the general resurrection, when the "dead, small and great, stand before God," the "books" of divine revelation are opened and they are judged upon the basis of the will of God thereby revealed to them. Those whose works conform to the will of God will live forever.—Rev. 20:11-15

The followers of Jesus in this age partake of a "heavenly calling." (Heb. 3:1) They will be with Jesus in the "place" he prepares for them. (John 14:2, 3) They are joint-heirs with Jesus, and will sit with him on his throne. (Rom. 8:17; Rev. 3:21) In the resurrection they partake of the "divine nature," of "glory and honor and immortality."—II Pet. 1:4; Rom. 2:7

Those awakened from death in the general resurrection will have the opportunity of being restored to perfection of human life here on earth as enjoyed by our first parents before they transgressed the law of God. These are the "sheep" class of Matthew 25:34, to whom it will be said, "Come, ye blessed of my Father, inherit the kingdom prepared for you from the foundation of the world." Peter describes this general restoration of all the willing and obedient of mankind as the "restitution of all things," adding that it had been foretold by the mouth of all God's holy prophets since the world began. In the "times of restitution," those who do not accept Christ and obey the laws of his kingdom will "be destroyed from among the people."—Acts 3:19-23

THE SECOND ADVENT. Christ came at his first advent to give his life a "ransom for all." For this purpose he was made flesh, and he gave his flesh, his humanity, "for the the life of the world." (John 6:51) He was raised from the dead in the "express image" of his Father's person, "whom no man hath seen, nor can see." (Heb. 1:1-3; I Tim. 6:15, 16) It is the divine Christ who returns and establishes his authority in the earth, and, for a thousand years, is both Ruler and Judge, his church being associated with him.—Isa. 9:6; II Tim. 4:1; I Pet. 4:5; I Cor. 6:2, 3; Rev. 2:26, 27; 3:21

PROPHECY. Prophecies descriptive of world conditions at the time of Christ's return are in process of fulfilment. These prophecies describe the destruction of "this present evil world," the social order over which Satan is prince, but "the earth abideth forever." (Gal. 1:4; Eccl. 1:4) God created the earth, "not in vain, he formed it to be inhabited."—Isa. 45:18

CHRISTIAN WORK. The present work of the church is to disseminate the Gospel for the perfecting of the saints for the future work of service; to develop in herself every grace; and to bear testimony to the world concerning the love of God through Christ, and the imminence of his long-promised kingdom.—Matt. 24:14

Notes: *This statement is in general agreement with that of the Pastoral Bible Institute from which the association is derived.*

*   *   *

TO US THE SCRIPTURES CLEARLY TEACH (PASTORAL BIBLE INSTITUTE)

Chartered in 1918, the Pastoral Bible Institute, Inc., was formed for the promotion of Christian knowledge. Its journal, *The Herald of Christ's Kingdom,* stands firmly for the defense of the only true foundation of the Christian's hope now being so generally repudiated—Redemption through the precious blood of "the man Christ Jesus, who gave himself a ransom [a corresponding price, a substitute] for all" (1 Pet. 1:19; 1 Tim. 2:6). Building upon this sure foundation the gold, silver, and precious stones (1 Cor. 3:11-15; 2 Pet. 1:5-11) of the Word of God, its further mission is to—"make all see what is the fellowship of the mystery which . . . has been hid in God . . . to the intent that now might be made known by the Church the manifold wisdom of God"—"which in other ages was not made known unto the sons of men as it is now revealed."—Eph. 3:5-10.

It stands free from all parties, sects, and creeds of men, while it seeks more and more to bring its every utterance into fullest subjection to the will of God in Christ, as expressed in the Holy Scriptures. It is thus free to declare boldly whatsoever the Lord hath spoken—according to the Divine wisdom granted unto us, to understand. Its attitude is not dogmatic, but confident; for we know whereof we affirm, treading with implicit faith upon the sure promises of God. It is held as a trust, to be used only in his service; hence our decisions relative to what may and may not appear in its columns must be according to our judgment of his good pleasure, the teaching of his Word, for the upbuilding of his people in grace and knowledge. And we not only invite but urge our readers to prove all its utterances by the infallible Word, to which reference is constantly made, to facilitate such testing.

TO US THE SCRIPTURES CLEARLY TEACH

THAT the Church is the "Temple of the Living God"—peculiarly "his workmanship"; that its construction has been in progress throughout the Gospel Age—ever since Christ became the world's Redeemer and the Chief Corner Stone of this Temple, through which when finished, God's blessing shall come to "all people" and they find access to him.—1 Cor. 3:16, 17; Eph. 2:20-22; Gen. 28:14, Gal. 3:29.

THAT meantime the chiseling, the shaping, and polishing of consecrated believers in Christ's atonement for sin, progresses; and when the last of these "living stones," "elect and precious," shall have been made ready, the Great Master Workman will bring all together in the First Resurrection; and the Temple shall be filled with his glory, and be the meeting place between God and men throughout the Millennium.—1 Pet. 2:4-9; Rev. 20:4, 6.

THAT the basis of hope for the Church and the world lies in the fact that "Jesus Christ by the grace of God, tasted death for every man," "a ransom for all," and will be "the true light which lighteth every man that cometh into the world," "in due time."—Heb. 2:9; John 1:9; 1 Tim. 2:5, 6.

THAT the hope of the Church is that she may be like her Lord, "see him as he is," be "partaker of the divine nature," and share his glory as his joint-heir.—1 John 3:2; John 17:24; Rom. 8:17; 2 Pet. 1:4.

THAT the present mission of the Church is the perfecting of the saints for the future work of service; to develop in herself every grace; to be God's witness to the world; and to prepare to be kings and priests in the next Age.—Eph. 4:12; Matt. 24:14; Rev. 1:6; 20:6.

THAT the hope for the world lies in the blessings of knowledge and opportunity to be brought to all by Christ's Millennial Kingdom—the restitution of all that was lost in Adam, to all the willing and obedient, at the hands of their Redeemer and his glorified Church—when all the willfully wicked will be destroyed.—Acts 3:19-23; Isa. 35.

Notes: *This statement is printed in each issue of* The Herald of Christ's Kingdom, *the periodical of the Pastoral Bible Institute, one of the earliest rivals of what is now known as Jehovah's Witnesses.*

Southcottites

SOME OF THE TRUTHS FOR WHICH THE CHRISTIAN ISRAELITE CHURCH STANDS

We believe the Holy Bible to be the Word of God. We believe in the Fall of man from an immortal life by the Spirit of God (in the image of God) to a mortal life of blood with an evil heart—which became the image of fallen man (Gen. 5: 3)—resulting from the disobedience of Adam and Eve, our first parents (Gen. 2:17). Death of the physical body was thus introduced because of the evil contamination. The Fall of man was permitted (Rom. 8:20), foreseen and provided for in God's plan of Salvation (Acts 15:18) to work out for mankind a greater weight of glory (2 Cor. 4:17).

By faith "we trust in the living God who is the Saviour of All men, specially of those that believe" (1 Tim. 4:10). Hence, the souls of all who die will rise again at God's appointed times, with spiritual (celestial) bodies; their physical bodies having returned to dust will be no more (Gen. 3:19). The dead in Christ (who have accepted Him as their personal Saviour) will enter upon their reward at the First Resurrection, they being "children of the Resurrection" equal unto the angels (Luke 20:36). The Unrepentant also will rise and be judged, but will be returned to their graves; this is the "Second death." They will remain there until the Second Resurrection, 1,000 years later (at the end of the Millenium), when they also will come forth and acknowledge Jesus Christ as their Saviour. For at the Name of Jesus, every knee shall bow, "of things in heaven and things in earth, and things under the earth" (Phill. 2:10). This great consummation has been made possible by the Obedience and Sacrifice of God's Son, Jesus Christ; for God required the shedding of the blood of a pure and sinless man for man's transgressions—and He alone could provide that requirement. He having died for the ungodly, and tasted death for every man (Rom. 5:6; Heb. 2:9), hence, "as in Adam all die, even so in Christ, shall ALL be made alive; but every man in his own order" (1 Cor. 15:22-23).

But we believe that besides celestial bodies there also are bodies terrestrial; "the glory of the celestial is one, and the glory of the terrestrial is another" (1 Cor. 15:40). God has an Elect number, whom He foreknew, and pre-destinated to be conformed to the image of His Son (Rom. 11:2 and 8:29). They will NOT DIE, for their physical bodies will be Cleansed of all evil, and changed like unto the glorified terrestrial body of "flesh and bone," as manifested by Jesus Christ (Phill. 3:21; Luke 24:39); blood not being their life, but living by the Abiding Presence of the Spirit of God.

We believe that in the year 1822 the Lord selected a "Messenger" to revive and preach the "Gospel of the Kingdom" embracing the abolition of death, overthrow of Satan, and the establishment of the Kingdom of God upon earth.

The Elect number (Rev. 7:4; Matt. 24: 22-24, 31) will be descendants of the Twelve sons of Jacob, whose name God changed to Israel; Two tribes of whom are the people known as Jews, and the other Ten tribes being at present in Christian churches—ignorant of the great destiny which is their inheritance. Hitherto they have been content with the assurance of the Salvation of the Soul alone (1 Peter 1:9), but when they hear the Gospel of the salvation of the whole being (spirit, and Soul and Physical Body, 1 Thess 5:23) and of Israel's Ingathering (Isa. 11:11-12) in these "latter days," they will come forth and surname themselves by the name of Israel, as foretold in Isaiah 44:5 and thereafter will be known as Christian Israelites. As the distinction implies, they will observe the dual obligation of both Gospel and Law as did Jesus Christ (Matt. 23: 2-3; Luke 10: 25-27; John 5: 46-47), who left us an example that we should follow in His steps (1 Peter 2:21). HE is the foundation upon whom we build; "for other foundation can no man lay than that is laid, which is Jesus Christ" (1 Cor. 3:11). This glorious manifestation of Faith in Action will be reinforced by God's Holy Spirit descending upon His "Chosen Remnant." The evil within their physical bodies will pass away, and their whole being will be preserved Alive unto the Second Coming of Jesus Christ, when they will be Purified (Dan. 12:10) and Glorified by their mortal bodies putting on PHYSICAL IMMORTALITY. In them will be fulfilled those words of Jesus in John 14: 12, "He that believeth on Me, the works that I do shall he do also." "They shall be known among the Gentiles, and all that see them shall acknowledge them that they are the seed which the Lord hath blessed" (Isa 61:9). When "Born again" by God's Holy Spirit being grafted "within" them, they then will possess the Kingdom of God within them; the Law of the Spirit of Life in Christ Jesus making them free from the law of sin and death (Rom. 8:2).

Notes: *Understanding the statement of the Christian Israelite Church requires some background of the movement begun by Joanna Southcott. The "messenger" mentioned in the text is John Wroe, a follower of Southcott. Following her failure to bear a child in 1814 as predicted, Southcott died, leaving her movement in disarray. She was succeeded in leadership by George Turner, who predicted the appearance of the child, Shiloh, in 1820, and then in 1821. John Wroe had stepped forward to denounce Turner's prophecies as false. He rose to leadership when Turner's predictions failed, and in 1822 reorganized the Southcott following.*

* * *

British Israelism

THE ANGLO-SAXON-CELTIC-ISRAEL BELIEF (ANGLO-SAXON FEDERATION OF AMERICA)

We believe in God—the God of the Bible (*Ex. 3: 6, 14*).

We believe in Jesus Christ, the only begotten Son of God (*John 1:14*).

We believe in the atoning sacrifice of Jesus Christ on Calvary (*Matt. 26:28; Rom. 5*).

We believe Christ died for us (*Rom. 5:8*); also that He was raised up from the dead (*Rom. 6:4*).

We believe He ascended into Heaven (*Mk. 16:19*).

We believe John 3:16—"For God so loved the world that He gave His only begotten Son, that whosoever believeth in Him should not perish, but have everlasting life."

We believe in the Holy Ghost and His mission (*John 14:26; Acts 2*).

We believe the whole Bible, both the Old Testament and the New Testament; that it is the inerrant Word of God (*II Pet. 1:19-21*). We believe its history; its covenants; its prophecies.

We believe in its Gospel of Grace (*Acts 20:24; Eph. 2:1-8*), which is the Gospel of Salvation for all men; that *personal* salvation by faith in the atonement of Jesus Christ is necessary for *all*, Israelite, Jew, Gentile (*Rom. 3:22-25*).

We also believe in the Gospel of the Kingdom (*Matt. 4:23, 24:14*).

We believe in the bodily return of Christ (*Acts 1:9-11*), who will take the Throne of David (*Isa. 9:6-7; Lk. 1:32*), and rule on this earth for a thousand years *(Rev. 20:1-6)*.

We believe the Bible contains God's plan for the remedy of all human ills, and we believe that plan is working out through the Bible people, called Israel (*II Sam. 7*).

We believe this people Israel, consisting of twelve tribes (*Ex. 28:21; Rev. 21:12*), the descendants of the twelve sons of Jacob (*Gen. 49*), were chosen of God to be His servant people (*Ex. 19:5; Deut. 7:6-8*), through whom all nations are to be blessed (*Gen. 22:18*).

We find that through Israel God has revealed Himself ever since the days of Moses (*Ex. 19; Matt. 15:24*). To them He gave the law (*Ex. 20*). Through their prophets came the inspired Scriptures. Our Lord was of that race (*Matt. 1*), and is Prophet, Priest and King. His Apostles also were of Israel, and we believe the Divine plan is still working through that appointed race.

Bible history shows that twelve-tribed Israel, after a checkered career covering some five centuries, came to its greatest historic development in Palestine under Kings David and Solomon (*II Sam. 7; I Kings 10*). Upon the death of King Solomon there was civil war among the tribes of Israel. Ten tribes revolted and set up the "House" or "Kingdom" of Israel, known as the Northern Kingdom, having its capital in Semaria. The remaining tribes became the "House" or "Kingdom" of Judah and were known as the Southern Kingdom (*I Kings 12*). The Royal line of the House of David remained for a time with the Southern Kingdom and its kings reigned from the throne in Jerusalem.

This divided condition continued for about two hundred and fifty years. Then, because of wicked conduct and defiance of God, the Northern Kingdom, or "House of Israel," was overthrown as the result of several military invasions by the Assyrian Empire and the people were driven into captivity in northern Assyria. Following that, as time went on, they disappeared from history (*II Kings 17*).

The Southern Kingdom, or "House of Judah," kept itself intact for approximately another hundred and thirty years. Then, because of national decadence and rebellion against God, it was repeatedly attacked by the armies of the Babylonian Empire and eventually conquered. Its people were taken into captivity by the Babylonians where they were destined to remain for a period of seventy years (*II Chron, 36:21; Jer. 25:9-11*). It was at the time of the captivity of the Southern Kingdom that the term "Jew" began to be used and it applied only to the remnant of Judah (*II Kings 18:26; Jer. 41:3*).

At the close of this exile period, a "remnant" of these Babylonian captives of the House of Judah were permitted to return to Jerusalem and establish themselves therein (*Ezra and Nehemiah*). During this resettlement of the land of Palestine the Nation of the Jews came into being. These returned captives were thereafter generally known as Jews (*Ezra 4:12*) and their descendants were the Jews of the time of Jesus (*Matt. 2:2*).

It will thus be seen that it is wholly erroneous to say that the Jews constitute all of Israel when they actually came only from the Southern Kingdom. Jews who can trace their ancestry through Judah to Abraham are of Israel, just as Georgia is a part of the United States. But just as it is absurd to say that all in the United States are Georgians, it is equally absurd to say that all Israelites are Jews.

The differentiation made in the Scriptures between "Israel" and "Judah" must not be overlooked or ignored (*see I Kings 12; Jer. 3:6-11; Ps. 114:1-2; Ex. 37; Zech. 11:7-14; II Chron. 10, 11, etc.*). They are by no means interchangeable terms. *To realize this is to possess the key to the identity of the true Israel of God in the world today.*

Diligent research into the Bible and historical records has disclosed the fact that the Anglo-Saxon-Celtic peoples are the lineal descendants of the House of Israel. Supporting proof is found in the records of heraldry, the findings of archaeology and in a study of ethnology and philology.

When the people of the Northern Kingdom went into Assyrian captivity, they did not remain there. During the subsequent dissolution of the Assyrian power through its involvement in foreign wars, the people of Israel escaped in successive independent waves, leaving the land of their captors when the opportunity came to do so. Under different names (*Scutai, Sak-Geloths, Massagetae, Khumri, Cimmerians, Goths, Ostrogoths, Visigoths, etc.*), they moved westward into the wilderness, across Asia Minor, then into Europe and eventually into the Scandinavian countries and the British Isles. From the "Isles of the Sea" they went further westward to the "desolate heritages" of the North American continent and to Australia, New Zealand, etc.

In the prophetic Scriptures many references are made to this Great Trek of the House of Israel. The records of medieval history reveal the emergence from time to time of bands of virile people of mysterious origin, who left their mark upon the course of empire wherever they appeared. These were the trekking tribes of Israel, whose identity had been lost to history but not to God (Amos 9:9).

The Gentile kingdoms are being broken, and heathen powers coming to judgment, while the time of Israel's punishment is terminating. The old Gentile social order is disintegrating, to be replaced by the restoration of the Kingdom of God on the earth. The world is being

THE ANGLO-SAXON-CELTIC-ISRAEL BELIEF (ANGLO-SAXON FEDERATION OF AMERICA) (continued)

prepared for the coming and reign of our Lord upon the Throne of David and the institution of the Age of Righteousness when "out of Zion shall go forth the law, and the word of the Lord from Jerusalem" (Isa. 2:2-5).

We believe the Israel peoples must and will, under God, lead the world out of the chaos which now afflicts mankind (Isa. 2:1-4). After much chastisement for their sins, the favor of God will again be upon them for the blessing of the world. "I do not this for your sakes, O house of Israel, but for mine holy name's sake" (Ez. 36:22-32).

We do not constitute a new sect or a new religion. We are Christians of many denominations who have formed a nonprofit educational center with the single purpose of getting the Bibles of America opened to permit them to present their entire revelation. We stress particularly the neglected fact of the modern identity of the Israel of God and the necessity to restore in our nation the administration of the Law of the Lord, for this is the Gospel of the Kingdom. We encourage a more complete grasp of the Biblical message of personal salvation and national redemption, for a consideration of the whole story the Bible tells will open to one's understanding the vast hemisphere of national and prophetic truths which we must all soon take into account.

Notes: *The British Israelite groups are distinguished by their belief in the identity of modern Anglo-Saxon people (especially those of the United States and Great Britain) as the literal descendents of the Ten Lost Tribes of ancient Israel, and thus heirs to all of the Old Testament prophecies given about Israel. Most groups have not committed their beliefs to a summary format.*

The statement of the Anglo-Saxon Federation of America details the understanding of the history of Israel and the Anglo-Saxon people held by most British Israelites.

*　　*　　*

WE BELIEVE (BRITISH ISRAEL WORLD FEDERATION)

AS ORTHODOX CHRISTIANS—OF ALL DENOMINATIONS—WE BELIEVE:

That our Lord Jesus Christ is the Son of God: that He spoke with the authority of Almighty God and that He meant what He said.

That our civilisation is approaching the Crisis so precisely foreseen and described by Him and that the End-of-the-Age sequence of events indicated by Him, revealing a tremendous upsurge of evil, has been reflected in the crescendo of visitations which have scourged mankind since the early days of the present century. We emphasize our positive conviction that the world at this moment stands on the threshold of a New Age and that this will be heralded by the promised Personal return of the King of kings. As a non-sectarian, interdenominational Movement, we urge Christians who truly accept the whole Gospel of

Christ to prepare themselves for His Imminent Second Coming.

That we—the English-speaking Nations—with our kinsfolk among the peoples of the North Sea fringe, embody the bulk of the present-day descendants of God's ancient people of Israel. As responsible servants He has commissioned us to form the core of His Kingdom on earth, bearing the Gospel of Jesus as our watchword, under the guidance of the Church of Christ.

We assert, therefore, that our associated peoples are none other than God's promised Company of Nations—the Commonwealth of Israel—which the Scriptures declare will be the nucleus of His earthly Kingdom, now open to all who will accept Jesus as Lord and Saviour, whatever may be their race or color.

We are able to adduce secular evidence to prove that the forebears of our kindred Celto-Saxon peoples originated in Bible lands. The Jewish folk of today contain only a residue of the people of Israel.

Notes: *This brief statement summarizes the British-Israel position.*

*　　*　　*

DOCTRINAL STATEMENT OF BELIEFS (CHRISTIAN IDENTITY CHURCH)

The following is a brief statement of our major doctrinal beliefs as taught by the Holy Scriptures. This list is not exhaustive, but a basic digest defining the true faith once delivered to the saints. For a further explanation of our beliefs and the implications of these truths, please contact us.

We believe in YHVH the one and only true and living eternal God (Isa. 44:6); the God of our fathers Abraham, Isaac and Jacob (Exo. 3:14-16), the Creator of all things (1 Cor. 8:6) who is omnipotent, omnipresent, unchangeable and all-knowing; the Great I Am who is manifested in three beings: God the Father, and God the Son, and God the Holy Spirit, all one God (Deut. 6:4).

We believe the entire Bible, both Old and New Testaments, as originally inspired, to be the inerrant, supreme, revealed Word of God. The history, covenants, and prophecy of this Holy Book were written for and about a specific elect family of people who are children of YHVH God (Luke 3:38; Psalm 82:6) through the seedling of Adam (Gen. 5:1). All scripture is written as a doctrinal standard for our exhortation, admonition, correction, instruction and example; the whole counsel to be believed, taught and followed (II Tim. 3:16, Act. 20:27).

We believe Yahshua the Messiah (Jesus the Christ) to be the only incarnate begotten son of God, the Word made flesh (John 1:14), born of the Virgin Mary in fulfillment of divine prophecy (Isa. 7:14; Luke 1:27) at the appointed time, having had His eternal existence as one with the Father before the world was (John 17:5, 21-22).

We believe in the personally revealed being of God the Holy Spirit, the Comforter (John 15:26, 16:7), who was sent by God the Son to glorify Him (John 16:14) and teach us all truth (John 14:26, 16:13; I Cor. 2:10-12) according to promise (Ezek. 36:25-27; Acts 2:33; Eph. 1:13-14). The Holy Spirit is sent to dwell in (I Cor. 3:16; John 14:17) the members of the body of Christ, giving unto each different gifts (1 Cor. 12) empowering them to witness (Acts 1:8) of sin, of righteousness, and of judgement (John 16:8-11). Natural man cannot know the things of the Spirit (John 14:17; I Cor. 2:14), which God sent forth to His sons (Gal. 4:6), thus identifying the children of Israel (Isa. 44:1-3, 59:20-21; Haggai 2:5; Rom. 8:16) in this world.

We believe that God the Son, Yahshua the Messiah (Jesus Christ), became man in order to redeem His people Israel (Luke 1:68) as a kinsman of the flesh (Heb. 2:14-16; Rom. 9:3-5); died as the Passover Lamb of God on the Cross of Calvary finishing His perfect atoning sacrifice for the remission of our sins (Matt. 26:28); He arose from the grave on the third day (1 Cor. 15:4) triumphing over death; and ascended into Heaven where He is now reigning at the right hand of God (Mark 16:19).

We believe in the literal return to this Earth of Yahshua the Messiah (Jesus Christ) in like manner as He departed (Acts 1:11), to take the Throne of David (Isa. 9:7; Luke 1:32) and establish His everlasting Kingdom (Dan. 2:44; Luke 1:33; Rev. 11:15). Every knee shall bow and every tongue shall confess that He is King of kings and Lord of lords (Phil. 2:10-11; 1 Tim. 6:14-15).

We believe Salvation is by grace through faith, not of works (Eph. 2:8-9). Eternal life is the gift of God through the redemption that is in our Saviour Yahshua (Jesus Christ) (Rom. 6:23) who will reward every man according to his works (Rev. 22:12).

We believe membership in the church of Yahshua our Messiah (Jesus Christ) is by Divine election (John 6:44, 65, 15:16; Acts 2:39, 13:48; Rom. 9:11, 11:7; II Thes. 2:13). God foreknew, chose and predestined the Elect from before the foundation of the world (Psalm 139:16; Jer. 1:5; Matt. 25:34; Rom. 8:28-30; Eph. 1:4-5; II Tim. 1:9; Rev. 13:8) according to His perfect purpose and sovereign will (Rom. 9:19-23). Only the called children of God can come to the Savior to hear His words and believe; those who are not of God, cannot hear his voice (John 8:47, 10:26-27).

We believe Yahshua the Messiah (Jesus the Christ) came to redeem (a word meaning purchase back according to the law of kinship) only His people Israel (Psalm 130:7-8; Isa. 54:5; Matt. 10:5-6, 15:24; Gal. 4:4-5) who are His portion and inheritance (Deut. 32:9).

We believe individual Israelites are destined for judgement (II Cor. 5:10; Heb. 9:27) and must believe on the only begotten Son of God, Yahshua the Messiah (Jesus Christ), in whom only there is salvation (Acts 4:12), that they be not condemned (John 3:18; Mark 16:16). Each individual Israelite must repent, putting off the old corrupt man and become a new creature (Eph. 4:22-24; II Cor. 5:17) walking in the newness of life (Rom. 6:4). This spiritual rebirth (John 3:3-6; I Peter 1:23) being necessary for a personal relationship with our Savior.

We believe in water baptism by immersion according to the Scriptures for all true believers; being buried into the death of Yahshua the Messiah (Jesus Christ) for the remission of our sins and in the likeness of His resurrection being raised up into the newness of life (Rom. 6:3-6). Baptism being ordained of God a testimony to the New Covenant as circumcision was under the Old Covenant (Col. 2:11-13).

We believe Yahshua the Messiah (Jesus Christ) to be our only High Priest (1 Tim. 2:5; Heb. 3:1, 6:20, 7:17, 24-25) and head over His body of called-out saints, the Church (Rom. 12:5; 1 Cor. 12:12, 27; Eph. 1:22-23, 4:12, 5:23, 30; Col. 1:18, 24). His bride, the wife of the Lamb, is the twelve tribes of the children of Israel (Isa. 54:5; Jer. 3:14; Hosea 2:19-20; Rev. 21:9-12).

We believe God chose unto Himself a special race of people that are above all people upon the face of the earth (Deut. 7:6; Amos 3:2). These children of Abraham through the called-out seedline of Isaac and Jacob (Psalm 105:6; Rom. 9:7) were to be a blessing to all the families of the earth who bless them and a cursing to those that curse them (Gen. 12:3). The descendants of the twelve sons of Jacob, called "Israel," were married to God (Isa. 54:5), have not been cast away (Rom. 11:1-2), have been given the adoption, glory, covenants, law, service of God, and promises; are the ones to whom the Messiah came (Rom. 9:4-5) electing out of all twelve tribes those who inherit the Kingdom of God (Rev. 7:4, 21:12).

We believe that the New Covenant was made with the Children of Israel, the same people the Old Covenant was made with (Jer. 31:31-33; Heb. 8:8-10) in fulfillment of the mercy promised our forefathers (Luke 1:72).

We believe the White, Anglo-Saxon, Germanic and kindred people to be God's true, literal Children of Israel. Only this race fulfills every detail of Biblical Prophecy and World History concerning Israel and continues in these latter days to be heirs and possessors of the Covenants, Prophecies, Promises and Blessings YHVH God made to Israel. This chosen seedline making up the "Christian Nations" (Gen. 35:11; Isa. 62:2; Acts 11:26) of the earth stands far superior to all other peoples in their call as God's servant race (Isa. 41:8, 44:21; Luke 1:54). Only these descendants of the 12 tribes of Israel scattered abroad (James 1:1; Deut. 4:27; Jer. 31:10; John 11:52) have carried God's Word, the Bible, throughout the world (Gen. 28:14; Isa. 43:10-12, 59:21), have used His Laws in the establishment of their civil governments and are the "Christians" opposed by the Satanic Anti-Christ forces of this world who do not recognize the true and living God (John 5:23, 8:19, 16:2-3).

We believe in an existing being known as the Devil or Satan and called the Serpent (Gen. 3:1; Rev. 12:9), who has a literal "seed" or posterity in the earth (Gen. 3:15) commonly called Jews today (Rev. 2:9; 3:9; Isa. 65:15). These children of Satan (John 8:44-47; Matt. 13:38; John 8:23) through Cain (1 John 3:12) are a race of vipers (Matt. 23:31-33), anti-Christs (1 John 2:22, 4:3) who have throughout history always been a curse to true Israel, the Children of God, because of a natural enmity between the two races (Gen. 3:15), because they do the works of their father the Devil (John 8:38-44), and because they please not God, and are contrary to all men (1 Thes. 2:14-15), though they often pose as ministers of righteousness (II Cor. 11: 13:15). The ultimate end of this evil race whose

DOCTRINAL STATEMENT OF BELIEFS (CHRISTIAN IDENTITY CHURCH) (continued)

hands bear the blood of our Savior (Matt. 27:25) and all the righteous slain upon the earth (Matt. 23:35), is Divine judgement (Matt. 13:38-42, 15:13; Zech. 14:21).

We believe that the Man Adam (a Hebrew word meaning: ruddy, to show blood, flush, turn rosy) is father of the White Race only. As a son of God (Luke 3:38), made in His likeness (Gen. 5:1), Adam and his descendants, who are also the children of God (Psalm 82:6; Hos. 1:10; Rom. 8:16; Gal. 4:6; 1 John 3:1-2), can know YHVH God as their Father, not merely as their creator. Adamic man is made trichotomous, that is, not only of body and soul, but having an implanted spirit (Gen. 2:7; I Thes. 5:23; Heb. 4:12) giving him a higher form of consciousness and distinguishing him from all the other races of the earth (Deut. 7:6, 10:15; Amos 3:2).

We believe that as a chosen race, elected by God (Deut. 7:6, 10:15; I Peter 2:9), we are not to be partakers of the wickedness of this world system (I John 2:15; James 4:4; John 17:9, 15, 16), but are called to come out and be a separated people (I Cor. 6:17; Rev. 18:4; Jer. 51:6; Exodus 33:16; Lev. 20:24). This includes segregation from all non-white races, who are prohibited in God's natural divine order from ruling over Israel (Deut. 17:15, 28:13; 32:8; Joel 2:17; Isa. 13:14; Gen. 1:25-26; Rom. 9:21). Race-mixing is an abomination in the sight of Almighty God, a satanic attempt meant to destroy the chosen seedline, and is strictly forbidden by His commandments (Exo. 34:14-16; Num. 25:1-13; I Cor. 10:8; Rev. 2:14; Deut. 7:3-4; Joshua 23:12-13; I Kings 11:1-3; Ezra 9:2, 10-12; 10:10-14; Neh. 10:28-30, 13:3, 27; Hosea 5:7; Mal. 2:11-12).

We believe sin is transgression of God's Law (I John 3:4; Rom. 3:31, 7:7) and that all have sinned (Rom. 3:23). Only through knowledge of God's Law as given in His Commandments, Statutes and Judgments, can we define and know what sin is. We are to keep and teach the laws of God (Matt. 5:17-19) on both a personal and national basis.

We believe God gave Israel His Laws for their own good (Deut. 5:33). Theocracy being the only perfect form of government, and God's divine Law for governing a nation being far superior to man's laws, we are not to add to or diminish from His commandments (Deut. 4:1-2). All present world problems are a result of disobedience to the Laws of God, which if kept will bring blessings and if disregarded will bring cursings (Deut. 28).

We believe men and women should conduct themselves according to the role of their gender in the traditional Christian sense that God intended. Homosexuality is an abomination before God and should be punished by death (Lev. 18:22, 20:13; Rom. 1:24-28, 32; I Cor. 6:9).

We believe that the United States of America fulfills the prophesied (II Sam. 7:10, Isa. 11:12; Ezek. 36:24) place where Christians from all the tribes of Israel would be regathered. It is here in this blessed land (Deut. 15:6, 28:11, 33:13-17) that God made a small one a strong nation (Isa. 60:22), feeding His people with knowledge and understanding through Christian pastors (Jer. 3:14-15) who have carried the light of truth and blessings unto the

nations of the earth (Isa. 49:6, 2:2-3; Gen. 12:3). North America is the wilderness (Hosea 2:14) to which God brought the dispersed seed of Israel, the land between two seas (Zech. 9:10), surveyed and divided by rivers (Isa. 18:1-2,7), where springs of water and streams break out and the desert blossoms as the rose (Isa. 35:1,6-7).

We believe the ultimate destiny of all history will be the establishment of the Kingdom of God upon this earth (Psalm 37:9, 11, 22; Isa. 11:9; Matt. 5:5, 6:10; Rev. 21:2-3) with Yahshua our Messiah (Jesus Christ) reigning as King of kings over the house of Jacob forever, of this kingdom and dominion there shall be no end (Luke 1:32-33; Dan. 2:44, 7:14; Zech. 14:9). When our Savior returns to restore righteous government on the earth, there will be a day of reckoning when the kingdoms of this world become His (Rev. 11:15; Isa. 9:6-7) and all evil shall be destroyed (Isa. 13:9; Mal. 4:3; Matt. 13:30, 41:42; II Thes. 2:8). His elect Saints will be raised immortal at His return (I Cor. 15:52-53; I Thes. 4:16; Rev. 20:6) to rule and reign with Him as kings and priests (Rom. 8:17; II Tim. 2:12; Rev. 5:10; Exodus 19:6; Dan. 7:18, 27).

Notes: *In its use of the names "YHWH" and "Yahshua" as the proper designations for God and Christ, this statement shows the influence of the Sacred Name Movement which has affected the theology of many modern British-Israel organizations. However, unlike most Sacred Name and British-Israel groups, the Christian Identity Church is trinitarian; its doctrinal statement contains a strong affirmation of the personality of the Holy Spirit. Baptism is by immersion. The statement highlights the beliefs of many modern British-Israel groups such as the church's position on the white race, the identity of present-day Israel, and the place of the United States in God's plan.*

* * *

ARTICLES OF FAITH AND DOCTRINE (CHURCH OF ISRAEL)

THE CHURCHES OF ISRAEL. Diocese of Manasseh, United States of America, issue the ARTICLES OF FAITH AND DOCTRINE which set forth the tenets of religious belief and conviction for the Covenant People, who combine and covenant themselves together under authority of Jesus Christ in pursuant to His Word in the historic Christian Faith and Birthright of our Fathers, under the protection of the United States Constitution and of the various State Constitutions under which religious freedom and association is guaranteed. These Articles of Faith and Doctrine provide the ground and foundation for the CHURCHES OF ISRAEL in the establishment of religious belief and conscience. These principles and tenets of faith will govern all Christian Israel people who covenant and combine themselves together under the name THE CHURCH OF ISRAEL.

RELIGIOUS LIBERTY

The Churches of Israel humbly acknowledge before Jesus Christ our appreciation of the inalienable rights of freemen to assemble before Almighty God and to read and interpret the Holy Scriptures in free religious association together. For the protection of these rights under the

United States Constitution, and the various State Constitutions where the Churches of Israel are organized, we give special and prayerful acknowledgement to Jesus Christ, and to the Christian Fathers, who bled and died that the Faith once delivered to the Saints would not perish from the earth. Moreover, we give thanks to Jesus Christ, that through him and pursuant to His Word, we have the right to organize a Church, and that such Churches receive their Christian Common Law Charter from the Holy Bible which is the ground and foundation of the Christian State.

CHRISTIAN PRESUPPOSITIONS

The Articles of Faith and Doctrine are set forth in terms of presuppositional statements. These presuppositions become the cornerstones of the religious tenets of faith espoused by Christian Israelites who seek to stand under the Blood of Jesus Christ, who seek to walk by His immutable Law Word, and who seek to walk in communion with the Holy Spirit. These presuppositions are intended to build a valid, consistent and systematic theology, a House of Faith, that will be built upon Jesus Christ the Rock and upon His Word in all of the Churches of Israel throughout the Diocese of Manasseh, the United States of America.

EPISTEMOLOGY

WE BELIEVE that all members of the CHURCH OF ISRAEL are required to have a valid Christian Epistemology (valid theory of knowledge). Yahweh must be the reference point for the beginning of all thought. The Christian presupposes God as the premise of knowledge. God, who alone created all factuality, and revealed it to His children (Deut. 29:29) must alone give the meaning for all revealed knowledge through His Holy Scripture. Apart from God, man can know nothing. The source of all truth is God. Only in His light can we see light. (Psm. 36.9) Only by thinking God's thoughts after Him (Holy Scripture) can we know truth. Scripture: Genesis 1.1-3, 3.1-5, Deut. 6.1-9, 30.15-20, Job 32.8, 42.1-3, Psa. 19.1-14, 33.11, 78.1-7, Provl. 1.1-7, 3.1-20, 4.1-5, 23.23, Eccl. 3.14, 12.13-14, Isa. 28.9-10, 55.8-11, Matt. 5.6, 16, 18, 6.22, 33, 7.24-29, Luke 4.4, John 14.26-27, John 16.13, 17.17, Acts 15.18, 17.28, Rom. 1. 18-20, I Cor. 2.6-16, 3. 11-13, I Cor. 12.5-11, Phil. 2.5, James 1.5-8, II Tim 3.7, Heb. 11.1-7, and I John 2.27.

DOCTRINAL IMPLICATIONS OF EPISTEMOLOGY: The Doctrine of Knowledge, The Doctrine of the Law of Faith, and the Doctrine of Conceptual Thinking.

BIBLIOLOGY

WE BELIEVE that the ultimate authority for Adam Man and the creation is the Revealed, Transcendent, Mediated Word of Yahweh, i.e., His Law Command Word as contained in the Holy Scriptures. The Holy Bible contains the infallible, inherent Word of God. The sufficiency of the Holy Scriptures for the Elect is certain; the sixty-six books of the historic canon are all that is necessary for building Christian Doctrine. The Books of the Apocrypha and the Pseudipigrapha are good for instruction and amplification and should, next to the Bible, be the chief source of all truth for the Christian. Scripture: Gen. 5.1, Deut. 4.2, 6.6-9, 8.3, 19.15, 29.29, Psalms 12.6, 119.89, 105, 142, 160,

Proverbs 30.5, Jer. 23.18, 29, Isa. 55.11, 59.21, Matt. 7.24-27, 18.16, Mark 14.49, Luke 21.33, John 1.1-14, 5.39, 10.35, 12.48, 17.17, Acts 17.11, Rom. 10.17, 15.4, Matt. 4.4, Eph. 6.17, Heb. 4.12, I Tim. 5.19, II Cor. 10.11, 13.1, John 20.31, I John 5.13, II Tim. 3.15-16, II Tim. 2.15.

DOCTRINAL IMPLICATIONS OF BIBLIOLOGY: The Doctrine of Scripture, The Doctrine of the Undivided Word, The Doctrine of Bible Numerics, The Study of Bible Hermeneutics, The Doctrine of Transcendance, and the History and Transmission of the Holy Scriptures. The Churches of Israel in the English-speaking world stand upon the Authorized King James Version of the Bible. This position is defended in a series of sermon lessons entitled "Defending the King James Version of the Bible," available on cassette tape.

COSMOLOGY

WE BELIEVE as the Elect in Christ that there exist two different kinds of being, i.e., the Uncreated and the Created, Yahweh is one kind, the UNCREATED. All the Created Universe (including the Angelic hosts) is the other Kind, the CREATED. The Universe and all that therein is was created and spoken into existence. The created cannot transcend into the Being of God. The line between the Uncreated and the Created cannot be transcended by the created. Scripture: Genesis 1.1-31, Genesis 2.1-7, Psalm 33.1-9, 95.5, Isaiah 45.12, 48.13, Jer. 51.15-16, and Hebrews 11.3.

DOCTRINAL IMPLICATIONS OF COSMOLOGY: The Doctrine of Creation, The Doctrine of Kind after His Kind, The Doctrine of Seed in Itself, The Law of the Sabbath, and The Divine Biblical Calendar.

THE BEING OF GOD

WE BELIEVE that Yahweh is one God, one God in three subsistences, God the Father, Son, and Holy Ghost. ALL ONE GOD! His relationship to Himself is ontological, and His relationship to His creation is transcendent, providential, and economical. The belief in the One, Holy, Triune God of Scripture is summarized in the words of the Schell City creedal statement, which reads, "I Believe in one true and everliving, self-existing and uncreated God, whose Name is YAHWEH, and in the Unity of His Being, there exist three subsistences of one essence, substance, power and eternity, God the Father, Son, and Holy Ghost, all one God, world without end." This One, Holy, and True God created the world, sustains the world, governs the world, and will one day judge His children in righteousness. The "unity" and the "triunity" of the one true God is of profound significance in building a House of Faith. Scripture: Genesis 1.1, 1.26, Es. 20.3, Deut. 6.4, Isa. 43.15, Isa. 6.3, Isa. 44.6-8, Mark 12.29-30, I Cor. 8.4-6, I Tim. 2.5, James 2.19, Matt. 3.16-17, Matt. 28.19, Mark 1.9-11, John 1.1-14, II Cor. 4.4, I Pet. 1.2, Num. 6.22-27, Isa. 6.9, Micah 5.2, Psa. 86.10, Isa. 45.6, John 17.3, II Cor. 13.14, John 2.28-29, 8. 17-18, 42, 58, 10.30, 10.38, 12.45, 14.9-10, 16.27-38, I John 5.7, Num. 6.24-26, I Pet. 1.2, Mark 1.9-11, Heb. 1.3, and Col. 1.15.

DOCTRINAL IMPLICATIONS OF THE BEING OF GOD: The Doctrine of the Triune God, The Doctrine of the Unity of Yahweh, The Doctrine of the Triunity of

Yahweh, The Doctrine of the One and the Many, and The
Doctrine of the Divine Name & Titles for the Unity and
the Triunity of Yahweh.

ANGELOLOGY

WE BELIEVE that Angels are created beings, one step
above Adam Man, who were all created to dwell in
immortal, celestial bodies. Angels are subject to all of the
Laws of God and were all created good. A portion of those
Angels participated in a rebellion against God in the
government of heaven (Rev. 12.4-9), were cast out into the
earth (Rev. 12.9), and then went after strange flesh (Jude
6-7, II Peter 2.4, Heb. 2.2, Gen. 6.1-4). The offspring of the
sinful Angels who cohabited with the daughters of Adam
were the giants or Nephilim (fallen ones). The spirits of
these out of kind beings are the demons or devils which
Jesus Christ cast out. Mark 5.1-20, Mark 1.23-34, 3.14-15,
3.22, 5.1-20, 6.7-13, 9.14-29, 16.9-17, Luke 8.2, Luke 4.3-4,
9.1, 10.17, 13.16, 32.

The angels are classified in the government of God
according to a rank or hierarchy. one order of Angels is
assigned to minister to those who are the heirs of salvation.
(Heb. 1.14, Psa. 34.7). Satan was, before his fall (Isa.
14.12-21, Rev. 12.7-9) the anointed cherub, standing at the
head of all the realm of Angels (Ezek. 28.13-19). Satan has
been defeated by the incarnation, atonement, and resurrection of Jesus Christ, and now holds dominion only when
Christians will it to so be. Scripture: Genesis 2.1, Psa. 8.3-
5, Job 1.6-7, 2.1, 38.7, Heb. 1.1-14, Rev. 12.7-9, Jude 6-13,
II Pet. 2.4, Heb. 2.1-9, Rev. 12.1-4, Gen. 6.1-4, Rev. 20.1-
2, Rev. Ch. 8, Rev. Ch. 16, I Cor. 6.2-3, Matt. 12.43-45,
Mark 5.1-13.

DOCTRINAL IMPLICATIONS OF ANGELOLOGY:
The Doctrine of Angels, The Government of Angels, The
Ministry of Angels, The Doctrine of Satanology, The
Doctrine of the Angels That Sinned, and the Doctrine of
Demonology.

ANTHROPOLOGY

The man, Adam, was made (asah) trichotomous. His being
was made from a created soul (Gen. 1.26-27), barah, a
formed body (yatsar), and an implanted spirit. (Gen. 2.7).
Adam was the particular of the Creation who was made in
the image and after the likeness of Yahweh, the Ontological Triune God (Isa. 43.7), I Thess. 5.23, Heb. 4.12, Luke
1.46-47 Matt. 10.28, Eph. 4.23, and Psa. 35.9. The man,
Adam, (Gen. 1.26) was made in the image and after the
likeness of ELOHIYM (God), was told to be fruitful,
multiply and replenish the earth, and was given the
dominion mandate to subdue the earth and rule over all
the creation. Scripture: Carefully study all of the following
scriptures to see that Genesis 1.26-28 and Genesis 2.7 have
reference to only Adam Kind Man. Genesis 5.1-3, 9.1-2,
Psalm 8.1-9, St. Matthew 19.4-6, St. Mark 10.6-9. The
Hebrew root word for the English word "man" is identical
in both Genesis 1.26 and Genesis 2.7. Only the "souls" of
Adam Kind Man were created in Genesis 1.27. The
created soul (Gen. 1.27) was placed into a formed body

(Genesis 2.7) and given an implanted spirit, that is, the
breath of life.

Adam was the father of only one race on this earth, that is
the caucasion race. The Hebrew root meaning for the
English man is #119, 120, and 121. These numbers are
catalogued in Strong's Exhaustive Concordance to the
Holy Bible. #119 Aw-Dam—To show blood in the face,
flush or turn rosey. Be dyed, made red (ruddy); #120 Aw-
Dawm—Ruddy, i.e., a human being (an individual or the
species, mankind, etc.) man, person; #121 Aw-dawm—
The same as #120 . . . Adam, the name of the first
man, also of a place in Palestine. All of the other races
preceded Adam in this earth. All of the non-Caucasion
races were on the earth before Adam was created. (Genesis
1.24-25). They were all created after the law of Kind after
His Kind, and were pronounced by ELOHIYM to be very
good. (Genesis 1.31). All races were created according to
the Law of Kind after His Kind, and were to remain
segregated in the habitat given each of them by the Eternal
God.

THE DOCTRINAL IMPLICATIONS OF ANTHRO-
POLOGY: The Doctrine of Adam Man, The Study of
Creationism, Traducianism and Pre-existence, The Exami-
nation of the Spirit, the Soul and the Body of Adam Man,
The Terrestrial-Celestial Hypostatic Union of Adam Man
before the Fall, The Doctrine of Adam Man and the
Dominion Mandate, and The Study of Anthropoidology.

HARMARTIOLOGY

WE BELIEVE that the man, Adam, by the act of Original
Sin, (Gen. 3.1-16) an act which follows a particular
pathology (I John 2.15-17), transgressed God's Law, and
by this act of disobedience, Adam lost his conditional
immortality and came under the *Dominion of Death.*
(Genesis 2.17, 3.22-24, Romans 5.12). By Adam's transgression he lost his hypostatic union of celestial-terrestrial
existence (I Cor. 15.40, Gen. 2.25, 3.7-11) and all men
came under the *Sentence of Death.* (Roman 3.9-23, 5.12,
Gal. 3.22, Psa. 51.5 and Psa. 58.3). The malignity of Sin
infected all the seed from Adam's loins (Romans 5.12, 17).
By the Act of Original Sin, Adam lost the dominion to
death and death reigned from Adam to Jesus Christ. (Col.
1.18, I Cor. 15.20, II Tim. 1.10, Rev. 1.18, Rom. 6.8-9,
Heb. 2.14).

The Fall of Adam from dominion into death resulted in
the fall of all the creation. (Rom. 8.19-23). Satan, being
created immortal (Ezek. 28.15) and not subject to the
organic laws of death, exercised the power of dominion by
his own progeny or offspring which he placed in this earth,
beginning with Cain. The serpent of Genesis 3.15 is Satan
(Rev. 12.9 and 20.2) and Satan appeared as an angel of
light in the Garden of Eden (Ezek. 28.13 and II Cor.
11.14). The two seeds of Genesis 3.15 are literal progeny or
offspring (Hebrew zera) and the same Hebrew root word
for the English word "seed" is used in the remainder of the
Old Testament. You cannot spiritualize the two seeds of
Genesis 3.15! To spiritualize the two seeds of Genesis 3.15
would do away with the existence of physical Israel
coming from the same Hebrew root word (zera) "seed" as
in Genesis 3.15. Cain was the progeny of the wicked one. I
John 3.11-12, St. Matthew 13.38, 23.29-35, St. Luke 11.51

and John 8.44. Adam was not the father of Cain. (Genesis 5.1-32). For additional scripture read: I John 3.4, Romans 7.7, Romans 3.20, Gen. 6.5, 8.21, Isa. 58.1, Isa. 59.1-2, Isa. 64.6-12, Jer. 17.9-10, II Cor. 5.14-15, Psa. 52.2-3, Rom. 8.5-8, I Cor. 2.14.

THE DOCTRINAL IMPLICATIONS OF HARMARTIOLOGY: The Doctrine of Original Sin, The Doctrine of the Pathology of Sin, The Doctrine of the Two Seedlines, Satan's Family Tree, Adam's Family Tree, The Rights of the Firstborn as a Consequence of Original Sin, The Doctrine of Blood Sacrifice and Atonement for Sin, and The Doctrine of Kinsman Redemption.

CHRISTOLOGY

WE BELIEVE that the second subsistence of the Godhead, Jesus Christ, is very God of very God and became very man of very man, in order to Redeem His people Israel and to deliver His creation. Scripture: Isa. 7.14, John 1.1-14, Jer. 31.22. Heb. 10.5, I Cor. 15.38, Matt. 1.18-25, Luke 1.26-35, Luke 2.21, Isa. 66.7, Matt. 12.46, Heb. 2.16, Heb. 7.3, John 7.42, Isa. 11.1, Rev. 5.5, Rev. 22.16, II Tim. 2.8, Acts 13.23, Psa. 132.11, Acts 2.30. Rom. 9.5.

We believe that Jesus Christ was born of the virgin Mary without taint or spot of sin (I Pet. 1.19-20 and Heb. 9.14). We believe in one Jesus Christ, eternally begotten of the Father, very God and very man, perfect God, perfect man, and in this one Jesus Christ there exist two perfect natures, inseparably united, without division, change, confusion or comingling. We believe that Jesus Christ made an all sufficient and perfect sacrifice for sin and that by His atonement upon the cross he fulfilled and made perfect the Law of Blood Sacrifice, making a sufficient payment for the ransom and redemption of those He came to save.

We believe that justification to salvation is by the blood of Jesus Christ. We believe that Jesus Christ is the paschal lamb who came to redeem His people from the bondage of sin. We believe that Jesus Christ descended into Sheol and that He led the Elect in Christ (Old Testament Saints) from the prison of Sheol-Hades. We believe that the souls of the righteous are now in Paradise, expectant and awaiting the redemption of their body. We believe that Jesus Christ rose for the dead on the third day as the firstborn from the dead and the firstfruits of them that slept. We believe in the Doctrine of Eternal Life. We believe that Jesus Christ is both the first and the last Adam. We believe that Jesus Christ is the only mediator between God and man, and that He stands as Prophet, Priest and King, making daily intercession for His saints.

THE DOCTRINAL IMPLICATIONS OF CHRISTOLOGY: The Doctrine of the Incarnation (Virgin Birth), The Doctrine of the Two Perfect Natures of the One Jesus Christ, The Doctrine of the Atonement (Justification), The Doctrine of Christ the Passover Lamb, The Doctrine of Christ into Sheol, The Doctrine of paradise, The Doctrine of the Resurrection, The Doctrine of Eternal Life, The Doctrine of the First and the Last Adam, The Doctrine of Mediatorial Intercession, The Doctrine of Christ as Prophet, Priest and King, and The Feast of Passover and Unleavened Bread.

PNEUMATOLOGY

WE BELIEVE that God the Holy Spirit is the third subsistence of the one true and everliving Triune God. God the Holy Ghost visited and empowered the Church on the day of Pentecost and He gave them the power, the authority, and the modus operandi to bring forth the government of God into the earth and this Body became the Church Militant. The Head, Jesus Christ, came forth to create a new Adamic Body, the Redeemed Israel, the Church Militant, to whom was given power and authority in the creation and in time to take Dominion of the whole earth and to establish the Kingdom for Jesus Christ, the King, and to defend His Crown Rights. God the Holy Ghost is the Comforter, Teacher, Counselor, and Sustainer of the Church and from Him come all the Spiritual Gifts and Fruits of the Spirit. Scripture: Num. 6.27, Lam. 1.16, Psa. 51.11, Isa. 6.3, Deut. 30.6, Ezek. 36.24-27, Jer. 31.31-34, Isa. 59.21, Joel 2.28-32, John 14.15-27, John 15.26, John 16.7-14, Acts Ch. 2, I Cor. Ch. 12, Gal. 5.22-23.

DOCTRINAL IMPLICATIONS OF PNEUMATOLOGY: The Doctrine of the Holy Spirit, The Doctrine of the Empowering at Pentecost, The Doctrine of Sanctification, The spiritual Gifts of the Holy Spirit, The Fruits of the Holy Spirit, The Apostolic Doctrine of Tongues (Languages), and the Feast of Pentecost or Feast of Weeks.

SOTERIOLOGY

WE BELIEVE that Yahweh, in the council of His own will, elected and chose (John 15.16 and Rom. 9.11, 11.7) as His vice regents before the foundation of the world (Eph. 1.4, II Tim. 1.90, Matt. 24.34) Priests and Kings on the earth and in His creation, a seed of a race by His Grace. (Gen. 12.1-3, 17.1-7, Psa. 22.30, Amos. 3.2, Psa. 135.4, Exod. 19.5-6, Jer. 31.1). The Elect in Christ from the Seed of Abraham (Gen. 17.7, 21.12, Rom. 9.7) were chosen by God the Father, (I Pet. 1.2). Redeemed by God the Son, (Gal. 4.4-5), and Sanctified and called by God the Holy Spirit, all one and holy triune God. (I Pet. 12). The elect in Christ are His workmanship (Eph. 2.8-10) and are passive in the matter of their salvation. They are made willing and repentent vessels of His mercy by the Grace of Jesus Christ, and are made holy by the atoning blood of Jesus Christ. (Psa. 65.4, 110.3, Rom. 2.4, I Cor. 1.29-31, II Cor. 4.6, Rom. 3.25, and Rev. 1.5).

The Elect were chosen in Christ and their names were written in the Lamb's Book of Life before the foundation of the world, to be born in the fulness of time, according to the perfect and sovereign will of God. (Rom. 9.6-7, Gal. 3.16, Rev. 13.8, 17.8, Phil. 4.3, Luke 10.20, John 10.3, Psa. 139.14-16, Dan. 12.1, Rev. 20.12-15, Rev. 21.27, and 22.19. We believe that the Election of God in the matter of salvation is unconditional, that the Atonement was definite with a people in view, that the Grace to effect this election is irresistible, and that the Elect in Christ will persevere and will be powerfully preserved. We believe that the Messianic Covenant of Grace was made from the foundation of the world (I Pet. 1.19-20). We believe that the Abrahamic Covenant of Promise was necessary to bring to pass the terms of the Messianic Covenant of Grace.

We believe that the Mosaic Covenant of Law was given that Israel might have a mirror from God to expose their

sin nature and see that salvation is not by law, not by any
work of man, but by atoning blood and righteousness of
Jesus Christ. We believe that the Israelites of the Scripture,
Old and New Testaments, are identified in the Caucasion
Nations of Europe, America, Canada, the British Isles,
Scandinavia, Australia, So. Africa, New Zealand and
wherever the seed of these people has been dispersed
throughout the whole earth. We believe that the everlast-
ing Birthright walks with Joseph, that the everlasting
Sceptre belongs to Judah, and that the Everlasting
Priesthood is in the possession of Levi. We believe that the
Birthright, the Sceptre, and the Priesthood are all present
on the world stage today as confirmation of the existence
of true Biblical Israel in this earth.

THE DOCTRINAL IMPLICATIONS OF SOTERIOL-
OGY: The Doctrine of Original Sin, The Doctrinal of
Unconditional Election, The Doctrine of Definite Atonement, The Doctrine of Irresistible Grace, The Doctrine of
the Preservation of the Saints, The Doctrine of the
Messianic Covenant of Grace, The Abrahamic Covenant
of Promise and the Mosaic Covenant of Law, The
Doctrine of the Children of Promise, The Doctrine of Law
and Grace, The History of Israel in the Bible beginning
with the call of Abraham, and ending with the divorce,
exile, captivity and dispersion into Asia Minor, Western
Asia, Europe, Scandinavia and the British Isles, The Study
of the Birthright, The Priesthood and the Sceptre, and The
Implication of These Promises upon Modern Israel.

ECCLESIOLOGY

WE BELIEVE that the Apostolic Church Militant is the
body of Jesus Christ in the creation and in time. The
Church Triumphant is those who have fought the fight,
won the victory, and are now expectant. The ecclesia
describes both the Church Militant on earth, and the
Church Triumphant, those who have conquered and
gained the victory. (Heb. Ch. 11). The doctrinal presuppositions of the Apostolic Faith of Christ's Church Militant
are articulated in the three historic creeds of the Apostolic,
i.e., The Apostles Creed, the Nicene Creed, and the
Athanasian Creed. In the Church Militant all worship
must be lawful and hallow His Name. Worship must serve
to exalt Jesus Christ (the One) and bring the Body (the
many) into a communion with the Head, thus effecting a
verticle communion with Jesus Christ (the Head), and a
horizontal communion of the saints (the body).

The Tree of Life containing the Holy Sacraments of the
Church enables the Elect in Christ (ecclesia) to walk in
hypostatic union with Jesus Christ, the Head, and walk
forth in Christian Dominion. From the Pulpit the Law and
the Doctrine of Jesus Christ is to be taught, and from the
Altar the Blood and Body of Jesus Christ (The Holy
Eucharist) serves to bring the Body into union with Christ
the Head.

We believe in the Doctrine of the Hypostatic Union of
Christ and His Church. We believe in an everlasting
Priesthood, in a Divine Pattern of Worship, and in the fact
that the Sacraments of the Church continue to be a vital
union of Christ with His Church. The seven historic

Sacraments of the Church include Holy Baptism, Holy
Communion, Holy Confirmation, Holy Matrimony, Holy
Ordination, Holy Repentance (penance), and Holy Unc-
tion (healing). We believe in the three historic creeds of the
Christian Faith, i.e., the Apostles Creed, the Nicene Creed,
and the Athanasian Creed. We believe in the doctrinal
work of the first Seven Councils of the Church: Jerusalem
A.D. 52 (waged a war against Judiasm), Nicea A. D. 325
(waged a war against Arianism), I Constantinople A. D.
381 (waged a war against semi-Arianism), Ephesus A. D.
431 (waged a war against Nestorianism), Chalcedon A. D.
451 (waged a war against humanism by setting forth the
truth of the two natures of Christ), II Constantinople A.
D. 553 (waged a war against the Monophysites), and III
Constantinople A. D. 680-681 (waged a war against the
introduction of humanity into the Deity of Jesus Christ).
We do not subscribe to much of the work accomplished at
the Councils after the date of 680-681, but do believe that
they should be studied for an evaluation of history from A.
D. 700 to the time of the Reformation.

We believe that the Christian Family is the basic unit of all
government, both for the Church and the State. It is the
duty of the parents in the home and the Clergy to teach
and practice those laws that will build strong Christian
family units of Government out of which the Church and
the Nation will be built.

DOCTRINAL IMPLICATIONS OF ECCLESIOLOGY:
The Doctrine of the Church, The Doctrine of the
Hypostatic Union of Christ and His Church, The Doctrine
of an Everlasting Priesthood, The Pulpit and the Altar,
The Doctrine of the Divine Pattern of Worship, The
Doctrine of Church Government, The Doctrine of the
Great Commission, The Doctrine of the Tree of Life & the
Holy Sacraments, The History of the Three Historic
Creeds of Christianity, The History of the Apostolic and
Church Fathers, The History of the First Seven Church
Councils, The Doctrine of the Christian Church and the
Dominion Mandate, and The Doctrine of the Christian
Family. The Writings of the Church Fathers should be
studied for the historical and doctrinal value to be gained
from these important writings.

THEOCRACY

WE BELIEVE that the Kingdom of God is the final goal
of all history, the event toward which the Elect in Christ
structure their lives and the event by which all priorities by
Jesus Christ (The Head) to His Apostles (the Body) must
be established in time and the creation. Scripture: Matt.
4.23, Matt. 10.7. Mark 1.14, Luke 8.1, Matt. 24.14, Isa.
9.6-7, Isa. 65.17-25, Micah 4.1-5. Micah 5.2, Luke 1.31-33,
Zach. 14.9, Rev. 11.15, and Rev. 21 and 22 (all). We
believe that the Church and the State represent the
undivided government of God and that they are equal
aspects of created reality. There is no separation between
Church and State in God's Word. Both the Church and
the State are under God and must be subject to Christ and
His Law as contained in the Holy Scriptures.

We believe that the law of God is immutable and without
change. (St. Matt. 5.17-20, Rom. 3.32, I Jn. 3.4, Mal. 3.6
and Heb. 13.8). We believe that the Commandments, the
Statutes, the Judgments and the Ordinances are all

immutable and eternal aspects of God's created reality. We believe that it is the moral responsibility of the Covenant Family, called into the saving knowledge of Jesus Christ, to make their lives relevant to the Law of God. We believe that parents, teachers, and all Ministers are under severe obligation to teach and practice the commandments and other vital personal and family areas of the law, and to demand that Civil Leaders make these laws relevant to all activities of government.

We believe in the Doctrine of the Tithe, and we believe in the Holy Feast Days of Yahweh, established in Holy Scripture. We believe that the Religious Festivals of Passover, Pentecost, The Feast of Trumpets, The Day of Atonement and Feast of Tabernacles are all vital to the Christian Dominion of this earth for Jesus Christ. We believe in the Holy Sabbath, and we believe that all aspects of God's Law must be honored by the Covenant people called into the saving knowledge of Jesus Christ. We believe in the Dietary Laws and all else that is in the Law that pertains to living life in terms of God's Law.

We believe that Jesus Christ will rule upon a literal throne, David's Throne, as the greater David of Prophecy, and that He will establish a theocratic government over all the earth at His Second Coming. (Ezekial 37.21-28, St. Matthew 19.28, 25.31-32, St. Luke 1.31-33, Rev. 11.15). We believe that there will be a literal regathering of Israel at the Second Coming of Jesus Christ, and that all of the Elect will be regathered, both of the Church Triumphant and of the Church Militant. (Matt. 24.31, Mark 13.27, Luke 13.29, Jer. 30.3, 33.7, Amos 9.13-15). We believe that a literal Kingdom will be restored to Israel at the Second Coming of Jesus Christ. Luke 1.31-33, Acts 1.6, I Cor. 15.24, Luke 12.32, Luke 19.11-13, Isa. 9.6-7, Dan. 2.44-45, Isa. 2.1-5, and Micah 4.1-7.

DOCTRINAL IMPLICATIONS OF THE STUDY OF THEOCRACY: The Doctrine of the Kingdom of God, The Doctrine of the Undivided Church and State, The Doctrine of an Everlasting Throne (Sceptre), The Doctrine of the Threefold Government of God, the Family, Church and State, The Doctrine of God's Immutable Law as Contained in the Commandments, Statutes, Judgments and Ordinances, The Doctrine of the Tithe, Tithe of the Firstborn and Firstfruits, The Poor Tithe, and The Festival Tithe, The Doctrine of Holy Feast Days, The Doctrine of Clean and Unclean, and all else that pertains to living in Sanctification before Yahweh, The Covenant God of Israel.

ESCHATOLOGY

WE BELIEVE that the consummation of history is to witness a time of great increasing world wide tribulation wherein the Living Church must occupy until Jesus Christ comes to establish His Kingdom upon this earth. (Luke 19.13 and Mark 13.34). The Second Coming of Jesus Christ will be climaxed by a time of great tribulation and judgment upon the wicked and the establishment of His Kingdom into the earth. (Matthew 24, Mark 13, Luke 21, and all of the Book of Revelation, I and II Chapters of Thess.). We believe that the white western Christian culture, the ninth culture to exist upon this earth, is now in the final stages of the Organic Culture Curve of history.

As this age comes to a close we believe that a time of increasing trouble and tribulation for all the Tribes of Israel, in all the countries of their dispersion, will take place. (Jer. 30.7-11, Ezek. 34.12, Dan. 12.1) We believe that the ending of this age will witness the Second Coming of Jesus Christ to rule upon a literal throne of David in this earth, that there will be a resurrection of the Elect in Christ (Rev. 20.6, I Thess. 4.16) and a regathering of all the Tribes of Israel to the land of their fathers, the promised land, and that the Kingdom will be "restored" again (Acts 1.6) to Israel. Since all the earth will be filled with the government of God, the Tribes of Israel will be apportioned throughout much of the globe with the capitol city the New Jerusalem, being the land deeded to Abraham, Isaac and Jacob-Israel by Covenant forever.

We believe that Hades or Sheol is the place of the departed souls of the wicked Adamites where they are taken following the death of the body, and that they will remain there until the resurrection of the body to stand in judgment at the Great White Throne Judgment. We believe that the souls of the righteous Elect go to be with Christ and are at rest with Christ, until the Second Coming. (I Thess. 3.13, 4.14, II Cor. 5.6-9, Phil. 1.23-24, John 14.3, John 17.24, John 12.26, Col. 3.4). We believe that the Elect in Christ, throughout all ages, will be resurrected at the first resurrection (Rev. 20.6) and that the rest of the dead will be resurrected following the thousand year millenium and little season. (Rev. Ch. 20). Following the Great White Throne Judgment we believe that the wicked will be cast into Gehenna, which is the second death. (Rev. 20.12-15). We believe that as the time of tribulation grows more severe (St. Matt. 24.21-22, John 16.1-4), all true Christians must stand firm in their religious conviction of faith and doctrine. We believe that Christians are absolutely prohibited from receiving any kind of mark, visible or invisible, of any kind or description, into the hand, forehead, or any part of the body. We believe that it is against the Word of God for Christians to be numbered or identified by government marking systems of any kind.

We believe that as we approach the ending of this age the counterfeit Kingdom of Satan and the reign of the antiChrist will seek to ensnare all Christian people into a false pseudo, and counterfeit Kingdom. As the Elect in Christ seek to make their lives relevant to Jesus Christ and His Word, they will be bound by their religious convictions to stand true to their conscience and not forfeit their spiritual inheritance in Jesus Christ. Where public policy affords Christian people no option to follow their religious convictions as established upon the Word of God, Christians will have no other choice but to obey God rather than men. (Acts. 5.29) It is the desire of all members of the Church of Israel to be the sons of God in the midst of a crooked and perverse world order (Phil. 2.15) and to be at peace with all men. When it is no longer possible to live by the terms of God's Word because of "public policy," Christians must be willing to cast their fate upon the mercy of God, and suffer whatever may come; they cannot forfeit their spiritual and moral convictions as established upon God's Word. (See Daniel 3.12-27, Daniel 6.4-23).

ARTICLES OF FAITH AND DOCTRINE (CHURCH OF
ISRAEL) (continued)

As a body of Christian people, bound to Jesus Christ and the Holy Scriptures, there is already a number of public policies which are offensive to God and to the Holy Scriptures. A listing of those "public policies" would be beyond the scope of this work. For the benefit of those Covenant Christian people who walk in the religious conviction of these tenets of Faith, the following specified areas of concern are clearly spelled out:

1.) We believe that it is a violation of God's Word to be marked or numbered in any way by a government agency at any level of operation. If, for example, the Social Security Number in the United States becomes the universal number of identification, then Christians have a moral responsibility to refuse or deny such a number as a matter of religious conscience. (See Revelation Chapters 7, 13, 14 and 15 and Ezekiel Chapter 9).

2.) We believe that it is a violation of God's Law to accept inoculations or vaccines into the body. Parents cannot allow their children to be made the subjects of vaccines and inoculations, and all parents living under these tenets of faith have a moral responsibility to oppose such inoculations as a violation of their religious conscience. (Leviticus 19.28, I Cor. 6.15, and I Thess. 5.23).

3.) We believe that Christians should abstain from harmful drugs of any kind or description and that the body must be kept holy for the indwelling of the Holy Spirit. (Romans 12.1-2, I Cor. 6.19-20).

4.) We believe that God's Law demands segregation of the races and that all races will be more happy living in the state which God assigned to them. Christians are thereby duty bound to practice segregation in their family life, dating and marriage relationships, pursuit of education, and wherever the safety and welfare of the family and Church are in question.

5.) The Church of Israel *DOES NOT* teach white supremacy. We do teach that the white people are the Israelites of the Bible and are called to be the *Servant People of God*. In this capacity they have built the churches, translated the Bible, clothed the world and provided food for the world. We do teach white separtism, black separtism, brown separtism and yellow separtism. We *Do Not* teach hatred toward non-white races. We as a Convenant people seek as per the Holy Scriptures to live and dwell, work and play, worship and educate our children separated and segregated as much as is humanly possible to do so in a multi-racial society. We likewise seek the same options for all races.

6.) We believe that Marriage is a Holy Sacrament of the Church, and that only the Church, acting in accordance with the requirements of Scripture, can establish two people, a man and a woman, together in the State of Marriage. To seek a license from the State is to allow the state to license the Holy Sacrament of Matrimony. This would be a violation of the religious conscience of all who stand under the tenets of these religious and moral teachings of Jesus Christ and the Holy Bible.

7.) We believe that healing is a Sacrament of the Church, and that people who are sick in mind or body should look to the Church for the divine healing that comes from Yahweh, through prayer, anointing with oil by the Elders of the Church, by following the Dietary Laws of Scripture, and through natural means of healing as outlined in the Holy Scriptures of truth.

8.) We believe that it is Biblically wrong for women to serve in the military service of the United States or any other country where Israelites may live. (Deut. Ch. 20). We believe that boys should be a minimum of 20 years of age before serving in the Military Service of the United States. We further believe that where war is being waged in violation of Bible Law (Deut. Ch. 20) they should register with the government as a conscientious objector.

9.) We *do not* advocate, nor do we believe in the use of violence for any cause. *We deplore all acts of terror* and believe that they that live by the sword will die by the sword. (St. Matthew 26.52). The weapons of our warfare are not carnal. (II Cor. 10.3-5 and Rev. 13.10). Christians do have a moral and Biblical right to keep and bear arms in defense of their lives and property. (St. Luke 22.36 and St. Matthew 12.29.).

10.) We believe that Abortion is murder of the unborn and innocent children of God. Life begins at conception and to destroy that life through any type of abortion amounts to an act of murder. Since abortion is an act of overt violence and terror of the unborn we oppose abortion and believe it is the duty of the family and the Church to oppose the murder of the unborn. (Exodus 21.22-25, Exodus 20.13, Deut. 5.17)

11.) We believe that it is the reponsibility of the parents to give their children a Christian Education as a fulfillment of the Baptismal vows and as required by the Word of God. Parents are responsible before God to see that their children are not offered to Molech in the form of brainwashing them and leading them away from Jesus Christ into humanism. Parents can fulfill their responsibility before God in the education of their children by providing home schooling or private Christian Education. (Deut. 6.7.20, Deut. 4.10, Deut. 11.19, Deut. 31.13, Prov. 22.6, Isa. 28.9, John 21.15, Lev. 18.21)

12.) We believe that Christians are called in Jesus Christ to take dominion of the earth to the glory of God. As Christians we stand as redeemed men under Jesus Christ and walk forth as Covenant Children of God, called into Christian Service in all areas of life. We stand under God as Covenant Men, called to walk in obedience to His Law Command Word. We are commissioned to Occupy till He comes. (St. Luke 19.13) The example of living for this age is established in the life and mission of Noah, who walked in fear before God, perfect in his generations and living in obedience to God. (Genesis 6:8-9, Heb. 11.7). Like Noah we seek to build an *Ark of Safety* in this time of national and world travail. We seek only to live in obedience to the Law of Yahweh, the Covenant God of Israel. We do not seek to impose our religious beliefs upon anyone and seek to cultivate peace and good will among all of God's people, and to walk as Covenant men, under Jesus Christ, and in obedience to His Laws throughout all our days.

13.) We do believe in the Constitution of the United States of America! We do believe in the Flag of the United States of America and we pledge our allegiance to the Republic for which it stands. We believe that this is a *Nation under God*, and that it is a great and wonderful privilege to live in these United States of America. We look with great pride upon the men who bled and died for this nation and we gratefully acknowledge the following documentation as proof of our Christian status as One Nation Under Jesus Christ.

In 1799, Justice Chase stated, "By our form of government, the Christian religion is the established religion; and all sects and denominations of Christians are placed upon the same equal footing, and are equally entitled to protection in their religious liberty." (Runkel v. Winemiller, 4 Harris & McHenry (MD) 429, I AD 311, 417).

In the 1892 Supreme Court case entitled "Church of the Holy Trinity v. United States," the Court found, "it is impossible that it should be otherwise: and in this sense and to this extent our civilization and our institutions are emphatically Christian . . . this is a religious people. This is historically true. From the discovery of this continent to the present hour, there is a single voice making this affirmation . . . we find everywhere a clear recognition of the same truth . . . this is a Christian Nation."

In the 1952 case of Zorach v. Clauson the liberal U.S. Supreme Court Justice William O. Douglas admitted, "The first amendment . . . does not say that in every and all respects there shall be a separation of Church and State . . . Otherwise, the state and religion would be aliens to each other—hostile, suspicious, and even unfriendly."

WE THE CHRISTIAN ISRAELITE PEOPLE OF THE CHURCHES OF ISRAEL DO COVENANT AND COMBINE OURSELVES TOGETHER IN SUPPORT OF THESE ARTICLES OF FAITH AND DOCTRINE, AND FOR AUTHORITY AND SUPPORT OF THESE TENETS WE DO LOOK TO JESUS CHRIST AND THE HOLY SCRIPTURES. FOR THE PROTECTION OF THESE TENETS OF RELIGIOUS LIBERTY WE GRATEFULLY ACKNOWLEDGE BEFORE ALMIGHTY YAHWEH, THE COVENANT GOD OF ISRAEL, OUR THANKSGIVING FOR THE UNITED STATES CONSTITUTION, AMENDMENT NO. 1. AND THE RELIGIOUS LIBERTIES GUARANTEED BY THE STATE CONSTITUTIONS OF THE MANY STATES WHICH COMBINED MAKE UP THE UNITED STATES OF AMERICA.

These Articles of Faith and Doctrine adopted and approved by The Board of Trustees, acting for and on behalf of the CHURCH OF ISRAEL at Schell City, Missouri, January 10, 1982.

Notes: *The Church of Israel began as a splinter of a Latter-Day Saint group, the Church of Christ (Temple Lot), and has moved into an acceptance of the British-Israel position, which is spelled out in detail in the church's statement of beliefs. The major remnant of Latter-Day Saint belief is evident in the discussion of priesthood in the section on ecclesiology. The church is also trinitarian. The discussion of racial issues is one of many public policy statements included at the end of this document. The church opposes abortion.*

* * *

FIRST PRINCIPLES (HOUSE OF PRAYER FOR ALL PEOPLE)

WE FOLLOW THE BIBLE IN ALL THINGS. Study your Bible and see if we are right. Name of Building—"HOUSE OF PRAYER FOR ALL PEOPLE" (Isa. 56:7, Matt. 21:13). A follower of Christ is—"A CHRISTIAN" (I Peter 4:16, Acts 26:28). All followers of Christ are—"CHRISTIANS" (Isa. 56:5, Isa. 62:2, Acts 11:26). All congregations of Christians are—"THE CHURCHES OF CHRIST" (Rom. 16:16). The officers of a local congregation are—ELDERS (Titus 1:5), DEACONS (I Tim. 3:1-5, Acts 6:1-6).

THE PLAN OF SALVATION—The true Bible way to be saved:

First: HEAR THE WORD OF YAHVEH PREACHED. (Rev. 2:7, Rom. 10:14). Second BELIEVE—have faith in Yahveh (Heb. 11:6). Third: REPENT OF YOUR SINS (Matt. 3:2, Matt. 4:17, Acts 2:38, Acts 17:30). Fourth: CONFESS FAITH IN YAHSHUA THE MESSIAH (Matt. 10:32, Rom. 10:9-10). Fifth: BE BAPTIZED IN WATER (Acts 2:28, Acts 22:16, I Peter 3:21). Hearing, Faith, Repentance, Confession and Baptism is the one and only complete plan of Salvation in the Bible.

HAVING OBEYED THE GOSPEL. THEN—YAHSHUA THE MESSIAH ADDS YOU TO HIS CHURCH (Acts 2:47, Eph. 2:19-22). And that is all there is to Church membership in the Church, which is His Body. (Eph. 5:30).

HOW TO WORSHIP ON SUNDAY—All believers in Yahshua the Messiah are to assemble for worship (Heb. 10:22-25). The services of a local congregation on every first day of the week (Sunday) consist of five parts.

THE KINGDOM MEAL (Gen. 14:18, Matt. 26:26, Lev. 24:5-9, I Chron. 9:32, Acts 20:7, I Cor. 10:2-4, John 6:53-56). 2. THE TITHE—Ten per cent of gross earnings (Gen. 14:20, Heb. 7:1-8, Mal. 3:10, I Cor. 16:2). 3. PREACHING THE GOSPEL (Matt. 28:18-20, Rom. 10:14-15, II Tim. 4:1-2). 4. SINGING HYMNS WITH INSTRUMENTAL MUSIC (Eph. 5:19, Col. 3:16, Psalm, 150:3-5, Psalm 87:7). 5. PRAYERS (I Thes. 5:17, James 5:13-16). The Kingdom Meal, Tithing, Preaching, Singing and Praying are the five parts that make a complete worship

FIRST PRINCIPLES (HOUSE OF PRAYER FOR ALL PEOPLE) (continued)

service on the first day of every week. By following this complete Bible program you will help to answer the prayer of Yahshua the Messiah for the unity of his people (John 17:11, 20-22, I Cor. 1:10-13).

Ephraim and Manasseh, the sons of Joseph, were exalted over all Israel (I Chron. 5:1). The names of Abraham, Isaac and Israel were called upon them. (Gen. 48:16, Gen. 49:22-26). Ephraim was to become a company of nations and Manasseh a Great Nation. (Gen. 48:19). This is fulfilled in Great Britain and the United States of America—the latter day Israel of Yahveh. We rule over the earth and no weapon that is formed against us shall prosper (Isa. 54:17). Read carefully all of Isaiah 54th chapter and Gal. 4:27-31, Deut. 28:1-44, Ezek. 34:25-31, Isa. 56:7, Matt. 21:13, Isa. 56:5, Isa. 62:2, Acts 11:26:26.

THE TRUE NAME of our Heavenly Father is YAHVEH and the name of His wife and our Heavenly Mother is KHAVEH the Holy Ghost. The name of their Son and our Saviour is YAHSHUA THE MESSIAH—We and all the sons of Yahveh are the ELOHIM (Gods) in ONENESS. The redemptive names are as follows: For your prosperity pray to YAHVEH—YIRETH (Gen. 22:14). For the healing of your body call upon YAHVEH - RAPHA (Ex. 15:26). For the restoration of the Kingdom on earth pray to YAHVEH - TSIDKENU (Jer. 23:6). For your protection the name is YAHVEH - NISSI (Ex. 17:8-15). For divine guidance the name is YAHVEH - RAAH (Ps. 23). For peace on earth use the name YAHVEH - SHALOM (Judges 6:24). For all present nearness and future hope call upon YAHVEH - SHAMMAH (Esek. 48:35). These are the true redemptive names of our Father. There is a contact and a power in these names.

Then realize that YAHVEH'S only true order is "The order of MELCHIZEDECK" (Gen. 14:18-20, Ps. 110:1-7, Heb. 6:13-20, Heb. 7:1-28). I have now revealed to you the true names of "OUR FATHER." Be very careful how you use them. The power of life and death is in those names.

We are Anglo - Saxon, Cymric, and Scandinavian Israelites and we are definitely interested in establishing the Kingdom politically and economically as the dominion of YAHVEH on earth as much as we are in establishing the Church as the temple of YAHVEH in the heart of Israel. With the Church and Israel restored, then will begin the gradual resurrection and restoration of all nations in their allotted places on earth and ultimately the reconciliation of all men and angels in ONENESS with YAHVEH.

Notes: *This statement, printed in most issues of the church's magazine, shows the House of Prayer to be one of the British Israel groups directly influenced by the Sacred Name movement (in accepting "Yahveh" and "Yahshua" as the names of the Creator and His Son). It is different in its designation of "Khaveh," the Holy Ghost, as our "Heavenly Mother."*

*　　*　　*

STATEMENT FROM THE PROPHETIC HERALD MINISTRY

The PROPHETIC HERALD proclaims Jesus Christ pre-eminent in all things (Col. 1:12-20). He is the only Saviour, Redeemer, Healer, Baptizer with the Holy Spirit (Acts 2), and only Mediator between God and man (1 Tim. 2:5). Atonement is possible only through His shed blood (Heb. 9:19-23).

The PROPHETIC HERALD advocates: the near return of Christ (Acts 1:11), and life only through Him (Col. 3:3); the literal resurrection of the dead (John 5:28); the immortalization of those in Christ (1 Cor. 15:53-54); the judgment of the wicked (Rev. 21:8); the final restoration of true Israel (Rom. 9:6, 11:7; Gal. 3:16) and true Judah (Rom. 2:28-29), as the *terrestrial* kingdom of God under the Kingship of Christ (Luke 1:32) and His *celestial* body (the "little flock" of overcomers) who will be *joint heirs* with Him (Rom. 8:17); restored true Israel and Judah (Ezek. 37 and Jer. 50:4-6; Gal. 3:26-29); to be *heirs* and head of nations over unrepentant Gentiles and heathen nations (Rev. 22:8-21); the "restitution of all things which God hath spoken by the mouth of all his holy prophets since the world began" ("Acts 3:21). It also firmly advocates repentance and immersion in the name of the Lord Jesus Christ for the remission of sins (Acts 2:38), and a consecrated life as essential to celestial glorification (1 Cor. 15:22-23).

Notes: *Though no longer in existence, this statement carried in most issues of the ministry's magazine would find approval among British Israelites. It carries some hint of the particular presentation of the International Church of the Foursquare Gospel in its affirmation of Christ as Saviour, Redeemer, Healer, and Baptizer with the Holy Spirit.*

Creed/Organization Name and Keyword Index

Creed names are indicated by italic type, while organizations and religious traditions appear in regular type. Page numbers are preceded by their volume numbers (roman numerals); boldface references indicate entries found in this volume.

305

B

C

E

H

I

J

K

L

M

N

O

T

Y

Z